AF522557

आ नो भद्राः क्रतवो यन्तु विश्वतः
Let noble thoughts come to us from every side
—Rigveda, I-89-i

BHAVAN'S BOOK UNIVERSITY

THE HISTORY AND CULTURE OF THE INDIAN PEOPLE
VOLUME IV

THE AGE OF IMPERIAL KANAUJ

BHAVAN'S BOOK UNIVERSITY

The History and Culture of the Indian People

THE AGE OF IMPERIAL KANAUJ

FOREWORD BY

K. M. MUNSHI

B.A., LL.B., D.LITT. LL.D.

Founder President, Bharatiya Vidya Bhavan

GENERAL EDITOR

R. C. MAJUMDAR

M.A.,PH.D., F.A.S., F.B.B.R.A.S.

Ex. Vice-Chancellor and Professor of History
Dacca University
Hon. Head of the Department of History
Bharatiya Vidya Bhavan

ASSISTANT EDITORS

A. D. PUSALKER

M.A., LL.B., PH.D.

Assistant Director and Head of the
Department of Ancient Indian Culture
Bharatiya Vidya Bhavan

AND

A. K. MAJUMDAR, M.A., D. PHIL

Director
Bharatiya Vidya Bhavan
Delhi Kendra

2023

BHARATIYA VIDYA BHAVAN

Kulapati K. M. Munshi Marg
Mumbai - 400007.

First Edition	:	1955
Second Edition	:	1964
Third Edition	:	1984
Fourth Edition	:	1993
Fifth Edition	:	2009
Sixth Edition	:	2018
Seventh Edition	:	2023

Price ₹ 1470.00

PRINTED IN INDIA

by Atul Goradia at Siddhi Printers, 13/14, Bhabha Building, 13th Khetwadi Lane, Mumbai - 400004, and Published by P.V.Sankarankutty, Director, for Bharatiya Vidya Bhavan, Kulapati K. M. Munshi Marg, Mumbai - 400007.

E-mail: publications@bhavans.info Website: http://www.bhavans.info

CONTRIBUTORS

A. S. ALTEKAR
M.A., LL.B., D.LITT.
Professor and Head of the Department of Ancient Indian History and Culture in the Patna University

R. C. MAJUMDAR
M.A., PH.D., F.A.S., F.B.B.R.A.S.

D. C. GANGULY
M.A., PH.D. (LONDON)
Secretary, Victoria Memorial Hall, Calcutta

D. C. SIRCAR
M.A., PH.D.
Superintendent for Epigraphy, Government of India, Ootacamund; formerly Lecturer in Ancient Indian History and Culture in the University of Calcutta

R. SATHIANATHAIER
M.A., L.T.
Professor of History and Politics in the Annamalai University

G. V. DEVASTHALI
M.A., B.T., PH.D.
Professor of Sanskrit in the H. P. T. College, Nasik

H. D. VELANKAR
M.A.
Joint Director, Bharatiya Vidya Bhavan; formerly Professor of Sanskrit, Wilson College, Bombay

A. D. PUSALKER
M.A., LL.B., PH.D.
Assistant Director and Head of the Department of Ancient Indian Culture, Bharatiya Vidya Bhavan

H. L. JAIN
M.A., LL.B., D.LITT.
Head of the Department of Sanskrit, Pali and Prakrit in the Nagpur University

K. R. SRINIVASA IYENGAR
M.A., D.LITT.
Professor and Head of the Department of English in the Andhra University, Waltair

U. N. GHOSHAL
M.A., PH.D.
Formerly Professor of History in the Presidency College, Calcutta

NALINAKSHA DUTT
M.A., B.L., P.R.S., PH.D., D.LITT. (LONDON)
Professor of Pali in the University of Calcutta

J. N. BANERJEA

M.A., PH.D.

Carmichael Professor of Ancient Indian History and Culture in the University of Calcutta

T. M. P. MAHADEVAN

M.A., PH.D.

Professor and Head of the Department of Philosophy in the University of Madras

H. D. BHATTACHARYYA

M.A.

Formerly Head of the Department of Philosophy, Dacca University, and Honorary University Professor of Indian Philosophy and Religion, Banaras Hindu University

I. J. S. TARAPOREWALA

B.A., PH.D., BAR-AT-LAW

Formerly Professor of Comparative Philology in the University of Calcutta, and Director, Deccan College Post-graduate and Research Institute, Poona

U. C. BHATTACHARJEE

M.A.

Formerly Professor of Philosophy in the Presidency College, Calcutta

FOREWORD

By Dr. K. M. Munshi

The Age of Imperial Kanauj, with which this Volume deals, deserves a more important place in Indian history than it has been given so far. I should, therefore, be forgiven if I gave in my own way a picture as I see it.*

The Age begins with the repulse of the Arab invasions on the mainland of India in the beginning of the eighth century and ends with the fateful year A.D. 997 when Afghānistān passed into the hands of the Turks.

With this Age, ancient India came to an end. At the turn of its last century, Sabuktigīn and Mahmūd came to power in Ghaznī. Their lust, which found expression in the following decades, was to shake the very foundations of life in India, releasing new forces. They gave birth to medieval India. Till the rise of the Hindu power in Mahārāshṭra in the eighteenth century, India was to pass through a period of collective resistance.

This Age of Imperial Kanauj, on the other hand, was an era of great strength and achievement for India. The Arabs who were on a march in three continents were repulsed. Throughout they were held on the frontiers. The Tibetan power was eliminated from Nepāl. The South emerged effectively in the political life of the country, as it had emerged in the earlier age in its religious and cultural life.

This Age saw the rise and fall of three great Empires in the country: of the Rāshṭrakūṭas, founded by Dantidurga (*c.* A.D. 733-757) and his successor, Kṛishṇa I (*c.* A.D. 757-773), which dominated the South till its collapse in the year A.D. 974; of the Pālas in the East, which saw its zenith under Dharmapāla (*c.* A.D. 770-810), though it revived a little at the end of the tenth century; of the Pratīhāras of the West and North, founded by Nāgabhaṭa I, which saw its zenith during the reigns of Mihira Bhoja (*c.* A.D. 836-885) and Mahendrapāla (*c.* A.D. 885-908), went under on account of the catastrophic blows dealt by the Rāshṭrakūṭa raids, but retained a shadowy imperial dignity to the end.

---

* I have incorporated without quotation marks several paragraphs from my study of the period in *The Glory that was Gūrjaradeśa* (2nd Ed. Revised and in part re-written).

II

It was the Age of Kanauj or, Kānyakubja, the imperial city of Īśānavarman, which dominated Madhyadeśa, the heartland of India. It was the coveted prize of the three imperial powers racing for all-India supremacy. Ultimately it passed into the hands of the Pratīhāra Gurjareśvaras about A.D. 815; remained the metropolis of power till A.D. 950, and continued to be the most influential centre of culture till A.D. 1018 when it was destroyed by Mahmūd of Ghaznī.

By inheritance Kanauj was the home of Indo-Aryan traditions. In the post-Vedic ages the region from Hardwar to Unnao, near Lucknow, was known as Āryāvarta. Later with the spread of Indo-Aryan culture, first, north India, and then the whole country, came to be called by that name. The original Āryāvarta, then come to be known as Brahmāvarta, with accretions, was called Madhyadeśa during this age.

When Hastināpura met with disaster due to floods, as the recent excavations at Hastināpura corroborative of the Puranic testimony show, Nichakshu, the descendant of Janamejaya Pārīkshita led the Kurus to Kauśāmbī. In the early sixth century when the Magadhan Age opened, it was the capital of a powerful Aryan kingdom; Vatsarāja, who could lure elephants by his music, was then its ruler. It remained such capital till the end of the sixth century of the Christian Era. Then North India was overrun by the Hūṇas. Kauśāmbī was destroyed. But with Īśānavarman, the liberator who drove out the Hūṇas, Kanauj came into prominence, as the centre of power in Madhyadeśa, no longer a principality of the Gupta Empire.

In the seventh century the kings of Bengal and Mālava destroyed the power of Kanauj, then in the hands of the descendants of Īśānavarman. On the ruins of the Maukhari kingdom, Śrī Harsha built his short-lived empire of Madhyadeśa. During his forty-two years' rule (A.D. 606-647), Kanauj grew into the foremost city of India. Śrī Harsha, however, could not create a hierarchy pledged to support his imperial structure. He left no able successor. His empire was dissolved soon after he died.

For more than half a century thereafter, the history of Kanauj is wrapt in obscurity. At the end of it, Yaśovarman, a great conqueror and the patron of Bhavabhūti and Vākpati, is found ruling Kanauj. Both Yaśovarman and Lalitāditya of Kāshmir joined hands against the inroads of the Arabs and Tibetans. But the allies soon fell out and Lalitāditya destroyed the power of Yaśovarman.

The Classical Age of India closed with the reign of Yaśovarman. This Age then opened with one Indrāyudha on the throne of Kanauj, which had retained its metropolitan and symbolic importance as the capital of India. And the stage was set for the triangular struggle for it between the Rāshṭrakūṭas of the South, the Pratīhāras of Gurjaradeśa and the Pālas of Bengal.

III

The first great conqueror to emerge on the scene, with the Age, was the Rāshṭrakūṭa Dantidurga. The son of Indra I by a Chālukyan princess of Gujarāt, he began his Napoleonic career in c. A.D. 733, became the master of the whole of Mahārāshṭra by 753, and destroyed the Chālukyan Empire to assume an imperial status. He was succeeded by his uncle Kṛishṇa I, the builder of the Kailāsa temple of Ellora. In a reign of fifteen years, he added to the empire what are the modern states of Hyderābād and Mysore.

About the same time, Gopāla, elected to the position of a chieftain, consolidated Bengal. His son Dharmapāla (*c.* A.D. 770-810) led his conquering army through the whole valley of Gaṅgā; reduced the ruler of Kanauj to a puppet; held courts at Kanauj and Pāṭaliputra. For long he commanded the allegiance of most of the kings of the north.

There was ferment also in the west. In A.D. 712 the Arabs conquered Sindh. About A.D. 725 Junaid, its governor, under the orders of Caliph Hasham of Baghdād, sent an army for the conquest of India. It overran Saurāshṭra, Bhillamāla, the capital of Gurjara (the Abu Region), and reached Ujjayinī.

Then arose an unknown hero, Nāgabhaṭa by name; possibly he belonged to a branch of the royal Pratīhāra family of Bhillamāla, the capital of Gurjaradeśa. He rallied to his banner the warriors of the allied clans of Pratīhāras, Chāhamānas and also, perhaps, Guhilaputras, Chālukyas and Paramāras, all of whom had their home in the region of Mount Abu. Nāgabhaṭa fought the invading army, flung it back, destroyed it.

This victory welded the clans of Gurjaradeśa into a hierarchy. It gave them self-assurance and the will to conquer. With a leader and a destiny, they laid the foundations of a new power that was destined to play an important part in history.

During Nāgabhaṭa's time Dantidurga with his conquering army swept over the north, captured Ujjayinī, where the Pratīhāra, his fortunes temporarily eclipsed, played the host to the conqueror.

Vatsarāja, the son of a nephew of Nāgabhaṭa I, styled "the preeminent among valiant Kshatriyas", waxed strong and entrenched himself in a strong position in north India. The allied clans were now a well-knit hierarchy. He, however, suffered a disastrous defeat at the hands of Rāshṭrakūṭa Dhruva and had to take refuge in some unaccessible region.

Under the Pratīhāras, Kanauj reached the zenith of power, learning and culture, between A.D. 815 and 940. Its rulers were called Gurjareśvaras; in a late inscription, Gurjara-Pratīhāras. One of them, as we know, was styled *Mahārājādhirāja* of Āryāvarta. One of the last emperors of the line, when the empire was no more than a symbol, was referred to as the *Raghukula-bhū-chakravartī*, Universal Overlord of Raghu's race; for these Pratīhāras claimed their descent from Lakshmaṇa, the brother of Śrī Rāmachandra of the Ikshvāku race. They were also called kings of Jurz or Gurjara by the Arab travellers, and their empire was called Gurjara.

Undaunted by reverses, the next ruler, Nāgabhaṭa II, consolidated the territory which comprised Mārwāḍ, Mālava and modern North Gujarāt. Having secured a base, he entered the race for all-India supremacy with the Pāla kings of Bengal and the Rāshṭrakūṭas of the South.

Dharmapāla marched on Kanauj, removed Indrāyudha from the throne of Kanauj and installed Chakrāyudha. Nāgabhaṭa II, in his turn, marched against Chakrāyudha, overthrew him and made Kanauj his capital. Soon after Rāshṭrakūṭa Govinda III invaded Kanauj and inflicted a defeat on Nāgabhaṭa which, however, did not cripple his strength. Ultimately Kanauj passed into the hands of the Pratīhāras. About A.D. 815 it became the capital of the Pratīhāra empire.

In c. A.D. 834 Nāgabhaṭa II died. Rāmabhadra, his son and successor, was in his turn, succeeded in c. A.D. 836 by Mihira Bhoja.

The new ruler of Kanauj was called Mihira Bhoja as he was born by the favour of God Sūrya; Ādi Varāha, because he uplifted the realm like the Divine Boar, the incarnation of Vishṇu; Vṛiddha Bhoja by later writers to distinguish him from the later Bhoja the Paramāra. The Arab travellers called him Bauūra, possibly a corruption of Varāha or Barāha; they also referred to him as the king of Jurz, an Arab corruption of the word Gurjara.

When he came to the throne, Mihira Bhoja, then a youth, was faced with a grave situation. Under the feeble rule of his father Rāmabhadra, the power and prestige of the empire had suffered. Its outlying parts had become independent. Even Gurjaradeśa, the homeland, was in open revolt. The imperial possessions extended no further than Kanauj and a small area surrounding it. Only a few of his father's feudatories stood loyal to the new ruler.

The first act of the young ruler was to restore his authority over his homeland; raise the morale of the allied clans of Gurjaradeśa and make them into a compact and invulnerable hierarchy. He did this with such success that the tenacity and vigour of the hierarchic dynasties survived more than a thousand years after the fall of the empire. Many of the Rajput rulers who surrendered power in the great integration of 1947-48 were descendants of the feudatories and generals of Mihira Bhoja.

The career of Mihira Bhoja, pieced together from stray references by modern scholars, was a great factor in making Kanauj a radiating centre of political and cultural activities which made for the integration of life.

In A.D. 836, Ral-pa-can, the Tibetan conqueror of Nepāl, died. A civil war followed. Nepāl shook off the foreign rule and became part of the political system of India. Sārasvata-*maṇḍala* in the Nepal Terai and other Himalayan areas were merged in the empire of Kanauj.

Bihār was also annexed to the empire of Kanauj. By A.D. 876, Mihira Bhoja had burnt 'the powerful people of Bengal in the fire of his rage', obtained a decisive victory over Nārāyaṇapāla and annexed considerable parts of the Pāla dominions to his empire. In the time of the next ruler, Mahendrapāla, the empire included parts of North Bengal.

During the reign of Mihira Bhoja, the Rāshṭrakūṭas, the inveterate enemies of Kanauj, were pre-occupied with troubled conditions in their own realm. And with occasional reverses, the armies of Bhoja and his allies pressed continually southwards till they dominated the whole of what is modern Gujarāt.

A Turkish Shāhiya family ruled in Kābul for a long time. The last king of this dynasty, Lagatūrmān, was overthrown by his Brāhmaṇa minister, Kallar or Lallīya Shāhi. He was possibly supported by Mihira Bhoja. Lallīya, however, lost Kābul to the Ṣaffārid Ya'qūb ibn Layth in A.D. 870 and transferred his capital to Udabhāṇḍa, on Sindhu near Attock.

The Arab conquest of Sindh was no more than 'a mere episode in the history of India which affected only a fringe of that vast country'. Within a year of Bhoja's accession, 'Imrān ibn-Mūsa, the Arab Governor of Sindh, tried to extend his hold over the adjoining territory. The Arabs, however, were driven out of Kutch between A.D. 833 and 842. A few years later, they lost the best part of Sindh.

Two petty principalities only remained to the Arabs of which Multān and al-Mansurah were the capitals. The Hindus, who had been forcibly converted to Islam, went back to their ancestral fold. Balādhurī says that in the time of al-Hākim ibn-'Awānah, "the people of al-Hind apostatised with the exception of the inhabitants of Qaṣṣah. A place of refuge to which the Moslems might flee was not to be found, so he built on the further side of the lake, where it borders on al-Hind, a city which he named al-Maḥfūzah (the guarded), establishing it as a place of refuge for them, where they should be secure and making it a capital."

Sulaimān who visited India in A.D. 851 refers to Bhoja in vivid terms. "Among them is the king of Jurz (Gurjara). This king maintains numerous forces and no other Indian prince has so fine a cavalry. He is unfriendly to the Arabs, still he acknowledges that the king of the Arabs is the greatest of kings. Among the princes of India there is no greater foe of the Muhammadan faith than he. His territories form a tongue of land (Saurāshṭra?). He has great riches, and his camels and horses are numerous. Exchanges are carried on in his state with silver (and gold) in dust, and there are said to be mines (of these metals) in the country. There is no country in India more safe from robbers."

In A.D. 916, Abū Zaid, while completing the *Silsilat-ut Tawārīkh* of Sulaimān, also attests to the excellent social conditions in India. "These observations", he says, "are especially applicable to Kanauj, a large country forming the empire of Jurz."

Al-Mas'udī of Baghdād, who visited India more than once between A.D. 900 and 940, refers to the Bauūra as 'the lord of the city of Kanauj' and as 'one of the kings of Sindh'. "He has large armies in garrisons on the north and on the south, on the east and on the west; for, he is surrounded on all sides by warlike kings. . . . Bauūra, who is the king of Kanauj, is an enemy of the Balharā (Vallabha Rāja, the title of Rāshṭrakūṭa emperors), the king of India." He adds: Bauūra, the king of Kanauj, "has four armies, according to the four quarters of the wind. Each of them numbers 700,000 or 900,000 men. The army of the north was against the prince of Mūltān, and with the Musulmans, his subjects, on the frontier. The army of the south fights against the Balharā, king of Mānkīr (Mānyakheṭa)." According to him, Balharā is at war with Jurz, "a king who is rich in horses and camels, and has a large army."

Sindh was evidently rescued by Mihira Bhoja. for, according to Mas'ūdī, the Indus ran right through one of the cities within the kingdom of Jurz (Gurjara).

The last known date of Bhoja is A.D. 882; possibly, he died in A.D. 888.

At the time of his death, the banner of the Ikshvāku Gurjareśvaras flew over an empire larger than those of the Guptas and Śrī Harsha. It comprised north India from the Himālayas to a little beyond the Narmadā, from East Punjāb and Sindh to Bengal. South was quiescent. The Pālas were no longer a power. The Arabs on the north-west frontier were kept at bay; Sindh had been wrested from them. Madhyadeśa was at the height of its power.

Bhoja, unlike ancient chakravartīs, did not rest content by establishing an evanescent military supremacy. His empire was built on the strength of regularly paid standing armies, the loyalty of his hierarchs and, it appears, the support of popular enthusiasm. Considerable parts of his empire were governed directly from Kanauj. What he conquered he consolidated as well.

IV

The Hūṇa incursions had a devastating effect. The Classical Age lost its vitality. The tottering Gupta Empire was dissolved. Its hierarchs were left with little cohesion and less vigour. The race of the Kshatriyas of Madhyadeśa, who formed its martial backbone, lost their vigour; perhaps it paid a heavy price in blood during the last heroic efforts it put forward to drive out the Hūṇas.

Vast social and cultural changes followed. *Varṇāśrama-dharma*, instead of being a social organisation of three higher castes more or less homogeneous in culture and traditions, became rigid. Intermarriages between the castes came to be looked upon with disfavour. Instead of being associated with the masses as its natural leaders, the Brāhmaṇas and the Kshatriyas became dominant minorities.

In the South, the Brāhmaṇas, from the beginning, were a dominant minority. Their vast influence imposed the Smṛiti pattern of social life there but in a form different from North India. In the South the dialects were alien in structure and vocabulary to Sanskrit. Sanskrit, therefore, from the beginning, was the language of the learned only influencing the development of the dialects.

Naturally Sanskrit, though still a powerful integrating force, instead of being the language of the educated throughout the land, developed a learned character, removed still further from the spoken dialects even in the North.

Dharma-śāstras, as the source of the fundamental law in the country, were looked upon as sacred and unifying factors. A new Śaivism had, through its strength derived from its popular contacts and beliefs, become the symbol of national resurgence. Āryāvarta consciousness, which related *dharma* to India as a whole, also continued as an effective group sentiment, particularly in north India.

The Age of Imperial Kanauj saw a vast religious and cultural resurgence in the country, of which the Purāṇas were the gospels. It harmonised beliefs and practices of most of the cults which accepted as the final source, also Buddhism. The temple architecture, which began with the majestic Kailāsa of Ellora and developed into the exquisite beauty of Chandella Dhaṅga's Śiva temple at Khajurāho, was its symbol. The cult of *tīrthas* as a fundamental institution of religio-social significance strengthened the unity of India, carrying forward the consciousness that Āryāvarta was the inviolate land of *dharma*. The sweeping movement of the spirit was led by Śaṅkarāchārya, the prophet of the Age and the intellectual architect of ages to come.

It was an age of catholicity. The different creeds joined hands to respect each other. The gods of differing cults were all worshipped; Śiva was worshipped with his whole family, and so were the Trimūrtis, the Pañchāyatana and the Mātṛikās. The kings generally patronised all religions and different rulers of the same dynasty are known to belong to different religious persuasions. Even the Arab traders were found happily settled in some parts of the country.

Though the Pāla Kings were great patrons of Buddhism, Buddhism was on the decline since the days of Harshavardhana. Its disappearance from India during this period was hastened by the growing unpopularity of the Tāntrik practices which it had adopted; by the Puranic pantheon accepting Buddha as an *avatāra* of Vishṇu and adopting several of its practices and beliefs; above all, by the evangelical triumphs of Śaṅkarāchārya.

The Pratīhāra emperors formed the spearhead of this religio-cultural upsurge. Some of them, like Mihira Bhoja, worshipped Bhagavatī as their guardian deity; others Vishṇu and Śiva. They were of the people and did not stand away from their hopes, aspirations and traditions. Like the Gupta Emperors, they received the full co-operation of the Brāhmaṇas, who, through their intellectual achievements and religious and social influence, could maintain a sense of identity between the dominant minorities and the people.

The ruling dynasties of Gurjaradeśa also maintained the tradition of being the protectors of *dharma*. They did not treat the old social order with contempt, nor did they deprive it of its inherent tenacity by imposing unfamiliar lines of development; in the result, they strengthened it. While they led the country to progress, they drew upon the social and spiritual energy of the people.

The reciters of the Purāṇas became as powerful, if not more, as Brāhmaṇas specialising in ritualism, philosophy, or literature. Particularly the Brāhmaṇas of Kānyakubja played a great role during this period. Even today after a thousand years, they are found all over Northern India. The Kulīna Brāhmaṇas of Bengal, for instance, and the Anavil Brāhmaṇas of South Gujarāt both claim their descent from the Brāhmaṇas of Kānyakubja.

An illustration of the prevailing Puranic atmosphere in royal courts is furnished by the Gwālior-*praśasti* of Mihira Bhoja composed by the poet Bālāditya on the occasion of the construction of a temple of Vishṇu. The whole poem pulsates with the fervour of a living belief. Manu, Ikshvāku, Kakutstha and Pṛithu provide the background. The primeval Nārāyaṇa is born twice, as Nāgabhaṭa I, and again as Nāgabhaṭa II, descended from Lakshmana the son of Daśaratha of the line.

The *praśasti* begins with an invocation to Vishṇu, to whom the temple is also dedicated, as the destroyer of the demon Naraka, the embodiment of evil.

The Gurjareśvaras, if the *praśasti* tells the truth, were cultured. Each possessed a distinct personality. Nāgabhaṭa I was a warrior; Kakkuka had a keen sense of humour; Vatsarāja was compassionate, generous and of flawless conduct. Nāgabhaṭa II, short and modest, was of resistless energy. He was virtuous, and worked for the welfare of the people and performed many sacrifices. He possessed *ātmavaibhava*, true greatness of soul. Rāmabhadra was brave and virtuous, a pure soul, opposed to worldliness and a defender of the faith.

But Bhoja was the greatest of all. Famous as he was, he was always unperturbed. Though an adept in rooting out evil, and wooed by Lakshmī, the guardian goddess of sovereignty, he was untainted by arrogance, and spotless in character. He was an ardent and unmatched administrator and a receptacle of pleasant and sweet words. When Brahmā himself wanted to discover another such man, whom else could he find but Śrī Rāmachandra himself?

So that his life may extend beyond the ordinary span everyone desired to serve him; the ascetics in return for his protection; the preceptors from affection, the servants from devotion; his many foes out of policy; all men in the interest of their own well-being and livelihood. And he was as worthy a recipient of these offerings as the Creator Himself.

Men of intellect, of honesty and of virtuous deeds helped to increase his prosperity, while enemies were scorched by the flame of his anger. The oceans were guarded by his valour. Like unto Kārttikeya, the god of war, he was of unbounded energy and the Earth waited upon him to hear her fate from his lips.

Thus, Bālāditya the poet sings of Bhojadeva with the vanity of the poet. He expresses the hope that his *praśasti* would last till the end of Creation. His prayer was granted. The *praśasti* will last till the end of time and through it Mihira Bhoja will live down the ages.

Mihira Bhoja was not merely a Caesar, nor a pontiff, as were imperators of Rome and Byzantium. He was a conqueror and a great emperor. He was the protector of *dharma.* He was an Ikshvāku, a family in which God Himself had chosen to be born.

Āryāvarta was thus a pyramid of culture. At its apex stood Vishṇu Himself, the upholder of an evenly ordered realm, the protector of happy and well-ordered governance. That is why Bhoja bore the epithet *'Ādi Varāha'.*

V

The Puranic Renaissance gave added sanctity to the Dharmaśāstras. In this Age, learning tended more and more to live on the past, the commentators and the writers of digests took the place of the law-givers. Of them, the most outstanding was Medhātithi, who wrote a commentary on the *Manu-smṛiti.*

The spirit of the Age found expression in relating *Varṇāśramadharma* which was dynamic to the virile concept of Āryāvarta. Āryāvarta, says Medhātithi, is not limited to geographical boundaries; it is not confined to the four corners of India; it is so called because the *mlechchhas*, though they frequently invade the country, are not able to abide in it.

If any prince of good character belonging to the Kshatriya or other castes subdues the *mlechchhas* and reduces them to the position of *chaṇḍālas,* as in Āryāvarta, and introduces *chāturvarṇya* in the conquered country, it would be fit for Vedic sacrifices to be performed. No sanctity attaches to Brahmāvarta as such; it would be *mlechchhadeśa* if the *mlechchhas* subjugated it and lived there.

Impurity does not attach to the land, but to the people. *Varṇāśrama-dharma* is a dynamic and expansive social organisation to be maintained and spread. Āryāvarta extended wherever the *dharma* is enforced and maintained.

This concept did not remain a mere theory; it was in active operation. The culture having come to dominate India was on a march to wider expansion. Indians crossed the frontiers and established kingdoms, carrying religious, literary and cultural traditions with them to far-off lands. In this way came into existence the Śailendra Empire in Java, Sumatra and Malay Peninsula (c. A.D. 778-13th century); the dynasty of Pāṇḍuraṅga (c. A.D. 757-860) and the Bhṛigu dynasty (c. A.D. 860-985) in Champā, the dynasties of Jaya-varman II (A.D. 802-877) and Indra-varman (c. A.D. 877-1001) in Kambuja, the dynasty of Sañjaya (c. A.D. 732-928) in Central Java, and the dynasty of Siṇḍok (c. A.D. 929-1007) in Eastern Java.

This dynamic outlook was followed in actual practice in India as would appear from the Arab chroniclers and the *Devala-smṛiti*. Even though converted to Islam, Brāhmaṇas, Kshatriyas, Vaiśyas and Śūdras, who had been forced to do forbidden or unclean things, could be reclaimed by purification. A woman carried away by the *mlechchhas* could become pure by abstention from food and sexual intercourse for three nights.

A king, says Medhātithi, has responsibility to maintain *dharma* in the land. He is under a paramount duty to resist foreign invasion at all cost. There can be no compromise with the invader: if his realm is invaded and its people massacred, the king must die fighting.

For a king, the law-giver says, fame should have no meaning; what matters is securing the submission of other kings. An enemy is an enemy; he should not be given time to prepare for war; his difficulties are no concern to a king. The best time for attack is when the king feels confident of his own strength; when the morale of his forces is high; when the crop in his country is plentiful; when the subjects of the enemy are in indifferent circumstances or are to be alienated.

Once a war is declared, there should be no weakening; no consideration for the enemy's weakness; no regard for consistency, for friend or foe. In pursuit of his aim he should, if necessary, dismiss or punish his minister.

Once an enemy is conquered, the form in which he submits is immaterial; what matters is effective surrender. A victorious king should take care to destroy his enemies, but he should penalise only the wicked and the treacherous. He should uproot the weeds, but spare, wherever possible, the inhabitants of the conquered realm.

It is not easy to consolidate gains after victory, says the political sage. The learned and the pious of the conquered country should be honoured; restraints on the subjects should be removed; the poor and ailing should be treated with kindness; sports and rejoicings should be initiated. Justice and sound finance must be restored. Wise methods of governance should be introduced. Above all, a policy of non-interference in the life of the people should be adopted.

Medhātithi lays stress on sound internal administration. Ambassadors should guard against the lure of women. The king should not part with the portfolios of finance and home to anyone and in making war and peace his should be the final voice. Services—both civil and military—should be paid their salaries regularly. Irrigation and other works must be carried out to make people independent of rains. On a small holding the taxes should be light; heavier taxes should be borne by larger profits. Then comes the dictum of a man who knows human nature well. "It is neither possible nor desirable to prohibit drinking, gambling or hunting absolutely".

The king owes his position to no divine sanction but to the wishes of the people. He is only an instrument of maintaining *daṇḍa* or sovereignty which is based on the fundamental law propounded by the Dharma-śāstras. This law is above the king and is inalienable; nor should custom be permitted to override it. The king must submit to the ordinances of the *Smṛitis*. At the same time Dharma-śāstras are not to be rigidly interpreted. Equity is an equal authority with the Vedas, *Smṛitis* and *āchāra* for determining the right principle of law. "Satisfaction of the learned and the virtuous," says Medhātithi, "is a vital test; it may find what appears to be *dharma* as *adharma* and what appears *adharma* as *dharma*. When those learned in the Vedas feel that a thing is pure, it is to be deemed as pure".

VI

Varṇāśrama-dharma of Medhātithi is a dynamic world force and not a static social order. A Brāhmaṇa can marry the daughter of a Kshatriya or a Vaiśya. An adopted son may be of a caste other than the father's; a Brāhmaṇa can adopt even a Kshatriya boy. A

Kshatriya and a Vaiśya have the right to recite the *Gāyatrī-mantra*. Brāhmaṇahood is not acquired by birth alone.

A Śūdra has the right to offer oblations to the fire, or to perform religious sacrifices, except the *Vaivāhika* fire at marriage. He may not be competent to pronounce judgment according to the *Smṛitis*, but he can be one of the *sabhyas* in a court of justice. If any *Smṛiti*, says Medhātithi, takes away the right of a Śūdra or lays down any prohibition, the injunction should be very strictly interpreted, and its scope is not to be enlarged by inferences from other texts. Those *smṛitis*, which are in favour of the Sūdras, should, therefore, be enforced. But these dicta are more in the nature of a protest against the growing rigidity of the social order and cannot be read as reflecting universal practice.

Medhātithi accords to women a position in refreshing contrast to some of the later authorities who wrote for the succeeding Era of Resistance. Women can perform all *saṁskāras;* only they should not recite Vedic *mantras*. At a partition an unmarried sister should be given one-fourth share of the dividing brothers.

A wife is obtained from God, not secured like cattle or gold, in the market; a husband, therefore, has no ownership over his wife. Before the wife could be compelled by the husband to serve him, he must have the necessary qualifications, among others, a loving attitude towards her. Medhātithi condemns the dictum of Manu that one is to protect oneself even at the cost of one's wife; even princes should not forsake their wives, says he. The practice of *Satī*, according to Medhātithi, is nothing but suicide, and as such, it is not permissible.

The position which the women occupied during this age, is also evidenced by other contemporary sources. The general level of their culture was high. Śīlamahādevī, wife of the Rāshṭrakūṭa Emperor, Dhruva, described as *parameśvarī* and *paramabhaṭṭārikā*, probably ruled jointly with her husband. She enjoyed the privilege of granting large gifts without her husband's consent. Several queens of the Kara dynasty ruled in Orissa. Sugandhā and Diddā of Kāshmir administered extensive kingdoms as dowager queens. There were learned women as well as women administrators. Avantisundarī, the wife of the poet Rājaśekhara, was an exceptionally accomplished woman. The poet quotes her thrice in the *Kāvyamīmāṁsā*. His *Karpūramañjarī* was produced at her request and Hemachandra quotes three of her Prakrit stanzas. Ubhayabhāratī or Sarasvatī, wife of Maṇḍanamiśra, who acted as an arbitrator in her husband's disputations with Śaṅkarāchārya, was a learned scholar herself.

We have a glimpse of the social conditions of imperial Kanauj in the works of Rājaśekhara, an ardent lover of Kanauj. Its women did not lag behind men in point of education. According to the poet, there were several poetesses in Kanauj. "Culture is connected with the soul and not with the sex" says the poet. The poet had met princesses and poetesses, daughters of prime ministers, courtesans and wives of court jestors who were well versed in science.

The dress worn by the ladies of the capital was adorable. "Women of other countries", says the poet, "should study the ways in which the ladies of Mahodaya dress and bedeck themselves, braid their hair and speak their words".

The women of Lāṭa were noted for their beauty and elegance. At the same time, it would be untrue to accept the position of women as portrayed by Rājaśekhara as reflecting the generally prevailing conditions under which women lived, for whatever it was, it was distinctly better than the position to which they were reduced under the painful pressure of the Era of Resistance.

VII

In the field of literature this Age cannot be compared with the Classical Age with its old masters like Kālidāsa and Bhavabhūti. Under the influence of the rhetoricians external features of literature rather than literary beauty came into fashion; scholarship replaced poetic fancy; Sanskrit acquired a learned character.

Even kings, as we find from some notable instances, were highly educated; several of them were accomplished poets. Most of them were patrons of learning as well as authors. All branches of literature were assiduously cultivated.

There were *kāvyas* in plenty; epics, romances and *champūs* were composed in large numbers. Lexicography was cultivated; so were grammar, poetics, metrics and rhetorics. Ānandavardhana wrote his famous *Dhvanyāloka,* propounding his famous theory of *Dhvani.* The favourite literary form of the Age was the Drama, though only one classical specimen survives in Viśākhadatta's *Mudrārākshasa.*

Literary activity in Sanskrit abounded even in the South. *Ṛigarthadīpikā* by Veṅkaṭa Mādhava, in the reign of the Choḷa king Parāntaka I, is one of the earliest of its kind in Sanskrit literature.

Śaktibhadra contributed the drama *Āścharyachūḍāmaṇi*, the first Sanskrit drama to be composed in the south, as known so far.

Literature was also cultivated in Prakrit, Haribhadra being the greatest master of the period. There was a vast non-canonical literature in Pāli and in Apabhraṁśa in which the works of several eminent Jain writers like Dhanapāla, Pushpadanta, Kanakāmara, Padmakīrti and Svayambhū have survived. During this period, several works of great value were composed in Kannaḍa and Tamil, forming landmarks in the development of these languages.

Philosophic literature was widely cultivated by the Bauddhas, the Jains and the Brāhmaṇas. Of them all, Śaṅkarāchārya was the greatest. He provided a philosophic theory which undermined the barren ritualism of the Mīmāṁsakas as well as the decadent Mahāyāna Buddhism and Jainism. He stood for monism; preached the superiority of *saṁnyāsa* over ritualism. He purged many religious beliefs of their grossness. He was also a practical reformer. His organizational work, which brought cults, practices and rituals under the direction of the four great Maṭhas which he founded and which stood for his Vedāntic monism, restored the cultural unity of the land. He also reorganized the monastic orders and infused a nobler sense of mission in them.

The *Bhāgavata Purāṇa* was the culminating point of the strong theistic movement started by the Āḻvārs and Nāyanārs in the South. It became the gospel of *bhakti*, the intense devotional ecstasy of the Āḻvārs as well as the teachings of *Bhagavadgītā*. Its deep emotion and creative beauty saved the soul of India duing the following Era of Resistance.

The last literary phase of the Age is represented by Rājaśekhara, who lived in the reign of Mihira Bhoja, for he was the court poet and teacher of Mahendrapāla and Mahīpāla.

Rājaśekhara's works give us a vivid glimpse of himself and the time. The poet was born in the family of Yāyāvaras, a family of poets. Though a Brāhmaṇa, he married into a Chāhamāna family and his wife, Avantisundarī, was therefore a Kshatriya.

His *Bālarāmāyaṇa* was staged at the court of Mahendrapāla at Kanauj. *Bālabhārata* was staged at Kanauj after Mahīpāla completed his campaign against the Rāshṭrakūṭa emperor Indra III, in about A.D. 916. The poet thus describes his patron who was present in the audience—

"In the family of Raghu, there was born a glorious Mahīpāladeva, who lowered the heads of the Muralas; who destroyed the Mekalas; who drove out the Kaliṅgas; who destroyed Kuntalas as if with an axe; who forcibly seized the royalty of the Ramaṭhas".

Rājaśekhara's *Kāvya-mīmāṁsā* is a work of great value and gives glimpses of the life and literature of the times.

The poet was a much travelled man, and has some very interesting remarks to make about the manners and speech of the people of different parts of the country. The Magadhas and those living to the east of Banaras spoke Sanskrit well but Prakrit badly. A Gauḍa could not speak Prakrit properly; he should, therefore, either give up the attempt or improve his Prakrit. The Karṇāṭakas recited poetry proudly with a twang at the end of each sentence irrespective of sentiment, style or quality. The Draviḍas recited prose and poetry both in a musical way. The people of Saurāshṭra and Travaṇa spoke Sanskrit but mixed it with Apabhraṁśa to add beauty to their speech. Kāshmirians were good poets but their recital sounded like a mouthful of *gaḍuchi*.

Rājaśekhara had a partiality for Lāṭa (South Gujarāt). According to him, it was the 'crest of the earth'. Its people, however, hated Sanskrit, but spoke elegant Prakrit in a beautiful way. Its women were noted for their beauty and elegance of speech. Its poets possessed distinctive literary traits; and favoured the style called 'Lāṭī'. Humour was its speciality.

The people of the region enclosed by the Gaṅgā and the Yamunā, the centre of which was Kanauj, according to the poet, were the ornaments of the land. They liked new and elegant literary works. The composition of its poets was well constructed and their recitation was sweet like honey. To him the city was the centre of the universe; a sacred place; the home of the imperial Ikshvākus; a centre from where radiated power, fashion and culture.

The whole country, therefore, in this period, had a unity of culture. Sanskrit was the language of the cultured, spoken and understood among the educated throughout the country, but was most prevalent to the east of Banaras.

VIII

Mihira Bhoja was succeeded by his son Mahendrapāla, a fearless military genius, who extended the empire of Mihira Bhoja adding to it the Karnal district in the Punjāb, the Nepalese terrain and the Rājshāhi district of Bengal. In A.D. 910 he was succeeded by Mahīpāla who also, like his father, was educated by the poet Rājaśekhara.

Within a few years of Mahīpāla's coming to the throne of Kanauj, however, Indra III, the Rāshṭrakūṭa emperor, marched to the north and occupied Kanauj. But he suddenly died, possibly in battle, and his army withdrew precipitately to the South. Though the Rāshṭrakūṭa empire was already disintegrating in A.D. 940, Kṛishṇa III again re-appeared in the north, overran Mālava and Gurjaradeśa, occupied Kālañjara and gave a shattering blow to the Pratīhāra empire.

The two raids of the Rāshṭrakūṭas had unfortunate results for the whole of India. Madhyadeśa lay mauled and bleeding. The empire of the South tottered to a fall. The feudatories of both declared independence one after the other. The country was prostrate and defenceless, and the Āryāvarta Consciousness was submerged by parochial sovereignties.

Out of the chaos, two powerful feudatories carved out independent kingdoms: the Paramāras of Mālava and the Chandellas of Jejākabhukti. Kanauj, however, continued to remain the metropolis of culture, but its emperor was no more than a shadow of his former self.

By about A.D. 974 the Empire of the Rāshṭrakūṭas was taken over by the Chālukya king, Taila II, a feudatory. A bitter and long drawn out war ensued between Taila II and Paramāra Muñja of Mālava. Ultimately, Muñja was captured and killed between A.D. 995-997. Taila followed him soon after in A.D. 997-998.

In the fateful year A.D. 997 Abū-l-Qāsim Mahmūd, son of Sabuktigīn, captured Ghaznī, developed a marvellous striking power and turned his attention to India.

Ancient India ended. Mediaeval India began.

IX

My thanks are due to Dr. R. C. Majumdar, the General Editor, and Dr. A. D. Pusalker, the Assistant Editor, for their indefatigable and conscientious labours, and to the scholars who have supplied their learned contributions for this volume. I am specially indebted to the Associated Advertisers & Printers Ltd., Bombay, who have, in such a short time, seen the volume through the Press, and to the staff of the Bhavan and the Press who looked after the preparation and printing of this volume with care and zeal. It is difficult to express adequately the deep debt of gratitude to Shri G. D. Birla, the Chairman, and other members of the Board of the Krishnarpan Trust who have so liberally financed the preparation of these volumes.

CONTENTS

CHAPTER IV

EASTERN INDIA DURING THE PĀLA PERIOD

By R. C. MAJUMDAR

CHAPTER V

CENTRAL AND WESTERN INDIA

By D. C. GANGULY, M.A., PH.D. (LONDON),

Secretary, Victoria Memorial Hall, Calcutta

CHAPTER VI

THE DECCAN

By D. C. SIRCAR, M.A., PH.D.,

Superintendent for Epigraphy, Government of India, Ootacamund; formerly Lecturer in Ancient Indian History and Culture in the University of Calcutta

CHAPTER VII

SOUTH INDIA

By R. SATHIANATHAIER, M.A., L.T.,

Professor of History and Politics, Annamalai University.

APPENDIX

The Genealogy and Chronology of the Pallavas

By D. C. SIRCAR

CHAPTER VIII

CEYLON

By D. C. SIRCAR

CHAPTER IX
LANGUAGE AND LITERATURE
A. *Sanskrit*

By G. V. Devasthali, M.A., B.T., Ph.D.,
Professor of Sanskrit in the H.P.T. College, Nasik

By H. D. Velankar, M.A.,
Joint Director, Bharatiya Vidya Bhavan, Bombay

C. *Non-canonical Pāli Literature*

By A. D. Pusalker

D. *Apabhraṁśa Language and Literature*

By H. L. Jain, M.A., LL.B., D. Litt.,
Head of the Department of Sanskrit, Pali and Prakrit, Nagpur University

E. *Dravidian Languages and Literature*

By K. R. Srinivasa Iyengar, M.A., D. Litt.,
Professor and Head of the Department of English in Andhra University

CHAPTER X

POLITICAL THEORY, ADMINISTRATIVE ORGANISATION, LAW AND LEGAL INSTITUTIONS

By U. N. GHOSHAL, M.A., PH.D.,
Formerly Professor of History in the Presidency College, Calcutta

CHAPTER XI

RELIGION AND PHILOSOPHY

By R. C. MAJUMDAR

B. *Buddhism*

By NALINAKSHA DUTT, M.A., B.L., PH.D, D.LITT.,
Professor of Pāli in the University of Calcutta

C. *Jainism*

By A. D. PUSALKER

CHAPTER XII

SOCIAL CONDITIONS

By U. N. Ghoshal

CHAPTER XIII

ECONOMIC LIFE

By U. N. Ghoshal

CHAPTER XIV

COLONIAL AND CULTURAL EXPANSION

By R. C. Majumdar

PREFACE

By Dr. R. C. Majumdar
General Editor

The preceding volume closed with an account of the shortlived empires in Northern India founded by Harsha-vardhana, Yaśo-varman, and Lalitāditya. But although they failed in their efforts to build up a stable empire, the imperial tradition handed down by them bore rich fruit during the period covered by this volume. The middle of the eighth century A.D., which marks its commencement, is a great landmark in Indian history. It saw the rise of three great dynasties which were destined to play the imperial role with far greater success than any of the three individual heroes mentioned above.

Of these three great dynasties the Gurjara-Pratīhāras were the earliest, and the foundation of their power in Western India, shortly before A.D. 750, has been described in the preceding volume. The two other powers, which suddenly came into prominence about the same time, were the Pālas of Eastern India and the Rāshṭrakūṭas of the Deccan. The rivalry and struggle between these three great powers forms the dominant theme of history dealt with in this volume.

The city of Kanauj was raised to the dignity of an imperial capital by Harsha-vardhana. But though his empire collapsed with his death, the glamour of Kanauj was revived by Yaśovarman. During the period under review it formed the centre of attraction of all the three great powers, and they regarded its possession as a consummation to be devoutly wished for. It was finally chosen as the capital by the Gurjara-Pratīhāras. Under them it rose to be the finest city in the whole of India, and continued as such till the end of the period covered by this volume. This circumstance has suggested the name of this volume, *viz. The Age of Imperial Kanauj.* It is hardly necessary to add that this nomenclature is only to be taken in a general sense, and is not intended to cover the entire history dealt with in this volume. Indeed no title could be devised which fulfils this condition, and no apology is perhaps needed to name any particular volume after its dominant theme.

The period covered by this volume witnessed the rise and fall of three empires. The Pālas under Dharmapāla and Devapāla established a mighty empire, and they claimed allegiance of nearly the whole of Northern India. Then came the turn of the Pratīhāras who, under Bhoja and Mahendrapāla, brought under their direct administration a vast extent of territory, from the Kāthiāwād Peninsula in the west to Northern Bengal in the east. No such empire flourished in North India after the Guptas. For there is no doubt that the Gurjara-Pratīhāra Empire was more extensive, more durable, and had a more stable and organised administration than the empire of Harsha-vardhana. The detailed account of this empire in the present volume will show the erroneous, almost ludicrous, character of the notion that Harsha-vardhana was the last empire-builder in Northern India, to which reference has been made in the Preface to the preceding volume.

Both the Pālas and Pratīhāras felt the full brunt of the Rāshṭrakūṭa power. Although the Rāshṭrakūṭas ruled over the Deccan, they were fired by the ambition of conquering Northern India. They defeated the Pratīhāra rulers Vatsarāja and Nāgabhaṭa and the Pāla king Dharmapāla. Under Dhruva and his son Govinda III they proved to be the greatest military power in India, and while the former carried his victorious campaign as far as the *doab* between the Gaṅgā and the Yamunā, the latter overran the whole country up to the Himālayas. Even a century later, one of their successors sacked the imperial city of Kanauj, then at the heyday of its glory, and forced the Pratīhāra Emperor to fly for his life.

The Rāshṭrakūṭas also successfully fought with the Pallavas and other powers of the South Indian Peninsula, and advanced even as far as Rāmeśvaram. From the political point of view the Rāshṭrakūṭa Empire constitutes the most brilliant episode in the history of the ancient Deccan. No other power, south of the Vindhyas, played such a dominant role in the history of North India, until the age of the Marāṭhā Peshwās in the eighteenth century.

The Pratīhāras, though never a match for the Rāshṭrakūṭas, played a dominant role in North Indian politics. They stood as bulwark against the Muslims of the Sindhu valley. It has been asserted by the Muslim writers that the Pratīhāras were the greatest foes of the Muslims, and could easily defeat the latter; but whenever the Pratīhāras advanced, the Muslims threatened to destroy the famous image of the Sun-god in Multān, and the Pratīhāras immediately retreated. The Muslims thus took advantage of the religious feelings of the Hindu Pratīhāras in order to save themselves from impending ruin.

It appears that the danger of Muslim menace was not yet fully realised by the Pratīhāras. Otherwise they should not have been deterred by religious scruples from exterminating Muslim rule in

India—a feat which was easily within their power. The Rāshṭrakūṭas went one step further. They befriended the Muslims and gave them all facilities for settling in their territory. They even allowed Muslim settlements to build mosques and to be ruled by their own governors. Whatever we might think of the political wisdom of the Rāshṭrakūṭas, their attitude is undoubtedly a manifestation of that spirit of religious toleration, which characterised India but was rare in that age elsewhere in the world, and offered a strange contrast to the iconoclastic fury of the Muslims.

To the west of the Pratīhāras lay the kingdom of the Shāhiyas. Originally ruled over by the Turkish chiefs who claimed descent from Kanishka, it was usurped by a Brāhmaṇa minister, and the new ruling family came to be known as the Hindu Shāhiyas. They became very powerful and ruled over an extensive territory from the Hindu Kush to the East Punjāb.

Although the Muslims were checked in Sindh they never gave up the idea of pushing their conquests to India. The Caliphs made repeated attempts to conquer Kābul and Zābul. Zābul made a prolonged and stubborn resistance against Arab aggression for more than two hundred years, and was not finally subdued till A.D. 870. Kābul, which was conquered at the same time, regained independence, and formed a part of the Shāhiya kingdom. The heroic resistance of these two states against the greatest military power in the world has not yet received the recognition it deserves, and has therefore been treated in some detail.

Tre rise of Ghaznī, towards the close of the period under review, was likely to be a great peril to India, and the Hindu Shāhiyas, who guarded her frontiers, were engaged in deadly conflict with the rulers of this state. The struggle began towards the very end of the period covered by this volume, and continued beyond it. A detailed account of this conflict, which inflicted untold miseries upon India and paved the way for its final conquest by the Muslims, will therefore be given in the form of a continuous narrative in the next volume.

The end of the first millennium, with which this volume closes, was a turning point in the history of India. India was on the verge of a great political transformation to which the nearest precedent is furnished by the invasion of the Aryans about three thousand years earlier. But the external invasion was not the only factor of importance. The internal change was also a momentous one. The collapse of the Pratīhāra Empire brought into prominence new powers, known later under the collective name of "Rājputs", who played a dominant part in Indian history throughout the Mediaeval period. They constituted a definite break with the old, and ushered in a new age both in political and cultural history of India.

The close of the tenth century A.D. also saw the final exit of the two great powers, the Rāshṭrakūṭas and the Pallavas, from the arena of politics in the south. The Chālukyas re-established their power in the Deccan after more than two centuries, while the Choḷas, one of the three ancient peoples in the Tamil land, once more emerged as a great power after ousting the Pallavas. But the main activities of both these dynasties really commence after the end of the period under review, and their history will be treated in the next volume.

Generally speaking, the period is one of decline and decadence in all spheres of cultural activity. Buddhism and Jainism lost their dominant position, and became gradually confined to particular regions. The rise of Tāntrik cults brought corruption both in Buddhism and Brahmanical religion. Literature became less creative and more artificial. The pursuits of science were less active. The age of original Smṛitis was passing away, ushering in the age of the commentaries. It was easily taken for granted that the era of authoritative creation, in the fields of religion, philosophy, law, manners, and morals, was now definitely closed, and all that remained for the people was to understand the past and follow it as scrupulously as possible. Nevertheless Indian genius occasionally shone forth in a brilliant manner. In the fields of religion and philosophy the name of Śaṅkarāchārya occupies an honoured place. Although he wrote only commentaries to existing works, the views he propounded through them entitle him to be ranked as one of the greatest philosophers of the world. Similarly Medhātithi, the commentator of *Manu-saṁhitā,* occupies a high place among the legal luminaries of India.

In literature Viśākhadatta and Rājaśekhara are great names, though far inferior to Kālidāsa and Bhavabhūti. But the period saw the highest development in one branch of literature, *viz.* theory of poetics. It was the age of the great rhetoricians like Udbhaṭa, Vāmana, Rudraṭa, Ānanda-vardhana, Abhinavagupta and Kuntaka. This period also witnessed the growth of a new type in Sanskrit literature *viz.* Champū, i.e. *Kāvya* written both in prose and verse. It may also be mentioned that the general output of literature during this period was not inconsiderable.

In medicine, Mādhavakara brought to perfection the branch of pathology in his masterly work *Rugviniśchaya* which, for the first time in the history of Indian medicine, treats of all diseases together in one volume. The treatise, now known as *Charaka-saṁhitā,* was also the result of considerable revision and enlargement of the original work by Dṛiḍhabala during this period. Mention may also be made of *Nighaṇṭu* of Dhanvantari, the oldest medico-botanical dictionary that we have at present.

In the domain of art, there is a noticeable decline in sculpture and painting. But there is a great development in architecture. The two main types of temple architecture, known as Nāgara (North Indian) and Drāviḍa, definitely emerge during this period, but are not fully developed till the next. Further, it is not always easy to assign the temples and images belonging to the same style or school to the one or the other of these periods. We therefore thought that it would perhaps be more convenient to deal with the last phase of Hindu art, from A.D. 750 to 1300, in a single chapter in the next volume. This will enable the reader to follow the continuous development of the temple architecture and get a comprehensive idea of the Mediaeval Indian sculpture in all its local varieties from beginning to end. The omission of the Chapter on art in this volume is a departure from the general plan, but was decided upon on the above grounds. The period under review is noted for some remarkable monuments such as the monolith Kailāsa temple at Ellora cut out of a hill-side, a unique achievement without any parallel in the history of art.

The colonial and cultural activities of the Indians outside India form a brilliant chapter of Indian history during the period under review. To complete the account in respect of China and Tibet, the activities in these regions have been traced down to the middle of the eleventh century A.D.

The policy and principles of editing, referred to in the preceding volumes, remain unchanged. I take this opportunity of thanking the contributors for their sincere co-operation. Dr. Pusalker has, as usual, rendered most valuable services in preparing this volume, and I am deeply grateful to him. In conclusion I must place on record my thanks for the appreciative reviews of the preceding volumes in different journals.

LIST OF MAPS

ABBREVIATIONS

Abh. Rat.	*Abhidhānaratanamālā of Halāyudha.*
ABORI.	*Annals of the Bhandarkar Oriental Research Institute, Poona.*
Apar.	*Aparārka.*
Āp. Dh. Sū.	*Āpastamba Dharma-sūtra.*
AR.	*Rāshṭrakūṭas and their times, by A. S. Altekar.*
ARSIE.	*Annual Report of South Indian Epigraphy.*
ASC.	*Archaeological Survey of India, Reports by Sir Alexander Cunningham.*
ASI.	*Archaeological Survey of India, Annual Report.*
ĀSS.	*Ānandāśrama Sanskrit Series, Poona.*
ASWI.	*Archaeological Survey of Western India.*
AUS.	*Allahabad University Studies.*
Bāla.	*Bālarāmāyaṇa of Rājaśekhara.*
BEFEO.	*Bulletin de l'École Française d'Extrême-Orient, Hanoi.*
BG.	*Bombay Gazetteer.*
Bhav.	*Bhavisayattakahā of Dhanapāla.*
Bh. List.	*A List of Inscriptions of Northern India by D. R. Bhandarkar (Appendix to EI, XIX-XXIII).*
BI.	*Bibliotheca Indica, Calcutta.*
BKO.	*Outline of the History of the Bhañja Kings of Orissa, by R. C. Majumdar (DUS, III. 2.137-170).*
BSOS.	*Bulletin of the School of Oriental Studies, London.*
BSS.	*Bombay Sanskrit Series.*
Bu-ston.	*History of Buddhism, by Bu-ston. Eng. trans by E. Obermiller. Heidelberg, 1932.*
BV.	*Bhāratīya Vidyā, Bombay.*
CCIM.	*Catalogue of the Coins in the Indian Museum, Calcutta.*
CII.	*Corpus Inscriptionum Indicarum.*
CP.	*Copper-plate.*
CW	*Collected Works of R. G. Bhandarkar. 4 vols. Poona, 1927-33.*
DHI.	*Development of Hindu Iconography, by J. N. Banerjea. Calcutta, 1942.*
DHNI.	*Dynastic History of Northern India, by H. C. Ray. 2 vols. Calcutta, 1931, 1936.*
DKA.	*Dynasties of the Kali Age, by F. E. Pargiter. Oxford, 1913.*
DLP Series.	*Sheth Devchand Lalbhai Jaina Pustakoddhara Series, Bombay.*
DUS.	*Dacca University Studies.*
Dyn. Kan.	*Dynasties of the Kanarese Districts, by J. F. Fleet.*
EC.	*Epigraphia Carnatica.*

EHI.	*Elements of Hindu Iconography*, by T. A. Gopinatha Rao. 2 vols. Madras, 1914-1916.
EI.	*Epigraphia Indica.*
EISMS.	*Eastern Indian School of Medieval Sculpture*, by R. D. Banerji.
ERE.	*Encyclopaedia of Religion and Ethics.* Ed. by J. Hastings.
Ferrand.	*Relations de voyages et Textes Géographiques Arabes, Persans et Turks—Relatifs a l' Extrême-Orient, du VIIIe au XVIIIe siècles.*, 2 vols. Paris, 1913-14.
Gaut.	*Gautama Dharma-śāstra.*
GIL.	*Geschichte der Indischen Literatur*, by M. Winternitz. 3 vols. Leipzig, 1905, 1909, 1920.
GOS.	*Gaekwad's Oriental Series*, Baroda.
GSAI.	*Giornale della Società Asiatica Italiana.*
HAL.	*History of Alaṁkāra Literature*, by P. V. Kane, Bombay, 1923.
HBR.	*History of Bengal.* Vol. I. Edited by R. C. Majumdar. Dacca, 1943.
HCSL.	*History of Classical Sanskrit Literature*, by M. Krishnamachariar. Madras, 1937.
HIED.	*History of India as told by its own historians*, Ed. by H. M. Elliot and John Dowson.
HIL.	*History of Indian Literature*, by M. Winternitz. Eng. trans. by Mrs. S. Ketkar. Calcutta University Press.
HISI.	*Historical Inscriptions of South India*, by R. B. Sewell.
Hir. Gṛ. Sū.	*Hiraṇyakeśī Gṛihya-sūtra.*
Hodivala.	*Studies in Indo-Muslim History*, by S. H. Hodivala.
HOS.	*Harvard Oriental Series.*
HSL.	*History of Sanskrit Literature.*
IA.	*Indian Antiquary*, Bombay.
IC.	*Indian Culture*, Calcutta.
ID.	*Das indische Drama*, by Sten Konow. Berlin, 1920.
IHQ.	*Indian Historical Quarterly*, Calcutta.
IS.	*Indische Studien.* Ed. by A. Weber.
JA.	*Journal Asiatique*, Paris.
JAHRS.	*Journal of the Andhra Historical Research Society*, Rajahmundry.
JAOS.	*Journal of the American Oriental Society.*
JASB.	*Journal of the Asiatic Society of Bengal*, Calcutta.
JAS,L.	*Journal of the Asiatic Society, Letters.* Calcutta.
JBBRAS.	*Journal of the Bombay Branch of the Royal Asiatic Society*, Bombay.
JBHS.	*Journal of the Bombay Historical Society.*
JBORS.	*Journal of the Bihar and Orissa Research Society*, Patna.
JBRS.	*Journal of the Bihar Research Society*, Patna.

JDL.	*Journal of the Department of Letters, Calcutta University.*
JDPS.	*Jaina Dharma Prasāraka Sabhā, Bhavnagar.*
JGJRI.	*Journal of the Ganganath Jha Research Institute, Allahabad.*
JIH.	*Journal of Indian History, Madras.*
JISOA.	*Journal of the Indian Society of Oriental Art, Calcutta.*
JKHRS.	*Journal of the Kalinga Historical Research Society, Balangir.*
JOI.	*Journal of the Oriental Institute, Baroda.*
JOR.	*Journal of Oriental Research, Madras.*
JPTS.	*Journal of the Pali Text Society.*
JRAS.	*Journal of the Royal Asiatic Society of Great Britain and Ireland, London.*
JRASB, L.	*Journal of the Royal Asiatic Society of Bengal, Letters. Calcutta.*
JUB.	*Journal of the University of Bombay.*
Kar.	*Karpūramañjarī of Rājaśekhara.*
Kāv.	*Kāvyamīmāṁsā of Rājaśekhara.*
KHDS.	*History of Dharma-śāstra, by P. V. Kane.*
KM.	*Kāvyamālā. NSP. Bombay.*
KSS.	*Kāmarūpa-śāsanāvali.*
Kuṭṭ.	*Kuṭṭanīmatam of Dāmodaragupta.*
List.	*See "Bh. List" above.*
Manu.	*Manu-smṛiti.*
MAR.	*Mysore Archaeological Report.*
MASB.	*Memoirs of the Asiatic Society of Bengal.*
MASI.	*Memoirs of the Archaeological Survey of India.*
Mbh(B).	*Mahābhārata, Bombay Edition.*
Mbh(Cr. Ed).	*Mahābhārata, Critical Edition, published by the Bhandarkar Oriental Research Institute, Poona.*
M.C.C. Magazine.	*Madras Christian College Magazine.*
MDJG.	*Māṇikachandra Digambara Jaina Granthamālā.*
Mrichchh.	*Mṛichchhakaṭika of Śūdraka.*
NIA.	*New Indian Antiquary, Bombay.*
NIS.	*New Imperial Series.*
NPP.	*Nāgarī Prachāriṇī Patrikā (in Hindi), Banaras.*
N.S. or NS.	*New Series.*
NSP.	*Nirṇaya-sāgara Press, Bombay.*
NUJ.	*Nagpur University Journal.*
Num. Chron.	*Numismatic Chronicle.*
OC.	*Transactions (Verhandlungen, Actes) of International Congress of Orientalists.*
OHRJ.	*Orissa Historical Research Journal. Bhubaneswar.*
ORLI.	*Outline of the Religious Literature of India. by J. N. Farquhar.*
Pag-sam-jon-zang.	*Ed. S. C. Das, Calcutta, 1908.*
Par Mādh.	*Parāśara-Mādhava (Comm. of Mādhavāchārya on Parāśara-smṛiti).*

PIHC.	*Proceedings of the Indian History Congress.*
PLC.	*Pali Literature of Ceylon,* by M. H. Bode London, 1909.
POC.	*Proceedings of the All-India Oriental Conference.*
P.S.	*Prākṛita-sarvasva of Mārkeṇḍeya.*
PTS.	*Pali Text Society, London.*
QJMS.	*Quarterly Journal of the Mythic Society, Bangalore.*
Rājat.	*Rājataraṅgiṇī of Kalhaṇa.*
Rati.	*Ratirahasya of Kokkoka.*
RT.	*Rājataraṅgiṇī of Kalhaṇa.*
SBE.	*Sacred Books of the East, Oxford.*
SBH.	*Sacred Books of the Hindus, Allahabad.*
Schiefner.	*Tāranātha. Geschichte des Buddhismus in Indien. German trans. by A. Schiefner.*
SD.	*Sanskrit Drama, by A. B. Keith. Oxford, 1924.*
SDar.	*Sāhitya-darpaṇa of Viśvanātha.*
Sel. Ins.	*Select Inscriptions bearing on Indian History and Civilization. Vol. I. By D. C. Sircar. Calcutta, 1942.*
SII.	*South Indian Inscriptions.*
SIS.	*Sino-Indian Studies, Calcutta.*
SJS.	*Singhi Jain Series.*
Sm. C.	*Smṛiti-chandrikā of Devaṇṇabhaṭṭa.*
SSG.	*Systems of Sanskrit Grammar, by S. K. Belvalkar. Poona, 1915.*
Tāranātha.	*See "Schiefner" above.*
TAS.	*Travancore Archaeological Series.*
THK.	*History of Kanauj, by R. S. Tripathi.*
TSS.	*Trivandrum Sanskrit Series.*
Upamiti.	*Upamitibhāvaprapañcha-kathā of Siddharshi.*
Vid.	*Viddhaśālabhañjikā of Rājaśekhara.*
Vish.	*Vishṇu-smṛiti.*
VRS.	*Varendra Research Society.*
VSS.	*Vizianagaram Sanskrit Series, Benares.*
Yāj.	*Yājñavalkya-smṛiti.*
ZDMG.	*Zeitschrift der Deutschen Morgenländischen Gesellschaft.*

CHAPTER I

THE RĀSHTRAKŪTA EMPIRE

We have already seen[1] how the Chālukya emperor was overthrown by one of his feudatories, Dantidurga, some time about A.D. 752. The family of the new ruler is known as Rāshṭrakūṭa. The origin of this name and the early history of the Rāshṭrakūṭas have been discussed above.[2] Dantidurga's family originally belonged to Laṭṭalūra situated in the Osmānābād District of the Hyderābād State, but it migrated to Ellichpur in Berār in c. A.D. 625, where it carved out for itself a small principality[3] and ruled as a feudatory of the Chālukya empire for several generations. The fortunes of the family began to rise during the reign of Dantidurga's father Indra I, who had married a princess of the Chālukya family.[4] Dantidurga, who is also sometimes referred to as Dantivarman, ascended the throne in c. A.D. 733.[5] He was able, ambitious, and sagacious; and managed to become the overlord of the Deccan in less than fifteen years.

1. DANTIDURGA

Two records of his reign, *viz.* the Samangad plates dated A.D. 754[6] and the undated Daśāvatāra cave inscription of Ellora[7] give a grandiloquent description of the triumphal career of Dantidurga. He is said to have fought on the banks of the Mahī, Mahānadī and Revā and won victories over Kāñchi, Kaliṅga, Kosala, Śrī-Śaila, Mālava, Lāṭa, and Ṭaṅka. He is also said to have made liberal rewards to various rulers at Ujjayinī and fixed his quarters in a Gurjara palace in that city. A later record[8] probably elaborates this when it says that Dantidurga performed *Hiraṇyagarbha* (or the Great Gift) at Ujjayinī in which "kings such as the Gurjara lord and others were made door-keepers". But his crowning act of glory was the overthrow of the Chālukya king, described in several records. According to contemporary records, he defeated with a small force the formidable Karṇāṭaka army and won victories over Vallabha, the lord of all kings. In later records he is credited with having wrested the supreme sovereignty from the Chālukyas[9] and "humbled the circle of proud kings from the Himālayas down to the limit of Setu" (*i.e.* Adam's Bridge).[10]

While these statements leave no doubt that Dantidurga was the real founder of the greatness of the family, it is difficult to reconstruct his history by arranging his victories in chronological sequence. It is probable that some of his victories were achieved while he was yet a feudatory of the Chālukyas, and on this basis we may provisionally reconstruct his history somewhat as follows:—

His first exploits were performed during the campaign organised by his feudal lord Vikramāditya II and the latter's Gujarāt feudatory Pulakeśin to repulse the Arab invasion. A sanguinary battle was fought near Navsāri in c. A.D. 738 in which the invaders were so completely overthrown that they never again dared to invade Gujarāt. The brunt of the battle was naturally borne by Pulakeśin and Dantidurga whose principalities lay in Gujarāt and Berār. The Chālukya emperor appreciated the heroism of his feudatories by conferring the titles of *Chālukyakulālaṁkāra* (the Ornament of the Chālukya family), *Pṛithvīvallabha* (the Lord of the Earth) and *Avanijanāśraya* (the Asylum of the People of the World) on Pulakeśin and those of *Pṛithvīvallabha* and *Khaḍgāvaloka* (one whose mere sight is as effective as sword) on Dantidurga.[11]

Dantidurga continued to be a loyal feudatory of Vikramāditya for some years more. He accompanied his Chālukya suzerain in his expedition against Kāñchī in c. A.D. 743 and shared the credit for the victory over the Pallavas.[12]

Dantidurga was ambitious; and he decided to take full advantage of the varied and valuable military experience he had gained in his campaigns in the north and south. When Vikramāditya II died in A.D. 747, he embarked upon a bold career of conquest, but took care to see that his annexations were, as far as possible, not at the cost of the Chālukya empire. He wiped out the Gurjara kingdom of Nāndīpurī (Nāndod) and appointed his nephew Karkka to rule over the region.[12a] Then he led an expedition into Mālwā; and proclaimed its conquest by performing *Hiraṇyagarbha-dāna* ceremony at its capital Ujjayinī. Next he proceeded against eastern Madhya Pradesh and brought it under his political influence. By c. A.D. 750 he had thus become the master of Central and Southern Gujarāt and the whole of Madhya Pradesh and Berār.

Kīrtivarman II, the Chālukya emperor, could now no longer ignore the rising power of his nominal feudatory and decided to challenge it. The armies of the two claimants to the overlordship of the Deccan probably met somewhere in Khāndesh and Dantidurga was victorious. As a result of this victory, he became the master of the whole of Mahārāshṭra by the end of A.D. 753. He now assumed full imperial titles *Mahārājādhirāja Parameśvara Paramabhaṭṭāraka*. He, however, did not survive his victory for long but died some time before A.D. 758. This is the earliest known date of his successor, his uncle Kṛishṇa I, who, we may presume, was a valued lieutenant of his ambitious nephew in his military conquests.[13]

2. KṚISHṆA I

Dantidurga had defeated Kīrtivarman, but had not extinguished his power. The Chālukya emperor retired to Karnātak and proceeded to reorganise his forces for a further trial of strength. The challenge was so successfully met by the new Rāshṭrakūṭa ruler that the Chālukya empire was wiped out of existence by c. A.D. 760. Kṛishṇa then proceeded against the Gaṅgas ruling in Mysore and occupied their capital Mānyapuram for some time. Later on he sent his son, the crown-prince Govinda, to invade the dominions of Vishṇuvardhana IV, the Chālukya king of Veṅgī, who being a ruler of a Chālukya branch was naturally hostile to the new power that had swept away the Chālukya supremacy from Western Deccan. The expedition was successful and, as a consequence, the whole of the former Hyderābād State was incorporated in the Rāshṭrakūṭa empire in c. 772. Śīlabhaṭṭārikā, a daughter of Vishṇuvardhana IV, is known to have been a queen of Dhruva, a younger brother of Govinda. Probably her marriage followed the conclusion of the peace.

Kṛishṇa I also defeated a king called Rāhappa, whose identity is uncertain. He brought under his sway southern Konkan and placed it in charge of Sanaphulla, the founder of the Śilāhāra family. The Bhandak plates prove that practically the whole of Marāṭhī-speaking part of Madhya Pradesh was under Kṛishṇa.

Kṛishṇa was great not only as conqueror but also as builder. The famous rock-cut Śiva temple at Ellora, which is justly regarded as a marvel of architecture, was constructed at his orders, and bears an eloquent testimony to the high level of skill attained by India in the arts of sculpture and architecture under the Rāshṭrakūṭa patronage. Kṛishṇa had the titles *Śubhatuṅga* and *Akāla-varsha.*

3. GOVINDA II AND DHRUVA[14]

Kṛishṇa I died about A.D. 773 and was succeeded by his eldest son Govinda II, *Prabhūtavarsha Vikramāvaloka.* He had been nominated as *yuvarāja* by his father and had distinguished himself on the battlefield by defeating Vishṇuvardhana IV of Veṅgī. He is also credited with some conquests after his accession; but he proved an utter failure as a ruler. Soon after his accession, he abandoned himself to a life of pleasure and debauchery and practically left the whole administration to his younger brother Dhruva. The latter took advantage of the situation to secure all power for himself. Govinda realised this and immediately removed Dhruva from the administration. Evidently it led to some confusion including a rebellion of feudatories and Dhruva made it an excuse for revolting openly against his brother. It has been stated in a record of the time of Dhruva that he proceeded to fight his brother, not so much to gain the throne for himself, as to prevent the danger of the Rāshṭrakūṭa family itself being ousted from the throne. Such excuses, however, should not be taken at their face value. In any case Govinda II refused to abdicate without resistance as he was urged to do. He sought help from the rulers of Kāñchī, Gaṅgavāḍī, Veṅgī and Mālwā. But Dhruva defeated his brother and usurped the throne before the other kings could come to Govinda's aid.

Dhruva must have ascended the throne before the end of A.D. 780. He assumed the titles *Nirupama Kali-Vallabha, Dhārāvarsha,* and *Śrī-Vallabha,* and is sometimes referred to as Dhora, a Prakrit form of Dhruva. Shortly after his accession, he proceeded to punish the kings who had supported his brother.

The Gaṅga king Śrīpurusha Muttarasa was defeated, his crown-prince Śivamāra was taken prisoner, and the whole of Gaṅgavāḍī was annexed to the Rāshṭrakūṭa empire, whose southern boundary was thus pushed to the Kāverī. The victor then proceeded against the Pallava ruler Dantivarman, who however conciliated him by offering an indemnity of elephants. The ruler of Veṅgī, Vishṇuvardhana IV, was also humbled and sued for peace.

These victories made Dhruva the undisputed overlord of the entire Deccan, but he was not satisfied with this achievement. He wanted to be the overlord of Northern India as well, and decided to make a bold bid to attain that position.[15]

Since the days of Harsha, Kanauj enjoyed the status of the premier city of Northern India, but Indrāyudha, who was ruling there at this time, was a mere titular emperor like Shah Alam II ruling at Delhi in the latter half of the eighteenth century. The Pālas of Bengal and the Gurjara Pratīhāras of Rājputāna were rising to prominence, and seeking to establish their own hegemony over Northern India by conquering Kanauj and making its nominal emperor a creature of their own. Vatsarāja, the Gurjara Pratīhāra ruler, first marched upon Kanauj and succeeded in occupying it. He, however, permitted Indrāyudha to rule as a puppet emperor under his protection as the Marāṭhās did with Shah Alam II towards the end of the eighteenth century. The success of Vatsarāja roused the jealousy of his Pāla rival Dharmapāla who challenged his power and marched into the Doāb, only to be defeated by Vatsarāja.

Dharmapāla, however, soon rallied his forces and proceeded to make a second bid for hegemony in the north. At this time when Dhruva had decided to try his luck as a third claimant to the kingdom of Kanauj in c. A.D. 786, the army of Dharmapāla was heading towards the Doāb and Vatsarāja was once again on the way to meet it.

Dhruva planned his northern expedition with great skill. He collected a strong force on the banks of the Narmadā and put his able and energetic sons Govinda and Indra in charge of the different sections. He could cross the Narmadā and occupy Mālava without much opposition, as the main army of Vatsarāja was in the Doāb. He then advanced towards Kanauj, and Vatsarāja had to withdraw his forces from the advanced position in the Doāb to meet this new danger from the south. The two armies met somewhere near Jhānsi, and the Deccan invader inflicted such a crushing defeat upon the forces of Vatsarāja that he had to fly to Rājputāna to take shelter in its sandy deserts. Flushed with this sensational victory, Dhruva decided to measure his strength with Dharmapāla as well, whose forces were hovering on the outskirts of the Doāb. The Goddess of Victory once more smiled on the Deccan emperor, and Dharmapāla had to flee from the battlefield leaving behind his white imperial umbrellas. The victor spent some weeks on the banks of the holy Gaṅgā and Yamunā and, as a memento of this sojourn, these famous rivers were incorporated in the Rāshṭrakūṭa Imperial banner.

Dhruva could not press home his victories by marching upon and occupying Kanauj. He was too far away from his base; he was also getting old and had to settle the problem of succession. He therefore returned to the south in c. A.D. 790, laden with rich booty.

At the close of Dhruva's reign the Rāshṭrakūṭa power had reached its zenith. The Gaṅga crown-prince was in the Rāshṭrakūṭa prison, and the Pallava king could save himself only by surrender; Vatsarāja had fled, and Dharmapāla had been overthrown. There was no power in the country to challenge the Rāshṭrakūṭa supremacy.

Dhruva had several sons, the names of four of whom are known. The eldest Stambha (or Kambha) Raṇāvaloka was the viceroy of Gaṅgavāḍī, and the other sons were also capable administrators. In order to prevent a struggle for succession after his death, Dhruva chose the third son Govinda as his successor. The latter was formally appointed as *yuvarāja* and invested with a *kaṇṭhikā* or necklace which was the insignia of the heir-apparent. But as the old emperor still apprehended trouble, he proposed to abdicate in favour of the heir-apparent. Though Govinda is said to have opposed this proposal, some records state that he was invested with the royal state by his father at a formal coronation. Unless we take these expressions to refer to his installation as a *yuvarāja*—though *rājādhirāja-parameśvaratā* would hardly bear that sense—we must conclude that in spite of Govinda's real or pretended opposition, Dhruva actually abdicated in favour of his son Govinda III who assumed the titles *Jagattuṅga, Prabhūtavarsha, Śrīvallabha, Janavallabha, Kīrtinārāyaṇa* and *Tribhuvanadhavala*.

According to an inscription of the time of Govinda III, Dhruva chose Govinda as his successor because he was the ablest and worthiest among his sons. Normally no great importance attaches to a statement like this, but the career of Govinda III fully justifies his father's choice if it was based upon any such consideration.

4. GOVINDA III

Govinda III ascended the throne in A.D. 793 and, as was expected, his accession did not go unchallenged. For a time Stambha kept quiet, but when he was assured of the support of a number of feudatories and neighbours, he broke out in open revolt against his brother. Govinda, however, quelled the rebellion of "twelve kings headed by Stambha" and took his brother prisoner. He, however, treated him leniently and, being convinced of his loyalty in future, Govinda took the magnanimous step of reinstating him in the Gaṅga viceroyalty. Throughout the rest of his life, Stambha remained loyal to his plighted word.

Śivamāra, the Gaṅga prince in the Rāshṭrakūṭa prison, had been released by Govinda soon after his accession, evidently to act as a check on Stambha's ambitions. Śivamāra, however, joined the side of Stambha, contrary to Govinda's expectations. When the two brothers became reconciled, they jointly marched against Gaṅgavāḍī, captured Śivamāra, and once again put him into prison. Next came the turn of the Pallava king Dantiga, who also was compelled to submit. Vishṇuvardhana IV of Veṅgī was the maternal grandfather of Govinda and so was not disposed to challenge his supremacy. When Govinda III thus became the undisputed overlord of the Deccan in c. A.D. 795, he decided to intervene in the political tangle of Northern India. Subsequent to the retirement of his father from the Gaṅgā valley in c. A.D. 790, considerable changes had taken place in the political situation. Dharmapāla recovered from his defeat earlier than Vatsarāja, and eventually succeeded in putting his own nominee Chakrāyudha on the Kanauj throne. Vatsarāja's successor Nāgabhaṭa II, however, soon turned the tables and reoccupied Kanauj after defeating Chakrāyudha and Dharmapāla. Such was the situation in the north on the eve of Govinda's invasion.

The northern expedition of Govinda was skilfully planned and boldly executed. Indra, the younger brother and loyal supporter of Govinda, was the viceroy of Gujarāt and Mālava; he was entrusted with the task of keeping watch over the Vindhyan passes in order to prevent Nāgabhaṭa from bursting into the Deccan, when the main Rāshṭrakūṭa army was away in the North. A number of detachments were kept in Central India to keep the local rulers in check and secure the lines of communication.

After taking these prudent precautions, Govinda marched into Northern India *via* Bhopāl and Jhānsi, Kanauj being his main objective. Nāgabhaṭa marched out to meet the invader. The two armies probably met in Bundelkhand. Victory once more favoured the southern army and Nāgabhaṭa fled to Rājputāna, leaving the Doāb at the mercy of the conqueror. Chakrāyudha, the puppet ruler of Kanauj, was quick to realise the futility of opposition and came forward with unconditional surrender. Govinda was satisfied and did not deem it necessary to march upon Kanauj. Dharmapāla also offered submission, as he too thought it politic and prudent to do so. He knew that Govinda could not long remain in Northern India and he was really grateful to him for having shattered the power of his mighty rival, Nāgabhaṭa II. Besides the powerful Gurjara-Pratīhāra and Pāla kings, other rulers of Northern India were also humbled by Govinda III. A detailed account of his conquests is given in the Sanjān plates of his son and successor which seem to describe the events in chronological order. Even at the risk of repetition, we may therefore sum up as follows the verses referring to the glorious conquests of Govinda III:—

After defeating Nāgabhaṭa and Chandragupta, a king whose identity is not certain, Govinda III uprooted other kings but afterwards reinstated them in their dominions. He then proceeded as far as the Himālaya mountains, and it was presumably on the way that Dharmapāla and Chakrāyudha submitted to him. He returned and "following again the bank of the Narmadā....and acquiring the Mālava country along with the Kosala, the Kaliṅga, the Vaṅga (or Veṅgi), the Ḍāhala, and the Oḍraka, that Vikrama (*i.e.* Govinda III) made his servants enjoy them". After having subjugated his enemies he returned to the banks of the Narmadā and established himself in a befitting manner in a capital city at the foot of the Vindhyas, performing pious deeds by constructing temples.

While he was encamped there, Mārāśarva or Śarva, the ruler of a small principality with his capital at Śrībhavana (modern Sarbhon in Broach District), submitted and presented to Govinda III valuable treasures which he had inherited from his ancestors.[16]

Govinda III stayed for some time in his capital and there his son and successor Amoghavarsha was born. It is somewhat curious that most of these details of the northern campaign are not found in the records of Govinda's reign and known only from an inscription recorded nearly 70 years later. But still, as they are substantially corroborated by contemporary records, we need not dismiss them as altogether fictitious though there may be some amount of exaggeration.

The date of the great northern campaign of Govinda III has been a subject of keen controversy among scholars. For a long time it was believed that it took place about A.D. 806 or 807. But it is now generally held that all these conquests were achieved before A.D. 802, most probably in A.D. 800.[17]

Vishṇuvardhana IV of Veṅgī died in A.D. 799 and was succeeded by his son Vijayāditya II. The new ruler challenged the Rāshṭrakūṭa supremacy, but Govinda defeated him and put his younger brother Bhīma Salukki on the Veṅgī throne in c. A.D. 802. The new ruler naturally enough became a loyal henchman of Govinda.

Taking advantage of Govinda's absence in the north, the Pallava, Pāṇḍya, Kerala and Gaṅga rulers formed a confederacy against him. Govinda marched against them with lightning speed and scattered them all before the end of A.D. 802. The occupation of Kāñchī by the Rāshṭrakūṭa forces created a tremor in the heart of the king of Ceylon, who tried to ingratiate himself into Govinda's favour by presenting him two statues, one of himself and the other of his premier. Govinda installed one of them in the Śiva temple at Kāñchī to serve as a column of victory to proclaim to the subjects of his enemy his great power and might.

Govinda III was undoubtedly the ablest of the Rāshṭrakūṭa emperors, unrivalled in courage, generalship, statesmanship, and martial exploits. His invincible armies had conquered all the territories between Kanauj and Cape Comorin, and Banaras and Broach. Veṅgī was governed by a nominee of his; and the power of the Dravidian kings in the extreme south was completely broken. Even the ruler of Ceylon was terrified into submission. Never again did the prestige of the Rāshṭrakūṭa empire rise so high.

5. ŚARVA OR AMOGHAVARSHA

Govinda III was succeeded by his son Śarva, better known as Amoghavarsha, in A.D. 814. He assumed the titles *Nripatuṅga*, *Mahārājashaṇḍa*, *Vīra-Nārāyaṇa*, and *Atiśaya-dhavala*. The new emperor was a boy of 13 or 14, and his father had arranged that Karkka, who had succeeded his father Indra as the viceroy of Gujarāt, should assume the reins of government during his minority.

The arrangement worked satisfactorily for two or three years, but a formidable revolt broke out in A.D. 817. It seems to have been led by the Veṅgī ruler Vijayāditya II who, though ousted from the throne by Govinda III, had subsequently managed to regain it.[18] A number of disgruntled officers, relations, and feudatories swelled the ranks of rebels; and they eventually gained the upper hand. The boy emperor had to flee and the Rāshṭrakūṭa power was for a time completely eclipsed about A.D. 818. Karkka, however, soon retrieved the situation and reinstated his ward upon the imperial throne some time before A.D. 821.

After spending five or six years in restoring order and authority in the different provinces of his empire, Amoghavarsha launched an attack on Vijayāditya of Veṅgī and inflicted a severe defeat upon him in c. A.D. 830. It appears that the Rāshṭrakūṭa forces were in occupation of Veṅgī for about a dozen years thereafter. The city was recaptured by Pāṇḍuraṅga, a general of Vijayāditya II, shortly before A.D. 845.

An almost continuous war was going on between the Rāshṭrakūṭas and the Gaṅgas during the first twenty years of the reign of Amoghavarsha. Eventually the latter were able to drive out the Rāshṭrakūṭa forces from the major part of their country. Amoghavarsha also did not make any serious effort to regain his ascendancy in that province. In c. A.D. 860 he married his daughter Chandrobalabbe to a Gaṅga prince named Būtuga, which put an end to the hostility between the two houses and ushered in an era of co-operation between them.

According to the Sirur plates the rulers of Aṅga, Vaṅga, Magadha, Mālava, and Veṅgī paid homage to him. The reference to the last is easily intelligible. As regards Mālava, it was a bone of contention between the Rāshṭrakūṭas and the Pratīhāras and. in spite of casual victories on either side, it ultimately passed into the hands of the latter. The first three countries in the list were included in the Pāla dominions, and it is interesting to note that the Pāla emperor Devapāla claims to have defeated the Draviḍa king who is usually identified with Amoghavarsha. It is probable. therefore, that hostilities occasionally broke out between these two: and that first Devapāla, and later Amoghavarsha had some success. It is difficult to believe that the latter actually invaded Aṅga and Vaṅga (Bengal and Bihār), though its possibility cannot be altogether ruled out.

Amoghavarsha built the city of Mānyakheṭa and established his capital there. This city is now represented by Mālkhed in the Hyderābād State, about 90 miles to the south-east of Sholapur. It is difficult to say where the capital was situated before this. Various suggestions have been made locating it at Mayūrakhiṇḍi or Morkhind (Nāsik District), Nāsik, Sooloobunjan near the Ellora caves, and Ellichpur. But there is no satisfactory evidence in support of any of these views.

The later part of the reign of Amoghavarsha was also full of rebellions. Even the crown-prince Kṛishṇa appears to have been involved in them. Baṅkeya, the great general of the king, who distinguished himself in the wars against the Gaṅgas, succeeded in crushing these rebellions. But the most unfortunate, and in some respects the most serious, rebellion was that of the Gujarāt Branch of the Rāshṭrakūṭas founded by Indra. When Amoghavarsha attained majority and assumed the reins of government in c. A.D. 821, his cousin Karkka, who was carrying on the regency administration, retired to Gujarāt as viceroy. His relations with Amoghavarsha continued to be cordial till his death in c. A.D. 830. He was succeeded by his son Dhruva I. The friendly relations between the two Rāshṭrakūṭa families terminated soon after the accession of Dhruva. Either Amoghavarsha was ungrateful or Dhruva became too overbearing, puffed up by the consciousness that it was his father who had won the throne for Amoghavarsha. Whatever the real cause, protracted hostilities raged between Amoghavarsha and his cousin which lasted for about 25 years. Dhruva I was eventually killed in this struggle and was succeeded by his son Akālavarsha in c. A.D. 845. The latter succeeded in winning back his throne, but the tables were soon turned against him when Baṅkeya, the famous general of Amoghavarsha, assumed the command of the imperial army. Eventually peace was concluded between the warring houses when Akālavarsha was succeeded by his son Dhruva II. By this time the Gurjara-Pratīhāra ruler Bhoja I had become very powerful and cherished designs to avenge the defeat inflicted upon his grandfather Nāgabhaṭa II by Govinda III, the father of Amoghavarsha I. Dhruva II could never hope to meet the Pratīhāra invasion single-handed, and Amoghavarsha had little chance to emerge victorious unless his viceroy in Gujarāt and Mālava gave him wholehearted support. The tragic and long-drawn war, therefore, came to an end in c. A.D. 860. The threatened Pratīhāra invasion did not materialise; there were only frontier skirmishes, and the Rāshṭrakūṭas were able to hold their own and confine the enemy to the other side of the Narmadā.

Amoghavarsha was no born military leader, but he was nevertheless able not only to reconquer his kingdom and establish peace and order but also to send an expedition against the Pālas. The arts of peace attracted him more than feats of war. He was a liberal patron of literature and his court was adorned by a number of famous Hindu and Jain writers such as Jinasena, the author of the *Ādipurāṇa*, Mahāvīrāchārya, the author of *Gaṇitasārasaṁgraha*, and Śākaṭāyana, the author of *Amoghavṛitti*. He was himself the author of *Kavirājamārga*, the earliest Kanarese work on poetics. He treated all creeds with impartiality and his own life was a striking synthesis of what was best in Hinduism and Jainism. He revered Mahāvīra as profoundly as Mahālakshmī, and on one occasion proffered to the latter a finger of his own in the belief that such sacrifice would abate a severe epidemic. Kings rarely bleed for others; usually they make others bleed for themselves. Towards the evening of his life from c. A.D. 860, he used off and on to retire from the work of administration in order to devote himself as much as possible to religious worship. Amoghavarsha's name will endure as of a ruler who established peace and order in his kingdom, encouraged art and literature practised the principles he preached, and did not flinch even from offering a limb of his body by way of sacrifice, when he thought that public welfare demanded it.

6. KṚISHṆA II

Amoghavarsha I died about A.D. 878 and was succeeded by his son Kṛishṇa II who, like his illustrious namesake, assumed the titles *Akālavarsha* and *Śubhatuṅga*. He married the daughter of the Chedi ruler Kokkalla I and received substantial help from his wife's relations in the arduous struggles of his reign.

Several Rāshṭrakūṭa records[19] make a bold claim on behalf of Kṛishṇa II that he terrified the Gurjaras, destroyed the pride of Lāṭa, taught humility to the Gauḍas, deprived the people on the seacoast of their sleep, and that his command was obeyed by the Aṅga, the Kaliṅga, the Gaṅga, and the Magadha, waiting at his gate. Much of this is, no doubt, mere conventional praise based upon a kernel of historical truth. But there is no doubt that his reign was full of wars.

The most arduous of his campaigns were those against the Pratihāras and the Eastern Chālukyas. Several records refer to his fight with the Gurjara-Pratīhāra ruler Bhoja[20], and the Begumra plates, dated A.D. 914, state that even then old men remembered the great battle and talked of it. It is clear from the records of the Lāṭa (Gujarāt) Branch of the Rāshṭrakūṭas that they, particularly their chief Kṛishṇarāja took a distinguished part in the campaign against the Pratīhāras. Although the advance of Bhoja was checked, the Lāṭa Branch seems to have come to an end shortly after. Kṛishṇarāja is known to have been on the throne till at least A.D. 888, but no successor of his is so far known. Whether he died without leaving any issue, leading to the lapse of his kingdom, or whether there was a further war between the main dynasty and the Lāṭa Branch which wiped out the existence of the latter, we do not know.

The war with the Eastern Chālukyas was a more serious affair, and at one time even threatened the very existence of the Rāshṭrakūṭa kingdom. The campaigns will be more fully described in connection with the Eastern Chālukyas in Chapter VI and a short summary here must suffice.

Vijayāditya III, the contemporary of Kṛishṇa II on the Veṅgī throne, had freed his kingdom from the Rāshṭrakūṭa yoke during the reign of Amoghavarsha; the advent of a new king on the Rāshṭrakūṭa throne emboldened him to take the offensive, and he was for a time successful. In the south he attacked the Noḷambas and the Gaṅgas, who were Rāshṭrakūṭa feudatories, and in the north his invading forces penetrated right into the heart of Berār. For a time Kṛishṇa was defeated all along the line. But in a few years he reorganised his forces, summoned the battalions of his feudatories, and hurled back the Chālukya invaders. His victory was decisive, and the Chālukya king Bhīma, who had succeeded his father, was taken prisoner. Eventually, Bhīma was released after a few years and permitted to rule his kingdom as a feudatory. In course of time, however, he once again challenged the Rāshṭrakūṭa overlordship, but was again defeated in a sanguinary battle, in which his crown-prince lost his life.

Kṛishṇa II seems to have had political relations with the Choḷas. One of his daughters was married to the Choḷa king Āditya I, and there was a son by this marriage named Kannara. On the death of Āditya, his other son Parāntaka ascended the throne. Thereupon Kṛishṇa II invaded the Choḷa kingdom in order to secure the throne for his grandson. But he was decisively defeated at Vallāla (modern Tiruvallam in North Arcot District).

The wars of Kṛishṇa II thus generally ended in failure and sometimes in disaster in spite of his initial brilliant victories against the Eastern Chālukyas.

7. INDRA III

Kṛishṇa II died towards the end of A.D. 914 after a reign of about 36 years. Like his father he had a leaning towards Jainism.

He was succeeded by his grandson Indra III, whose father Jagattuṅga predeceased Kṛishṇa. Indra assumed the titles *Nityavarsha, Raṭṭakandarpa, Kīrttinārāyaṇa,* and *Rājamārtaṇḍa.*

Indra III was a youth of 30 at the time of his accession, and he had inherited the military dash and daring of Govinda III. Soon after his accession, he emulated his great ancestor by declaring war against the Gurjara-Pratīhāra emperor Mahīpāla. It has been suggested by some writers that he did this in sympathy with his Chedi relations,[21] who had espoused the cause of Mahīpāla's rival and half-brother Bhoja II. There is, however, no positive evidence in support of this, and Indra's expedition against the Gurjaras may be merely a phase of the long-standing hostility between the two powers. The southern army followed the Bhopāl-Jhānsi-Kālpi route, crossed the Yamunā at the last mentioned place, and marched upon Kanauj and occupied it. The capture of Kanauj, the imperial city of Northern India, was a sensational achievement and immensely enhanced the prestige of the Rāshṭrakūṭa arms. Mahīpāla fled and Indra sent his own Chālukya feudatory, Narasiṁha II of Vemulavāḍa, in pursuit. This campaign has been dealt in detail in the next chapter.

The war with the Veṅgīs continued in the reign of Indra also, but with no conspicuous success on either side. Indra died some time after A.D. 927[22] and was succeeded by his son Amoghavarsha II. The latter fell a prey to the foul play of his younger brother Govinda IV; his widow fled to Veṅgī, and lived under the protection of its ruler Amma I, as she did not feel that either her honour or her son would be safe anywhere within the empire over which her husband once ruled. Govinda naturally did not like this action of Amma I, and when the latter died in 925, he intervened in the war of succession for the Veṅgī throne that ensued, and eventually succeeded in putting his own nominee Tāḍapa upon it.

8. GOVINDA IV AND AMOGHAVARSHA III

Govinda was a youth of about 25 at the time of his accession, and soon gave himself up to a life of vicious pleasures. His administration became tyrannical and unpopular, and his ministers and feudatories felt that his removal was necessary in the interests of the empire. They therefore made overtures to Amoghavarsha, an uncle of Govinda, and requested him to displace Govinda. Amoghavarsha had a high reputation for character and integrity, and when he marched against Mālkhed with the assistance of his Chedi relations, he was openly welcomed by the distressed people who had become disgusted with Govinda's vices and excesses.

Amoghavarsha found no difficulty in overthrowing Govinda and ascending the throne in A.D. 936.[23] Whether Govinda was killed in battle or was put in prison, we do not know.

Amoghavarsha III was aged about 50 at the time of his accession. He was religious by temperament and did not take any active interest in administration. During his short reign of three years, therefore, the government was entirely carried on by his able and ambitious son Kṛishṇa. The latter sent an expedition into Gaṅgavāḍī, and deposed its king Rājamalla with a view to enthrone the latter's younger brother Būtuga, who had married a sister of Kṛishṇa. As crown-prince, Kṛishṇa also led an expedition into Bundelkhand and captured the important forts of Kālanjar and Chitrakūṭa. During this expedition a misunderstanding and possibly a conflict arose between him and his Chedi relations, which put an end to the long-standing *entente cordiale* between the two royal families.[24]

9. KṚISHṆA III

Kṛishṇa III *Akālavarsha* succeeded to the throne as the *de jure* emperor on his father's death towards the end of A.D. 939. Soon after his accession he planned an invasion of the Choḷa kingdom in collaboration with his brother-in-law Būtuga, ruling in Gaṅgavāḍī. The two brothers-in-law led a lightning expedition to the south and captured the important cities of Kāñchī and Tanjore some time in A.D. 943. Parāntaka, the Choḷa king, soon rallied his forces and repulsed the invaders, who could retain effective possession only of Toṇḍamaṇḍalam, consisting of Arcot, Chingleput and Vellore Districts. In A.D. 949 the Choḷa army penetrated into Arcot District with a view to drive out the invader, but sustained a signal defeat at the battle of Takkolam, in which the Choḷa crown-prince Rājāditya, who was leading his forces, was killed in his *howdah* by Būtuga. Kṛishṇa pressed home his victory by marching down to Rāmeśvaram, where he set up a pillar of victory; then he came back to North Arcot and encamped for some years at Melpāḍi. He built the temples of Kṛishṇeśvara and Gaṇḍamārtaṇḍāditya at or near Rāmeśvaram to shine there 'as resplendent hills of fame.' Kṛishṇa eventually decided to annex only Toṇḍamaṇḍalam which remained an integral part of his empire to the end of his reign.

In recognition of the valuable help rendered by his brother-in-law, the Gaṅga king, Kṛishṇa bestowed upon him the governorship of Banavāsi 12000, Belvola 300, Purigere 300, Kinsukāḍ 70, and Bagenāḍ 70.

In c. A.D. 963 Kṛishṇa led a second expedition into Northern India in which Mārasiṁha, the successor of the Gaṅga ruler Būtuga, offered valuable assistance. Kṛishṇa seems to have marched into Bundelkhand; but his objective is not definitely known.[24a] Later on he led an expedition into Mālwā against the Paramāra ruler Sīyaka and occupied Ujjayinī.

Kṛishṇa succeeded in bringing Veṅgī effectively under his control by championing the cause of Bāḍapa against Amma II, and putting him on the Veṅgī throne in A.D. 956. Though Bāḍapa remained a loyal Rāshṭrakūṭa feudatory till the end of his life, Amma II soon regained the throne and put an end to the Rāshṭrakūṭa influence.

Kṛishṇa III was one of the ablest monarchs of the Rāshṭrakūṭa dynasty. Possibly he was not as successful in his northern campaigns as Dhruva, Govinda III, or Indra III. But there is no doubt that, unlike any of his predecessors, he was the lord of the whole of Deccan (*Sakala-dakshiṇa-dig-adhipati*) in the full sense of the term. Govinda III conquered Kāñchī, but could not penetrate to Rāmeśvaram and thus effectively break the power of the Draviḍa kings. Veṅgī was a source of trouble to him; during the latter half of Kṛishṇa's reign, it was ruled by a submissive feudatory. Kṛishṇa was in effective possession of a large part of the Choḷa kingdom and his temples of Kṛishneśvara and Gaṇḍamārtaṇḍāditya at or near Rāmeśvaram proclaimed his conquest of the extreme south of the Peninsula. No other Rāshṭrakūṭa king was the overlord of the entire Deccan in so complete a sense of the term as Kṛishṇa was in c. A.D. 965.

10. KHOṬṬIGA AND KARKKA II

Kṛishṇa III apparently had no issue living at the time of his death, since he was succeeded by his younger brother Khoṭṭiga in A.D. 967. The new ruler was an old man at the time of his accession and seems to have lacked military capacity. At any rate he was unable to repulse the invasion of the Rāshṭrakūṭa dominions by the Paramāra king Sīyaka, who was keen on avenging his defeat by the previous Rāshṭrakūṭa emperor. Sīyaka crossed the Narmadā and advanced straight upon Mālkhed. The Rāshṭrakūṭa capital was captured and plundered in the spring of A.D. 972. The imperial treasury was completely sacked and the raider carried away even the office copies of copper-plate charters lodged in the record office. Khoṭṭiga died of a broken heart soon after this calamity, probably in September, A.D. 972.

Khoṭṭiga was succeeded by his nephew Karkka II, son of Nirupama. The prestige of the empire had been already shattered by the sack of its capital, and matters were worsened by the maladministration of the new emperor and his two vicious ministers. This naturally aroused imperial ambitions in the minds of the feudatories, and one of them eventually deprived Karkka of his sovereignty over the Deccan within eighteen months of his accession.

This feudatory was Taila II of the Chālukya family. He was ruling over a small fief at Tarddavāḍi in Bijāpur District as a submissive feudatory of the Rāshṭrakūṭas from the time of Kṛishṇa III down to A.D. 965. He, however, believed that he was a direct descendant of the Imperial Chālukya family of Bādāmi, and his ability and military capacity urged him to make a bid for the imperial status snatched from his ancestors by the Rāshṭrakūṭas. He made elaborate but secret preparations, and by the end of A.D. 973 openly revolted against the authority of Karkka. The latter marched against him, but was signally defeated in a sanguinary battle fought somewhere in northern Karṇāṭaka. The notorious ministers of Karkka were killed in the battle, but Karkka himself escaped and managed to carve out a small principality for himself in Sorab *tāluk* of Mysore State, where he continued to rule up to A.D. 991. Though Karkka gave up the task of restoring Rāshṭrakūṭa supremacy as hopeless, it was attempted by the Gaṅga ruler Mārasiṁha on behalf of his nephew Indra, a grandson of Kṛishṇa III. This effort also failed, as Taila succeeded in crushing his enemy's forces in A.D. 974. Both Mārasiṁha and Indra turned Jain monks and died by the *Sallekhanā* vow, and Taila became the overlord of the Deccan by A.D. 975. His reign and the history of his family will be described in the next volume.

11. RETROSPECT AND REVIEW

The period of Rāshṭrakūṭa ascendancy in the Deccan from about A.D. 753 to 975 constitutes perhaps the most brilliant chapter in its history. No other ruling dynasty in the Deccan played such a dominant part in the history of India till the rise of the Marāṭhās as an imperial power in the eighteenth century. No less than three of its rulers, Dhruva, Govinda III, and Indra III carried their victorious arms into the heart of North India, and by inflicting severe defeats upon its most powerful rulers changed the whole course of the history of that region. Their success in the south was equally remarkable, and Kṛishṇa III literally advanced as far as Rāmeśvara in course of his victorious career. All the great powers of India, the Pratīhāras and the Pālas in the north, and the Eastern Chālukyas and Choḷas in the south, were subjugated by them at one time or another. They, no doubt, suffered reverses at times but on the whole their military campaigns against powerful adversaries were repeatedly crowned with brilliant success.

The Rāshṭrakūṭas also excelled in arts of peace. The Kailāsa Temple at Ellora, to be described elsewhere, will keep alive for ever the name of its builder Kṛishṇa I. Amoghavarsha, though not renowned like his father and grandfather as a conqueror, was a remarkable personality. By virtue of his literary accomplishments and religious temperament he occupied a unique position among contemporary sovereigns. The Arab writers who visited Western India for trade or other purposes speak very highly of the Rāshṭrakūṭa kings whom they refer to as Balharā, no doubt an abbreviation of Ballaha-rāya, a Prakrit form of Vallabha-rāja. According to these foreigners the Balharā was recognised as the greatest king in India and homage was paid to him by all the other princes. It is further said: "He gives regular pay to his troops and has many horses and elephants and immense wealth". On the other hand Mas'ūdī says: "His troops and elephants are innumerable, but his troops are mostly infantry, because the seat of his government is among the mountains."[25] Both the king and his subjects are described as being friendly to the Muslims, and according to some writers Muslims were appointed even as governors of cities in the kingdom.[26] Mas'ūdī says: "There is none among the rulers of Sindh and Hind who in his territory respects the Muslims like Rāja Balharā. In his kingdom Islam is honoured and protected. And for them mosques and congregational mosques, which are always full, have been built for offering prayers five times."[27] All these undoubtedly testify to the liberal and progressive views of the Rāshṭrakūṭa kings.

1. Vol. III, pp. 248-9.
2. Vol. III, pp. 198-202. In later times the Rāshṭrakūṭas regarded themselves as having been descended from Yadu, and one record describes them as belonging to the Sātyaki branch of Yaduvaṁśa. There is hardly any doubt that these Rāshṭrakūṭas were of Kannaḍa origin; at least Kannaḍa was their mother tongue.
3. According to Mirashi, Dantidurga's "ancestors were ruling, not over Vidarbha, but over the Aurangābād District (ancient Mūlaka) where the earliest inscriptions of the family have been found." (*POC.* XV Summary of Papers, p. 98).
4. It is said in the Sanjān Plates of Amoghavarsha that "Indrarāja, in the (marriage) hall, namely Khetaka, seized in battle the daughter of the Chālukya king by the *rākshasa* form of marriage" (*EI*, XVIII 252). This is also referred to in other records which give the name of the princess as Bhavagaṇā. Kheṭaka is modern Kaira, where a battle must have taken place, though we do not know the cause of it. The princess probably belonged to the Gujarāt branch of the Chālukyas. The circumstances relating to the battle and the forced marriage are shrouded in obscurity.
5. The Ellora plates of Dantidurga, the earliest record of the family, are dated in *Saṁ.* 663. This has been referred to the Śaka era, and the resulting date is A.D. 742 (*EI*, XXI. 26). Prof. V. V. Mirashi, however, reads the date as 463 and refers it to the Kalachuri era of A.D. 250-51 (*POC.* XV. Summary of

Papers pp. 97-8). The equivalent Christian date being A.D. 715, it pushes back the accession of Dantidurga by more than 25 years. If we accept this interpretation, Dantidurga must have had a long reign of more than 40 years, as his other known record, Samangad plates, is dated A.D. 754.

6. *IA*, XI. 111.
7. *ASWI*, V. 92.
8. *EI*, XVIII. 252.
9. *EI*, IV. 287.
10. *EI*, XVIII. 252.
11. This para is based upon the inference suggested by the Navsāri plates of Pulakeśin and Ellora plates of Dantidurga.
12. Vol. III, pp. 247-8, 263.

12a. For a different view on this point, cf. next chapter (pp. 20-21. fn. 14).

13. According to some records (*IA*, XII. 264) Dantidurga died without a son, and Kannara (i.e. Kṛishṇa) succeeded him. According to the Baroda plates of A.D. 812-13 (*IA*, XII. 158), Kṛishṇa I had replaced a relative who had gone astray. The view that Dantidurga was deposed by his uncle Kṛishṇa for oppressing his subjects cannot be upheld. For a full discussion of the point, cf. Altekar, *Rāshṭrakūṭas*, pp. 41-2.
14. For the reign of Govinda II, cf. Alas Plates (*EI*, VI. 208), Daulatābād Plates (*EI*, IX. 195), and Bhor State Museum Plates (*EI*, XXII. 176).
15. A large number of inscriptions refer to the conquests of Dhruva and Govinda III. Among them may be specially mentioned:
    (i) Rādhanpur and Wani plates of Govinda III (*IA*, XI. 157).
    (ii) Baroda Plates (*IA*, XII. 158).
    (iii) Nilgund, Sirur, and Sanjān plates of Amoghavarsha (*EI*, VI. 98; VII. 203; XVIII. 244).
16. This detail is found in Rādhanpur and other plates, but not in Sanjān plates which merely refer to the birth of his son in Śarva's kingdom.
17. The vexed problem of the chronology of the campaigns of Govinda III was discussed by the author of this chapter and Mirashi, in *D. R. Bhandarkar Volume*, pp. 153 ff. and *EI*, XXIII. pp. 214-7, 293-7. The views given above are slightly different from those held previously by the author. Cf. also *EI*, XXXII, 159 (Ed.).
18. This will be described more fully in Chapter VI.
19. Karhad Pl. (*EI*, IV. 287).
20. This will be described more fully in Chapter II.
21. Indra himself, his father Jagattuṅga, grandfather Kṛishṇa II, and son Amoghavarsha II had all married princesses of the Chedi family of Tripurī.
22. According to one view, he ruled till at least A.D. 927 and was succeeded by his elder son Amoghavarsha who was removed by Govinda IV in A.D. 930 (*EI*, XXVI. 162-3). Some scholars believe that he ruled till the end of A.D. 928 (*EI*, XXXII. 50). The date 922, for the death of Indra III as given in the first edition (p. 13) by the late Dr. Altekar has been proved to be wrong by epigraphic records and has been changed to 927 (Ed.).
23. Some authorities place it in A.D. 934 (*EI*, XXVI. 163-4).
24. This is denied by Prof. K. A. N. Sastri (*JOR*, XVI. 155).

24a. For a different view, cf. Ch. V, Section II.

25. *HIED*, I. 3, 13, 21.
26. Al Istakhrī (*ibid*. 34) says: "There are Musalmans in its (land of Balharā) cities, and none but Musalmans rule over them on the part of the Balharā. There are Jama *Masjids* in them (where Muhammadans assemble to pray)." The bracketed portion is added by Ibn Haukal (*ibid*) who repeats the rest.
27. *POC*, X. 406.

CHAPTER II

RISE AND FALL OF THE PRATĪHĀRA EMPIRE

The early history of the Gurjara-Pratīhāras has been dealt with in the third volume.[1] We have seen how the Pratīhāra dynasty, founded by the Brāhmaṇa Harichandra, carved out a powerful kingdom in Rājputāna, and various other Gurjara families, probably branches of the same dynasty, set up small principalities to the south and east. The southern branches ruled in Lāṭa with its capital at Nāndīpurī,[2] but we have no definite information about the capital of the eastern branch or the exact locality and extent of its dominions. Some scholars hold the view that Bhillamāla was the early capital of this family, as they identify it with the capital city of the Gurjara kingdom mentioned by Hiuen Tsang. But apart from their identification being doubtful, that kingdom was ruled, as has been shown already,[3] by the main branch. As a matter of fact, the eastern branch did not come into prominence till about a century later, and as the main branch in Jodhpur continued to rule for 150 years more after that, there is no valid ground for taking Bhillamāla as the original capital of the eastern branch.[4] The only clue to the original location of the family is furnished by the details available about the fourth king Vatsarāja. There are grounds to believe that he ruled over both Jālor and Avanti. But these are disputed points and will be treated more fully later, in connection with that ruler. For the present we may accept as a probable hypothesis, though not as a proved fact, that he and his ancestors ruled over Avanti and had their capital at Ujjayinī.

1. NĀGABHAṬA I

The family came into prominence in the second quarter of the eighth century A.D. by the successful resistance it offered under Nāgabhaṭa I to the Arabs. He is described in the Gwālior Inscription as "having crushed the large armies of the powerful Mlechchha king." It has already been noted above[5] how he saved Western India from the Arabs and gradually brought under his sway a large number of states that had been overrun by them. In particular, he established his supremacy over the Gurjara kingdom of Nāndīpurī, and probably also over the Pratīhāra family of Jodhpur. A new feudatory family the Chāhamānas—was set up in Broach, but the old dynasty of Harichandra continued at Jodhpur. Śīluka, whose history has been related above,[6] was perhaps the last independent ruler of this family. His two successors Jhoṭa and Bhillāditya are said to have proceeded respectively to the Bhāgīrathī and Gaṅgādvāra, and no martial glory is ascribed to them.[7] This would indicate that the Jodhpur family was politically insignificant during the latter half of the eighth century A.D. It is obvious that Nāgabhaṭa and his descendants now attained the supremacy and leadership of the Gurjara confederacy, so long enjoyed by the Jodhpur chiefs.

It is unfortunate that we know practically nothing of the ancestors of Nāgabhaṭa I. Very likely they had carved out a kingdom in Eastern Rājputāna and Mālwā about the same time as the other branch had conquered the region round Broach. Like the latter, they too probably acknowledged the suzerainty of the Jodhpur Pratīhāras until Nāgabhaṭa established the independence of his kingdom on a firm footing in the wake of the political disruption that followed the disastrous Arab raids.

The date of Nāgabhaṭa's accession is not definitely known, but since he successfully opposed the Arabs, he must have ruled in the second quarter of the eighth century A.D. Whether he defeated Junaid or his successor Tamin[8] it is difficult to say, but in any case, he must have ascended the throne within a few years of A.D. 730. He ruled probably till A.D. 756 as will be noted below.

About the time when Nāgabhaṭa was laying the foundations of the future greatness of his family, another powerful dynasty arose in the Deccan, immediately to the south of Mālwā. These were the Rāshṭrakūṭas whose history has already been dealt with in the preceding chapter. The Rāshṭrakūṭa king Dantidurga, who reigned between c. A.D. 733 and 758, is said to have defeated the Gurjara king and made him serve as a door-keeper (*pratīhāra*) when he performed the *Hiraṇyagarbha-dāna* ceremony at Ujjain.[9] It has been suggested by some scholars[10] that there is a pun on the word *pratīhāra* and an allusion to the Pratīhāra king of Avanti. Though this view is not accepted by all,[11] there is no doubt that a Gurjara king had to submit to Dantidurga, who went to the extent of occupying the palace of the vanquished ruler.[12]

Dantidurga also claims to have conquered Lāṭa (Southern Gujarāt) and Sindh. Since Dantidurga died before A.D. 758, it is more or less certain that his Gurjara adversary could not have been anybody else but Nāgabhaṭa I. But since the latter is acknowledged as suzerain by Bhartṛivaḍḍha, the Chāhamāna ruler of Broach, in A.D. 756,[13] it does not appear that Dantidurga's military victory was followed by any permanent conquest.[14] Both Nāgabhaṭa I and Dantidurga fished in the troubled waters caused by the Arab raids.

Though Dantidurga gained some initial successes, he could not conquer permanently the territory north of the Kim river, *i.e.* the old Gurjara principality of Nāndīpurī. Perhaps the impending conflict with his Chālukya overlord forced him to abandon his aggressive designs in the north. In any case there are good reasons to believe that in spite of initial discomfiture Nāgabhaṭa was able to leave to his successors a powerful principality comprising Mālwā and parts of Rājputāna and Gujarāt. The Gwālior Inscription describes him as the image of Nārāyaṇa, and there can be no doubt whatever that he achieved distinction as a great national hero by defeating the Arabs

2. VATSARAJA

Nāgabhaṭa I was succeeded by his brother's sons, Kakkuka and Devarāja, of whom nothing is known. Devarāja's son Vatsarāja was, however, a powerful ruler. The author of a Jain work, *Kuvalayamālā,* says that he composed the work in the year 700 (= A.D. 778) at Jāvālipura (modern Jālor) which was at the time ruled by the *Raṇahastin* (war-elephant) Vatsarāja.[15] This Vatsarāja has been generally identified with the Pratihāra ruler. Another Jain work, Jinasena's *Harivaṁśa-purāṇa*, contains a reference to Vatsarāja and his kingdom, but unfortunately the interpretation of the passage is not free from difficulty, and has given rise to a keen controversy.[16] Jinasena gives the names of kings who flourished in different directions when he finished his work at Vardhamāṇapura in the year 705 (= A.D. 783). The first two lines of the verse tell us that in that year Indrāyudha was ruling in the north, and Śrī-Vallabha, son of king Kṛishṇa, in the south. The next two lines of the verse run as follows:—

Pūrvvāṁ Śrīmad=Avanti-bhūbhṛiti nṛipe Vatsādirāje=parām |
Saurāṇām=adhimaṇḍale(laṁ) jaya-yute vīre Varāhe=vati ||

According to some scholars[17] it means that Vatsarāja, the ruler of Avanti, was the king in the east, while victorious Varāha (or Jaya-Varāha) was ruling over the Sauras in the west. Others,[18] however, point out that Avanti-*bhūbhṛit* (king of Avanti) must be distinguished from Vatsarāja, as otherwise the word *nṛipa* (king) is redundant. They accordingly infer from the passage that the ruler of Avanti was the king of the east and Vatsarāja of the west, while Varāha was ruling over the Sauras. This interpretation is, however, open to serious objections. In the first place, the name of the eastern king is omitted, while the names of all other kings are given. No purpose is served by saying that the ruler of Avanti was the eastern king, which would be almost tantamount to stating that the ruler of the eastern kingdom is the king of the east. Secondly, it appears from the general tenor of the verse that the author proposes to name the four rulers in the four directions. The proposed translation adds a fifth without indicating its connection or relevancy to the context. It is urged by some that the fifth ruler has been named because he reigned over Vardhamānapura where the work was composed. But if we accept the identification of Vardhamāna with Wadhwān in Kāthiāwār Peninsula, we can hardly regard Vatsarāja as a western ruler, even though his kingdom was in Rājputāna, as is argued by scholars who do not accept the other translation locating it in Avanti. To obviate this difficulty one scholar proposes to identify Vardhamāna with Badnawar, about 40 miles to the south-west of Ujjain.[19] But in that case, we cannot assign any reason why the fifth king should be mentioned at all. Thus there are difficulties in the second translation which are of a more serious nature than those of the first. For, as regards the redundance of the word *nṛipa*, it should hardly surprise us if we remember such expression as *Gurjareśvara-pati* used with reference to the son of the same Vatsarāja, in a record dated A.D. 812,[20] *i.e.* less than thirty years after Jinasena wrote. On the whole, therefore, it is a more reasonable view to regard Vatsarāja as the king of Avanti in A.D. 783. This view is also corroborated by what has been said above regarding the Gurjara king defeated by Dantidurga.

The two Jain works would thus prove that the Pratīhāra king Vatsarāja ascended the throne in or before A.D. 778, and his kingdom comprised both Mālwā and eastern Rājputāna. That he ruled over Central Rājputāna also is proved by two epigraphic records.[21] Some idea of the extent of his kingdom may be gained from the fact that the northern king named by Jinasena as his contemporary was Indrāyudha, who was probably king of Kanauj.[22] There is no doubt that Vatsarāja gradually extended his dominions in the north. The Gwālior inscription of his great-grandson records that he forcibly wrested the empire from the famous Bhaṇḍi clan. This Bhaṇḍi clan has been taken by some to refer to the ruling family founded by Bhaṇḍi, the maternal uncle of Harsha.[23] It would then follow that this clan wielded imperial power, probably with its seat of authority in Kanauj, though we have no independent evidence of this. But whatever we might think of these probabilities, there is no doubt that Vatsarāja was ambitious of establishing an empire in Northern India and attained a great deal of success. We learn from the Rāshṭrakūṭa records[24] that he defeated the Lord of Gauḍa, who must be identified with a Pāla king of Bengal, probably Dharmapāla; and carried away his umbrellas of state. Vatsarāja was aided in this expedition by his feudatory chiefs, one of whom, the Chāhamāna Durlabharāja of Śākambharī, is said to have overrun the whole of Bengal up to the confluence of the Gaṅgā and the sea.[25] But as this occurs in a poetical work composed about four centuries after the event described, it is difficult to take it as literally true. As the kingdom of Gauḍa at that time extended up to the Gaṅgā-Yamunā Doāb, it cannot be said definitely whether Vatsarāja actually invaded Bengal, or met and defeated the lord of Gauḍa somewhere in the Doāb.[26] Be that as it may, Vatsarāja must have established his supremacy over a large part of Northern India and laid the foundations of a mighty empire. He thus appears to have scored over Dharmapāla who was equally ambitious of founding an empire. Unfortunately the imperial dreams of both were rudely shattered by the invasion of the Rāshṭrakūṭa king Dhruva. While Vatsarāja and Dharmapāla were fighting for the empire in the north, the Rāshṭrakūṭa king Dhruva seized the opportunity to emulate Dantidurga by renewing the attempt to conquer the north. The details of his campaign are not known, but, according to the Rāshṭrakūṭa records,[27] Dhruva inflicted a crushing defeat upon Vatsarāja, who was forced to put the desert of Rājputāna between him and the invading army. Dhruva next turned against Dharmapāla and defeated him somewhere between the Gaṅgā and the Yamunā.

Thus began that triangular struggle between the Gurjaras, the Pālas and the Rāshṭrakūṭas for supremacy in Northern India which was destined to be an important factor in Indian politics for more than a century. The city of Kanauj, which was raised to the position of imperial dignity by Harsha-vardhana, seems to have been the prize coveted and won by each, with a varying degree of success. It is very likely, though not known with certainty, that Vatsarāja took possession of it before marching towards Gauḍa. Dharmapāla, the king of Gauḍa, was also proceeding towards the west with the same object, and thus ensued the fight between the two rival claimants, probably somewhere in the Doāb. Although both Dharmapāla and Vatsarāja were defeated by Dhruva, the Pratihāra king seems to have fared worse. For Dharmapāla, in spite of his successive defeats, was in possession of Kanauj not long afterwards, and held a *durbar* there in the presence of a host of rulers of northern states including Avanti, all of whom acknowledged his imperial position.[28]

As we have seen above, Indrāyudha was the ruler of the north in A.D. 783. As Dharmapāla is expressly said to have conquered Kanauj by defeating Indrarāja and others, it is generally held that Indrarāja was the same as Indrāyudha. If, as is presumed, Vatsarāja had conquered Kanauj before Dharmapāla, he, too, must have defeated Indrāyudha and permitted him to rule as a vassal. But

Dharmapāla placed on the throne a new ruler Chakrāyudha, whose name-ending shows that he was probably connected with the ruling family.

3. NĀGABHAṬA II

After his defeat at the hands of Dhruva, Vatsarāja passes completely out of our view. Nothing is known of him or of his kingdom during the palmy days of Pāla imperialism under Dharmapāla. It is probable that his power was confined to central Rājputāna. His son and successor Nāgabhaṭa II, however, retrieved the fortunes of his family. The Gwālior Inscription of his grandson tells us that the rulers of Andhra, Saindhava, Vidarbha and Kaliṅga succumbed to him, that he defeated Chakrāyudha and the lord of Vaṅga, and forcibly seized the hill-forts of the kings of Ānartta, Mālava, Kirāta, Turushka, Vatsa, and Matsya.[29] The records of some of the families feudatory to him corroborate and supply details of these conquests. On the other hand, the Rāshṭrakūṭa records categorically assert that Nāgabhaṭa was defeated by Govinda III who overran his dominions and reached the Himālayas.

Although we thus know a great many details of the eventful career of Nāgabhaṭa II, it is not easy to arrange then chronologically, and view his reign in a correct perspective. We do not know, for example, whether his discomfiture at the hands of the Rāshṭrakūṭas preceded or followed his victories,—in other words, whether his reign began in disaster and ended in glory, or whether the reverse was the case. No wonder, therefore, that different views have been adopted by different scholars about the life and career of this great emperor.[30] The following reconstruction of his history may be regarded as merely provisional:—

The forcible seizure of the hill-forts of Ānartta, Mālava, etc. is said to have begun even in his boyhood. It has been suggested that some of these events might actually have taken place in the reign of Vatsarāja.[31] But as the same record refers to the achievements of Vatsarāja, and is silent about them, this view is not probable. They may, therefore, be regarded as the earliest military exploits of Nāgabhaṭa II. The geographical position of the rulers shows that Nāgabhaṭa advanced towards North Gujarāt (Ānartta) and Mālwā in the south and east, and this probably brought him into conflict with the Rāshṭrakūṭas, which is referred to in the records of both the parties. Indra, the Rāshṭrakūṭa ruler of Lāṭa, is said to have defeated the Gurjara king who fled to distant regions.[32] On the other hand Vāhukadhavala, a feudatory chief of Nāgabhaṭa II, is said to have defeated the Karṇāṭas, which apparently refer to the Rāshṭrakūṭas (Inscription No. 3).[32a] It may be concluded, therefore, that no party gained a decisive victory, though Nāgabhaṭa probably retained some of the captured hill-forts. His similar enterprises in the north (Matsya), east (Vatsa), and west (Turushka) were probably more successful, but we possess no details of these campaigns. The Turushkas undoubtedly refer to the Muslim rulers of the west against whom he scored some success,[33] and the Kirātas represent some primitive tribes, probably of the Himālayan region.

The initial successes of Nāgabhaṭa in these military raids emboldened him to carry on further campaigns which resulted in the submission of the Saindhava chiefs, ruling in Western Kāthiāwār, and the rulers of Andhra, Kaliṅga and Vidarbha. It is difficult to believe that Nāgabhaṭa actually advanced as far as Andhra or even Kaliṅga country on the eastern coast of the Deccan.[34] It is not, therefore, unlikely that he entered into a confederacy with them, though, as usually happens in such cases of unequal alliance, they became, for all practical purposes, subordinate, rather than independent, allies. Although this view has been challenged,[35] it seems to be true at least in the case of the Saindhavas of whom alone we possess any contemporary records. It appears from the contemporary copper-plate grants[36] of the Saindhava chiefs that while they were devoted and loyal to the Pratīhāras, they did not invoke their name as suzerains as was done by the Chāpas and Chālukyas of the Kāthiāwār Peninsula—the other feudatories immediately to their east.

Nāgabhaṭa's next move seems to have been to reconquer Kanauj. As already noted, its ruler Indrāyudha had probably acknowledged Vatsarāja's suzerainty and was, perhaps for that very reason, defeated by Dharmapāla, who put instead Chakrāyudha on the throne. Nāgabhaṭa defeated Chakrāyudha and conquered his kingdom.[37] He probably occupied Kanauj which later became the permanent capital of the Pratīhāras. It was a challenge to the power of Dharmapāla, and both sides made preparations for the inevitable conflict. Nāgabhaṭa was joined by at least three of his feudatory chiefs in this momentous struggle for the empire. These were Kakka, of the Jodhpur Pratīhāra family, Vāhukadhavala, the Chālukya chief of Southern Kāthiāwār, and the Guhilot Śaṅkaragaṇa. The family records (Ins. 2-4) of these three refer to the first as having fought the Gauḍas at Monghyr, the second as having defeated king Dharma, and the third as having defeated Gauḍa and made the whole world, gained by warfare, subservient to his overlord. All the three evidently refer to the great battle between Nāgabhaṭa and the lord of Vaṅga, described in the Gwālior Inscription, in which the latter, though possessed of "crowds of mighty elephants, horses, and chariots", was vanquished by the former. There is no reference to this encounter in the Pāla records, but the combined testimony of the four different records, coming from four different sources, and particularly the fact that the Pratīhāras advanced as far as Monghyr, almost in the heart of the Pāla dominions, leave no doubt that Nāgabhaṭa scored a great victory over his Pāla rival Dharmapāla.

But Nāgabhaṭa's success was not destined to be more permanent than that of his father. Once more the hereditary enemies from the south upset the grandiose imperial scheme of the Pratīhāras. Nāgabhaṭa, as noted above, had already come into conflict with the Rāshṭrakūṭas in the early part of his reign. This took place probably about A.D. 794-95, early in the reign of Govinda III, when the new king was engaged in the south in putting down the rebellion of his brother and fighting with the Gaṅga ruler. The brunt of the attack fell upon his viceroy of the north, Indra, who *'alone'* is said to have defeated the Gurjara lord. But, as noted above, the Pratīhāras also claimed victory, and probably gained some hill forts in Mālwā. The northern frontier was, however, guarded effectively by Indra and his son Karkka, who says in one of his records that the Rāshṭrakūṭa king had "caused his arm to become an excellent door-bar of the country of the lord of Gurjaras."[38]

But the Rāshṭrakūṭa king Govinda III could not be content merely with a defensive policy against the Pratīhāras. As soon as he was free from internal troubles, he made preparations to invade the north as his father Dhruva had done before. Like the latter he achieved phenomenal success, though probably more than one campaign was necessary for the purpose. He "destroyed the valour of Nāgabhaṭa", who "in fear vanished nobody knew whither", and then having "devastated his home" and overrun his dominions, proceeded up to the Himālayas.[39] Even making allowance for exaggerations, there can be hardly any doubt that Govinda III inflicted a crushing blow on Nāgabhaṭa and shattered his dreams of founding an emipre.

A Rāshṭrakūṭa record[40] informs us that Dharmapāla and Chakrāyudha surrendered of their own accord to Govinda III. If we remember that both of them were defeated by Nāgabhaṭa II, it is difficult to avoid the conclusion that they had invited the Rāshṭrakūṭa king, or at least made common cause with him against Nāgabhaṭa II, their common foe. This would satisfactorily explain the triumphant march of Govinda III right up to the Himālayas and the complete discomfiture of the Pratīhāras for some time to come.

If the success of Govinda III matched his father's in brilliance, it was equally ephemeral. He was called to the Deccan on account of internal troubles that had broken out during his long absence in the north, and for nearly half a century the Rāshṭrakūṭas ceased to play any dominant part in north Indian politics. The field was thus left free to the two rival powers, the Pālas and the Pratīhāras. The reverses of Nāgabhaṭa II gave an opportunity to Dharmapāla and his son Devapāla to re-establish the power and supremacy of the Pālas, and there was a decline in the Pratīhāra power for the time being.

It is difficult to fix the date of the great victory of Govinda III over Nāgabhaṭa II, but it must have taken place before A.D. 809-10.[41] Although Nāgabhaṭa's imperial ambitions were curbed, his power was not destroyed. A record,[42] dated A.D. 815, found at Buchkalā in Bilada District, Jodhpur, gives him all the imperial titles and describes the locality as *sva-vishaya,* or his dominions proper. In addition to the three feudatories who helped him in his wars against the Pālas, we know of another, Gūvaka I, the founder of the Chāhamāna dynasty of Śākambharī (near Ajmer), who was his vassal (Ins. 6). Whether they threw off their allegiance to him after his discomfiture we cannot say, but this does not appear very likely. For, though the record (Ins. 2) of Bāuka, the Pratīhāra king of the Jodhpur dynasty, dated A.D. 837, would lend some colour to such a supposition, we should remember that Nāgabhaṭa's grandson Bhoja was able to enlist the support of his feudatories within a few years of his grandfather's death. On the whole we may conclude that Nāgabhaṭa II continued to exercise his sway over the greater part, if not the whole, of Rājputāna and Kāthiāwār Peninsula. In the east his sway extended up to Gwālior,[43] and probably further east so as to include Kanauj and Kālañjara.[44]

We learn from a Jain book, *Prabhāvaka-charita,*[45] that king Nāgāvaloka of Kānyakubja, the grandfather of Bhoja, died in 890 V.S. (=A.D. 833). This Nāgāvaloka is undoubtedly Nāgabhaṭa II, and if we can rely on this passage, his death must have taken place in A.D. 833. It would also appear that Nāgabhaṭa II had fixed his capital at Kanauj. But although Kanauj was the capital of Bhoja, we have no independent evidence that it was the Pratīhāra capital before his time. The reference to Kānyakubja in *Prabhāvaka-charita* may be explained by the fact that Kanauj had been the well-known capital of the Pratīhāras long before the thirteenth century A.D. when this book was composed. The reference to *svavishaya* in the Buchkalā record, noted above, and the claims of Dharmapāla and Devapāla in the Pāla records cannot be easily reconciled with the renewed imperialist ambition of Nāgabhaṭa II as would be necessarily indicated by his permanent transfer of capital to Kanauj. The admittedly inglorious reign of his son is also against such a supposition. The fact that the grandson of Nāgabhaṭa II was on the throne within three years of the date of his death, as given in *Prabhāvaka-charita,* throws doubt on the whole passage, but even if we accept it as true, we can only presume that the capital was changed towards the very end of his reign. The same passage in *Prabhāvaka-charita* also tells us that Nāgabhaṭa II put an end to his life by immersion in the holy waters of the Gaṅgā—a religious process adopted in later years by Rāmapāla of the Pāla dynasty and Amoghavarsha, the Rāshṭrakūṭa king. This shows his religious temperament, which is also testified to by his performance of religious ceremonies enjoined by the Vedas. An active religious sentiment is further proved by the eclectic spirit of the royal family—for four generations of Pratīhāra kings beginning from Devarāja were devotees respectively of Vishṇu, Śiva, Bhagavatī, and Sūrya.[46]

In spite of doubts and uncertainties, due to the paucity of data, the reigns of Vatsarāja and Nāgabhaṭa II occupy a prominent place in the contemporary history of India. Both of them were remarkable personalities and had a high degree of military skill; and the ultimate reverses at the hands of the Rāshṭrakūṭas cannot minimise the glory they had achieved by extensive military conquests from one end of north India to the other. They raised a provincial principality into a first-rate military and political power, and although their dreams of founding a stable empire were not actually realised, they laid its foundations so well that ere long king Bhoja succeeded in the great task even in the face of very strenuous opposition from his hereditary foes, the Pālas and the Rāshṭrakūṭas.

Nāgabhaṭa II was succeeded by his son Rāmabhadra, who had a very short and inglorious reign of probably three years. His kingdom, which certainly extended up to Gwālior in the east,[47] but probably no further, seems to have been overrun by hostile forces.[48] It is curious, as two copper-plate charters[49] record, that two grants, made by his father, had lapsed during his reign, and had to be confirmed by his successor. All this shows a period of weakness and trouble, probably brought about by the aggressive policy of the Pāla emperor Devapāla as will be noted in the next chapter.

4. BHOJA

With the accession of Rāmabhadra's son and successor Bhoja, a new and glorious chapter begins in the history of the Pratīhāras. The earliest record of the king is the Barah copper-plate[50] which he issued in A.D. 836 from his camp (*skandhāvāra*) at Mahodaya in order to confirm an endowment in the Kālañjara subdivision (*maṇḍala*) of the division (*bhukti*) of Kānyakubja which had been obstructed during the reign of his father. It shows that Bhoja had ascended the throne in or before A.D. 836, and was already in possession of the region round Kālañjara (Bāndā District, U.P.). If Mahodaya denoted Kanauj, as is generally supposed, we must further presume that he was also in occupation of that city and probably had his capital there. It has been urged, however, against this view, that Mahodaya, in this record, was not identical with Kānyakubja which is mentioned separately as such, and that the epithet *skandhāvāra* or camp could not have been appropriate for a *rājadhānī* (capital) like Kanauj. The latter objection may be easily ruled out, as even famous capital cities like Pāṭaliputra and Vikramapura have been referred to as *skandhāvāra* in the records of the Pāla and Sena kings. The other objection, though more valid, is also not decisive. For the older name might have been used for the big Division, while the city proper could be referred to by the alternative name. On the whole it is likely, though not certain, that as early as A.D. 836, Bhoja had fixed his capital at Kanauj, and obtained mastery of the region round it, which had been probably lost during his father's reign.

The Jodhpur Pratīhāras, whose history has been dealt with above,[51] also came into prominence and probably regained independence during the inglorious reign of Rāmabhadra. This seems to follow from the family records of both the branches. The Jodhpur Inscription, as noted above,[52] describes the two successors of Śīluka as practising austerities, an unmistakable indication of the decline in their political and military authority. But the next king Kakka is described as a great fighter who, as noted above, accompanied Nāgabhaṭa II in his expedition against the Pāla king of Bengal. But although he acknowledged the suzerainty of Nāgabhaṭa II at first, he seems to have practically behaved like an independent king in later years. In the Jodhpur Inscription dated A.D. 837 (Ins. 2), Kakka's queen-consort is called a *Mahārājñī*, and the career of their son Bāuka is described in terms which make him out to be an independent king, at least *de facto*, if not *de jure*. This conclusion is corroborated by the Daulatpura copper-plate of Bhoja[53] which records that a piece of land in Gurjaratrā, the home-territory of the Jodhpur Pratīhāras, which was originally granted by Vatsarāja and continued by Nāgabhaṭa II, fell into abeyance, and was renewed by Bhoja in A.D. 843. This indicates like the Barah copper-plate, that there was obstruction in the enjoyment of land during the reign of Rāmabhadra, and this fits in well with the view that the Jodhpur

Pratīhāras threw off the yoke of this king. The copper-plate further shows that by A.D. 843 Bhoja had reasserted his authority over Gurjaratrā or Central and Eastern Rājputāna. The success of Bhoja was undoubtedly due to the loyal devotion of some of his feudatories, one of whom, the Guhilot prince Harsharāja, son of Śaṅkaragaṇa,[64] is said to have overcome the kings in the north and presented horses to Bhoja (Ins. 4).

It is thus clear that Bhoja succeeded, within a few years of his accession, in re-establishing, to a considerable extent, the fortunes of his family. But soon he had to measure his strength with the Pāla king Devapāla. Bhoja was defeated, and his triumphant career was arrested, as will be related in the next chapter. He now turned his attention to the south, no doubt tempted by the distracted condition of the Rāshṭrakūṭas.[55] Some time between A.D. 845 and 860 he seems to have invaded the Rāshṭrakūṭa dominions, but was defeated by Dhruva, the Rāshṭrakūṭa chief of the Gujarāt branch.[56] Thus the growing power of the Pratīhāras was once more checked by their two hereditary enemies. Bhoja was also defeated by the Kalachuri king Kokkalla (c. 845-880).[57] It is interesting to note that the Rāshṭrakūṭa inscription, which records the defeat of Bhoja, refers to him in very flattering terms, and describes him as "united to fortune and surrounded by crowds of noble kinsmen," and having "conquered all the regions of the world." This shows that Bhoja had already raised his kingdom to a position of eminence. But there is no doubt that the defeat at the hands of the Pālas, the Rāshṭrakūtas, and the Kalachuris was a great blow to his rising power which perhaps declined to a considerable extent.

An indication of this decline is seen in the renewed power of the Jodhpur Pratīhāras. Bāuka's step-brother and successor Kakkuka refers in two of his inscriptions, dated A.D. 861,[58] to Gurjaratrā and other provinces as forming part of his own dominions. Thus Bhoja must have lost his hold over this part of Rājputāna some time between A.D. 843 and 861. It appears that after some initial successes Bhoja's attempt to re-establish the glory of his family proved a failure.

But Bhoja did not lose heart and bided his time. An inscription,[59] dated A.D. 876, refers to his resolve "to conquer the three worlds", and there is no doubt that he renewed his aggressive career some time in the third quarter of the ninth century A.D. The death of Devapāla removed a thorn in his side, for the next two kings of the Pāla dynasty, who ruled during the second half of the ninth century A.D., were weak and peace-loving. Fortunately for him the Rāshṭrakūṭa king Amoghavarsha, who ruled from A.D. 814 to c. A.D. 878, was also of a religious disposition, and did not have the aggressive imperialism or military ambition of his two illustrious predecessors, Dhruva and Govinda III. Nevertheless Amoghavarsha came into conflict with the Pāla rulers, and probably, after his conquest of Veṅgī, invaded the Pāla dominions from the south and gained some successes. Perhaps taking advantage of the weakness of the Pāla rulers and their distracted condition due to the Rāshṭrakūṭa raids, Bhoja planned a campaign against Bengal. The combined testimony of several records indicates that he was helped in this enterprise by Guṇāmbhodhideva, the Chedi ruler of Gorakhpur, and the Guhilot chief Guhila II, son of Harsharāja.[60] Assisted by these powerful chiefs Bhoja appears to have inflicted a crushing defeat upon the Pāla king Nārāyaṇapāla and conquered a considerable part of his western dominions.

Bhoja was also engaged in a prolonged struggle with the Rāshṭrakūṭas.[61] Reference has already been made to his fight with Dhruva of Gujarāt. It was renewed during the reign of Kṛishṇa II (c. A.D. 878-914). Bhoja probably took the offensive and gained considerable success. A Pratīhāra record[62] refers to the defeat of Kṛishṇa II, probably on the banks of the Narmadā, and his retreat to the south of the river. After having thus occupied Mālwā, Bhoja advanced towards Gujarāt. The Rāshṭrakūṭa records admit that not only Kheṭaka (Kaira District) but also the region round it fell into his hands. They, however, assert that Kṛishṇa II recovered them, and there was a sanguinary battle between the two hosts at Ujjayinī which made a deep impress even upon posterity.[63] It is generally held that Bhoja lost Mālwā as a result of this defeat, which took place some time between A.D. 878 and 888. But this is by no means certain. An inscription[64] at Partābgarh, in Southern Rājputāna, refers to a local Chāhamāna dynasty which was a source of great pleasure to king Bhojadeva. It has been suggested, with a great degree of plausibility, that these Chāhamānas helped their overlord Bhoja in his wars against the Rāshṭrakūṭas. This Chāhamāna dynasty acknowledged the suzerainty of the Pratīhāras in the time of Mahendrapāla II (A.D. 946), and asked for some favours from the representatives of their overlord at Ujjayinī and Maṇḍapikā (Māṇḍu) about the same time. It would thus appear that Mālwā formed a part of the Pratīhāra dominions even so late as A.D. 946, and as we know that it was conquered by Bhoja, it is more reasonable to suppose that it continued to be in the possession of the Pratīhāras rather than that it was reconquered by his successors all of whom, except his son Mahendrapāla I, were too weak to be credited with any such new acquisition. In any case, we may take for granted that the Partābgarh region formed a part of the dominions of Bhoja, and Mālwā, even if lost, was reconquered by Mahendrapāla I.

Although Bhoja lost his hold upon Kheṭaka or Kaira District, he maintained supremacy over probably the whole of Kāthiāwār Peninsula.[65] In the north-west his dominions extended to the Punjāb. In the east the Kalachuris of Gorakhpur were his feudatories, and probably the whole of Awadh (Oudh) was included in his dominions. The Chandellas of Bundelkhand also acknowledged his overlordship. Bhoja thus consolidated a mighty empire in Northern India for which Vatsarāja and Nāgabhaṭa had fought in vain, and raised Kanauj, his capital, once more to the position of an imperial city.

Bhoja had a long reign of more than 46 years, two of his known dates being A.D. 836 and 882.[66] An Arab account of India, composed in A.D. 851 and generally attributed to Sulaimān, refers to the great power and resources of the king of Juzr. As Juzr undoubtedly stands for Gurjara, the Arab account may be taken to refer to Bhoja. As such it is an interesting commentary upon his reign and personality and may be reproduced in full:—

"This king maintains numerous forces and no other Indian prince has so fine a cavalry. He is unfriendly to the Arabs, still he acknowledges that the king of the Arabs is the greatest of kings. Among the princes of India, there is no greater foe of the Muhammadan faith than he. His territories form a tongue of land. He has got riches, and his camels and horses are numerous. Exchanges are carried on in his states with silver (and gold) in dust, and there are said to be mines (of these metals) in the country. There is no country in India more safe from robbers."[67]

It is thus evident that Bhoja had the reputation of a strong ruler, able to maintain peace in his kingdom and defend it against external dangers. He stood as a bulwark of defence against Muslim aggression, and left this task as a sacred legacy to his successors.

Bhoja was undoubtedly one of the outstanding political figures of India in the ninth century, and ranks with Dhruva and Dharmapāla as a great general and empire-builder. Unfortunately, we know very little of his personal history,[68] except that he was a devotee of Bhagavatī and was known by various names such as Prabhāsa, Ādivarāha, and Mihira, in addition to Bhoja which was most commonly used.

5. MAHENDRAPALA

Bhoja probably died about A.D. 885, and was succeeded by his son Mahendrapāla I, whose earliest known date is A.D. 893 (Ins. 3). A verse in *Rājataraṅgiṇī*, the meaning of which is obscure, seems to indicate that he lost some territory in the Punjāb, gained by his father, to Śaṅkaravarman king of Kāshmir.[69] But, with this doubtful exception, Mahendrapāla not only maintained intact the vast empire inherited by him, but also further expanded it towards the east. No less than seven of his records have been found in South Bihār and North Bengal with dates ranging from years 2 to 19. These indicate that shortly after his accession he conquered Magadha and even a part of Northern Bengal, the home territory of his hereditary enemy, the Pālas. Mahendrapāla's records have also been found in Kāthiāwār Peninsula, Eastern Punjāb, Jhānsi District and Awadh (Oudh), and we may say, without much exaggeration, that his empire extended from the Himālayas to the Vindhyas and from the Eastern to the Western ocean.

The name of Mahendrapāla is also written in slightly varying forms such as Mahīndrapāla and Mahendrāyudha, and he was also known as Nirbhaya-narendra or Nirbhayarāja.[70] His *guru*, or spiritual preceptor, Rājaśekhara, is a famous personality in Indian literature. Although his writings do not throw any light on the career or personality of Mahendrapāla, they refer in unmistakable terms to the glory and grandeur of the imperial city of Kanauj.

6. MAHĪPALA

Mahendrapāla's last known date is A.D. 907-8,[71] and he probably died not long afterwards. The succession to the throne after him is a matter of dispute, as the available data lend themselves to various interpretations. He had at least two queens, Dehanāgādevī and Mahīdevī (or Mahādevī).[72] The son of the former, Bhoja II, ascended the throne before Vināyakapāla, the son of the latter, one of whose known dates is A.D. 931 (Ins. 9). Mahīpāla,[73] a son of Mahendrapāla, is known to have ruled in A.D. 914[74] and A.D. 917 (Ins. 8), while a king Kshitipāla is known to be the father of king Devapāla ruling in A.D. 948-9 (Ins. 7). There are good grounds to believe that the last two kings also belonged to the same family. A king Devapāla, with the epithet *Hayapati* (lord of horses), son of Herambapāla, is mentioned in another contemporary inscription,[75] and it is held by some that this Devapāla is identical with his namesake, ruling in A.D. 948-9. Thus his father would be Herambapāla *alias* Kshitipāla, and as these are synonymous respectively with Vināyakapāla and Mahīpāla, the identity of all the four is generally presumed, and the genealogy is drawn up as follows[76]:—

Dehanāgādevī = Mahendrapāla I = Mahīdevī (or Mahādevī)

Bhoja II

Vināyakapāla
(*alias* Mahīpāla
alias Kshitipāla
alias Herambapāla)
(A.D. 914, 917, 931)

Some scholars, however, do not accept the identification of the two kings named Devapāla, and therefore regard Vināyakapāla as different from Mahīpāla *alias* Kshitipāla.[77] Others again identify the latter with Bhoja II.[78] It is impossible, with the insufficient data now available, to prove or disprove any of these hypotheses. So we may provisionally accept the genealogy drawn up above.

It is significant that while the Grant of Vināyakapāla, dated A.D. 931, refers to his elder brother Bhoja II as his predecessor, the earlier Grant, dated A.D. 917, makes no reference to Bhoja II, and represents Mahīpāla as having succeeded Mahendrapāla. It has been suggested that this omission may be due to short duration of Bhoja's reign or to a struggle for succession between the two.[79] But it may be easily explained by the not uncommon practice of tracing only the direct descent of the ruling king by omitting all references to collateral line. The short duration of reign is not a satisfactory explanation, and if we accept the identification of Mahīpāla and Vināyakapāla, we can hardly explain the omission in one Grant and not in the other as due to rivalry. It has been urged that with the lapse of time the memory of the old rivalry faded away, and hence the reference to the reign of the elder brother was made in A.D. 931 but not in A.D. 917. But this is questionable.

A struggle for succession to the throne has been inferred from the statement in the Kalachuri records that Kokkalladeva I "set up Bhojadeva" and "granted him freedom from fear." These expressions have been taken to mean that Bhoja II invoked the aid of Kokkalla in the war of succession against his brother.[80] But apart from the fact that it is uncertain whether Bhoja here refers to the father or son of Mahendrapāla,[81] we need not assume that any help that Kokkalla might have rendered to Bhoja II was necessarily against his brother. For a Rāshṭrakūṭa record seems to imply that Kṛishṇa II invaded the dominions of the Pratīhāras and occupied the Yamunā-Gaṅgā Doāb. The veracity of this claim has been doubted by many scholars, but there may be some truth in it,[82] and if Bhoja II sought the help of Kokkalla, it might have been on such an occasion.

On the whole, we have no definite knowledge of the events that followed the death of Mahendrapāla. The weakness of the empire, as revealed by the advance of the Rāshṭrakūṭas to the very gates of the imperial city and its destruction by them, not much later, about A.D. 916, undoubtedly lends colour to the theory of internal dissensions, but we must remember that the Rāshṭrakūṭas achieved similar successes even during the reigns of powerful kings like Vatsarāja and Nāgabhaṭa II.

In any case there are no good grounds against the view that when Mahīpāla ascended the throne, about A.D. 912, the empire enjoyed peace and prosperity. An inscription, dated A.D. 914, proves his suzerainty over the Kāthiāwār Peninsula. Al Mas'ūdī, a native of Baghdād, who visited India in the year A.D. 915-16, refers to the great power and resources of the Pratīhāra king of Kanauj, and the wide extent of his kingdom, which touched the Rāshṭrakūṭa kingdom in the south, and the Muslim principality of Multān in the west, with both of which he was at war. He was, we are told, rich in horses and camels, and maintained four armies in four directions, each numbering 700,000 or 900,000 men.[83]

The poet Rājaśekhara, who graced the court of Mahīpāla, as that of his father, refers to the former as "the pearl-jewel of the lineage of Raghu" and "the *Mahārājādhirāja* of Āryāvarta". He also describes the conquests of Mahīpāla in a grandiloquent verse according to which the emperor defeated the Muralas, Mekalas, Kaliṅgas, Keralas, Kulūtas, Kuntalas, and Ramaṭhas.[84] This would mean the suzerainty not only of nearly the whole of Northern India, but also of a part of the Deccan where the Rāshṭrakūṭas ruled. Even making due allowance for the panegyrical exaggerations of the court-poet, it may be reasonably held that Mahīpāla not only maintained intact the empire inherited by him, but probably even extended it in the early part of his reign.[85]

But once more the eternal enemies, the Rāshṭrakūṭas, were to prove the doom of the Pratīhāra empire. Leaving aside the boast of the Rāshṭrakūṭa king Kṛishṇa II that he advanced up to the Gaṅgā, there is no doubt that his successor Indra III conducted a campaign against the Pratīhāra dominions some time between A.D. 915 and 918. According to a Rāshṭrakūṭa record,[86] Indra III advanced through Mālwā, crossed the Yamunā, and completely devastated the city of Kanauj. According to a Kanarese poem, *Pampabhārata*, Indra's feudatory Narasiṁha (Chālukya) took a prominent part in inflicting a crushing defeat upon Mahīpāla. It is said that "Mahīpāla fled, as if struck by thunderbolts, staying neither to eat, nor rest, nor pick himself up; while Narasiṁha, pursuing, bathed his horses at the junction of the Gaṅgā."[87]

Thus according to the Rāshṭrakūṭa version Indra III had a complete victory. He occupied the capital city of his enemy and sacked it, while Mahīpāla fled for his life, hotly pursued by the hostile forces as far as Allāhābād. But, as on previous occasions, the Rāshṭrakūṭas did not stay long enough to consolidate their conquests in the north.

It redounds to the credit of Mahīpāla that he survived this terrible shock and re-established the fortunes of his family. This was due mainly to the help of his powerful feudatories. According to a Chandella record,[88] king Harsha placed Kshitipāla on the throne. It refers most probably to the help rendered by the powerful Chandella chief to Kshitipāla or Mahīpāla in regaining the throne after the Rāshṭrakūṭa debacle.[89] The Guhilot chief Bhaṭṭa, grandson of Harsharāja, who helped Bhoja I, is said to have defeated in battle the king of the south, at the command of his paramount lord, at a time of great danger when the kingdom was invaded by foreign soldiers and everything was in confusion (Ins. 4). This also probably alludes to the defeat inflicted upon the Rāshṭrakūṭas after they had overrun the Pratīhāra dominions. The recovery of Mālwā is hinted at by the vainglorious claim made by Bhāmāna, the feudatory Kalachuri chief of Gorakhpur, that he conquered Dhārā (Ins. 5).

Whether Mahīpāla succeeded in recovering all the territories he had lost is difficult to determine. But we have literary and epigraphic records to show that in A.D. 931 the empire of Mahīpāla-Vināyakapāla extended up to Saurāshṭra (Kāthiāwār Peninsula) in the west[90] and Banaras in the east (Ins. 9), and in A.D. 942-3 up to Chanderi (Narwar) in the south.[91] Even so late as A.D. 946, the Pratīhāra empire included Mālwā (Ins. 10). It would thus appear that Mahīpāla recovered at least a large part, if not the whole, of his dominions, but there can be no doubt that the prestige of the Imperial Pratīhāras suffered a severe blow from which they never fully recovered.[92] The feudatory chiefs and provincial governors slowly asserted independence, and new dynasties rose to power. This will be evident from the history of the Chandellas, Chedis, and Paramāras dealt with in a separate chapter. The decline and the process of disintegration of the Pratīhāra empire offer a close parallel to the fate which overtook the Mughal empire in the eighteenth century.

Towards the close of Mahīpāla's reign the Rāshṭrakūṭas seem to have again invaded the north. It is said in a Rāshṭrakūṭa record,[93] dated A.D. 940, that "on hearing of the conquest of all the strongholds (by Kṛishṇa III) in the southern regions simply by means of his angry glance, the hope about Kālañjara and Chitrakūṭa vanished from the heart of the Gurjara." It has been inferred from this that these two forts of the Pratīhāras were occupied by the Rāshṭrakūṭa army shortly before A.D. 940.[94]

7. MAHĪPĀLA'S SUCCESSORS

Vināyakapāla ruled till at least A.D. 942,[95] and was succeeded by his son Mahendrapāla II,[96] whose known date is A.D. 945-6 (Ins. 10). During the next 15 years there is a succession of no less than four kings, *viz.* (1) Devapāla (A.D. 948-9), son of Kshitipāla (Ins. 7); (2) Vināyakapāla II (A.D. 953-4); (3) Mahīpāla II (A.D. 955);[97] and (4) Vijayapāla (A.D. 960), successor of Kshitipāla (Ins. 11). Whether all these were distinct rulers or two or more of them were identical, it is difficult to say. Dr. Bhandarkar identifies Mahendrapāla II with Devapāla, and takes the kings Nos. 2, 3 and the predecessor of No. 4 to be the same person.[98] Dr. N. Ray[99] takes No. 1 to be son of Bhoja II, whom he identifies with Mahīpāla *alias* Kshitipāla, but distinguishes him from Vināyakapāla. He also suggests that No. 2 was probably a son of Mahendrapāla II, No. 3 a son of No. 1, and No. 4 a son of No. 3, who was also called Kshitipāla. Dr. Tripathi[100] regards Nos. 1 and 2 respectively as a brother and a son of Mahendrapāla II, and No. 4 as a brother or half-brother of No. 1. He argues that there is not sufficient ground to hold that No. 3 was a Pratīhāra emperor, and he might have been a vassal ruler who, as Rajor Inscription (Ins. 11) shows, often assumed imperial titles.[101] It is also doubtful whether No. 2 is a separate king ruling in A.D. 953-4, or is to be identified with Vināyakapāla I whose name appeared in a record long after his death.[102]

The different views are quoted above just to indicate the great uncertainty prevailing about the succession to the imperial throne between A.D. 945 and 960. There is, however, no doubt that there was a steady decline in the power and authority of the empire during this period. The Chāhamānas of Partābgarh, in south-east Rājputāna, acknowledged Mahendrapāla II as overlord, and the imperial officers were posted at Ujjayinī and Maṇḍapikā (Māndu) in A.D. 945-6 (Ins. 10). But in a record dated A.D. 954, we find the Chandellas taking credit for defeating the Gurjaras and forcibly taking possession of the famous fort of Kālañjara, though they still refer to Vināyakapāla as protecting the earth.[103] An inscription dated A.D. 960 (Ins. 11), found at Rajorgarh, about 28 miles southwest of the town of Alwar, records an order issued by the *Mahā-*

rājādhirāja, Parameśvara, the illustrious Mathanadeva of the Gurjara-Pratīhāra lineage, residing at Rājyapura (*i.e.* Rajor), to his officials. This record leaves no doubt that although, like the Chandellas, he invoked the name of the Pratīhāra Emperor Vijayapāladeva as his suzerain, yet he ruled as a *de facto* independent king.

Most probably the Rāshṭrakūṭa king Kṛishṇa III led a second expedition to Northern India about A.D. 963. His feudatory, Gaṅga chief Mārasiṁha, distinguished himself so much in this northern campaign that he came to be known as the king of the Gurjaras. This proves that the main brunt of the attack fell upon the Pratīhāras. The great success of the Rāshṭrakūṭa king is proved by his Kanarese record incised on a stone slab found at Jura, 12 miles from Maihar Railway Station in Bundelkhand.[104]

Although the Rāshṭrakūṭas could not achieve any permanent success they probably gave the final blow to the Pratīhāra domination in Central India. The Chandella ruler Dhaṅga (A.D. 950-1000) claims to have attained "supreme lordship after inflicting a defeat over the king of Kānyakubja." Even Gwālior, which was a stronghold of the Pratīhāras ever since the time of Rāmabhadra, if not earlier still, fell into the hands of the Chandellas. A few years later the Kachchhapaghāta chief Vajradāman conquered it after defeating the Pratīhāra Emperor.[105]

The Chāhamānas of Śākambharī, many of whose chiefs helped their Pratīhāra overlords as noted above,[106] asserted their independence, and so did also the Guhilas[107] and perhaps some other vassals. While the feudatories were gradually defying the imperial authority, there arose new powers like the Kalachuris in Central India, the Paramāras in Mālwā, and the Chaulukyas in Gujarāt to weaken still further the declining authority of the Pratīhāras.

The history of these powers, which is related in detail in a subsequent chapter, leaves no doubt that about the middle of the tenth century A.D. the Pratīhāra empire disintegrated and was gradually reduced to the territory round about Kanauj. We do not possess any record of the Pratīhāra emperors for nearly half a century after Vijayapāla, who was on the throne early in A.D. 960. When the curtain rises again in A.D. 1019, the Pratīhāra empire had vanished and North India presented the same political features as inevitably followed the disruption of an empire. Rājyapāla, the successor of Vijayapāla, ruled over the small kingdom of Kanauj, but the old imperial name and fame still lingered for a decade, to be finally swept away by the invasions of Sultān Mahmūd. Trilochanapāla,[108] the successor of Rājyapāla, ruling in A.D. 1027, is the last of the Imperial Pratīhāras known to us.

Attention may be drawn to the fact that three of the powerful succession states that arose out of the ruins of the Pratīhāra empire were those of the Chāhamānas (Chauhāns) in Rājputāna, Chaulukyas (Solankis) in Gujarāt, and the Paramāras (Pawārs) in Mālwā. It is interesting to note that these three, along with the Parihāras (Pratīhāras), are described in bardic traditions as Agnikula, originating from a sacrificial fire-pit (*agnikuṇḍa*) on Mount Abu. Whatever we might think of this mythical legend, it is not unlikely that these four tribes were connected by ethnic ties or some other close association, and we may therefore hold that a considerable part of the empire of the Pratīhāras, specially their home-territory and original dominions, passed into the hands of kindred peoples who had hitherto accepted their suzerainty.

8. THE PRATĪHĀRA EMPIRE—A GENERAL REVIEW

The Pratīhāra empire, which continued in full glory for nearly a century, was the last great empire in Northern India before the Muslim conquest. This honour is accorded to the empire of Harsha by many historians of repute, but without any real justification; for the Pratīhāra empire was probably larger, certainly not less in extent, and its duration was much longer. It recalled, and to a certain extent rivalled, the Gupta empire, and brought political unity and its attendant blessings upon a large part of Northern India. But its chief credit lies in its successful resistance to the foreign invasions from the west. From the days of Junaid (*c.* A.D. 725) to those of Mahmūd of Ghaznī, the Pratīhāras stood as the bulwark of India's defence against the aggression of the Muslims. This was frankly recognised by the Arab writers themselves. Historians of India, since the days of Elphinstone, have wondered at the slow progress of Muslim invaders in India, compared to their rapid advance in other parts of the world. Arguments of doubtful validity have often been put forward to explain this unique phenomenon. But now there can be little doubt that it was the power of the Pratīhāra arms that effectively barred the progress of the Muslims beyond the confines of Sindh, their first conquest, for nearly three hundred years. In the light of later events this must be regarded as the chief contribution of the Pratīhāras to the history of India.

The Pratīhāra empire was the logical end of the tripartite struggle for power that characterised the history of India for nearly a century (A.D. 750-850). Dhruva and Govinda III, as well as Dharmapāla and Devapāla, played the imperial role, and then came the turn of the Pratīhāras under Bhoja and Mahendrapāla. Though in each case the empire, like waves of the sea, rose to the highest point only to break down, the Pratīhāras had a longer spell of success than either of their rivals.

The Pratīhāra line was distinguished for its long succession of able rulers. Apart from the hero who founded the royal dynasty, four such remarkable personalities as Vatsarāja, Nāgabhaṭa II, Bhoja, and Mahendrapāla, ruled almost uninterruptedly for a century and a half with a short break of three years. They created the tradition of an imperial glory which long endured and survived many rude shocks. It is reflected in the literary works of Rājaśekhara, the last Indian poet who could, with justifiable pride, refer to his royal patron as "the *Mahārājādhirāja* of Āryāvarta" (King-Emperor of Northern India). But the best testimony to the power and glory of the Pratīhāras is the eloquent tribute paid to their wealth and resources by their inveterate enemies, the Arabs.

GENERAL REFERENCES

1. R. C. Majumdar, The Gurjara-Pratīhāras. *JDL*. X. 1-76 (abbreviated as *GP*).
2. R. S. Tripathi, *History of Kanauj* (abbreviated as *THK*).
3. A. S. Altekar, *The Rāshṭrakūṭas and their times* (abbreviated as *AR*).
4. D. Sharma, The Imperial Pratīhāras—a revised study. (*JIH*, XXII. 93).
5. N Ray, A note on the chronology of the Later Pratīhāras. (*IA*, LVII. 230).

IMPORTANT INSCRIPTIONS (Referred to in the text by the serial No.)

1. Gwālior Stone Inscription of Bhoja, *EI*, XVIII. 99.
2. Jodhpur Inscription of Bāuka, *EI*, XVIII. 87.
3. Two Grants of Chālukya Chiefs of the Time of Mahendrapāla, *EI*. IX. 1.
4. Chatsu Inscription of the Guhilot chief Bālāditya, *EI*, XII. 13.
5. Kahla Plate of Kalachuri Soḍhadeva, *EI*, VII. 88.
6. Harsha or Haras Stone Inscription of the Chāhamāna Vigraharāja, *EI*, II. 119 ff; *IA*, XLII. 60 ff.
7. Siyadoni Inscription, *EI*, I. 162.
8. Asni Inscription of Mahīpāla (A.D. 917), *IA*, XVI. 173.
9. Bengal Asiatic Society's CP of Vināyakapāla (A.D. 931), *IA*, XV. 138.
10. Partābgarh Inscription of Mahendrapāla II (A.D. 946), *EI*, XIV. 176.
11. Rajorgarh Inscription of Vijayapāla (A.D. 960), *EI*, III. 263.
12. Barah CP of Bhoja, *EI*, XIX. 15; XXIII. 242.
13. Daulatpura CP of Bhoja, *EI*, V. 208; *JBBRAS*, XXI. 410.
14. Gwālior Ins. of Bhoja, dated V. 932. *EI*. I. 154.

1. Ch. X, pp. 153 ff.
2. Cf. Vol. III, p. 155.
3. Cf. Vol. III, p. 153.
4. Cf. *JDL*, X. 10 and the authorities referred to therein.
5. Vol. III, pp. 155, 173.
6. Vol. III, p. 154.
7. Cf. Ins. No. 2, given above.
8. Vol. III, p. 173.
9. Sanjān CP. *EI*, XVIII. 235.
10. *JDL*, X. 25; *EI*, XVIII. 239; *THK*. 226-7; *AR*. 40 (fn. 32).
11. *IHQ*, VI. 753; *ABORI*, XVIII. 396; *IC*, XI. 161.
12. Curiously enough this fact, mentioned in the Ellora Ins. (*ASWI*, V. 87), is not referred to by any of those who oppose the view that Vatsarāja ruled in Mālwā.
13. Cf. Hansot Pl. EI, XII. 197. The name of the suzerian king is given as Nāgāvaloka, but he is generally identified with Nāgabhaṭa I (*ibid*, 200). The grant was issued from Broach and records the gift of a village in Akrūreśvara-*vishaya* which has been identified with Anklesvar *tāluk* on the left bank of the Narmadā. We may, therefore, regard the Chāhamāna principality as extending up to the Kim river and thus corresponding to the old Gurjara kingdom of Nāndīpurī.

14. It has been urged (*JIH*, XXII. 94) that according to Antroli-Chharoli pl. (*JBBRAS*, XVI. 105), dated A.D. 757, "Karka II, a feudatory Rāshṭrakūṭa chief of Gujarāt, gave away villages from practically the same region, showing thereby that sometime between A.D. 756 and 757 the Rāshṭrakūṭa ruler Dantidurga had succeeded in defeating the Praṭīhāras and ending their supremacy in Lāṭa." But the villages granted lay to the south of the Kim river. Dr. Altekar argues (*AR*. 11) that "since the donee hailed from Jambusāra in the Broach District" this region was included in the dominions of Karka II. But this assumption can hardly be justified. On the whole, there is nothing to indicate that Nāgabhaṭa lost his supremacy over the feudatory principality of Broach which extended up to the Kim river in the south (see preceding note).
15. *ABORI*, XVIII. 397-8.
16. For various opinions, cf. *JDL*, X. 23-25. Also, *IC*, XI. 161 ff.
17. Fleet (*EI*, VI. 195); Bhandarkar (*EI*, XVIII. 238-9); Altekar (*AR*. 39); Tripathi (*THK*. 225-6).
18. J. C. Ghosh (*IHQ*, VI. 755); Dasaratha Sarma (*ABORI*, XVIII. 396; *JIH*, XXIII. 43); H. L. Jain (*IC*, XI. 161).
19. H. L. Jain, *op. cit.* But in the map on p. 165, Badnawar is placed to the *north-west* of Ujjain.
20. Baroda Pl. of Karkarāja, *IA*, XII, 163.
21. Daulatpura CP. (*EI*, V. 208); Osia Ins. (*ASI*, 1908-9, p. 108; *JRAS*, 1907, p. 1010).
22. *THK*. 213.
23. I proposed the identification of the Bhaṇḍis with the Bhaṭṭis (*JDL*, X. 28), and this view was accepted by Tripathi (*THK*. 229). Their identification with Bhaṇḍi's family was proposed by Ojha and is accepted by many. Bhaṇḍi is referred to in *Harsha-charita*, but we do not know anything about him or his successor, not even whether he was a ruling chief.
24. Rādhanpur and Wani Grant of Govinda III (*EI*, VI. 248; *IA*, XI. 157).
25. *IHQ*, XIV. 844.
26. Cf. *HBR*. 105, fn. 1, 2 and also Ch. III. §2, below.
27. Cf. fn. 24.
28. *Vide infra*, Ch. III, § 2.
29. The identification of these places has been discussed in *JRAS*, 1909, pp. 257-8. Anartta is northern part of Kāthiāwār Peninsula, and Vatsa probably represents the region round Kauśāmbī, or Rewa country, further to the south, which is associated with the name of Vatsa.
30. Cf. *JIH*, XXII. 99 ff, *PIHC*, XI. 141.
31. *JIH*, XXII. 103.
32. Baroda Pl. *IA*, XII, 163; Sisavai Grant, v. 15; *EI*, XXIII, 209.
32a. References are to the list of "Important Inscriptions" given at the end of this Chapter.
33. *Vide infra*, Ch. V, § VI.
34. For a possible conflict or alliance between Nāgabhaṭa II and the E. Chālukya king Vijayāditya II, cf. Ch. VI.
35. *JIH*, XXII. 102-3.
36. *EI*, XXVI. 185.
37. The Barah CP (EI, XIX. 15) shows that the Kālañjara-*maṇḍala* in the Kānyakubja-*bhukti* was included in the dominions of Nāgabhaṭa II.
38. Baroda Pl. *IA*, XII, 163.
39. The victory of Govinda III is referred to in many Rāshṭrakūṭa records of the main and Gurjara branches. Nāgabhaṭa is mentioned by name in Sanjān CP. (*EI*, XVIII. 235) which also refers to Govinda's advance up to the Himālayas. The Pathari Pillar Ins. (*EI*, IX. 255) refers to the 'hasty retreat' and 'devastated home' of Nāgāvaloka, who has been identified with Nāgabhaṭa II. Karkka, to whom the credit for this achievement is given, probably accompanied the Rāshṭrakūṭa king Govinda III (*IA*, 1911, 239).
40. Sanjān CP. v. 23 (*EI*. XVIII. 245).
41. Dr. Altekar has shown good grounds for the belief that Govinda III led more than one expedition to Northern India, and has given a revised chronology of his campaigns (*D. R. Bhandarkar Vol*. 153). But he has somewhat changed his views in the preceding chapter.
42. *EI*, IX. 198.
43. EI, I. 156-7.
44. *EI*, XIX. 15.
45. *THK*. 236; *JIH*, XXII. 104.

46. This appears from the epithets given to the various kings in the official genealogy contained in the royal charters.
47. *EI*, I. 154.
48. This seems to be hinted at in v. 12 of the Gwālior Ins. (No. 1).
49. *EI*, XIX. 15; v. 208.
50. *EI*, XIX. 15; XXIII. 242.
51. Vol. III. pp. 153 ff.
52. See p. 20.
53. *EI*, V. 208.
54. See above p. 25.
55. See above, p. 10.
56. Begumra Pl. *IA*, XII. 179.
57. See later, Ch. V. §II.
58. *JRAS*, 1895. 513; *EI*, IX. 277.
59. *EI*, I. 156.
60. Tripathi thinks that Guhila II accompanied Mahendrapāla I in his expedition against Bengal (*THK*. 250-255; cf. also Ch. V. §VII. 2). The question cannot be definitely decided one way or the other.
61. For a detailed account, cf. *PIHC*, VI. 166.
62. *EI*, XIX. 174.
63. Begumra Grant of Kṛishṇa (*IA*, XIII. 66); Begumra Grant of Indra III, No. I, v. 15, *EI*, IX. 31.
64. *EI*, XIV. 176.
65. This follows from the description of Arab writer Sulaimān that Bhoja's territory formed a tongue of land. It is also confirmed by a tradition in the *Skanda Purāṇa* to which Dr. Raychaudhuri drew attention (*IHQ*. V. 129-133).
66. Pehoa Ins. (*EI*, I. 184).
67. *HIED*, I. 4.
68. According to the story in the *Skanda Purāṇa*, referred to in fn. 65 above, Bhoja, king of Kānyakubja, abdicated his throne and went on a pilgrimage to the holy sites of Saurāshṭra. But this story, mixed up with myths and fables, can hardly be regarded as historical. Dr. Raychaudhuri has sought to prove the abdication by reference to epigraphic data, but without success (cf. *THK*. 245).
69. For full discussion on this point, cf. *JDL*, X. 55.
70. The name read by Fleet as Mahishapāla in the Asni CP. (*IA*, XVI. 173) is obviously a misreading for Mahīndrapāla.
71. Siyadoni Ins. (*EI*, I. 162).
72. This form occurs in Partābgarh Ins. (*EI*, XIV. 182).
73. Tripathi is wrong in his statement that according to Asni Ins. Mahīpāla was born of Mahīdevī (*THK*. 254). This (or any other) inscription does not give the name of Mahīpāla's mother.
74. Haddala CP. *IA*, XII. 190; XVIII. 90.
75. Khajurāho Ins. *EI*, I. 122.
76. *JDL*, X. 58-63; *THK*. 257.
77. *EI*, XIV. 180.
78. *IA*, LVII. 230.
79. *THK*. 255.
80. *Ibid*.
81. See later, Ch. V, §II.
82. *PIHC*, VI. 169.
83. *HIED*. I. 21.
84. For full discussion, cf. *JDL*. X. 63; *THK*. 263.
85. As Rājaśekhara was the *guru* of Mahendrapāla also, it is likely that he wrote his poems in the early part of Mahīpāla's reign.
86. *EI*, VII. 38.
87. *AR*. 101-2; *THK*. 260; *JDL*, X. 66.
88. Khajurāho Ins. EI, I. 121.
89. Some scholars hold that the incident refers to the help that Mahīpāla received in his struggle against his brother (*THK*. 256). But, as already noted above. we have no evidence of any such struggle for the throne.
90. Harisena associates Vinayādikapāla, in A.D. 931, with Vardhamānapura, usually identified with Wadhwan (above, p. 22). Cf. *IC*, XI. 162.
91. *ASI*, 1924-25, p. 168.
92. This is strongly denied by Tripathi (*THK*. 262, 270). He, however, observes that the Chandella ruler Yaśovarman gave 'a great blow to the prestige of the Pratīhāras' (*ibid*. 272).

93. Deoli Pl. (v. 25). *EI*, V. 188.
94. *THK*. 267-8; *AR*. 113. But this does not seem very likely. Possibly the two forts were conquered by a third power (Kalachuris or Chandellas) allied to the Rāshṭrakūṭas, and the Gurjara-Pratīhāras gave up all hopes of recovering them (cf. *JOR*. XVI. 155-58). For a critical discussion of Mahīpāla's reign cf. *JIH*, XXXVIII, 611-26.
95. *ASI*, 1924-25, p. 168.
96. Bhandarkar infers from Ins. 10 that Vidagdha was an epithet of Mahendrapāla II (List No. 61. fn. 3).
97. Bayna Ins. (*EI*, XXII. 122).
98. List of Ins. p. 400.
99. *IA*, LVII. 234.
100. *THK*. 271-4.
101. *Ibid*. 275.
102. The Khajurāho Ins. of Dhaṅga, dated A.D. 954 (*EI*, I. 122), mentions, in the last line, Vināyakapāladeva as protecting the earth. There is no doubt that he was the Pratīhāra ruler of Kanauj to whom the Chandellas still paid at least nominal allegiance. He was formerly identified with Vināyakapāla I whose last known date is A.D. 942. But as he must have died before A.D. 946, the known date of his son and successor Mahendrapāla II (ins. 10), it was held that the inscription, though originally drafted earlier than A.D. 946, was actually set up in A.D. 954, without any modification of the suzerain's name. But this explanation is not accepted by some scholars who regard him as a different ruler Vināyakapāla II (*THK*. 273; *IA*, LVII. 232).
103. See preceding note. If, as noted above, the fort of Kālañjara had been seized by the Rāshṭrakūṭas, the Chandellas probably recovered it from them. But even then they conquered it on their own account and not on behalf of their Gurjara-Pratīhāra overlord. It is possible that the successful reconquest of this region from the Rāshṭrakūṭas made the Chandellas virtually an independent power.
104. *EI*, XIX. 287. Altekar takes quite a different view of the expedition (*AR*. 121), but does not meet the argument of Mr. N. L. Rao (*EI*, XIX. 289) that the northern campaign of Kṛishṇa III took place in A.D. 963-4. The reference to the Gurjaras makes it unlikely that the campaign was directed against a Paramāra king, as Altekar thinks. Evidently Altekar has changed his view; cf. above p. 14.
105. *IA*, XV. 36. This must have taken place before A.D. 977 when Vajradāman was already in possession of Gwālior (*JASB*, XXXI. 393).
106. See pp. 22, 27, 31.
107. *Vide infra*, the history of the Guhilas and Chāhamānas in Ch. V.
108. Jhusi CP. *IA*, XVIII. 33. Another king Yaśaḥpāla is known from Kara Ins. (*JRAS*, 1927, p. 692), but it is not definitely known whether he belonged to the Imperial Pratīhāra family.

CHAPTER III

THE PĀLAS

1. THE RISE OF THE PĀLAS

Reference has been made above[1] to the political disintegration of Bengal resulting in anarchy and confusion for more than a century after the death of Śaśāṅka. But about the middle of the eighth century A.D. a heroic and laudable effort was made to remedy the miserable state of things. The people at last realized that all their troubles were due to the absence of a strong central authority and that this could be set up only by the voluntary surrender of powers to one popular leader by the numerous chiefs exercising sovereignty in different parts of the country. It reflects no small credit upon the political sagacity and the spirit of sacrifice of the leading men of Bengal that they rose to the occasion and selected one among themselves to be the sole ruler of Bengal to whom they all paid willing allegiance.[2] It is not every age, it is not every nation, that can show such a noble example of subordinating private interests to public welfare. The nearest parallel is the great political change that took place in Japan in A.D. 1870. The result was almost equally glorious and the great bloodless revolution ushered in an era of glory and prosperity such as Bengal has never enjoyed before or since.

The hero who was thus called to the throne by the popular voice was named Gopāla. We do not know anything of his early history, but may very well presume that he was a leading chief who had already made his mark as a ruler and a general.[3] His father Vapyaṭa is said to have destroyed his enemies, and was perhaps a military chief of renown, but we cannot say whether he was a ruling chief. Dayitavishṇu, the grandfather of Gopāla, is only described as a learned man and evidently had no military achievements to his credit. Gopāla was thus the real founder of the ruling dynasty which came to be known as Pāla, from the last part of his name which formed the name-ending of all his successors —affording an almost exact parallel to the Gupta dynasty. Gopāla was a Kshatriya, or at least came to be regarded as such, and it was only at a very late age that his family claimed any mythical pedigree such as descent from the Sun or the Ocean. Gopāla was a Buddhist and so were all his successors. According to Tibetan tradition, Gopāla founded a monastery at Nālandā.

In a poetical work *Rāmacharita*[4], written by a court-poet of a later Pāla king, Varendrī or North Bengal is said to be the fatherland (*janakabhū*) of the Pālas. At the same time, there are good grounds to believe that Gopāla's original kingdom was in Vaṅga or East Bengal. We may, therefore, readily accept Tāranātha's account according to which Gopāla was born of a Kshatriya family near Puṇḍravardhana (Bogra District), but was subsequently elected ruler of Bhaṅgala, which was undoubtedly a corrupt form of Vaṅgāla or Vaṅga. Tāranātha seems to imply that the election was only in respect of this kingdom which formed a part of Bengal. But the Khālimpur copper-plate (No. 1)[4a] of Gopāla's son Dharmapāla speaks of his having been elected without any such geographical limitations. But whatever might have been the original limits of his kingdom, it is probable that before his death he consolidated his rule over the whole of Bengal.[5] His reign-period is not definitely known but probably extended from A.D. 750 to 770.[6]

2. DHARMAPALA (c. A.D. 770-810)

When Dharmapāla ascended the throne of Bengal, the political horizon was gloomy in the extreme. The Pratīhāras, who had established their power in Mālwā and Rājputāna, were gradually extending their territories in the east, and the newly established Rāshṭrakūṭa power in the Deccan also cast covetous eyes on the rich fertile plains of the north.[7] Dharmapāla was shortly involved in a struggle with these two powers—whether deliberately out of imperial designs, or as a means of defence against aggressive enemies, we cannot say. The course of events in this long-drawn struggle cannot be definitely traced in chronological order, but some of the main incidents can be broadly noted. The first encounter took place between the Pratīhāra ruler Vatsarāja and Dharmapāla, probably somewhere in the Gangetic Doāb,[8] in which the former gained a complete victory. He is said to have "appropriated with ease the fortune of royalty of the Gauḍa" and "carried away Gauḍa's umbrellas of state." But before Vatsarāja could collect the spoils of his victory, he was defeated by the Rāshṭrakūṭa king Dhruva and forced to take refuge in the deserts of Rājputāna. Dhruva then advanced to the Doāb[9] and defeated Dharmapāla, but shortly after his victory he retreated to the Deccan.

It would appear that Dharmapāla gained more than he had lost by the incursions of the Rāshṭrakūṭas. For while Vatsarāja's power was effectively destroyed, Dharmapāla did not suffer much either in power or prestige. The Rāshṭrakūṭas not only freed him from the Pratīhāra menace, but left in the harried and devastated Northern India a free field for his military ambitions. He was not slow to take full advantage of the situation, and by a series of victorious campaigns, made himself the suzerain of nearly the whole of Northern India.

Although the details and chronology of Dharmapāla's campaigns are not known to us, we can form some idea of their nature and extent from the description of the *durbar* which he held at Kanauj. His main object in convoking the great assembly was to proclaim himself as the suzerain and install Chakrāyudha on the throne of Kanauj in place of Indrāyudha whom he had defeated.[10] The *durbar* was attended by a number of vassal chiefs among whom are mentioned the rulers of Bhoja, Matsya, Madra, Kuru, Yadu, Yavana, Avanti, Gandhāra and Kīra, who uttered acclamations of approval, "bowing down respectfully with their diadems trembling." This categorical and specific statement, occurring in a contemporary record, cannot be lightly brushed aside,[11] and we must hold that Dharmapāla must have enjoyed, at least for some time, the unique position of a paramount lord in Northern India. This view is supported by the fact that even in a poetical work composed by a Gujarāti poet[12] in the eleventh century A.D., Dharmapāla is referred to as the "Lord of Northern India" (*Uttarāpathasvāmin*).[13]

We know very little of the different states, mentioned above, which acknowledged the suzerainty of Dharmapāla, but most of them are well-known names. Gandhāra represents the Western Punjāb and the lower Kābul valley. Madra was in the Central Punjāb, while Kīra, Kuru, and Matsya correspond respectively to Kāngra, Thāneswar and Jaipur regions. Avanti denotes the whole or a part of Mālwā, and the Yavana must be taken to refer to a Muslim principality in the Sindhu valley. The location of Yadu and Bhoja, though these are very well-known in ancient Indian history, offers some difficulty. The Yadus or Yādavas had various settlements such as Siṁhapura (Punjāb), Mathurā, and Dvārakā (Kāthiāwār Peninsula), and probably the first is meant here. The Bhojas probably ruled over Berār or a part of it.

These states were not annexed by Dharmapāla, but their rulers acknowledged his suzerainty, and were evidently left undisturbed so long as they paid homage and fulfilled the other conditions imposed on them.[14] The kingdom of Kanauj was, however, on a different footing. Its ruler Indrāyudha, who was probably a vassal of Vatsarāja,[15] was defeated and dethroned, and another ruler, Chakrāyudha, probably a member of the same royal family, was placed on the throne by Dharmapāla. It was the visible symbol of the most significant change in the political situation of the time, *viz.* the transfer of supreme power in Northern India from the Pratīhāras to the Pālas and the formal assumption of imperial authority by the latter. Kanauj thus became once more the seat and symbol of imperialism,[16] though it was ruled directly not by Dharmapāla, but by his nominee Chakrāyudha.

The empire of Dharmapāla may thus be broadly divided into three distinct parts. Bengal and Bihār, which formed its nucleus, were directly ruled by him. Beyond this, the kingdom of Kanauj, roughly corresponding to modern U.P., was a close dependency, whose ruler was nominated by, and directly subordinate to, him. Further to the west and south, in the Punjāb, Western Hill States, Rājputāna, Mālwā and Berār, were a number of vassal states which did not form an integral part of the dominions ruled over by Dharmapāla, but whose rulers acknowledged him as their overlord and paid him homage and obedience. According to a tradition preserved in the *Svayambhū-Purāṇa*, Nepāl was also a vassal state of Dharmapāla.[17]

The position of supremacy attained by Dharmapāla must have been the result of a series of victorious military campaigns. We are told that, in the course of these, Dharmapāla's army visited such holy places as Kedāra and Gokarṇa. The former is even now a famous place of pilgrimage on the Himālayas in Garhwāl and may be regarded as a landmark in the northern campaign of Dharmapāla in course of which he subdued Kuru, Madra, Kīra and probably other neighbouring states. The location of Gokarṇa is somewhat uncertain. It has been identified with a holy place of that name in the North Kānarā District of the Bombay State,[18] as well as with a sacred site in Nepāl[19] on the bank of the Bagmati river. The latter view is more probable. If we accept the other, we have to presume that Dharmapāla marched over the whole of the Deccan right across the entire length of the Rāshṭrakūṭa dominions. We have no independent evidence of such a brilliant military campaign, and if there was any basis for it, it would surely have been prominently mentioned in the Pāla records.

Dharmapāla's triumphant career did not remain unchallenged for long. Nāgabhaṭa II, the son and successor of Vatsarāja, revived the fortunes of his family and adopted an aggressive imperialist policy like his father. He achieved great success and even conquered Kanauj and drove away Chakrāyudha. This was really a challenge to Dharmapāla whose protégé Chakrāyudha was. A struggle for supremacy between the two rivals was inevitable, and Nāgabhaṭa made extensive preparations.[20] According to the Pratīhāra records, a pitched battle was fought, probably near Monghyr, in which Nāgabhaṭa defeated the mighty lord of Vaṅga "who appeared like a mass of dark, dense cloud in consequence of the crowd of mighty elephants, horses, and chariots".[21]

The Pāla records make no reference to this struggle, but the very fact that the Pratīhāras advanced up to Monghyr supports their claim to a great victory. Unfortunately, Nāgabhaṭa II had to suffer the same fate as his father. Once more it was the Rāshṭrakūṭas who decided the political issue in Northern India. Govinda III completely defeated Nāgabhaṭa II and forced him to give up the dream of founding an empire in India.[22]

The Rāshṭrakūṭa records tell us that both Dharmapāla and Chakrāyudha submitted of their own accord to Govinda III.[23] Considering the great advantages which these two had derived from the timely intervention of the Rāshṭrakūṭa king, this is by no means surprising or improbable. Indeed it is even possible that they appealed to Govinda III for aid to save themselves from Nāgabhaṭa's domineering power, and secured it by a formal acknowledgment of his suzerainty. But in reality this meant nothing, for, as they could have easily anticipated, Govinda III soon left for the Deccan and Dharmapāla was once more free to pursue unchecked his imperial ambitions.

On the whole there are good grounds to believe that the great success of Nāgabhaṭa II was a passing phase that ended with the Rāshṭrakūṭa invasion, and Dharmapāla continued to rule as a mighty emperor till the end of his life. When he died at an advanced age, after a reign of 32 years or more, he left intact[24] his extensive dominions to his son Devapāla.

Although we know so little of the personal history of Dharmapāla, there is enough to indicate that his career was a remarkable one. He was the hero of a hundred fights and passed through many crises, when not only his own fortunes, but the fate of Bengal hung in the balance. But he never faltered; he overcame all difficulties, and in the end achieved phenomenal success. His triumph in the political field seems almost miraculous. Bengal, which had lost all political homogeneity and had almost been eliminated as a factor in Indian politics, suddenly emerged under him as the most powerful state in Northern India. The country, which was hopelessly divided by internal dissensions and trampled upon by a succession of foreign invaders for more than a century, was raised by him to the position of a strong integrated state exercising imperial sway over a considerable part of Northern India. Śaśāṅka's dream of founding a great Gauḍa empire was at last fulfilled. The new imperial status attained by Bengal is reflected in the records of Dharmapāla. He assumed full imperial titles *Parameśvara, Paramabhaṭṭāraka,*

Mahārājādhirāja. Reference has been made above to the great imperial *durbar* which he held at Kanauj. A grandiloquent description is also given (Ins. No. 1) of the pomp and splendour of the court which he held at the other imperial city Pāṭaliputra, "where the bed of the Gaṅgā was covered by his mighty fleet and the daylight was darkened by the crowd of his mighty elephants and the dust raised by the hoofs of numberless horses presented by the kings of the north, some of whom also attended in person with their innumerable infantry." These are no doubt poetic embellishments, but they reflect the new spirit of the people.

The credit for this great transformation of Bengal is no doubt mainly due to the spirit of self-sacrifice and the sense of political wisdom displayed by her people and leading chiefs when they voluntarily surrendered their power and authority to their elected chief, Gopāla. Verily a remarkable act produced a remarkable result, of which there are few parallels in the history of India. But king Dharmapāla is also entitled to a large share of the credit. He personified the new energy and vision of the people, and led them to the Promised Land. His grateful subjects fully realized what they owed to him, and his name and fame were sung all over the country. It is a strange irony of fate that he should have been forgotten in the land of his birth but his memory should be kept green in Tibet. According to Tibetan tradition,[25] he was a great patron of Buddhism and founded the famous Vikramaśila monastery which developed into a great centre of Buddhist learning and culture,[26] second only to that of Nālandā. It was located at the top of a hill, on the banks of the Gaṅgā in Magadha, and most probably the hill at Pātharghāta near Bhāgalpur represents the site of this great university. It was named after the great emperor who had a second name Vikramaśila. Dharmapāla also founded a great *vihāra* at Somapurī in Varendra, the ruins of which have been recently excavated at Pāhārpur in the Rājshāhi District.[27] According to Tibetan authority, Dharmapāla also founded a big and splendid monastery at Odantapurī in Bihar. but others give the credit for this achievement to Devapāla or Gopāla. Dharmapāla was the patron of the great Buddhist author Haribhadra and, according to Tāranātha, founded fifty religious schools. He thus distinguished himself also in the peaceful pursuits of life in spite of his untiring activities in the field of war and politics.

Dharmapāla married Raṇṇādevī, the daughter of the Rāshṭrakūṭa king Parabala. A Rāshṭrakūṭa king of this name is known to have ruled in Central India in A.D. 861.[28] Although he is usually regarded as the father-in-law of Dharmapāla, it seems very doubtful in view of the fact that Dharmapāla must have died more than half a century before this date. It is not, of course, beyond the range of possibility that out of political considerations Dharmapāla married at a fairly advanced age a young lady of the Rāshṭrakūṭa royal family. The issue of this marriage was Devapāla who succeeded his father about A.D. 810. The last known date of Dharmapāla is his 32nd regnal year (Ins. No. 1). According to Tāranātha he ruled for 64 years; but such a long reign is not supported by any other positive evidence. We may, therefore regard Dharmapāla as having ruled from c. A.D. 770-810.

3 DEVAPĀLA (c. A.D. 810-850)

Devapāla was a worthy son of a worthy father. Not only did he maintain intact the great empire inherited by him, but he even appears to have extended its boundaries. He is said to have exacted tributes from the whole of Northern India from the Himālayas to the Vindhyas and from the eastern to the western ocean.[29] More specifically we are told that his victorious campaigns led him as far as Kāmboja in the west and Vindhyas in the south,[30] and that he exterminated the Utkalas, conquered Prāgjyotisha (Assam), curbed the pride of the Hūṇas, and destroyed the haughtiness of the lords of the Draviḍas and Gurjaras. In these victories he was considerably helped by the diplomacy and wise counsels of his ministers, Darbhapāṇi and his grandson Kedāramiśra, and the bravery and military skill of his cousin, Jayapāla.[31]

It would appear from these statements that Devapāla, like his father, followed an aggressive imperialist policy and spent a great part of his life in military activities. He was materially helped by his cousin Jayapāla, son of Dharmapāla's younger brother Vākpāla. Jayapāla was the commander of the army, and we are told that on his approach the king of Prāgjyotisha (Assam) submitted without any fight and the king of Utkala fled from his capital city.[32] It is likely that both the kingdoms acknowledged the suzerainty of the Pāla empire but, as will be shown below, threw off the yoke within a short time.

On the opposite extremity of the empire lay the Hūṇas. They had several principalities, one of which was situated in Uttarāpatha near the Himālayas. This was probably subjugated by Devapāla, who then proceeded to the Kāmboja territory which lay still further to the west in the North-West Frontier Province. Unfortunately, we do not know the details of his campaign or the extent of his success.

The Gurjara lords against whom Devapāla fought must have been the Pratīhāra rulers. It is possible that Nāgabhaṭa II tried to assert his power after the death of Dharmapāla and if, as some scholars believe, he transferred his capital to Kanauj, he must have achieved some success. But Devapāla soon re-established the Pāla supremacy, and it was possibly after his successful campaign against the Pratīhāras that he advanced to the Hūṇa and Kāmboja principalities. Nāgabhaṭa's son, Rāmabhadra, probably also had his kingdom invaded by Devapāla. The next Pratīhāra king Bhoja also, in spite of his initial success, suffered reverses at the hands of Devapāla, and could not restore the fortunes of his family so long as the Pāla emperor was alive. Thus Devapāla successfully fought with three generations of Pratīhāra rulers,[33] and maintained the Pāla supremacy in Northern India.

The Draviḍa king defeated by Devapāla is generally supposed to be the Rāshṭrakūṭa ruler Amoghavarsha. This view is not unlikely in view of the part played by Dhruva and Govinda III in Northern India, and the weakness and pacific disposition of Amoghavarsha. But Draviḍa, it should be remembered, normally denotes the land of the Tamils in the south and not the Deccan, the territory of the Rāshṭrakūṭas. From this point of view, it has been suggested that the Draviḍa king defeated by Devapāla was most probably his contemporary Pāṇḍya king Śrī-Māra Śrī-Vallabha who claims in an inscription to have defeated a hostile confederation consisting of the Gaṅgas, Pallavas, Choḷas, Kaliṅgas, Magadhas and others.[34] The Magadhas in this list obviously refer to the Pāla forces, and it is not unlikely that the conquest of Utkala brought Devapāla into contact with the southern powers. As the Rāshṭrakūṭas were common enemies of these powers and the Pālas, an alliance between them might have been dictated by political exigencies. Unfortunately, we know little of this phase of Pāla diplomacy, and cannot say anything definite about the expedition of Devapāla to the far south. But some victorious campaign in this region may be the basis of the claim put forward in the Monghyr copper-plate (No. 2) that the empire of Devapāla extended from the Himālayas in the north to Rāmeśvara Setubandha in the south.

But whatever we might think of Devapāla's victory in the extreme south, there cannot be any doubt that he occupied the position of a paramount ruler in North India. It does not appear that his direct rule extended beyond Bengal and Bihār, but as his victorious arms reached the frontier both in the east and the west, there is no reason to doubt that he effectively maintained the suzerainty which he had inherited from his father. His great rivals, the Pratīhāras, in spite of some initial successes, could not re-establish their power till after his death. The Rāshṭrakūṭas left North India alone during his reign, and Devapāla probably carried the fight to their dominions. He certainly led his army as far as the Sindhu and claimed an imperial position in North India, a feat to which no other ruler of Bengal could lay claim during the next thousand years.

Devapāla had a long reign of about forty years.[35] He was a great patron of Buddhism like his father, and his fame spread to many Buddhist countries outside India. About this time a powerful Buddhist dynasty, the Śailendras, ruled over an extensive empire in the East Indies.[36] Bālaputradeva, a king of this dynasty, sent an ambassador to Devapāla, asking for a grant of five villages in order to endow a monastery at Nālandā. Devapāla granted the request.[37] Another record informs us that a learned Buddhist priest, hailing from Nagarahāra (Jelālābād), received high honours from Devapāla and was appointed the head of Nālandā monastery.[38]

The reigns of Dharmapāla and Devapāla constitute the most brilliant chapter in the history of Bengal. Never before, or since, till the advent of the British, did Bengal play such an important role in Indian politics. A brief but interesting account of the Pāla empire at the height of its glory is given by the Arab merchant Sulaimān who visited India and wrote his account in A.D. 851.[39] He refers to the Pāla kingdom as Ruhmi,[40] a name which cannot be satisfactorily explained. According to him the Pāla ruler was at war with his neighbours, the Gurjaras and the Rāshṭrakūṭas, but his troops were more numerous than those of his adversaries. We are told that the Pāla king took 50,000 elephants in his military campaigns, and ten to fifteen thousand men in his army were "employed in fulling and washing cloths."

The Tibetan records claim that some of their rulers, who were contemporaries of Dharmapāla and Devapāla, conquered the dominions of the Pālas, and specifically refer to Dharmapāla as submitting to Tibetan supremacy. This is not, however, corroborated by any independent evidence, and we cannot say how far the claims can be regarded as historically true. It is not unlikely that Tibet exercised some political influence in Eastern India during the period A.D. 750-850, and the occasional reverses of the Pāla rulers at the hands of the Pratīhāras and the Rāshṭrakūṭas may be partly due to Tibetan aggression.[41]

4. FALL OF THE PĀLA EMPIRE

Devapāla was succeeded by Vigrahapāla. He was most probably a nephew, descended from Vākpāla, the younger brother of Dharmapāla, but some scholars regard him as a son of Devapāla.[42] After a short reign of probably three or four years he abdicated the throne and retired to an ascetic life. His son and successor Nārāyaṇapāla, who ruled for more than half a century,[43] was also of a pacific and religious disposition. During the reigns of these two unmartial kings the Pāla empire fell to pieces. Some time after A.D. 860 the Rāshṭrakūṭas defeated the Pāla rulers.[44] The Pratīhāras took advantage of the distress and weakness of their rivals; and their rulers Bhoja and Mahendrapāla gradually extended their power to the east. Nārāyaṇapāla not only lost Magadha (South Bihār), but for a time even North Bengal, the homeland of the Pālas, passed into the hands of the Pratīhāra king Mahendrapāla.[45]

The triumph of the Pratīhāras encouraged the subordinate chiefs to throw off the yoke of the Pālas. King Harjara of Assam assumed imperial titles and is credited with many victories; and the Śailodbhavas established their power on a firm footing in Orissa.[46]

The disintegration of the Pāla empire was thus almost complete, and for a time the rule of Nārāyaṇapāla was probably confined to a part of Bengal. He, however, recovered North Bengal and South Bihār from the Pratīhāras some time before the year 54 of his reign,[47] which probably corresponds to about A.D. 908. This was probably due to the Rāshṭrakūṭa invasion of the Pratīhāra dominions —the factor which had saved the Pālas more than once in the past. The Rāshṭrakūṭa king Kṛishṇa II, who defeated the Pratīhāras, however, also claims success against the Gauḍas and it is not unlikely that Nārāyaṇapāla was defeated by him.[48] But peace was established and probably cemented by a marriage alliance. For the Rāshṭrakūṭa Tuṅga, whose daughter was married to Nārāyaṇapāla's son Rājyapāla (Ins. No. 5), is most probably to be identified with Jagattuṅga,[49] the son of Kṛishṇa II. In any case, Nārāyaṇapāla re-established the Pāla supremacy in Bengal and Bihār before his death which took place about A.D. 908. He was succeeded by his son Rājyapāla.

The Pāla kingdom steadily declined during the reigns of Rājyapāla and his two successors, Gopāla II and Vigrahapāla II, which covered a period of about eighty years.[50] The collapse of the Pratīhāra empire might have offered some respite to the Pālas, but they suffered equally from the new powers that arose out of the ruins of that empire. The records of both the Chandellas and the Kalachuris[51] refer to the defeat inflicted by their rulers upon Gauḍa, Rāḍhā, Aṅga, and Vaṅgāla. The mention of these separate units[52] indicates a disintegration of the Pāla kingdom into a number of independent or semi-independent principalities. And we definitely know the existence of at least two such states within the boundaries of Bengal.

The first is a kingdom in West Bengal ruled by a Kāmboja family. We know the names of three rulers of this family, *viz.* Rājyapāla and his two sons Nārāyaṇapāla and Nayapāla. In a charter[53] issued by Nayapāla in which both he and his father are given imperial titles, *Parameśvara, Paramabhaṭṭāraka* and *Mahārājādhirāja,* lands are granted in the Vardhamāna-*bhukti, i.e.* Burdwān division in West Bengal. The Kāmboja rule in North Bengal is testified to by an inscribed pillar found in Dinājpur District which mentions a lord of Gauḍa belonging to the Kāmboja family.[54] The date of this record has been interpreted as 888 (Śaka), though this is doubtful. But there is no doubt that both the records belong to the latter half of the tenth century A.D. and probably refer to the same family. The names of the three kings who thus ruled over both North and West Bengal were all borne by the Pāla kings of Bengal and, what is curious, Rājyapāla's queen is named Bhāgyadevī, as is also the case with the Pāla king Rājyapāla. Nevertheless we cannot identify the two without more evidence. It is held by some scholars that the Kāmbojas, a hill tribe from Tibet or other regions, conquered Bengal. But it is more likely that some high official of the Pālas, belonging to the Kāmboja family or tribe, took advantage of the weakness of the Pāla kings and set up an independent kingdom. Its capital was Priyaṅgu which cannot be identified.

A copper-plate found at Chittagong[55] mentions a Buddhist king of Harikela named *Mahārājādhirāja* Kāntideva. Harikela primarily denotes Eastern Bengal, or a part of it comprising the Sylhet and portions of neighbouring districts, though it was sometimes used in a wider sense, as a synonym of Vaṅga (East and South Bengal).[56] The capital of Kāntideva was Vardhamānapura. If it denotes the modern city of Burdwān then his kingdom must have comprised a portion of West Bengal also, but this is very doubtful. The date of Kāntideva is not definitely known, but he probably reigned during the century following the death of Devapāla.

Kings with names ending in *-chandra* also ruled in East Bengal as independent kings after Kāntideva. One of them is Layahachandra[57] whose record dated in his 18th regnal year has been found near Comilla. Two Buddhist kings, Trailokyachandra and his son Śrīchandra, ruled over Harikela and Chandradvīpa (Bākarganj District). Śrīchandra, who ruled for no less than 46 years,[58] probably flourished towards the close of the tenth and the beginning of the eleventh century A.D. Later, this dynasty extended its power to South Bengal. The original home of this dynasty was Rohitāgiri which has been identified by some with Rohtasgaḍh, and by others with Lalmai or Maināmati hills near Comilla in Bengal.

Gopāla II is known to have ruled in East Bengal in the first, and North Bengal in the sixth year of his reign.[59] But gradually he or his son and successor Vigrahapāla II lost hold of nearly the whole of Bengal and ruled only in Bihār. The Pāla kingdom had thus reached the very nadir when Mahīpāla I, the son of Vigrahapāla II, ascended the throne about A.D. 988. The new king was, however, made of sterner stuff, and succeeded to a large extent in recovering the old glory of his family. A full account of his reign will be given in the next volume, and it will suffice here to state that before he had reigned for three years he had reconquered nearly the whole of North and East Bengal "after defeating the usurpers who had seized his ancestral kingdom" (Ins. No. 5). Thus by the year A.D. 1000, with which this volume closes, the Pālas had once more become a powerful ruling family in Eastern India. Mahīpāla, who is justly described as the second founder of the Pāla kingdom, gave it a new lease of life which continued, with strange vicissitudes, for nearly another century and a half.

GENERAL REFERENCE

1. *HBR*. Ch. VI. (It contains a full reference to authorities for topics discussed in this chapter).

IMPORTANT INSCRIPTIONS

1. Khālimpur CP of Dharmapāla, year 32. *EI*, IV. 243.
2. Monghyr CP of Devapāla, year 33. *EI*. XVIII. 304.
3. Bhāgalpur CP Nārāyaṇapāla, year 17. *IA*, XV. 304.
4. Bādāl Pillar Inscription. *EI*. II 160.
5. Bāngadh Grant of Mahīpāla. *EI*. XIV. 324.
(All the above inscriptions are edited in *Gaudalekhamālā* a Bengali work, by Akshaya Kumar Maitreya).

1. Vol. III, pp. 142 ff.
2. The election of a ruler by the *prakṛitis* or people of Bengal in order to remove misrule and anarchy is referred to in Ins. No. 1. and also described by the Tibetan historian Lāmā Tāranātha (*History of Buddhism in India*. Tr. by A. Schiefner). Tāranātha's work was written in A.D. 1608, but he had evidently access to old traditions and records now lost. His statements about the Pāla kings, though interesting and informative, should not be accepted as historical unless corroborated by independent evidence.
The common meaning of the word *prakṛiti* is '*subjects*', and hence it is generally held that Gopāla was elected king by the general body of the people. But we cannot think of a general election in the modern sense. The choice was evidently made by the leading chiefs and endorsed by the people.
3. Military skill and administrative capacity must have been the indispensable qualifications of a leader in those troublous times.
4. A fuller account of this work will be given in connection with the history of Rāmapāla in the next volume.
4a. References are to the list of "Important Inscriptions" given above.
5. It is said in Ins. No. 2 (v. 3) that his conquests extended up to the sea.
6. The chronology of the Pāla kings is not yet definitely settled. The view adopted here is based on *HBR* (Ch. VI, App. II, p. 176).
7. The history of the Rāshtrakūṭas and the Pratīhāras has been dealt with in Chapters I and II.
8. Some scholars take the view that Vatsarāja advanced as far as Bengal and actually conquered it up to the sea. This does not seem likely, and the only evidence in support of it is a casual verse in a poetical work composed four centuries after this event.

9. It is definitely said in the Rāshṭrakūṭa records that Dhruva met the king of Gauḍa between the Gaṅgā and the Yamunā and carried off his umbrellas of state (Sanjān CP. v. 14; *EI*, XVIII. 244). It has been recently urged by a scholar (*IHQ*, XX. 84) that Dhruva did not defeat the king of Gauḍa, but really got his state umbrellas from Vatsarāja when the latter was returning from his expedition to Bengal. In his opinion, it was Vatsarāja whom he met and defeated between the Gaṅgā and the Yamunā, but the writer of the Rāshṭrakūṭa records, who knew that Dhruva captured the white umbrellas belonging to the Gauḍa king, naturally, but erroneously, thought that the Gauḍa king was defeated by Dhruva. This theory is no doubt ingenious and even plausible, but cannot be accepted in view of the categorical statement in Sanjān CP, so long at least as we have no evidence in support of it.
10. The full significance of v. 12 of Ins. No. 1 which contains an account of this assembly has been discussed in *HBR*, 107.
11. Cf. *e.g. THK*. 216, 230.
12. The *Udayanasundarī-kathā* by Soḍḍhala (G. O. S. edition), pp. 4-6.
13. Uttarāpatha technically means the western part of North India, but applied to Dharmapāla, ruler of Bengal and Bihār, it evidently means the overlordship of North India.
14. This is clearly indicated by Ins. No. 2, v. 8.
15. Cf. Ch. II, p. 23 above.
16. It is significant that all three contending powers, the Pālas, the Pratīhāras, and the Rāshṭrakūṭas, had their eyes fixed upon Kanauj. The Pratīhāras finally transferred their capital to this city. The Rāshṭrakūṭa king Dhruva and Govinda III overran this region, and one of their successors, Indra III, captured and ruthlessly sacked this city which was then the imperial capital of the Pratīhāras.
17. *IC*, IV. 266.
18. *IA*, 1892, p. 257, fn. 6.
19. *IC*, IV. 266. The capital of the Kirātas was situated in the jungles of Gokarṇa to the north-east of Paśupati (Levi, *Le Nepal*. II. 83).
20. For Nāgabhaṭa's history and military campaigns, cf. Ch. II, pp. 24 ff.
21. Gwālior Ins. of Bhoja, v. 10 (*EI*, XVIII. 112). The description shows the strength of the Pāla army and may be contrasted with the 'easy victory' obtained by Vatsarāja against the king of Gauḍa referred to above.
22. Cf. Chapters I and II.
23. According to Sanjān CP. "Dharma and Chakrāyudha surrendered of themselves" to Govinda III (*EI*, XVIII. 253). There is no evidence in support of the view that Dharmapāla was defeated in a battle by Govinda III (*JBORS*. XII. 362).
24. Ins. No. 2, v. 12.
25. For authorities, cf. *HBR*. 115.
26. It consisted of a central temple surrounded by 107 others—all enclosed by a boundary wall. It provided for 114 teachers in different subjects (*JASB*, N. S. V (1909), pp. 1 ff.).
27. For detailed description, see Vol. V, Ch. XVI.
28. *EI*, IX. 248.
29. Ins. No. 4, v. 5.
30. Ins. No. 2, v. 13.
31. Ins. No. 4, v. 13; No. 3. v. 6. Darbhapāṇi's father Garga was a minister of Dharmapāla.
32. Ins. No. 3, v. 6.
33. For details see Ch. II.
34. For a full discussion of this point, cf. *POC*, VIII. 537; *S. K. Aiyangar Com. Vol.* 197; *HBR*. 120-21. But K. A. N. Sastri opposes this view (*India Antiqua*, 254).
35. The last known date of Devapāla depends upon the reading of the figure for his regnal year in the Nālandā CP. It is usually read as 39 (*EI*, XVII. 318), but seems to be really 35 (*JRASBL*. VII. 215).
36. *Vide infra*, Ch. XV.
37. Nālandā CP. (*EI*, XVII. 318).
38. Goshrāwā Stone Ins. (*IA*, XVII. 307).
39. *HIED*, I. 5, 25. But some scholars doubt whether the account was really written by Sulaimān (cf. *Arab Geographers' Knowledge of Southern India* by S. M. H. Nainar, pp. 7 ff).
40. *IHQ*, XVI. 232.
41. *HBR*. 124. Cf. also Ch. IV, §1.

42. The whole question has been fully discussed in *HBR.* 188.
43. His latest known date is year 54 (*IA*, XLVII. 110).
44. According to Sirur Ins. dated A.D. 866 (*IA*, XII. 218), Aṅga, Vaṅga and Magadha paid homage to king Amoghavarsha, who could not possibly have undertaken an expedition against the Pālas before his conquest of Veṅgī which took place about A.D. 860.
45. Several inscriptions of Mahendrapāla have been found in South Bihār (*Pālas of Bengal*. 64) and one in Pāhārpur (North Bengal) (*MASI*, 55. 75).
46. See next Chapter.
47. This is proved by an image found in Bihār with an ins. dated in the year 54 (*IA*, XLVII. 110). Inscription No. 3 shows that Nārāyaṇapāla was in possession of Bihār in the year 17. So the Pratīhāras conquered it propably during the interval between these years (c. A.D. 870-908). As Mahendrapāla did not ascend the throne till after A.D. 882, his conquest of Bihār and North Bengal may be placed between A.D. 890 and 900.
48. According to v. 5 of the Ḍeoli CP, Krishṇa II was the preceptor "charging the Gauḍas with the vow of humility" and that "his command was obeyed by Aṅga, Kaliṅga, Gaṅga and Magadha" (*EI*, V. 193). The Rāshṭrakūṭa king was probably accompanied by Malla, a chief of Velanāṇḍu (in Krishnā District), for the latter claims to have subdued the Vaṅgas, Maghdhas and the Gauḍas (Pithāpuram Ins. v. 11; *EI*, IV. 40).
49. For other views, cf. *HBR*, I. 131, fn. 4.
50. The Pāla records have nothing to say about them except that Rājyapāla dug tanks deep like the sea and constructed temples high as the mountains (cf. Ins. No. 5, vv. 7-10). In a verse applied to Gopāla II and Vigrahapāla II in two different records (No. 5 and Jājilpārā CP of Gopāla II. *JASL*, XVII. 137) their elephant forces are said to have wandered in the eastern regions, western deserts, Malaya mountains in the south and the Himālaya in the north. These aimless wanderings were formerly regarded by some scholars as a covert allusion to the loss of ancestral kingdom by Vigrahapāla, but as the same verse is now known to apply to the earlier king Gopāla II also, this interpretation is doubtful (cf. *HBR*. 136). But the verse may indicate the hopelessly weak position of both the kings.
51. For the history of these dynasties, cf. Ch. V. For the effect of Chandella invasions on Bengal, cf. *IHQ*. XXVIII. 177.
52. As noted above, some of these units are separately mentioned also in the Rāshṭrakūṭta records (cf. fn. 44 and 48 above).
53. Irdā CP. *EI*, XXII. 150; XXIV. 43.
54. *JASB*, VII. 619.
55. *EI*, XXVI. 313.
56. Cf. *IC*. XII. 88.
57. *EI*, XVII. 349.
58. *HBR*. Ch. VII. The year 46 is found in Madanpur Plates (*EI*, XXVIII. 51, 337).
59. Cf. Mandhuk (Tippera District) Ins. of Gopāla II year 1 (*IHQ*, XXVIII. 55) and Jājilpārā CP. of the same king (*JASL*, XVII. 137).

CHAPTER IV

EASTERN INDIA DURING THE PĀLA PERIOD

Having dealt with the history of the Pālas who were the leading political power in Eastern India, we may now turn our attention to the several independent kingdoms which flourished in Nepāl, Kāmarūpa (Assam) and Utkala (Orissa).

I. NEPĀL

The history of Nepāl, during the two centuries following the death of Jayadeva II,[1] is very obscure, as the *Vaṁśāvalīs* (chronicles are hopelessly confused and there are no epigraphic records to help us. One strange episode at the beginning of this period has been preserved in *Rājataraṅgiṇī*.[2] It tells us how, in the course of his victorious campaign, Jayāpīḍa, the grandson of Lalitāditya,[3] came to Nepāl, was captured by its king Aramuḍi, effected his escape through the self-sacrifice of his minister, and conquered the kingdom. Like his other adventure concerning Jayanta,[4] this also reads more like a romance than real history, and Stein rejects it as mythical. Lévi has, however, pointed out that the name Aramuḍi is Tibetan, and as we know from Tibetan sources that Nepāl was at this time under the political subjection of Tibet, and there was hostility between this country and Kāshmir, there may be some basis for the story. According to the *Chronicles of Ladakh*, the Tibetan king Khri-sroṅ-lde-btsan (A.D. 755-97) carried his victorious arms to India.[5] According to another Tibetan text, composed in the ninth century A.D., his son conquered a large part of Jambudvīpa.[6] The next important king Ral-pa-can (A.D. 817-836) is said to have conquered India as far as the confluence of the Gaṅgā and the sea.[7] As noted above,[8] there is no independent evidence in support of these claims. But, according to some Nepālese chronicles, the Tibetan king Namoyāti ruled over Nepāl after the reign of Vasantadeva, and we may regard the Tibetans as having exercised a general supremacy over Nepāl. This Namoyāti may be identified with king Aramuḍi who defeated and imprisoned Jayāpīḍa, as mentioned above. But it is very doubtful if Aramuḍi is a Tibetan name.[8a] In addition to the Tibetans, the Pālas also appear to have exercised some sort of supremacy over Nepāl.[9]

These foreign conquests may explain the political confusion in Nepāl which is reflected in its chronicles. The year A.D. 879, the epoch of the Newārī era, which is current even now in Nepāl, probably marks an important political event in its history. According to Prinsep and Cunningham the new era, dating from October 20, A.D. 879, was inaugurated by king Rāghavadeva. S. Lévi however, rejects this view, as this king does not occupy any prominent place in the local chronicles. He suggests that the new era was simply the Śaka era with the omission of the eight hundred. In his opinion, after the end of the Śaka year 800, the Nepālese, who had a superstitious dread for the figure 8, began to count the year afresh as 1, 2, etc. without any reference to the figure for hundred. This view gains additional strength from the fact that we have now good grounds to believe that of the two earlier Nepālī eras, the first one was really the Śaka era, and the second, the same era with the omission of 500.[10] It would thus appear that the Nepālese adopted the Śaka era before the end of its fourth century, and continued to use it ever since, dropping the hundredth figure, first after 500 and then, again, after 800 years of that era. The last-named era probably came into use during the reign of Rāghavadeva, and hence he was regarded by posterity as the founder of that era.

Rāghavadeva is mentioned in two old Chronicles, which assign to him a reign-period respectively of 43 and 63 years. The names of his successors are also given differently in them. It is not unlikely that the two Chronicles refer to two different lines of kings ruling simultaneously over two regions. King Vikramadeva and his three successors are, however, common names in both the lists. Narendradeva, who succeeded Vikramadeva, is known from the colophon of a manuscript to have ruled in A.D. 999. Henceforth the royal lists in the Chronicles can be checked with the help of colophons and epigraphic records. Thus we reach a firm ground in the history of Nepāl only at the close of the period dealt with in this Volume.[11]

A great deal of uncertainty, however, prevails in respect of the chronological and genealogical position of king Guṇakāmadeva, who is mentioned in all the Chronicles as having played a great role in the history of Nepāl. His name is placed in the two old Chronicles immediately after Narendradeva. These assign him a reign of 85 years while the modern Chronicles give it as 51. All this is impossible, for Guṇakāmadeva's reign must have come to an end by A.D. 1000, as his successor is said to have ruled for 5½ years, and the next king Nirbhaya is known to have jointly ruled with Rudra in the year 128 (= A.D. 1007).[12] Guṇakāmadeva was evidently a king of some eminence, and a great many traditions have gathered round his name. He probably extended the boundaries of his dominions beyond the valley towards the east. He is said to have been owner of fabulous wealth, and to have spent a large amount in religious endowments, including many benefactions to the God Paśupati. He is the reputed founder of the capital city of Kātmāndu, where he instituted a religious festival in honour of Lokeśvara Khasarpaṇa. Lévi thinks that Kāntipura, the old name of this city, is derived from Guṇakāma, both *kāma* and *kānti* being derived from the same root. The other cities, Patan and Sanku, are also said to have been founded about the same time. The foundation of new cities probably indicates the growth of trade and commerce. Nepāl was at first mainly an agricultural country, but its contact with Tibet and China made it a valuable highway for trade between India and these countries. Whereas the epigraphic records of the earlier period refer only to villages and rural community, the Chinese History of the T'ang dynasty (A.D. 618-905) shows that merchants were numerous, and cultivators scarce, in Nepāl. There was also a development of arts and crafts. This transformation from rural to industrial economy probably explains the great wealth of the king.

GENERAL REFERENCES

1. Lévi—*Le Nepal*, Vol. II, 172-187.
2. *DHNI*, I. Ch. IV.

II. KĀMARŪPA

King Harsha of Sālastambha family[13] was followed by Balavarman, and probably one or two others,[14] after whom we find a king Sālambha on the throne of Kāmarūpa. He is referred to in several inscriptions as belonging to the dynasty of Sālastambha,[15] but at least one record[16] seems to imply that he restored the sovereignty of the Naraka dynasty, *i.e.* the family to which Bhāskara-varman belonged, though it draws prominent attention to the somewhat strange character of the name. Another record, however, omits the name of this king and clearly states that after many rulers of the family of Sālastambha had reigned, Harjara became king of Kāmarūpa.[17]

It is, therefore, difficult to say definitely whether Sālambha founded a new family, and if so, whether it was connected in any way with the earlier rulers of Kāmarūpa ending with Bhāskaravarman. We are not also quite sure about the name of the ruler, for another copper-plate gives the name as Prālambha.[18] He probably flourished about the end of the eighth or the beginning of the ninth century A.D.[19] It is, therefore, probable that the change in the royal dynasty of Kāmarūpa was caused by the successful invasion of the Pālas referred to above,[20] for it is not unlikely that Devapāla drove away or killed the king and put his own nominee on the throne. He might have selected a scion of the old ruling family in order to make the political change less unacceptable to the people.

Nothing is known of Sālambha, but his son or nephew[21] Harjara-varman was a king of some eminence. One of his records (No. 1),[22] dated in the year 510 of the Gupta era (= A.D. 829), gives him the full imperial titles *Mahārājādhirāja Parameśvara Paramabhaṭṭāraka*. It is also probably not without significance that in another record of this family (No. 4) the name of Sālambha or Prālambha is omitted, and the royal line begins with Harjara. On the whole, it would be fair to conclude that Harjara-varman threw off the yoke of the Pālas and ruled as an independent king. It is not unlikely that as his predecessors had to acknowledge the suzerainty of the Pālas, their names were omitted in the records of later kings who did not like to recall those inglorious days of the family.

No particulars of the reign of Harjara are known. He was succeeded by his son Vanamāla-varman who was probably associated in the government as *yuvarāja* during his father's rule.[23] Vanamāla-varman is said to have had a long reign (No. 5). One record (No. 3) of his reign refers to a grant of land to the west of the Trisroṭā river. This is undoubtedly represented by the modern Tistā, and we must, therefore, conclude that the kingdom of Kāmarūpa included a part of North Bengal. This supports the traditional account that the river Karatoyā formed the western boundary of Prāgjyotisha or Kāmarūpa.

Vanamāla was succeeded by his son Jayamāla, who assumed the name of Vīravāhu after his accession to the throne.[24] Nothing is known of him or of his son and successor Bala-varman. But we know from a later inscription[25] that when Tyāgasiṁha, the twenty-first king after Sālastambha, died without any issue, the people chose Brahmapāla, a kinsman of the deceased ruler, as king. Tyāgasiṁha was probably the last king of the dynasty of Sālambha.

The dynasty of Sālambha ruled from A.D. *c.* 800 to *c.* 1000. The kings were devotees of Śiva, and their capital was Harūppeśvara on the bank of Lauhitya or the Brahmaputra river. Although no detailed account of their reign is known, it may be presumed that under Harjara and his descendants Kāmarūpa flourished as a powerful independent kingdom.

GENERAL REFERENCES

1. *DHNI*, I. Ch. V.
2. *KSS*—All the inscriptions are edited in this work.

LIST OF IMPORTANT INSCRIPTIONS

1. Tezpur Rock Inscription of Harjara-varman, dated 510 G.E., *JBORS*, III: 508.
2. Hāiyunglhal CP. of Harjara-varman (Noticed in *IHQ*, III. 838, 841, 844. Edited in *KSS*).
3. Tezpur CP. Vanamāla, *JASB*. IX. (1840), p. 766.
4. Parbatiya Plates of Vanamalavarmadeva, *EI*. XXIX, 145.
5. Nowgong CP. of Bala-varman, *JASB*. LXVI. 121, 285; LXVII. 103.
6. Howraghat Plates of Bala-varman, *EI*, XXXII. 283.

III. UTKALA (ORISSA)

We have already discussed[26] the history of the Śailodbhavas whose rule terminated probably about the middle of the eighth century A.D. or somewhat later. During the two centuries and a half that followed, we find several dynasties ruling in different parts of Orissa. Unfortunately, neither their chronology nor the boundaries of their kingdoms can be definitely ascertained, nor do we know anything of their exact status and mutual relations. The most powerful of them were the Karas, who ruled along the eastern seaboard, exercising authority in the districts of Balasore, Cuttack and Puri, and a part of the corresponding hinterland. The Bhañjas set up several states which covered a large part of what were till lately known as the feudatory Orissa States. In addition to these two, several minor dynasties ruled in these regions from time to time. Whether the Śailodbhavas continued to rule over Koṅgoda cannot be exactly determined, but this region, corresponding to the northern part of Ganjām, not only passed from time to time under the political authority of both the Karas and the Bhañjas, but we find there other dynasties such as the Gaṅgas of Śvetaka who occasionally acknowledged the supremacy of the Karas. Towards the middle of the tenth century A.D. the Somavaṁśī kings of South Kosala conquered Orissa and continued to rule it till the advent of the Eastern Gaṅgas more than a century later.

The history of Orissa during this period offers certain peculiarities. An unusually large number of inscriptions have come to light, far exceeding those we have for a bigger province like Bengal during the corresponding period. But apart from royal names, they hardly ever give any details of historical interest. Although many of them are dated, the years are more often regnal or refer to an era which is unknown. Their palaeography, too, is often of no great help in determining their age, as the letters, even of the same time and locality, are sometimes written in different styles which give erroneous impressions about their antiquity. As a matter of fact, in the case of no other region in India do we notice such a wide difference of opinion among scholars regarding the age of the records. To add to the difficulty, we have very often the same name borne by a number of kings, and several alternate names borne by the same king which are indiscriminately used in official records. All this makes it almost impossible to arrive at any conclusion which would be generally acceptable, and all that we can do is to arrange the known facts under some system of chronology, which appears to be the most reasonable. With these preliminary remarks we proceed to give a short account of the different dynasties with the exception of the Somavaṁśīs whose history will be dealt with in the next volume.

1. *The Karas*

About the time when the Pālas established their power in Bengal we find a new dynasty ruling in Orissa. It was called both Bhauma and Kara. The former designation shows that the dynasty claimed descent from Bhūmi or Earth, and the latter was no doubt derived from the fact that the names of all the kings of the family ended in *-kara*. There is nothing to show that the Bhauma dynasty of Orissa was connected in any way with the dynasty of Kāmarūpa[27] to which Bhāskara-varman belonged, though that was also descended from Naraka, the son of Bhūmi (Earth). The *Vishṇu Purāṇa* refers to Mahendra-Bhauma along with Kaliṅga and Māhishika as being protected (?) by Guha (or Guhas).[28] These Bhaumas living in Mahendra hill may be regarded as the ancestors of the Bhaumas of Orissa, and the conclusion is strengthened by the fact that the capital of the latter was called Guhadeva-pāṭaka or Guheśvara-pāṭaka, apparently named after Guha (or the Guhas) with whom the Bhaumas are associated in the *Vishṇu Purāṇa*. It has been suggested that the Bhūñās, now inhabiting the northern hill tracts of Orissa, are the representatives of the Bhaumas, and in this connection attention has been drawn to the fact that a class of people, living to the south of the Mahānadī river, call themselves Māṭi-vaṁsa or family sprung from the Earth.[29]

No less than seventeen records of this family have so far come to light. They enable us to draw the following genealogy of the family. Many of these contain dates which, however, cannot all be read with certainty. These are put in brackets after the names. Most of the kings had one or more alternative names which are added after the name ending in Kara, though in some records these alternative names alone are used. The order of succession is shown by Roman figures.

I. Kshemaṅkaradeva
|
II Śivakaradeva I *alias* Unmaṭṭasiṁha *alias* Bharasaha (20 or 50)[30]
|
III. Śubhākaradeva I (54 ?)[31]
|
(sons of III:)
IV. Sivakaradeva II (73 ?) — **V. Śāntikaradeva I *alias* Gayāḍa I *alias* Lalitahāra I (93)** = **VIII. Tribhuvana-Mahādevī I (110)**
|
VI. Subhākaradeva II (100)[32] (son of IV)
VII. Śubhākaradeva III *alias* Siṁhaketu *alias* Kusumahāra I (103) (son of V and VIII)

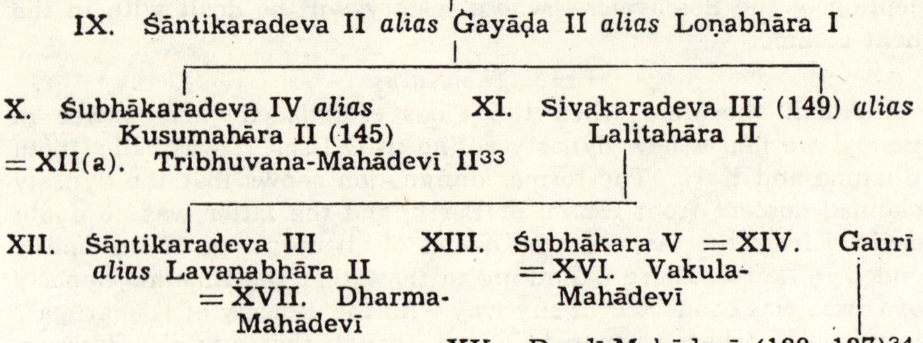

As will be seen from the above table, there were five kings bearing the name Śubhākara. The first king of that name is known from Neulpur plate, but as the characters of the newly discovered Khaḍipadā (now Cuttack Museum) inscription of Śubhākara seem to be older than those of the former, it has been suggested that there was an earlier king bearing that name.[35] On the other hand, it has been pointed out that the palaeographical differences between the two inscriptions are "not so great as to render the identification of these two Śubhākaras impossible."[36] The identity of these two kings has been assumed in the above table, but it is not unlikely that there was an earlier king of that name, who even preceded No. I.

It has been stated in Hindol Plate that when kings like Lakshmīkara and others of the Bhauma family "had gone to heaven," there flourished in that family king Śubhākara (No. III). It may be inferred from this that there was a king called Lakshmīkara, who was either identical with No. I or his predecessor, immediate or remote. But there is nothing to justify the assumption that Lakshmīkara was the father of No. I.[37]

The chronology of these kings has been a matter of dispute. At a time when the relation between these rulers was not definitely known, it was held on palaeographic grounds that the king No. III flourished about eighth century A.D.[38] and the Queen No. XIV, as late even as thirteenth century A.D.[39] In spite of uncertainty in the reading of some figures, there is now no doubt that all the monarchs ruled in an unbroken line of succession, and as their known dates extend from 20 (or 50) to 187 of the same era, the rule of the entire dynasty must be placed within a period of two centuries, notwithstanding indications of palaeography to the contrary.

Fortunately, there is some independent evidence in support of the conclusion, based on palaeography, that the first three kings flourished about the eighth century A.D. Professor Lévi drew attention to the fact that in the year A.D. 795 the Chinese Emperor Te-tsong received an autographed Buddhist manuscript from the king of Wu-ch'a (Uḍra=Orissa) whose name is translated as "the fortunate monarch who does what is pure, the lion." Lévi has shown that a name like Śubhakara corresponds very well with the Chinese translation, and he accordingly identifies Śubhākara (No. III) as the king who sent the manuscript.[40] It has been argued that the name is really Śubhākara which means 'the store of purity' and that the emendation of the name to Śubhakara "one who does what is pure" is unwarranted.[41] This difficulty can be avoided if we identify the king of Uḍra (Orissa), who sent the manuscript in A.D. 795, not with Subhākara, but with his father Śivakaradeva, as *Śiva* and *Subha* mean the same thing. Besides, Śivakaradeva had another name Unmaṭṭasiṁha. and the last part of this means 'the lion', which forms a part of the name in the Chinese translation. It would thus follow that king No. II flourished in the latter half of the eighth century A.D. and the dynasty was evidently founded about the middle of that century.

This view goes against the assumption that the dates of the Kara kings are to be referred to the Harsha era.[42] This theory is open to several objections. In the first place, the ruler of Orissa about A.D. 795 would be a queen (Nos. XIV-XVI) who was a Śaiva and not a Buddhist. The Buddhist ruler of Orissa in A.D. 795, who, according to the Chinese source, "had a deep faith in the Sovereign Law", must be identified with one of the first three Kara kings who are called respectively '*Paramopāsaka*', '*Paramatathāgata*' and '*Paramasaugata*', and not with any of their successors who were devotees of Maheśvara. Secondly, according to Tāranātha, there was political disintegration both in Bengal and Orissa shortly before the time when Gopāla was elected to the throne. As his statement has proved to be true with regard to Bengal, we may give credit to it in respect of Orissa as well. It is more probable, therefore, that the Karas, who ruled for two centuries in an unbroken line of succession, established a powerful kingdom about the middle of the eighth rather than the seventh century A.D. Thirdly, if we refer the date of the Kara records to Harsha era, king No. III would flourish about the middle of the seventh century A.D., but the scripts of his plate are so distinctly later than the Ganjām plate of Śaśāṅka that it has been assigned to the latter half of the eighth century A.D[43] Fourthly, if the date of king Unmaṭṭakesarī, recorded in the Ganjām grant, is really 20, we can hardly refer it to the Harsha era as Orissa had not yet been conquered by Harsha.

On these and other grounds it is more reasonable to refer the foundation of the Kara dynasty to the middle of the eighth century A.D. In that case we cannot refer the dates in their records to any known era, and must presume that it was a case of continuous reckoning of the regnal year of the first king by his successors which has given rise to so many local eras, including the Gaṅga era in Kaliṅga.

Very little is known of the detailed history of the long line of rulers belonging to the Kara dynasty. As mentioned above, kings Nos. I-III were all devout Buddhists. The Neulpur plate, issued by No. III, refers to the first two as kings and gives the title *Mahārāja* to the third. In a record of No. IV, however, both Nos. III and IV are given the higher imperial titles *Paramabhaṭṭāraka Mahārājādhirāja Parameśvara*. These titles were borne by all their successors, whose charters have so far come to light, and these charters are also drawn in characteristic imperial style, the royal order being addressed to *Mahāsāmantas, Mahārājas, Rājaputras* and a host of high officials. This shows that the kings were independent and powerful, but we have no reason to believe that their permanent authority extended beyond the boundaries of Orissa or even over the whole of it.

The Talcher plate, dated 149, tells us that Unmaṭṭasiṁha (No. II) defeated in battle the king of Rāḍhā and carried away his daughter, while his son Śubhākara I (No. III) subjugated the Kaliṅgas. It is somewhat singular that neither the Neulpur plate issued by Śubhākara I himself nor any other record refers to any such exploits.

But some corroboration about the conquests of the Kara kings at this time is obtained by the Ganjām Grant of Jayavarmadeva. This record indicates that Jayavarman of the Śvetaka Branch[44] of the Gaṅgas, who ruled in the northern part of Ganjām District, acknowledged the supremacy of king Unmaṭṭakesarī of Virajas. This Unmaṭṭakesarī may be identified with the Kara king No. II. It would then follow that even in his time a part of Koṅgoda was included within the dominions of the Karas. and the next king Śubhākara had probably extended his conquests further south to Kaliṅga. But as Koṅgoda formed a part of the dominions of the Gaṅgas of Kaliṅga, it is also not unlikely that Śubhākara himself achieved a victory over them in his father's reign. and hence his name was associated with the conquest of Kaliṅga in later days.

Although the dates of Śubhākara I and his son Śivakara II. read respectively as 54 and 73, are somewhat doubtful, we may take as certain the date 93 of Śāntikaradeva I. He therefore flourished in the second quarter of the ninth century A.D. It was perhaps during his reign, or that of his brother and predecessor Śivakaradeva II, that Devapāla subjugated Utkala.[45] There is perhaps a covert allusion to it in the Dhenkanal Plate dated 110. It distinctly says that after the death of eminent *Mahārājas* like Unmattakesarī (No. II) and Gayāḍa (No. V), "the Kara family had to depend upon nothing but their past glory", and "the kingdom looked like the sky bereft of refulgent stars and a female with distressful heart." Tribhuvana-Mahādevī (No. VIII), the daughter of Rājamalla, a renowned Nāga chief of the south, and the queen of Lalitahāra (No. V), then ascended the throne being "entreated by a great circle of chiefs to be pleased to protect the fortunes of Kara kingdom," as Devī Gosvāminī did in old days. In the Talcher plate, dated 141, it is said that after the death of Kusumahāra (No. VII) his mother Tribhuvana-Mahādevī took up the burden of administration of the entire kingdom and abdicated in favour of her grandson Loṇabhāra when he had come of age. None of these plates mention king Śubhākara II (No. VI) who evidently ruled during this period. All these would indicate that some time before A.D. 860 the Kara kingdom was visited by a great calamity and suffered much in power and prestige, but the situation was saved by the queen-mother, probably with the aid she received from her father Rājamalla. It is not unlikely that the invasion of the Pāla ruler Devapāla was the cause of the calamity, but then the boast of the Pālas that the Utkalas were exterminated can only be regarded as the usual exaggeration of court poets, for the Kara dynasty soon re-established its power, and the kings continued to use the imperial titles. Possibly the collapse of the Pāla empire after Devapāla gave Utkala the requisite opportunity. It is worthy of note that shortly before the Pāla invasion the Kara kings gave up the Buddhist religion. and henceforth the sovereigns were mostly Śaiva, though Tribhuvana-Mahādevī was a devotee of Vishṇu. Whether this change of religion had any political significance in the relations between the Pālas and the Karas, it is difficult to say.

Nothing is known of the four successors of Loṇabhāra (Nos. X-XIII). The last of them, Śubhakara V, was succeeded on his death by his queen, named Gaurī. After her. her daughter Daṇḍī-Mahādevī ascended the throne. Two of her charters dated 180 and 187 are known. According to the newly discovered Taltali plate[46] she was succeeded by her step-mother Vakula-Mahādevī. and the latter by Dharma-Mahādevī, queen of Lavaṇabhāra. undoubtedly a Sanskritized form of Loṇabhāra. As we know from the Angul plate that Dharma-Mahādevī was the name of the queen of Śāntikaradeva III, we must presume that Lavaṇabhāra was another name of Śāntikaradeva III. It is no doubt very singular that there was a regular succession of four queens on the throne, which passed after Daṇḍī-Mahādevī to two senior ladies of the royal family. All the three ruling queens of the family whose charters have so far come to light, *viz.* Tribhuvana-Mahādevī (No. VIII), Daṇḍī-Mahādevī (No. XV) and Dharma-Mahādevī (No. XVII), assumed imperial titles *Parama-bhaṭṭārikā*, and *Mahārājādhirāja-Parameśvarī.*

It is interesting to note that Vakula-Mahādevī is described in a verse as "an ornament like a flag with insignia in the family of the Bhañja kings." This verse is a verbatim copy of one applied to Daṇḍī-Mahādevī in the Kumurang plate, with the substitution of Bhañja for Kara. There is hardly any doubt that Vakula-Mahādevī belonged to the Bhañja family, and it is also not unlikely that her paternal relations played some part in the politics of the Kara kingdom at this period. The succession of four queens one after another probably indicates troublesome times for the Kara dynasty which led to its downfall at no distant date, and the Bhañjas might have played a prominent part in the final stage.

Nothing is known of the Karas after Dharma-Mahādevī who probably flourished about the year 200 of the Kara era, *i.e.* about A.D. 950. Probably the family was ousted by the Somavaṁśīs, who are known to have conquered Orissa about the middle of the tenth century A.D.[47]

We can get a fair idea of the dominions of the Karas from the names of villages mentioned in their land-grants. In addition to the coastal territories comprised in the modern districts of Balasore, Cuttack and Puri, their dominions included Angul, the old feudatory states of Hindol, Dhenkanal, Talcher, Pal Lahara, a part of Keonjhar, and the northern part of Ganjām District. These territories are sometimes referred to as included in North and South Tosalī, but the name Utkala also occurs in the records.

The northern part of the Ganjām District is referred to as Koṅgoda-*maṇḍala* in South Tosalī. It is definitely known from their land-grants that the rulers Nos. II, VII, and XV exercised authority in this region, but, as we shall see later, we find there also the records of the Bhañjas as well as of a branch of the Gaṅgas of Kaliṅga. As noted above, one of the latter, Jayavarman, refers to Unmattavarman as his overlord, but neither the other rulers of this family nor the Bhañjas refer to the Kara overlord in their land-grants. There can be hardly any doubt that some of these Bhañja and Gaṅga rulers were contemporaries of the Karas. Either, therefore, this region must have frequently changed hands, or the feudatories issued land-grants without any reference to their Kara overlords.

All the land-grants of the family are issued from the same place, which is called Guhadeva-pāṭaka in the earlier records and Guheśvara-pāṭaka in the later ones. This town was evidently the capital of the family. A late tradition places the foundation of the Kara kingdom in Jājpur. The Ganjām grant also refers to the second king of the dynasty as king of Virajas, evidently a variant of Virajā, which is a well-known name of Jājpur. It may be presumed therefore that this town represents the site of the ancient capital of the Karas.[48]

GENERAL REFERENCE

Binayak Misra—*Orissa under the Bhauma Kings.*

Section I of this book gives a list of Kara inscriptions, and either edits or contains a short account of them. The historical discussion in Section II is, however, not always helpful or reliable. Five new inscriptions have been discovered since the above work was published. They are referred to in the footnotes.

2. *The Bhañjas*

More than thirty records of kings with names ending in Bhañja have so far come to light. The task of arranging them in a genealogical or chronological order has proved a difficult one and scholars differ widely on the subject. But we can easily distinguish two important branches, one ruling at Khiñjali, and the other at Khijjiṅga. The latter is undoubtedly the same as Khiching in Mayurbhanj whose ruins still testify to its great antiquity. Khiñjali, which lay far to the south, cannot be definitely identified. The records refer to two Khiñjalis, and it has been suggested that one lay to the north and the other to the south of the Mahānadī. But there is no doubt that the kingdom of Khiñjali corresponded, at first, to the old feudatory states of Baud and Sonpur in Orissa and its immediate neighbourhood, though later its boundaries extended further south to the northern part of the Ganjām District.[49]

Whether the Bhañja ruling chiefs of Khiñjali and Khijjiṅga belonged to the same family, or were connected in any way, is not definitely known to us. Some scholars held this view and tried to draw up a genealogy of them all on this basis,[50] but the result has been very unsatisfactory. On the whole, although it is quite possible that the different Bhañja chiefs had a common ancestor, there is no evidence in support of it and the question must be left open.

A. The Bhañjas of Khiñjali

The rulers of this family, so far known from their records, are represented in the following genealogical table:—

I. Yathāsukha
|
II. Mallagambhīra
|
III. Śilābhañja I (Aṅgaddi)
|
IV. Śatrubhañja (Gandhaṭa; Maṅgalarāja)
|
V. Raṇabhañja

(Kalyāṇakalaśa I)

VII. Digbhañja Diśābhañja)
|
VIII. Śilābhañja II (Tribhuvanakalaśa)
|
IX. Vidyādharabhañja (Amoghakalaśa)
|
X. Neṭṭabhañja II (Kalayāṇakalaśa II)

The first four rulers are known from the Tekkali plates of Śatrubhañja.[illegible] The rulers Nos. III-X are known from other records. While there is no doubt about the genealogy of these rulers (III-X), doubts have been entertained regarding the identity of Śilābhañja, and his son Śatrubhañja, mentioned in the Tekkali plates, with the rulers bearing the same names and the same relation in the other list.[illegible] Their identity has been challenged on the ground that the opening verses of the Tekkali plates resemble those of the later, and not earlier, Bhañja rulers of the family. But as Nos. III to X ruled in an unbroken line of succession, the four rulers mentioned in the Tekkali plates can only be regarded as collateral (i.e. contemporary) or posterior to No. X. The latter view is untenable as the characters of the Tekkali plates are undoubtedly much earlier than those of No. X, and there are not sufficient grounds for the former view. The identity of names of two generations naturally leads to the presumption of the identity of the persons, and the genealogy has accordingly been drawn on this basis.

Even the identity of Raṇabhañja mentioned in the different records has been challenged, and *Rāṇaka* Raṇabhañja and *Mahārāja* Raṇabhañja have been held to be different persons.[illegible] But here, again, there are not sufficient reasons to reject the normal presumption about their identity.

A recently discovered plate, not yet published, adds the name of another Bhañja king, who evidently flourished after No. X, and probably belonged to the same family. It was issued in the 13th regnal year of *Rāṇaka* Neṭṭabhañja Tribhuvanakalaśa, sòn of Rāyabhañja and grandson of Pṛithvībhañja. It has been surmised that the last named was not far removed from No. X and might have been his brother, son or grandson.[54]

There can be hardly any doubt that the name-ending Bhañja of No. III was adopted by his successors and gave rise to the name "Bhañja dynasty," even as we find in the case of Guptas, Pālas and Karas. It may be presumed, therefore, that Śilābhañja was the real founder of the kingdom. A charter of the Somavaṁśī king Mahāśivagupta Yayāti refers to a village called Śilābhañja-pāṭi in the Oḍra country.[55] It has been reasonably inferred that the village was named after king Śilābhañja who must, therefore, have been earlier than the Somavaṁśī king.

The earliest known charter of the royal family is that issued by Śatrubhañja.[56] He is called *Rāṇaka*, but the seal in his charter is referred to as *Mahārājakīya mudrā*. There is, therefore, no reason to doubt that both he and his father were at least *de facto* independent kings, whatever might have been the status of the first two rulers. The charter may be referred to the eighth or ninth century A.D. on palaeographic grounds.

Raṇabhañja, the son and successor of Śatrubhañja, had a long reign of more than 58 years. His death marks the end of one epoch and the beginning of another in the history of this family. Both Raṇabhañja and his father are styled in their charters 'Lord of Khiñjali', but this title is not applied to their successors. That this is no mere accidental omission, but denotes a great change, is indicated by the fact that whereas the charters of Raṇabhañja and his father were issued from Dhṛitipura, those of his successors were issued from Vijaya-Vañjulvaka. Further, while all the villages granted by the former, so far as they have been identified, are situated in the States of Sonpur and Baud, those granted by the latter are situated in the Ganjām District or its immediate neighbourhood. All these seem to indicate that after the death of Raṇabhañja his successors shifted to the south and changed their capital. Their kingdom seems to have been confined to the northern part of Ganjām District and the Nayagadh State. Reference may be made in this connection to a ruler named Neṭṭabhañja, who is known from the Baud Grant[57] to have ruled in the region corresponding to Angul and Athmallik States. The date of his charter has been read as 98, but it seems to be really 85. It may be referred to the era used by the Kara kings, and the date would then be equivalent to about A.D. 835. It is thus quite probable that he drove out the dynasty of Raṇabhañja from the northern part of Khiñjali. Neṭṭabhañja is not given any royal title in his Grant, but issues commands to *Sāmantas, Mahārājas,* and others without any reference to any overlord. He was thus a *de facto* independent ruler, but not unlikely a feudatory, either of the Karas or the Pālas, who defeated the Bhañjas and set him up as their protégé. He might have been related to Raṇabhañja.

We do not know what became of this kingdom during the period when the descendants of Raṇabhañja (Nos. VI-X) were ruling in Ganjām. Some light is thrown by the Jurada charter[58] of *Mahāmaṇḍaleśvara* Neṭṭabhañjadeva, son of Raṇabhañja, and grandson of *Mahāmaṇḍaleśvara* Neṭṭabhañja, granting a village, within the jurisdiction of Khiñjali-*maṇḍala.* This village, as well as the place from which the charter was issued, has been located in the Ganjām District. This region was not perhaps originally included in the Khiñjali kingdom, at least in the time of the immediate successors of Rāṇabhañja (No. V), for otherwise they would not have given up the title of Lord of Khiñjali. It is highly probable, therefore, that the family of Neṭṭabhañja, who ousted Raṇabhañja's family from Khiñjali, ultimately conquered the southern region also and included it within the bounds of the Khiñjali kingdom. If this view be accepted we may identify Neṭṭabhañja, the grandfather of the donor of the Jurada charter, with the king of the same name who issued the Baud grant in the year 85.[59] In that case we must suppose that he and his two successors were ruling in Khiñjali proper while the five successors (Nos. VI-X) of Raṇabhañja were ruling in the Ganjām District. The last of these was defeated by Neṭṭabhañja who issued the Jurada grant.

Another Bhañja family of six kings is known from two copper-plates[60] issued by the last two rulers, Yaśobhañja and his brother Jayabhañja. No grants of the first four kings have come to light, but Devabhañja, the founder of the family, is called *Rājādhirāja*, and Yaśobhañja is described as the lord of the whole of Khiñjali. As these rulers flourished after Neṭṭabhañja of the Jurada grant, they probably obtained possession of the kingdom by defeating him or his family.

The date of these Bhañja kings cannot be determined with certainty. The date of the Tekkali plates of Śatrubhañja, the earliest charter of the family, was read as Saṁvat 800 (= A.D. 742) by R. D. Banerji, but this is very doubtful.[61] On palaeographic grounds this charter may be referred to the ninth century A.D., but Orissan epigraphs of this period, on account of the variety of scripts employed even in contemporary records, cannot be relied upon as a very safe guide in matters of chronology. The only positive clue in this respect is furnished by the fact that Vijyā, the queen of Raṇabhañja, was the daughter of *Rāṇaka* Niyārṇama. This Niyārṇama has been identified with the Kadamba chief Niyārṇṇava, grandfather of *Rāṇaka* Dharmakheḍi, who is mentioned in a charter dated in the year 520 of the Gaṅga Era.[62] The epoch of this era is not yet definitely determined, but is generally placed at the end of the fifth century A.D. Dharmakheḍi may thus be taken to have lived in the early part of the eleventh century A.D., and his grandfather, about the middle of the tenth century A.D. If we accept the identification of the latter with the father-in-law of Raṇabhañja, this Bhañja king may be placed in the second half of the tenth century A.D.

In spite of some uncertainties this date may be provisionally accepted as a working hypothesis. Śilābhañja I, who seems to have laid the foundations of an independent Bhañja kingdom, may therefore be placed at the beginning of the tenth century A.D.

Although Raṇabhañja had a long reign of at least fifty-eight years, his five successors must have reigned for short periods as the same goldsmith served under all of them.[63] The reigns of the Bhañja kings of Khiñjali, discussed above, some of whom might have been contemporaries, may thus be regarded as having covered the tenth and eleventh centuries A.D. The dynasty may be regarded as having risen to power on the decline of the Karas, and, as already noted above,[64] might have played an important part in the last stage of their history.

If the dates proposed above be accepted, we may regard the removal of the Bhañja capital from Dhṛitipura to Vañjulvaka, as due to the invasion of Orissa by the Somavaṁśīs who forced them to take shelter in the south.

It is quite probable that the Bhañjas continued to rule even beyond A.D. 1100, either as independent or as feudatory chiefs. In any case, their rule in Khiñjali can be traced down to the mediaeval period. A copper-plate[65] found at Baud introduces us to a line of three kings, *viz.* Solaṇabhañja, his son Durjayabhañja, and the latter's son Kanakabhañja, who ruled in the neighbourhood of the Tel river, *i.e.* in old Khiñjali, about the fifteenth century A.D. There are still Bhañja families living in a place called Kinjili between Aska and Berhampore in the Ganjām District.[66] This Kinjili might be an echo of the old Khiñjali.

On the other hand there are good reasons to believe that many Bhañja chiefs flourished before those rulers whose history we have discussed above. A verse in the copper-plates of the early Bhañja kings[67] says that many Bhañja kings, thousands in number, flourished in the past, and in their family was born Śilābhañja (No. III).

Even allowing for the obvious exaggerations, this verse may be taken to testify to the existence of one or more Bhañja ruling families long before the eighth century A.D. This theory is supported by a short record below a tempera-painting on a rock-shelter in the village of Sitābhinji, Keonjhar District. "The subject-matter of the painting is a procession relating to a king on elephant who is preceded by footmen, a horseman, and a dancing woman and followed by an attendant woman. A painted inscription below the king gives the name of the king as "*Mahārāja* Śrī Diśābhañja".

Mr. T. Ramachandran, from whose account the above description is quoted; refers the inscription to the fourth century A.D. and says that this date is "corroborated by an ensemble of evidence furnished by other associative antiquities."[68]

Dr. D. C. Sircar, on the other hand, thinks that the characters of the epigraph belong to a much later date, between the eighth and eleventh centuries A.D.[69]

There is no doubt that the Orissan inscriptions, even of the same king, employ a variety of scripts, so that palaeography is a very uncertain factor in determining chronology. This is amply illustrated by the widely differing views about the dates of Kara, Śailodbhava and Bhañja kings. Nevertheless, it has to be admitted that the characters of the short record at Sitābhinji can by no means be regarded as later than those of the charters of the early kings of Kaliṅga who have been unanimously referred to the fifth century A.D.[70] Dr. D. C. Sircar's proposed identification of Diśābhañja of the Sitābhinji record with the king Digbhañja-Diśābhañja (No. VII), mentioned above, cannot therefore be upheld, and until more definite evidence is available, Diśābhañja of Sitābhinji may justly be regarded as the earliest Bhañja king who flourished in the fourth or fifth century A.D. The painted scene and the locality seem to indicate that he was a powerful ruler whose kingdom included the Keonjhar State. If we accept this view, we may well believe that the Bhañjas had been ruling in Orissa almost continuously since the fourth or fifth century A.D., though their power and status must have varied in different ages. The territory called Bhañjabhūmi or Bhanjbhūm, which includes the present Mayūrbhanj, was evidently named after the Bhañjas.

B. The Bhañjas of Khijjiṅga

The records of this dynasty closely resemble each other and are distinguished in some essential respects from those of other Bhañjas described above. They are issued from Khijjiṅga and give a traditional account of the origin of the family. The Ādi-Bhañja or the first Bhañja, called Vīrabhadra Gaṇadaṇḍa, is said to have come out of the egg of a pea-hen and to have been brought up by the sage Vasishṭha. They refer next to Koṭṭabhañja who may be regarded as the first historical ruler of the family. The names of the successors of Koṭṭabhañja are, however, given differently in different records. But since all the kings ruled in Khijjiṅga it is probable that the differences are due mainly to the same king having different names as we find in the Kara dynasty. On this assumption we may tentatively draw the following gnealogy of the kings known to us.[71]

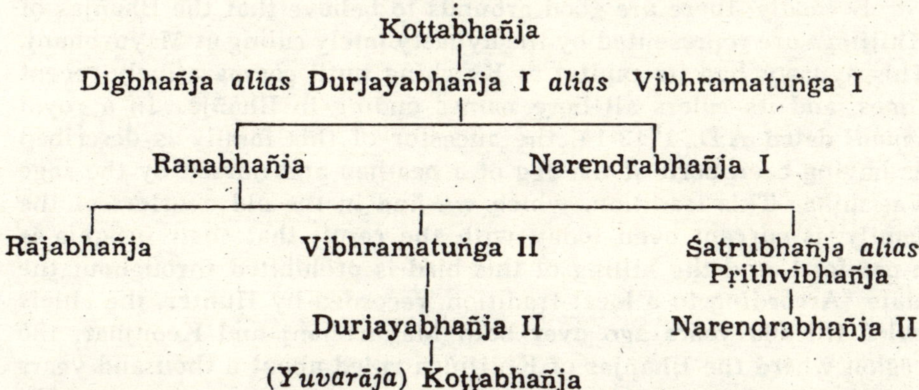

Vīrabhadra is described as '*Chakravartisamaḥ*' (like an emperor), and Śatrubhañja is called *Mahāmaṇḍal-ādhipati-Mahārājādhirāja-Parameśvara*. Raṇabhañja is called both *Mahārāja* and *Mahārājādhirāja*. These titles and the fact that they issued charters without reference to any overlord indicate that they were at least *de facto* independent rulers.

As regards chronology, we have two specific dates for Raṇabhañja, *viz.* 288 and 293.[72] These cannot be referred to the era used by the Karas. as the royal Kara dynasty is not known to have continued beyond the year 200 of that era, and there is nothing to indicate that their era was in use after them. The other possibilities are the Harsha and the Gaṅga eras. If we assume the former, which appears more probable, Raṇabhañja flourished towards the close of the ninth century A.D., and the dynasty must have ruled roughly between A.D. 850 and 1000. We may then assume that it rose to power out of the chaos and confusion in Orissa caused by the invasion of the Pālas under Devapāla, and took full advantage of the downfall of the Pāla empire.

Although we know very little of the history of this dynasty, special interest attaches to it for more than one reason. In the first place, the ruins of temples and images at Khiching, the old capital of the dynasty, testify to a very high development of art and architecture under the Bhañjas.[73] Indeed some of the sculptures found here have been justly regarded as among the best products of mediaeval sculpture in India. This rich artistic treasure gives us a clear idea of the high culture and civilization of the people of Utkala under the Bhañjas. It may also be noted that the art of Khiching shows close affinity with the art of the Pālas rather than of Orissa, and this may be easily explained by its geographical position as well as the political influence of the Pālas which was naturally more effective in this region than that lying further south.

Secondly, there are good grounds to believe that the Bhañjas of Khijjiṅga are represented by the dynasty lately ruling at Mayurbhanj. This dynasty had its capital at Khiching until comparatively recent times, and its rulers all bore names ending in Bhañja. In a royal *sanad*, dated A.D. 1713-14, the ancestor of this family is described as having been born of the egg of a pea-hen and nursed by the sage Vasishṭha. This tradition, which we find in the old charters of the family, is current even today with the result that their insignia is a pea-fowl, and the killing of this bird is prohibited throughout the state. According to a local tradition, recorded by Hunter, the chiefs ruled till 200 years ago over both Mayurbhanj and Keonjhar, the region where the Bhañjas of Khijjiṅga ruled about a thousand years ago.[74]

This striking agreement in respect of the family name and tradition, the capital, and extent of the kingdom leaves no doubt that the modern ruling chiefs of Mayurbhanj are linked up with the old Bhañja rulers of Khijjiṅga; and makes it highly probable that they form one continuous royal line which has ruled for more than a thousand years in an uninterrupted line of succession. Such a phenomenon is very rare in Indian history, and the case of Mayurbhanj may be regarded as almost unique.

GENERAL REFERENCES

1. R. D. Banerji—*Orissa.*
2. R. C. Majumdar, *Outline of the History of the Bhañja Kings of Orisa* (*Dacca University Studies*, Vol. III, No. 2, pp. 137-70). It contains a complete list of the inscriptions of the dynasty with references. This article is abbreviated as *BKO*. Inscriptions discovered since then are referred to in the footnotes, and in *IHQ*, XXVIII. 225 ff.
3. Binayak Misra, *Dynasties of Mediaeval Orissa.*

3. *The Minor Dynasties*

In addition to the Karas and Bhañjas several minor dynasties flourished in Orissa during the period under review. One of them, the Śvetaka branch of the Gaṅgas, has been dealt with in connection with Kaliṅga. Another is the Tuṅga dynasty[75] comprising two kings, Salāṇatuṅga and his son Gayāḍatuṅga, born in the line of Rājā Jagattuṅga who came from Rohitāgiri (Rohtāsgarh in Shāhābād District). Gayāḍatuṅga, who is described as *Samadhigata-pañcha-mahāśabda* and the ruler of Yamagarta, has been identified by some with king Gayāḍa of the Kara dynasty,[76] but this is not very likely. Perhaps the dynasty was at first feudatory to the Karas and assumed independence after their decline. The Talcher Plate of Śivakaradeva,[77] dated 149 (=c. A.D. 900), records a grant of land in Pūrvarāshṭravishaya by the Kara king at the request of *Rāṇaka* Śrī Vinītatuṅga. This *Rāṇaka* is probably the same as is mentioned in the Bonai Grant[78] together with his son Khaḍgatuṅga and grandson Vinītatuṅga II, ruler of Eighteen Gondamas including Yamagarta. Gayāḍatuṅga probably belongs to this family[79] which is also said to have migrated from Rohitāśva and ruled in parts of Talcher, Pal Lahara and Keonjhar State. A ruler, Jayasiṁha, with feudatory titles, issued a Grant[80] from the banks of the Mandākinī river. As the donated lands belonged to Yamagarta-*maṇḍala*, he ruled in the same region as the Tuṅgas.

Another Bonai Grant refers to the Buddhist Mayūra-vaṁśa which originally came from the Chitrakūṭa mountain and ruled over Vaṇāi-*maṇḍala*, which is evidently the same as Bonai. It mentions Uditavarāha, his descendant Tejavarāha, and the latter's son Udayavarāha with the titles *Paramasaugata Samadhigata-pañcha-mahāśabda Mahārāja Rāṇaka.*[81] This, too, was probably a feudatory line, assuming *de facto* independence. As the Grant of this family has some verses in common with those of the Tuṅga plates, the two families were probably closely connected and ruled over the same or neighbouring territories.

More importance attaches to the Śūlkis (called also Śūlkikāṁśa-family) who are probably identical with the "Śūlikas with an army of countless horses" referred to in the Haraha Inscription of the Maukhari king Īśānavarman.[82] A number of records[83] give us the genealogy of the family, but there are some variations. It is not easy to reconcile them, and different views have been entertained by different scholars. The following genealogy may be tentatively offered as the most satisfactory:—

Kāñchana-stambha
|
Kalaha (or Kaṇada) -stambha *alias* Vikramāditya
|
Raṇa-stambha *alias* Kula-stambha[84]
|
Jaya-stambha
|
Nidaya-stambha

It is probable that the second king was known as Kula-stambha. A Grant of Raṇa-stambha contains a date which has been interpreted as 103. It may be referred to the era of the Kara kings. Raṇa-stambha had the title *Mahārājādhirāja* as well as *Samadhigata-pañcha-mahāśabda*, denoting a feudatory rank.[85] Like Vinītatuṅga II, Raṇa-stambha is described as lord of Gondama, and the Śūlki family probably ruled in Talcher and Dhenkanal States. They might have acknowledged the suzerainty of the Karas, but were *de facto* independent rulers. The name Śūlki has been regarded by some as variation of the name Chālukya or Solāṅki. Others have identified Śūlkis with the modern Śūlkis of Midnapore and the Śaulika of the *Bṛihat-saṁhitā and Mārkaṇḍeya Purāṇa*.[86]

The Tuṅga kings, Jayasiṁha, and the Śūlkis all claim to have ruled over the whole of Gondama (or Gondrama) which is sometimes specifically referred to as Eighteen Gondamas. Gondama has been taken to mean the Gond tribe, but it probably denotes a territory which cannot be exactly defined.[87] It has been suggested that Gondama denoted the entire hilly tract extending from Bonai and Bamra in the north up to Jeypore in the Viśākhapatnam District in the south, but this is very doubtful.[88]

Another dynasty, called the Nanda, ruled over the same region, Gondama, probably at a somewhat later date. Four inscriptions supply us with the names of the following kings:—[89]

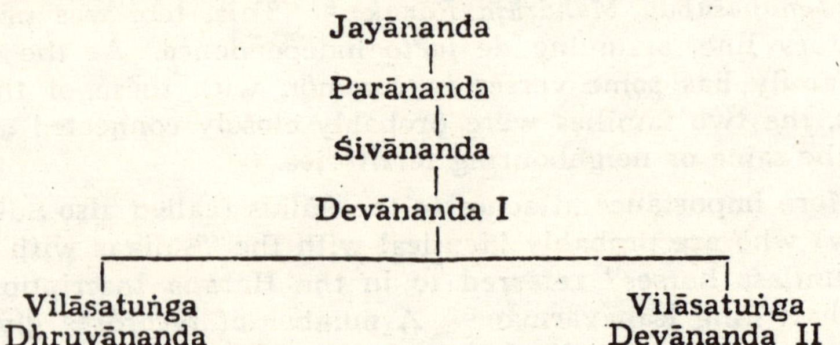

Dhruvānanda is said to be *Parama-saugata* (*i.e.* a Buddhist) while Devānanda was a *Parama-māheśvara* (*i.e.* Śaiva).

The name or surname Vilāsatuṅga and the sovereignty over Gondama indicate some relationship with the Tuṅgas. The plates are issued from Jayapura which has been identified with Jaipur in the old Dhenkanal State, and mention the *maṇḍala* of Airāvatā which has been located in the Cuttack District.[90] The Talmul plates of Dhruvānanda contain a date which has been variously read,[91] but the correct reading seems to be Saṁvat 383. It may be referred to the Gaṅga Era, though this is by no means certain.

A copper-plate Grant, now in the Madras Museum, gives us the name of a king named Narendra-dhavala, who is not known from any other source. Some internal evidence shows that he was either a contemporary of the Bhañja king Śilābhañja I or ruled before his time, and his reign may be placed in the tenth century A.D.

Kings with names ending in 'dhavala' are known to have ruled in Medieval Orissa, and even now the members of the Dompara Raj family of the Cuttack District have similar name-endings. There was evidently a 'Dhavala' ruling family of whom the only ancient ruler so far known is Narendra-dhavala. The territory known as Dhavalabhūmi or Dhalbhum may be presumed to have derived its name from this ruling family.[92]

GENERAL REFERENCES

1. *DHNI*, I. Ch. VII.
2. B. Misra, *Dynastics of Mediaeval Orissa.*

FOOTNOTES

1. Vol. III, p. 138.
2. IV. 529-80.
3. Vol. III, p. 135.
4. Vol. III, p. 143.
5. Francke, *Antiquities of Tibet*, Part II, p. 87; Dr. Petech in *IHQ*, XV. Supplement, 65. The name of the king is written as K'ri-sroṅ-lde-btsan (by Petech) and Khri-Sroṅ Lde-Brtsan (*JRAS*, 1952. p. 149).
6. F. W. Thomas, *Tibetan Literary Texts and Documents concerning Turkestan*, p. 270.
7. Francke, *op. cit.*, 89-90. According to Francke Ral-pa-can ruled from A.D. 804 to 816, but Dr. Petech (*op. cit.* 81) gives the date A.D. 817-836.
8. See p. 52.

8a. Petech, *Mediaeval History of Nepal*, 29.

9. See above p. 47.
10. *JAS*, vol. I. No. I, 1959, p. 47.
11. Petech, *Mediaeval History of Nepal*, 28-32.
12. *A Catalogue of Palm-leaf and Selected Paper Manuscripts belonging to the Durbar Library of Nepal* by H. P. Sastri, p. 21.
13. Cf. Vol. III, p. 141.
14. This is implied by the Hāiyungthal plate of Harjara-varman, though, on account of some lacunae, the meaning of the passage is not quite clear.
15. Hāiyungthal Plate and the Bargaon CP. of Ratnapāla (v. 9).
16. Tezpur CP. of Vanamāla, vv. 6-7.
17. Nowgong CP. of Bala-varman, v. 10.
18. According to the published reading of the Tezpur CP. of Vanamāla the name is Prālamba. But as this reading goes as far back as 1840, and the original plates are lost, we have adopted the reading Sālambha which is quite clear in the newly discovered Pārbatiyā Plate of Vanamālā. (*EI.* XXIX, 145).
19. For, as noted below, his son or nephew was on the throne in A.D. 829.
20. See p. 50.
21. Harjara-varman has been hitherto regarded as the son of Prālambha. But the newly discovered Pārbatiyā plate of Vanamāla, referred to in fn. 6 above, shows that Harjara was the son of Ārathi, brother and successor of Sālambha. This was first pointed out in *PIHC*, XII. 157-9 by Sri K. Dutta.
22. References are to the "List of Important Inscriptions" given on p. 61.
23. This is inferred from Ins. No. 2 which contains an order issued by *Yuvarāja* Vanamāla.
24. Ins. No. 4. Hoernle took Jayamāla and Vīravāhu to be separate kings, but Kielhorn regards the two as identical. This view is also accepted in *KSS* (cf. *DHNI*, I. 246).
25. Bargaon CP. of Ratnapāla, *JASB*, LXVII. 99.

26. Vol. III, pp. 141 ff.
27. Mr. R. D. Banerji thinks that "most probably they (the Karas) also claimed descent from Naraka, like the early kings of Kāmarūpa." (*EI.* XV. 2.) Cf above, Vol. III, p. 88.
28. *DKA.* 54.
29. Misra, *op. cit.* 80-82.
30. For the date, cf. Ganjām Grant of Jayavarma-deva (*IHQ*, XII. 489). The date of this inscription has been read as 50 by Mr. Misra who edited the Plates, but the facsimile published by him shows that the symbol should be read as 20. Mr. Misra does not seem to notice that the symbol is different from that in Neulpur Plate which he reads as 50 (*op. cit.* 7; cf. also the chart facing p. 56).
31. The date has been read as 8 by Mr. R. D. Banerji (*EI*, XV. 1), 54 by Misra (*op. cit.* 7), and 204 by Bhandarkar (List No. 1751).
32. The name and date of this king are known from a newly discovered plate, now in the Utkal University, Cuttack. Dr. D. C. Sircar, while announcing this discovery (*JOR*, XVIII. 49), considered it possible, though not very likely, that this king might be identical with No. VII. But later he seems to have excluded this possibility and definitely regarded the two as separate rulers (*JASL*, XVII. p. 16, fn. 1). This seems to be the more reasonable view.
33. An unpublished article of Dr. D. C. Sircar refers to the recently discovered Baud plates of Tribhuvana-Mahādevi II, dated in the year 158. According to these, the kings Nos. X and XI having died without leaving any issue, the throne passed to Tribhuvana-Mahādevi II, the queen of No. X. This statement is in conflict with the later records which vouch for the existence of two sons of No. XI (Nos. XII, XIII), who actually ascended the throne after XI. The only reasonable explanation seems to be that there was a party in the state who, for some reason or other, did not recognise Nos. XII and XIII to be legitimate sons of No. XI and set up Tribhuvana-Mahādevi II as a rival claimant to the throne after the death of No. XI. Evidently she was overthrown, probably after a short reign, and No. XII obtained undisputed possession of the kingdom. For further discussion about her reign, cf. the section on Somavaṁśis, Ch. VI. III.
34. The dates have been read as 280 and 287 by Bhandarkar (*Lists:* Nos. 1413. 1416). The second date was read as 387 by Panday (*JBORS*, V. 571). But cf. EI, XXIX, 81.
35. *EI*, XXVI. 248.
36. *PIHC*. XII. 69.
37. Mr. Misra has made this assumption; cf. the genealogical table on p. 71 of his book.
38. EI, XV. 1.
39. EI, VI. 136.
40. *EI*, XV. 363. Mr. S. C. De, who supports this view, even goes further and regards Śubhākara as the king of Orissa who initiated Rāhulabhadra in Mantrayāna (*PIHC*, XII. 69).
41. Misra, *op. cit.* 76. In the Neulpur plate the *ākāra* is indistinct, but it is quite clear in the other inscriptions. There is no doubt that the name should be read as Śubhākara.
42. Misra, op. cit. 72 ff. Misra's statement that Kielhorn took the 'era of the Ganjam Plate of Daṇḍi-Mahādevi as the Harsha era' is wrong. Keilhorn referred the plate dated 187 to the thirteenth century A.D. (*EI*, VI. 136). Dr. D. C. Sircar also refers the date of the Karas to Harsha Era (*JKHRS*, II. 103-4). But he has recently informed me in a private letter that a newly discovered inscription in Orissa "seems to suggest that the era used in the inscriptions of the Bhauma-Karas started from a date about the beginning of the 9th century A.D."
43. Cf. R. D. Banerji's view about the date of the Neulpur Plate (*EI*. XV. 1). On the other hand, Mr. A. Ghosh thinks that the characters of the Khaḍipadā inscription "are more or less similar to those of the Ganjam plates of Śaśāṅka" (*EI*, XXVI. 247). This would support the theory of Harsha Era.
44. There can be hardly any doubt that Jayavarman of the Ganjām Grant (*IHQ*, XII. 489) is to be identified with the king, one of whose copper-plates has been published in *EI*, XXIII, 261. For the Śvetakas, cf. Vol. III. p. 217.
45. See above, p. 50.
46. *IHQ*, XXI. 218.
47. Mr. P. Banerjee points out the "striking similarity" between the scripts of the Taltali Plate of Vakula-Mahādevī and those of the Somavaṁśī kings which can be dated about the middle of the tenth century A.D. (*JASL*, XVII. 247).

48. Misra. *op cit.* 87. This view is supported by Dr. D. C. Sircar who has discovered a fragmentary inscription of Śubhākara I amid the ruins of the Haṁseśvara temple at Sivadāsapura, not far from the celebrated Virajā temple of Jājpur. This is the only record of the Karas so far found within the boundaries of modern Jājpur (*JASL.* XVII. 15).
49. *JBORS,* XVII. 105; XV. 83-4; BKO. 147.
50. *EI,* XVIII. 286.
51. Edited by R. D. Banerji (*JBORS.* XVIII. 387) and S. Rajaguru (*JKHRS,* I. 181), and commented upon by Dr. D. C. Sircar (*IHQ,* XXVIII. 229). The name Yathāsukha was read as Pathāsukha by Rajaguru, and the name of Mallagambhīra as Pallagambhīra by R. D. Banerji. The date was read as 800 by Banerji, as 1012 by Rajaguru, 17 by Dr. B. Misra (*op. cit.* 105), and 14 by Dr. Sircar. The first figure may be easily read as 10, but the second one is very unusual and cannot be read with certainty. In any case, the date seems to be a regnal year and not one in Saṁvat or Śaka era as held respectively by Banerji and Rajaguru.
52. Dr. Sircar (*op. cit.*) regards the rulers, mentioned in the Tekkali plates, as belonging to a collateral line, ruling contemporaneously with the Bhañjas of Vañjulvaka. But his chronological ideas are not very clear. In one place (p. 229) he says that Śatrubhañja flourished considerably after the reign of Raṇabhañja (about the middle or the third quarter of tenth century). But on the very next page he remarks that "the use of the numerical symbols instead of decimal figures in the record of Śatrubhañja Maṅgalarāja (i.e. Tekkali Plates) would, however, suggest that he flourished before the eleventh century."
53. *ABORI,* XVII. 393.
54. *IHQ,* XXVIII. 228.
55. *JBORS,* XV. 85.
56. Tekkali Pl. cf. fn. 51 above.
57. *JBORS,* XVII. 104.
58. *EI,* XXIV. 15.
59. It is, however, possible to identify him also with king No. VI or X. In that case we shall have a new branch or a continuation of the old family.
60. Antirigan CP. *EI,* XVII. 282, 298.
61. See above, fn. 51.
62. This was originally suggested by B. Misra (*op. cit.* 104) and Dr. Bhandarkar (*List* No. 2053, fn. 2), and later by Dr. D. C. Sircar (*PIHC,* XII. 128).
63. Cf. *IHQ,* XXVIII. 228.
64. See above, p. 67.
65. Baud Plate, *JBORS,* II. 356.
66. *JAHRS,* VII. 109.
67. Cf. Sonpur CP. of Śatrubhañja (*EI,* XI. 99) and Chakradharpur (Daspalla) CP. of Raṇabhañja (JBORS, VI. 269).
68. *JAHRS,* XIX. 191.
69. *IHQ,* XXVIII. 227-8.
70. Above, Vol. III, pp. 221 ff.
71. For detailed discussion and alternate views, cf. *BKO.* 137 ff.
72. *JASB,* XL (1871), 161; *EI,* XXV. 147.
73. *ASI,* 1922-3, p. 124; 1923-4, p. 85; 1924-5, p. 111. Generally speaking, the architecture and sculpture of Orissa during this period show a far greater progress and development than we could reasonably expect from the petty principalities ruling there. We have, therefore, devoted more space to its history than would be justified by its political importance.
74. It may be more than a thousand years if we regard Diśābhañja of Sitābhinji ins. as flourishing in the fourth century A.D. (see fn. 68 above).
75. For inscriptions, cf. *JASB,* V (1909). 347; XII. 291.
76. *DHNI,* I. 420.
77. Misra, *Orissa under the Bhauma Kings,* p. 41.
78. *JBORS,* VI. 236. Bhandarkar thinks that the record refers only to Vinītatuṅga, the donor, and his son Khaḍgatuṅga. (*Bh. List* No. 1747).
79. There are striking resemblances between the wordings of the Bonai Grant and the Tuṅga charters. Both again refer to the king Vānāryaśatru.
80. *JBORS.* II. 417. The Editor reads the date of the Grant as 99, but this is very doubtful.
81. *JBORS.* VI. 241; XXXI 159. Bhandarkar thinks that the plate only mentions Uditavarāha or Udayavarāha and his son Tejavarāha (*List* No. 1754).
82. Vol. III, p. 68.

83. For the inscriptions of this dynasty, cf. *EI*, XII. 156; *JASB*, LXIV (1895). 123 ff; *JBORS*, II. 168 ff; 395 ff. All the plates are issued from Kodālaka or Kodāloka which has been identified with Kuālu in the Dhenkanal State (*JBORS*, XVI. 453).
84. H. P. Sastri takes Raṇa-stambha I as son of Kula-stambha (*JBORS*, II.. 400), but cf. *EI*, XII. 158.
85. According to MM. H. P. Sastri he made a land-grant in Rāḍhā-*maṇḍala* or West Bengal. The village granted, named Jara, according to Sastri, still exists in the Hooghly District, and a section of its inhabitants still call themselves Sukli (*JBORS*, II. 168-71). But as Dr. D. C. Sircar has shown, this view is erroneous and there is no reason to suppose that Raṇa-stambha conquered any part of West Bengal as Sastri supposed (*JOR*, XVIII. 45).
86. *EI*, XIV. 112; *JASB*, 1895, p. 124; 1911, pp. 443, 447; *DHNI*, I. 439.
87. The Bonai Grant refers to Yamagartta-*maṇḍalu* as situated in the *Vishaya* of Eighteen Gondamas (*JBORS*, VI. 237, 239).
88. *JBORS*, XVI. 462-3.
89. *JBORS*, XV. 87; XVI. 457. *EI*, XXVI. 74; *Ancient India*, No. 5, p. 50; Misra (*op cit.* 35) takes Dhruvānanda (or Dhṛivānanda as read by him) as another name of Devānanda. The relation between the last three kings is not certain. For the views adopted, cf. *EI*, XXVI. p. 76, fn. 2.
90. *Ancient India*, No. 5, p. 50.
91. See references under footnote 89. Misra (*op. cit.*) reads the date as 193 on p. 35 and 183 in the plate facing p. 96. Dr. Bhandarkar reads the date as 293 (*List*, No. 2043). The hundredth figure, however, seems to denote 300, as there are two distinct adjuncts, one above and one below the letter *l* which is usually read as 100. The decimal figure resembles the one used in the plate of Daṇḍī-Mahādevī, read as 80. If we read the date as 183, the date may be referred to the era used by the Kara kings, and we may assume that the family was feudatory to the Karas but assumed *de facto* independence towards the end of their rule. Bhandarkar refers the date 293 to the Harsha Era.
92. *PIHC*, XII. 127.

CHAPTER V

CENTRAL AND WESTERN INDIA

I. THE CHANDELLA DYNASTY

After the break-up of the Pratihāra Empire a number of dynasties rose to power in Central and Western India. One of them, known as Chandella or Chandrātreya, held sway over the country now called Bundelkhand.

The Chandellas trace their descent from the sage Chandrātreya, who was born of the Moon. Their social status was equal to that of the Chāhamānas. The bards mention them as one of the thirty-six Rājput clans. The dynasty was founded by Nannuka in the first quarter of the ninth century A.D. Epigraphic records connect the early kings of the family with Kharjuravāhaka, the modern village of Khajrāho, in old Chhatarpur State, Bundelkhand. Nannuka appears to have ruled over the country around this place, which was the early capital of his family. At this time the Pratihāra Empire under Nāgabhaṭa II extended up to Kālañjara-*maṇḍala* (Kālinjar) which is nearly forty miles north-east of Khajrāho and is situated in the Bāndā District, in Uttar Pradesh. Deogarh, in the Jhānsi District, Uttar Pradesh, was within the kingdom of the Pratihāras. Khajrāho, which lies between Deogarh and Kālinjar, was obviously under the supremacy of the Pratihāra kings, and the early rulers of the Chandella dynasty may therefore be regarded as vassals of the Pratihāras of Kanauj. Nannuka was succeeded by his son Vākpati, who probably flourished in the second quarter of the ninth century. The Vindhya hill is said to have been the "pleasure ground" of Vākpati. It probably means that he fought battles in this region, for at this time the Vindhya hill was the target of attacks of a number of kings, *viz.* the Pratihāra Bhoja, the Pāla Devapāla, and the Kalachuri Kokkalla I. Vākpati had two sons, Jayaśakti and Vijayaśakti. Jayaśakti, who was also known as Jejjāka and Jejā, succeeded him on the throne. Henceforward the country ruled by the Chandellas was called Jejākabhukti after his name. Jayaśakti appears to have had a daughter named Naṭṭā who was given in marriage to the Kalachuri Kokkalla I. Jayaśakti was succeeded by his younger brother Vijayaśakti, also known as Vijjaka. Both these brothers may be taken to have flourished in the third quarter of the ninth century. The Khajrāho inscription states that Vijaya subdued the neighbouring countries, and "on his warlike expeditions reached even the southernmost point of India." This has led Dr. R. C. Majumdar to suggest that Vijaya was probably an ally of king Devapāla of Bengal and accompanied him in his southern expedition.[1] Vijaya was succeeded by his son Rāhila. There is a village named Rāhilya, two miles south-west of Mahobā, in the Hamirpur District, Uttar Pradesh. A tank in this village, on the bank of which stands an old ruined temple, is known as Rāhilyasāgara, and tradition ascribes the foundation of both to Rāhila-varmā. If Rāhila-varmā is identical with the Chandella king of this name, Mahobā, the ancient Mahotsava-nagara, must have been included in the Chandella kingdom during this period. After the death of Rāhila, his son Harsha ascended the throne.

Harsha ruled approximately from A.D. 900 to 925. The Chandellas evidently exercised greater political power during the reign of this king. The Khajrāho inscription reports that Harsha established king Kshitipāladeva on the throne. As has been mentioned above,[2] it is generally held that Kshitipāladeva is identical with the Pratīhāra Mahīpāla I, and Harsha helped him to recover his throne of Kanauj after it was captured by the Rāshṭrakūṭa Indra III about A.D. 914. This valuable military service, rendered by Harsha, won for his family a high political status.[3] Harsha married a Chāhamāna lady named Kañchukā, who probably belonged to the Chāhamāna family ruling in the Mālava region.

After the close of Harsha's reign (c. A.D. 925), his son Yaśovarman, also known as Lakshavarman, assumed the royal state. As noted above, the disintegration of the Pratīhāra Empire began about this time, and Mahendrapāla II's successor Devapāla[4] was unable to keep in check the revolutionary forces. Yaśovarman, who was a contemporary of Devapāla, made use of this opportunity for enhancing his political power and defied the authority of the Pratīhāras. The Khajrāho inscription states that he was a scorching fire to the Gurjaras. He conquered Kālañjara, which had been in the possession of the Imperial Pratīhāras, and pushed the northern boundary of his kingdom up to the banks of the Yamunā. He is said to have made the Yamunā and the Gaṅgā his pleasure lakes when he went out for the conquest of the regions. After consolidating his position in Bundelkhand, Yaśovarman directed his army against his southern neighbours. About this time, the Kalachuri Yuvarāja I was ruling the Chedi country from his capital Tripurī near Jubbulpore, and the Paramāra Sīyaka II was governing the adjoining country of Mālava as a vassal of the Rāshṭrakūṭa Krishna III. Yaśovarman fought successfully with both Yuvarāja I and Sīyaka II, and pushed the southern boundary of his kingdom up to the borders of

Chedi and Mālava. In the course of these campaigns he seems also to have come into conflict with the Somavaṁśī kings of Southern Kosala, who suffered defeat at his hands. He is also known to have led expeditions against distant countries.

In the middle of the tenth century Bengal was passing through a period of stress and strain. The Kambojas deprived the Pālas of their sovereignty of Gauḍa and established their supremacy over that country. The Pāla king Gopāla II was forced to take shelter in Magadha and Mithilā. During this period of turmoil Yaśovarman invaded the territories of the Pālas and the Kambojas. He is said to have conquered Gauḍa and Mithilā. The Khajrāho inscription states that Yaśovarman "equalled[5] the forces of the Khaśas, the Kāśmīrī warriors perished before him, and he was to the Kurus what a storm is to the trees." Yaśovarman's contemporary kings of Kāshmir were Yaśaskara, Saṁgrāmadeva, and Parvagupta. Lohara, modern Lohrin, in Kāshmir, was under the rule of the Khaśa chiefs. About this time Chandurāja seems to have been on the throne of Lohara, and the Tomaras of Delhi were in possession of Kurukshetra. It does not seem likely that Yaśovarman, in the course of conquest, went as far as Kāshmir forcing his way through the Punjāb. This statement may, therefore, be taken as a vain panegyric of the poet.

Yaśovarman was undoubtedly a general of high order. He appears to have come to terms with his overlord Devapāla, whose nominal sway he continued to acknowledge. He received an image of Vishṇu from Devapāla, which in turn had been received by Devapāla's father Herambapāla[6] from Sāhi, king of Kīra or Kāngrā Valley. Sāhi obtained it from the lord of Bhoṭa or Tibet. Yaśovarman erected a magnificent temple at Khajrāho, which is now identified with the Chaturbhuja temple, and installed in it this image of Vishṇu. He also dug a beautiful tank. He was succeeded by his son Dhaṅga.

Dhaṅga and his successors took pride in calling themselves the lords of Kālañjara. Dhaṅga acknowledged the supremacy of Vināyakapāla, the successor of the Pratīhāra Devapāla, at least up to A.D. 954.[7] At this time the Chandella kingdom extended "as far as Kālañjara and as far as Bhāsvat, situated on the banks of the river of Mālava; from here also to the river Kālindī, and from here also to the frontiers of the Chedi country and even as far as that mountain called Gopa." Bhāsvat is the modern Bhilsa on the Betwā river in old Gwālior State, Kālindī is the Yamunā, and Gopa is Gwālior. Thus in the early part of the reign of Dhaṅga, Gwālior, the Yamunā, Kālañjara, northern border of the Jubbulpore District, and Bhilsa were the extreme limits of his kingdom. He obviously inherited this kingdom from his father Yaśovarman. He could not, however, retain Gwālior for a long time as some time before A.D. 977 Vajradāman, son of Lakshmaṇa, of the Kachchhapaghāta family, invaded Gwālior and forced Dhaṅga and his overlord, who seems to have been the Pratīhāra Vijayapāla, to surrender it to him. It is claimed that Vajradāman conquered Gopagiri by defeating the king of Gādhinagara, *i.e.* Kanauj. A stone inscription of the reign of the *Mahārājādhirāja* Vajradāman, dated V. S. 1034 (= A.D. 977) has been found at Gwālior. This discomfiture of the king of Kanauj seems to have encouraged Dhaṅga to rise against him. He invaded his kingdom and inflicted a crushing defeat on him. The eastern portion of the Pratīhāra kingdom to the north of the Yamunā now passed into the hands of the Chandellas. In A.D. 998 Dhaṅga issued an inscription from Kāśikā (Banaras). Probably from the base at Banaras, Dhaṅga led a successful military campaign against Aṅga or Bhāgalpur, which was within the kingdom of the Pālas, and Rāḍhā or West Bengal. The Pāla kings Vigrahapāla II and Mahīpāla I were his contemporaries. In the first quarter of the eleventh century Southern Rāḍhā was under the rule of Raṇaśūra of the Śūra family. Raṇaśūra's predecessor probably had to bear the brunt of Dhaṅga's attack. The Somavaṁśī kings of Kosala had also to yield to his forces. During his southern campaigns he seems to have come into conflict with the kings of Andhra and Kuntala. Andhra was under the rule of the Eastern Chālukyas. The Rāshṭrakūṭa supremacy in Kuntala was put to an end by Taila II of the Chālukya dynasty in *c.* A.D. 972. The king of Kuntala, who was an adversary of Dhaṅga, cannot be identified. The claim of the court-poet that Dhaṅga defeated the kings of Kratha, Siṁhala, and Kāñchī seems to be a hyperbole.

Firishta relates that Jayapāla, king of the Punjāb, in order to save his kingdom from the attack of Amir Sabuktigīn, sought help from the kings of Northern India, and the *Rājā* of Kālinjar was one of those who responded to his call. The confederacy of the Hindu chiefs met Sabuktigīn near Lamghan and was badly defeated about A.D. 989. The *Rājā* of Kālinjar was evidently Dhaṅga. The authenticity of the statement that the chiefs of Hindusthān joined in this battle has been called in question, as it does not find mention in the records of earlier authorities. There is, however, definite evidence to prove that Dhaṅga came into conflict with the Muslims. An inscription from Mahobā states that he, "by the strength of his arms, equalled even the powerful Haṁvīra." It is obvious that Haṁvīra refers to a Yamīnī king of Ghaznī, who bore the title Amir. So Firishta's report may be accepted as historical.

Dhaṅga was the first independent king of the Chandella dynasty. He bore the title *Mahārājādhirāja*, which indicates his independent sovereign status. A number of temples were erected at Khajrāho during his reign. Prabhāsa, born in the lineage of Gautama Akshapāda, who was competent to explain the Nyāya doctrine, was appointed his chief minister. The dates of the inscriptions of Dhaṅga's reign range from A.D. 954 to 1002. He died shortly after A.D. 1002, at the age of one hundred, at Prayāga. He was succeeded by his son Gaṇḍa.

II. THE KALACHURIS

1. *The Kalachuris of Tripurī*

The kingdom of the Chandellas was bordered on the south by that of the Kalachuris of the Chedi country. The Kalachuris, also known as the Haihayas, were an ancient race.[8] The Kalachuris of Chedi are sometimes referred to as the kings of Ḍāhala-*maṇḍala*, the capital of which was Tripurī, now a village known as Tewar, six miles west of Jubbulpore, Madhya Pradesh. The earliest known king of this Kalachuri dynasty is Kokkalla I.[9] Ḍāhala-*maṇḍala* was ruled by a king named Lakshmaṇarāja in A.D. 841-2. It is known from the Sanjān copper-plate of Amoghavarsha that the Rāshṭrakūṭa Govinda III (A.D. 794-814), after conquering the Ḍāhala country, placed one of his servants there. This Rāshṭrakūṭa officer, who was made the governor of Ḍāhala, was probably Lakshmaṇarāja or his predecessor. Kokkalla I, whose relationship with Lakshmaṇarāja is not known, ascended the throne of Ḍāhala shortly after A.D. 842.[10] The date of his accession may be fixed approximately at A.D. 845. Kokkalla was one of the greatest generals of his age. Shortly after his accession he involved himself in a war with the Pratīhāras of Kanauj and their feudatories. The Pratīhāra Bhoja I failed to check the invading Kalachuri army. The Kalachuri Śaṅkaragaṇa (of Sarayupāra in U.P.) the Guhila Harsharāja (of Ḍhavagartā, i.e. Dhoḍ in Mewār) and the Chāhamāna Gūvaka II of Śākambharī (near Ajmere), all of whom were vassals of Bhoja, yielded to the forces of Kokkalla, who is said to have carried away their treasures. Kokkalla granted Bhoja and his feudatories 'freedom from fear', which probably means an assurance that he would not lead any more aggressive campaign against their territories.[11] In the course of his marauding excursions in Rājputāna Kokkalla seems to have come into clash with the Turushkas, who were obviously Turkish soldiers in the service of the Arab governors of Sindh. The Turushkas had to acknowledge defeat at his hands. To the east Kokkalla is said to have reached Vaṅga or East Bengal in the course of his military campaign, and plundered the wealth of that country. The king of Vaṅga at this time was in all probability Kāntideva,[12] who was in possession of Harikela, which is a synonym for Vaṅga. In the latter part of his reign Kokkalla was engaged in a war with the Rāshṭrakūṭas of the Deccan. Kokkalla vanquished the Rāshṭrakūṭa king Kṛishṇa II (A.D. 878-914) who was his son-in-law, and invaded Northern Konkan. Konkan was at this time ruled by a feudatory of the Rāshṭrakūṭas named Kapardin II of the Śilāhāra dynasty, who readily submitted to the Kalachuri army. A treaty was ultimately concluded between the Kalachuris and the Rāshṭrakūṭas.

All these conquests made by Kokkalla, though they did not enable him to acquire new territories, certainly raised the Kalachuri dynasty to the rank of the imperial ruling families of the age. Kokkalla married a Chandella princess, who seems to have been the daughter of King Jayaśakti.[13] He had eighteen sons, all of whom, except the eldest, were made rulers of different *maṇḍalas* or Divisions. A descendant of one of these younger sons of Kokkalla subsequently founded a kingdom in Dakshiṇa-Kosala, the capital of which was Tummāṇa. Kokkalla had a daughter who was given in marriage to the Rāshṭrakūṭa Kṛishṇa II during the reign of Amoghavarsha I. The names of only two sons of Kokkalla are know[n] Śaṅkaragaṇa and Arjuna. Śaṅkaragaṇa, also known as Śaṅkila an[d] Śaṅkuka, was evidently the eldest and succeeded him to the throne Kokkalla was a contemporary of the Rāshṭrakūṭa king Kṛishṇa I[I] who ascended the throne in c. A.D. 878. Śaṅkaragaṇa was on the throne of Ḍāhala when Guṇaka-Vijayāditya III of the Eastern Chālukya dynasty, whose reign terminated in A.D. 888, was the king of the Andhra country. Hence Kokkalla must have been succeeded by Śaṅkaragaṇa some time between A.D. 878 and 888.

Śaṅkaragaṇa assumed the titles *Mugdhatuṅga*, *Prasiddhadhavala*, and *Raavigraha*. He fought with a Somavaṁśī king of Kosala, and conquered from him Pāli, twelve miles north-west of Ratanpur, in the Bilāspur District, Madhya Pradesh. He could not utilise his energies for further conquests as his help was sought by his brother-in-law, the Rāshṭrakūṭa Kṛishṇa II, against the Eastern Chālukya king Vijayāditya III, who had invaded the Deccan. Śaṅkaragaṇa, at the head of the Kalachuri army, joined Krishṇa II at Kiraṇapura, now a small town in the Bālāghāt District, Madhya Pradesh. A great battle was fought there with the Eastern Chālukyas in which both Śaṅkaragaṇa and Kṛishṇa II were worsted. The Kalachuris and the Rāshṭrakūṭas were forced to retreat, and Kiraṇapura was burnt by the Chālukya general, Pāṇḍuraṅga. The Maliyapundi grant of Amma II states that Vijayāditya III "terrified Śaṅkila, the lord of the excellent Ḍāhala, who was joined by the fierce Vallabha, and burnt Kiraṇapura." The Pithāpuram inscription reports that Vijayāditya frightened Śaṅkila, residing in Kiraṇapura and joined by Kṛishṇa. Thus Śaṅkaragaṇa's engagement with the Eastern Chālukyas resulted in his complete discomfiture. The claim of the Bilhari inscription that he raided the Malaya country does not seem to have any historical basis. He had two sons, Bālaharsha and Yuvarāja I, and a daughter named Lakshmī. Lakshmī was married to Jagattuṅga, son of the Rāshṭrakūṭa Kṛishṇa II. Lakshmī gave birth to Indra III, who succeeded to the throne of his grandfather. Vijambā, the grand-daughter of Śaṅkaragaṇa's younger brother Arjuna, was given in marriage to Indra III. Śaṅkaragaṇa died in the latter part of the ninth century and was followed on the throne by Bālaharsha. Nothing particular is known about the reign of Bālaharsha. He was succeeded by his younger brother Yuvarāja I, who assumed the title *Keyūravarsha.*

Yuvarāja flourished in the second quarter of the tenth century. He inherited the military skill of his father and grandfather. In the course of his conquests, he reached the Gauḍa country and defeated its king, who was either Rājyapāla or his son Gopāla II of the Pāla dynasty. Kaliṅga, which was at that time ruled by the Gaṅgas, had to bear the brunt of his attack. In the latter part of his reign he had, however, to suffer some military defeats. The Chandella Yaśovarman, in his endeavour to push the boundary of his kingdom further south, came into conflict with him. Though the Chandellas claimed to have won a victory over him, they did not seem to have been able to acquire any part of the Kalachuri kingdom. At this time the Rāshṭrakūṭas reduced him to a very critical situation. He gave his daughter Kundakadevī in marriage to the Rāshṭrakūṭa Amoghavarsha III Vaḍḍiga, who ruled from A.D. 936 to 939. Amoghavarsha's son by this Kalachuri princess was Kṛishṇa III, who ascended the throne of the Deccan in A.D. 939-40. Kṛishṇa III led a successful expedition against Kālañjara during the reign of his father. Some time after his accession Kṛishṇa III invaded the kingdom of his maternal grandfather Yuvarāja I. The Kalachuris failed to rise equal to the occasion and suffered a heavy defeat with a disastrous result. The whole of Ḍāhala-*maṇḍala* was now at the mercy of Kṛishṇa III. The Karhād inscription of this Rāshṭrakūṭa king, dated A.D. 959, states that he "conquered Sahasrārjuna (*i.e.* the Kalachuri king), though he was an elderly relative of his mother and his wife." A stone inscription at Jura, in old Maihar State, Baghelkhand, proves that the Rāshṭrakūṭa Empire extended at least for some time up to Maihar during the reign of Kṛishṇa III. The Rāshṭrakūṭas could not, however, keep the kingdom of the Kalachuris under their subjugation for long. Yuvarāja I rallied his forces and succeeded in driving them out of Ḍāhala. The Bilhari inscription mentions his victory over the Karṇāṭas and the Lāṭas. Lāṭa or the Southern Gujarāt formed part of the Rāshṭrakūṭa Empire. The great poet Rājaśekhara evidently refers to this battle when he states that "Yuvarāja (I) won a victory over Vallabha, who formed a confederacy with other chiefs." This achievement of Yuvarāja was a memorable event in the history of the Kalachuris. To celebrate this victory Rājaśekhara staged his drama *Viddhaśālabhañjikā* at the court of Yuvarāja. The authenticity of the statement in the Bilhari inscription that Yuvarāja I raided Kāshmir and the Himālaya may well be doubted. It has been noticed above that the Khajrāho inscription puts forward similar claims on behalf of the Chandella Yaśovarman, the northern adversary of Yuvarāja I.

Yuvarāja I helped the Śaiva ascetics in preaching their doctrine in his kingdom. There was a famous Śaiva monastery known as Golaki-maṭha in the Ḍāhala-*maṇḍala*, which was founded by Durvāsa. Sadbhāvaśambhu, a remote successor of Durvāsa, and the high priest of the Golaki-maṭha, received from Yuvarāja a large number of villages for the maintenance of that monastery. Yuvārāja I married Nohalā, the daughter of the Chaulukya Avanivarman, who resided at the city of Mattamayūra. There was a Śaiva monastery in this city, which exercised tremendous influence over that part of the country during this period. Yuvarāja I invited Prabhāvaśiva of this monastery to his kingdom and entrusted to him the charge of a monastery, which was built at great cost, and which was richly endowed by the king. At Chandrehi, twenty-nine miles south of Rewā, Baghelkhand, there are remains of a temple of Śiva and a monastery. This might have been the monastery over which Prabhāvaśiva had been placed in charge. Yuvarāja built a magnificent temple at Gurgi, twelve miles east of the Rewā town. The place is now in ruins. The queen Nohalā erected a temple of Śiva at Bilhari, in the Jubbulpore District, and granted seven villages for its maintenance.

The poet Rājaśekhara, who lived for some time at the court of the Pratīhāra Mahendrapāla and his son Mahīpāla of Kanauj, was also intimately connected with the Kalachuri kings of his time. The poet remarks that "of rivers the Mekalasutā (*i.e.* Narmadā), of kings Raṇavigraha, and of poets Surānanda are the ornaments of the country of Chedi." This obviously refers to the poet's association with the court of Tripurī during the reign of Śaṅkaragaṇa Raṇavigraha, the father of Yuvarāja I. Rājaśekhara says that he wrote the drama *Viddhaśālabhañjikā* to please Yuvarājadeva, and as already mentioned, it was staged in the court of the Kalachuris at the orders of the assembly of Yuvarāja (*Yuvarāja-parishad*). He seems to be identical with the 'wonder-struck poet Rājaśekhara,' mentioned in the Bilhari inscription of the time of Yuvarāja II, grandson of Yuvarāja I. Bhākamiśra was the chief minister of the king. Yuvarāja I was succeeded by his son Lakshmaṇarāja, who probably flourished in the third quarter of the tenth century.

Lakshmaṇarāja pursued the traditional expansionist policy of his predecessors. His father, as has been noticed, plundered Gauḍa. He raided the Vaṅgāla country or East Bengal, which was at this time probably ruled by Trailokya-chandra of the Chandra dynasty. It was apparently during this eastern campaign that he came in contact with the king of Oḍra or Orissa, and obtained from him an effigy of the serpent Kāliya, wrought in jewels and gold. About the same time Lakshmaṇarāja won laurels by inflicting a defeat on the king of Kosala, who may be identified with Mahābhavagupta, son of Śivagupta, of the Somavaṁśa. After finishing his eastern conquests, Lakshmaṇarāja invaded the western region with all his infantry, cavalry, elephant forces and feudatory chiefs. He humbled the chief of Lāṭa, who seems to have been a feudatory of the Rāshṭrakūṭas of the Deccan, and won a victory over the king of Gurjara, who was evidently Mūlarāja I, the founder of the Chaulukya dynasty in Aṇahilapāṭaka, modern Pātan in Northern Gujarāt. Thereafter he reached Somanāthapattana, probably defeating Grāharipu of the Ābhīra family, ruling in Junāgadh, in his way. On that occasion he dedicated the effigy of Kāliya, which he had received from the king of Oḍra, to the god Someśvara. The statement of the Gaharwa inscription of Karṇa that Lakshmaṇarāja conquered Kāshmir and the Pāṇḍya country is obviously an exaggeration.

Like his father Lakshmaṇarāja also extended his patronage to the Śaiva teachers. He handed over the monastery of the holy Vaidyanātha, which was situated at Bilhari or in its neighbourhood, in the Jubbulpore District, to the Śaiva teacher Hṛidayaśiva of the Mattamayūra sect. His minister Bhaṭṭa Someśvara Dīkshita, son of Bhākamiśra, prime-minister of Yuvarāja I, built a temple of Vishṇu at Karitalai, in the Mudwara sub-division of the Jubbulpore District. Lakshmaṇarāja himself, his queen Rāhaḍā, and his son Śaṅkaragaṇa made donations for its maintenance. The Lakshmaṇasāgar tank at Bilhari was probably dug by this king. Besides Śaṅkaragaṇa, he had another son named Yuvarāja II, and a daughter named Bonthādevī, who was married to the Chālukya Vikramādityā IV. Bonthādevī's son Taila II put an end to the rule of the Imperial Rāshṭrakūṭas, and re-established the sovereignty of the

Chālukyas in the Deccan. Lakshmaṇarāja was succeeded by his son Śaṅkaragaṇa, who was a great devotee of Vishṇu (*parama-Vaishṇava*). His reign was uneventful and he appears to have ruled for a very short period. He was succeeded by his younger brother Yuvarāja II.

Yuvarāja II ruled in the last quarter of the tenth century. He reconstructed the city of Tripurī in order to enhance its beauty and grandeur. Both Yuvarāja II and his brother Śaṅkaragaṇa lacked that military prowess which brought success to their predecessors. The enemies of the Kalachuris took advantage of this situation and declared war on them. Chālukya Taila II, the king of the Deccan, notwithstanding the fact that Yuvarāja II was his maternal uncle, attacked his kingdom and carried on raids in the Chedi country. Muñja, the Paramāra king of Mālava, who made a bid for paramount position in Central and Western India, also fell upon the Kalachuris. In vain did Yuvarāja II try to defend his capital. Muñja made a triumphal entry into the city of Tripurī and held it for some time. Some Kalachuri generals lost their lives in the battle, and Yuvarāja appears to have fled from his capital. After the withdrawal of the Paramāras from the Chedi country the chief ministers did not allow Yuvarāja II to assume royalty owing to the abject cowardice he had shown on the approach of the Paramāras, but placed his son Kokkalla II on the throne.

Yuvarāja II is said to have made donations to the holy Someśvara. His reign appears to have come to a close before the death of Muñja, which took place between A.D. 993 and 998. The Kalachuris regained their power and prestige under the guidance of Kokkalla II. Kokkalla led an expedition against the Gurjara country, and defeated its king, who may be identified with the Chaulukya Mūlarāja or his son Chāmuṇḍarāja. He also avenged the defeat inflicted by the Chālukya king Taila II on his father by a successful invasion of the Deccan. He is said to have forced the king of Kuntala to live in Vanavāsa. About this time Kuntala (Deccan) seems to have been ruled by the Chālukya Satyāśraya. There seems to be a pun in the word Vanavāsa, which may be referring to Banavāsi, modern Shimoga Taluq in Mysore, which was situated in the kingdom of the Chālukyas of the Deccan. To the east, Kokkalla advanced up to the Gauḍa country, which was then ruled by the Pāla Mahīpāla I. Kokkalla is said to have forced the Gauḍa king to take shelter in the watery fort of the sea. Thus Kokkalla succeeded in re-establishing the authority of his family, which had suffered an eclipse during the reign of his father.

2. *Kalachuris of Sarayupāra*

At the time when Kokkalla I and his successors were on the throne of Tripurī, a collateral branch of the Kalachuri family was ruling on the banks of the Sarayu, modern Gogrā, which flows by the Bahraich and Gondā Districts, U.P. The territory over which it ruled was known as Sarayupāra. The earliest king of the family is Rājaputra, who flourished in the latter part of the eighth century. Rājaputra captured the Turagapati Vāhali, destroyed the fame of Kirīṭin and other princes, and curbed the power of the kings of Prāchī (east). Vāhali and Kirīṭin cannot be identified. The leader of the kings of Prāchī might have been Dharmapāla of Bengal. Rājaputra probably defended his kingdom successfully when Dharmapāla was making conquests in Uttar Pradesh, Rājaputra's son and successor was Śivarāja I. Śivarāja I was succeeded by Śaṅkaragaṇa, who suffered a defeat at the hands of the Kalachuri Kokkalla I. Śaṅkaragaṇa flourished in the middle of the ninth century. He was succeeded by his son Guṇāmbhodhideva, also known as Guṇasāgara I, who ruled in the second half of the ninth century. Guṇāmbhodhideva defeated the king of Gauḍa. It has been suggested that he joined the Pratīhāra Bhoja when the latter invaded the kingdom of the Pālas.[14] It might have been in recognition of this service that Bhoja granted some territories to this Kalachuri chief.

To the east of the territory of the Kalachuris lay the kingdom of the Malayaketu dynasty. Two inscriptions of this family have been found in the Gorakhpur District, U.P. The capital of the dynasty was Vijayapura, which was situated in the Uttara-girikaṭaka. The city seems to have been situated at the foot of the Himālayas in the northern part of the Gorakhpur District. Three kings of this dynasty are known, *viz. Mahārājādhirāja* Jayāditya I, his son *Mahārājādhirāja* Dharmāditya, and the latter's son *Mahārājādhirāja* Jayāditya II. Jayāditya II was ruling in A.D. 870. Later members of the Kalachuris of Sarayupāra are found ruling over the territories up to the banks of the Gandak, which included the Gorakhpur District. It is not unlikely that the Pratīhāra Bhoja I, after putting an end to the rule of Jayāditya II, handed over the latter's kingdom to Guṇāmbhodhideva. After Guṇāmbhodhideva's death, his two sons Ullabha and Bhāmānadeva successively occupied the throne. Bhāmānadeva distinguished himself in a war with the king of Dhārā, the capital of Mālava, which was at this time ruled by the Paramāra Vairisiṁha II as a vassal under the Rāshṭrakūṭas of the Deccau. In the second quarter of the tenth century Mālava passed into the hands of the Pratīhāras for some time.

Bhāmānadeva seems to have helped the Pratīhāra Mahīpāla I in wresting Mālava from the Paramāras.[1] He was followed on the throne in succession by Śaṅkaragaṇa II Mugdhatuṅga, Guṇasāgara II, Śivarāja II Bhāmāna, Śaṅkaragaṇa III, and Bhīma, each being the son of his predecessor. Bhīma, who flourished in the early part of the eleventh century, is said to have lost his kingdom by the decree of fate. The cause of his dethronement is not known, but probably he was worsted in a civil war. In A.D. 1031 Vyāsa, son of Guṇasāgara II, was raised to the throne. Vyāsa's son and successor was the *Mahārājādhirāja* Soḍhadeva. who was ruling in A.D. 1079. Soḍhadeva's kingdom extended from the Sarayu or Gogrā to the Gandak, and comprised the Bahraich, Gondā, Basti, and Gorakhpur Districts, in U.P. Nothing is known of the dynasty after Soḍhadeva.

III. THE PARAMĀRAS

The kingdom of the Paramāras of Mālava was conterminous with that of the Kalachuris of Chedi. It is generally assumed that the original home of the Paramāras was Mount Abu, in the Sirohi State, Rājputana. This assumption is based on a story related by Padmagupta Parimala in the latter part of the tenth century, and repeated in the later inscriptions of the Paramāras. According to this story the sage Vasishṭha had a Kāmadhenu (wish-granting cow) which was stolen by the sage Viśvāmitra. In order to recover it. he made some offerings to the sacrificial fire on Mount Abu with holy incantations. A hero sprang out of the fire, forcibly carried the cow from Viśvāmitra, and returned it to his creator. Vasishṭha, in recognition of this service, gave him the name Paramāra, which means 'Slayer of the Enemy,' and made him king. In the lineage of this hero was born Upendra, who is the earliest known king of the Paramāra dynasty. This story of the origin of the Paramāras is not mentioned in the inscriptions of the family issued prior to the second quarter of the eleventh century. The earliest known epigraphic record of the Paramāras, *viz.* the Harsola grant, which was issued nearly half a century before the time of Padmagupta, relates on the other hand, that the kings of the Paramāra dynasty were born in the family of the Rāshṭrakūṭas of the Deccan.

Dhārā, modern Dhār, in Madhya Bhārat, was the capital of the main branch of the Paramāras. Since it is known that Vākpati-Muñja, the seventh king of the dynasty, commenced his reign about A.D. 972, Upendra, who was also known as Kṛishṇarāja, may be taken to have flourished in the first quarter of the ninth century. Shortly before A.D. 812 the Rāshṭrakūṭa Govinda III conquered Mālava by defeating the Pratīhāra Nāgabhaṭa II and handed it over to one of his followers. As the early Paramāra chiefs are known to have been vassals of the Rāshṭrakūṭas of the Deccan, the follower of Govinda III, who was made the ruler of Mālava, was probably Upendra. Govinda III realised that Nāgabhaṭa II would make an attempt to reconquer his home-territory of Mālava and Upendra would not be able to resist him. So he commissioned Karkkarāja, the chief of Lāṭa, to defend Mālava against the incursion of the Pratīhāras. Nāgabhaṭa II could not reconquer Mālava though he succeeded in capturing some of its outlying hill fortresses.

Upendra had two sons, Vairisiṁha I and Ḍambarasiṁha. Ḍambarasiṁha and his successors ruled in Vāgaḍa, corresponding to modern Banswara and Dungarpur, until the early part of the twelfth century, as vassals of the main branch at Dhārā. Vairisiṁha I ascended the throne of his father. He was succeeded by his son Sīyaka I, whose son and successor was Vākpati I. Padmagupta does not mention the names of Vairisiṁha and Sīyaka I, but merely states that there ruled in the Paramāra dynasty more than one king between Upendra and Vākpati I. The Rāshṭrakūṭa Amoghavarsha I, who was a contemporary of Upendra, Vairisiṁha, and Sīyaka I, claims that he was worshipped by the king of Mālava. The Udepur Praśasti mentions Vākpati I as the king of Avanti. It was probably during his reign that the Rāshṭrakūṭa Indra III halted at Ujjain while advancing with his army against the Pratīhāra Mahīpāla I. It is not unlikely that Vākpati I accompanied Indra III in that expedition. The Udepur Praśasti mentions that he led his army up to the banks of the Gaṅgā. Vākpati's son and successor was Vairisiṁha II, also known as Vajraṭa. The successors of Indra III were busy with their own affairs at home till the accession of Kṛishṇa III in A.D. 939. Mahīpāla I, who had suffered an ignominious defeat at the hands of Indra III, took advantage of the situation and invaded the Rāshṭrakūṭa Empire. Vairisiṁha II could not resist the invading army. Mahīpāla and his subordinate, the Kalachuri Bhāmānadeva, the chief of the Gorakhpur Division, conquered all the territories up to the banks of the Narmadā including Ujjayinī and Dhārā. A Pratīhāra governor was posted at Ujjayinī. The Paramāra sovereignty in Mālava had ceased till after A.D. 946 when Mahendrapāla II, son of Mahīpāla I, was on the throne of Kanauj. Shortly after this date Vairisiṁha II reconquered Mālava, apparently with the help of the Rāshṭrakūṭa Kṛishṇa III. The Udepur Praśasti avers that Vairisiṁha proved by the strength of his sword that Dhārā belonged to him. He was succeeded by his son Sīyaka II, who was known also as Harsha.

Sīyaka II owed allegiance to the Rāshṭrakūṭa Kṛishṇa III. He ascended the throne at a time when the Pratīhāra Empire was gradually disintegrating. His kingdom extended on the west up to the Sābarmati river beyond which lay the kingdom of the Chaulukya Mūlarāja I. The chief of Kheṭaka-*maṇḍala*, modern Kaira, in Gujarāt, was his ally. Sīyaka defeated a chief named Yogarāja and, while returning to his capital, encamped on the banks of the Mahī river. This vanquished chief may be identified with the Chālukya Avanivarman Yogarāja II, the ruler of Saurāshṭra. To the north-west of Mālava was situated Hūṇa-*maṇḍala*, which was ruled by a chief named Jajjapa in the second half of the ninth century. Sīyaka II claims to have defeated a Hūṇa chief, who was obviously one of the successors of Jajjapa. On the north-east, Sīyaka II had to acknowledge defeat at the hands of the Chandella Yaśovarman of Khajrāho. Yaśovarman pushed the boundary of his kingdom up to the Mālava river, which is probably identical with the Vetravatī, modern Betwā.

In the latter part of his reign Sīyaka II decided to throw off the yoke of the Rāshṭrakūṭas, and the death of the Rāshṭrakūṭa Kṛishṇa III presented a favourable opportunity. He refused to avow allegiance to Khoṭṭiga, successor of Kṛishṇa III, and openly revolted. Khoṭṭiga marched against the rebel, and was opposed by the latter at a place known as Kalighaṭṭa, on the banks of the Narmadā. In this fateful battle Sīyaka was assisted by the Paramāra Kaṁka, also known as Chachcha, the ruler of Vāgaḍa, and the successor of Dhanika, a descendant of Ḍambarasiṁha. Kaṁka died fighting bravely with the enemy. Sīyaka succeeded after a hard fight in dispersing his adversaries. He pursued Khoṭṭiga up to Mānyakheṭa, the capital of the Rāshṭrakūṭas, which for the first time experienced the invasion of a foreign army. The city was plundered by the Paramāras without encountering any opposition (A.D. 972). The encampment of the Emperor was, however, bravely defended by the Gaṅga Mārasiṁha II. Sīyaka had eventually to withdraw from the Deccan, but he pushed the southern boundary of his kingdom up to the Tāpti. He deserves credit for achieving the independence of his dynasty. On the north Sīyaka's kingdom was bounded by that of the *Mahārājādhirāja* Chāmuṇḍarāja, who was ruling in old Jhālāwār State in A.D. 971.

Sīyaka had two sons, Muñja and Sindhurāja. Merutuṅga relates that Muñja was not the son of Sīyaka. Sīyaka was, we are told, without any issue for a long time. Once, while touring the countryside, he picked up a new-born child from a tuft of Muñja grass. He gave him the name Muñja and adopted him as his heir. Subsequently a child was born to him who was named Sindhurāja. The birth of the child did not, however, lead Sīyaka to lessen his affection towards Muñja. He arranged that he should be succeeded by Muñja and Sindhurāja successively. In the latter part of his reign he adopted the life of an ascetic and "clothed himself in the grass-robe of a royal sage." Muñja succeeded him to the throne some time between A.D. 972 and 974.

Muñja was also known as Utpala and Vākpatirāja II, and assumed the titles *Śrīvallabha, Pṛithvīvallabha,* and *Amoghavarsha.* He inherited a kingdom which extended on the north up to the southern border of Jhālāwār, on the east up to Bhilsa, on the south up to the Tāpti and on the west up to the Sābarmati. He directed his energies towards its further expansion. On the east, he defeated the Kalachuri Yuvarāja II and plundered his capital Tripurī, but could not annex any part of the Kalachuri kingdom. He led an extensive campaign against numerous states in Rājputāna. The Hūṇas of Hūṇa-*maṇḍala* yielded to his sword. The Guhilas of Medapāṭa were the next victims of his attack. He destroyed the elephant forces of the king of the Guhilas, who was either Naravāhana or his son Śaktikumāra, and plundered his capital Āghāṭa, modern Ahar, in Udaipur, Rājputāna. The vanquished chief saved his life by taking shelter with the Rāshṭrakūṭa Dhavala of Hastikuṇḍī. This success brought Muñja on the border of the kingdom of the Chāhamānas of Naḍḍula, modern Nadol, in Jodhpur. He wrested from the Chāhamāna Balirāja Mount Abu and the southern part of Jodhpur up to Kirādu, sixteen miles north-west of Balmer. His attempt to conquer Naḍḍula was, however, foiled by this Chāhamāna king. The conquered territories were divided between the princes of the Paramāra dynasty for efficient administration. Muñja's sons Araṇyarāja and Chandana were made the governors respectively of Mount Abu and Jābālipura, modern Jālor, in Jodhpur. His nephew Dusala, son of Sindhurāja, was placed in charge of Bhillamāla or Śrīmāla, modern Bhinmāl, in Jodhpur. Successors of these princes ruled their respective territories for many years. Muñja invaded the kingdoms of Aṇahilapāṭaka and Lāṭa on the west. Mūlarāja of the Chaulukya dynasty, king of Aṇahilapāṭaka, being worsted, fled with his family to the desert of Mārwār. His army had at last to take shelter with the Rāshṭrakūṭa Dhavala of Hastikuṇḍī for safety. Muñja's adversary in Lāṭa was the Chaulukya Bārappa, the general of the Chālukya Taila II of the Deccan. Taila II, who had established his authority over the Deccan after overthrowing the Rāshṭrakūṭas, considered himself the master of the whole of the Rāshṭrakūṭa Empire. In order to recover the territories, which seceded from it, he sent his general, Bārappa, to Lāṭa and himself led successive campaigns against Mālava. Muñja defeated Bārappa and repulsed Taila's attacks six times. Then, in order to get rid of this menace once for all by crushing the military power of his sworn enemy, he thought of an aggressive campaign. His veteran minister Rudrāditya did not approve of this, and tried to dissuade him from it. On being unsuccessful he requested the king not to cross the Godāvarī under any circumstances. Muñja led his army to the Deccan and crossed the Godāvarī in pursuit of the enemy, totally disregarding the advice of his minister. On receipt of this news Rudrāditya, who had a premonition that a dire calamity would befall his master, committed suicide. The faithful minister preferred death to the shock of seeing the dismal fate of his master. Muñja was soon entrapped in the country of his enemy and taken prisoner. Taila II took possession of the southern part of the Paramāra kingdom, possibly up to the banks of the Narmadā, and kept his adversary confined in the prison of his capital. Muñja's officers went there in disguise, and made a secret plan for his rescue. But the plan was detected and on the orders of Taila the captive king was executed. Such was the tragic end of a great king, who was not only a great general and a great poet, but also a great patron of art and literature. The poets Dhanañjaya, Bhaṭṭa Halāyudha, Dhanika, Padmagupta, Amitagati and many others benefited from his munificence. He also dug many tanks and built a number of temples.

The death of Muñja took place between A.D. 993 and 998. He was succeeded by his younger brother Sindhurāja, who assumed the titles of *Kumāranārāyaṇa* and *Navasāhasāṅka*. He defeated the Chālukya Satyāśraya, king of the Deccan, and recovered the territories which Muñja had to surrender to Taila II. The poet Padmagupta, who lived in his court also, composed a book *Navasāhasāṅkacharita* or the life of *Navasāhasāṅka* Sindhurāja. The book narrates how a king of the Nāga dynasty, whose kingdom lay two hundred miles south of the Narmadā, sought help from Sindhurāja against a neighbouring demon-king named Vajrāṅkuśa. Sindhurāja, along with the Vidyādharas, reached the country of the demons after crossing the Godāvarī and killed the demon-king in a battle. In gratitude the Nāga king gave his daughter Śaśiprabhā in marriage to the victor. That the outline of this story, narrated by Padmagupta, is based on historical facts is admitted on all hands. It has been suggested that the Nāga king was a chief of the Nāga dynasty ruling in old Bastar State, and the demon-king was a chief of the Non-Aryan Māna tribe of Vajra, modern Wairagarh, in the Chāndā District, Madhya Pradesh. The Vidyādharas were the Śilāhāras of Thānā, whose ruler at that time was Aparājita. Sindhurāja is known to have conquered Aparānta. It was probably during his campaign against Wairagarh that Sindhurāja plundered the territory of the Somavaṁśī kings of Kosala. On the north Sindhurāja scored a victory over the chief of the Hūṇa-*maṇḍala*. The Paramāra Chaṇḍapa, son of Kaṁka, ruler of Vāgaḍa, tried to assert his independence, but was readily put down by Sindhurāja. Sindhurāja was also involved in wars with the Chaulukyas of Lāṭa and Aṇahilapāṭaka. Though he could easily subjugate Lāṭa, which was then ruled by Bārappa's successor Goṅgirāja, his attempt to assert supremacy over northern Gujarāt was frustrated by Chāmuṇḍarāja, son of Mūlarāja I. His reign came to an end about A.D. 1000 and he was succeeded by his son Bhoja.

IV. THE MINOR DYNASTIES OF GUJARAT AND KATHIAWAR

During the period under review, Saurāshṭra was ruled by a number of dynasties like the Saindhavas, the Chālukyas, the Chāpas, and others, whose history may now be briefly related.

1. *The Saindhavas*[16]

The Saindhava dynasty, also known as the Jayadratha dynasty, ruled the Western Saurāshṭra (*apara-Saurāshṭra-maṇḍala*) from its capital Bhūtāmbilikā, also mentioned as Bhūmilikā, modern Bhumili or Ghumli, in Kāthiāwār, twenty-five miles north-east of Porbandar, in a gorge of the Bardā hills. The earliest known king (*kshitipati*) of the dynasty is Pushyadeva, who flourished in the second quarter of the eighth century. It was probably during the reign of this king, in or before A.D. 739, that the Arabs of Sindh invaded the kingdom of the Saindhavas.[17] Pushyadeva appears also to have suffered a defeat at the hands of the Rāshṭrakūṭa Dantidurga. He was succeeded by his son Kṛishṇarāja, whose son and successor was the Mahāsāmanta Agguka I. Agguka ruled in the last quarter of the eighth century. During the reigns of these two chiefs the Arabs made fresh attempts by sea to establish their supremacy over Saurāshṭra. About A.D. 756 Hishām was appointed governor of Sindh. Hishām sent "Amru bin Jamāl with a fleet of barks to the coast of Barada." Barada obviously is the tract of the country along the Bardā hills. The fact that the Saindhavas called themselves masters of the western sea (*apara-samudrādhipati*) indicates that they had strong naval forces. As the Muslims do not claim any victory on this occasion they were certainly routed by the Saindhavas under the leadership of Kṛishṇa. Twenty years after this incident, about A.D. 776, the Arabs sent another naval expedition against Barada. It is stated that they captured a city there but had to withdraw from the country because of the outbreak of an epidemic, which carried away a large number of their soldiers. After this disaster the Caliph Mahdī "gave up the project of conquering any part of India." The town which was conquered by the Arabs may be identified with Ghumli. The real cause which forced the Arabs to withdraw from the shores of Bardā was not, however, the outbreak of epidemic in their military camps. That was probably the report which the Arab generals sent to the Caliph to save their skin. There is evidence to prove that Agguka I inflicted a defeat on them and freed his country from their designs. An inscription states that Agguka I "showed the greatness of Varāha when he easily rescued his country, which was being drowned in an ocean of naval force sent by powerful enemies." This obviously refers to Agguka's victory over the Arabs.

Agguka I was succeeded by his son Rāṇaka, who seems to have ruled in the first quarter of the ninth century. During this period the Partīhāra Nāgabhaṭa II led an expedition against Saurāshṭra and won a victory over the Saindhavas. Rāṇaka had by his two queens two sons, Kṛishṇarāja II and Jāika I. The king (*rājā*) Kṛishṇarāja II succeeded his father to the throne. From this time there was a protracted war between the Saindhavas and the Chāpas of Vardhamāna. Kṛishṇa II fought successfully with the chief of the Chāpas, who may be identified with Vikramārka. He is stated to have brought happiness to the inhabitants of Parvata, which probably refers to the Bardā hills. Kṛishṇa II died at an early age and was succeeded by his young son Agguka II. Jāika I, the step-brother of Kṛishṇa II, acted as a regent of this young prince. Jāika issued a charter as regent in A.D. 832 and professed that "though Kamalā (Royal Fortune) was anxious to be united to him in preference to Agguka, her rightful lord, he spurned her wily overtures and decided to be the disinterested guardian of his young and inexperienced nephew." But later Jāika is found occupying the throne of Bhūtāmbilikā, and it is not unlikely that he deposed his nephew. He is credited with a victory over the Chāpas of Vardhamānapura. He had two sons, Chāmuṇḍarāja and Agguka III. Chāmuṇḍarāja ascended the throne after his father, and was succeeded by his younger brother Agguka III, whose son was Rānaka II. It is stated that after being on the throne for a long time Agguka III decided to crown his son, noticing how "Lakshmī, the goddess of Royal Fortune, had become eager to be united with his son Rāṇaka, who had become quite capable of bearing the burden of administration." It appears that Agguka III abdicated in favour of his son Rāṇaka II in order to establish the right of the latter to the throne in supersession of the claim of his nephew Agguka IV, son of Chāmuṇḍarāja. Rāṇaka II's known date is A.D. 874. His son Jāika assumed the position of the *Yuvarāja*, but after Rāṇaka II, Agguka IV is found occupying the throne. This suggests that he succeeded in overthrowing his cousin. He was ruling in A.D. 886. After his death his son *Mahāsāmantādhipati* Jāika II came to the throne whose known dates are A.D. 904 and 915. He is the last known king of his family. His successors were probably overthrown by the Ābhīra chief, Grāharipu.

The Saindhavas ruled Western Saurāshṭra as feudatory chiefs, but we cannot definitely say who their suzerain lords were. It is not unlikely that they acknowledged the suzerainty of the Pratīhāra Nāgabhaṭa II and his successors, whose Empire is known to have extended at least up to Junāgadh, which bordered the kingdom of Bhūtāmbilikā on the west.

2. *The Chālukyas*

A Chālukya dynasty ruled in some part of Saurāshṭra, possibly in Junāgadh, contemporaneously with the Saindhavas. Their history is based entirely on two copper-plate inscriptions[18] found in the town of Una, in Junāgadh. The earliest known king (*mahīpati*) of this dynasty is Kalla, who was succeeded by his brother Mahalla. These two royal brothers flourished in the latter part of the eighth century. The successor of Mahalla was Kalla's son. This ruler, whose name cannot be deciphered from the inscription, was succeeded by his son Vāhukadhavala. Vāhukadhavala ruled in the first quarter of the ninth century. About this time the Chālukyas came under the sway of the Pratīhāras of Kanauj, whose king Nāgabhaṭa II conquered all the territories up to Western Saurāshṭra. Vāhukadhavala claims to have defeated Dharma, Karṇāṭa army, and many other imperial kings. Dharma was evidently Dharmapāla of Bengal, and the Karṇāṭa army refers to the forces of the Rāshṭrakūṭas of the Deccan. It is obvious that Vāhukadhavala fought these battles under the leadership of the Pratīhāra Nāgabhaṭa II. Vāhukadhavala's son and successor was Avanivarman I, who was succeeded by his son *Mahāsāmanta* Balavarman. Balavarman acknowledged the supremacy of the Pratīhāra Mahendrapāla I, and was ruling in A.D. 893. He won a victory over Jajjapa of the *Hūṇa-maṇḍala* to the north-west of Mālava. After Balavarman, his son Avanivarman II, also known as Yoga, ascended the throne. Avanivarman was ruling in A.D. 899 as a vassal of the Pratīhāra Mahendrapāla I. He led an army against the Chāpas of Vardhamānapura, and defeated their king Dharaṇīvarāha, who was a feudatory of the Pratīhāra Mahīpāla I, son of Mahendrapāla. This clash between the feudatories of the Pratīhāras shows that about this time the latter had lost effective control over the outlying provinces of their Empire. Avanivarman had to acknowledge defeat at the hands of the Paramāra Sīyaka II in the latter part of his reign which extended up to the middle of the tenth century. The rule of the Chālukyas in Saurāshṭra was put an end to by the Ābhīras in the third quarter of the tenth century.

3. *The Ābhīras*

The Ābhīras established their supremacy over the Southern and Western Saurāshṭra under their king Grāharipu in the second half of the tenth century. Their capital was Vāmanasthali, modern Vanthali, nine miles west of Junāgadh. Grāharipu, who is described as a Mlechchha chief, carried on anti-Brahmanical activities. He ate beef, and plundered the pilgrims to Prabhāsa *tīrtha* (Somanātha). In order to end this menace, the Chaulukya Mūlarāja, king of Aṇahilapāṭaka, marched with his army against Grāharipu. Grāharipu strengthened his position by securing assistance from Laksha, son of Phula, king of Kachchha-*deśa,* also known as Jartra-*deśa,* modern Kutch. A great battle was fought on the banks of the Jambumāli river in which Laksha lost his life and Grāharipu was taken prisoner.[19]

4. *Varāhas (?) of Saurya-Maṇḍala*

In the third quarter of the eighth century a king named Mahāvarāha was ruling somewhere in Saurāshṭra. He came into clash with the Rāshṭrakūṭa Kṛishṇa I (c. A.D. 758-773) of the Deccan. The Baroda plate, dated A.D. 812, states that he attacked Kṛishṇa I, but was repulsed.[20] A fragmentary stone inscription, now deposited in the Barton Museum, Bhāvnagar, states that Kṛishṇa was made to retreat along the banks of the Narmadā by a king whose name ends in Varāha. Dr. Bhandarkar is inclined to restore the name as Mahāvarāha, who, in his opinion, was identical with the chief of this name, referred to above.[21] The battle between Kṛishṇa and Mahāvarāha was indecisive. Mahāvarāha seems to have been succeeded by Jayavarāha, who, as noted above,[22] is known to have been ruling in A.D. 783 in the territories of the Sauryas to the west of Vardhamāna, modern Wadhwān, in Kāthiāwār. Nothing is known of this dynasty after Jayavarāha.

5. *The Chāpas*

The Chāpas were also known as Chāvaḍās, Chāvotkaṭas, and Chāpis. There were two branches of the Chāpa dynasty. One of them ruled from Vardhamāna and the other from Aṇahilapāṭaka, modern Pātan, in Northern Gujarāt, which was the capital of the Sārasvata-*maṇḍala*. The first known king of the family at Vardhamāna is Vikramārka, who ruled in the first quarter of the ninth century. He had apparently to bear the brunt of an invasion by the Pratīhāra Nāgabhaṭa II. He was succeeded by his son Aḍḍaka, after whom the country around Wadhwān, including Limbdi, came to be known as Aḍḍaṇaka-*deśa*. Aḍḍaka's son and successor was Pulakeśi, who had two sons, Dhruvabhaṭa and Dharaṇīvarāha. Dhruvabhaṭa ascended the throne in the closing years of the ninth century. Dhruvabhaṭa and his predecessors fought a series of battles with the Saindhavas of Western Saurāshṭra. After Dhruvabhaṭa, his younger brother Dharaṇīvarāha became king. Dharaṇīvarāha, who was ruling in A.D. 914 as a vassal of the Pratīhāra Mahīpāla I, had to submit to the forces of the Chālukya Avanivarman II Yogarāja. His kingdom was invaded by the Chaulukya Mūlarāja, who captured his throne and drove him out of Saurāshṭra. In his distress, he saved his life by taking shelter with the Rāshṭrakūṭa Dhavala of Hastikuṇḍī.[23] Aḍḍaṇaka-*deśa* was annexed to the kingdom of the Chaulukyas.

Vanarāja was the founder of the other branch of the Chāpa dynasty ruling in Aṇahilapāṭaka. It is stated that Vanarāja built this city and established there the supremacy of his family in A.D. 745. After him ruled Yogarāja, Ratnāditya, Kshemarāja, Ākaḍadeva, and Bhūyaḍadeva or Bhūyagaḍadeva, also known as Sāmantasiṁha. The story runs that once Sāmantasiṁha held a cavalry parade. It was attended by three brothers Rāji, Bīja, and Daṇḍaka, sons of Bhuvanāditya, king of Kalyāna-kaṭaka, in Kanauj, who halted at Aṇahilapāṭaka in the guise of beggars on their way back to Kanauj from Somanātha. Rāji, by his wise criticism of the cavalry movement, attracted the attention of the king who, taking him to be a member of a royal family, gave his sister Līlādevī in marriage to him. Līlādevī died while giving birth to her son, who was given the name Mūlarāja. Mūlarāja served his maternal uncle as a general for some time and then usurped his throne after putting him to death in A.D. 942. The authenticity of this story, narrated by the Gujarāt chroniclers, may reasonably be doubted. But that Mūlarāja put an end to the rule of the Chāpas admits of no doubt. The Vadnagar Praśasti states that Mūlarāja carried away "the fortune of the kingdom of the Chāpotkaṭa princes." The traditional date of the end of the rule of the Chāpas and the accession of the Chaulukya Mūlarāja in A.D. 941-42 is corroborated by an epigraphic record.

V. THE CHAULUKYAS

It is generally assumed that the names Chālukya and Chaulukya are synonymous. But the traditional belief of the Chālukyas in regard to their origin is different from that of the families calling themselves Chaulukyas. The existence of at least three branches of the Chaulukya dynasty is known. The oldest of them ruled at Mattamayūra, which was situated in Central India in the neighbourhood of Mālava and Chedi. The earliest known chief of this branch is Siṁhavarman, whose son and successor was Sadhanva. Sadhanva's son and successor was Avanivarman, who ruled in the last quarter of the ninth century. Avanivarman gave his daughter in marriage to the Kalachuri Yuvarāja I. He was a patron of the Śaiva ascetics residing in his kingdom.

Mūlarāja I, as has already been noticed, was the founder of another branch of the Chaulukya dynasty, which in course of time rose to imperial eminence. He established his capital at Aṇahilapāṭaka, which was also known as Aṇahilapura, Aṇahilanagara, Aṇahila-pattana, and Aṇahilavāḍa. His inscription states that he conquered Sārasvata-*maṇḍala* (*i.e.* the country on the banks of the Sarasvatī river) with his own arms and resided in the city of Aṇahilapāṭaka. He was an ambitious king, and chose Saurāshṭra as the field of his first military excursion. He forced the Chāpa Dharaṇīvarāha to flee from his capital Vardhamāna, and annexed his kingdom. He led successive invasions against Kachchha-*deśa*, modern Cutch, but was repulsed by its ruler Laksha or Lākhā. About this time the anti-Brahmanical activities of the Ābhīra chief Grāharipu of Vāmanasthali prompted him to lead an army against him. In this religious war he is said to have been helped by contingents from the chiefs of Ābu, Srīmāla, Māravāḍa and other places. Lākhā, king of Kachchha, came with his army to assist Grāharipu. In the battle that followed Lākhā lost his life and Grāharipu was taken prisoner. Mūlarāja brought Kachchha-*deśa* under his sway.

Mūlarāja had to fight defensive wars in other directions. Once his kingdom was invaded on the north by the Chāhamāna Vigraharāja, king of Śākambharī. To make the situation worse, the Chaulukya Bārappa, the chief of Lāṭa, and a general of the Chālukya Taila II, made an onslaught on the southern border of his kingdom. In this predicament he, on the advice of his ministers, retired to the fort of Kanthā, modern Kanthakot, in Cutch, to bide his time, hoping that Vigraharāja would withdraw to his own country during the following rainy season. But contrary to his expectation Vigraharāja, disregarding the obstacles caused by the rains, overran Sārasvata-*maṇḍala* and Lāṭa and reached the banks of the Narmadā. Being thus hard pressed, Mūlarāja concluded a treaty with the Chāhamānas.[24] After the departure of the Chāhamāna army he sent his son Chāmuṇḍarāja against Bārappa who was killed in the battle. Mūlarāja's fight with the Paramāra Muñja proved disastrous for him. He, along with his family, had to withdraw to Mārwār, and his army had to take shelter under the Rāshṭrakūṭa Dhavala. Though Mūlarāja eventually succeeded in recovering his kingdom, he had to suffer another defeat at the hands of the Kalachuri Lakshmaṇa. The historical value of the report of the Gujarāt chroniclers that he fought successfully with Sindhurāja and the king of North Kosala cannot be ascertained.

Mūlarāja's kingdom extended on the north up to Sānchor in Jodhpur, and was bounded on the east and south by the Sābarmati river. He founded a temple at Maṇḍali, modern Mandal, in the Viramgām *Tāluk*, Ahmadābād District. He also built two temples at Aṇahilapāṭaka. The dates of his reign, known from epigraphic sources, range between A.D. 942 and 994. Merutuṅga's *Vichāraśreṇī* mentions V.S.1052 (=A.D. 995) as the date of the end of his reign. He abdicated his throne in favour of his son Chāmuṇḍarāja.

Chāmuṇḍarāja defended his kingdom against the incursion of the Paramāra Sindhurāja, the brother of Muñja. But he had to yield to the forces of the Kalachuri Kokkalla II, the son of Yuvarāja II. He committed a grave social crime and, being penitent, started for Banaras for expiation after handing over the charge of the government to his son Vallabharāja. While passing through Mālava, he was forced to give up the insignia of royalty by the king of that country, who was evidently the Paramāra Bhoja, son of Sindhurāja. On his return from Banaras he asked his son to punish the king of Mālava for his impudence. Vallabharāja marched with an army against Mālava, but died of small-pox on the way. Chāmuṇḍarāja then handed over the sovereignty to his second son Durlabharāja. According to the Gujarāt chroniclers, Chāmuṇḍarāja's reign ended in A.D. 1008.

Bārappa founded the supremacy of another line of the Chaulukya dynasty in Lāṭa, the capital of which was Bhṛigukachchha, modern Broach in Southern Gujarāt. A collateral branch of the Rāshṭrakūṭa dynasty ruled in Lāṭa till the first half of the tenth century. In A.D. 948 Kheṭaka-*maṇḍala*, modern Kaira, was ruled by a feudatory of the Rāshṭrakūṭas, who was an ally of the Paramāra Sīyaka II. Bārappa, who is described as a general of Taila II, king of the Deccan, established his supremacy over Lāṭa by defeating the feudatories of the Rāshṭrakūṭas after the fall of Mānyakheṭa. Bārappa could not enjoy his throne peacefully. His kingdom was invaded by the Paramāra Muñja. He tried to gain some advantage over his northern neighbour, the Chaulukya Mūlarāja, when the latter's kingdom was invaded by the Chāhamāna, Vigraharāja. Eventually he lost his life in an encounter with *Yuvarāja* Chāmuṇḍarāja, son of Mūlarāja, who took possession of his territory for some time. Bārappa's son and successor Goṅgirāja succeeded in recovering the territory from his northern rival, for he claims to have relieved his country, which had been seized by powerful enemies.

VI. THE CHAHAMANAS

There were several branches of the Chāhamāna dynasty. The earliest known branch ruled in Lāṭa up to the middle of the eighth century.[26] Another branch established its supremacy in the Śākambharī-*pradeśa,* the capital of which was Śākambharī, modern Sāmbhar, in Jaipur, in the early years of the seventh century. The territory over which this branch ruled was also known as Sapādalaksha country. Vāsudeva was the founder of this line. In his lineage was born Sāmanta, who was followed on the throne by Pūrṇatalla, Jayarāja, and Vigraharāja I in succession. Vigraharāja's son and successor was Chandrarāja who flourished in the middle of the eighth century. After Chandrarāja, his younger brother Gopendrarāja ascended the throne. Gopendrarāja's successor was his nephew Durlabharāja I, son of Chandrarāja I, who ruled in the last quarter of the eighth century. About this time, the country of Śākambharī was included in the kingdom of the Pratīhāra Vatsarāja, which extended from Avanti to Didwana, in Jodhpur. Durlabharāja is said to have defeated the king of Gauḍa, and to have reached Gaṅgā-sāgara in the course of conquest. This seems to refer to his participation in the battle between his overlord Vatsarāja and Dharmapāla of Bengal. Durlabharāja's son and successor was Govindarāja I, also known as Gūvaka I, who is said to have attained pre-eminence in the court of Nāgāvaloka, *i.e.* the Pratīhāra Nāgabhaṭa II. The *Prabandhakośa,* a work of a later period, mentions that the Chāhamāna Govindarāja repulsed an attack of the Sultan Vega Varisa. Vega Varisa is identified with Bashar, son of Da'ūd, who was the governor of Sindh under the Caliph Al-Ma'mūn (A.D. 813-833). It is also known from *Khummāṇa-Rāso* that the Guhila Khommāṇa II, along with many other Indian chiefs, resisted the onslaught of the Arabs under the Caliph Al-Ma'mūn. The Pratīhāra Nāgabhaṭa II, as has already been noticed, came into conflict with the Muslims. It seems that Bashar, the Arab governor of Sindh, during the Caliphate of Al-Ma'mūn, attacked the western part of the Pratīhāra Empire, but Nāgabhaṭa II with the help of his feudatories, Govindarāja I and Khommāṇa II, succeeded in repulsing him. After the close of Govindarāja's reign, his son Chandrarāja II, also known as Śaśinṛipa, ascended the throne. Chandrarāja had a son named Gūvaka II and a daughter named Kalāvatī. Gūvaka II, after his accession to the throne, gave his sister in marriage to the king of Kanauj, who seems to have been the Pratīhāra Bhoja I. The king of Śākambharī, who was worsted by the Kalachuri Kokkalla I,[26] seems to have been Gūvaka II. Gūvaka II's son and successor Chandana killed in battle Rudrena, a king of the Tomara dynasty. Chandana's queen laid the foundation of some religious buildings at Pushkara-*tīrtha*. His son and successor was Vākpatirāja, who ruled in the first quarter of the tenth century. Vākpatirāja I is stated to have harassed Tantrapāla, who was on his way to Anantagochara with a message from his overlord. The overlord of Vākpatirāja I was apparently the Pratīhāra Mahīpāla I. Anantagochara seems to have been the name of the country round Sikar. The above statement makes it clear that about this time the Chāhamānas had acquired enough power to defy the authority of the Pratīhāras. Vākpatirāja built a temple of Śiva at Pushkara. He had three sons, Siṁharāja, Vatsarāja, and Lakshmaṇa. Lakshmaṇa founded a kingdom at Naḍḍula, in Southern Mārwār, where his successors ruled for several centuries. Siṁharāja ascended the throne after Vākpatirāja.[27] He defeated a Tomara leader named Salavana, and put into prison a number of princes, who were feudatories of the Pratīhāras of Kanauj. In order to liberate them, the king of the Pratīhāra dynasty, who was one of the successors of Mahīpāla I, possibly Devapāla, came to his house in person. Subsequently Siṁharāja freed his territory from the suzerainty of the Pratīhāras, who had about this time lost their imperial position. He is the first among the Chāhamāna kings of Śākambharī to assume the title *Mahārājādhirāja*. He granted a number of villages to the temple of Harshanātha, which was constructed in A.D. 956, and lies near the village of Harshanāth, about seven miles south of Sikar, in the Shaikhawati Province of Jaipur. He was succeeded by his son Vigraharāja II, who was ruling in A.D. 973. Vigraharāja invaded Gujarat, forced the Chaulukya Mūlarāja to take shelter in the fort of Kanthakot, in the Kachchha-*deśa*, and led his victorious army up to the banks of the Narmadā. He built a temple of the Goddess Āśāpurī at Bhṛigukachchha on the bank of the Narmadā. Subsequently Mūlarāja came to terms with him and regained his kingdom. After Vigraharāja II, his younger brother Durlabharāja, also known as Durlaṅghyameru, came to the throne. He was ruling in A.D. 999, and his kingdom extended up to Parbatsar, in Jodhpur, on the west. He conquered Rāsośittana-*maṇḍala*, which cannot be identified. He also invaded the territory of the Chāhamāna Mahendra, king of Naḍḍula.

Mahendra failed to stand up to his adversary and sought protection under the Rāshṭrakūṭa Dhavala of Hastikuṇḍī.

In the closing years of the tenth century, the kingdom of the Chāhamānas of Śākambharī extended at least up to Sikar on the north, the town of Jaipur on the east, Pushkar near Ajmere on the south, and Parbatsar, in Jodhpur, on the west.

It has been noticed above that Lakshmaṇa, the youngest son of the Chāhamāna Vākpatirāja I of Śākambharī, founded a kingdom at Naḍḍula, modern Nadol, in Jodhpur. Lakshmaṇa was succeeded by his son Śobhita, who annexed Mt. Abu in Sirohi to his kingdom. His son and successor was Balirāja, who had to surrender Mt. Abu and the adjoining territory to the Paramāra Muñja. Muñja, as has already been noticed, established the princes of his family to rule over Mt. Abu, Jālor and Bhinmāl, which lay to the southern border of the Chāhamāna kingdom of Nadol. After Balirāja's death his cousin Mahendra, also known as Mahendu, son of Śobhita's brother Vigrahapāla, ascended the throne. During this time the Chāhamānas of Śākambharī became hostile to their kith and kin at Nadol. It has been mentioned above that when king Durlabha of Śākambharī overran the kingdom of Nadol, Mahendra saved his life by taking shelter under the Rāshṭrakūṭa Dhavala. Mahendra, however, regained his position within a short time. He had two sons, Aśvapāla and Aṇahilla, and was succeeded by the former.

A branch of the Chāhamāna family ruled in Dholpur in the ninth century, apparently as a feudatory of the Imperial Pratīhāras of Kanauj. Three chiefs of this family are known. They were Īsuka, his son Mahisharāma, and the latter's son Chaṇḍamahāsena. Chaṇḍamahāsena was ruling in Dhavalapuri, modern Dholpur, in A.D. 842. He claims to have been served by the Mlechchha lords, who settled on the banks of the Charmaṇvatī, *i.e.* the Chambal river. These Mlechchha lords cannot be identified. Chaṇḍamahāsena built a temple at Dhavalapurī. Nothing is known of his successors.

Another branch of the Chāhamāna family ruled in Partābgarh as a feudatory of the Imperial Pratīhāras.[28] The first known chief of this family is Govindarāja, one of whose predecessors is said to have been a source of great pleasure to the Pratīhāra Bhoja. After Govindarāja, his son Durlabharāja occupied the throne. Durlabharāja's son and successor was the *Mahāsāmanta* Indrarāja. Sometime before A.D. 942 Indrarāja built a temple of the Sun-god in the village of Ghoṇṭavarshikā, in the Western *Pathaka* of Daśapura. The village is identified with Ghotarsi, seven miles east of Partābgarh. It is not known how the rule of this family came to an end.

VII. THE GUHILAS

1. *Guhilas of Mewār*

Adjoining the kingdom of the Chāhamānas of Naḍḍula to the south-east lay that of the Guhilas of Medapāṭa or Mewār, whose early history up to the reign of Bappā has been discussed in the third volume.[29] Bappā is said to have abdicated the throne in A.D. 753, and this date may be regarded as approximately correct. As noted above, Bappā's name does not occur in the genealogical list given in the epigraphic records of the dynasty, but he may be regarded as identical with either Kālabhoja or Khommāṇa of that list. After the close of Khommāṇa I's reign, Mattaṭa, Bhartṛipaṭṭa I, Siṁha, and Khommāṇa II occupied the throne one after another. It has been noticed above that Khommāṇa II joined hands with the Pratīhāra Nāgabhaṭa II and the Chāhamāna Guvāka I in a battle with Bashar, the Arab governor of Sindh. Khommāṇa II was followed in succession by Mahāyaka, Khommāṇa III, and Bhartṛipaṭṭa II. Bhartṛipaṭṭa is given the title *Mahārājādhirāja*, which signifies that he enjoyed independent position. A stone inscription of his reign, bearing the date A.D. 943, has been found in Ahar, ancient Āghāṭa, a few miles north of Udaipur. From this time, Āghāṭa is known to have been the capital of Medapāṭa. In A.D. 942 the *Mahārājādhirāja* Bhartṛipaṭṭa granted a field in the village Palāśakūpikā to the temple of the Sun-god Indrādityadeva, founded by the Chāhamāna Indrarāja in Ghoṇṭavarshikā, modern Ghotarsi, seven miles east of Partābgarh. His kingdom, therefore, seems to have extended on the south-east up to the border of Partābgarh.[30] His son and successor was Allaṭa, whose known dates are A.D. 951 and 953. Allaṭa killed Devapāla in battle. This adversary of the Guhilas might have been the Pratīhāra king of this name ruling in Kanauj, whose known date is A.D. 948, and whose reign ended before A.D. 954. About this time a Pratīhāra king of Kanauj, who was apparently Devapāla, came to Śākambharī to liberate his feudatories, who were imprisoned by the Chāhamāna Siṁharāja. On that occasion Devapāla seems to have come into conflict with Allaṭa and lost his life in the encounter. Allaṭa married a Hūṇa lady named Hariyadevī. During this time Āghāṭa became a great centre of trade frequented by merchants from Karṇāṭa, Lāṭa, Madhyadeśa, and Ṭakka. After Allaṭa, his son Naravāhana ascended the throne and ruled till at least A.D. 971. His queen belonged to the Chāhamāna family. He was succeeded by his son Śālivāhana, whose son and successor was Śaktikumāra. Three stone inscriptions of Śaktikumāra's reign have been found at Ahar. One of these bears the date V.S. 1034 (=A.D. 977). It was probably during the reign of Śaktikumāra that the Paramāra Muñja destroyed Āghāṭa, the pride of Medapāṭa. Śaktikumāra had five sons, Ambāprasāda, Śuchivarman, Naravarman, Anantavarman, and Kīrttivarman. He ruled up to the close of the tenth century. It appears from the inscriptions of Śaktikumāra and his predecessors that Samoli, in the Bhumat District, Ahar, and Ekalingaji, north of Udaipur, were included in the kingdom of the Guhilas which extended up to the border of Partābgarh on the south-east. Chitrakūṭa, modern Chitor, nearly sixty miles north-east of Ahar, is not known to have been included in the kingdom of this branch of the Guhilas at least up to the tenth century.

2. *Guhilas of Dhoḍ*

Reference has been made above[31] to another branch of the Guhila dynasty ruling in the north-eastern part of Udaipur and to its ruler Dhanika with his capital at Dhavagartā, modern Dhoḍ in the Jahāzpur District, Udaipur. After Dhanika, his son Āuka and his grandson Kṛishṇa ruled one after the other. Kṛishṇa, who flourished in the last quarter of the eighth century, seems to have acknowledged the supremacy of the Pratīhāra Vatsarāja, whose kingdom extended from Mālava to Jodhpur. Kṛishṇa's son and successor was Śaṅkaragaṇa, who defeated a general of the Gauḍa king, and presented the latter's kingdom to his overlord. The Gauḍa king was Dharmapāla, and the king, who was Śaṅkaragaṇa's overlord, was apparently the Pratīhāra Nāgabhaṭa II. Śaṅkaragaṇa obviously helped Nāgabhaṭa II in wresting the kingdom of Kanauj from Dharmapāla. Śaṅkaragaṇa was succeeded by his son Harsha, who was a feudatory of the Pratīhāra Bhoja. Harsha claims to have conquered the kings of Udīchya, *i.e.* Uttarāpatha, and presented to Bhoja horses, which were expert in traversing the Sindhu. This seems to refer to Harsha rendering assistance to Bhoja in conquering the Eastern Punjāb. Harsha had to suffer defeat at the hand of the Kalachuri Kokkalla I. If Chitrakūṭā-*bhūpāla*, mentioned in the Banaras copper-plate of the Kalachuri Karṇa, really refers to Harsha, Chitrakūṭa or Chitor is to be taken to have been the capital of this branch of the Guhila dynasty.

As regards the history of Chitrakūṭa during this period, it is known that it was in the possession of the Gurjaras during the reign of the Rāshṭrakūṭa Govinda III. The place was also under the sway of the Gurjaras when it was invaded by the Rāshṭrakūṭa Kṛishṇa III shortly before A.D. 939. As there is no evidence to prove that the early Guhila kings of Medapāṭa were in any way connected with Chitor, there is nothing against the view that Harsha was the ruler of Chitrakūṭa. Harsha is mentioned in the inscription of his great-grandson as a *dvija, i.e.* Brāhmaṇa. He was succeeded by his son Guhila II, who is said to have conquered the king of Gauḍa and levied tribute from the princes of the east. He seems to have joined Bhoja[32] or helped Mahendrapāla in conquering the Gauḍa country by defeating king Nārāyaṇapāla of the Pāla dynasty. Some silver coins, discovered at Agra, bearing the legend Śrī-Guhila, are ascribed to him. He married a Paramāra princess, who gave birth to a son named Bhaṭṭa. Bhaṭṭa, who succeeded his father, seems to have been a contemporary of the Pratīhāra Mahīpāla I. He defeated the king of the Deccan at the behest of his master. He apparently joined hands with the Chandella Harsha to help Mahīpāla in his war against the Rāshṭrakūṭa Indra III. Bhaṭṭa's son and successor was Bālāditya, who married a Chāhamāna princess, the daughter of king Śivarāja. Bālāditya erected a temple of Vishṇu at Chātsu, in Jaipur, where an inscription of his reign has been found. The history of the predecessors of Bālāditya is known mainly from this epigraph. He is the last known king of his family, and although he had three sons, nothing is known about his successors.

VIII. THE TOMARAS

The kingdom of the Chāhamānas of Śākambharī seems to have been bordered on the north-east by that of the Tomaras. Tomaras are included in the thirty-six Rajput clans by the bards. They ruled the Hariyāṇa country from their capital Ḍhillikā, modern Delhi. The tradition runs that the Tuars, a contraction of Tomaras, founded Delhi in A.D. 736. The earliest reference to the Tomaras is found in an inscription at Pehowa, ancient Pṛithūdaka, in Karnāl District, Punjāb, of the reign of the Pratīhāra Mahendrapāla I. It states that there was the king (*rāja*) Jāula of the Tomara dynasty, who "obtained prosperity by looking after the affairs of a king." He was apparently in the service of an unknown king in the early years of his life, and subsequently attained royal position. In the lineage of Jāula was born Vajraṭa, who seems to have flourished in the middle of the ninth century. About this time the Tomaras of Delhi must have acknowledged the supremacy of the Pratīhāra Bhoja, whose kingdom extended up to Sirsa and Karnāl Districts in the Punjāb. Vajraṭa's son and successor was Jajjuka, who was again succeeded by his son Gogga. Gogga, who is known to have been a feudatory of the Pratīhāra Mahendrapāla I, is described as *bhūnātha* or the lord of the earth. Gogga and his two step-brothers Pūrṇarāja and Devarāja, built at Pṛithūdaka, on the banks of the Sarasvatī, three temples of Vishṇu, during the reign of Mahendrapāla I. Kielhorn remarks that these three Tomara princes were probably connected with Delhi, and they might not have any political connection with Pehowa, a place of pilgrimage, where they, like many others from different parts of India, founded religious establishments. According to Firishta Thāneswar, about 20 miles east of Pehowa, was within the kingdom of Delhi in the early part of the eleventh century. In the tenth century the Tomaras came into conflict with the Chāhamānas of Śākambharī. A Tomara chief named Rudrena (Rudra?), who was probably a descendant of Gogga, lost his life in a battle with the Chāhamāna Chandana, son of Gūvaka II. Chandana's grandson Siṁharāja, who flourished in the third quarter of the tenth century, won a victory over the Tomara leader (*nāyaka*) Salavana, and captured a large number of his soldiers. The Tomaras continued to rule the Hariyāṇa country till the middle of the twelfth century when they were overthrown by the Chāhamāna Vigraharāja III Vīsaladeva.

IX. THE SHAHIS (OR SHAHIYAS)

It has been noticed in a previous chapter that the Eastern Punjāb, up to Sirsa, if not up to the Sutlej, was within the Pratīhāra Empire in the second half of the ninth century. In the early years of the tenth century, Śaṅkaravarman, king of Kāshmir, deprived the Pratīhāra Mahendrapāla of his territories in the Punjāb and handed them over to one of his officers, who belonged to the Thakkiya family.[33] In the latter part of this century a king (*rāja*) named Śatrughnadeva is found ruling from Tribhāṇḍapura, modern Bhatinda, in Patiāla, where a stone inscription of his reign has been discovered.

A Turkish Shāhiya family ruled the Kābul Valley and the Gandhāra country for a long time. Kallar, a Brāhmaṇa minister of king Lagatūrmān of this dynasty, overthrew his master and occupied the throne. Kallar, who thus founded the Hindu Shāhi dynasty in the second half of the ninth century A.D., is identified with Lalliya Shāhi referred to in the *Rājataraṅgiṇī*. Lalliya could not keep Kābul under his control for a long time. It was taken possession of by the Ṣaffārid Ya'qūb ibn Layth in A.D. 870. Lalliya then fixed his capital at Udabhāṇḍa, modern village of Und, on the right bank of the Sindhu, fifteen miles above Attock, in Rāwalpindi District. Lalliya's kingdom is stated to have been situated between those of the Turushkas (Kābul valley) and the Darads (Kishangangā valley in Kāshmir). Alakhāna, the king of Gurjara, who ruled the "upper portion of the flat Doāb between the Jhelum and the Chenāb rivers, south of Dārvābhisāra, and probably also a part of the Punjāb plain further east," was his protégé. King Śaṅkaravarman (A.D. 883-902) of the Utpala dynasty of Kāshmir invaded the kingdom of Alakhāna and wrested from him Ṭakka-land, which was the country adjoining the lower hills east of the Chenāb. Next the Kāshmir king invaded the territory of Lalliya but failed to gain any advantage. Kalhaṇa highly praises the valour and achievements of Lalliya, and states that Lalliya's glory outshone that of all the rulers in the north, and many kings found safety in his town Udabhāṇḍa. Lalliya had a son named Toramāṇa. After his death, his throne was usurped by a scion of the Shāhi family named Sāmanta. Some coins, found in Afghānistān, bearing the legend Śrī-Sāmanta, are ascribed to him. Prabhākara, a minister of Śaṅkaravarman's son and successor Gopālavarman, plundered Udabhāṇḍa, dethroned the rebellious Shāhi, and placed Toramāṇa on the throne of that country.[34] He gave Toramāṇa a new name Kamaluka. Kamaluka is mentioned by Al-Bīrūṇī as Kamalū, and is called Kala(Kamala)varman in an inscription of his successor. Muhammad 'Aufi (c. A.D. 1211) mentions him as the Rai of Hindustān. Fardaghān, the governor of Zābulistān (region round Ghaznī) under 'Amr ibn Layth (A.D. 879-900), the brother and successor of Ṣaffārid Ya'qūb ibn Layth, plundered Sakāwand, a place of Hindu pilgrimage, which was within the kingdom of the Shāhis. Kamaluka organised a large army against the Muslims in retaliation. But he abandoned the project on receipt of the news that the Muslims had collected a strong force to oppose him. Baihakī (A.D. 1059) mentions Sakāwand as a pass to Kābul from India. It was situated at or near Jalālābād.

After the death of Kamaluka his son Bhīma ascended the throne. A stone inscription of the reign of *Mahārājādhirāja Parameśvara* Shāhi Śrī-Bhīmadeva has been discovered at Dewai, Gadun territory.[35] Bhīma gave his daughter in marriage to Siṁharāja, king of Lohara, identified with the valley of Lohrin, comprising the mountain Districts, south-west of Kāshmir, in the hill state of Punch. Diddā, the queen of Kshemagupta (A.D. 950-958) of Kāshmir, was the daughter of Siṁharāja and daughter's daughter of Bhīma. On account of this relationship it was possible for Bhīma to exercise influence over the royal court of Kāshmir. He built a magnificent temple of Vishṇu, richly endowed it and called it the shrine of Bhīmakeśava. It is identified with an old temple at Bumzu, near the sacred springs of Mārtāṇḍa (Bavan), which has now been converted into a Muslim Ziārat. The temple possessed valuable treasures even during the reign of Harsha (A.D. 1080-1101). Some silver coins bearing the legend Śrī-Bhīmadeva, found in Kābulistān, are assumed to have been issued by the Shāhi Bhīma.

The fact that Bhīma's grand-daughter (daughter's daughter) Diddā was married to Kshemagupta, who ruled from A.D. 950 to 958, shows that Bhīma must have been born not later than A.D. 900. It is also clear from the Kāshmir Chronicle that he was on the throne at least during a part of the reign of Kshemagupta. But the dates of his accession and death are not definitely known.

The Muslim chroniclers refer to Jaipāl or Jayapāla as the next king. But the *Rājataraṅgiṇī* is silent about him, though it mentions another Shāhi king named Thakkana in the reign of Abhimanyu (A.D. 958-72), the son of Diddā. Some scholars take the name-ending of Jayapāla as indicating a change of dynasty, but this view is refuted by well-known examples of similar changes in royal names in the same family. The fact, however, that Firishta describes Jaipāl as the son of Ishtpāl (probably Ishṭapāla) may be taken to indicate that Jayapāla was not the son of Bhīmapāla and there might have been one or more kings between the two. Jayapāla probably ascended the throne in the last quarter of the tenth century A.D.

A fragmentary stone inscription of the reign of *Paramabhaṭṭāraka Mahārājādhirāja* Śrī-Jayapāladeva has been found on a hill north of Bari Kot, in Upper Swāt.[36] It records that some persons founded something at Vajirasthāna. Rai Bahadur Daya Ram Sahni identified the king, mentioned above, with the Shāhi Jayapāla, and Vajirasthāna with Waziristān. Vajirasthāna seems to have been the country round Bari Kot, where the stone inscription has been found. This proves that the Shāhi kingdom during this period extended up to the Swāt valley.

The *Adāb ul Mulūk wa Kifāyat ul Mamlūk,* composed by Muḥammad bin Manṣūr during the reign of the Sultān Iltutmish (A.D. 1210-1236), gives an account of Jayapāla's war with the chiefs of Lahore. It relates that Ḥaḥ, son of Bhadrā, founded the town of Lohūr, and ruled there for seventy-five years. He was overthrown by his son Bharat, who imprisoned him in the fort of Kahlūr. Bharat built a fort at Lohūr, and founded a village on the bank of the river Biyāh. He made an audacious bid to conquer the salt mines of Nanduṇa, the district of Jhelum, and Tākeshar, which were in the possession of Jayapāla. He crossed the Chandrāhah river with his army and attacked Tākeshar where he was opposed by Jayapāla's son, Ānandapāla. After a short engagement, Bharat was defeated and made a prisoner. Ānandapāla marched towards Lohūr and captured the town. On receipt of a large sum of money, he allowed Bharat to rule his territory as a feudatory. After the departure of Ānandapāla, Bharat was dethroned by his son Ḥandrat, who usurped the throne. Jayapāla sent Ānandapāla with an army to chastise Ḥandrat. Ḥandrat was defeated and imprisoned and his sons took refuge with Sāmah Kora Rāy of Jālandar. Jayapāla annexed the kingdom of Lohūr in A.H. 389 (= A.D. 999).[37]

Jayapāla thus ruled over a large kingdom extending from Sirhind to Lamghan (or Laghman) and from the borders of Kāshmir to Multān. Roughly speaking it included the Western Punjāb, N.W.F. Province and Eastern Afghānistān. Unfortunately for him a powerful Muslim kingdom was establised about this time in the immediate vicinity with Ghaznī as capital. The history of Jayapāla and his successors is, practically speaking, the history of a long-drawn struggle with this kingdom. They fought with valour and tenacity for nearly half a century, but in vain, and the great Shāhi kingdom ultimately collapsed before the repeated onslaughts of Sultān Mahmūd of Ghaznī. That story will be told in the next volume.

X. KASHMIR

1. *Kārkoṭa Dynasty*

Lalitāditya Muktāpīḍa of the Kārkoṭa dynasty, whose career has been described above,[38] was followed on the throne of Kāshmir by his two sons Kuvalayāpīḍa and Vajrāditya Bappiyaka one after the other. Vajrāditya, who ruled from c. A.D. 762, is said to have sold many men to the Mlechchhas and introduced into his kingdom practices which befitted only the Mlechchhas. These Mlechchhas seem to have been the Arabs of Sindh. It is known that Hishām ibn 'Amr at-Taghlibī, the governor of Sindh (A.D. 768-772), raided Kāshmir and secured many prisoners and slaves. This invasion is likely to have taken place during the reign of Vajrāditya, who thus came in contact with the Mlechchhas. Vajrāditya had three sons: Pṛithivyāpīḍa, Saṁgrāmāpīḍa I, and Jayāpīḍa. Pṛithivyāpīḍa, who ascended the throne after the death of his father, was overthrown by his step-brother Saṁgrāmāpīḍa. Saṁgrāmāpīḍa died seven days after his accession, and the sovereignty was then assumed by Jayāpīḍa. Jayāpīḍa, who was also known as Vinayāditya, was a valiant general like his grandfather Lalitāditya. In the early part of his reign he launched an expedition against the eastern countries. Kalhaṇa narrates that during Jayāpīḍa's absence from Kāshmir, his brother-in-law named Jajja usurped his throne. The soldiers who accompanied him gradually deserted his camp in large numbers and returned to Kāshmir. At Prayāga he left the remainder of his troops who were still with him, and began to travel incognito from country to country. Once, while residing in the city of Puṇḍravardhana, he earned the good grace of its king named Jayanta by killing a big lion. Jayanta, who soon discovered his identity, gave his daughter in marriage to him. Jayāpīḍa defeated the five chiefs of Gauḍa and honoured his father-in-law by making him their sovereign. Kalhaṇa's narrative of Jayāpīḍa's adventure in Gauḍa contains obviously a touch of romance. The report that the king won victories over some chiefs of that country, however, seems to have a historical foundation. From Gauḍa he is said to have gone back to Prayāga to meet his troops and thence started for Kāshmir. On his way he defeated the king of Kānyakubja, who seems to have been Indrarāja. As soon as he reached the Kāshmir valley he was opposed by the usurper Jajja, who was easily defeated and slain. After a period of three years' absence from his country, he made a triumphant entry into his capital.

Kalhaṇa states that some time afterwards Jayāpīḍa again went out for conquests. He invaded the kingdoms of Bhīmasena of the eastern region and Aramuḍi of Nepāla. On these occasions he fell a captive into the hands of his adversaries, though he eventually succeeded in effecting his escape. His last expedition was against the 'Strī-rājya'. The authenticity of this report of Jayāpīḍa's military excursions may be doubted, for the existence of a king named Bhīmasena in the eastern region or of a king named Aramuḍi in Nepāl is not known from any other source.[39] Jayāpīḍa's court was graced by learned scholars like Kshīra, Bhaṭṭa, Udbhaṭa, Dāmodaragupta, and others. In the later years of his life, he is said to have incurred unpopularity by oppressive taxes. A conspiracy of the Brāhmaṇas brought about his end in the thirty-first year of his reign. He ruled from c. A.D. 770 up to the closing years of the eighth century. Thereafter his sons Lalitāpīḍa and Saṁgrāmāpīḍa II occupied the throne in succession. After the death of Saṁgrāmāpīḍa, who bore another name Pṛithivyāpīḍa, Lalitāditya's son Chippaṭajayāpīḍa, born of a concubine named Jayādevī, became king. Chippaṭajayāpīḍa, who was also called Bṛihaspati, was very young at the time of his accession. Important offices of the State were held by his maternal uncles, Utpalaka and four others, who were sons of a spirit-distiller. Chippaṭajayāpīḍa was killed in c. A.D. 813 through the intrigue of his maternal uncles, who then began to fight among themselves for power. They ruled Kāshmir without hindrance by setting up puppet kings for nearly forty years. Thus Utpalaka placed Ajitāpīḍa, grandson of Vajrāditya Bappiyaka, on the throne by force of arms. Ajitāpīḍa was overthrown by a rival faction, which set up Anaṅgāpīḍa, son of Saṁgrāmāpīḍa II, as king. Sukhavarman, son of Utpalaka, removed Anaṅgāpīḍa and placed Utpalāpīḍa, son of Ajitāpīḍa, on the throne. During this time the merchant Nara of the Khaśa tribe established his authority over Dārvābhisāra and the neighbouring territories. Sukhavarman, who became the *de facto* ruler, was killed by his own relative. The minister Śūra thereupon dethroned Utpalāpīḍa and declared Avanti-varman, son of

Sukhavarman, as king in A.D. 855-56. Thus the rule of the Kārkoṭa dynasty came to an end.

2. *The Utpala Dynasty*

Avanti-varman was the founder of the Utpala dynasty. He devoted his energies to the amelioration of the economic condition of his subjects, who had suffered badly during the last few decades. The overflowing water of the Mahāpadma (modern Vulur) lake caused frequent floods, damaging crops in the neighbourhood. Lalitāditya had tried to get over this difficulty by draining off the surplus water, but his successors did not take any interest in the matter. Avanti-varman engaged his able minister Suyya to remove this danger permanently. Suyya undertook the work in right earnest, and removed the boulders which had rolled down from the mountains into the bed of the Vitastā, obstructing the normal flow of the water. Stone embankments were built along the banks of the river to prevent further landslides from the mountains. He shifted the place of the confluence of the Vitastā (Jhelum) with its tributary the Sindhu by diverting their courses, and thereby made the extensive lands in the neighbourhood fit for cultivation. As a result of these engineering operations the annual output of grains increased to an enormous extent, and their prices correspondingly fell.

The prime minister Śūra exercised great influence over the king. He killed a powerful Ḍāmara (a feudal land-owner) named Dhanva for misappropriating temple funds in the Lahara District. The king extended his patronage to men of learning like Muktākaṇa, Śivasvāmin, Ānandavardhana, and Ratnākara. His death in A.D. 883 was followed by a civil war between a number of the descendants of Utpala. The chamberlain Ratnavardhana declared Avanti-varman's son Śaṅkara-varman as king. Karṇapa, a councillor, set up Sukhavarman, a nephew of Avanti-varman. as Yuvarāja. Śaṅkara-varman, after a strenuous fight. put down Sukha-varman and other rivals, and made himself the absolute ruler of the country.

Śaṅkara-varman made an attempt to restore Kāshmir to its former position as a great political power by launching expeditions against the neighbouring chiefs in the south. He subjugated Dārvābhisāra, the territory between the Jhelum and the Chenāb to the north of Gujrāt, in the Punjāb. Its king Naravāhana, son of the Khaśa Nara. was allowed to rule for some time, but was subsequently killed together with his followers by Śaṅkara-varman, who suspected him of treachery. After being deprived of his sovereignty, Naravāhana's son Phulla founded a kingdom in Lohara, where he was followed in succession by Sātavāhana, Chanda, Chandurāja, Gopāla and Siṁharāja. About this time Pṛithivīchandra, the king of Trigarta, modern Kāngrā, acknowledged Śaṅkara-varman's supremacy without opposition. Śaṅkara-varman next invaded the Gurjara country, modern Gujrāt in the Punjāb, and forced its king Alakhāna to surrender to him the Ṭakka-land which was to the east of the Chenāb. His military operation against Lalliya Shāhi of Udabhāṇḍa, who lent his support to Alakhāna against him, did not meet with success. The Pratīhāra Mahendrapāla also had to cede his territories in the Punjāb to Śaṅkara-varman who handed them over to a member of the Thakkiya family. After finishing his conquests, Śaṅkara-varman returned to his capital with glory. However, he was addicted to vices and did not prove an efficient adminiśtrator. He oppressed his subjects by numerous exactions. His son Gopālavarman tried to save the people from his father's greed, but failed. Taking advantage of the disturbed state of things, the Kāyasthas appropriated a large slice of territory.

Śaṅkara-varman met his death under tragic circumstances. His officer in charge of the passes leading into Kāshmir in the western border of his kingdom lost his life in an affray at Vīrānaka, the seat of the Khaśas, identified with the village Viran, in the Vitastā Valley between Muzaffarābād and Kathai. This led Śaṅkara-varman to march with an army to punish the offenders. After destroying Vīrānaka he proceeded to Uttarāpatha and compelled a number of chiefs ruling on the banks of the Sindhu to submit to him. When he was passing through Uraśā, modern Hazāra, the inhabitants of the country objected to the quartering of his army there. In the conflict that ensued, an arrow discharged by the enemies from the summit of a hill pierced his neck, and he succumbed to the injuries within a short time. For the safety of the army, the news of his death was kept concealed by the Kāshmiri officers. After six days' march, the minister Sukharāja, along with the army, reached Bolyāsaka, which was within the borders of Kāshmir. The place is identified with the village of Buliāsa on the old route from Muzaffarābād to Kāshmir, on the right bank of the Jhelum, four marches below Bāramula. There the funeral rites of the king were performed.

Śaṅkara-varman's son Gopāla-varman ascended the throne shortly before A.D. 900.[40] As he was still young, his mother Sugandhā carried on the administration of the State. She fell in love with the minister Prabhākara. Prabhākara led an expedition against the Shāhi kingdom and secured the throne of Udabhāṇḍa for Lalliya Shāhi's son Toramāṇa-Kamaluka by defeating the usurper Sāmanta. Prabhākara killed Gopāla-varman by a stratagem and placed Saṅkaṭa, an alleged son of Śaṅkara-varman, on the throne. This new king died ten days after his accession. As there was no direct heir to the throne, the queen Sugandhā assumed the royalty at the wishes of the people. At this time, the Tantrin infantry formed a powerful political organisation in Kāshmir and made their power felt in making and unmaking kings. The queen tried to secure the throne for Nirjita-varman, also known as Paṅgu, who was the grandson of Śūra-varman, a half-brother of king Avanti-varman. But the Tantrins deprived the queen of her sovereignty, and placed Pārtha, the son of Nirjita-varman, who was ten years old, on the throne in A.D. 906. Sugandhā left the royal palace and took her residence at Hushkapura. Eight years later, in A.D. 914, with the help of the Ekāṅga troops, a military body, rival to the Tantrins, she advanced towards the capital to regain her power. But the Tantrins defeated the Ekāṅgas and put Sugandhā to death. Nirjita-varman, with the sanction of the Tantrins, became the guardian of his son Pārtha. He maintained his position by paying heavy bribes to the Tantrins, and oppressed the people with numerous fiscal exactions. At this time, in A.D. 917, a great famine broke out in Kāshmir, causing the death of a large number of people. In A.D. 921 Nirjita-varman deposed Pārtha with the help of the Tantrins and himself assumed the royalty. In A.D. 923 he placed his other son named Chakra-varman on the throne, and died soon after. Chakra-varman ruled for ten years under the guardianship of his mother and grandmother. The Tantrins, eager for more money, overthrew him and placed his half-brother Śūra-varman I on the throne. After a year, Śūra-varman had to yield his throne to Pārtha, who had regained the favour of the Tantrins. A year later, in A.D. 935, Chakra-varman got back the sovereignty by paying a higher price. Shortly afterwards Chakra-varman, having failed to meet the demands of the Tantrins, fled in fear. Thereupon the minister Śambhuvardhana, by offering handsome bribes, purchased the throne for himself. Chakra-varman sought the help of the Ḍāmaras (feudal landowners) who were hostile to the Tantrins. The Ḍāmara Saṁgrāma took up his cause and inflicted a crushing defeat on the Tantrins near Padmapura. Chakra-varman entered the capital Śrīnagara, where he was received with honours by the feudal lords, chiefs, ministers and the Ekāṅgas. Śambhuvardhana was taken prisoner and executed. Chakra-varman abandoned himself to vicious pleasures, and alienated the sympathy of the people. In A.D. 937 he lost his life at the hands of robbers. Unmattāvanti (Mad Avanti), son of Pārtha, was then raised to the throne by the ministers. He was one of the most vicious and tyrannical kings that ever occupied the throne of Kāshmir. At his instigation, his subordinates killed his father in a most diabolical manner.

He had an able minister in Kamalavardhana whom he feared. Just before his death in A.D. 939 he declared a child named Śūra-varman II as his son and placed him on the throne. After the death of the king, Kamalavardhana put down the Ḍāmaras, who had been exercising great influence over the rulers of Kāshmir from the time of Chakra-varman, entered the capital with his army after overcoming all opposition offered by the Ekāṅgas, Tantrins and the feudal chiefs. and dethroned Śūra-varman II. He could have secured the throne for himself without any difficulty. But he foolishly left the election of the king to the assembly of the Brāhmaṇas, fondly hoping that the choice would fall on him. But the assembly offered the crown to a Brāhmaṇa named Yaśaskara, son of Prabhākaradeva, treasurer of the kings Śaṅkara-varman and Gopāla-varman, who had earned great reputation as a man of learning. The rule of the Utpala dynasty thus came to an end in A.D. 939.

3. *Dynasties of Yaśaskara and Parvagupta*

Yaśaskara restored peace and order in the country. Though his career was occasionally marred by vicious actions, he administered his kingdom with success. He built a *maṭha* (monastery) for the residence of the students coming from Ārya-deśa to Kāshmir for higher education. Once when he became seriously ill, he wanted to place Varṇaṭa, the son of his paternal grand-uncle, on the throne in preference to his son Saṁgrāmadeva, who however as a matter of fact was not begotten by himself. But the designing minister Parvagupta ultimately persuaded the king to hand over the sovereignty to Saṁgrāmadeva. After the installation of Saṁgrāmadeva, Yaśaskara left the royal palace unceremoniously and took his residence in his *matha* where he was poisoned by his attendants in A.D. 948. A year after the death of Yaśaskara, Parvagupta killed the young king Saṁgrāmadeva and captured the throne for himself.

Parvagupta was the son of Saṁgrāmagupta and grandson of Abhinava, who was a writer. He died in A.D. 950 leaving the throne to his son Kshemagupta. Kshemagupta married Diddā, the daughter of the Khaśa Siṁharāja, king of Lohara, modern Lohrin valley in the territory of Punch, and the daughter's daughter of Bhīma Shāhi of Udabhāṇḍa.[41] Diddā, who was a woman of keen intelligence, played an important rôle in Kāshmir politics in the second half of the tenth century. Kshemagupta died after an inglorious reign of eight years, and was succeeded by his young son Abhimanyu. Diddā. who became the regent for her son, tried to assume all the royal power into her hands and had no scruples in removing anybody who stood in her way. She quarrelled with the prime minister Phalguṇa and dismissed him. She put down the revolt of Yaśodhara and his associates and won over some of them to her side by offering them high posts in the government. Yaśodhara was made the commander-in-chief of her army. He led an expedition against the Shāhi Thakkana and forced him to submit. But he soon fell into the ill graces of the queen and was dismissed. His old associates again revolted and besieged the royal palace. The queen, with the help of her faithful minister Naravāhana and some other officers, brought the situation under control. Shortly after this the queen, on the report of malicious persons, lost confidence in Naravāhana who, in order to avoid disgrace and humiliation, committed suicide. About this time the Ḍāmaras were also trying to raise a revolt. The situation was made worse for the queen by the death of Rakka, the commander of the army. In order to cope with the situation Diddā recalled Phalguṇa and made him the chief of the army. Phalguṇa conquered Rājapurī, the modern hill state of Rajauri.

King Abhimanyu died in A.D. 972 after a rule of fourteen years, leaving behind three sons Nandigupta, Tribhuvana and Bhīmagupta. Nandigupta assumed the royalty. Diddā received a severe shock by the death of her son. For a year she kept her evil propensities under control and engaged herself exclusively in establishing religious foundations and building new cities. But soon after, she resumed her vicious activites. She brought about the death of Nandigupta. He was succeeded by Tribhuvana, who also shared the same fate two years later (A.D. 975). The young Bhīmagupta was then placed on the throne. He was allowed to enjoy this position for onlv five years. About this time Phalguṇa died. The queen then killed Bhīmagupta and ascended the throne in A.D. 980.

Diddā made the Khaśa Tuṅga of the Parṇotsa country her prime minister. The appointment of Tuṅga, who was formerly a herdsman of buffaloes, caused great resentment among the people. Vigraharāja and Saṁgrāmarāja were the two sons of king Udayarāja of Lohara, the brother of Diddā. The refractory elements brought the prince Vigraharāja to Kāshmir to help them against Tuṅga. Vigraharāja rallied the Brāhmaṇas against the queen. But Diddā succeeded in bringing the Brāhmaṇas back to her side by heavy bribery. All attempts to dislodge Tuṅga failed. Tuṅga earned great renown by leading a successful expedition against Pṛithvīpāla, the king of Rājapurī, who had become hostile. As Diddā had become fairly old she appointed her nephew Saṁgrāmarāja of Lohara as her successor. She died in A.D. 1003 and was followed on the throne by Saṁgrāmarāja. The supremacy of the Lohara dynasty was now established in Kāshmir.

XI. THE HILL STATES OF CHAMBA

A number of dynasties were ruling in the hill states of Rājapurī, Dārvābhisāra, Trigarta (Jālandhar), Kīra (Kāngrā), Chambā, Kulu (Kulūta), etc. during this period. Of them the history of the Mūshaṇa family of the Chambā State can be traced chronologically with the help of the *Vaṁśāvalī* and the epigraphic records.

The Mūshaṇa dynasty established its supremacy over Chambā in the sixth century A.D. The capital of its early kings was Brahmapura, modern Brahmaur, about twenty-five miles south-east of the Chambā town. The king Ajita-varman of this family flourished in the middle of the eighth century. After him ruled Suvarṇa-varman, who was succeeded by Lakshmī-varman. The *Vaṁśāvalī* narrates that during the reign of Lakshmī-varman a large number of people died as the result of an epidemic. Taking advantage of this situation the Kīras (of the Kāngrā valley) killed the king and took possession of the country. Lakshmī-varman's son Mūshaṇa-varman recovered his throne after defeating the Kīras. Mūshaṇa-varman was followed on the throne by Haṁsa-varman, Sāra-varman, Sena-varman, and Sajjana-varman in succession. According to Dr. Vogel, Sajjana-varman founded the city of Chanpakā (Chambā) and transferred his capital there.

An inscription of the tenth century, engraved on a rock at Proliragala on the Dhauli Dhar, belongs to the reign of a king Mrityuñjaya-varman, who is not mentioned in the *Vaṁśāvalī*. Dr. Vogel suggests that this king succeeded Sajjana-varman. Epigraphic records refer to another king Sāhilla-varman who fought successfully against a confederacy of the Kīra forces, the lord of Durgara (Jammu State), and the Saumatikas. The king of Trigarta (Jālandhar) sought his alliance after suffering a defeat at his hands, and the chief of Kulūta (Kulu) sought his favour for granting him royalty for services rendered. The *Vaṁśāvalī* states that the war between Sāhilla-varman and the Kulu chief continued for twelve years. It is also known from an inscription that Sāhilla-varman routed the forces of the Turushkas in a battle. He probably joined with the Shāhis in repulsing an attack of the Turks in the Kābul valley during the reign of Alptigīn. After achieving all these victories, he assumed the epithets *Sāhasāṅka, Niśśaṅkamalla,* and *Maṭamaṭasiṁha.* He is also said to have assumed the title *Karivarsha* after making a gift of elephants to the Sun-god at the time of a solar eclipse at the holy Kurukshetra. His reign came to a close in the middle of the tenth century, and he was succeeded by his son Yugākara-varman, whose son and successor was Vidagdha-varman. Both Yugākara-varman and Vidagdha-varman issued inscriptions from their capital at

Chaṇpakā granting lands in the *Maṇḍalas* of Brahmaputra and Tāvasaka. Vidagdha-varman's successor Dodaka-varman, known from a single inscription, ruled in the closing years of the tenth century. In the eleventh century, Sālavāhana, his son Soma-varman, and the latter's son Āsaṭa of the family ruled the Chambā State.

XII. KUMAUN AND GARHWAL

A detailed analysis of six ancient inscriptions of Kumaun and Garhwāl is available to scholars,[42] although it is not based on quite satisfactory transcripts of the original records. Only one of these records has been satisfactorily edited,[43] while the rough transcript of another has also been published.[44] The texts of the remaining four inscriptions still await publication.

The inscription, of which only a tentative transcript was published in 1838, is the one on a stone-slab in the temple of Śiva called Bāgeśvar (Vyāghreśvara) situated at the junction of the Gomati and Sarju in Poṭṭī Katyūr in Kumaun (Almora). The inscription contains no less than three grants made by three different kings in favour of the god Vyāghreśvaradeva. The defective nature of the published transcript renders it difficult to be definite about the names of the two kings mentioned in the first and probably the earliest of the three charters as they are given in the absurd forms *Śrī-Bhasantanadeva* (also *Masantanadeva* or *Basantanadeva*) and *Śāya-svairaṁ-svairaṁ-dadau.*[45] The names of the kings mentioned in the second of the three charters have been read as Śrī-Kharparadeva, his son Śrī-Kalyāṇarājadeva, and his son Śrī-Tribhuvanarājadeva. It seems that these rulers flourished later than those mentioned in the first charter referred to above, but before the kings known from the third charter. The third and last grant incorporated in the Bāgeśvar inscription mentions four generations of kings. The third name in this list of four kings is that of Lalitaśūradeva who is also known from two other of the six ancient inscriptions from Kumaun and Garhwāl referred to above. These are two copper-plate grants dated in the 21st and 22nd years of Lalitaśūradeva's reign, preserved in the temple of Yogabadari at Pāṇḍukeśvar in the Garhwāl District. Both the charters were issued from the city of Kārttikeyapura by *Paramabhaṭṭāraka Mahārājādhirāja Parameśvara* Lalitaśūradeva, the son of *P.M.P.* Ishṭagaṇadeva and *Mahādevī* Vegādevī and the grandson of Nimbara and *Mahādevī* Nāśudevī. Nimbara, who is not endowed with imperial titles in the records, was probably the founder of this line of kings. Their capital was probably at the city of Kārttikeyapura which has been identified with modern Baijnath or Vaidyanātha in the Almora

(Kumaun) District. According to tradition, the city was built by a Katyūrī king of the Katyūr valley in Kumaun on the ruins of an ancient city named Karavīrapura. It is not improbable that the name of Kārttikeyapura is a Sanskritized form of the aboriginal name Katyūr. Possibly Kartṛipura of the Allāhābād pillar inscription of Samudra-gupta was just another Sanskritized form of the same name.

The astronomical details of the dates of Lalitaśūradeva's grants appear to suggest that his 21st and 22nd regnal years corresponded respectively to A.D. 853 and 854. The reigns of his father and grandfather may thus be ascribed roughly to the period A.D. 790-832. According to the Bāgeśvar inscription Lalitaśūradeva was succeeded by his son Bhūdevadeva whose reign may be tentatively assigned to the third and fourth quarters of the ninth century.

The three remaining inscriptions out of the six ancient records of Kumaun and Garhwāl disclose the names of five generations of rulers who belonged to a different dynasty and apparently succeeded the house of Nimbara. The earliest of the three records of this new family is a copper-plate charter preserved at the temple of Bāleśvar in East Kumaun (Almora). It was issued from Kārttikeyapura in the fifth regnal year of *P.M.P.* Desaṭadeva who was the son of *P.M.P.* Ichchhaṭadeva and the grandson of Saloṇāditya. The two other charters of the family are preserved in the temple at Pāṇḍukeśvar. One of them was issued from the same Kārttikeyapura in the 25th regnal year of *P.M.P.* Padmaṭadeva, son of Ichchhaṭadeva, while the other was issued from the city of Subhikshapura in the fourth regnal year of *P.M.P.* Subhiksharājadeva, son of Padmaṭadeva. Subhikshapura, apparently named after Subhiksharājadeva, was probably the name of a new city built by this king in the vicinity of the old city of Kārttikeyapura. These five kings seem to have ruled about the last quarter of the ninth as well as in the tenth century It appears that the last member of Nimbara's family was overthrown by Saloṇāditya who founded a new dynasty; but the events leading to this dynastic revolution are unknown. Little is known about the history of Kumaun and Garhwāl after Subhiksharāja's death.

An earlier line of kings of the Kumaun-Garhwāl region is known from two plates found at Tāleśvar in Almora District.[46] The records have been assigned on palaeographical grounds to the sixth century A.D. One of the copper-plate grants was issued in the fifth regnal year of *Paramabhaṭṭāraka Mahārājādhirāja* Dyutivarman. In the legend on the seal attached to the plate, the king is represented as the son of Agnivarman, gradson of Vṛishavarman and great-grandson of Vishṇuvarman I. The other charter was issued in the twenty-eighth regnal year of *Paramabhaṭṭāraka Mahārājādhirāja* Vishṇuvarman II, son of Dyutivarman. The family to which the kings belonged is described as 'the lunar dynasty' as well as 'the lineage of the moon and the sun', while it is also specifically called 'the Paurava line of kings.' Both the charters were issued from the city of Brahmapura which was apparently the capital of the Paurava kings of the Almora region. They record certain grants of the kings made in favour of the god Vīraṇeśvara who is described as an incarnation of Ananta or Vishṇu. The god was apparently installed in a temple at Brahmapura and was probably the family deity of the Pauravas. In the seventh century A.D. the celebrated Chinese pilgrim Hiuen Tsang visited the country of Brahmapura, no doubt meaning the kingdom of which the city of the same name was the capital. The same country is also mentioned in Varāhamihira's *Bṛihat-saṁhitā* composed in the sixth century A.D. Both Varāhamihira and Hiuen Tsang appear to refer to the kingdom of the Pauravas of Brahmapura, although the inscriptions apply the name Parvatākara to their *rājya*. Little is known about the relation of the Paurava kings mentioned in the Tāleśvar plates with the later rulers of the Kumaun-Garhwāl region known from other sources and discussed above.

XIII. THE ARABS IN INDIA

1. *Kābul and Zābul*

The early attempts of the Arabs to conquer Kābul, Zābul and Sindh have been noted in the preceding volume, and we have seen that, by the middle of the eighth century A.D., although they maintained a precarious hold on Sindh, they could not establish their authority in the other two kingdoms.

This was partly due to the decline in power of the central authority in the Islamic world. The Caliphs of the Umayyad dynasty were gradually weakened by internal dissensions and other causes and were supplanted by a new dynasty, the 'Abbasids, in A.D. 749. Under a few able rulers the 'Abbasids restored the power and glory of the Caliphate and its effect was also felt in India. During the reign of Al-Manṣūr, the second Caliph of this dynasty, who ruled from A.D. 754 to 775, Kandahār was conquered, and the Muslim governor of Sijistān again demanded tribute from the king of Zābul. The latter sent some camels, tents, and slaves, but reckoned each article at double its value. The Muslim governor thereupon invaded Zābul but evidently could not subdue its ruler. For we are told that during the next three Caliphates (A.D. 775-809) the Muslim officers collected tribute as best as they could (or according to their strength and weakness). When Caliph Al-Ma'mūm (A.D. 813-833) visited the eastern region, the ruler of Zābul paid double tribute to him.

It is said that the Caliph sent an army against Kābul and forced its ruler to submit and pay taxes. But evidently both Kābul and Zābul regained independence. Two more expeditions were probably sent against Kābul in A.D. 769 and 786, but without any conspicuous success. It was not till about A.D. 870 that both Kābul and Zābul were conquered by Ya'qūb ibn Layth, the founder of the Ṣaffārid dynasty, who began his life as a brigand in Sijistān and ultimately became the ruler of Persia and the neighbouring regions in the east. The king of Zābulistān was killed and the people embraced Islam. Henceforth this petty state, that had carried on a prolonged and heroic resistance against the Arab aggression for more than two hundred years, ceased to belong to India either politically or culturally. But Kābul probably regained independence and formed a part of the Hindu Shāhiya kingdom, whose history has been narrated above.[47]

The story of the successful resistance of the tiny states of Kābul and Zābul against the Arabs has not obtained its due place in the history of India. It is worthy of note, however, that they defied the conquerors of the world and ultimately succumbed, not to the political power of the Caliphate, but to the local principalities that arose on its ruins.

2. *Sindh*

The 'Abbasid Caliphs made a determined effort to consolidate the power of Islam in India. They sent expeditions to drive away the old officers of the Umayyad dynasty who refused to recognise the new authority. Hishām, who was appointed governor of Sindh by Al-Manṣūr (A.D. 754-775), took possession of Multān and Kunduhar, usually identified with Kandahār. He is also said to have conquered Kāshmir, but this must be regarded as extremely doubtful. For it has been reasonably inferred from a statement in the *Rājataraṅgiṇī* that Lalitāditya Muktāpīḍa thrice defeated a ruling chief of the Arabs. Possibly the Arabs made a successful border raid into Kāshmir, but the fact that we do not hear of any further Arab invasion of that country seems to indicate that Lalitāditya successfully defended his kingdom against Arab aggression.

According to Al Idrisi, the famous city of Mansura, which became the capital of Sindh, was founded by the 'Abbasid Caliph Al-Manṣūr; but Balādhurī tells us that it was built by a son of Muḥammad ibn-Qāsim when Hakam was the governor of Sindh under the Umayyads. Probably the town was founded in the time of Hakam but finished in the time of the 'Abbasid Caliph Al-Manṣūr. This great and opulent Muslim capital of Sindh, of which we get a detailed account from Muslim writers, was founded on the ruins of the Hindu city of Brāhmanābād and lay 43 miles north-east of the modern city of Haidarābād and eight miles south-east of the railway station of Shadadpur.

Caliph Al-Mahdi (A.D. 775-785), who succeeded Al-Manṣūr, sent a naval expedition against India but it could not gain any success.[48] During the Caliphate of Harun Al-Rashīd (A.D. 786-809), his governor is said to have conquered a few places in Western Sindh. The Muslim army had also to fight with the hardy Jaths of Kikānan who are known to have resisted the Arabs as far back as A.D. 662. Evidently they were not completely subdued even during this long interval. There were also frequent conflicts between the Muslims on the one side and the Jaths and Meds on the other in the neighbourhood of Alor, the old capital of Sindh. Sometimes we hear of a successful Hindu rising. Thus the Hindu chiefs of Sindan, a place conquered during the Caliphate of Al-Ma'mūn (A.D. 813-833), rose against its ruler and killed and crucified him. According to Balādhurī the Hindus became masters of the city but "left its mosque for the Muslims to assemble in and pray for the Caliph."

On the whole, it would appear from a study of the Muslim chronicles that the 'Abbasids, even in their palmiest days, could not gain any conspicuous success in their Indian expeditions. They not only failed to extend their dominions beyond Sindh, but were even unable to consolidate their conquests in this province. This was undoubtedly due to the active vigilance of powerful Indian states bordering on Sindh. The Pratīhāras, whose chief Nāgabhaṭa I saved Western India from Arab aggression[49] in the eighth century A.D., founded a strong principality which proved to be a bulwark against any further Arab aggression. King Nāgabhaṭa II of this dynasty,[50] who was a contemporary of the great Caliphs Harun Al-Rashīd and Al-Ma'mūn, is described in an almost contemporary record as having captured the strongholds of the Turushkas. The reference is probably to the Muslim rulers of Sindh some of whom originally belonged to Tukhāristān. The Pāla king Dharmapāla, who also belonged to the same period, claims in his own record that a *Yavana* vassal chief made obeisance to him. Here again the reference seems to be to a Muslim ruler of Sindh. An inscription, dated A.D. 842, states that powerful Mlechchha rulers on the river Chambal made obeisance to the Chāhamāna king. These and similar other isolated references[51] point to the fact that since the initial success of the Arabs in Sindh, in the first quarter of the eighth century A.D., they were unable to make much headway in India owing to the vigour and alertness of the Indian chiefs.

The decline of the 'Abbasid power about the middle of the ninth century A.D. had its natural repercussions on Sindh. During the Caliphate of Al-Ma'mūn (A.D. 813-833), Bashar, the governor of Sindh, rebelled but was defeated by Ghassan. The latter took Bashar as captive to Baghdad, leaving Musa as his deputy in Sindh. Musa nominated his own son as his successor, and henceforth the governors of Sindh ruled practically as independent chiefs. Later, it formed a part of the dominions of the Ṣaffārids (A.D. 872-903). After the fall of the Ṣaffārids the Muslim territories in Sindh were divided into two independent states, *viz.* those of Mansura and Multān. The former extended from the sea to Alor, and the latter comprised the upper valley of the united Sindhu up to this city. Little is known of their history, but it appears that the greater part of the administrative authority was left in the hands of the Hindus.

Neither of the two states was very powerful. Multān was always in dread of the mighty Pratīhāra power. The Pratīhāra army frequently marched gainst Multān, and its Muslim ruler secured his safety by playing upon the religious sentiments of the Hindus. There was a famous image of the Sun-god in the city of Multān which was venerated all over India. We learn from Al-Ma'sūdī that "when the unbelievers march against Multān and the faithful do not feel themselves strong enough to oppose them, they threaten to break their idol and their enemies immediately withdraw." Iṣtakhrī, who makes a similar statement, adds that "otherwise the Indians would have destroyed Multān."

The other Muslim state in Sindh, *viz.* Manṣura, was equally exposed to the attacks of the Hindus. According to Al-Ma'sūdī, "it was constantly at war with a nation called the Meds, who are a race of Sind, and also with other races on the frontiers of Sind."

The older generations of historians like Elphinstone felt surprised at the slow progress of the Islamic conquest of India, and sought to explain it by various hypotheses which have no foundation in fact. The real matter for surprise, however, is that the vestige of Arab authority continued in Sindh for three hundred years. Even according to the testimony of the Muslims, the Pratīhāras could have easily conquered Multān that guarded the flank of every possible route which a future Muslim conqueror from the outside would have to follow. That they were deterred from doing this by the fear that the holy images at Multān might be broken by the Muslim ruler of the place, only shows a lack of foresight and statesmanship and a deplorable want of rationality on the part of the Hindu leaders. If they had possessed even a general knowledge of the political condition of the lands immediately outside the borders of India on the west, they would have made serious efforts to defend India against the almost inevitable danger of Muslim invasion. The first steps in this direction should have been to drive away the Muslims from the petty principalities which they still held in Sindh and to establish a strong garrison in Multān and other strategic places in the Punjāb. The Shāhis and the Pratīhāras were both powerful ruling dynasties who could have easily accomplished this task. But they did not do so. Either they were ignorant of the new political situation created by the rise of strong Muslim states on the frontiers of India, and of the consequent dangers threatening their country, or they were too parochially minded to take a broad view of the interests of India as a whole. This, however, can hardly apply to the Shāhis, who were too near the danger to ignore it and whose own interest, in this case, coincided with that of India. The united stand made at a later date by the Indian chiefs on the invitation of the Shāhi rulers proves that a real sense of patriotism was not altogether absent in them. We can, therefore, only conclude that the lack of knowledge of the outside world, or failure to grasp the real significance of contemporary events, was the principal cause of the indifference of the Hindu chiefs to the great danger that was destined to overwhelm them at no distant date.

The danger was brought home to the Shāhi rulers by the foundation of the state of Ghaznī in the last quarter of the tenth century A.D. Ere long the inevitable conflict broke out and the Shāhi rulers were worsted in the fight. Then the horrors of Muslim invasions, inspired by greed and animated by fanatic religious zeal and iconoclastic fury, were let loose on the fair temples and cities of India. She paid dearly for her remissness in the past, but somehow escaped the great doom which had overtaken Persia, Egypt and other countries. The history of this great crisis will be dealt with in the next volume.

1. *HBR*, 121. Cf. above, pp. 50-52.
2. See pp. 33-4.
3. Harsha, the adversary of Kalachuri Kokkalla I, is wrongly identified with the Chandella king of this name. He is identical with Guhila Harsha of Dhavagartā. Cf. *IHQ*, XIII. 485.
4. See p. 37.
5. This is the translation of Kielhorn (*EI*, *I*. 122); but Dr. R.C. Mazumdar suggests that the correct translation would be 'defeated' (*IHQ*, XXV. 213).
6. See pp. 33-4.
7. See p. 37.
8. Vol. I, pp. 274, 278 ff, etc.
9. The name is also written as Kokkala and Kokalla.
10. Prof. Mirashi thinks that Lakshmaṇarāja belonged to the Kalachuri Dynasty and was a predecessor of Kokkalla I.—*EI*, XXIII. 255.
11. The Bilhari inscription (*EI*, I. 264) mentions that Kokkalla I set up two columns of his fame—Krishṇa on the south and Bhoja on the north. The Benares copper-plate (*Ibid*, II. 306) states that Kokkalla granted freedom from fear to Bhoja, Vallabharāja, Śrī-Harsha, king of Chitrakūṭa, and the king Śaṅkaragaṇa. These two reports are taken to imply that Kokkalla helped the Rāshṭrakūṭa Krishṇa II and the Pratīhāra Bhoja I in consolidating their sovereign position, which was threatened by their enemies. But in view of the information supplied by the Amoda plates (EI, XIX. 78) that Kokkalla I raided the treasuries of Karṇāṭa, Gurjara, and those born of the Raghu family, this king of the Kalachuris cannot be regarded as an ally of the Rāshṭrakūṭas and the Pratīhāras. As Kokkalla I is known to have been succeeded by his son Śaṅkaragaṇa before A.D. 888, his adversary Harsha cannot be assumed to have been the king of this name of the Chandella dynasty, who ruled from c. A.D. 900-925. It has been suggested that Chitrakūṭa, referred to, is the hill of this name in the Bāndā District, U.P., 25 miles north-east of Kālinjar, and its king was evidently the Chandella Harsha. The Chandella Harsha, the king of Khajrāho, was not, however, in possession of even Kālinjar, about 40 miles north-east of Khajrāho. Chitrakūṭa hill was outside the Chandella kingdom, at least up to A.D. 954, when it was bounded on the east by Kālinjar. The expression 'Chitrakūṭa-*bhūpāla*' may not, therefore, be referring to the Chandella Harsha. This king, whose name has not been mentioned, and who was the ruler of Chitor, might have been another adversary of Kokkalla. For detailed discussion, *cf*. *IHQ*, XIII. 482 ff.

   Dr. R. C. Majumdar has recently expressed a different view on the subject (*PIHC*, XII. 123 ff). He points out that 'not a single record of the 9th or 10th century A.D. refers to the Kalachuris as a great power in the period of Kokkalla I, and that the posthumous military glories of this king gradually grew with passing years'. He holds the view that Kokkalla was a dashing military chief who joined with one great power against another as suitable opportunity offered itself, and that far from exercising supremacy over the Pālas, Pratīhāras and the Rāshṭrakūṭas he probably owed allegiance first to the Rāshṭrakūṭas and then to the Pratīhāras. He also points out that Kokkalla's daughter was married to Krishṇa II long before the latter ascended the Rāshṭrakūṭa throne. On the other hand we have to remember the following facts. Harsha, king of Chitrakūṭa, Śaṅkaragaṇa (king of Sarayupāra), kings of Gurjara and Śākambharī, mentioned in the Benares and Amoda plates as adversaries of Kokkalla, are known to have been feudatories of the Pratīhāra Bhoja, and the king of Koṅkaṇa mentioned as another adversary of Kokkalla in the Amoda plates only, was a feudatory of the Rāshṭrakūṭa Krishṇa. It appears that when Kokkalla fought with Bhoja and Krishṇa, his adversaries were assisted by their feudatories. It is thus obvious that when Bilhari inscription mentions only the two chief adversaries of Kokkalla, the Benares and Amoda plates furnish more details of the conflicts by mentioning the names of the feudatories of those two adversaries who participated in them. Amoda plates, however, mention two new military adventures of Kokkalla, *viz*. that he won victories over the king of Vaṅga and the Turushkas, which are not found referred to in the Bilhari and Benares inscriptions. Dr. Majumdar has virtually accepted elsewhere (*HBR*, I. 196) the statement of the Amoda plates that Kokkalla conquered Vaṅga as authentic.

12. See above, p. 54.
13. See above, p. 83.
14. See above, p. 31.
15. See above, p. 36.
16. The history of this family is principally based on the copper-plates (*EI*, XXVI. 185) discovered at Ghumli in 1936.
17. See above, Vol. III, p. 173.
18. *EI*, IX. 1 ff.
19. This account is based on chronicles only and is not supported by epigraphic evidence. Cf. *DHNI*, II. 941.
20. *IA*, XII. 159, l. 13. The inscription states that Mahāvarāha, kindled with the rays of the sun, attacked Krishṇa I (*Sauryy-oshma-saṁdīpitam=āpatantam)*. Kielhorn corrects Sauryya as Śauryya, meaning bravery. But there is no difficulty in accepting the reading of the passage as it occurs. In my opinion there is a pun on the word Saurya, which may be taken to mean also the people of this name (cf. *Sauryāṇām = adhimaṇḍale* etc., in Jain *Harivaṁśa*). The verse purports to say that Mahāvarāha, being strengthened by the support of the Sauryas, attacked Krishṇa I.
21. *EI*, XIX. 175. Also cf. *Bh. List.* No. 2106 fn. 1
22. See p. 21.
23. The Rāshṭrakūṭa Dhavala's grandfather Vidagdha was ruling in A.D. 916, and his father's known date is A.D. 939. In his old age Dhavala abdicated his throne in favour of his son Bālaprasāda, who is found ruling in A.D. 997. So it is not unlikely that the Chāpa Dharaṇīvarāha was a contemporary of both Dhavala and the Chaulukya Mūlarāja, who ascended the throne in A.D. 942.
24. According to Nayachandra Sūri's *Hammīra-Mahākāvya*, Mūlarāja was killed by the Chāhamāna Vigraharāja. This seems to be unlikely.
25. Cf. Vol. III, pp. 162-3.
26. See p. 87.
27. The Bijoli Rock Ins. (*EI*, XXVI. 91) mentions Vindhyanṛipati as the successor of Vākpati I. For the account of Siṁharāja and his predecessors, cf. *EI*, II. 116 ff.
28. *EI*, XIV. 176.
29. Ch. X, pp. 158 ff.
30. The nature of the political relation of Bhartṛipaṭṭa II with the Imperial Pratihāras cannot be ascertained from the Partābgarh inscription (*EI*, XIV. 176). All that can be gathered from it is that the *Mahārājādhirāja* Bhartṛipaṭṭa made a grant to the temple of Indrādityadeva in A.D. 942 and the *Mahārāja* Mahendrapāla II from his residence at Mahodaya donated land to the same temple in A.D. 946.
31. Vol. III, p. 160.
32. See p. 31.
33. See pp. 33, 118.
34. Kamalu ascended the throne in or before A.D. 900. As he obtained the sovereignty during the reign of Gopāla-varman who, according to Kalhaṇa, began his rule in A.D. 902, the date of the latter's accession is to be shifted back by a few years.
35. *EI*, XXI. 298.
36. *EI*, XXI. 301.
37. Firishta mentions Lahore as the capital of Jayapāla. This does not seem to be correct. Al-Bīrūnī describes Luhavur (Lahore) as a country, the capital of which was Mandahukur (Sachau, I. 206).
38. Vol. III, pp. 133-136.
39. S. Lévi (*Le Nepal*, II. 176-77), however, thinks that there may be some historical basis of the story of Jayāpīḍa's fight with Nepāl. Nepāl was at that time a protectorate of Tibet and there was a long-standing hostility between this kingdom and Kāshmir. According to Lévi a story-teller would hardly invent an uncouth and barbarous name like Aramuḍi, who was perhaps a Tibetan general sent to oppose Jayāpīda. The river Kāla Gaṇḍika, on the banks of which the battle is alleged to have taken place, almost certainly represents the Kāla Gandaki, the westernmost branch of the seven Gandakis, which was the first natural barrier against an invader coming from the west.

40. For the date of Gopāla-varman, see fn. 34 above.
41. See above, p. 113.
42. E. T. Atkinson, *The Himalayan Districts of the North-Western Provinces of India*, Vol. II (forming Vol. XI of the Gazetteer, N.W.P.), 1884, pp. 496-85. Cf. *BV*, XII. 149-52.
43. *IA*, XXV. 177 ff.
44. *JASB*, Vol. VII, 1838, pp. 1056-58.
45. This name apparently begins with *śri* or *śrimat* and ends with *deva*.
46. *EI*, XIII. 109. The editor of the inscription regarded them to be forged without sufficient justification. Cf. Bhandarkar, *List* Nos. 1786-7. Bhandarkar does not notice all the inscriptions analysed by Aktinson.
47. See pp. 112-115.
48. See pp. 99-100.
49. Vol. III, p. 155.
50. See pp. 24 ff.
51. See pp. 20, 25, 39.

CHAPTER VI

THE DECCAN

I. THE EASTERN CHALUKYAS

When Vijayāditya I died after a rule of 18 or 19 years about A.D. 764, his son Vishṇuvardhana IV became king and ruled the Veṅgī country for 36 years, *i.e.* down to about A.D. 799. Shortly before A.D. 769-70, the Rāshṭrakūṭa king Kṛishṇa I sent his son, the crown-prince Govinda II, to invade the Veṅgī country. According to the Alas grant[1] of the Rāshṭrakūṭa crown-prince, issued in A.D. 769-70 from the camp of his victorious army at the confluence of the Kṛishṇaveṇā and the Musī, the king of Veṅgī was humbled and ceded his treasury, forces and kingdom. Soon after A.D. 779, there was a struggle for the Rāshṭrakūṭa throne between Govinda II and his younger brother Dhruva, in which the former managed to get the assistance of the rulers of Mālava, Kāñchī, Gaṅgavāḍi and Veṅgī, all of whom had been previously subdued by the Rāshṭrakūṭas and were apparently eager to improve their position by exploiting the situation arising out of the fratricidal war. But Govinda II was defeated by Dhruva who next ascended the Rāshṭrakūṭa throne. Govinda II having been eliminated, Dhruva now set himself with full vigour against his brother's allies. An epigraph of A.D. 802,[2] supported by the Rādhanpur grants[3] of A.D. 808, says that "at half a word from the mouth of Dhruva's letter-bearer, the king of Veṅgī, wherever he was, constantly performed his service without intermission, by his own wish, and built for him an outer wall, lofty as the sky, of marvellous splendour, with the constellations around its head like a garland of pearls." Although the exact nature of the claim is difficult to determine and although the capital city of Mānyakheṭa is said to have been built by Amoghavarsha, some writers go so far as to suggest that Vishṇuvardhana IV was himself compelled to construct a wall for Mānyakheṭa (modern Mālkhed in Hyderābād State). It is, however, probable that the Veṅgī king was forced to become a subordinate ally of the Rāshṭrakūṭa monarch. The Jethwai grant[4] dated A.D. 786 speaks of his daughter Śīlamahādevī who was married to Dhruva.

Vishṇuvardhana IV had several sons, *viz.* Vijayāditya II, Bhīma-Sālukki (*i.e.* Bhīma-Chālukya) and Nṛiparudra (born of a Haihaya or Kalachuri princess). About A.D. 799, Vijayāditya II became king and assumed the titles *Narendramṛigarāja, Chālukyārjuna* and

Tribhuvanāṅkuśa. The duration of his rule is variously given in different records as 40, 41, 44 or 48 years. Fleet accepted 44 years as the proper duration of the reign although from the actual date of the accession of the king's great-grandson Chālukya-Bhīma I, it now appears that Vijayāditya II ruled for 48 years and died about A.D. 847. The real cause of the discrepancy regarding his regnal period seems to be that for some years during this reign the Eastern Chālukya throne was occupied by a rival. The king built a large number of Śiva temples in different parts of his dominions.

Vijayāditya II, who assumed the titles *Paramabhaṭṭāraka Mahārājādhirāja-Parameśvara*, was one of the most powerful rulers of the family. But his early years witnessed a series of failures. His brother Bhīma-Sālukki deserted him and joined the Rāshṭrakūṭas. The king was utterly defeated by the Rāshṭrakūṭas under Govinda III and their allies the Gaṅgas, and Bhīma-Sālukki was raised to the throne of Veṅgī. But Vijayāditya II continued the struggle and, when after the death of Govinda III (A.D. 814) his minor son Amoghavarsha I ascended the Rāshṭrakūṭa throne and was facing a rebellion of his officials and feudatories, the Chālukya king succeeded in recovering his throne by overthrowing Bhīma-Sālukki in spite of the assistance the latter received from the Rāshṭrakūṭas and Gaṅgas. This success was pursued by Vijayāditya II with redoubled vigour. The Eastern Chālukya army now overran considerable portions of the Rāshṭrakūṭa empire and reached the city of Stambha (modern Cambay in Gujarāt)[5] which they plundered and devastated. In the records of his successors, Vijayāditya is said to have fought 108 battles in a continuous struggle of 12 years with the Rāshṭrakūṭas and Gaṅgas, to have destroyed the Dakshiṇa Gaṅga (the southern Gaṅgas), and to have taken possession of Veṅgī-*maṇḍala* by extirpating his younger brother Bhīma-Sālukki. The records of the Rāshṭrakūṭas themselves cf. Navsāri grant[6] of Indra III) admit that, in the early part of the reign of Amoghavarsha I, the glory of the Raṭṭa (Rāshṭrakūṭa) kingdom "was drowned in the ocean of the Chālukyas" who had "completely devastated the city of Stambha."[7] But the success of the Eastern Chālukyas against the Rāshṭrakūṭas was shortlived. Amoghavarsha I, who received considerable help from Karkka, the Rāshṭrakūṭa viceroy of Gujarāt, is said to have later raised the glory of the Rāshṭrakūṭas once again. The rebellious feudatories were subdued and the Eastern Chālukya army was driven out of Rāshṭrakūṭa territory. In the records of his successors, Amoghavarsha I is described as having destroyed a large host of the Chālukyas at the battlefield of Viṅgavalli. The hostilities continued in spite of the marriage of a Rāshṭrakūṭa princess named Śīlamahādevī (probably a daughter of Dhruva by Śīlamahādevī who was a sister of Vijayāditya II) to Vishṇu-vardhana V, son of Vijayāditya II. The Eastern Chālukyas had to acknowledge Rāshṭrakūṭa supremacy.

Vijayāditya II came into conflict with a Nāga king probably of the Bastar region. But the reference may also be to Nāgabhaṭa II of the Gurjara Pratīhāra dynasty, with whom he fought, according to the Gwālior inscription[7] of Bhoja I, probably in connection with his Gujarāt expedition.

The next king of Veṅgī was Vijayāditya's son Vishṇuvardhana V, also called Kali-Vishṇuvardhana (Kali-Biṭṭarasa), Sarvalokāśraya and Vishamasiddhi. He ruled only for 18 or 20 months and died about A.D. 848. He left several sons, *viz.* Vijayāditya III (born of the Rāshṭrakūṭa princess Śīlamahādevī), Ayyaparāja, Vikramāditya (I) and Yuddhamalla (I). Vijayāditya III succeeded him on the throne of the Veṅgī country and ruled for 44 years (A.D. 848-92). The new king had a number of *virudas* such as *Guṇaka* (*Guṇaga*), *Parachakrarāma, Raṇaraṅgaśūdraka, Manujaprakāra, Vikramadhavala, Nṛpatimārtaṇḍa, Virudaṅgabhīma, Bhuvanakandarpa, Arasaṅkakeśarin, Tripuramartyamaheśvara* and *Tribhuvanāṅkuśa.*

Like his grandfather, Vijayāditya III was bent upon *Digvijaya* in which he was assisted by his able minister Vinayāḍiśarman and by two reputed generals, namely Kaḍeyarāja and his son Paṇḍaraṅga. In the south, he conquered the city of Nellūra (Nellore), probably from the Pallavas of Kāñchi. Vijayāditya III is said to have carried away gold from the Pallavas. He is further credited with a victory over the Pāṇḍyas and with giving shelter to the Choḷa king. Having been goaded to retaliation by the Raṭṭa or Rāshṭrakūṭa king (*raṭṭeśa-saṁchodita*), he cut off the head of Maṅgi, king of Nolambarāshṭra in Mysore, in a great battle, and also defeated the Gaṅgas completely in the west. Next turning to the north, the Eastern Chālukya king defeated the combined forces of the Rāshṭrakūṭa king Kṛishṇa II[8] and the latter's brother-in-law (wife's brother) and ally, the Kalachuri king Śaṅkila or Śaṅkuka (Śaṅkaragaṇa), lord of Ḍāhala (the Jubbulpore region), at the great battle of Kiraṇapura, probably modern Kiranpur in the Bālāghāt District, Madhya Pradesh. Like his grandfather, Vijayāditya III overran the Rāshṭrakūṭa empire and burnt Achalapura (modern Ellichpur in Berār). Vijayāditya III is also said to have defeated Baḍḍega, very probably the Chālukya chief of Vemulavāḍa who was the grandfather of Narasiṁha (a feudatory of Indra III, grandson and successor of Kṛishṇa II). He is further said to have burnt the city of Chakrakūṭa in the old Bastar State, captured the elephants of the king of Kosala (South Kosala in Chhattisgarh and the adjoining area), and taken by force the gold of the

Gaṅga king of Kaliṅga, from whom he also received elephants as tribute. Vijayāditya III appointed his younger brother Vikramāditya his heir apparent, but the latter probably predeceased him. After Vijayāditya's death the throne passsed to Chālukya-Bhīma I, son of Vikramāditya.

Fleet suggested that Chālukya-Bhīma I ascended the throne in A.D. 888; it is however now known from the Attili inscription[9] that this king's coronation took place in Śaka 814 corresponding to A.D. 892. Chālukya-Bhīma I was also known as Vishṇuvardhana and had the *virudas Tribhuvanāṅkuśa, Drohārjuna, Sarvalokāśraya* and *Ṛitasiddhi*. He is often called *Paramabrahmaṇya*. He ruled for 30 years and died about A.D. 922. He is said to have fulfilled the desires of distressed and helpless persons and of the ascetics just like their parents, friends and preceptors.

The Aṇakapalle inscription[10] of Chālukya-Bhīma I proves his control over Devarāshṭra in Elāmañchi-Kaliṅgadeśa, *i.e.* the Yellamanchili tract of Viśākhapatnam District. He made Paṇḍaraṅga his general. Another general of Chālukya-Bhīma I was Mahākāla who was the son of a daughter of the king's foster-mother.

During this reign, the struggle with the Rāshṭrakūṭas continued. According to the *Pampa-Bhārata* or *Vikramārjuna-vijaya* by the Kanarese poet Pampa, the Chālukya chief Baḍḍega (probably feudatory of Kṛishṇa II) defeated Bhīma, apparently Chālukya-Bhīma, and took him prisoner. The forces of Kṛishṇa II overran the Andhra country as far south as Guntur and Nellore Districts and the Rāshṭrakūṭa king actually appointed his own officials in charge of various forts in the Eastern Chālukya country. Paṇḍaraṅga, general of Chālukya-Bhīma I, made attempts to overthrow the domination of the foreigners. At the battle of Niravadyapura—one of the many that took place between the Rāshṭrakūṭas and the Eastern Chālukyas—Chālukya-Bhīma's son killed a Rāshṭrakūṭa *Daṇḍeśa* (general) named Guṇḍaya, but was also himself killed. Paṇḍaraṅga captured some 12 strongholds from Vaso-Boya, probably a Rāshṭrakūṭa partisan, and also the hill-forts of Veṅgīnāṇḍu (the Veṅgī country). Chālukya-Bhīma I, who was evidently released after some time, is said to have illumined the Veṅgī country which had been overrun by Raṭṭa (Rāshṭrakūṭa) chieftains "just as by dense darkness after sunset" and to have defeated the army of Kṛishṇavallabha (Kṛishṇa II) and his allies, the kings of Karṇāṭa and Lāṭa. Chālukya-Bhīma's successes may have been achieved during the latest years of the reign of Kṛishṇa II.

Chālukya-Bhīma I had at least two sons, *viz.* Vijayāditya IV and Vikramāditya, of whom the former succeeded him about

A.D. 922. Hostilities with the Rāshṭrakūṭas continued unabated. Vijayāditya IV defeated the Rāshṭrakūṭa forces but lost his life after a reign of 6 months, at the battle of Virajāpurī to the south of the Kṛishṇā. The city is said to have been the capital of a viceregal family known as the Parichchhedins who ruled "the country of 6000" lying on the southern bank of the Kṛishṇaveṇā (Kṛishṇā).

Vijayāditya IV had at least two sons, *viz.* Amma I, *alias* Vishṇuvardhana, and Chālukya-Bhīma II (born of Melambā), of whom the former succeeded him about the end of A.D. 922 with the *virudas Rājamahendra* and *Sarvalokāśraya.* Amma I ruled for 7 years, *i.e.* till about A.D. 929. The Pulivarru inscription[11] records the grant of a village by the king in favour of Indaparāja, grandson of Indaparāja of the Mahā-Raṭṭavaṁśa who was the lord of the city of Mānyakheṭa. There is apparently reference here to a grandson (named Indra) of the Rāshṭrakūṭa king Indra III of Mālkhed. It has been suggested that the donee may have been a son of Amoghavarsha II (*c.* A.D. 927), who might have taken shelter at the Eastern Chālukya court when his father was overthrown by the latter's younger brother Govinda IV (*c.* A.D. 927-36). The non-mention of Amoghavarsha II in the Eastern Chālukya record may, however, suggest that the father of the donee was not a crowned monarch.

Two sons of Amma I, *viz.* Vijayāditya V and Bhīma, are known from records; the former succeeded (A.D. 929) him under the name Kaṇṭhika-Vijayāditya or Kaṇṭhika-Beta. A fortnight after the installation of Vijayāditya V, the young king was overthrown by Tāla (Tāḷapa, Tāḍapa or Tāḍa), son of Yuddhamalla and grandson of Vishṇuvardhana V. Tāla's success was specially due to the assistance he received from the Rāshṭrakūṭa king Gojjiga or Govinda IV and from Ayyappa, king of Nolamba-rāshṭra. Vijayāditya V was imprisoned and Tāla declared himself king (A.D. 929). Vijayāditya however escaped from captivity and took shelter at the court of the Chālukya ruler Arikesarin II (great-grandson of Baḍḍega and patron of the poet Pampa), ruler of Vemulavāḍa and a feudatory of the Rāshṭrakūṭas.

The new king Tāla was, however, ousted after only a month by another claimant to the throne named Vikramāditya (II) who was a son of Chālukya-Bhīma I. Vikramāditya is said to have ruled over the Veṅgī country together with Trikaliṅga for nine or eleven months or for a year (A.D. 929) when he was himself overthrown by Bhīma II who was a son of Amma I and a brother of Vijayāditya V. But after a rule of 8 months (A.D. 930) Bhīma II was killed by one Malla, Mallapa or Yuddhamalla (II), who was a son of Tāla and a protégé of the Rāshṭrakūṭa king Govinda IV. This king, who ruled for seven years (A.D. 930-36), built the Malleśvarasvāmī temple at Vijayawāda. During Yuddhamalla's rule, the Rāshṭrakūṭas were all powerful in the Andhra country. An inscription[12] of Amma II naively admits that the Śabara chiefs, the commanders of the army of Vallabha (the Rāshṭrakūṭa king), and others apportioned the Eastern Chālukya kingdom among themselves for seven years (*i.e.* the duration of Yuddhamalla's reign). With Rāshṭrakūṭa help, however, Yuddhamalla succeeded in holding his position against a number of rival claimants to the throne, including Chālukya-Bhīma II who was a son of Vijayāditya IV and a step-brother of Amma I; but Yuddhamalla was ultimately ousted by Chālukya-Bhīma II. According to the Maliyapundi grant,[13] the five years following the death of Vikramāditya II witnessed the princes of the family who coveted the kingdom, *viz.* Yuddhamalla, Rājamārtaṇḍa, Kaṇṭhika-Vijayāditya (V) and others, fighting for supremacy and oppressing the people like Rākshasas; then Chālukya-Bhīma "slew Rājamayya in battle, made Kaṇṭhika-Vijayāditya and Yuddhamalla go to foreign country and despatched to the abode of death many others who, though respectable kings, had shown themselves puffed up by evil conduct and were causing distress to the country." Another record[14] says that Bhīma (Chālukya-Bhīma II) ruled for 12 years (A.D. 935-46) after having extirpated Yuddhamalla and other claimants to the throne. The Kalachumbarru inscription[15] of Amma II says that Chālukya-Bhīma II slew the glorious Rājamayya, the mighty Dhaḷaga the fierce Tāta Bikki (or Tāta-Vikyana, *i.e.* Tāta Vikramāditya), Bijja always ready for war, the terrible Ayyapa (the Nolamba king), the army of Govinda (Govinda IV Rāshṭrakūṭa), Lova-Bikki who was the ruler of the Choḷas, and Yuddhamalla. Western Gaṅga records[16] refer to a struggle between the Nolamba king Ayyapa and Mahendra (*i.e.* Chālukya-Bhīma II).

Chālukya-Bhīma II was also known as Bhīma, Rāja-Bhīma and Vishṇuvardhana. He bore the *virudas Sarvalokāśraya, Tribhuvanāṅkuśa, Rājamārtaṇḍa* and *Gaṇḍa-Mahendra.* One of his feudatories was Vijjaya of the Pānara dynasty. An important official was the Velanāṇḍu chief Malliya. Chālukya-Bhīma II had several sons, *viz.* Amma II (born of Lokamahādevī), Dānārṇava (born of Aṅkidevī) and Kāma. Of these Amma II, who was younger than Dānārṇava, became king (probably because he was the son of the chief queen) after his father's death in Śaka 867 corresponding to A.D. 946.

Amma II, who became *yuvarāja* at the age of 8 and king at 12, was also known by the name Vijayāditya and bore the *virudas*

Rājamahendra, Tribhuvanāṅkuśa and *Samastabhuvanāśraya*. There is a tradition which connects the foundation of the city Rājamahendrī or Rājamahendrapura (which probably became the capital or a secondary capital of the later Eastern Chālukyas) with a Chālukya king named Vijayāditya-Mahendra. This king seems to have been no other than Amma II who was known both as Vijayāditya and Rājamahendra. He married the daughter of Nṛipakāma, lord of Saras or Kolanu (Colair lake) in Godāvarī District. Durgarāja, great-grandson of the celebrated warrior Paṇḍaraṅga, was the king's general. His minister was Kuppanayya (son of Tūrkkiya-Yajvan) who was also known as Vipranārāyaṇa. Amma II is described as lord of both Veṅgī and Kalinga and is known to have made grants of lands in the Bārupunāṇḍu-*vishaya* in Elāmañchi-Kaliṅga, *i.e.* the Yellamanchili tract of Viśākhapatnam District. One of his records refers to the *yuvarāja* Ballāladeva Velābhaṭa, surnamed Boḍḍiya, son of Pammavā of the Paṭṭavardhinī family. At the request of Chāmekā (a courtesan loved by the king) of the same family, the king granted a village in favour of the Jain temple of Sarvalokāśraya Jinavallabha. He is also known to have made gifts to the Jain temples at Vijayavāṭikā (Bezwāda). One of his grants was in favour of the temple of Śiva Samastabhuvanāśraya built by Narendramṛigarāja at Vijayavāṭa (Bezwāda).

After Amma II had ruled for eleven years, *i.e.* about A.D. 956, he was driven out of the Veṅgī country by Bādapa, son of king Yuddhamalla. Bādapa became king with the help of the Rāshṭrakūṭa king Karṇa or Kannara, *i.e.* Kṛisha III (*c.* A.D. 939-67), and Amma II proceeded to the Kaliṅga country (Elāmañchi-Kaliṅga) owing to Kṛishṇa's (Kṛishṇa III Rāshṭrakūṭa) wrath against him. Shortly afterwards, Amma II regained his kingdom.

Bādapa styled himself Vijayāditya and *Samastabhuvanāśraya*. One of his officers appears to have been Gaṇḍanārāyaṇa, son of Nṛipakāma of Saras (father-in-law of Amma II). This Gaṇḍanārāyaṇa, who was a famous archer, earned the appellation Kārmukārjuna and Satyavallaṭa.

Bādapa was succeeded by his younger brother *Mahārājādhirāja* Tāla (II), surnamed Vishṇuvardhana. His minister was Kuppanayya, son of Makariyarāja and grandson of Kalivarman of the family of Pallavamalla (probably king Nandivarman of Kāñchī). Tāla was slain in battle after a short reign by Amma II, who was slain in turn by his elder brother Dānārṇava in A.D. 970. Amma's death was avenged by his wife's brother Jaṭā Choḍa-Bhīma who defeated and killed Dānārṇava in A.D. 973 and made himself king of Veṅgī. The sons of Dānārṇava went into exile at the Choḷa court until Rājarāja conquered Veṅgī for them from Jaṭā Choḍa-Bhīma in A.D. 999.[17]

The inscriptions of the descendants of Dānārṇava do not recognise the rule of Bādapa and his successors. They record that "after Dānārṇava, through the evil action of fate, the country of Veṅgī was without a ruler for 27 years (c. A.D. 973-99), after which the son of king Dāna (Dānārṇava), that glorious Śaktivarman who resembled the king of gods, having overcome the enemies by force of his valour, protected the earth for 12 years (c. A.D. 999-1011)". Śaktivarman, also called Chālukya-Nārāyaṇa, Chālukya-chandra and Vishṇuvardhana, is said to have risen to fame even in his youth by his victory in a battle with the Choḷas (probably the Telugu-Choḍas). He put to flight one Badyema-Mahārāja and killed Choḷa-Bhīma (*i.e.* the Telugu-Choḍa chief, Jaṭā Choḍa-Bhīma). As Bhīma is also said to have been killed by Rājarāja I, it is clear that Śaktivarman joined Rājarāja I in his campaign against Veṅgī in A.D. 999. Jaṭā Choḍa-Bhīma was defeated and killed, and Śaktivarman became the ruler of Veṅgī in that year.

GENERAL REFERENCES

A. S. Altekar—*The Rāshṭrakūṭas and their Times.*
J. F. Fleet—I.A., XX; *Bombay Gazetteer,* I, ii.
D. C. Ganguly—*The Eastern Chālukyas.*
B. V. Krishna Rao—*JAHRS,* X. 16.
H. C. Ray—*Dynastic History of Northern India,* Vol. I.
R. Sewell—*The Historical Inscriptions of Southern India.*
N. Venkataramanayya—*The Eastern Chālukyas of Veṅgī; The Chālukyas of Le (Ve)mulavāḍa.*

II. THE EASTERN GAṄGAS (c. A.D. 750-1000)

The Early Eastern Gaṅgas of Kaliṅganagara were rulers of a small territory in Srikākulam District. At a later date, the members of a branch of this family, who are usually called the 'Later Eastern Gaṅgas' but may be styled the 'Greater or Imperial Gaṅgas', extended the Gaṅga power over wide regions of the coastal area from the lower course of the Bhāgīrathī in the north-east to that of the Godāvarī in the south-west. The history of the Eastern Gaṅgas till the middle of the eighth century has already been narrated.[18]

1. *Later Members of the Early Gaṅga Family*

Of the later rulers of the Early Gaṅga dynasty mention may be made of Rājendra-varman I (who seems to have been the successor of Devendra-varman II, c. A.D. 747-52) and his son Anantavarman II known from records dated in the Gaṅga years 284 (A.D. 780-82) and 304 (A.D. 800-02).[19] Ananta-varman II was succeeded by his brother Devendra-varman III who issued charters in the Gaṅga years 308 (A.D. 804-06) and 310 (A.D. 806-08).[20] The successor of Devendra-varman III was Rājendra-varman II, son of the former's brother Ananta-varman II. King Rājendra-varman II is known from his records with dates ranging between the Gaṅga years 313 (A.D. 809-11) and 342 (A.D. 838-40).[21] This king was succeeded by his cousin Satya-varman who was a son of Devendra-varman III and issued a charter in the Gaṅga year 351 (A.D. 847-49).[22] The next three rulers appear to have been Ananta-varman III (Gaṅga year 358), another son of Devendra-varman III, Bhūpendra-varman Mārasiṁha,[23] and his son Devendra-varman IV who issued the Cheedivalasa grant in the Gaṅga year 397 (A.D. 893-895).[24] A grant issued by the son of a king named Devendra-varman in the year 393 (A.D. 889-91) has been recently published.[25] This king's name has been taken to be Manujendra-varman, although the reading intended may be Rājendra-varman.

No definite history of the Eastern Gaṅgas is available for about a century after Devendra-varman IV. The earliest records of the Greater Gaṅgas have to be assigned to the close of the tenth century. There is some evidence to show that during this century, the Gaṅga kingdom was split up into five tiny principalities, mostly under different branches of the royal family. One of these appears to have been under the Gaṅga house of Śvetaka and another was probably under the Kadambas of Jayantyāpura. During this period the Eastern Chālukyas appear to have encroached upon the Gaṅga territories. King Vijayāditya III (A.D. 844-92) is said to have taken by force the gold of the Gaṅga king of Kaliṅga and received elephants as tribute from that country. Eastern Chālukya influence seems to have been at the root of the introduction of the Śaka era in the land that had previously used the era of the Gaṅgas themselves.

2. *Rise of the Greater Gaṅgas*

The earliest definite and undisputed date in the history of the Greater Gaṅgas is the 9th of April, 1038 A.D.[26] when Vajrahasta-Ananta-varman, father of Rājarāja and grandfather of the great Ananta-varman Choḍagaṅga, was crowned. The records of Vajrahasta and his son as well as the earlier ones of his grandson give the following information about the early history of this branch of the Gaṅga family.[27] In the Ātreya *gotra* and the Gaṅga family (a Brāhmaṇa family according to Muslim chroniclers) was born Guṇamahārṇava who acquired the glory of *sāmrājya;* his son Vajrahasta united the earth which had been divided into five kingdoms and ruled for 44 years; the next rulers were his three sons, *viz.* Guṇḍama (3 years), Kāmārṇava (35 years) and Vinayāditya (3 years); thereafter Kāmārṇava's son Vajrahasta-Aniyaṅkabhīma became king and ruled for 35 years; he was followed by his three sons, *viz.* Kāmārṇava (6 months) who married Vinayamahādevī of the Vaidumba family (holding sway in the land about Arcot, Cuddappa and Nellore Districts from the ninth to the thirteenth century), Guṇḍama (3 years) and Madhukāmārṇava (19 years). Vajrahasta-Ananta-varman, who was crowned in A.D. 1038, was the son of Kāmārṇava by the Vaidumba princess. This account evidently suggests that Guṇamahārṇava was the first king of this branch of the Gaṅga family, that the Gaṅga kingdom had been divided into five principalities apparently owing to the weakness of the central government, and that Guṇamahārṇava's son Vajrahasta succeeded in reuniting the diverse units under his sole sway. But though this account of the rise of the Greater Gaṅgas is not altogether improbable, at least in regard to the broad outline, it has to be noted that the tradition recorded in the later records[28] of the family, from the latter part of the reign of Ananta-varman Choḍagaṅga, is somewhat different.

The later account represents the Gaṅga family as a branch of the lunar dynasty and reminds us of the fabricated genealogy of the Pallavas, Eastern Chālukyas and others. It traces the descent of the family from Ananta (Vishṇu), Brahman born of Vishṇu's navel, his mind-born son Atri (the *gotrarshi* of the Gaṅga family), and Atri's eye-born son Śaśāṅka (Moon). From the moon to Yayāti's son Turvaśu, the Puranic account of the lunar dynasty is followed. It is then said that Turvaśu had, through the favour of the goddess Gaṅgā, a son named Gāṅgeya whose descendants were known as Gaṅga. The seventeenth descendant of Gāṅgeya, as enumerated in the list, was Kolāhala (also called Ananta-varman) who is said to have built Kolāhalapura (modern Kolār in Mysore) in the Gaṅgavāḍi *vishaya*. Here is an attempt to trace the descent of the Eastern Gaṅgas of Orissa from the Western Gaṅgas of Mysore, who however claimed to have belonged to the Kāṇvāyana *gotra* and the solar dynasty of Ikshvāku.[29] Kolāhala's son was Virochana in whose lineage, after 81 kings had ruled at Kolāhalapura, flourished Vīrasiṁha. Vīrasiṁha's son Kāmārṇava presented his own territory to his paternal uncle and set out to conquer the earth with his four brothers, *viz.* Dānārṇava, Guṇārṇava, Mārasiṁha and Vajrahasta. He came to Mount Mahendra in Kaliṅga (in Ganjām District) and worshipped the god Gokarṇasvāmin (Gokarṇeśvara). Through the god's favour, Kāmārṇava obtained the *Vṛishabha-lāñchhana* (bull crest) and the insignia of sovereignty. He then took possession of the Kaliṅga country after having defeated Śabarāditya and ruled for

36 years at Jantāvura (Dantapura or Jayantyāpura?). He was succeeded by his brother Dānārṇava, who ruled for 40 years, while to his other brothers were assigned the districts called *Ambavāḍi-vishaya* (Ambavalli in Parlākimedi), Sodāmaṇḍala (Soda in Parlākimedi) and Varāhavartanī (Tekkali-Chicacole area). Dānārṇava's son Kāmārṇava, who ruled for 50 years, built a city named Nagara and a temple of Īśa (Śiva) under the name Madhukeśa. His son Raṇārṇava ruled for five years and was succeeded by his two sons, *viz.* Vajrahasta (15 years) and Kāmārṇava (19 years). The son and successor of this Kāmārṇava was Guṇārṇava, who is said to have ruled for 27 years and is apparently the same as Guṇamahārṇava mentioned in the earlier account as the founder of the Greater Gaṅga family. But in the present account the successor of Guṇārṇava (Guṇamahārṇava) is said to have been his son Potāṅkuśa (15 years), who was himself succeeded by his brother's son Kaligalāṅkuśa (12 years), followed by Potāṅkuśa's brothers Guṇḍama (7 years), Kāmārṇava (25 years) and Vinayāditya (3 years). It has been suggested that this Kāmārṇava and Vinayāditya are mentioned in the Conjeeveram inscription of Jaṭā Choḍa-Bhīma, dated A.D. 982, as having been killed by that chief.[30] The next king was Kāmārṇava's son Vajrahasta who is the same as Vajrahasta-Aniyaṅkabhīma of the first account. It will be seen presently that we are on surer grounds from this reign. The account of the predecessors of this king up to Guṇārṇava (Guṇamahārṇava) is extremely doubtful at least in regard to details, while the tradition about the earlier history of the family, not found in the earlier account, seems to have been entirely fabricated. Some scholars find in the reference to the construction of the city called Nagara a historical allusion to the foundation of Kaliṅganagara. This is impossible in view of the fact that the builder of Nagara is placed about eight generations before a king who was crowned in A.D. 1038, while the city of Kaliṅganagara is known to have existed at least as early as the sixth century A.D.

If Vajrahasta-Aniyaṅkabhīma (35 years) was succeeded by his three sons, Kāmārṇava (6 months), Guṇḍama (3 years) and Madhukāmārnava (19 years) who was followed by Vajrahasta-Anantavarman, crowned in A.D. 1038, the regnal periods of these kings may have been as follows: Vajrahasta-Aniyaṅkabhīma, A.D. 980-1015; Kāmārṇava, A.D. 1015-16; Guṇḍama, A.D. 1016-19; Madhukāmārṇava, A.D. 1019-38. This chronology appears to be supported by epigraphic evidence. To Vajrahasta-Aniyaṅkabhīma (son of Kāmārṇava), A.D. 980-1015, no doubt is to be assigned the Ponduru grant issued by king Vajrahasta, son of Kāmārṇava, in the Gaṅga year 500 (A.D. 996-998).[31] The Mandasa grant of the Kadamba chief Dharmakheḍi, son of Bhīmakheḍi, was issued during the reign of the

Gaṅga king Ananta-varman in the Saka year *navaśatakasaptaraśa*. *Navaśataka* no doubt indicates 900 and *saptaraśa* is probably a hybrid Sanskrit-Prakrit word standing midway between Sanskrit *saptadasa* and Prakrit *sattarasa* meaning 17.[32] This epigraph, dated in Śaka 917 (A.D. 995) and referring to the Gaṅga king Ananta-varman, suggests that Vajrahasta-Aniyaṅkabhīma, like his grandson, was also known as Ananta-varman. The suggestion seems to be supported by the Chicacole grant of the Gaṅga year 526 (A.D. 1022 24) which was issued by the Gaṅga king Madhukāmārṇava represented in the record as the son of Ananta-varman. This king is apparently no other than Madhukāmārṇava who was the son of Vajrahasta-Aniyaṅkabhīma and ruled in A.D. 1019-38. The Kadamba chief Dharmakheḍi, who issued the Mandasa grant in A.D. 995, later issued the Santa-Bommali charter[33] in the Gaṅga year 520 (A.D. 1016-18) during the reign of the Gaṅga king Devendra-varman, son of Ananta-varman (Vajrahasta-Aniyaṅkabhīma). Devendra-varman seems to have been a second name of either Kāmārṇava (A.D. 1015-16) or Guṇḍama (A.D. 1016-19) who were both sons of Vajrahasta-Aniyaṅkabhīma-Ananta-varman.

The later history of the family from Vajrahasta-Ananta-varman (crowned in A.D. 1038), who is styled Vajrahasta III (according to the genealogy given in his own records) or Vajrahasta V (according to the fabricated genealogy found in the later records of his successors) and was the real founder of the family's greatness, will be discussed in the next volume. But we might consider here the plausible suggestion that the rise of the Greater Gaṅgas was a result of the Choḷa expedition against Kaliṅga in the reign of Rājarāja Choḷa (A.D. 985-1016). Rājarāja Choḷa claims to have conquered Kaliṅga some time before A.D. 1003,[34] while his son Rājendra is known to have set up pillars of victory,[35] probably during his father's reign, on Mount Mahendra in Kaliṅga. The omission of Kaliṅga in the list of countries conquered by Rājendra Choḷa's generals shortly before A.D. 1023[36] seems to suggest that the Gaṅga king was then regarded as a subordinate ally of the Choḷas. The Greater Gaṅgas, who gained power probably under the patronage of the Choḷa conquerors, are known to have employed Choḷa officials and contracted matrimonial alliances with the Choḷas. The Vaidumba relative of Vajrahasta-Aniyaṅkabhīma-Ananta-varman might have been Vishṇudeva Duraiaraśan who was a feudatory of Rājarāja Choḷa and is known from an inscription of A.D. 992.[37]

3. *The Gaṅga House of Śvetaka*

Reference has already been made to the rise of the viceregal Gaṅga house of Śvetaka, no doubt at the expense, and owing to the weakness, of the Gaṅga kings of Kaliṅganagara.[38] The earliest known rulers of the Śvetaka house were Jaya-varman (Gaṅga years 100 and 120 falling in A.D. 596-616) and Sāmanta-varman (Gaṅga year 165 or 185). A group of later rulers of Śvetaka were Mahīndra-varman, his son Pṛithvī-varman, and the latter's sons Indra-varman and Dānārṇava. King Bhūpendra-varman, son of Kailāsa, seems to be a later member of the same house which probably continued its separate existence till the last quarter of the eleventh century. The last ruler of the Śvetaka house appears to have been king Devendra-varman mentioned as the overlord of Kadamba Udayāditya, son of Dharmakheḍi, in the Kambakaya grant probably dated in Śaka 1003 (A.D. 1081).[39] He is also known from the Gara inscription[40] of an uncertain date, the Drākshārāma inscription[41] of Kulottuṅga Choḷa's 33rd regnal year (A.D. 1103), and the *Kaliṅgattuparaṇī*. A recently discovered copper-plate grant was issued in Śaka 988 (A.D. 1066) during this king's reign. The Śvetaka house appears to have been completely extirpated by Anantavarman Choḍagaṅga about the close of the eleventh century.

4. *The Kadambas of Jayantyāpura*

We have referred to the Mandasa and Santa-Bommali grants of the Kadamba chief Dharmakheḍi issued during the reigns of Vajrahasta-Aniyaṅkabhīma-Ananta-varman and Devendra-varman (Kāmārṇava or Guṇḍama) in the period A.D. 995-1018. Like their overlords, these Eastern Kadambas appear to have represented a branch of a western ruling house, *viz.* the Kadamba family of the Kanarese country. *Rāṇaka Mahāmaṇḍaleśvara* Dharmakheḍi, son of Bhīmakheḍi and grandson of Niyārṇava, ruled over five districts from his capital at Jayantyāpura. Dharmakheḍi's grandfather Niyārṇava seems to be no other than the *Raṇaka* Niyārṇama mentioned as the father of *Mahādevī* Vijyā in a record of *Rāṇaka* Raṇabhañja (son of Śatrubhañja and grandson of Śilābhañja) who ruled Khiñjali-*maṇḍala* from Dhṛitipura. Reference has already been made to Udayāditya who was a son of Dharmakheḍi and a feudatory of Gaṅga Devendra-varman, probably of Śvetaka, and issued the Kambakaya grant in A.D. 1081. A Parlākimedi inscription[42] of the time of Vajrahasta (crowned A.D. 1038) refers to a feudatory named Ugrakheḍi of the Nidusanti clan and the Kadamba family. This epigraph also contains a later record of *Rāṇaka* Udayakheḍi who is possibly the same as Udayāditya of the Kambakaya grant. A recently discovered copper-plate grant of A.D. 1066 mentions Bhīmakheḍi, son of Dharmakheḍi, as a feudatory of Gaṅga Devendra-varman, probably of Śvetaka. Nothing is known about these Eastern Kadambas after the eleventh century A.D.

III. THE SOMAVAMŚĪS

The early history of the Pāṇḍuvaṁśa, also called the family of the Moon (*Somavaṁśa*), which ruled in South Kosala with Śrīpura (modern Sirpur in Raipur District) as the capital, has been already discussed.[43] The rulers of this family were called lords of Kosala, although their records have been mostly found in the western part of this *janapada*.[44] Their early charters had the Vaishṇavite emblem of Garuḍa on their seal while the later ones bore the Śaiva symbol of the couchant bull. Little is known of this family after king Śivagupta (Mahāśivagupta) Bālārjuna, who seems to have flourished at the close of the sixth and the first half of the seventh century A.D.[45] Another group of kings, some of whom bore the names Śivagupta and Mahāśivagupta and had names ending in the word *kesarin* (like some members of the Pāṇḍuvaṁśa), is also known to have claimed descent from the Somavaṁśa (family of the Moon) and suzerainty over Kosala. The records of the early members of this family, which have been found in the Sambalpur tract in the eastern part of the ancient South Kosala country, cannot, however, be assigned to any date earlier than the tenth century. The kings moreover have the distinctive epithet *Trikaliṅgādhipati*, and never claim to have been descended from the Pāṇḍuvaṁśa. The seal of their early records bears not the Garuḍa or the bull emblem but the Gajalakshmī symbol (although they were Śaivas) like that of the Śarabhapurīyas and the Kalachuris. The relations of the Somavaṁśīs under discussion with the earlier ruling families of South Kosala cannot be definitely determined in the present state of insufficient information.

The founder of this later Somavaṁśa was king Śivagupta. His records have not yet been discovered but he has been assigned imperial epithets in the records of his son. That the later members did not regard him as the founder of the family seems to indicate that his son and not he was the real founder of the family's greatness. His reign may be roughly assigned to the first half of the tenth century (c. A.D. 915-35). It has been suggested that he was possibly the Kosala king from whom Mugdhatuṅga, the Kalachuri king of Tripurī (in Ḍāhala or the Jubbulpore region), claims to have conquered a locality called Pālī which has been identified with a village of that name near Ratanpur in the Bilāspur District. If the early members of the Somavaṁśa actually held sway over Chhattisgarh, they must have been gradually ousted from that area by the Kalachuris of Ḍāhala, although permanent occupation of Chhattisgarh by the Kalachuris has to be assigned to the eleventh century.

Śivagupta was succeeded by his son Janamejaya Mahābhavagupta I *alias* Dharma-kandarpa (*c.* A.D. 935-70) whose earliest and latest records (dated in the regnal years 3 and 34) were issued from Suvarṇapura (modern Sonpur in the old Sonpur State). Some other charters of the king were issued from such places as Murasīma (modern Mursinga in the old Patna State) and Ārāma (supposed to have been a pleasure garden near Suvarṇapura). The king who was a devout worshipper of Maheśvara (Śiva) is sometimes specifically mentioned as king of Kosala, and some of the villages granted by him are said to have been situated in Kosaladeśa. According to the Bhuvaneswar inscription of Uddyotakesarin, Mahābhavagupta I captured the royal fortune of the king of the Oḍra country, roughly corresponding to the lower part of modern Orissa, which was in this age under the rulers of the Kara dynasty. This king, like other members of the family, called himself "the lord of Trikaliṅga."[46] As has been pointed out above, it is not definitely known whether the name Trikaliṅga indicated three countries *(e.g.* Kosala, Kaliṅga, and Utkala or Oḍra) collectively, or a particular tract of land lying probably between Kaliṅga and South Kosala. But, as has been indicated above, the country of Utkala or Oḍra was in this age comprised in the dominions of the Karas with whom the Somavaṁśī monarch may have come into conflict. The exact boundaries of the dominions of Janameyaja Mahābhavagupta I cannot be determined. Kalachuri Lakshmaṇarāja, who ruled about the third quarter of the tenth century and claimed to have defeated the lord of Kosala, possibly came into conflict with this king.

An important official of the king was his minister for war and peace, named Malladatta, who was the son of Dhāradatta and served the Somavaṁśī ruler at least from the sixth to the thirty-first year of his reign. Malladatta was succeeded in the office by a second Dhāradatta who was probably his son. The history of the ministerial family of the Dattas, which solves a number of problems in the genealogy of the Somavaṁśī rulers, illustrates the interesting ancient Indian custom of the hereditary appointment of ministers referred to in the Udayagiri inscription of Chandra-gupta II of the Gupta dynasty.

Janamejaya Mahābhavagupta I was succeeded, some time after his thirty-fourth regnal year, by his son Yayāti Mahāśivagupta I, who assumed the title Paramamāheśvara like his father, and seems to have ruled in the second half of the tenth century (*c.* A.D. 970-1000). The earlier records of this king were issued from Vinītapura which has been identified with modern Binka in the old Sonpur State; but the charters dated in his twenty-fourth and twenty-eighth regnal years are found to have been issued from Yayātinagara on the Mahānadī, a city apparently founded by, and named after, the king. Some writers believe that Yayātinagara was the name given by king Yayāti Mahāśivagupta I to Vinītapura. His charters, like those of his father, often record gifts of land specifically in Kosala or Dakshiṇa Kosala, although an inscription[47] of his ninth regnal year is known to record the grant of a village in South Tosala which formed an integral part of the dominions of the Karas. In one of his charters, an official of the king is specially mentioned as the *Sandhivigrahin* of Kosaladeśa. Dhāradatta II, who served Janamejaya as minister for war and peace during the later years of his reign, continued in office till at least the twenty-fourth regnal year of Yayāti, and was later succeeded as minister for war and peace by another member of the Datta family, named Siṁhadatta, who was the son of Harshadatta and probably a grandson of Dhāradatta II.

The latest known record of Yayāti Mahāśivagupta I is dated in his twenty-eighth regnal year. The later records of the king describe him as having captured 32 big elephants and defeated a certain ruler named Ajapāla of whom nothing is known.

A short supplement, comprising three verses, engraved at the end of a charter of Yayāti Mahāśivagupta,[48] tells us that a king of Kosala of the lunar dynasty *(soma-kula)*, named Svabhāvatuṅga, defeated the Chaidyas or Kalachuris of Ḍāhala (modern Jubbulpore region). It seems further to say that certain lieutenants of the Chedi (Kalachuri) king, headed by Bhaṭṭa-Peḍi, were honoured by their master for invading the Somavaṁśī kingdom and carrying away a number of women, but that the Somavaṁśī monarch, aided by a general named Lakshmaṇa, pursued the Chedi forces into the enemy's territory, killed Bhaṭṭa-Peḍi and rescued the captured women. It also describes how Svabhāvatuṅga's son (whose name is not mentioned) cared little for the Chaidya (Kalachuri king) named Durgarāja and burnt the land of Ḍāhala (the Chedi country) rendering it depopulated.

As the only Somavaṁśī king mentioned in these supplementary verses is Svabhāvatuṅga, it may be regarded as another name of Yayāti Mahāśivagupta I himself. If this identity be presumed, we get valuable information regarding the political relations between the Somavaṁśīs and the Kalachuris in the latter half of the tenth century A.D.

The unpublished Baud plates of the Kara queen Pṛithvīmahādevī *alias* Tribhuvanamahādevī II, dated in the year 158 of the Kara era, state that she was the daughter of king Svabhāvatuṅga of the lunar dynasty of Kosala, who may be none other than the Somavaṁśī monarch mentioned above, and therefore identical with Yayāti Mahāśivagupta I. We have seen above how this Somavaṁśī king granted in his ninth regnal year a village in the Kara territory. Another inscription of the same king records the grant of a village in the Gandhaṭapāṭī (modern Gandharadhi in the old Baud State) *maṇḍala* (district), apparently named after Śatrubhañja I Gandhaṭa of the Bhañja dynasty of Dhṛitipura, which owed allegiance to the Karas. This seems to suggest that it was Yayāti Mahāśivagupta I who was responsible for driving the descendants of Śatrubhañja's son Raṇabhañja from Dhṛitipura in Upper Orissa to Vañjulvaka in the Ganjām region.[49] These two facts, pointing to the success of Yayāti Mahāśivagupta I against the Karas, do not appear to be unconnected with his daughter's accession to the Kara throne which, as noted above, was a disputed one. It is very probable that Pṛithvīmahādevī succeeded in occupying the Kara kingdom with the active help of her father Yayāti Mahāśivagupta I. Possibly in connection with his successful campaign against his daughter's rivals for the Kara throne the Somavaṁśī monarch granted the village of Chandragrāma in Dakshiṇa-Tosala, identified with modern Chandgan, about 32 miles from Cuttack.[50] It may be pointed out in this connection that the year 158 of the Kara era, when Pṛithvīmahādevī was on the throne, does not appear to have been far removed from the ninth regnal year of Yayāti Mahāśivagupta I.[51]

1. *EI*, VI. 208.
2. *Eastern Chālukyas*, 44.
3. *EI*, *VI*. 242.
4. *EI*, XXII. 105.
5. Some scholars, however, identify it with modern Cunbum in Kurnool District.
6. *EI*, IX. 39.
7. *EI*, XVIII. 107.
8. Some scholars interpret *raṭṭeśa-saṁchodita* as "ordered by the Rāshṭrakūṭa king" whom they identify with Amoghavarsha I. They hold that after the death of this king, Vijayāditya threw off his allegiance to the Rāshṭrakūṭas and thus war ensued with Kṛishṇa II.
9. *ARSIE*, 1913, p. 131.
10. *Ibid*, 1909, p. 108.
11. *Ibid*, 1924, pp. 10, 98.
12. *Ibid*, 1917, p. 117.
13. *EI*, IX. 47.
14. *IA*, VII. 18.
15. *EI*, VII. 177.
16. *EC*, VI. 49.
17. This is based on the reconstruction of the history of Jaṭā Choḍa-Bhīma by Dr. N. Venkataramanayya (*PIHC*, III. 605 ff). See now the same author's *The Eastern Chālukyas of Veṅgī*, pp. 200 ff. Cf. also B.V. Krishna Rao, *JAHRS*, X. 16.
18. See Vol. III, pp. 215 ff.
19. *EI*, III. 18.
20. *EI*, XVIII. 312.
21. *Bh. List*, No. 2051.
22. *IA*, XIV. 11.

23. He is said to have been the son of Vajrī (Vajrahasta). See *Bh. List*, p. 386.
24. *JASL*, XVIII. 77.
25. *JAHRS*, XX. 161.
26. *Bh. List*, No. 1090.
27. *Ibid*, No. 1091.
28. *Ibid*, No. 1103. See *EI*, XXVIII. 235 ff; *ARSIE*, 1935-6, pp. 61-3.
29. There is absolutely no evidence in favour of the conjecture that the Gaṅgas were the descendants of the ancient people called Gangaridae by classical writers. For the Indian name of the Gangaridae, see Sircar, 'The City of Gaṅgā', *PIHC*, 1947, pp. 91-98.
30. The two kings, who are also mentioned in the earlier account, lost their lives respectively about A.D. 977 and 980. They probably fought with the Telugu-Choḍa king on behalf of the Eastern Chālukyas.
31. *JKHRS*, I. 219.
32. The expression is usually taken to be a combination of the words *sapta* (7) and *rasa* (6). In that case the date may be Śaka 913 (A.D. 991). But I have no doubt that *saptarasa* stands for 17. See *JKHRS*, I. 219-21.
33. *Bh. List*. No. 2053.
34. *EC*, X. Mb. 123.
35. *EI*, VI. 347.
36. *EI*, IX. 229.
37. Sewell, *HISI*, 54.
38. See Vol. III, p. 217.
39. *JKHRS*, I. 219.
40. *ARSIE*, 1932-3, pp. 56-7. If the inscription is really dated in Śaka 1005 (A.D. 1083) and in the 7th regnal year of the king, his name *Devendravarman* may be regarded as a mistake for *Anantavarman* (i.e. Chodagaṅga, son of Rāja-rāja I Devendra-varman, c. A.D. 1070-78).
41. *EI*, XXII. 138 ff.
42. *EI*, III. 223.
43. Vol. III, pp. 220 ff.
44. A recently discovered record, dated in the 57th regnal year of Bālārjuna, contains the names of two villages which have been located in the old Kalahandi State. This probably suggests that the rule of the *Pāṇḍuvaṁśīs* extended over the eastern part of the *janapada* as well (*JKHRS*, I. 265-6). In *EI*, XXVIII. 322-3, the villages have been located in Sambalpur District, Orissa.
45. Vol. III, p. 222.
46. The published eye-copy (*JRASB*, L. XIII. 74) of the Bhuvaneswar Inscription (1.2) suggests the reading of a word in a damaged section as *triliṅg-ādhipa* in connection with this king. It is uncertain whether Janamejaya is himself called the lord of Triliṅga or one who defeated the Triliṅga king.
47. *EI*, III. 351; Misra, *Dynasties of Medieval Orissa*, pp. 63 ff.
48. It was originally published in *JPASB*, 1905, pp. 14-16. See now *JASL*, XIX. 117 ff.
49. *IHQ*, XXVIII. 227; also cf. above, Ch. IV. III. 2.
50. Misra, *Dyn. Med. Orissa*, p. 68.
51. The Daspalla plates of Śatrubhañja, recently edited in *EI*, offer astronomical details suggesting the beginning of the era in A.D. 831. Cf. *IHQ*, XXIX. 148 ff. [This is not compatible with the view of Kara chronology adopted above on p. 63. Cf. also p. 79, fn. 33.—Ed.]

CHAPTER VII

SOUTH INDIA

I. THE PALLAVAS

1. *Danti-varman and Nandi-varman III*

Danti-varman, whose inscriptions range from his second to his fifty-first regnal year and cover a large part of the Pallava dominions, was the son of Nandi-varman II Pallavamalla by Revā (Revakā), the Rāshṭrakūṭa princess. Danti-varman, who was thus the grandson of Dantidurga Rāshṭrakūṭa, married a Kadamba princess. About A.D. 804 Rāshṭrakūṭa Govinda III invaded Kāñchī which had earlier been attacked by his predecessor, Dhruva. We do not know how the relations between the Pallavas and the Rāshṭrakūṭas changed for the worse. An inscription in Tamil of Danti-varman in the Pārthasārathi temple, Triplicane (Madras), describes him as "the ornament of the Pallava family," belonging to the Bhāradvāja *gotra*, the *gotra* of the previous Pallava sovereigns as well. This record proves the antiquity of that temple which was built by an earlier Pallava ruler. The reign of Danti-varman witnessed a recrudescence of the Pāṇḍya aggression, and Varaguṇa I occupied the Kāverī region. The inscriptions of Danti-varman are significantly absent from that region from his sixteenth regnal year to the end of his reign, while some records of the Pāṇḍya king are found there. The Bāṇas were feudatory to Danti-varman.

Danti-varman's son, Nandi-varman III, known by his conspicuous surname of Teḷḷāṟṟerinda, worshipped Śiva, patronised Tamil literary savants like Perundevanār, author of the *Bhāratavеṇbā*, and married Śaṅkhā, the daughter of Amoghavarsha I Rāshṭrakūṭa. Nandi-varman's other surnames like Avani-nāraṇan, Varatuṅgan and Ugrakopan are mentioned in a contemporary Tamil work, the *Nandikkaḷambakam*. It throws a flood of light on his military activities—his achievements at Teḷḷāṟu (North Arcot District) and several other battle-fields. It is clear that Nandi-varman III heroically rolled back the swelling tide of Pāṇḍya aggression, which had come to a head during his predecessor's reign; he inflicted a decisive defeat on the enemy at Teḷḷāṟu and pursued him, it is said, to the banks of the Vaigai. The battle of Teḷḷāṟu must have been fought early in the reign of Nandi-varman, seeing that it is described in his Velūrpāḷaiyam plates issued in his sixth regnal year. The literary work referred to above mentions him as the ruler of the

Kāverī region, the Koṅgudeśa, etc., and enumerates his chief cities Kāñchī, Mallai (Mahābalipuram) and Mayilai (Mylapore, Madras). Like Danti-varman, Nandi-varman was the overlord of the Bāṇas.

2. *Nṛipatuṅga-varman and Aparājita*

Nṛipatuṅga-varman, the son of Nandi-varman III by the Rāshṭrakūṭa princess, maintained the integrity of his empire and received the allegiance of the Bāṇas. His inscriptions are found as far south as Pudukkoṭṭai. His warlike policy towards the Pāṇḍyas was successful. His Bāhūr (Vahur, near Pondicherry) plates record his victory over them on the banks of the Arichit (Ariśil or Araśalār, a distributary of the Kāverī). This battle is regarded by Jouveau Dubreuil to have taken place at Kuḍamūkku or Kumbhakonam. The Bāhūr plates mention the grant of three villages by the minister of Nripatuṅga-varman in the eighth regnal year to a *Vidyāsthāna* or Vedic college as a *Vidyābhogam i.e.*, for the promotion of learning, and as *Brahmadeya*. According to one interpretation of verses 24 to 26, the college made provision for the study of fourteen divisions of learning, *viz.* four Vedas, six Aṅgas, Mīmāṁsā, Nyāya, Purāna, and Dharmaśāstra. Whatever may be the correct interpretation of the word in question *viz. chaturddaśa-gana*, there is no doubt that the *Ghatikā* of the earlier period developed into the *Vidyāsthāna* of the ninth century A.D. In the sphere of education, as in other fields, the Pallavas anticipated the great achievements of the Cholas of Tanjore and Gaṅgaikoṇḍacholapuram.

Aparājita is the last known prince belonging to the imperial line of the Pallavas. His name is connected with a great victory and a decisive defeat. The campaign against the Pāṇḍyas culminated in their defeat at Śrīpuṛambiyam near Kumbhakonam about A.D. 880. The victorious Pallavas were aided by their feudatories Pṛithvīpati I (Western Gaṅga) and Āditya I (Choḷa). "At the head of the great battle of Śrīpuṛambiyam this hero (Pṛithvīpati I) quickly defeated Varaguṇa II, the lord of the Pāṇḍyas, and having, at the expense of his own life, secured that his friend was Aparājita (unconquered) in fact as in name, he ascended to heaven."[1] The battle of Śrīpuṛambiyam or Tiruppuṛambiyam is an epic event in South Indian history. The imperial position of the Pāṇḍyas was completely lost, but their imperial successors were not the Pallavas, who were soon after overthrown by the Choḷas under Āditya I. At his hands the victorious Aparājita suffered defeat about A.D. 893 and the victor became master of Toṇḍamaṇḍalam.

With Aparājita, the Pallava imperial line came to an end. There were branches of the dynasty like the Nolamba-Pallavas or

Nolambas holding sway over the region called Nolambavāḍi. But in Toṇḍamaṇḍalam, the main theatre of Pallava glory, we find in the thirteenth century a great chieftain named Ko-Peruñjiṅga who defied the Choḷa authority in the days of its decline. He claimed Pallava descent, but we cannot connect him genealogically with the imperial Pallavas.

II. THE CHOḶAS OF TANJORE

1. *Vijayālaya and Āditya I*

The founder of the Choḷa dynasty of Tanjore was Vijayālaya, a feudatory of the Pallavas. His dynasty rose to high eminence and lasted for more than two centuries. Vijayālaya rose to power near Uṟaiyūr, the capital of the Choḷas of the Śaṅgam Age. An inscription at Tiruneḍuṅgaḷam (Tiruchirapalli District) records a gift of land in accordance with the orders of Parakesari Vijayālaya Choḷadeva. The titles Parakesari and Rājakesari were alternately assumed by the Choḷa sovereigns from the time of Vijayālaya. Though he cannot be connected genealogically with the Choḷas of Uṟaiyūr (Karikāla and his successors), his rise in the Uṟaiyūr region is not without significance. He may be assigned to the period, c. A.D. 850-871, and his son and successor Āditya I to c. A.D. 871-907. Vijayālaya captured Tanjore from the Muttaraiyar, who had their headquarters at Śendalai, near Tanjore. They were for long feudatories of the imperial Pallavas and were now under the Pāṇḍyas. As there was hostility and open conflict between the Pallavas and the Pāṇḍyas, Vijayālaya, a feudatory of the Pallavas, felt justified in seizing Tanjore from the Muttaraiyar on behalf of his overlord. It is also probable that he took advantage of the political confusion in the Kāverī region, the borderland between the Pallava and Pāṇḍya kingdoms, in order to promote his own interests. After the conquest of Tanjore, Vijayālaya built a temple there for Durgā; and his successors also were staunch Śaivas. The territory acquired by him extended between the North and South Veḷḷār rivers along the lower course of the Kāverī and the Coleroon.

Āditya I (c. A.D. 871-907), the son and successor of Vijayālaya, took part in the great battle of Śrīpuṟambiyam in which, as mentioned above, the Pāṇḍyas were defeated by his Pallava suzerain. He reaped the fruits of the victory and obtained additions to his territory near Tanjore from the grateful king Aparājita. But Āditya's loyalty did not long endure. Not long afterwards he fought with his overlord and defeated him. An inscription states that in a battle Āditya "pounced upon and slew the Pallava king who was seated on the back of a tall elephant" and that he earned the surname of Kodaṇḍarāma. This event, which may be assigned to about A.D. 893, gave Āditya mastery over Toṇḍamaṇḍalam. Subsequently he conquered the Koṅgudeśa (the districts of Coimbatore and Salem) from the Pāṇḍyas and the Western Gaṅgas probably with the aid of the Chera king, Sthāṇu Ravi, with whom he maintained cordial relations. Āditya is also credited with the seizure of Taḷakāḍ the capital of the Western Gaṅgas. Pṛithvīpati II recognised the overlordship of Āditya, whose kingdom now stretched from Kāḷahasti and Tirukkaḷukkunṛam to Pudukkoṭṭai and Coimbatore and included Taḷakāḍ. Āditya married a Pallava princess and had two sons Parāntaka and Kannaradeva. He built several temples for Śiva. Though the nucleus of the Choḷa kingdom was created by Vijayālaya, the real founder of its power was Āditya I, a prince of striking ability, energy, and wisdom.

2. *Parāntaka I*

Āditya was succeeded by his son Parāntaka who ruled for more than forty-five years (A.D. 907-953). The date of his accession is definitely known and may be said to be the bed-rock of Choḷa chronology. The reign of Parāntaka was an eventful one and he led numerous military campaigns with the help of his allies, *viz.* the Western Gaṅgas, the Kerala ruler and the Koḍumbāḷūr chiefs. By these successful wars he built up the Choḷa Empire which attained the pinnacle of fame and glory under his successors.

The most important among the conquests of Parāntaka was Madura, and it was achieved gradually during the first half of his long reign. Soon after his accession to the throne he raided Madura and won the title of *Madhurāntaka* or destroyer of Madura. In his third regnal year he assumed the title of *Maduraikoṇḍa* or captor of Madura. Consequent on his defeat, the Pāṇḍya king, Rājasiṁha II, sought and obtained the aid of the Ceylonese ruler. About A.D. 915 a famous battle was fought at Veḷḷūr (south-west of Madura) where the Pāṇḍyas and the Sinhalese were beaten. A third campaign effected the expulsion of Rājasiṁha about A.D. 920, and three years later Parāntaka described himself as *Maduraiyum Īḻamum Koṇḍa* or captor of Madura and Ceylon. But towards the close of his reign, he failed in his attempt to obtain from the Ceylonese ruler the insignia of Pāṇḍya royalty left with him by Rājasiṁha, who had fled to Kerala. The conquest of Madura was, however, by no means easy, and Parāntaka was engaged throughout the latter half of his reign in reducing the conquered country to order and obedience. In subduing Madura, he received the help of the Kerala ruler and of the Koḍumbāḷūr chiefs.

About A.D. 915 the Bāṇas were 'uprooted' by Parāntaka with the aid of Pṛithvīpati II, the Western Gaṅga ruler, upon whom were conferred the titles of *Bāṇādhirāja, Hastimalla* and *Śembiyan Māvalivāṇarāyan*. About A.D. 915 Parāntaka also defeated the Vaidumbas of the Renāṇḍu country who were the allies of the Bāṇas. The coalition was perhaps headed by Rāshṭrakūṭa Kṛishna II, and the decisive victory was won by Parāntaka in a battle at Vallāla (Tiruvallam, N. Arcot District). Parāntaka smashed the remains of the Pallava power and conquered the country as far north as Nellore. By these successive victories, he enlarged his empire which extended from the North Peṇṇār to Cape Comorin and was bounded on the west by the Chera and Western Gaṅga kingdoms.

Not long after the Choḷas had thus extended their power far and wide, the Rāshṭrakūṭa king Kṛishṇa III invaded Toṇḍamaṇḍalam with the support of Būtuga II, the Western Gaṅga chief. A decisive engagement took place at Takkolam in A.D. 949 in which the Choḷas were completely defeated and the crown-prince Rājāditya lost his life. It was the death knell of the imperialist ambitions of Parāntaka, who lost Toṇḍamaṇḍalam as well as his control over the Pāṇḍya country.

Eleven queens of Parāntaka are mentioned in his inscriptions, and one of them was a Kerala princess. He had five sons—Rājāditya, Gaṇḍarāditya, Arikulakesari, Uttamaśīli and Ariñjaya, the last being the son of the Kerala princess. Parāntaka had also two daughters. He was devoted to Śiva and constructed many temples. He provided the Naṭarāja shrine at Chidambaram with a gold roof. Some of his titles have been mentioned; his other titles are *Parakesari-varman, Vīranārāyaṇa, Devendra Chakravartī, Paṇḍitavatsala* (one fond of learned men), *Kuñjaramalla* or wrestler with elephants, and *Śūraśūlāmaṇi* or the crest-jewel of heroes.

3. *The Rāshṭrakūṭa Interregnum in Toṇḍamaṇḍalam*

The Rāshṭrakūṭa invasion of Toṇḍamaṇḍalam was not a bolt from the blue. It was the result of many factors such as the rapid territorial expansion of the Choḷas, the aggressive policy of Parāntaka I towards the Bāṇas and the Vaidumbas, the death of Pṛithvīpati II in A.D. 940, followed by the accession to the Western Gaṅga throne of Būtuga II, the husband of Kṛishṇa III's sister, and above all, the growing power of Kṛishṇa III, the last great Rāshṭrakūṭa ruler who possessed ability and enterprise and aimed at avenging the defeat of Kṛishṇa II at Vallāla and rivalling the achievements in South India of Govinda III, the greatest of the

Rāshṭrakūṭas. The Bāṇas and the Vaidumbas also appealed to Kṛishṇa against the rising tide of Choḷa aggression and imperialism. Parāntaka I was not oblivious of the dangers inherent in his own policy and concentrated on the defences of Toṇḍamaṇḍalam by entrusting its administration to his eldest son, Rājāditya.

Kṛishṇa III's invasion of Toṇḍamaṇḍalam took place some time before A.D. 949, the date of the battle of Takkolam, fixed with reference to the Ātakūr inscription of Butuga II. The Ātakūr record says that "when Kannaradeva was fighting the Choḷa, Būtuga made the howdah battle-field, and aimed at, pierced and killed Rājāditya." Consequently the Choḷas lost the battle, and Būtuga II was lavishly rewarded with grant of territory by his grateful brother-in-law. We have already detailed the consequences of the Choḷa disaster at Takkolam. The Rāshṭrakūṭa occupation of Toṇḍamaṇḍalam must have taken a few years and we have no genuine inscriptions of Kṛishṇa III in Toṇḍamaṇḍalam earlier than A.D. 953. The Rāshṭrakūṭa interregnum must have lasted for at least fifteen years,—A.D. 953 to 968. During this period, over a dozen inscriptions of Kṛishṇa III testify to the activity of the village assemblies at Uttaramerūr, Ukkal, Kāvanūr, Tirukkaḻukkunṛam, Bāhūr, etc. This seems to indicate that the rule of the Rāshṭrakūṭas was not prejudicial to the progress of the Mahāsabhā in Toṇḍamaṇḍalam, the activity of which was characteristic of the reign of Parāntaka I. Several inscriptions of Kṛishṇa found in Toṇḍamaṇḍalam describe him as the captor of Kāñchī and Tanjore. Some records refer to the progress of the Rāshṭrakūṭas southwards through the Choḷa dominions as far as Rāmesvaram, where a pillar of victory is said to have been erected. It is difficult to estimate the truth contained in such statements. Probably there were occasional raids into the southern Choḷa territory. But there are no inscriptions of Kṛishṇa III or of his feudatories, south of Pondicherry. Therefore the Rāshṭrakūṭa interregnum was most probably confined to Toṇḍamaṇḍalam.

4. *Gaṇḍarāditya, Parāntaka II, and Uttama Choḷa*

The interval between the death of Parāntaka I (c. A.D. 953) and the accession of Rājarāja I in A.D. 985 is a confused period in Choḷa history. The dynastic genealogy and chronology during that period are largely uncertain and the course of history is not sufficiently clear. Parāntaka I was succeeded by his second son Gaṇḍarāditya, his eldest son having perished at Takkolam. Gaṇḍarāditya's queen, Śembiyan Mahādevī, who died in A.D. 1001, was a pious and charitable lady fond of building temples and esteemed by all the members of the royal family, including Rājarāja I, who was the brother of

Āditya II and son of Sundara Parāntaka II (son of Gaṇḍarāditya's brother, Ariñjaya). Uttama Choḷa was the son of Gaṇḍarāditya. During the short reign of the latter (A.D. 953-957) the need for recovering Toṇḍamaṇḍalam was not lost sight of. He is regarded as the author of a single hymn on the Chidambaram temple.

Gaṇḍarāditya was succeeded by Ariñjaya and the latter in his turn by Sundara Choḷa or Parāntaka II (A.D. 957-973). He was active against the Pāṇḍyas, who were independent under Vīra Pāṇḍya, and the latter was defeated in spite of the Sinhalese aid he had secured. The Pāṇḍya war led to an expedition to Ceylon. In these military expeditions, the Koḍumbāḷūr chiefs[2] played an important part, and inscriptions portray the active role of prince Āditya II. In spite of the Choḷa success, the Pāṇḍya campaigns were, on the whole, indecisive. But Toṇḍamaṇḍalam was recovered from the Rāshṭrakūṭas. It is significant that Sundara Choḷa died at Kāñchī, and Vānavan Mahādevī, the mother of Rājarāja I, committed *sati*. Another queen of Sundara Choḷa belonged to Kerala. He was a patron of literature, both Tamil and Sanskrit. A little before his death, his son Āditya II was murdered at the instigation of Uttama Choḷa, who coveted the throne, as he belonged to the senior branch of the royal family.

Uttama Choḷa (A.D. 973-985) was the wicked son of his admirable parents, Gaṇḍarāditya and Śembiyan Mahādevī. Toṇḍamaṇḍalam enjoyed peace after its recovery from the Rāshṭrakūṭas. The earliest Choḷa coin is a gold piece belonging to the reign of Uttama Choḷa. Five of his queens are mentioned in his inscriptions. His son was Madhurāntaka Gaṇḍarāditya, but Rājarāja had been made the heir apparent of Uttama Choḷa.

The reign of Rājarāja, which extended beyond the period under review, marks the beginning of that ascendancy which made the Choḷas the paramount power over a large part of India. It will be therefore convenient to treat his history along with that of his successors in the next volume.

III. THE FIRST PĀṆḌYA EMPIRE

1. *Neḍuñjaḍaiyan*

Neḍuñjaḍaiyan, the son of Māṟavarman Rājasiṁha I, is also known as Māṟañjaḍaiyan, Parāntaka, Jaṭila or Jaṭilavarman and Varaguṇa I. His inscriptions range from his third to his forty-third regnal year, and it is not unreasonable to assign to him a regnal period of fifty years, A.D. 765-815. The Veḷvikuḍi grant dated in his third regnal year possesses a unique importance. It gives an account of the vicissitudes of the Pāṇḍya country from the time of its invasion and occupation by the Kaḷabhras. It tells us how Kaḍuṅgon effected their overthrow and was followed by Avaniśūlāmaṇi and Śendan; of Arikesari Māṟavarman and his great victory at Nelveli; his destruction of the Paravas and the people of Kuṟunāḍu and his triumphs over the Chera king at Puliyūr; Kochchaḍaiyan's victories at Marudūr and Mangalore; and Māṟavarman Rājasiṁha I's numerous victories and his pre-eminent position. This account is followed by a description of the greatness of Neḍuñjaḍaiyan, who is called *Paṇḍitavatsala* and *Parāntaka* (destroyer of his enemies); he won a great victory over the Kāḍava (Pallava) at Peṇṇagaḍam near Tanjore, on the southern bank of the Kāverī and crushed a rising of petty chieftains headed by Āyo-veḷ, the ruler of the mountainous country between Tirunelveli and Travancore. Then follows an account of the revival of the old grant of the village of Veḷvikuḍi, which had been abrogated by the Kaḷabhras.

The Madras Museum plates of the seventeenth regnal year of Jaṭilavarman (Neḍuñjaḍaiyan) mention his further military successes. He conquered the Aḍigamāns of Tagaḍur (Dharmapuri, Salem District) and brought Koṅgudeśa under his control in spite of the aid they had obtained from the Chera and Pallava rulers. He also annexed Veṇāḍ or southern Travancore after the conquest of Viḻiñam, but the conquered country was a source of trouble for a long time. He therefore strengthened his position by fortifying Karavandapuram or Kaḷakkāḍ (Tirunelveli District). He thus waged several wars during the first half of his reign. He was the greatest imperialist of his dynasty, and successfully encountered the opposition of the Pallavas and the Cheras. His conquests made him the master of Tanjore, Tiruchirapalli, Salem and Coimbatore districts and also of Southern Travancore. He was an enthusiastic builder of temples for Śiva and Vishṇu, and some scholars connect his name with the Śaiva saint, Māṇikkavāśagar. The king's *uttaramantri* or chief minister was Madhurakavi, who was succeeded by his brother; the other members of his family were also in the service of Neḍuñjaḍaiyan.

2. *Śrīmāra Śrīvallabha and his Successors*

Śrīmāra Śrīvallabha, the son of Neḍuñjaḍaiyan, may be assigned to the period A.D. 815-862. According to the larger Śinnamanūr plates of Rājasiṁha II, Śrīmāra won victories over a number of enemies. He assumed the titles *Ekavīra* and *Parachakrakolāhala* and combated a destructive invasion of the Pāṇḍya country caused by the intrigues of Māyāpāṇḍya or the Pāṇḍya pretender. Śrīmāra is said to have fought at Viḻiñam and triumphed over the Kerala ruler.[3]

Above all, the Pāṇḍya king won a great victory at Kuḍamūkku or Kumbhakonam against a combination of the Gaṅgas, Pallavas, Choḷas, Kaliṅgas, Magadhas and others. He was, however, subsequently defeated at Teḷḷāṟu by Nandi-varman III Pallava and at the Arichit by his successor Nṛipatuṅga-varman. Śrīmāra was succeeded by Varaguṇa or Varaguṇa-varman II (*c.* A.D. 862-880)[4] who as noted above, sustained a crushing defeat about A.D. 880 at Śrīpuṟambiyam at the hands of Aparājita Pallava, assisted by Pṛithvīpati I Western Gaṅga and Āditya I Choḷa. It ruined Varaguṇa and the Pāṇḍya empire.

Varaguṇa II was followed by Parāntaka Vīranārāyaṇa (*c.* A.D. 880-900). He triumphed at Kharagiri, destroyed Peṇṇāgaḍam, and waged war in Koṅgudeśa, according to the larger Śinnamanūr plates. His queen was Vānavan Mahādevī, a Kerala princess. His son and successor was Māṟavarman Rājasiṁha II, the donor of the larger Śinnamanūr record, who ruled from c. A.D. 900 to c. A.D. 920. We have narrated above Parāntaka I Choḷa's conquest of Madura and the defeat of Rājasiṁha II followed by his flight first to Ceylon, where he left his crown and other valuables, and then to his mother's home in Kerala. "Encircled by the fire of his (Parāntaka's) prowess, the Pāṇḍya, as if desirous of cooling the heat caused by it, quickly entered the sea (embarked for Ceylon), abandoning his royal state and the kingdom inherited from his ancestors."[5]

The battle of Takkolam in A.D. 949 created unrest in the Pāṇḍya country and led to the overthrow of the newly established Choḷa authority. Vīra Pāṇḍya assumed the title of 'one who took the head of the Choḷa' and triumphed for some time. It is suggested that the Choḷa king who was beheaded was Gaṇḍarāditya or Sundara Choḷa. But the expression *Talaikoṇḍa* may only mean that the defeated king fell at the feet of the victor, and consequently Vīra Pāṇḍya's title may indicate no more than his victory over the Choḷa. He succeeded in frustrating Gaṇḍarāditya's attempt to re-establish Choḷa authority in the Pāṇḍya country. But Sundara Choḷa defeated Vīra Pāṇḍya in the battle of Chevūr and forced him to seek refuge in the forests. The Tiruvālaṅgāḍu plates say that he was killed by Āditya II but according to the larger Leiden plates of Rājarāja I, "that young boy (Āditya) played sportively in battle (at Chevūr) with Vīra Pāṇḍya just as lion's cub (does) with a rutting mad elephant proud of (its) strength." There are not convincing reasons for believing that a Choḷa king's head was cut off by Vīra Pāṇḍya nor for accepting the statement that the latter was killed by Āditya II. We do not know whether Uttama Choḷa's title of

Madhurāntaka was inherited by him, or whether he undertook any campaign against the Pāṇḍyas. The fact that they were independent and powerful till their reconquest by Rājarāja I is clear from his Tanjore inscription (twenty-ninth regnal year) which states that he "deprived the Śeḻiyas (Pāṇḍyas) of (their) splendour at the very moment when (they were) resplendent (to such a degree) that (they were) worthy to be worshipped everywhere."

IV. THE WESTERN GAṄGAS

1. *Śivamāra II to Pṛithvīpati II*

Although the Western Gaṅga kingdom became most prosperous under Śrīpurusha and deserved the name of *Śrīrājya,* he did nothing to remove the danger to it from the rise of the Rāshṭrakūṭas in the Deccan. Kṛishṇa I invaded Gaṅgavāḍi, was encamped at Maṇṇe in A.D. 768, and effected a military occupation of the country. Śrīpurusha had four sons: Śivamāra II (A.D. 788-812), Vijayāditya, Duggamāra and Śivagella, the last predeceasing his father. Duggamāra disputed Śivamāra's succession but the latter triumphed with the support of his feudatory, Noḷamba Siṅgapota. Kṛishṇa I Rāshṭrakūṭa was succeeded by Govinda II, whose vicious life and neglect of royal duties resulted in his supersession by his younger brother, Dhruva (A.D. 780-793). Śivamāra had espoused the cause of Govinda II. Therefore Dhruva invaded Gaṅgavāḍi, imprisoned Śivamāra and appointed his own son Stambha as the Viceroy of Gaṅgavāḍi. Govinda III Rāshṭrakūṭa (A.D. 793-814) was confronted at his accession with the hostility of his elder brother Stambha in league with a number of neighbouring princes. The former released Śivamāra from "the burden of his cruel chains" and sent him back to his country. But he asserted his independence and supported Stambha. Govinda overcame his brother but treated him generously by re-appointing him to the Western Gaṅga Viceroyalty and thus secured his loyalty permanently. Śivamāra again became a prisoner but was released and reinstated as ruler of Gaṅgavāḍi so that his co-operation might be secured in Govinda's campaigns against the Eastern Chālukyas. Śivamāra was a very learned man. He mastered several subjects such as logic, philosophy, drama, grammar, etc., and composed the *Gajasataka* in Kannaḍa. The vicissitudes of his fortunes during the time of Dhruva and Govinda III resulted in the partition of the Western Gaṅga kingdom between the son and the brother of Śivamāra,—Mārasiṁha and Vijayāditya. Thus was founded the collateral line of Mārasiṁha I, whose brother was Pṛithvīpati I. The latter's son and grandson were Mārasiṁha II and Pṛithvīpati II.

Govinda III was succeeded by Amoghavarsha I (A.D. 814-878), a young boy. Consequently the Rāshṭrakūṭa feudatories, including the Western Gaṅgas, revolted, and the boy-king was dethroned. From this anarchy the Rāshṭrakūṭa Empire was saved, as noted above, and Amoghavarsha regained his regal position in A.D. 821. Though he waged war successfully with the Eastern Chālukyas about A.D. 860, he practically acquiesced in Western Gaṅga independence.

Sivamāra II was followed by his nephew (his brother Vijayāditya's son) Rājamalla I (A.D. 817-853),[6] who continued the main branch of the Western Gaṅgas. He allied himself with the Noḷambas by dynastic marriages and tried to exploit the difficulties of Amoghavarsha I, who failed to achieve his ambitious project of "uprooting the lofty forest of fig trees of Gaṅgavāḍi difficult to be cut down." The Rāshṭrakūṭa force invading Gaṅgavāḍi was withdrawn, and Rājamalla succeeded in restoring the integrity of his kingdom. Therefore in his inscriptions he is likened to "Vishṇu in the form of a Boar, rescuing the earth from the infernal regions."

Rājamalla I was succceeded by his son Nītimārga I (A.D. 853-870) who continued with success the struggle for Western Gaṅga independence. He triumphed over the Bāṇas and the Rāshṭrakūṭas. Amoghavarsha gave his daughter, Chandrobelabbā, in marriage to Būtuga I, the younger son of Nītimārga I. His elder son, Rājamaḷḷa II (A.D. 870-907), was ably assisted by his younger brother, Būtuga I, in the wars with the Eastern Chālukyas. The two brothers helped the Pallavas against the Pāṇḍyas. Būtuga predeceased his brother, who was consequently succeeded by Nītimārga II (A.D. 907-935), the son of Būtuga I. Nītimārga II consolidated his position in Gaṅgavāḍi, and had three sons, Narasiṁha, Rājamalla III, and Būtuga II. After a short reign, Narasiṁha was followed by Rājamalla III, who was ousted by Būtuga II in A.D. 937.

The collateral line of the Western Gaṅgas was represented by Pṛithvīpati I (A.D. 853-880), son of Śivamāra II, and by the former's son Mārasiṁha II (A.D. 880-900), and grandson, Pṛithvīpati II (A.D. 900-940), ruling over Kolār and the north-eastern portions of Gaṅgavāḍi. A Bāṇa king married Kundavvai, daughter of Pṛithvīpati I. This Gaṅga ruler acquired fame by co-operating with the Pallavas against the Pāṇḍyas in the battle of Śrīpuṛambiyam and dying on the battle-field. We have referred to Parāntaka I's campaign against the Bāṇas and the help rendered to him by Pṛithvīpati II, who gained the titles of *Bāṇādhirāja*, *Hastimalla*, and *Sembiyan Māvalivāṇarāyan*. According to his Udayendiram plates, Parāntaka "uprooted two Bāṇas." The death of Pṛithvīpati II in

A.D. 940 after the passing away of his son, Vikkiyaṇṇa or Vikramāditya, led to the enthronement of Būtuga II in Gāṅgavāḍi with the aid of Kṛishṇa III Rāshṭrakūta, their alliance resulting in the Choḷa catastrophe at Takkolam in A.D. 949.

2. *Būtuga II to Rakkasa Gaṅga*

The Rāshṭrakuṭa king Amoghavarsha III (A.D. 936-939) was of a religious turn of mind, and consequently he handed over the administration to his energetic son, Kṛishṇa III (A.D. 939-967). His sister Revakā was married to Būtuga II, who killed his brother Rājamalla III, and became king of Gaṅgavāḍi. We have mentioned the part played by Būtuga in the battle of Takkolam by killing Rājāditya, and this service was rewarded by Kṛishṇa with the gift of the province of Banavāsi. Būtuga was proficient in Jain philosophy and is said to have triumphed over a Buddhist in doctrinal disputation. In short, Būtuga II played an active and successful role in the annals of Gaṅgavāḍi for more than twenty years, though he fully acknowledged the overlordship of the Rāshṭrakūṭas. He had a son named Maruladeva by Revakā; Marula died soon after his father and was succeeded by Mārasiṁha III, Būtuga's son by another queen.

Mārasiṁha III (A.D. 960-974) was faithful to the Gaṅga-Rāshṭrakūṭa alliance and co-operated with Kṛishṇa III in his campaigns in Gujarāt and Mālava, but failed in his attempt to restore Indra IV to the Rāshṭrakūṭa throne against the opposition of Taila II, the Western Chālukya king. Chāmuṇḍa Rāya, the Gaṅga general, captured Uchchangi, the chief stronghold of the Noḷambas. Mārasiṁha's campaign against them secured for him the title of *Noḷambakulāntaka* or destroyer of the Noḷamba family. Finally, he committed *Sallekhanā*, or suicide by starvation, in the Jain fashion.

Mārasiṁha III was succeeded by his elder son Rāchamalla or Rājamalla IV (A.D. 974-985). Attempts at usurpation of the throne were foiled by Chāmuṇḍa Rāya, the great minister who was a good Jain and a famous general with the title of *Vīramārtaṇḍa* or sun among heroes, and *Raṇaraṅga-siṁha* or lion on the battle-field. He had distinguished himself in the campaign against the Noḷambas during the previous reign. He was a master of Kannaḍa, Sanskrit and Prakrit. In A.D. 978 he wrote the Kannaḍa work, the *Chāmuṇḍa Rāya Purāṇa* which contains, among others, an account of the twenty-four Jain *Tīrthaṅkaras* or prophets. About 982 he erected a *basti* or Jain temple named after himself, at Śravaṇa Beḷgoḷa. Above all, he executed about A.D. 983 a colossal statue of Gommaṭeśvara, "larger than any of the statues of Rameses in Egypt," which "in daring conception and gigantic dimensions (56½ feet in height) is without a rival in India." He truly earned the title of Rāya.

Rājamalla IV was followed by his younger brother, Rakkasa Gaṅga, during whose reign (A.D. 985-1024) the Choḷas captured Taḷakāḍ (A.D. 1004). His inscription, dated A.D. 1024, mentions Rājendra Choḷa as his overlord, but gradually the Gaṅga rule came to an end. Some later Gaṅga chiefs are, however, known. A Gaṅga Rāja was the minister of Vishṇuvardhana Hoysaḷa in the twelfth century, and another Gaṅga Rāja of Śivasamudram defied Kṛishṇadeva Rāya of Vijayanagar early in the sixteenth century.

V. THE BĀṆAS

The Bāṇas were feudatory to the Pallavas under the successors of Nandi-varman Pallavamalla. The Western Gaṅgas and the Noḷambas combined against the Bāṇas, though Kundavvai, the daughter of the Gaṅga ruler Pṛithvīpati I, was married to Vikramāditya I Bāṇa or Bāṇavidyādhara. He may be assigned to the period A.D. 868-890. In the battle at Soremaṭi or Soremaḍi (Anantapur District) about A.D. 878 the Western Gaṅgas and the Noḷambas were defeated by the Bāṇas and the Vaidumbas. An inscription of A.D. 892-93 records that the Noḷamba chief Mahendra I, called Mahendrādhirāja, destroyed the Bāṇas, but the latter continued to be active. Their inscriptions of A.D. 898, 905 and 909 during the period of Vijayāditya II Bāṇa are dated in the Śaka era, and mention no overlord. He and his successor, Vikramāditya II, must have enjoyed an independent status. But soon the Bāṇas came into conflict with Parāntaka I and we have narrated how he dealt with them and the consequences of his aggressive policy. Vikramāditya III Bāṇa, described as the friend of Kṛishṇa (III), secured the support of the Rāshṭrakūṭa power against the Choḷas, and joined the battle of Takkolam which resulted in the complete discomfiture of the Choḷas in A.D. 949. Therefore Parāntakta I's 'extirpation' of the Bāṇas did not close their story. Their chiefs appear in South Indian history up to the sixteenth century and their movement from district to district (originally from Āndhradeśa) took them to the far south, *viz.* the Pāṇḍya country where they were Governors of Madura under the Rāyas of Vijayanagar. The history of the Bāṇas during more than a thousand years possesses a singular interest in that it illustrates the survival of a tribe or dynasty by migration.

VI. THE NOḶAMBAS AND THE VAIDUMBAS

The Noḷambas or Noḷamba Pallavas (Noḷambas claiming Pallava descent) ruled mainly over Noḷambavāḍi 32,000 or the Chitaldrug district of Mysore. Their principal cities were Uchchangi, Henjeṟu (Hemāvati) and Chitaldrug. The Noḷamba chief Siṅgapota was feudatory to Śivamāra II and the latter's imprisonment by the Rāshṭrakūṭas led to their control of the Noḷambas. We have noticed Rājamalla I's policy of dynastic marriages with them. Polalchora, the grandson of Siṅgapota, married the daughter of Rājamalla I, and their son was Mahendra I. With the support of the Western Gaṅgas, he sent his general Kāḍuveṭṭi Muttarasa to invade the Pulināḍu belonging to the Bāṇas. They and the Vaidumbas were attacked at Soremaṭi about A.D. 878 but the Noḷambas were repulsed. Mahendra was subsequently killed in battle by Nītimārga II, who consequently assumed the title of *Mahendrāntaka* or destroyer of Mahendra. His great-grandson, Nanni Noḷamba, came into conflict with Mārasiṁha III, who conquered and annexed Noḷambavāḍi, and assumed the title of *Noḷambakulāntaka*. The Gaṅga victory was followed by a general massacre of the Noḷambas, but three princes escaped and revived the fortunes of their dynasty after the death of Mārasiṁha III in A.D. 974.

The Vaidumbas were in possession of the Renāṇḍu (7000 country) in the ninth century. The first known chief was Irigaya. Gaṇḍa Triṇetra led the Vaidumba forces to the aid of the Bāṇas against the Western Gaṅgas and the Noḷambas at Soremaṭi about A.D. 878. Apparently the Vadumbas were feudatory to the Bāṇas. To the tenth century belongs Śandayan Tiruvayan I. Probably he was the Vaidumba chief defeated by Parāntaka I Choḷa after his subjugation of the Bāṇas. Sandayan Tiruvayan II was known as Śrīkaṇṭha. Like the Bāṇas, after their defeat by the Choḷas, the Vaidumbas appealed for help to the Rāshṭrakūṭas. Thus the Vaidumbas also had their share in compassing the ruin of the Choḷa empire at Takkolam in A.D. 949. Subsequently they entered the service of the Choḷas. Ariñjaya Choḷa married a Vaidumba princess, and their son was Sundara Choḷa.

VII. ĀLUVAKHEḌA, KOṄGUDEŚA AND KERALA

Chitravāhana II (c. A.D. 800) and his successors ruled over Āluvakheḍa for several centuries till it was annexed to the Hoysaḷa kingdom in the fourteenth century. Koṅgudeśa became the bone of contention between the Western Gaṅga, Pallava and Pāṇḍya imperialists, and we have noticed the overthrow of the Aḍigamāns of Tagaḍūr by Neḍuñjadaiyan Pāṇḍya and the establishment of his authority in the Salem and Coimbatore Districts. Āditya I Choḷa annexed Koṅgudeśa by overcoming the Western Gaṅgas and the Pāṇḍyas.

The last of the Perumāḷs of Kerala was Cheraman Perumāḷ, and the end of his rule may be connected with the origin of the Kollam or Malayāḷam era in A.D. 824-25, though some scholars would explain it as marking the foundation of Kollam or Quilon. The latest writer on Cheraman Perumāḷ assigns him to A.D. 742-826, rejects the story of his conversion to Christianity or Islam, and maintains that his pilgrimage towards the close of his life was not to Mylapore or Mecca but to Chidambaram. The Arabs, who settled in Malabar in the ninth century, married the women of the country, and thus the Moplah population came into existence. Sthāṇu Ravi was on very friendly terms with Āditya I Choḷa. Though the immigration of the Jews is assigned to the first century A.D. the first definite proof of their colony near Cranganore on the west coast is the Tamil charter of Bhāskara Ravivarman (A.D. 978-1036) to Joseph Rabban giving him and his descendants certain lands and privileges. Kerala princesses graced the Pāṇḍya and Choḷa courts as queens, like the queen of Parāntaka I who was the mother of Ariñjaya. Several Choḷa officers, including a general named Veḷlaṅgumaran, belonged to Kerala, and Chaturānana Paṇḍita was the *guru* of Rājāditya.

SELECT BIBLIOGRAPHY

1. Arokiaswami, M., *The Early History of the Veḷḷār Basin.* Madras, 1954.
2. Ayyar, V. Venkatasubba, *SII*, XII. Madras, 1943.
3. Gopalan, R., *History of the Pallavas of Kanchi.* Madras, 1928.
4. Jouveau-Dubreuil, *The Pallavas.* Pondicherry, 1917.
5. Mahalingam, T. V., The Bāṇas in South Indian History (*JIH*, XXIX. 153-81, 277-305).
6. Pandarathar, T. V. Sadasiva, *Pirkālach-Cholar-Charittiram* Part I (in Tamil), Annamalainagar, 1949.
7. Pandarathar, T. V. Sadasive, *Pāṇḍiyar Varalāṟu* (in Tamil). Madras, 1950.
8. Rao, M. V. Krishna, *The Gangas of Talkad.* Madras, 1936.
9. Rice, B. L., *Mysore and Coorg.* London, 1909.
10. Sastri, K. A. Nilakanta, *The Pandya Kingdom.* London, 1929.
11. Sastri, K. A. Nilakanta, *The Cholas*, I. Madras, 1935.
12. Sewell, R. *Hist. Ins.* Madras, 1932.
13. Venkayya, V., Five Bāṇa Inscriptions from Guḍimallam (*EI*, XI. 222-40). Calcutta, 1911-12.

1. Udayendiram Grant, *SII*, II. 382.
2. Arokiaswami, M., *The Early History of the Veḷḷār Basin* (Madras, 1954), pp. 108-10. For a different view, cf. Pandarathar, T. V. Sadasiva, *Pirkālach-Cholar-Charittiram* (in Tamil) Part I (Annamalainagar, 1949), pp. 76-78.
3. For his victory in Ceylon, cf. Chapter VIII.
4. For an account of his accession, cf. Ch. VIII.
5. Tiruvālaṅgāḍu Pl. of Rājendra Choḷa I. For the help rendered to the Pāṇḍya king by the Ceylonese ruler, Kāśyapa V, cf. Ch. VIII.
6. The last known date of Śivamāra II is A.D. 812, and the earliest known date of Rājamalla is A.D. 817.

APPENDIX

THE GENEALOGY AND CHRONOLOGY OF THE PALLAVAS

1. *The Successors of Nandi-varman Pallavamalla*

Nandi-varman Pallavamalla was succeeded by his son Danti-varman, whose latest known date is the regnal year 51. As stated above,[1] he ascended the throne some time before April 4, A.D. 804, when Govinda III was returning from the Pallava country after having levied tribute from Dantiga (Danti-varman) king of Kāñchī. Danti-varman's successor was his son Teḷḷāṟṟerinda Nandi-varman (*i.e.* Nandi-varman who defeated his enemies at Teḷḷāṟu in the Wandiwash *tāluk* of North Arcot District), whose latest known date is the year 22 of his reign. This king married the Rāshṭrakūṭa princess Śaṅkhā (probably a daughter of Amoghavarsha I Nṛipatuṅga, son of Govinda III) and was succeeded by his son by her, called Nṛipatuṅga-varman (probably named after his maternal grandfather). The latest known date of king Nṛipatuṅga-varman is his 41st regnal year.[2] Thus we find that the four generations of Pallava kings, *viz.* Nandi-varman Pallavamalla, Danti-varman, Teḷḷāṟṟerinda Nandi-varman, and Nṛipatuṅga-varman ruled for 179 (65 + 51 + 22 + 41) years, *i.e.* nearly 45 years per generation. This is rather abnormal. It may be that, like many of the Choḷa rulers, the reigns of the Pallava kings and their successors often overlapped. If, however, the above regnal periods be regarded as successive, and if the latest known dates of the kings in question be regarded as the last years of their reigns, Nṛipatuṅga-varman probably ceased to reign in A.D. 910 (731 + 179). Nṛipatuṅga's inscriptions have been found all over the region from Guḍimallam in the north to Pudukkoṭṭai in the south. The Bāṇa king Bāṇavidyādhara, *i.e.* Vikramāditya I, was a feudatory both of Nandi-varman Teḷḷāṟṟerinda and of Nṛipatuṅga.[3]

Inscriptions disclose the names or *virudas* of several Pallava rulers such as Aparājita-varman (regnal years 3 to 18), Kampa-varman (regnal years 6 to 25), Vayiramegha-varman (regnal year 2), Narasiṁha-varman (regnal years 3 to 24), Īśvara-varman (*i.e.* Parameśvara-varman, regnal years 12 and 17), Chandrāditya and Kāṭṭirai. Of these Kampa-varman (probably named after Rāshṭrakūṭa Stambha or Kamba who may be supposed to have been his maternal grandfather) was possibly also known as *Nandikampa* which has been interpreted as "Kampa-varman son of Nandi-varman (Teḷḷāṟṟerinda)", although it very probably indicates "Nandi-varman surnamed Kampa-varman." The second suggesion (involving another that Danti-varman Pallava married a daughter of Stambha) is probably supported by the tendency of cross-cousin marriages between two royal families in successive generations among South Indian rulers. Kampa-varman may thus be regarded as identical with Nandi-varman Teḷḷāṟṟerinda (whose latest known date in that case would be the regnal year 25 instead of year 22). Vayiramegha-varman may have been another name of Danti-varman who was apparently named after the Rāshṭrakūṭa king Danti-varman (Danti-durga) surnamed Vairamegha. Narasiṁha-varman and Īśvara-varman may be the same respectively as Narasiṁha-varman II and Parameśvara-varman I; but these may also have been secondary names of two of the later kings. Kāṭṭirai and Chandrāditya were probably local Pallava chiefs under Pallava or Choḷa overlords.

According to Choḷa records, the Choḷa king Āditya I overthrew Pallava Aparājita and killed him towards the end of the ninth century A.D. From an inscription at Tirumalpuram near Kāñchī we learn that Toṇḍaiman Āṟṟur-tuñjina-uḍaiyar (Āditya I) granted a village in the heart of the Pallava empire in the 21st year of his reign. The date of Āditya's accession is now usually believed to have been A.D. 871, which would make his 21st year correspond to A.D. 892-93. But as there is no evidence regarding the nature and duration of the Pallava-Choḷa struggle of this period, it is impossible to say that Aparājita was already extirpated by A.D. 892-93.

According to the Udayendiram grant, the Gaṅga king, Pṛithvīpati I, in order to help his friend (overlord) Aparājita, defeated Pāṇḍya Varaguṇa II at the battle of Śrīpuṟambiyam (near Kumbhakonam) but lost his life in the engagement. As the same Gaṅga king is referred to in the Ambur inscription of the 26th year of Nṛipatuṅga as one of the Pallava king's feudatories, Aparājita could not have ceased to rule before this year. If Nṛipatuṅga-varman ruled till A.D. 910, as noted above, we cannot regard the two as identical and can only presume that they ruled over different parts of the Pallava dominions. It would also then follow that the Pallava sovereignty was not extinguished with Aparājita's death, but continued till at least A.D. 913. This view is supported by the Karandai Plates of Rājendra I which refer to the success of Parāntaka I against the Pallavas.[4]

2. *Tentative genealogy of the Later Pallavas*

Hiraṇya-varman (great-great-grandson of Bhīma-varman who was a brother of the Greater Pallava king Siṁhavishṇu)

1. Nandi-varman Pallavamalla (married Revā, probably the daughter of Dantidurga-Danti-varman-Vairamegha), c. A.D. 731-96.

2. Dantiga-Danti-varman-Vayiramegha-varman (probably married the daughter of Stambha or Kamba, son of Dhruva, who was a cousin of Dantidurga-Danti-varman-Vairamegha), c. A.D. 796-847.

3. Teḷḷāṟṟerinda Nandi-varman-Kampa-varman (married Śaṅkhā, probably the daughter of Amoghavarsha I, son of Govinda III, who was a brother of Stambha or Kamba), c. A.D. 847-72.

4. Nṛipatuṅga-varman (A.D. 872-913).

It has to be admitted that the reigns of the four kings may have overlapped to a considerable extent. It is also uncertain whether the latest known dates of these kings were actually the last years of their reigns.

1. Vol. III, p. 282.
2. *Ancient India*, No. 5, p. 54.
3. *JIH*, XXIX. 174.
4. *JOR*, XIX. 148.

CHAPTER VIII

CEYLON

I. POLITICAL HISTORY

Agrabodhi VI was succeeded, after a rule of about 40 years, by his brother Agrabodhi VII (A.D. 759-65). He was famous for his sense of justice and knowledge of medical science. After he had reigned for six years, Mahendra II Śilāmeghavarṇa (A.D. 765-85), son of Agrabodhi VI, seized the throne. The new kings's authority was, however, challenged by Dappula, who was the son of a sister of king Agrabodhi VI and became a constant source of trouble throughout the 20 years' reign of Mahendra II. Anarchy prevailed almost throughout the land. The next king Udaya (sometimes styled Dappula II, A.D. 785-90) was a son of Mahendra II. The new ruler is said to have helped his son-in-law Mahendra to conquer Rohaṇa in South Ceylon, and to drive out the latter's father Daṁshṭrāśiva, collector of revenue at Rohaṇa, to take shelter in India. Udaya died after a reign of about five years and was succeeded by his son Mahendra III Śilāmeghavarṇa (A.D. 790-94) who ruled for about four years. The next king was Agrabodhi VIII (A.D. 794-805), a brother of Mahendra III. This ruler was exceptionally devoted to his mother whom he allowed to offer his own person as a gift to the Buddhist church and then freed himself by paying to the church a sum considered equal to his own value. He died after a rule of 11 years, and his younger brother Dappula II (or III, A.D. 805-21) next reigned for 16 years. The successor of Dappula II (or III), his son Agrabodhi IX (A.D. 821-24), had to fight with Mahendra (son of king Mahendra III) who was the real heir to the throne according to the Ceylonese law of inheritance.[1] Prince Mahendra was compelled to flee to South India. After a short rule of three years, Agrabodhi IX was succeeded by his younger brother Sena (A.D. 824-44), surnamed Śilāmegha. Sena removed a potential danger by having Prince Mahendra killed by his agents in India. But he had to face an attack of the Pāṇḍya king of Madura in South India, who had probably given shelter to Mahendra.

The Pāṇḍya king, who led an expedition against Ceylon, conquered the northern part of the island, and the defeated king Sena fled to the mountainous region of Malaya. The victorious Pāṇḍyas took away all the valuables in the Ceylonese king's treasury and elsewhere in the island, including gold images and plates belonging to the monasteries. Then king Sena submitted to the Pāṇḍya king, and the latter returned to his own country. The Pāṇḍya king was probably Śrīmāra Śrīvallabha who gained a victory in the island of Ceylon according to the Sinnamanūr grant.[2] Sena died after a reign of about 20 years, and was succeeded by his brother's son Sena II (A.D. 844-79). During his reign a rebel son of the Pāṇḍya king took shelter at the Ceylonese court. In retaliation for the Pāṇḍya invasion during the rule of Sena I, Sena II sent a large army against the Pāṇḍya country. Ceylonese forces besieged Madura and completely defeated the Pāṇḍya king who lost his life. The Pāṇḍya capital was plundered and the valuables, including the golden images brought from Ceylon, were all taken back to the island. The son of the deceased Pāṇḍya king was placed on the throne. It may be suggested that the reference is probably to the accession of Śrīmāra's son Varaguṇa II in A.D. 862. The successful war of Sena II against the Pāṇḍyas is mentioned in a number of inscriptions. The king died in the 35th year of his reign, and was succeeded by his youngest brother Udaya II (or I, A.D. 879-90), surnamed Śilāmeghavarṇa. Kīrtyagrabodhi, a member of the royal family, rebelled against the new king and made himself master of Rohaṇa; but the rebellion was soon quelled. The king died after a rule of about 11 years, and his brother Kāśyapa IV Śrīsaṅghabodhi (A.D. 890-907) succeeded him. One of the new king's ministers was Choḷarāja whose name seems to connect him with the Choḷa country in the Tanjore-Tiruchirapalli region in South India. Kāśyapa IV is said to have ruled for 17 years and was succeeded by a son of Sena II named Kāśyapa V (A.D. 907-17), called Abhaya Śilāmeghavarṇa in his inscription.

During the rule of Kāśyapa V, the Pāṇḍya king of the Madura-Ramnad-Tirunelveli region was vanquished by his neighbour, the king of the Choḷas, and he applied for help to the Ceylonese ruler. Kāśyapa V sent an army to the Pāṇḍya king's help; but the expedition was unsuccessful. The Choḷa king appears to be no other than Parāntaka I, who ascended the throne in A.D. 907 and claimed victories over the Pāṇḍya king Rājasiṁha (Māṟavarman Rājasiṁha III) and over an army of the king of Ceylon.[3] Kāśyapa V died in the 10th year of his reign. His successor Dappula III (or IV, A.D. 917-18), who ruled for a few months, was probably one of his step-brothers. The next king was Dappula IV (or V) Śilāmeghavarṇa (A.D. 918-30), who was probably a brother of the preceding ruler. During his rule, the Pāṇḍya king, whose country was subjugated by the Choḷas, took shelter at the Ceylonese court; but having failed to secure any help, the Pāṇḍya ruler left his diadem and other valuables behind and betook himself to the Kerala country in the Malabar coast of South

India, although there is a tradition about the Ceylonese king's victorious fight with the Damilas who came from the Choḷa country. Dappula IV (or V) died in the 12th year of his rule, and was succeeded by Udaya III (or II, A.D. 930-33), who was a brother's son of Sena II and died in the 3rd year of his reign.

The next king Sena III (A.D. 933-42), probably a brother of the preceding ruler, died in his ninth regnal year, and was succeeded by Udaya IV (or III, A.D. 942-50) whose relation to his predecessors is unknown. During this king's rule the Choḷa king, who had conquered the Pāṇḍya country, demanded from the Ceylonese monarch the diadem and other valuables left in the island by the Pāṇḍya ruler in the reign of Dappula IV (or V). The demand not having been complied with, a mighty Choḷa army invaded Ceylon and occupied large tracts of the island. King Udaya IV (or III) fled with the crown and other valuables to Rohaṇa. The Choḷa king can be no other than Parāntaka I (A.D. 907-53) who calls himself "conqueror of Ceylon" in his records.[4] It is claimed in the Ceylonese chronicles that the Ceylonese king's general now laid waste the borderland of the Choḷa monarch and compelled him to restore all the valuables carried away from the island as booty. But the invading Choḷa army appears to have actually left Ceylon owing to the Rāshṭrakūṭa invasion of the Choḷa country under Kṛishṇa III about A.D. 949, the year of the great battle of Takkolam. Udaya IV (or III) died in his eighth regnal year, while his successor Sena IV (A.D. 950-53) ruled for three years. The next king Mahendra IV Śrīsaṅghabodhi (A.D. 953-69), who was probably his predecessor's brother, married a princess of the royal house of Kaliṅga in India. During his rule, the Vallabha king sent a force to Nāgadvīpa (identified by some writers with north-western Ceylon, but by others with Jaffna) to subjugate Ceylon; but the war was concluded by a peace between the two powers. The Vallabha is apparently king Kṛishṇa III (A.D. 939-67) of the family of the Rāshṭrakūṭas, who were the successors of the Chālukya Vallabharājas and were known to the Arabs as the Balharās of Mānkīr (Vallabharājas of Mānyakheṭa). There are epigraphic and literary records[5] referring to the subjugation of Ceylon by Kṛishṇa III before A.D. 959. although the Rāshṭrakūṭa expedition appears to have been merely a raid. Mahendra IV is also said to have repulsed a Choḷa invasion under Parāntaka II, who led an attack against the island as its ruler had helped the Pāṇḍya king in his revolt against the Choḷas.

Mahendra IV restored certain monasteries that had been previously burnt by the Choḷas. After his death in the 16th year of his reign, his 12-year-old son, Sena V (A.D. 969 79), became king.

During his rule, there was a rebellion headed by a general, also named Sena, as a result of which the king had to flee to Rohaṇa. The country was ravaged by Damila forces whose help was requisitioned by the rebellious general. Ultimately the king and the rebel entered into a pact; but the former died in the 10th year of his reign, still young in years. The next king was his younger brother Mahendra V (A.D. 979-1027)[6] who had to face numerous difficulties owing to the disturbed condition of the country. He made his brother's widow his queen and, on her death which took place shortly afterwards, raised his brother's daughter to the rank of *Mahishī*. The new king was unable to keep his troops contented by regular payment. The Kerala (Malayali) mercenaries in the king's army once besieged the royal residence at Anurādhapura, although the king managed to escape by an underground passage to Rohaṇa. In other parts of the country complete anarchy prevailed, and Kerala and Karṇāṭa (Kanarese) as well as Ceylonese chieftains carried on the government as they pleased. On hearing of this anarchical condition of Ceylon from a horse-dealer, the Choḷa king sent a strong army to invade the island. The Choḷa king was no doubt the mighty Rājarāja, who not only conquered the northern part of Ceylon but gave it the name Mummuḍi-Choḷa-maṇḍalam (cf. the names Rājarājapuram and Jagannāthamaṅgalam applied respectively to Māntai or Mātoṭa and Polonnaruva) and even granted Ceylonese villages to the great temple at Tanjore.[7] The southern part of the island appears to have been conquered by the Choḷa king Rājendra, son and successor of Rājarāja, in or shortly before A.D. 1017, when, according to Ceylonese chronicles, the Choḷas captured not only the Ceylonese king's *Mahishī*, but also "the jewels, the diadem that he had inherited, the whole of the royal ornaments, the priceless diamond bracelet which was a gift of the gods, the unbreakable sword, and the relic of the torn strip of cloth."[8] The king, who had fled to the jungle, was captured on "the pretence of concluding a treaty." Mahendra V was then sent with all his treasures to the Choḷa king in India where the Ceylonese monarch died 12 years later. According to the inscriptions of the Choḷas, Rājendra, after heavy fighting in Ceylon, captured "the crown of the island" (indicating the capture of the king), "the beautiful crown of the queen of Ceylon" (indicating the capture of the queen) and "the crown of Sundara and the pearl necklace of Indra" which the Pāṇḍya king had given to the king of Ceylon. The Choḷas carried away many costly images of gold, destroyed the Buddhist monasteres, and stripped the island of all valuables. With Pulatthinagara (modern Polonnaruva) as their base, the Choḷas held complete sway over Rājarāshṭra or North Ceylon.

The people of the island were secretly bringing up the young prince Kāśyapa in the southern country due to fear of the Choḷas. When the Choḷa king heard that the boy had reached his 12th year, he sent a force to seize him. An army of 95,000 men now ravaged South Ceylon.

In the meantime king Mahendra V died at the Choḷa court in the 48th year after his coronation. Kāśyapa, the young son of Mahendra V, was then made king under the name Vikramabāhu (A.D. 1027-39); but he declined to undergo formal consecration so long as Rājarāshṭra was in the occupation of the foreigners. He continued to rule at Rohaṇa and died in the 12th year of his reign. Thereupon an official named Kīrti exercised royal authority for a few days after which he was murdered by Mahālānakīrti (A.D. 1039-42) who became ruler of Rohaṇa, He was defeated by the Choḷas and lost his life in his third regnal year. The Damilas took away his treasures, diadem, and other valuables which were sent to the Choḷa country. Mahālānakīrti's son Vikramapāṇḍya (probably connected with the Pāṇḍya royal house of Madura on the mother's side) carried on the government in a small tract from his headquarters at modern Kalutara at the mouth of the river Kalugaṅgā in south-western Ceylon, for about one year (A.D. 1042) according to the Pāli chronicle, but three years, according to the Sinhalese sources on which Geiger relies. He was slain in battle by Jagatīpāla, said to have been a Sūryavaṁśī prince coming from Ayodhyā; but Jagatīpāla (A.D. 1042-46) was himself killed by the Choḷas, probably after a rule of four years. His queen and daughter, together with all valuables, were sent to the Choḷa country. Parākrama or Parākramapāṇḍya (A.D. 1046-48), who is often regarded as the son of a Pāṇḍya king of Madura but may have actually been a son of Vikramapāṇḍya, was also slain by the Choḷas, probably after a rule of two years. The Choḷa king Rājādhirāja, son of Rājendra, claims in a record of A.D. 1046[9] that he had deprived four Ceylonese kings of their crowns, namely (1) Vikramabāhu, (2) Vikramapāṇḍya, (3) Vīraśilāmegha hailing from Kanauj (apparently the same as Jagatīpāla), and (4) Śrī-vallabhamadanarāja (possibly another name of Parākramapāṇḍya or of some other unknown Ceylonese chief) who is said to have lived for some time at the court of Kannara, *i.e.* the Rāshṭrakūṭa king Krishṇa III. Another ruler killed by Rājādhirāja was Mānabharaṇa, who may have been a Ceylonese chief, although Hultzsch takes him to be a scion of the Pāṇḍya royal family. The Choḷa king also claims to have captured the queen-mother of Ceylon and to have cut off her nose, the reference probably being to the capture of Jagatīpāla's queen. The Choḷa records would thus suggest that the rule of Jagatīpāla, if not also of Parākramapāṇḍya, ended in or shortly before A.D. 1046. The records of Rājendra, younger brother and successor of Rājādhirāja, say that some time before A.D. 1057 the Choḷa king killed Vīraśilāmegha, "king of the Kaliṅgas" (probably a Ceylonese prince connected with Kaliṅga on his mother's side), and captured the two sons of Mānabharaṇa, "king of the people of Laṅkā." Vīraśilāmegha and Mānabharaṇa, mentioned here should be identified with the princes of these names referred to in the records of Rājādhirāja, although they are usually supposed to be different. In an inscription[10] of A.D. 1069, Rājendra's successor, Vīrarājendra, also claims to have subdued Ceylon.

Towards the middle of the eleventh century, when the whole island was under Choḷa occupation, the Ceylonese chronicles place the rule of two chiefs named Lokeśvara (six years, A.D. 1048-54) and Keśadhātu Kāśyapa (six months, A.D. 1054-55), who had their headquarters at Kājaragrāma (modern Kataragām on the Menikgaṅgā not far from Magama, the chief city of Rohaṇa or Southern Ceylon). These chiefs had a rival in the person of a scion of the Ceylonese royal family named Kīrti, later styled Vijayabāhu I Śrīsaṅghabodhi (A.D. 1055-1110),[11] one of the greatest generals of Ceylon, who succeeded in extirpating Choḷa rule from the island in the 15th year of his reign. Vīrarājendra's claim of subjugating Ceylon about A.D. 1069 seems to refer to the great Choḷa victory over Vijayabāhu's forces in a battle near Anurādhapura in the 12th year of the Ceylonese king's reign which probably corresponds to a date not much earlier than A.D. 1069. A Śiva Devale (temple) at Polonnaruva contains inscriptions of Rājendra Choḷa I and of Adhirājendra who ruled for some time about A.D. 1070. The liberation of Ceylon by Vijayabāhu thus seems to have taken place shortly after A.D. 1070 in the 15th year of his reign.

II. FINE ARTS

Ceylon is an offshoot of India not only geographically but also culturally. The literary[12] and art traditions of the island as well as its religious, political, social and economic life show how deeply they were regulated by the conventions of Indian life and thought.

In early times Indian *Bhikshus* in Ceylon lived in very simple monasteries, mostly stone caves such as those of Mihintale, Vessagiriya, and Isurumuniya in Anurādhapura, and Situlpahuva (Chittalaparvata) near the Menikgaṅgā, and in groves like the Mahāmeghavana in Anurādhapura. Although information about the exact nature of the buildings used by the early inhabitants and ruling chiefs is meagre, there is evidence of the gradual growth of a grand monastic architecture inspired by Indian tradition. The great Stūpārāma was built at Anurādhapura in the middle of the third century B.C., and an offshoot of the Bodhi tree was planted in the island. Unfortunately remnants of the early structures are usually found enclosed in later additions. Numerous *Vihāras* or Buddhist monasteries were built in the early period, some of the most famous of them being the Tishyamahārāma (dating from the second or third century B.C. according to some scholars) at Magama or Mahāgrāma, capital of Rohaṇa (South-West Ceylon), and the Stūpārāma, Mahāvihāra, Abhayagirivihāra (built by Vaṭṭagāmaṇī Abhaya or Vaḷagambā in the first century B.C.), and the Jetavanārāma (built by Mahāsena in the fourth century A.D.). The monasteries usually covered wide areas, and were meant for accommodating a large number of *Bhikshus*. The Jetavanārāma is 251 feet high and stands on a stone platform nearly 8 acres in extent, while the space within the walled enclosure measures nearly 14 acres. Generally the monasteries had stone foundations, the upper structures being always of wood, clay or brick. There were residential quarters, a refectory, and an Uposatha house where the Saṅgha assembled on the fortnightly fast day of the new moon and the full moon. The Vihāras had a *Chaitya* or *Stūpa*, called *Dāgaba* in Ceylon. In the first century B.C. the great builder Duṭṭhagāmaṇī built the Lohaprāsāda (Lohamahaseya) or Brazen Palace (so called from the gilt bronze dome that once crowned it) and the Ruvaṇavaliseya in the Mahāvihāra at Anurādhapura, the former being the Uposatha house and the latter the *Dāgaba*. The Ceylonese *Dāgabas* were usually built essentially on the pattern of the Indian *Stūpas* like those of Sānchī, although they differed a good deal in details. They had the shape of a heap of paddy or a hemisphere, and were erected on three circular terraces, standing on a round or square basement, approached by one or four stairways. Above the hemispherical dome there was a square called *Hataras koṭuva*, on which stood the round *Devata koṭuva* ("citadel of the gods" corresponding to the Indian *Harmikā*), forming the base of the pointed ringed spire. The spire represented an earlier *chhatrāvalī* (umbrellas).

The early extant examples of Ceylonese sculptures are usually made of limestone and belong to the style of Amarāvati and Nāgārjunikoṇḍa. The specimens representing the great miracle of Śrāvastī and Māyā's dream in the Colombo Museum may be actually the work of South Indian artists. But other specimens representing Buddha, Bodhisattvas, and Nāgas were apparently works of local artists inspired by Indian tradition. Many of the Ceylonese images were originally plastered and coloured, and "the rough, weatherworn blocks, now visible, do not produce the effect designed by the artists."

In the following period Ceylonese shrines of simpler structures, consisting of two sections (one forming the real shrine and the other used for the beating of drums) standing on two platforms connected by a huge slab, were giving way to great vaulted buildings with massive brick walls and door-posts of stone. These "huge masses of masonry" had usually a *Maṇḍapa* or porch, a nave, a communication passage, and a *Dāgaba*. The *Dāgabas* were sometimes small in size and stood on square platforms. The celebrated temple, called the Gedige, at Nalanda (an old military post between Malaya and Anurādhapura) is built entirely of stone in South Indian style. Some writers believe that it was built for the use of the Pallava troops who accompanied Māna-varman to Ceylon in the sixth century, but others ascribe its construction to the age of Choḷa occupation in the first half of the eleventh century.

A number of Hindu temples, called Devales and Kovils, were built at Polonnaruva and other places (*e.g.* Kotaragāma, Kandy and Ratnapura) in the time of Choḷa occupation and in Choḷa style. One of them, a Śiva temple originally known as Vaṇuvaṇmādevī Īśvaramudaiyar and made of granuilite and limestone, consists of a *Garbhagṛiha, Antarāla, Ardhamaṇḍapa*, and *Maṇḍapa* with a four-storied *Vimāna.*

King Kāśyapa I built, in the fifth century, the great rock fortress of Sigiriya or Siṁhagiri, so called from its façade in the form of a huge seated lion. This rock fortress, on the top of which the king erected a large number of buildings, its galleries and the wall round them covered with white plaster, and the celebrated frescoes done in the Ajaṇṭā style, have immortalised the name of Kāśyapa I in the cultural history of Ceylon.

Some of the sculptures of this period are made in gneiss. The influence of the Gupta style is clearly marked in the bas-relief of "the man and woman" and in the meditating Buddha images at Isurumuniya (Anurādhapura), as well as in the Moon-stone (a semicircular slab carved elaborately in low relief and placed at the foot of a staircase in Ceylonese art) at the entrance of the queen's palace at Anurādhapura. The carving of the elephant figures on the rock of Isurumuniya and the sage Kapila with horse's head (representing Sagara's sacrificial horse) show great influence of the Pallava style, especially of the famous bas-reliefs at Māmallapuram.

A number of bronze and copper images dating from the fifth century A.D. have been found. The Badulla Buddha (fifth or sixth century) in the Colombo Museum exhibits pure Gupta style. The fine small figures of Avalokiteśvara and Jambhala (Kuvera), now in the Boston Museum, have been assigned to the eighth century. Numerous bronze or copper images of various Hindu deities and

South Indian saints in pure Dravidian style have been recovered from the Devales and Kovils. These include images of Śiva, especially of the Naṭarāja type, Pārvatī, Gaṇeśa, Kārttikeya, Vishṇu, Lakshmī, Bālakṛishṇa, Hanuman and Sūrya, as well as of Sundaramūrtisvāmī, Māṇikka Vāśagar, Tirujñāna Sambandhasvāmī and Apparasvāmī. There is no doubt that these were works of South Indian artists; but whether most of them were cast in South India or at Polonnaruva, the Chola headquarters in Ceylon, cannot be determined with certainty. Some of the specimens are very fine. An excellent bronze image is that of the goddess Pattinī Devī which is now in the British Museum. Pattinī is the guardian of female chastity, but has power also over epidemics. Her cult went to the island from South India.

The frescoes of Sigiriya closely resemble in style those in the Ajaṇṭā caves. They portray, either singly or in couples, twenty-one figures and probably represent celestial damsels (all covered by clouds below the waist), though some writers would take them to be queens and princesses with their ladies in waiting. Colours used by the artists are red, yellow, green, and black. The figures are graceful and sensual, and the brush work exhibits sound knowledge of modelling and technique. But their standard compares rather unfavourably with that of the best frescoes in the Ajaṇṭā caves. The painting in the Pulligoda Galkomde near Polonnaruva, representing five nimbate seated male figures, may date from the seventh century; but the rock-paintings at Hindagale, representing Buddha in the thirty-third heaven, appears to be of a later date.

1. The rule of succession was that the next younger brother of the king succeeded him on the throne. Only when there was no brother did the crown pass to the next generation, and in that case also the eldest son of the eldest brother of the preceding generation became king. The sister's son of the king enjoyed a certain preference. This remnant of an earlier matriarchy was at times a disturbing factor in the right of succession. A conflict between matriarchy and patriarchy is noticeable in the rivalry of Mahendra II and Dappula for the throne.
2. *SII*, III. 461.
3. *JRAS*, 1913, p. 526.
4. Sastri, *Colas*, I. 148.
5. Altekar, *Rāshṭrakūṭas*, 118-9.
6. The accession of Mahendra V is assigned by Geiger to A.D. 981 but by Hultzsch to A.D. 978. Considering the fact that his 36th regnal year corresponded to a date in A.D. 1016 or 1017, it seems that he ascended the throne in A.D. 979 or more probably in A.D. 980.
7. *SII*, II. 241, 424 ff. Rājarāja's inscription at Padariya in Ceylon is dated in his 27th year corresponding to A.D. 1011-12 (*SII*, II. p. v.).
8. Sewell, *HISI*. 62.
9. *SII*, III. 51 ff.
10. *Ibid*. 202-3.
11. The accession of Vijayabāhu is assigned by Hultzsch to A.D. 1054, and Geiger to A.D. 1059. But the fact that he was defeated by the Choḷas in his 12th regnal year, probably falling shortly before A.D. 1069, and that he recovered the island from the Choḷas in his 15th regnal year or shortly after A.D. 1070 would suggest that he ascended the throne in A.D. 1055-56.
12. For an account of the Pāli literature of Ceylon, cf. Vol. III, pp. 394 ff.

CHAPTER IX

LANGUAGE AND LITERATURE

A. SANSKRIT

I. BELLES-LETTRES

The famous poets of the sixth and the seventh centuries A.D., such as Bhāravi and Māgha, presented a queer combination of real poetic merit with pedantry or artificiality. Of the two sides thus displayed the latter was not only the easier to imitate but was also the more attractive owing to the external show that it could present. The lesser poets that followed these masters, therefore, naturally fell a prey to the temptation and produced works which are noted more for their artificiality than for any intrinsic merit. This love of pedantry was increased to no small extent by the fact that Sanskrit literature was mainly composed not only by the *Paṇḍitas* but also for them. It is, therefore, no wonder if we find pedantry and artificiality to be the general characteristics of the great bulk of literature produced during this and the following ages. It would, however, be wrong to suppose that this age had nothing of real value to contribute to Sanskrit literature. It saw the rise of a special form of prose composition—the *Champū*. It is this age, again, that gives us our earliest anthology, a class of works of no mean importance to the student of Sanskrit literature. But by far the most important contribution of this age to Sanskrit literature is in the field of poetics which reached its high watermark of development during this period.

1. *Drama*

Great importance attaches to the politico-historical play, the *Mudrārākshasa,* of Viśākhadatta, son of the *Mahārāja* Bhāskaradatta or minister Pṛithu, and grandson of Vaṭeśvaradatta, a feudatory, of what prince we are not expressly told. The attempt to place Visākhadatta in the fifth century A.D. on the hypothesis that Vaṭeśvaradatta was a *Sāmanta* of Chandra-gupta II is not well founded. Nor is there any solid ground to assume that he belonged to Bengal. On the strengh of the variant "Avantivarman" occurring in the *Bharatavākya* of the play, some place him in the seventh century at the court of the Maukhari Avantivarman, while others would place him under the Kāshmirian Avantivarman in the middle of the ninth century A.D. But both these theories are considerably weakened by the fact revealed in Hillebrandt's critical edition of the play that the variant is in all probability spurious.[1] Nor is there any definite proof for Jacobi's identification of the eclipse referred to in the play as that of December 2, A.D. 860 when, according to him, the play was enacted.[2] Viśākhadatta is certainly earlier than the tenth century A.D. as he is referred to by Dhanañjaya in his *Daśarūpaka* and also by Abhinavagupta[3] in his commentary on Bharata's *Nāṭyaśāstra*. Viśākhadatta is, therefore, to be assigned very probably to the seventh or the eighth century A.D.

The *Mudrārākshasa*[4] is a play in seven acts, unique in Sanskrit literature as being wholly based on some political or historical theme, and avoiding not only the erotic feeling but also the erotic atmosphere. It is a drama without a heroine. Its author must rank very high indeed owing to the great success he has achieved in creating a highly captivating play out of the dry historical material; and that, too, without the aid of the most inspiring of sentiments—the *śṛiṅgāra*. The play deals with the astute manoeuvres of Chāṇakya to win over Rākshasa, the faithful, clever and honest minister of the exterminated Nandas, to the side of Chandragupta.

There are two other plays ascribed to Viśākhadeva who is very probably the same as Viśākhadatta. One of these, the *Devīchandragupta,* dealing with the story how Dhruvadevī was saved by Chandra-gupta from the ignominy of being surrendered to a Śaka ruler,[5] is known to us only from citations in the *Nāṭyadarpaṇa* by Rāmachandra and Guṇachandra. Abhinava and Bhoja similarly quote from another play, the *Abhisārikāvañchitaka* (or *bandhitaka*) based on a love legend of Udayana, which tells us how Padmāvatī regained the lost love of her husband by playing the role of an *abhisārikā* in the guise of a Śabarī.

On apparently the same theme as that of the *Mudrārākshasa* is based the *Pratibhāchāṇakya* of Bhīma, or Bhīmaṭa. This is only one of the five dramas composed by Bhīma of which the *Svapnadaśānana* won him chief fame. As the *Pratibhāchāṇakya* is modelled after the *Mudrārākshasa,* Bhīma may be placed somewhere in the ninth century A.D There is positive ground for connecting him with the Chandella king Harsha.[6]

To the end of the eighth or the beginning of the ninth century belongs Murāri, son of Vardhamāna of the Maudgalya *Gotra* and Tantumatī. Some scholars place Murāri between A.D. 1050 and 1135 on the strength of the fact that no rhetorician earlier than Maṅkha refers to him.[7] But Ratnākara (middle of the ninth century) makes a clear reference to him in his *Haravijaya,* and the author of the *Prasannarāghava* also seems to have imitated him.[8] The attempt to make him a contemporary of Rāmachandra, a pupil of Hemachandra, is, therefore, futile.[9] From the reference to Māhishmatī as "*agra-mahishī*" in act VII of his play, Konow[10] infers that Murāri was a protégé of a Kalachuri prince at Māhishmatī. This suggestion, if accepted, would place his date prior to the middle of the eighth century A.D. when Māhishmatī ceased to be the capital of the Kalachuris.[11] His work, the *Anargha-rāghava*, is a play in seven acts depicting the early life of Rāma up to his return from the forest, and bears ample testimony to the linguistic abilities of its author, though as a drama its defects are too obvious.[12]

Śaktibhadra, the author of a play called the *Chūḍāmaṇi* (or *Āścharya-Chūḍāmaṇi*), also probably belongs to the end of the eighth or the beginning of the ninth century A.D. To the ninth century belongs the Jain author Hastimalla,[13] son of Govinda of Śrīvatsa *Gotra*, who was a remote disciple of Guṇabhadra. He seems to be a voluminous writer; besides several poems he has given us no less than eight plays including the *Vikrānta-kaurava* (also called the *Sulochanā Nāṭaka*), the *Subhadrāharaṇa*, and the *Maithilīkalyāṇa*.

Slightly later is the polymath Rājaśekhara, who certainly is a great master of words but lacks originality and polish, and cannot, therefore, rank high as a playwright.[14] He has, among other works, composed four dramas. The *Bālarāmāyaṇa* is a Rāma play (a *mahānāṭaka*) in ten acts with an embryo act (*Garbhāṅka*) in the third. The *Bālabhārata*, his next, is only fragmentary. Then comes the *Nāṭikā*—the *Viddhaśālabhañjikā*—in four acts, which is followed by the *Karpūramañjarī*,[15] a *saṭṭaka* wholly in Prakrit (the only play of its type that has come down to us), composed and staged at the request of Avantisundarī. These works were followed by the *Bhuvanakośa*, purporting to be a detailed geography of the then known universe, which is known to us only from a reference made to it by the author in his *Kāvyamīmāṁsā*, an elaborately planned work on poetics. Besides these, Rājaśekhara is known to have composed one more work, the *Harivilāsa* which, as we know from Hemachandra, is a *Svanāmāṅka Kāvya* (an epic bearing the name of its author). This, from citations by Hemachandra and Ujjvaladatta, seems to be a *Mahāprabandha* and may, as such, be taken to be a product of Rājaśekhara's mature age.

Rājaśekhara was the "son of the minister Darduka and Śīlavatī, grandson of Akāla-jalada, and descendant of Surānanda, Tarala, and Kavirāja, all poets of name". He belonged to the Yāyāvara family of Mahārāshṭra, and was a moderate Śaiva by faith. His wife, Avantisundarī, was an accomplished princess of the Chāhamāna family and Rājaśekhara's great regard for her is evinced by his references to her views in his *Kāvyamīmāṁsā*. Rājaśekhara was the *guru* of king Nirbhaya *alias* Mahendrapāla; while his *Bālabhārata*[16] was composed for his successor, Mahīpāla.[17] Again, on the one hand he quotes from Vākpatirāja, Udbhaṭa, and Ānandavardhana, and praises Bhavabhūti; while he himself is referred to by Somadeva and Dhanañjaya and eulogised by Soḍḍhala. He must, therefore, be placed at about A.D. 900.

Kshemīśvara[18] composed his *Chaṇḍakauśika* for Mahīpāla[19] whom H. P. Shastri identifies with the Pāla prince of that name, and Pischel with the Pratīhāra Mahīpāla of Kānyakubja, the patron of Rājaśekhara. According to the former identification Kshemīśvara would belong to the eleventh century, while the latter would take him back to the tenth. His grandfather Vijayakoshṭha or Vijayaprakoshṭha also was a man of learning. The *Chaṇḍakauśika* in five acts deals with the Hariśchandra legend of the *Mārkaṇḍeya Purāṇa* without displaying any distinct dramatic merit or even high poetical ability. His other work is the *Naishadhānanda*[20] in seven acts based on the story of Nala.

To the tenth century belongs also the *Mahānāṭaka* which holds a unique position in Sanskrit literature in more respects than one. It is found in two recensions differing very widely from each other. The Bengali version has fourteen acts and gives the name as *Mahānāṭaka;* while the Devanāgarī, which gives the name as *Hanumannāṭaka,* has only ten. The latter ascribes the work to the monkey of the Rāmāyaṇa fame. Several and varied indeed are the legends[21] current about this play; and though differing in details they are agreed that what is now extant of this unique work is only a recast or reconstruction of the original which is lost. According to one legend it was revised by Madhusūdana at the command of Vikramāditya, while another makes one Dāmodara revise it at the command of Bhoja. The chronology of these versions is hard to fix with any definiteness. It is clear, however, that in its present form the work contains verses not only from the *Rāmāyaṇa* and the *Hitopadeśa,* but also from the *Bālarāmāyaṇa* and the *Anargharāghava;* and is in its turn drawn upon by Subhaṭa of the thirteenth century. But it must be noted that a great portion of this work must be much older, as is suggested by the legends, and also by the fact that three verses from this play have been quoted by Ānandavardhana in his *Dhvanyāloka.*[22]

The *Mahānāṭaka* is not a *Nāṭaka* in the exact sense of the term. It is something between an epic and a dramatic composition comparable to Jayadeva's *Gītagovinda,* which can be enjoyed simply as such, and is at the same time capable of a quasi-dramatic presentment. It is often described as a *Chhāyā-nāṭaka* (shadow-play) on the ground that it resembles in many respects the *Dūtāṅgada,* a *Chhāyā-nāṭaka,* which was acted on the stage on March 7, 1243, at the command of the Chaulukya king Tribhuvanapāla.[23] It is, however, doubtful whether the play can be called a shadow-play at all. In fact the exact meaning of the term *Chhāyā-nāṭaka* is unhappily uncertain; and while Pischel and Konow take it to mean shadow-play, it may also denote a "drama in the state of a shadow."[24] According to Subandhu,[25] this is a *Samagra* type of dramatic composition which, he says, combines in itself all the different characteristics of all the types of *Nāṭaka.* But for want of any further elucidation on this point, the view of Subandhu must remain vague and uncertain. The only statement, therefore, that we may safely make about this play for the present, is that it is a literary drama, a play never intended to be acted, as seems to be shown by the several peculiar features such as the prevalence of verse over prose, absence of Prakrit, the large number of characters, the omission of the Vidūshaka, and its plagiarisms from earlier Rāma dramas.[26]

In conclusion, a brief reference may be made to *Bhāṇa* or monologue play. Four Bhāṇas *viz. Ubhayābhisārikā, Padmaprābhṛitaka, Dhūrtaviṭasaṁvāda* and *Pādatāḍitaka,* ascribed on the strength of a traditional verse respectively to Vararuchi, Śūdraka, Īśvaradatta and Śyāmilaka, have been published under the title *Chaturbhāṇī.* Contrary to Keith[27] who holds none of these plays to be older than A.D. 1000, De fixes the lower limit for *Pādatāḍitaka* (and the rest), by references of Abhinavagupta, Kuntala, and Kshemendra before the end of the tenth century, and takes these plays to be much earlier than Dhanañjaya.[28] Thomas[29] takes the *Pādatāḍitaka* to be considerably older than Abhinavagupta, and places it "in the time of Harsha of Kanauj or even that of the latter Guptas," *i.e.,* sixth or seventh century. These Bhāṇas are different from the later Bhāṇas.

2. *Kāvya*

In the field of *Kāvya* notable contributions have been made during this period by both Buddhist and Jain authors. The Buddhist Śivasvāmin has given us epic, the *Kapphaṇābhyudaya* in twenty cantos, describing the conversion of king Kapphaṇa who had marched against king Prasenajit of Śrāvastī. He wrote under Avantivarman of Kāshmir and is highly influenced by Bhāravi and Māgha.

The Digambara Jain, Jinasena, a disciple of Vīrasena of the Senasaṅgha, is referred to in *Harivaṁśa,* composed in A. D. 783 by another Jinasena, disciple of Kīrtisena, and may thus be referred to the eighth century A.D.[30] He has given us the *Pārśvābhyudaya-*

kāvya which embodies within it the whole text of Kālidāsa's *Meghadūta*, and has also composed the first forty-two chapters of *Ādipurāṇa*. To this *chūlikā*, comprising five chapters, has been added by the author's own pupil Guṇabhadra, who has also composed the *Uttarapurāṇa*, a continuation of the *Ādipurāṇa* giving the lives of the Tīrthaṅkaras after Ṛishabha. Lokasena added a further continuation in A.D. 898. Ravisheṇa's *Padmapurāṇa* was composed in A. D. 678.[31] Asaga is another Jain author who has given us a long epic in eighteen cantos called the *Vardhamānacharita* or the *Mahāvīracharita* or the *Sanmitracharita*. According to the *Praśasti*[32] occurring at the end of a MS. of this work, Asaga composed eight works, including the present one, at Dharalā in Choḷadeśa, in Saṁvat 910 (c. A.D. 853). Mention may also be made of another Jain author Kanakasena Vādirāja, whose *Yaśodharacharita* was composed prior to A.D. 950.[33]

The *Haravijaya*, a long epic in fifty cantos, narrating the story of Śiva killing the demon Andhaka, shows a strong influence of Māgha. It is composed by Rājānaka Ratnākara, son of Amṛitabhānu, who flourished under Jayāpīḍa and Avantivarman of Kāshmir. In spite of the presence of some good stanzas the work betrays a deplorable lack of proportion and excessive fondness for *Yamakas*. The last four cantos of this work are held to be spurious on the ground that Alaka, the author's pupil, has commented only up to the middle of the forty-sixth canto. The *Vakroktipañchāśikā* is another small poem of the same author.

Another Kāshmirian poet of this period is Abhinanda, son of Jayanta, whose fifth ancestor Śaktisvāmin was a minister of Lalitāditya Muktāpīḍa. He refers to Rājaśekhara as a contemporary[34] and is quoted in his *Lochana* by Abhinavagupta. His father Jayantabhaṭṭa in his *Nyāyamañjarī* refers to Śaṅkaravarman as the ruling prince of Kāshmir.[35] Abhinanda must, therefore, belong to the close of the ninth century A.D. His *Kādambarī-Kathāsāra* is an epitome of Bāṇa's *Kādambarī* in an epic form. In the introduction to this work he tells us that his ancestors hailed from Gauḍadeśa. This suggests his identification with another poet of whom we know only from anthologies where he is styled Gauḍa Abhinanda. Although there is no chronological difficulty in the way of this identification it cannot be regarded as certain.[36]

Quite different, however, is the author of the *Rāmacharita*, a long epic in thirty-six cantos, also named Abhinanda, son of Śatānanda. The date of this author is sought to be fixed on the strength of the reference he makes in his epic to Hāravarsha Yuvarāja, son of Vikramaśīla, probably identical with Dharmapāla of Bengal.[37]

There is one more Abhinanda, also styled Gauḍa, who has given us an epitome of the *Yogavāsishṭha* in forty-eight cantos divided into six *prakaraṇas*. His identity with the author of the epitome of the *Kādambarī* is also not yet definitely proved.[38]

One more name that must be mentioned here is that of Vāsudeva, son of Ravi and pupil of Bhārataguru, who has given us three long epics. The *Yudhishṭhiravijaya,* narrating the story of Yudhishṭhira up to his coronation in eight *āśvāsas,* was composed during the reign of Kulaśekhara; while the *Śaurikathodaya* and the *Tripuradahana* mention Rāma as the ruling prince. All these poems very well display their author's fondness for *Yamakas* which has led scholars to ascribe to him even the *Nalodaya.*[39] It is difficult to fix the date of Vāsudeva, for we have no definite clue regarding the identity of his patron Kulaśekhara. Pisharoti and Ayyar would place him in the ninth century A.D, but Keith declares this date to be improbable.[40]

Dhanañjaya, the Jain author of Dvisandhāna (or *Rāghavapāṇḍavīya*), has wrongly been identified by Keith and Winternitz with Dhanañjaya Śrutakīrti, the author of *Nāmamālā* (A. D. 1123-1140); for Dhanañjaya Śrutakīrti, the author of *Dvisandhāna*, is quoted by Vardhamāna and eulogised by Somadeva and Jalhaṇa.[41]

The historical *kāvya* is very meagrely represented in Sanskrit literature as a whole, and causes of this phenomenon are perhaps to be found in the peculiarities of the Indian mind. The inscriptions, which form an important source of our knowledge of the history of the ancient days, and particularly the *Praśastis* or encomia, are often metrical in form and sometimes contain no little poetical merit. But the value of these compositions as poetry varies enormously. It must, however, be said that they represent a first step towards *Praśastis* of the eighth century A. D. composed by Rāmachandra who styles himself Kavīśvara. He displays his mastery over language in a poem of fourteen stanzas applying equally well to Śiva and Pārvatī. A similar phenomenon is observed in the inscription of Lalitasuradeva of the ninth century A. D.[42]

The only important historical *kāvya* belonging to this period is the *Navasāhasāṅkacharita* of Padmagupta *alias* Parimala, son of Mṛigāṅkagupta. This work in eighteen cantos narrates a purely imaginary story of the winning of the princess Śaśiprabhā with a covert reference to the history of king Sindhurāja Navasāhasāṅka of Mālava. Padmagupta is mentioned by Bhoja, Kshemendra and Vardhamāna. He must, therefore, be placed about A.D. 1000.[43]

In the field of lyrical poetry very little has been preserved for us between Kālidāsa and Govardhana, a contemporary of Jayadeva.

In fact the only source of our knowledge of this branch of literature during this age is the anthologies which naturally enough have preserved for us only fragments of the works of poets of whom again nothing more than mere name has been told. There are also cases where even the names have been lost. Thus from anthologies we know of one Pāṇini whose skill as a poet of love is evident from the poems ascribed to him. The grammatical inaccuracies noticeable in these, however, clearly show that he is not to be identified with the great grammarian. To Vākkūṭa and Laḍahachandra are ascribed elegant stanzas voicing forth the condition of the lover at various situations. Śilābhaṭṭārikā is yet another poetess having pretty stanzas ascribed to her, and having the unique honour of being ranked with Bāṇa in point of style.

We are, however, more fortunate in the case of hymns *(stotras)*. After the *Mayūraśataka* and the *Chaṇḍīśataka* of Mayūra and Bāṇa respectively, and after several very pithy hymns ascribed (in some cases rightly) to Śaṅkara the philosopher, we have the *Devīśataka* of Ānandavardhana. In these hundred stanzas addressed to goddess Bhavānī, the author, even against his own theories so ably expressed in his *Dhvanyāloka,* pays more attention to the embellishments than to suggestion, in keeping with his own admission again that the latter is only of secondary importance in hymns. To the first quarter of the tenth century belongs Utpaladeva's *Stotrāvalī* consisting of twenty short hymns addressed to Śiva. About the same period was composed the *Mukundamālā* which is a hymn in honour of Vishṇu by Kulaśekhara,[44] who very probably is dfferent from the patron of Vāsudeva, the author of the *Yudhishṭhiravijaya.* The date of the *Śyāmalādaṇḍaka* as well as its authorship is now fortunately settled on the strength of the evidence supplied by a MS. which leaves no doubt that the work was composed, not by Kālidāsa to whom it is traditionally ascribed, but by one Purāntaka, son of Mahādeva, a worshipper in the temple of Mahākālī. From the same source we learn that king Bhoja of Dhārā showed his appreciation of the work by granting a hundred *agrahāras* in A.D. 1001.[45] This work is in a peculiar variety of prose called *Daṇḍaka* which has a fixed melody. Mention may here be made of two Jain authors, Śobhana and Mānatuṅga. The former, also known as Śiromaṇi, was a staunch Jain of the court of Dhārā in the tenth century, and has given us a hymn in honour of Tīrthaṅkaras variously called *Chaturviṁśati-Jinastuti,* or *Tīrtheśastuti* or *Śobhanastuti.* This has been commented upon by his brother Dhanapāla.[46] Mānatuṅga, the famous author of the *Bhaktāmarastotra,* was, according to a *Paṭṭāvalī* of the Bṛihad-Gachchha, a minister of Vairisiṁha of the Paramāra dynasty of Mālava. In the *Prabhāvakacharita* his life is given after that of Bappabhaṭṭi who died in Saṁvat 895; but at the same time we are told that he was a contemporary of Mayūra and Bāṇa at the court of king Harsha.[47] It is thus difficult to fix the date of this author, though we may be sure that he was earlier than A.D. 1000.[48]

Of the didactic poems we may note only three. The earliest is the *Kuṭṭanīmata* of Dāmodaragupta, a minister of king Jayāpīḍa of Kāshmir. This is a very highly interesting small poem and may be said to be a sort of manual for the guidance of the *hetaerae.* To the ninth century belongs the *Bhallaṭaśataka* of Bhallaṭa who wrote under king Śaṅkaravarman of Kāshmir. This is a collection of a hundred stanzas in different metres carefully elaborated. Curiously enough it contains one stanza of Ānandavardhana. The Jain Somadeva, author of the *Yaśastilaka champū* (tenth century), composed the *Nītivākyāmṛita* which, though definitely more moral in its tone, is yet almost entirely based on Kauṭilya's *Arthaśāstra* to which it may well serve as a sort of commentary. It advises kings to behave well and prudently rather than with cunning.

The *Kīchakavadha,*[49] narrating in five cantos the story of Bhīma killing Kīchaka and his followers, is one of the earliest specimens of *Ślesha* and *Yamaka* and similiar devices pressed into the service of poetry. It has been quoted, as is but natural, by grammarians, rhetoricians, and also lexicographers, the earliest being Namisādhu who composed his commentary on Rudraṭa's *Kāvyālaṁkāra* in A.D. 1069. But beyond his name, Nītivarman, we know nothing about the author of this work. Similar, though of poor workmanship, is the *Rākshasakāvya* (or *Kāvyarākshasa*) which is variously ascribed to Kālidāsa, Ravideva, and Vararuchi, though Keith[50] is inclined to accept Ravideva as its author. Winternitz[51] sees stylistic and other similarities of this poem with the *Nalodaya,* and ascribes both to Ravideva, son of Nārāyaṇa. The *Nalodaya,* narrating in three cantos the story of Nala, is again a highly elaborate poem ascribed to Kālidāsa. There can, however, be no doubt that it is not from the pen of the author of *Raghuvaṁśa,* who never indulges in elaborate metres or rhymes. Keith[52] ascribes this work to Vāsudeva, the author of the *Yudhishṭhiravijaya.* Whoever be the author of the *Rākshasakāvya,* its date can tolerably be fixed on the strength of the fact that a manuscript of some anonymous commentary thereon was copied in Saṁvat 1215 (*c.* A.D. 1159). It may, therefore, be presumed that the poem itself was composed much earlier than the twelfth century.[53]

The anthologies, as a class of literary works, first make their appearance in the tenth century. These, of course, are collections of stanzas composed by poets of old, arranged according to various principles. It is, therefore, futile to seek any originality in these and yet they are important since they preserve, at least in parts, the work of many early poets that would otherwise have been totally lost to us. The only work of this class that we have to note here is the *Kavīndravachana-samuchchaya*,[54] the earliest anthology as yet known to us. It differs from some other anthologies only in having one section devoted to Buddha and another to Avalokiteśvara. It is noteworthy that none of the poets, whose stanzas have been preserved in this collection of 525 stanzas, flourished later than about A.D. 1000. Among the royal poets[55] revealed by these anthologies may be mentioned Yaśovarman of Kanauj, Jayāpīḍa and Avantivarman of Kāshmir, and Vākpatirāja II of Dhārā.

Budhasvāmin's *Ślokasaṁgraha*[56] (an abridgement in verse of Guṇāḍhya's *Bṛihat-kathā*) is an important poem. For it is more faithful to Guṇāḍhya's work than the well-known collections of tales in *Kathāsaritsāgara* and *Bṛihatkathāmañjarī* which can now be regarded as representing only the Kāshmirian recension of the original. Unfortunately, however, we have only a fragment of this works so that it is difficult to form an exact estimate of Budhasvāmin's workmanship. It is, however, apparent that he has shown considerable art in his work and deserves praise. He is definitely earlier than Kshemendra and Somadeva. Nor can the gulf of time removing him from Guṇāḍhya be very wide. There is, however, no strong ground on which to fix the date of this author; and Lacôte's view that he belongs to the eighth or the ninth century is only a conjecture based on the manuscript tradition.

3. *Romance*

In the field of romance, we have to note two works, the *Mādhavānala-Kāmakandalā-Kathā* and the *Tilakamañjarī*. The former is the well-known love story of the Brāhmaṇa Mādhavānala and the dancer Kāmakandalā who, after a long and painful separation, were at last married to each other through king Vikramāditya. The story is narrated in simple artless prose in Sanskrit interspersed with numerous verses in Sanskrit as well as Prakrit, many of which appear in the *Vetālapañchaviṁśatikā* and also in anthologies.[57] It is composed by Ānanda, a pupil of Bhaṭṭa Vidyādhara about whose date, however, we know nothing definitely. The *Tilakamañjarī* is a romance composed admittedly in imitation of Bāṇa's *Kādambarī* by Dhanapāla,[58] son of Sarvadeva, brother of Śobhana who converted him to Jainism. He was a contemporary of Halāyudha, Padmagupta, Dhanañjaya and Devabhadra and enjoyed the patronage of kings Sīyaka and Vākpati of Dhārā. Before his conversion he composed the Prakrit Lexicon *Pāïyalachchhī*[59] in A.D. 972-3, and it was after becoming a Jain that he composed the *Ṛishabhapañchāśikā*[60] in fifty Prakrit stanzas. Merutuṅga, in his *Prabandhachintāmaṇi,* has narrated the incident which induced Dhanapāla to name his romance after his daughter.

4. *Champū*

Whatever may be said to be the origin of the *Champū,* it is certain that it is the most elaborate and artificial form in Sanskrit literature, calculated to afford to the poet the amplest opportunities to display not only his erudition but also his command over prose as well as verse in one and the same composition. Up to the tenth century, compositions were either in prose or in verse almost exclusively; and even when they were in prose and verse intermingled, the latter was used only occasionally and for some definite purposes. But the yearning of poets to display their mastery over both simultaneously seems to be responsible for the rise of this altogether new form in Sanskrit literature. Though the earliest traces[61] of this form can be found in the *Jātakamālā* and the inscription of Harisheṇa, yet the earliest work of this class, written in full *Kāvya* style, belongs to the tenth century A.D., so that the *Champū* may be said to be one of the contributions of this age to Sanskrit literature.

The word *Champū* itself is of obscure origin. Nor has the form any very definite technique. Viśvanātha defines it merely as a *Kāvya* in prose and verse,[62] which shows that its technique was apparently the same as that of *Kāvya,* but for the intermingling of prose and verse. Nor is there any fixity as regards the purposes which are to be served by prose and verse respectively.

The earliest work of this class that has come down to us is the *Nalachampū,* also called *Damayantīkathā,* of Trivikramabhaṭṭa. It is only a torso in seven chapters narrating the famous epic story of Nala. Trivikrama does not seem to be a very good poet in spite of his own boasts, though his erudition and linguistic art must be admitted as being pretty high. The *Madālasāchampū* is another work of this class composed by this very Trivikrama, son of Nemāditya[63] and grandson of Śrīdhara of Śāṇḍilya *Gotra.* He belonged to the beginning of the tenth century and was a poet at the court of the Rāshṭrakūṭa king Indra III, for whom he composed the text of the Navsāri inscription in A.D. 915.

To the middle of the tenth century belongs the Digambara Jain Somadeva, the author of the *Yaśastilakachampū* composed in Śaka 881 (c. A.D. 959) during the reign of the Rāshṭrakūṭa king Kṛishṇa III. Though Somadeva is known from his work as belonging to Devasaṁgha, Yaśodeva of the Gauḍasaṁgha is mentioned in the Lemulavāḍa grant as his grand-preceptor. Again in the *Champū*, Somadeva twice addresses the king as Dharmāvaloka which title was borne by Tuṅga of the Bodh-Gayā branch of the Rāshṭrakūṭas. It would, therefore, appear that Somadeva was originally a pupil of the Gauḍasaṁgha in the Gauḍadeśa and was probably patronised by the Bodh-Gayā Rāshṭrakūṭas, from whom he went to Lemulavāḍa under the Rāshṭrakūṭa feudatories Arikesarin and his successors. And as the Rāshṭrakūṭas had intimate contact with the Chedis and the Gurjara Pratīhāras of Kanauj, it is not unlikely that Somadeva came into contact with Mahendrapāla (probably II) of Kanauj, and at his instance composed the *Nītivākyāmṛita* as is declared in some anonymous commentary.[64] Before this, however, Somadeva had composed the *Shaṇṇavatiprakaraṇa*, the *Yuktichintāmaṇi* and the *Mahendramātalisañjalpa* as we know from the colophon of his *Nītivākyāmṛita*. All these, however, are to us no more than mere names as yet.

The *Yaśastilakachampū* narrates the story of the legendary king Yaśodhara of Ujjain in seven chapters in full *Kāvya* style, and shows the great erudition and linguistic attainments of its author. From it again we learn that Somadeva, from his childhood, had made a deep study of *Tarkaśāstra*,[65] which, however, did not banish all poetic abilities from him. But our main interest in this work centres round the fact that its last three chapters are devoted to a discussion of the Jain dogmas, so much so that this part is often taken to be a manual of Jainism for laymen.

Lastly, mention may be made of *Udayasundarīkathā*, which is sometimes regarded as a *Champū*. It was composed by Soḍḍhala who describes himself as a Vāllabha Kāyastha of Lāṭa. He flourished about A.D. 1000 and lived in the court of king Mummuṇirāja of Konkan.[66]

II. SCIENTIFIC LITERATURE

1. *Lexicography*

The *Dhanvantari Nighaṇṭu*, the earliest extant medical lexicon in its present form belongs to this period, though in its original form it may be much older. Of the ordinary dictionaries (*kośa*) only one can with some accuracy be assigned to this period, and that is the *Abhidhāna-ratnamālā* of Halāyudha who has followed the authority of Amaradatta, Vararuchi, Bhāguri and Vopālita.[67] The arrangement of the work is almost like that of the *Amarakośa*. The synonymous portion extends over four *kāṇḍas* called *Svarga, Bhūmi*.

Pātāla and *Sāmānya,* and is followed by the *Anekārthakāṇḍa,* the fifth and the last, which forms the homonymous portion including the indeclinables. The earliest author to quote from this *Kośa* is Maṅkha who lived in the first half of the twelfth century A.D. It may also be noted that though Kshīrasvāmin, in his commentary on the *Amarakośa,* quotes a very large number of works and authors, he has not quoted Halāyudha or his *Kośa.* This Halāyudha has been identified[68] with the author of the *Kavirahasya* and the commentary called the *Mṛitasañjīvinī* on Piṅgala's *Chhandaḥsūtra.* The latter was composed in honour of king Muñja Vākpati of Dhārā between A.D. 974 and 995; while the former is an elaborate poem, meant to illustrate the modes of the formation of the present tense in Sanskrit literature, and is at the same time a eulogy of king Kṛishṇarāja III of the Rāshṭrakūṭa dynasty, who ruled over the Deccan between A.D. 939 and 967.

2. *Grammar*

In grammar we come across the name of Maitreyarakshita, a Buddhist, who wrote a commentary on the *Nyāsa* of Jinendrabuddhi under the title of *Tantrapradīpa,* and has also to his credit the *Dhātupradīpa,* based on the *Dhātupāṭha* of Pāṇini. It is difficult to fix the date of this author; for the only thing we know about him is that Sarvānanda (A.D. 1159), the commentator of the *Amarakośa,* is the earliest writer to quote him by name. His *Dhātupradīpa* refers to, and is therefore later than, the *Tantrapradīpa.* Another rival commentary on Jinendrabuddhi's *Nyāsa* is the *Anunyāsa* composed by Indu or Indumitra who may have flourished earlier than Maitreyarakshita. One more writer, of the ninth century, is Vimalamati who is known to have composed the *Bhāgavṛitti.*[69]

Śākaṭāyana,[70] the founder of a new school, belongs to the ninth century. There can be no doubt regarding the historicity of the writer; and his date also has been fixed beyond all dispute on the strength of a reference made by him in his *Amoghavṛitti* to an historical event of the reign of king Amoghavarsha, the great Rāshṭrakūṭa king who ruled between A.D. 814 and 878. His main work is the *Śabdānuśāsana,* which, however, has little originality though at one time it seems to have attained very high popularity, not only among the Śvetāmbara Jains for whom it was intended, but also among other non-Jain authors.

Durgasiṁha, who probably flourished about A.D. 800, is the oldest known commentator on Kātantra grammar or Kālāpa, as it is otherwise known. In addition to his *Vṛitti,* on which he himself wrote a *Ṭīkā,* we have also another commentary, *viz. Śishyahitanyāsa* by Ugrabhūti (c. A.D. 1000). Though *Kātantra* may have been very old in its origin, we have at present no work of this school earlier than that of Durgasiṁha. This school spread over Bengal and Kāshmir. Among the Kāshmirian writers may be mentioned Bhaṭṭa Jagaddhara and Chhichhubhaṭṭa who composed the *Bālabodhinī* and the *Laghuvṛitti* respectively about A.D. 1000.[71]

3. *Poetics*[72]

Greater and more fruitful activity was evinced during this age in the field of poetics.[73] To this age belonged great rhetoricians like Udbhaṭa, Vāmana, Rudraṭa, Ānandavardhana, Abhinavagupta, and Kuntaka (or Kuntala). It is this age again that saw the rise and growth of the various theories of poetics laying stress respectively on factors like *Alaṁkāra* (ornament or poetic figures), *Rīti* (style), *Dhvani* (tone, suggestion), and *Vakrokti* (crooked speech) as the essence of poetry. This age may, therefore, be said to be the golden age of Sanskrit poetics.

The mightiest champion and representative of the *Alaṁkāra* school is Udbhaṭa whose name is associated with several doctrines in *Alaṁkāraśāstra*. Thus the theory of *arthabhedāt śabdabhedaḥ* or the twofold division of *Ślesha* (double meaning), its inclusion among figures of sense, and regarding it as stronger than other figures are often referred to as peculiar to Udbhaṭa, who also seems to have elaborated for the first time the divisions of *Upamā* (simile) on the basis of grammar. He often differs from Bhāmaha, the earliest exponent of the *Alaṁkāra* school, on some important matters. He exercised such great influence on Sanskrit poetics, and attained such high celebrity, that he easily eclipsed his predecessor Bhāmaha and threw him into oblivion for a long period. His *magnum opus* is the *Alaṁkārasārasaṁgraha*, defining forty-one figures in about seventy-nine verses, and illustrating them in about a hundred illustrative stanzas, taken mostly, as we know it from the commentator, from his own *Kumārasambhava* which, to judge from the verses we have before us, very much resembled Kālidāsa's poem of that name. The work is divided into six chapters (*varga*) and was commented upon by Pratīhārendurāja about the middle of the tenth century A.D. Udbhaṭa is often quoted in the *Dhvanyāloka*, and Kalhaṇa tells us that he was *Sabhāpati* of king Jayāpīḍa of Kāshmir.[74] Udbhaṭa must, therefore, have flourished in the second half of the eighth century A.D.

Next to Udbhaṭa comes Rudraṭa, the author of the *Kāvyālaṁkāra* which, in seven hundred and thirty-four verses, divided into sixteen chapters, deals with all the important topics of the *Sāhityaśāstra*, and reviews the whole field of that science. He declares that Kāvya must have *Rasa* (sentiment), and thus indicates his acquaintance with the *Rasa* theory. But this does not prove that he belongs to the *Rasa* school. The *Rītis* (styles) he refers to only casually, and neglects *Guṇas* (qualities) altogether. But to *Alaṁkāras* he attaches great importance which may justify the view that he was a writer of the *Alaṁkāra* school. His partiality to figures appears not only from the fact that he defines a greater number of them than is done by Bhāmaha, Daṇḍin, and Udbhaṭa, but also from his exposition of the figures which is more systematic and scientific than theirs. No predecessor has been mentioned by name by Rudraṭa, though he seems to refer to Bharata and to Mayūra, the author of the *Mayūraśataka*. This shows that he must be later than these two writers. He must again be much earlier than A.D. 1068-69 when a commentary on his work was composed by Namisādhu, a Śvetāmbara Jain and pupil of Śālibhadra. Again he is quoted by numerous writers from the tenth century onwards. Thus he is quoted or referred to by Rājaśekhara, Pratīhārendurāja, Dhanika, Abhinavagupta, and Mammaṭa. Thus Rudraṭa cannot be later than A.D. 900, and his acquaintance with the *Dhvani* theory coupled with his great affinity with Bhāmaha and Udbhaṭa shows that he must have flourished between A.D. 800 and 850. It appears from Namisādhu's commentary on *Kāvyālaṁkāra*[75] that Rudraṭa was also known by the name Śatānanda, and that his father's name was Vāmuka.

Mention may be made of another work which is based on Rudraṭa's *Kāvyālaṁkāra*. It is the *Śṛiṅgāratilaka* which, in three chapters called *Parichchhedas*, deals with the *Rasas*, the *Bhāvas* (emotions), the kinds of *Nāyaka* (hero) and *Nāyikā* (heroine), the *Vipralambha Śṛiṅgāra* in its various stages, the six *upāyas* (means) of winning one's offended beloved, the other *Rasas*, and the four *vṛittis*. Very often the author of this work, whose name is Rudrabhaṭṭa, is confounded with the author of the *Kāvyālaṁkāra*. But there seems to be very little solid ground for the identification of these two authors. Thus, for example, while Rudraṭa has not one word to say in favour of the courtesans, Rudrabhaṭṭa, even after admitting all strictures against them, has yet to offer some defence on their behalf. But on the whole there is a remarkable similarity between the two, not only of thought but even of phraseology, which can be accounted for only on the assumption of one of the two being the borrower. Rudrabhaṭṭa must, therefore, be placed after Rudraṭa and as such may be said to have lived between A.D. 900 and 1000 the lower limit being roughly determined on the strength of the fact that the earliest writer to quote from the *Śṛiṅgāratilaka* is Hemachandra.

A marked advance over the *Alaṁkāra* school is made by the *Rīti* school, the foremost champion of which is Vāmana, the author of the *Kāvyālaṁkārasūtravṛtti.* The representatives of the former looked upon the *Alaṁkāras* as the soul of poetry, and were thus yet far away from the real essence of poetry. Vāmana, however, for the first time emphatically asserted that the soul of poetry was *Rīti*, which consists in such a peculiar arrangement of words that they would exhibit *Guṇas.* The real essence of poetry had not yet been discovered, for the *Rīti* school was not yet aware of what the *Guṇa* belong to. But credit is due to Vāmana for having made a very close approach to the soul of poetry which it was left for his successors to realise in full. Vāmana's work comprises three hundred and nineteen *Sūtras,* divided into five parts (*parichchheda*), which are subdivided into twelve *adhyāyas,* with a *vṛitti* thereon composed by the author himself and illustrations derived from various sources. Besides the main theory of *Rīti* being the soul of poetry, there are other doctrines which are recognised as being peculiar to Vāmana. Such, for example, are the distinction between *Guṇas* and *Alaṁkāras,* the inclusion of *Vakrokti* among figures of sense, and the peculiar definition of *Viśeshokti* and *Ākshepa.* Vāmana quotes from Māgha and Bhavabhūti among others, and is himself quoted by Rājaśekhara and Pratīhārendurāja. Kalhaṇa mentions Vāmana as one of the ministers of king Jayāpīḍa of Kāshmir. Vāmana would thus appear to be a contemporary and perhaps even a rival of Udbhaṭa who was a *Sabhāpati* of the same king.

But by far the most important school of poetics that arose in this age is the *Dhvani* school championed emphatically by Ānandavardhana, the author of the famous *Dhvanyāloka.* Like many other works on poetics this also comprises three parts, the *Kārikā,* the *Vṛitti* and the *Udāharaṇa.* The last is derived from the vast field of Sanskrit literature; but there is a keen controversy regarding the authorship of the other two. According to Winternitz, Keith, De, and others, the author of the *Kārikā* is to be distinguished from that of the *Vṛitti.* The former is, according to them, in all probability Sahṛidaya, while the latter is Ānandavardhana or simply Ānanda. Dr. Satkari Mookerjee,[76] on the other hand, has argued in favour of the identity of authorship of the *Kārikā* and the *Vṛitti* with no fresh material to adduce in support of his view. The problem therefore remains unsolved. According to Kalhaṇa, Ānandavardhana lived at the time of Avantivarman of Kāshmir. He may, therefore, be said to have flourished about the middle of the ninth century A. D. Besides the epoch-making *Dhvanyāloka,* Ānandavardhana has also composed the *Devīśataka,* before which, however, he had already composed the *Tridaśānanda* and the *Ānandakathā,* which are only other names of the *Arjunacharita* and the *Vishamabāṇalīlā* respectively.[77] From Abhinavagupta again we learn that Ānandavardhana had also written the *Dharmottamā* which is a commentary on the *Pramāṇaviniśchaya* of Dharmakīrti. The *Tattvāloka* is yet another work in which he has discussed the relation between *Śāstranaya* and *Kāvyanaya.* About Ānandavardhana himself, however, we know hardly anything beyond the fact that he was the son of Noṇa, and that the author of the *Kārikās* in the *Dhvanyāloka,* if at all he was different from Ānandavardhana, was in all probability his *guru.*

In the *Dhvanyāloka,* comprising one hundred and twenty-nine *Kārikās* divided into four chapters (*Uddyota*), Ānandavardhana has stated several views regarding *Dhvani* (tone or suggestion), including his own, given its classification on the basis of *Vyaṅgya* and also on that of *Vyañjaka,* tried to fix the place of *Guṇas* and *Alaṁkāras* in poetry, and ultimately stated his view regarding *Pratibhā* and the province of poetry. It was in this work that the theory of *Dhvani* in rhetorics found its first expression in clear and definite terms, though it might have been in the air for some time before it.

It must, however, be noted that even this admirable work, propounding an equally admirable theory, had to pass through the ordeal of very severe criticism before it found general acceptance. In due course, however, it established itself to such an extent, that even a fastidious author like Jagannātha declared that Ānandavardhana had settled all the important problems of poetics. Before dealing with the critics, however, we must note its commentator Abhinavagupta, who refers to and criticises an older commentary called *Chandrikā* composed by someone belonging to Abhinava's own family. Abhinavagupta was the son of Chukhala and grandson of Varāhagupta and elder brother of Manoratha, as he himself tells us in his *Parātriṁśikīvivaraṇa.* He has several works to his credit, and appears to have at least three *gurus.* In his *Lochana* he refers to Bhaṭṭendurāja and Utpala as his *guru* and *paramaguru* respectively. Bhaṭṭa Tauta, the author of the *Kāvyakautuka,* is also referred to in the same work as his *guru;* while Lakshmaṇagupta seems to have been his teacher in Śaiva philosophy. His literary activity may be said to have extended from A.D. 990 to 1020, since we know that he composed his *Bhairavastotra* in A.D. 993, and his *Pratyabhijñāvimarśinī* in A.D. 1015.

Pratīhārendurāja, Kuntaka, Bhaṭṭanāyaka and Mahimabhaṭṭa made very severe criticisms against the views of the *Dhvani* school. Pratīhārendurāja is the commentator of Udbhaṭa, and is one of the oldest commentators in the field of poetics. He has taken up all the examples of *Dhvani* given by Ānandavardhana, and has shown that they are one and all merely examples of *Alaṁkāras*. Bhaṭṭanāyaka, the author of the *Hṛidayadarpaṇa*, flourished between A.D. 900 and 1000; while Mahimabhaṭṭa came shortly after A.D. 1000. Kuntaka is perhaps the mightiest of the critics of the *Dhvani* school, and is the founder of a new theory called *Vakrokti* (figurative speech). This theory he has explained in his *Vakroktijīvita* in four parts (*unmesha*). Like many other works on poetics it contains *Kārikās*, *Vṛitti*, and *Udāharaṇas*, the two former being his own work and the last being borrowed from various authors. In this work he defines *Vakrokti* as a speech that charms by the skill of the poet, and then goes on to give the several varieties of *Vakrokti* together with illustrative examples. His contention is that *Dhvani* cannot have an independent existence as the soul of poetry. It comes only under *Vakrokti* which, therefore, must be admitted as the soul of poetry. Kuntaka quotes Ānandavardhana, Rudraṭa, and Rājaśekhara, and is himself quoted by Mahimabhaṭṭa in his *Vyaktiviveka*, and his views are summarised in the *Alaṁkārasarvasva*. He would thus belong to the latter half of the tenth century A.D., slightly later than Abhinavagupta who makes no reference to *Vakroktijīvita*.

The *Kāvyamīmāṁsā* of Rājaśekhara, whose works have been already noticed above, is important and interesting not so much for the theory it preaches, but from various other points of view. Instead of dealing with the *Rasas*, *Guṇas* and *Alaṁkāras* directly, it treats of various topics which are very useful to the poet. This work may be said to be a practical handbook of a poet. From the introductory chapter it would appear that the extant work is only the first part of what was originally planned by Rājaśekhara. Two more authors whose names may be mentioned are Mukulabhaṭṭa and Bhaṭṭa Tauta. The former, the son of Kallaṭa and a contemporary of Rājaśekhara, flourished in the reign of king Avantivarman of Kāshmir. In his *Abhidhāvṛittimātṛikā*, the only work that has come down to us, he discusses in fifteen *Kārikās*, with *Vṛitti* thereon, the two powers of words, *viz. abhidhā* and *lakshaṇā*. Bhaṭṭa Tauta is known to us as Abhinavagupta's *guru* and the author of the *Kāvyakautuka*, known only from citations. Abhinavagupta in his *Lochana* tells us that he had written a *Vivaraṇa* on his work. Kshemendra, Hemachandra, and Someśvara refer to and quote from him. He is credited with the famous definition of *Pratibhā* as '*Prajñā navanavonmeshaśālinī pratibhā matā*.' He held the *Śānta* as the most important of the *Rasas*, and one more peculiar doctrine of his that may be mentioned is that *Kavi*, the *Nāyaka* and the reader (*Śrotā*) pass through the same experience so far as *Rasa* is concerned. Evidently again, he was against the view of Śaṅkuka, *viz.* '*anukaraṇarūpo-*

rasaḥ.' He must have flourished about A.D. 960-990 and had greatly influenced Abhinavagupta.

On dramaturgy there are, indeed, very few works that have come down to us; and almost all that we know at present, with the exception of Bharata's *Nāṭyaśāstra,* is later than about A.D. 1000. Only two works that are slightly earlier than A.D. 1000 are the *Daśarūpaka* and *Nāṭakaratnakośa* (or *Nāṭaka-lakshaṇaratnakosa*). The former belongs to the latter half of the tenth century A.D. approximately, since we are told that the *Kārikās* were composed by Dhanañjaya at the time of king Muñja (A.D. 974-994). Dhanika, very probably his younger brother, commented on this work slightly later. The *Nāṭakaratnakośa*[78] is a similar work composed by Sāgaranandin. From the views expressed in his work, Sāgaranandin would seem to be earlier than Dhanañjaya. Besides this work he seems to have written another work, a play named *Jānakīharaṇa.*

In conclusion, even at the risk of some repetition, we may make a general survey of the development of the theory of poetics and show how rhetoricians began by emphasizing the purely external constituent of poetry, *viz.* the figures of speech, and ultimately succeeded in discovering the real soul of poetry in suggestion or *Dhvani.* The *Rasa* theory was evolved by Bharata mainly with reference to dramatic works and could be applied to complete poetical compositions alone. But nobody ever knew then how it could be applied to single verses also. It was only after a lapse of some centuries that the *Dhvani* school arose and extended the *Rasa* theory to even stray verses. The earliest rhetoricians, however, looked upon the *Alaṁkāras* as the most important constituent of poetry. Thus Bhāmaha, Udbhaṭa, Daṇḍin, Rudraṭa, and Pratīhārendurāja not only devoted a major portion of their works to *Alaṁkāras,* but also gave a very systematic and detailed treatment thereof. They were not quite unaware of the *Rasa* theory or even of the suggested sense or *Dhvani.* But they could not apply that theory to poetry and naturally subordinated *Rasa* to *Alaṁkāras,* thus giving figures like *rasavat, preyas,* and *ūrjasvī.* Another important result of the *Alaṁkāra* theory was the exuberant growth of figures of speech in general and the *śabdālaṁkāras* in particular. The importance gained by the *śabdālaṁkāras* naturally gave a sort of impetus to what is known as the *Chitra kāvya. Alaṁkāra,* however, is only an external matter and has little to do with the soul of poetry as is suggested by the name itself. Vāmana, therefore, set aside the *Alaṁkāras* and hit upon something more internal—more essential—, *viz. Rīti* and declared it to be the soul of poetry. That the *Rīti* school wielded great influence is evident from the fact that *Rīti* forms an important topic in almost every work on rhetorics after Vāmana. It must, however, be observed that the importance already gained by the *Alaṁkāras* was never on the wane. This is evident from the fact that every rhetorician of note has devoted a major portion of his work to them. Vāmana has certainly made a real advance over his predecessors, but yet even he could not reach the goal and was only groping in the dark. He could see that the *Alaṁkāras* were too extraneous to deserve the title of the soul of poetry. But he could not discover the real soul thereof, which it was left for Ānandavardhana to do. The *Dhvani* school founded by Ānandavardhana is, in fact, an extension of *Rasa* theory. Taking his cue from the tenet that *Rasa* is only *vyaṅgya,* he propounded the theory that *vyaṅgya artha, i.e. Dhvani,* is the soul of poetry; and further based his classification of poetry on the relative prominence enjoyed by the *vāchya* and the *vyaṅgya arthas* therein. Thus though, while classifying poetry Ānandavardhana admits *Chitra* as the third variety, he holds that poetry in the real sense of the term can be only of one type, and that is *Dhvani kāvya.* He runs down *Chitra kāvya* in very strong terms with the natural result that the prominence enjoyed by it along with *Alaṁkāras,* both of sound as well as sense, dwindled into insignificance. And had no later rhetorician like Kuntaka said something calculated to revive it, *Chitra kāvya* in all probability would not have waxed so strong at all in Sanskrit literature. The views of Ānandavardhana had, however, to pass through the fiery ordeal of penchant criticism at the hands of Pratīhārendurāja and others before they found general acceptance. The influence and importance of the *Dhvanyāloka* is evident from the fact that it has been looked upon as almost the last word on poetics by no less a rhetorician than Jagannātha Paṇḍita. About a century later Kuntaka with all his critical acumen tried to criticise the *Dhvani* theory and founded a separate school of his own declaring *vakrokti* as the soul of poetry. From Kuntaka's definition of *vakratā* and its classification it is evident that Kuntaka wanted to make his *vakratā* as comprehensive as possible so as to include all classes of *kāvya* within its purview. According to Ānandavardhana *Chitra kāvya* is *kāvya* only by courtesy; but Kuntaka would admit it as *kāvya* without any grudge. For according to him any composition that is possessed of *vakratā* in any of its six varieties deserves the name of *kāvya.* Kuntaka thus, it would appear, tried to effect a compromise among all the three different schools before him; and in this he seems to have succeeded very well as can be seen from the fact that in the later centuries we find the *Chitra* aspect of the *kāvya* also receiving great attention. From this point of view, however, one cannot help thinking that Kuntaka did more harm than good to Sanskrit *kāvya* when one finds that once *Chitra kāvya* and the *śabdālaṁkāras* got a sort of sanction at the hands of Kuntaka, they cropped up in such exuberance as to stifle real poetry or *Dhvani kāvya.* It is true that Kuntaka had very few followers among the rhetoricians; and yet it cannot be denied that poets of the later centuries finding *Dhvani kāvya* perhaps much beyond their capacities, for want of the most important requisite, *pratibhā,* turned their attention more to the other type of *kāvya* which afforded better opportunities for a display of learning and scholarship and which it was easier to compose even in the absence of *pratibhā.* In fact even writers possessed of *pratibhā* did not remain satisfied by composing simple suggestive poetry without any display of the various feats with the help of words and their sounds. This is evident from works like the *Gītagovinda.* Later rhetoricians right from Mammaṭa down to Jagannātha Paṇḍita championed the *Dhvani* theory, no doubt; but even they could not deny a place to *Chitra kāvya* in their classification of poetry, with the result that its growth could not be retarded. There was, indeed, little in the field of poetics after Ānandavardhana (or perhaps after Kuntaka) which can be said to be new; and the reasons for such a state of things are perhaps to be sought in the social, religious and even political condition of India during these centuries.

4. *Metrics*

As regards metrics, the only important writer on Sanskrit Metres is Utpala who lived in the latter half of the tenth century A.D. In his commentary to chapter 103 of Varāhamihira's *Bṛihatsaṁhitā,* he has given us about sixty definitions of the Sanskrit Akshara-Gaṇa Vṛittas. About forty of these definitions have been bodily reproduced from Jayadeva's work.[79] Utpala also quotes two illustrations from Prakrit which contain the name of the metre as well as its illustration. This would show that Prakrit metrics too had well developed by that time, so much so that the Prakrit metricians had begun to compose their own illustrations like the Sanskrit metricians, instead of quoting stanzas from already existing Prakrit poems. This naturally indicates a late stage in the development of Prakrit metrics.

Svayambhūchhandas is a very important[80] work so far as the history of Prakrit poetry is concerned. The author Svayambhū is an early Jain writer and is known to have composed two long poems in the Apabhraṁśa language. He is later than Mayūra and Śrīharsha and probably lived in the tenth century A.D. He is respectfully mentioned by Hemachandra in his *Chhandonuśāsana,* and by Pushpadanta in his *Mahāpurāṇa* in A.D. 965.

5. *Medicine*

Though the principal *Saṁhitās* of medicine had already been composed, it was left to this age to bring to perfection the branch of pathology in the masterly work called *Rugviniśchaya*, known also as *Mādhava-nidāna* after its author, or simply *Nidāna*. This work of Mādhavakara, son of Indukara, for the first time in the history of Indian medicine, treats of all diseases together and has often been laid under contribution by later writers on this subject such as Chakrapāṇidatta and Vaṅgasena. The numerous commentaries on this work show that it enjoyed high popularity. It is not clear whether Mādhavakara is earlier than Dṛiḍhabala, son of Kapilabala, who is said to have revised and enlarged the *Charaka-saṁhitā* of Agniveśa in the eighth or the ninth century A.D. He is generally assigned to the ninth century A.D.[81]

The *Siddhiyoga* (also called *Vṛindamādhava*) is another curious work belonging to the same period which closely follows the order of diseases and treatment as found in the *Mādhava-nidāna*. Its author Vṛinda himself admits his indebtedness to the work of Mādhavakara with whom he need not be identified;[82] and since he is drawn upon by Chakrapāṇidatta in the eleventh century he may be placed about A.D. 1000.

Interesting again is the *Nighaṇṭu* of Dhanvantari, the oldest medico-botanical dictionary that we have at present. Older works of this class, if there were any, have all been lost to us. The *Dhanvantarīya Nighaṇṭu* itself is found in two recensions comprising seven and nine chapters respectively. Amara is said to have used this work in his *Kośa*. But what was used by Amara must be some older version of the extant work which cannot be older than about the eighth century A.D. since it refers to quicksilver. The idea of the earlier and the later editions of this *Nighaṇṭu*, thus suggested, finds some corroboration in a stanza found in a manuscript of the work stating that the original work of Dhanvantari was revised by Kāśyapa.[83]

Another important branch that was just cropping up in the medical science is the one dealing with the preparations of quicksilver and other metals. The importance of quicksilver grew to a large extent, because its preparations were deemed to give perpetual youth, life for thousand years, invisibility, invulnerability, and other goods things. The earliest work on this topic that can be dated fairly accurately is the *Rasaratnākara* of Nāgārjuna, who is placed in the seventh or the eighth century by Ray, and in the tenth century by Winternitz.[84]

6. *Mathematics, Astronomy and Astrology*

In mathematics[85] we read of Srīdhara who had written a work similar to the *Līlāvatī* of Bhāskarāchārya. He is perhaps the same as the author of the *Gaṇitasāra* who is referred to by Mahāvīra in his *Sārasaṁgraha*. The date of this latter can be fixed at about A.D. 850, since he tells us that he enjoyed the patronage of the Rāshṭrakūṭa king Amoghavarsha I. To the last quarter of the ninth century belongs the *Bṛihanmānasa* of Manu on which, according to Al-Bīrūnī, is based the *Laghumānasa* which Muñjāla composed about A.D. 932. From Al-Bīrūnī again we know of Balabhadra, a resident of Kanauj, as the author of several independent works on all the branches of *Jyotiḥśāstra*, and also commentaries on several works including the *Yogasūtra* of Patañjali. Another writer of the same period is Vaṭeśvara (Vitteśvara of Al-Bīrūnī) probably belonging to Kāshmir. But the most important author of this age is Āryabhaṭa II, the author of the *Āryasiddhānta*, who is certainly later than Brahmagupta, but earlier than Bhāskarāchārya, who mentions him. As Bhaṭṭotpala does not cite any passage from this *Āryasiddhānta*, Āryabhaṭa II cannot be much earlier than A.D. 966. Among other writers of the tenth century may be mentioned Pṛithusvāmī (a mere name to us), Bhaṭṭotpala, and Vijayanandī, the author of the *Karaṇatilaka*, all of whom are noted by Al Bīrūnī. Of these Bhaṭṭotpala made a deep and accurate study of his predecessors in the field. He has commented upon several works and possibly also composed an independent work on the *Gaṇitaskandha*. His commentaries are all learned and prove the accuracy of their author. But more interesting and important than the rest is, perhaps, that on the *Bṛihatsaṁhitā*, a study of which is calculated to give its reader a good idea of the history of this science in India in the earliest stages. This commentary was composed in *Śaka* 888 (c. A.D. 966). The only other work that remains to be noted is the *Sārāvalī* of Kalyāṇavarman. This work is perhaps the same as that referred to by Bhaṭṭotpala, so that Kalyāṇavarman must be earlier than the tenth century A.D. On the strength of the fact that he calls himself Vateśvara[86] he is said to have lived in the last quarter of the ninth century A.D. But from internal evidence of the *Sārāvalī* itself it appears that in A.D. 966 Bhaṭṭotpala revised the original work of Kalyāṇavarman which at that time was about three hundred years old. It would, therefore, seem to belong to the seventh century A.D.[87]

7. *General Review of Secular Literature*

We may now close this survey by a few critical observations on the mass of literature produced during this age. The first thing that we have to notice is that Sanskrit was steadily losing its position as a spoken language, *pari passu* with the growth of the canonical languages of the Buddhists and the Jains and of the various other *Deśabhāshās.* It is true that Sanskrit continued to be used as the chief language for exchange of thought among the learned down to a very late date. But this very fact, it may be observed, led to its estrangement from the generality of the people, so much so that the literature that came to be composed in Sanskrit had its appeal more or less to the *Paṇḍitas* rather than to the common people of India. It is this gulf that arose between the language of the people and that of literature that seems to be responsible for the several features noticeable in Sanskrit literature of this age. Thus in *Kāvya* we notice the sameness of theme in several works. More often than not the theme is drawn from the epics or the Purāṇas, so that by itself the theme being too well known has but little interest for the poet or the erudite reader. What interests the poet now is a display of his erudition, of his mastery over sound and sense, his infinite vocabulary, and his power to execute some wonderful and intricate devices. The readers of these works, naturally *Paṇḍitas,* also do not care for the theme so much as for these extraneous factors. This explains how there arose a tendency in Sanskrit literature to be pedantic and artificial,—a tendency which, as is natural, grew stronger and stronger as the gulf between the language of the people and that of the learned gradually widened. The natural effect of this is that Sanskrit literature and the Sanskrit speaking *Paṇḍitas* were as a class torn away from the masses and remained for long an object of awe and admiration, but hardly of love and sympathy. As a natural result, therefore, the poet always sought to appeal to the *Paṇḍitas* by rigidly following the poetical canons and, within the limits set by them, to exercise his talents. This rigidity in its turn practically eliminated the personal element of the poet, so much so that in Sanskrit literature we miss the revelation of the poet's personality in their poems. This impersonal character of the *Kāvya* is further enhanced by the theory of the rationality of the world order which was recognised in India from very early ages. To balance these defects, however, there are qualities such as mastery over emotions and sentiments in all their shades, intimate and real love of nature, a sympathetic outlook, power of description, and capacity to produce fine word pictures in a short space beautified by appropriate metre. This is why we find many poets producing exquisite lyrics though they may be no good at epic poetry or even dramas. For dramas were composed, later, not for the stage, but merely as linguistic and poetical exercises.

All this weakness in *belles lettres* was, however, more than compensated by the theory of poetics which saw its fullest development in this age at the hands of these very *Paṇḍitas.* This shows that the age as such was the age of critics and not of poets, and explains the marked difference in quality between artistic and scientific literature during the period as a whole. We have already seen how medicine, philosophy, and even astronomical science were steadily growing and producing some special branches in their fields. The *Paṇḍitas* naturally took greater and keener interest in the sciences, and directed their attention to expounding fresh theories and exploring new avenues of thought.

It may thus be seen that *belles lettres* had little living interest for the masses. Nor had it any such interest for the learned specialists or original thinkers who worked upon it as merely a means to an end. Literature to them was merely a hand-maid to poetics. The scientific literature, however, had a living interest for the specialists, though the masses in general were certainly averse to it. Hence we observe that in the mass of literature surveyed here the scientific side is more living and dynamic than the other which was slowly and gradually freezing to a static condition.

III. RELIGIOUS AND PHILOSOPHICAL LITERATURE

The two great epics had now practically reached their final form, though interpolations of isolated verses, passages, and even entire chapters possibly continued till quite a late date. The Dharmaśāstras and the Purāṇas had no doubt attained a sanctity which should have normally made its rank closed to new accessions. But as these texts served as sources of civil law as well as religious beliefs and practices, there was always the vital need of keeping them abreast with changing times. This led to the composition of pseudo-Smṛitis and Upa-Purāṇas passing under the names of renowned sages or rather their namesakes who were even older or greater than they, such as Greater or Older Manu, Nārada, etc. But there were other ways of attaining the same object, *viz.* extensive additions to the existing Purāṇas, and commentaries on the Dharmaśāstras. If we add to these the compilations and digests of the latter we shall practically complete the picture of these two branches of literature.

1. *Purāṇas*

It is now agreed on all hands that large additions were made to the Purāṇas during the period under review. To the texts of the original Purāṇas, which may be pretty old, were added several topics, at different times by different hands, *i.e.* whenever need for these was felt. Thanks to the patient researches of Dr. Hazra,[88] we are now in a position to assign approximate dates to several sections of these works. Thus sections on the consecration of *Liṅga,* the *Pāśupata-vrata,* the *Pañchāksharī mantra, Dīkshā, Puraścharaṇa. Yatidharma,* great gifts, and mystical rites and practices were added to the *Liṅga Purāṇa* between A.D. 800 and 1000. During the same centuries again the *Varāha Purāṇa* got into its text sections on holy places, *Dīkshā,* penances, and funeral sacrifices, while those on hells, *Karmavipāka,* gifts, and *Strīdharma* (duties of women) were interpolated into it in the tenth century. Sections on *Yugadharma,* vows, worship, *tithis,* and funeral rites, however, seem to be as old as A.D. 800. Similar sections were introduced in the *Bṛihannāradīya* between A.D. 850 and 950; while the *Nāradīya* got them between A.D. 875 and 1000. It was again during the ninth century that sections on holy places, *Varṇāśramadharma,* marriage, *Āchāra, Grahamakha, Grahaśānti, Rājadharma* and similar other topics were added to the *Agni Purāṇa;* while sections on *Dīkshā, Nyāsa, Mauñjībandhana, Pratishṭhā,* funeral sacrifices, *Yugadharma,* etc., got into the *Garuḍa Purāṇa* during the tenth; and the *Vāmana Purāṇa* took in sections on *Karmavipāka, Varṇāśramadharma,* vows, *Vishṇupūjā* etc. during the ninth and the tenth centuries. Similar sections were again added to the *Kūrma Purāṇa* during the eighth century; while sections on *Janmāshṭamīvrata* and *Ekādaśīvrata* were added to the *Brahmavaivarta* during the eigth century, and were again recast by Bengali authors between A.D. 1000 and 1500. On the whole it may be observed that the sections thus added to the Purāṇas have hardly any counterpart in the older Smṛitis like those of Manu and Yājñavalkya. This explains why these sections were interpolated into several Purāṇas almost simultaneously. The topics dealt with in these may be designated Puranic rites and ritual which seem to have dominated the society in India during this period.

2. *Dharmaśāstras or Smṛitis*

The two compilations *Chaturviṁśatimata* and *Shaṭtriṁśanmata* probably belong to this age since they have been quoted by Vijñāneśvara in his *Mitāksharā* and also by Aparārka, but not by Viśvarūpa and Medhātithi.[89] The first contains a summary of the teachings of 24 sages. The second, known only from quotations, was also probably a work of the same type. It is interesting to note that both are decidely anti-Buddhist, and the latter even prescribes a bath for touching Bauddhas, Pāśupatas, Jains, atheists, and followers of Kapila. On the whole, however, it has to be observed that the age of original literature in *Dharmaśāstra* is now over and that commentators and writers of digests have taken up the field. Viśvarūpa wrote his *Bālakrīḍā* on the *Yājñavalkya-smṛiti* before Vijñāneśvara who thrice refers to it in his *Mitākasharā.* Viśvarūpa quotes, among others, the *Ślokavārttika,* and is very probably to be identified with Bhavabhūti.[90] He is generally sought to be identified with his namesake, the disciple of Śaṅkara. But that does not appear to be a correct view.

The next great name of this period is that of Medhātithi who is the oldest commentator of the *Manu-smṛiti* whose commentary has come down to us. A northerner, probably a Kāshmirian, he was erudite and was throughly conversant not only with *Dharmaśāstra* but also with *Mīmāṁsā.* He quotes Asahāya and Kumārila by name, and most probably cites the view of Śaṅkarāchārya. Vijñāneśvara looks upon him as an authority on *Dharmaśāstra.* His activity must, therefore, fall somewhere between A.D. 825 and 900. Among other writers on *Dharmaśāstra* may be mentioned Bhāruchi, Śrīkara, and Yogloka who are known only from quotations. The last named is often criticised and taunted by Jīmūtavāhana who appears to be much junior to him. Bhāruchi's date probably falls between A.D. 950 and 1050. Slightly older than Bhāruchi is Śrīkara who probably lived in the ninth century.

3. *Philosophy*

The greatest name of this age in philosophy is that of Vāchaspatimiśra, the versatile and erudite genius that shows himself an adept in every branch of the orthodox systems of Indian Philosophy. Richly, therefore, does he deserve the epithet *Sarvatantrasvatantra* or *Sarvadarśanavallabha* that is generally applied to him. Before composing his commentary on the *Nyāyavārttikatātparya* he composed an index to the *Nyāyasūtras* which he himself has dated A.D. 841.[91] This date is confirmed by other considerations. Besides commenting on several works, he has also written some independent treatises on some of the *darśanas.* The *Tattvakaumudī* and the *Tattvaśāradī*[92] are the names of his commentaries on Īśvarakṛishṇa's *Sāṁkhyakārikā* and *Vyāsabhāshya* on Patañjali's *Yogasūtra* respectively. His *Nyāyavārttikatātparyaṭīkā* contains a brilliant defence of the orthodox logicians against Buddhistic onslaughts. The *Nyāyasūchini-bandha* and the *Nyāyasūtroddhāra* are two more *Nyāya* works from the same pen. The *Nyāyakaṇikā* is his commentary on the *Vidhiviveka* of Maṇḍanamiśra, while the *Taṭṭvabindu* is an independent work on the *Bhāṭṭa Mīmāṁsā* in which, it may be noted, Vāchaspati distinguishes between two schools of the Prabhākaras as old and new *Bhāmatī* on Śaṅkara's *Bhāshya* on the *Brahmasūtras,* of course, is too well known. One more Vedānta work of Vāchaspati is the *Tattvasamīkshā* which is a commentary on the *Brahmasiddhi,* a Vedantic work of Maṇḍanamiśra *alias* Sureśvara. From Vāchaspati's own statement[93] in the *Bhāmatī* it appears that before it he had already composed several of these works. Vāchaspati wrote under the patronage of king Nṛiga whose munificence was unsurpassed. It has not yet been possible to identify this king, though it is certain that Vāchaspati flourished in the first half of the ninth century A.D.

In *Yoga* there are only three works belonging to this age, *viz.* the *Rājamārtaṇḍa,* the *Yogavārttika,* and the *Yogasārasaṁgraha.* The first is an excellent commentary on Patañjali's *Yogasūtra* composed by Bhoja, who probably is to be placed in the tenth century A.D. The other two are works of Vijñānabhikshu who probably belongs to the same period. The former is a running commentary on the *Yogabhāshya* of Vyāsa while the latter is an independent tract aiming at a brief exposition of the *Yoga* system. It may be noted that in both these Vijñānabhikshu has criticised some views of Vāchaspati.

Next to Vāchaspati stands Udayana who composed the *Tattvaśuddhi* (*Tātparyapariśuddhi*), a commentary on the *Nyāyavārttikatātparyaṭīkā,* in A.D. 984. Like his illustrious predecessor, Udayana also has defended the orthodox views in his *Ātmatattvaviveka,* which is a defence of the doctrine of the eternity of soul; while in his *Bauddhadhikkāra* he has assumed even the offensive and taken cudgels against Buddhistic views. The *Nyāyapariśishṭa,* which is a sort of commentary on the *Nyāyasūtra,* is also ascribed to the same author. Two more authors of the Nyāya school deserve to be mentioned here. Jayanta, the author of the *Nyāyamañjarī,* which is an independent commentary on the *Nyāyasūtras,* stands between Vāchaspati whom he quotes and Ratnaprabha and Devasūri who quote him. He also refers to Śaṅkaravarman as the ruling prince of Kāshmir. He must, therefore, belong to the last quarter of the ninth century A.D. The other writer is Bhāsarvajña whose *Nyāyasāra* is a survey of the Nyāya philosophy. He belongs to the tenth century A.D.

The literary activity of the *Vaiśeshikas* in this period is restricted mainly to the commentaries of which the earliest is *Lakshaṇāvalī* composed by Udayana in A.D. 984.[94] His *Kiraṇāvalī,* found in two sections, *viz.* Dravyakiraṇāvalī and Guṇakiraṇāvalī, is a sort of running commentary on Praśastapāda's Bhāshya on the *Vaiśeshikasūtra.* On the same text was composed in A.D. 991 a commentary under the title *Nyāyakandalī* by Śrīdhara Bhaṭṭa, son of Baladeva and Abbokā and grandson of Bṛihaspati, who lived at Bhūriśreshṭhi in Dakshiṇarāḍhā (West Bengal) and enjoyed the patronage of one Pāṇḍudāsa. The other works that Śrīdhara refers to in this commentary as his own are no more than mere names to us for the present. The *Nyāyakandalī*, however, is highly important, since Śrīdhara has therein, for the first time in the history of the system, given us a theistic interpretation of the *Nyāyavaiśeshika.*[95] The *Vyomavatī* is another commentary on the same text composed by Vyomaśekhara; while the fourth commentary on the same text again is the *Līlāvatī* of Śrīvatsa who probably belongs to the eleventh century A.D. One important work of Udayana that must be mentioned here is the *Kusumāñjali* or the *Nyāyakusumāñjali*, comprising seventy-two *Kārikās* together with the author's own commentary thereon, in which the existence of soul is established from the Nyāya point of view. In this work Udayana criticizes not only the aesthetic doctrine of the Mīmāṁsakas, but also the theories of causation propounded by the Sāṁkhyas, the Vedāntins, and the Buddhists.[96]

Vāchaspati's works in the field of Mīmāṁsā have been already noticed. In Vedānta, besides Vāchaspati we have Sarvajñātmamuni, the pupil of Sureśvara and the author of the *Saṁkshepaśārīraka* which is only an epitome of Śaṅkara's Bhāshya on the *Brahmasūtra*. Among writers of other schools of Vedānta may be mentioned two of the predecessors of Rāmānuja. One is Nāthamuni, the author of the *Nyāyatattva* and the *Yogarahasya;* while the other, Yāmunāchārya, the uncle of Rāmānuja, has given us the *Āgamaprāmāṇya, Mahāpurusha-Nirṇaya, Siddhitraya, Gītā-Saṁgraha,* and several other works. The *Yogavāsishṭhasāra* of Gauḍa Abhinanda also belongs to the same period. It is, of course, like the original text, partly philosophical and partly theological. Śaivism was also developing systematic schools, along the lines of Vaishṇavism, in great affinity with the Vedānta. Thus in Kāshmir we get two schools of Śaivism, the *Spandaśāstra* and the *Pratyabhijñāśāstra.* The former was founded about the ninth century by Vasugupta to whom god Śiva revealed the *Śivasūtra,* the main *sútra* work of the school. Another equally important work of this school is the *Spandakārikā,* comprising fifty-one verses, composed by Kallaṭa on the basis of the instructions imparted by his preceptor Vasugupta. Kallaṭa lived in the reign of Avantivarman (A,D. 854). The important works of the *Pratyabhijñā* school, are the *Śivadṛishṭi* and the *Pratyabhijñāsūtra,* composed by Somānanda and his pupil Utpala respectively in the beginning of the tenth century A.D. The latter of these is more important and has been commented upon by the famous rhetorician Abhinavagupta, the commentary being called the *Pratyabhijñāvimarśinī* (composed between A.D. 991 and 1015). Abhinavagupta has also given us two more works of this school; the *Tantrāloka* and the *Paramārthasāra.* In the latter, it may be noted, Abhinavagupta has combined the monistic teaching of *Advaita* with the practices of the *Yoga* and the *Bhakti* of Śaivism and Vaishṇavism in such a manner that it can be said to strike a new path altogether. In this work of a hundred *Kārikās* he has laid under contribution what he calls the *Ādhārakārikās* ascribed to Ādiśesha (Patañjali), a work which has not come down to us.[97]

B. PRAKRIT

During this period, the Prakrits had already passed beyond the stage of a spoken language on the one hand, and were being supplanted by Sanskrit on the other, both in the field of exegesis and enlightenment, among the learned of all classes and sects. The result was their comparative negligence even among the Jains. The Jains respected the Prakrits as their holy language, since their Āgamas were composed in them. Yet they could not wholly keep themselves aloof from Sanskrit, which had still retained its influence on the minds of the learned and was respected as the cultural language of the nation as a whole. Any new religious worships, philosophical dogmas or spiritual experiments had to be submitted through the medium of this language to the circles of the free-thinking leaders of the society for their judgment and approbation. Without their sanction no system had any hope or chance of being respected or continued in the higher strata of the community. Indians in ancient and middle ages were a highly free-thinking people by their nature, education and equipment. They would not accept anything on the mere recommendation of this or that person, howsoever great he may be. Everything had to be proved by means of reasoning on the generally accepted lines of argumentation which had been developed through a long period. So that when the wise men of Jainism clearly saw that the learned circles would not care even to look at their precious theories unless and until they were presented through this cultural language of the nation, they gradually took to writing in Sanskrit for establishing their claim to a place in the midst of the respectable philosophers of the land. They not merely explained their Prakrit Āgamas in Sanskrit, but also wrote independent treatises in that language, either for conversion of intelligent men to their faith or at least for their thoughtful consideration. Siddhasena Divākara was probably the first among the Jain *Paṇḍitas* who thus turned to Sanskrit for the propagation of his faith and philosophy. Haribhadra, pupil of Jinabhaṭa and known also as Virahāṅka, was the next great writer of this school. He describes himself as the son of Mahattarā Yākinī, who, an ordinary nun, had become instrumental in his conversion to Jainism according to tradition. He lived in the latter half of the eighth century A.D. and wrote many commentaries in Sanskrit on the Āgamas, which before him were generally explained by means of Prakrit commentaries like Niryukti, Chūrṇi and Bhāshya. Haribhadra's example was followed by others and the tendency found its culmination in the great Hemachandra of Gujarāt, who lived at the court of king Kumārapāla in the twelfth century A.D.

In spite of this growing tendency to neglect the Prakrits and to adopt Sanskrit for their literary works among the Jain *Paṇḍitas,* the inherent beauty of the Prakrit languages and a sense of sanctity attached to them by the Jains prevented them from falling into oblivion. Naturally the simplicity and homeliness which characterized the early Prakrits gradually disappeared from them and artificiality and ornamentation took their place. Haribhadra was the first great Prakrit writer of this period. His principal Prakrit works are *Ṣamarāditya-Kathā* (*Samarāichcha-kahā*) and *Dhūrtākhyāna*. But his Sanskrit commentaries on the Āgamas often contain illustrative stories narrated in simple Prakrit and probably reproduced from the floating mass of the Prakrit story literature orally transmitted among the followers of Jainism.

Samarāditya-kathā is a religious tale (*Dharmakathā*), divisible into nine parts, which describe the cycle of nine lives through which the hero Samarāditya and his antagonist have to pass in succession as a result of their actions. In addition to this main story many popular legends find their place in the work by way of illustration or corroboration. *Samarāditya-kathā* is written in a simple and fluent narrative prose rarely interspersed with long descriptive passages in the ornate style of the Sanskrit writers. Here and there it contains short and long metrical passages usually in the Gāthā metre, but written in a slightly more artificial style than that of the prose. *Dhūrtākhyāna,* on the other hand, is composed entirely in verse, containing 485 Gāthās in a simple style. It is a collection of absurd-looking tales narrated with a good deal of wit and ironical humour with the obvious intention of disparaging the religious legends of the Brāhmaṇas found in their Epics and Purāṇas. It is divided into five chapters called the Ākhyānas where five professional cheats (*Dhūrta*), a woman being one of them, narrate their imaginary experiences about some strange events which they may have seen. Before they began, they made a condition that any one who did not believe what was being narrated, saying merely 'It is a lie', must admit defeat and supply food to all who had gathered there. But any one who supported it by quoting parallel stories from Epics and Purāṇas shall be deemed to have won and shall not give any thing to any one. Ultimately, the woman-cheat is represented to have outwitted the rest by telling them in the course of her story that they all were her slaves who had run away from her, two days back, with the clothes which they wore but which were her property According to the condition the other rogues could either corroborate it and actually be her slaves, or admit defeat by saying 'it is a lie', and supply food to all. They were naturally silenced by this dilemma and accepted her as their undisputed leader, openly confessing that woman was wiser than man by her very nature. The tales of the cheats are fantastic and extremely amusing owing to their imaginativeness. But their cutting sarcasm becomes quite apparent when similar tales from the Epics and Purāṇas, suspposed to contain the truths of the Brahmanical religion, are placed side by side with them. Both this and the other work of Haribhadra amply prove his close acquaintance with folk-tales and legends of all kinds. But in addition they also show his creative genius which admirably fills up the gaps left by the existing story literature.

The next important work of this period is *Kuvalayamālā,* which is a religious tale (*Dharmakathā*) narrated in Prakrit prose and verse on the pattern of the Sanskrit *Champū-kāvya.* Its author is Uddyotanasūri, also called Dākshiṇyachihna, pupil of Tattvāchārya. He was very well versed in all Prakrits and pretty well acquainted with the important provincial languages current in his times. He mentions 18 such provincial tongues, quoting some 2 or 3 characteristic words from each, in the course of the story of his hero when he visits a busy market of a great commercial town. The principal Prakrit employed in the work is the Māhārāshṭri, but short and long passages, usually of a descriptive nature, are also found in the Apabhraṁśa and even in Paiśāchī language. For the metrical parts of the work Gāthā, Dvipadī, Dohā and Daṇḍaka metres are employed, the first being the most predominant one. Uddyotana describes Haribhadra as one of his Vidyāgurus and mentions Pādalipta, Sātavāhana, Jaṭāchārya and Ravisheṇa as his predecessors in the art of story-telling. The work takes its name from the heroine like Bāṇa's *Kādambari.* It was composed in the Śaka year 700, *i.e.* A.D. 778. An abridged version of this story in Sanskrit was made in the fourteenth century by one Ratnaprabhasūri.

Upadeśamālā of Dharmadāsagaṇi consists of over 500 stanzas in the Gāthā metre. It is a work of a very early origin, but a Prakrit commentary on it was composed in Saṁ. 913 (about A.D. 857) by Jayasiṁhasūri, pupil of Kṛishṇarshi. Maheśvarasūri, pupil of Sajjana Upādhyāya, composed a religious tale called the *Jñānapañchamīkathā* in the latter half of the tenth century A.D. It is a poem in Prakrit containing about 2000 Gāthās and illustrates the religious importance of the Jñānapañchamī, which is a name given to the fifth day in the first ḥalf of the month of Kārttika. Śīlāchārya, pupil of Mānadeva of the Nivṛitti Kula, composed another religious poem on the life of 54 important men of Jainism (Mahāpurushas or Śalākā-purushas as they are generally called) in Sam. 925 (A.D. 869-70). Similarly, Vijayasiṅha, pupil of Samudrasūri of the Nāgila Kula composed a *Bhuvanasundrīkathā* in A.D. 975. It is composed in the Gāthā metre and contains a total of about 9000 stanzas. To this period also belongs Nandisheṇa, the author of *Ajita-Śānti-stava,* a Prakrit poem in various rare and artificial metres. The work glorifies Ajita, the second, and Śānti, the 16th Tīrthaṅkara together, because both are said to hāve spent the rainy season in the caves of the Śatruñjaya mountain. This hymn is recited by special singers at the confession festivals. In all these Prakrit works, whether written in prose or in verse, a great change in style is noticeable when compared with the earlier works written in Prakrit. The old simple conversational style is abandoned in favour of a flowery one characterized by *Alaṁkāras* like Ślesha, and other literary devices of an artificial nature in partial imitation of the Sanskrit writers of that period.

There are many stray Prakrit stanzas attributed to different authors numbering more than fifty, and quoted by Svayambhū in his metrical work called *Svayambhūchchandas* composed before A.D. 1000, for illustrating the various metres defined by him. Most of these authors are non-Jain and otherwise unknown, two being women among them.

C. NON-CANONICAL PĀLI LITERATURE

The period dealt with in this volume is one of decadence, so far as Pāli literature is concerned, both in India and Ceylon. There is hardly any work from continental India, and the political conditions in Ceylon adversely affected literary productions in Pāli in the island. The advent of Mahinda IV (A.D. 953-69), who encouraged the study of Dhamma by patronising monks well versed in the *Vinaya,* kept the torch of learning from being extinguished and brought about some revival in the study of Pāli literature. A few of the authors who flourished during this period are noted below.[98]

(i) Chulla Dhammapāla

Though assigned to Ānanda in the *Saddhamma-Saṁgaha,*[99] the *Sachchasaṅkhepa* (Elements of Truth) has been ascribed to Chulla Dhammapāla, a pupil of Ānanda, in the *Gandhavaṁsa*[100] and the colophon supports this ascription. The *Sachchasaṅkhepa* is a short treatise of 387 stanzas dealing in five chapters with the *Abhidhamma* topics *rūpa* (form), *vedanā* (feeling), *chitta* (thought), *khandha* (miscellanea), and *nibbāna* (nirvāṇa). Chulla Dhammapāla appears to have been earlier than Anuruddha (twelfth century) as the latter's work is said to have superseded the *Sachchasaṅkhepa* as a *vade mecum*.[101]

(ii) Mahānāma

Mahānāma is said to be the author of *Saddhammappakāsinī*, a commentary on the Patisambhidāmagga. In the epilogue the author states that he finished the work in the third year after the death of king Moggalāna, while residing in the Uttaramanthiparivena of the Mahāvihāra. Though some scholars identify this Moggalāna with Moggalāna I in the first half of the seventh century, B.C. Law prefers to identify him with Moggalāna III, father and predecessor of Vijayabāhu I (A.D. 1055-1110).[102] Malalasekera believes this Mahānāma to be the second Mahānāma appearing in Bodh-Gayā inscription after Upasena II and to have been later than the earlier Mahānāma by a couple of centuries.[103]

(iii) Khema

Khemappakaraṇa (also called *Paramattha-dīpa*) by Elder Khema contains short descriptions of the *chitta*, and definitions of *kusalā* and *akusalā dhammā*, a list of twenty-eight mnemonic verses briefly giving the meaning of some *abhidhamma* terms. It is more appropriately called *Nāma-rūpa-samāsa* in Ceylon. With its short disquisitions on various subjects concisely written in simple, easy style, the work serves as a little handbook for the study of medieval *Abhidhamma*. References to the author in the *Nikāyasaṁgraha* and the *Saddhamma-ratnākara*, the latter calling him Tipiṭaka-pariyattidhara (versed in the text of Tipiṭaka), indicate that the book was held in high esteem in Ceylon. Vāchissara Mahāsāmi of Ceylon wrote a commentary on it in the twelfth century.

(iv) Upatissa

Though the book itself says nothing regarding its authorship, the *Bodhivaṁsa* (or *Mahābodhivaṁsa*, History of Bodhi tree) has been ascribed to Upatissa of Ceylon by several authors. It is a prose work, there being gāthās only at the ends of chapters and towards the end of the whole book. Beginning with a history of Buddha Dīpaṁkara, it gives a brief account of the life of Bodhisattva under previous Buddhas, life of Gotama, his enlightenment, planting of Bodhi tree at Jetavana by Ānanda, *parinibbāna*, three councils, landing of Mahinda in Ceylon and establishment of Buddhism there, planting of the tree, and starting of ceremonies connected with its worship.

The *Mahābodhivaṁsa* has largely drawn on the *Nidānakathā* for its first chapter, and its account is usually shorter. The *Samanta-pāśādikā* and *Mahāvaṁsa* serve as sources for the later chapters, there being identity in the concluding verses of some chapters of the *Mahābodhivaṁsa* and the closing chapters of the *Mahāvaṁsa.* Though thus borrowing from other works, the *Mahābodhivaṁsa* has a style different from them, more artificial and affected. The author is fond of long periods and ornamental epithets. The work shows distinct traces of the influence of Sanskrit on Pāli and may be regarded as inaugurating the era of Sanskritised Pāli.

Identifying Dāṭhānāga at whose instance the *Mahābodhivaṁsa* was written, with Dāṭṭha who is said to have induced Buddhaghosha to write *Sumaṅgala-vilāsinī,* Strong assigns the author to the period of Buddhaghosha. But Dāṭhānāga and Dāṭṭha are not identical. Dāṭhānāga has been identified with his namesake who was appointed by Mahinda IV (A.D. 953-69) to discourse on *Abhidhamma,* and Geiger and Wickremasinghe place the work in the tenth century.[104]

(v) *Telakaṭāhagāthā*

Reference may be made in conclusion to *Telakaṭāhagāthā* (stanzas of the oil cauldron), a short poem in 89 stanzas, purporting to be religious exhortations of Kalyāṇīya Thera, condemned to be cast into a cauldron of boiling oil on suspicion of complicity in the intrigue with the queen-consort of Kalāṇī Tissa (third century B.C.). It appears that a Vihāra was built later on the spot where the Thera was put to death.

The *Mahāvaṁsa* relates the story in brief, but instead of the boiling cauldron, speaks of the Thera as being slain with his attendant and thrown into the sea. The *Rasavāhinī* by Vedeha (*c.* fourteenth century) gives greater details of the story.

There is no reference to the name of the author or his date in the work. The language and style most definitely disclaim the pretensions of the work to be the stanzas uttered by the Thera (*c.* third century B.C.) in the boiling cauldron, and point to a much later date. Fervently exhorting men to lead a good life, the work incorporates fundamental tenets of Buddhism and shows a great depth of religious and metaphysical learning. Though well acquainted with Sanskrit, the author does not overburden his Pāli with Sanskritisms. Malalasekera assigns the work to the tenth or the earlier part of the eleventh century, while Winternitz regards it hardly earlier than the twelfth century.[105]

D. APABHRAMŚA LANGUAGE AND LITERATURE

1. *Origin of Apabhraṁśa*

The last stage of the Prakrit languages is represented by the Apabhraṁśa, which has considerable importance on account of the fact that the modern Aryan languages like Hindī, Gujarātī, Marāṭhī and Bengali have all evolved from it. The earliest mention of Apabhraṁśa in relation to language is found in the *Mahābhāshya* of Patañjali when he says: "Each pure word has several corrupt forms—'Apabhraṁśas' such as *Gāvī, Goṇī, Gotā, Gopotalikā* and others for a single word *'Go'*." It is obvious from this that Apabhraṁśa was not yet the name of any particular language or dialect, but was used to denote all deviations from the normal Sanskrit. As such, even Pāli and Prakrit were probably known as Apabhraṁśa about 150 B.C.

In the *Nāṭyaśāstra* of Bharata we find a lot of information about the languages of the time. It tells us that language is of two kinds, namely, Sanskrit and Prakrit, the latter being only the corrupted or unrefined form of the former. Prakrit, again, has expressions of three kinds, namely, Similar, Corrupt, and Local (*Samāna, Vibhrashṭa* and *Deśī*). We have then a scheme of the distribution of Sanskrit and various Prakrits or *Deśī Bhāshās* amongst the actors of play. The *Deśī Bhāshās* mentioned are seven in number, namely, *Māgadhī, Āvantī, Prāchyā, Śaurasenī, Ardhamāgadhī, Bālhīkā*, and *Dākshiṇātyā*. In addition to these, we are told, there are the languages used by the *Śabaras, Ābhīras, Chāṇḍālas Sacharas, Draviḍas, Oḍras*, and *Vanacharas* which are of an inferior type and are known as *Vibhāshā*. The distribution of these languages in a drama according to professions and regions is interesting. Pulkasas, charcoal-makers, hunters, and wood- or grass-sellers use *Pāñchālī* with the sibilants. Those who trade in elephants, horses, goats, camels and the like, and those who dwell in pastoral settlements use the *Śabara* language. The countries between the Vindhya and the sea have a language abounding in the nasal sound. *Ābhīras* speak Śābarī and *Draviḍas* the Drāviḍī. The countries between the Gaṅgā and the sea have a language abounding in *e*. Surāshṭra, Avantī and the regions situated on the Vetravatī have a language abounding in *ch*. People belonging to Himavat, Sindhu, Sauvīra, and others use a language abounding in *u*.

The comprehensive view of the languages presented by Bharata is very useful and important for linguistic studies. What, however, interests us particularly in connection with our study of the Apabhraṁśas is that the Himālaya-Sindhu region is said to possess a language in which the *u* sound was predominant. It is well known that amongst all the Prakrits it is the Apabhraṁśas alone that have their nominative and accusative termination *u,* and in several positions *o* is reduced to *u;* therefore they abound in this sound. North-Western India appears, therefore, to be the original home of the Apabhraṁśas.

But the Apabhraṁśa known to the author of *Nāṭyaśāstra* as Vibhrashṭa or Vibhāshā was only a dialect: it had not yet developed a literary standard. The exact date of the *Nāṭyaśāstra* is not known, but there is no doubt that it belongs to the early centuries of the Christian era. By the sixth century the Apabhraṁśa had developed to such an extent that rhetoricians like Bhāmaha and Daṇḍin had to recognise it as a vehicle of poetic literature almost as exalted as Sanskrit and Prakrit, in which both prose and verse compositions were produced. Daṇḍin throws some welcome light upon the position of Apabhraṁśa in his time. According to him, theorists continued to call all linguistic vehicles other than Sanskrit by the name of Apabhraṁśa, while, in the realm of poetry, the languages of the Ābhīras and others were known as Apabhraṁśa. There is no doubt that Daṇḍin had in his mind the view of Patañjali when he called all non-Sanskrit forms Apabhraṁśa. The view of Bharata about the language of the Ābhīras has been noticed above. It is this language, according to Daṇḍin, which, amongst others, came to be utilised for poetic compositions. The history of Ābhīras is important, but it is not yet fully and properly explored. From the scattered notices of the Ābhīras referred to above[106] it is clear that they spread from the North-West and Punjāb to Central India and further south between the first and the fourth centuries A.D. The language of the Ābhīras must have grown in importance along with their political power and influence. Besides the testimony of Bhāmaha and Daṇḍin, we find a copper-plate inscription praising the proficiency of king Guhasena of Valabhī (A.D. 559-567) in Sanskrit, Prakrit and Apabhraṁśa poetry.

Rudraṭa in his *Kāvyālaṁkāra* (ninth century) not only includes Apabhraṁśa among his six languages of poetry, but also says that Apabhraṁśa has several varieties according to countries.

2. *Nature of Apabhraṁśa*

The Apabhraṁśa language that prevailed in the early centuries of the Christian era in the Himālaya-Sindhu region possessed the following characteristics:—

(1) Retention of *ṛi.*

(2) Retention of *r* as second member of a conjunct.

(3) Retention of the intervocalic consonants in their original or softened form.

(4) Nominative singular termination *u*, and possessive *ssa*.

(5) Use of rhymed metre.

This language might be called ancient Ṭhakkī. As the language spread towards south to Sindh with the expansion of the people who spoke it, the Ābhīras, it developed the tendency of *ch* and *j* being indistinctly pronounced with *y* sound preceding them (as laid down by the grammarians for *Vrāchaḍa*).

Apabhraṁśa had attained the literary form before the time of Hemachandra, as is proved by the illustrations in his Prakrit Grammar, and by the literature available so far and known to be of an earlier date. It is probably for this reason that Hemachandra has not noticed the varieties which have been enumerated by the grammarians who followed him and who went by the conventional dialect distinctions rather than by the actual literary form that held the field.

The word Apabhraṁśa literally means corrupt, and the grammarians regarded the language as such. But the poets themselves never admitted this and they have called their language, not Apabhraṁśa but *Deśī, i.e.* of the land.

3. *Apabhraṁśa in Sanskrit Dramas*

We know that the sixth case-ending *'ho'* is a peculiarity of Apabhraṁśa. In the *Sāriputraprakaraṇa* of Aśvaghosha (second century A.D.) we come across a form *makkaḍaho* (Sk. *markaṭasya*). In the *Pañcharātra* of Bhāsa (c. fourth century), the Māgadhī put into the mouth of the cowherds contains the nominative and accusative suffix *u* which is known to be the characteristic of Apabhraṁśa, *e.g. Śadamaṇḍalu śuyyo* (Sk. *Śatamaṇḍalaḥ sūryaḥ*), *Śavvam ghoshum viddavanti choḷā* (Sk. *Sarvaṁ ghoshaṁ vidravanti chaurāḥ*). If scholars doubt the genuineness of these readings, it is only because they hesitate to accept such an ancient date for Apabhraṁśa. But the history of the language, as traced above, shows, beyond doubt, that the occurrence of Apabhraṁśa forms in dramas during that period is not at all surprising. The language used by Māthura in the second act of *Mṛichchhakaṭika* abounds in *u* and so it may be called the Māgadhī Apabhraṁśa. The Māthura is presumably a person hailing from Mathurā, the centre of the western part of the country, and he has obviously imported the tendency of his homeland into the eastern language. The commentators have called the language *ḍhakkī* which is probably a mistake for *ṭhakkī*. Mārkaṇḍeya calls it *Ṭakki* and remarks that Hariśchandra likes to call this language Apabhraṁśa which the learned use in their dramas and other compositions.[107] There are sixteen verses in Apabhraṁśa in Kālidāsa's *Vikramorvaśīya* which can now safely be accepted as early examples of Apabhraṁśa lyric.

4. *Apabhraṁśa Dohās*

The earliest poetry in pure Apabhraṁśa appears to have been produced in the *Dohā* metre, *i.e.* couplets of varying measure. In the available Apabhraṁśa poetry the *Dohā* verses are more universal and less grammatically regulated than the other forms of poetic compositions. This metre has been adopted by almost all the modern languages of North India, where the medieval saints used it as their favourite vehicle of expression. The *Dohā* compositions fall into two classes according to their subject-matter, the *romantic*, and the *dscetic*. The former class is represented by single verses depicting the sentiment of love, pathos, or heroism. They appear to be mostly the compositions of bards. Examples of these occur in the grammar of Hemachandra.

The latter class is represented by a large number of works composed by Jain and Buddhist saints. *Paramappayāsu* and *Jogasāru* of Joindu (sixth century), *Pāhuḍa-Dohā* of Rāmasiṁha Muni, *Sāvaya-dhamma-Dohā* of Devasena (tenth century), and *Vairāgyasāra* of Suprabhāchārya are some of the best examples of *Dohā* works in Jain literature. The theme is the spiritual unity of the universe which discountenances all differences of caste and creed. In Devasena's *Nayachakra,* a Prakrit work on logic, we are told that the work was originally composed in the *Dohā* metre; but it was subsequently transformd into *Gāthās* by Māilla-dhavala because a critic remarked that *Dohā* metre was not suitable for a serious subject like logic. The date of Devasena, as recorded in one of his works, is V. S. 990 (=A.D. 933). It appears that up to his time the learned *Paṇḍitas* had not reconciled themselves to the use of the *Dohā* form of composition.

The Buddhist saints who wrote *Dohā* verses are Tillopāda, Sarahapāda, Kaṇhapāda and others. Their works are found collected in the *Dohākośa,* first compiled by Haraprasad Sastri and later re-edited by Dr. Shahidullah and by Dr. P. C. Bagchi. Many more examples have been brought to light by Rāhula Samkrityayana. Their subject-matter may be termed mysticism, showing the same traits as the Jain *Dohās* mentioned above, as well as the compositions of the later saints like Kabīr, Dādu, and Nānak. The traditional name for the language of these works is *'Sandhyā Bhāshā,' i.e.* Twilight Tongue, which is very significant when we remember that

Apabhraṁśa forms a link between the older classical languages Sanskrit and Prakrit on the one hand, and the modern languages on the other.[107a] The period of these *Dohā* compositions may be fixed from the sixth to the twelfth centuries A.D.

5. *Epic Poems*

Epics form a very important, well-developed and voluminous part of ancient Indian literature. The same is true of Apabhraṁśa literature as well. In form and style epic poems in Apabhraṁśa are as highly polished and conventionalised as the Sanskrit and Prakrit Mahākāvyas. But they possess some very characteristic features. The *Kaḍavaka,* consisting of about 8 rhymes in *Alillaha* or *Pajjhaṭikā* metre followed by a *Ghattā* or *Duvaī* verse, is the normal unit of this poetry. This style could easily be recognised as the forerunner of the *Chaupāī-Dohā* style of Hindī poems like the Padmāvata of Jāyasi and the *Rāmacharita-Mānasa* of Tulasīdāsa. A number of *Kaḍavakas,* normally ten to fifteen, constitute a *Sandhi* or canto which sometimes opens with a *Dhruvaka* verse, and the metre and the style frequently change in consonance with the movement of the narrative, so as to harmonise with the sentiment to be expressed. The rhetorical qualities of Sanskrit and Prakrit poetry are fully reproduced in Apabhraṁśa as well.

The subject-matter of the epic poems so far discovered is mostly the lives of the 63 super-men called *Śalākā-Purushas* (*i.e.* remarkably great men) in Jainism, the purpose being entertainment as well as social and religious instruction.

The earliest epics available in Apabhraṁśa are the *Paüma-chariu* and *Harivaṁśa Purāṇa* of Svayambhūdeva, which are the Jain versions of the *Rāmāyaṇa* and the *Mahābhārata,* respectively. The former contains 90 *Sandhis* arranged in five *Kāṇḍas,* the total number of *Kadavakas* being about 1300, calculated to be equal to 12000 *ślokas.* The latter contains 112 *Sandhis* and about 2000 *Kaḍavakas,* being equal to 18000 *ślokas.* In the introductory part of the *Harivaṁśa Purāṇa,* the poet admits his indebtedness to Indra, Bharata, Vyāsa, Piṅgala, Bhāmaha, Daṇḍin, Bāṇa, Harsha and Chaumuha for the diverse requisites of excellent poetry. His debt to Chaumuha is of particular interest, since it was from him that the poet derived his style of *Paddhaḍiā* metre with *Duvaī* and *Dhruvaka.* Obviously Chaumuha was either the originator of this Apabhraṁśa style or he was the first to make extensive use of it. In a few old verses found prefixed to the *Paüma-chariu,* Chaumuha is praised for his excellent diction, Dantī for his charming meaning, and Svayambhū as excelling in both. We also find Chaumuha extolled for his *Goggahakahā,* and Bhadda for his *Goggahaṇa* and

Machchhaveha. It appears that the three were the precursors of Svayambhū and they probably wrote the *Mahābhārata* story partly or fully in Apabhraṁśa poetry. Unfortunately, their works have not yet been discovered. Svayambhū is also credited with works on Apabhraṁśa prosody, rhetoric and grammar.[108] Svayambhū left *Paüma-chariu* and *Harivaṁśa Purāṇa* incomplete, but they were ably completed by his worthy son Tribhuvana-Svayambhū, and a few chapters at the end of *Harivaṁśa Purāṇa* were added by Yaśaḥkīrti about A.D. 1500. Perhaps the greatest Apabhraṁśa poet so far come to light is Pushpadanta who wrote his *Mahāpurāṇa*, *Jasahara-chariu* and *Ṇāyakumāra-chariu* at Mānyakheṭa under the patronage of the ministers of the Rāshṭrakūṭa Kṛishṇa III and his successor. Pushpadanta carries to perfection the possibilities of Apabhraṁśa as a vehicle of poetry. His charming style, striking figures of speech and occasional double *entendres* recall the best traditions of classical Sanskrit poetry. In his *Mahāpurāṇa* he has beautifully delineated the lives of the 63 great men, while in the other two works he has narrated the lives of two other religious heroes. The poet himself tells us that his parents were originally Brāhmaṇas and belonged to the Śaiva faith, but later on they got converted to Jainism. The poet lived at the court of some prince; but some calamity befell him there which compelled him to undertake the long journey to Mānyakheṭa where his poetic genius was rekindled by Bharata, the minister of king Kṛishṇa. In one of the verses prefixed to various *sandhis* of his *Mahāpurāṇa*, the poet makes mention of the ravages of Mānyakheṭa by the king of Dhārā. Obviously, this event is no other than the invasion by Sīyaka II of Dhārā during the reign of the Rāshṭrakūṭa king Khoṭṭigadeva, the successor of Krishṇa III. This event, according to the author of *Pāiyalachchhi-nāma-mālā*, took place in V.S. 1029 (=A.D. 972), and the mention of it by Pushpadanta proves that his literary activity continued for at least seven years after the completion of his *Mahāpurāṇa* in Śaka 887 (=A.D. 965).

The *Karakaṇḍa-chariu* of Kanakāmara, admittedly inspired by the poetry of Pushpadanta, is noteworthy for its subject-matter and historical references. In ten *sandhis* it narrates, in comparatively easy and lucid style, the life of Karakaṇḍa who is recognised as a *Pratyekabuddha* by the Jains and the Buddhists alike. The hero's compaign in the south gives occasion to the description of the Jain caves at Terāpur which are identifiable with the existing caves at Dhārāśiva in the vicinity of Osmānābād, which, according to the details furnished by the poet, may belong to the time of the early Śilāhāra princes. The author gives a short account of himself according to which he was a Brahmin of the Chandra-ṛishi *gotra*, but adopted the Digambara Jain faith on account of a feeling of renunciation. The work may be assigned to the tenth century A.D.

The *Bhavisayattakahā* of Dhanapāla is a poem in twenty-two *sandhis*, and narrates the life of a merchant who suffered immensely on account of the jealousy of his step-brother. Though there is no evidence to determine the age of the composition, Dr. Hermann Jacobi assigns the work to the tenth century A.D.

Ṇemiṇāha-chariu of Haribhadra is an Apabhraṁśa poem of high merit. The prominent metre here is *Raḍḍā* as distinguished from the normal *Paddhaḍiā*. Only a portion of this work called *Saṇakumāra-chariu* has been edited and published. It contains 343 *Raḍḍā* verses which constitute verses 443 to 785 of the original. The whole book contains more than 8000 *ślokas*. The hero of the poem is one of the twelve Chakravartins, and the poet names his teacher as Chandra and mentions the date of his work as V.S. 1216.

Paümasiri-chariu of Dhāhila is a poem in four *sandhis*, and narrates the life of a female devotee to illustrate the evil results of deceitful conduct. Though the editor assigns the work to the twelfth century, the evidence on which he has relied is rather weak.

Kīrtilatā of Vidyāpati (fourteenth century) narrates the life of Kīrtisiṁha who was a contemporary of Nawab Ibrahim Shah of Jaunpur. Thus, it is of much historical importance as well. Linguistically, it illustrates the Māgadhī tendencies of Apabhraṁśa, makes use of *Raḍḍā* and other metres, divides itself into *pallavas* instead of *sandhis*, and thus indicates the advent of modern linguistic tendencies. The epics described above, except the *Harivaṁśa Purāṇa*, have all been critically edited and published.

Pāsaṇāha-chariu or *Pāsapurāṇu* of Padmakīrti, which still remains in manuscript and for the most part critically unexamined, deals with the life of the twenty-third Tīrthaṅkara in eighteen *sandhis*, equal to more than 3300 *ślokas*. The spiritual precursors of the poet were Chandrasena, Mādhavasena, Jinasena and Padmakīrti of the *Sena Saṁgha*. He completed the poem, according to his own statement, on the new moon day of Kārttika in V.S. 999 (=A.D. 942).

6. *Short Stories*

Another important and interesting branch of Apabhraṁśa literature is short stories meant for entertainment as well as moral and religious instruction. We know that the Pāli literature is dominated by tales and legends, such as the Jātakas and Avadānas intended to point a moral. The Jain literature from the earliest time is replete with parables and anecdotes exemplifying religious principles. Ethical works, in particular, make frequent mention of persons who observed the rules in spite of much suffering and thus reaped the reward in this life or the next. The ethical principle laid down for the monks is that they should observe non-violence and perfect equanimity of body and mind even at the risk of their lives. The laity are recommended to observe the same in a less rigorous form, and to discipline and train themselves gradually for higher spiritual life. Religious instruction was imparted in two ways. Those professing a different faith were sought to be converted by stories revealing the absurdities and incongruities of the other creeds; while those who belonged to the true faith had to be strengthened in the same and persuaded to observe the religious vows and practices by inspiring examples from the past.

The earliest literature of the first kind in Apabhraṁśa is the *Dhamma-Parikkhā* of Harisheṇa, who acknowledges his debt to the work of his predecessor Jayarāma in *Gāthā* metre. Evidently, Jayarāma's *Dharma-Parīkshā* was written in Prakrit verses and it became the source of similar works in Apabhraṁśa and Sanskrit. Harisheṇa's work is satirical and is of the same kind as the *Dhūrtākhyāna* of Haribhadra Sūri written in Māhārāshtrī Prakrit during the eighth century. But until Jayarāma's work in *Gāthās* is brought to light and its date is determined, it is difficult to say who was the originator and who the imitator of this style. The *Dhamma-Parikkhā* of Harisheṇa is composed in eleven *sandhis* comprising in all 234 *Kaḍavakas,* equal to more than 2000 *ślokas.* The poet admits that he was originally a resident of Chitor in Mewād and belonged to the Dhakkaḍa family. He migrated to Achalapura (probably modern Ellichpur in Amraoti District), where he studied metrics and rhetoric, and wrote his *magnum opus* in A.D. 987. As his predecessors in the field of Apabhraṁśa poetry, he mentions Chaturmukha, Svayambhū, and Pushpadanta. The subject-matter of the poem is didactic, with a number of stories and fables intervening, and is similar to that of the *Dharma-Parīkshā* of Amitagati in Sanskrit composed in A.D. 1014. This latter work is known to bear in its language marked traces of Prakritism, which cannot all be traced to the present work. It may, however, be presumed that Amitagati, when writing his work, had before him the present poem composed a quarter of a century earlier.

E. DRAVIDIAN LANGUAGES AND LITERATURE

I. *Kannaḍa Literature*

With the exception of Tamil, Kannaḍa is the most ancient of the Dravidian languages. The word "Canarese," the Europeanized corrupt form of "Kannaḍa," owes its origin to the early Portuguese settlers on the West Coast. The word "Kannaḍa" itself is apparently derived from "Karṇāṭaka," a popular name for the great Empire of Vijayanagar, or from the more ancient name "Karunāḍu". There are a couple of references to "Karunātar" in the second century Tamil classic, the *Silappadikāram,* and this fact may be taken as a proof that Karṇāṭaka started on its independent existence, with its own local variation of the parent Dravidian tongue, nearly two thousand years ago. The word "Kannaḍa" is construed in various ways—the country of the black soil, the big or the high country, the sweet or fragrant country, etc.[109]

Next to the Telugu and Tamil speaking peoples, the Kannaḍa speaking people are the largest unit among the Dravidians. The vast bulk of the Kannaḍa population is comprised within the geographical boundaries of Mysore, Western Hyderābād, Kanara, the Dhārwār, Belgaum, and Bijāpur districts of the Bombay State, and a few outlying regions as well. We owe to Nṛipatuṅga, a ninth century rhetorician and poet, the following account of the Kannaḍa country and its people:

'Twixt sacred rivers twain it lies—
From famed Godāvarī,
To where the pilgrim rests his eyes
on holy Kāverī...
The people of that land are skilled
To speak in rhythmic tone;
And quick to grasp a poet's thought,
So kindred to their own.
Not students only, but the folk
Untutored in the schools,
By instinct use and understand
The strict poetic rules.[110]

The Jains, Vīraśaivas, and Vaishṇavas have all enriched Kannaḍa literature, and hence it is often divided into three periods, called the Jain, Vīraśaiva, and Vaishṇava periods respectively. But this is misleading, for the so-called periods overlap considerably and hence this classification is chronologically not of much value. If we take the *Kavirājamārga* of Nṛīpatuṅga as our starting-point, for about three centuries (A.D. 850 to A.D. 1150) Jain predominance seems to be clear enough; for the next three centuries, Jain and Vīraśaiva writers flourish together; and from A.D. 1450 onwards, Vaishṇava authors also are increasingly in evidence, and Kannaḍa literature accordingly gains in length, breadth and depth. Muslim and Christian influences are by no means imperceptible in the literature of recent times, while it is likely that the early Jain period was itself preceded by a Buddhist period, although no works of that period have come down to us. Buddhism, Śaivism, Vaishṇavism, Islam, Christianity—the major world religions, in fact—have all thus played a part in shaping Kannaḍa literature, just as they have played a part in shaping Tamil literature.

A characteristic member of the Dravidian group, Kannaḍa nevertheless owes a good deal to Sanskrit. Its script is not dissimilar to the *Tamil-Grantha* script, and both ultimately derive from the Aśokan Brāhmī script. The Tamil alphabet and the Kannaḍa alphabet differ in certain particulars, e.g. Tamil has no aspirated letters, it has two different letters for the "n" sound and it uses the same symbol for surds and sonants (the two 'p's and two 'b's for instance). Sanskrit seems to have influenced even the pronunciation of the Kannaḍa language, and certain old Dravidian sounds like "ḻ" (as in "Āḻvār") and strong "ṟ" are no longer current in Kannaḍa. "The chief reason for the differences between the Tamil and Kannaḍa alphabets", says R. Narasimhacharya, "is to be found in the fact that the grammar of the Tamil language was, to a great extent, systematized independently of Sanskrit influence, and that Sanskrit modes of pronunciation being almost unknown to the Tamilians, their alphabet, though originally derived from the same source, was greatly altered so as to suit their peculiar phonetic system. The same independence of Sanskrit influence cannot be claimed for the alphabet of the Kannaḍa language, which has mostly adhered to the alphabetical system of Sanskrit. The same is the case with grammar. . . Nevertheless, the grammatical structure of the two languages (Tamil and Kannaḍa) will be found to be essentially similar."[111] From this it is natural to conclude, not only that Kannaḍa and Tamil are sister languages, but also that "Kannaḍa was less developed than Tamil when it received the impact of Sanskrit."[112] Generally speaking, Kannaḍa writers are apt to incline more towards Sanskrit, though not quite as much as Telugu or Malayālam writers. Many of the Kannaḍa men of letters were good Sanskritists also, and in some respects Kannaḍa can lay claim to be a bridge between Aryan and Dravidian, between the North and the South.

A prose work, *Vodda-ārādhana,* recently discovered, is probably the earliest of all extant Kannaḍa works. Its author, Śivakoṭyāchārya, was a Jain, and its prose style has been much praised. Like many Jain works, *Vodda-ārādhana,* too, has a professedly didactic aim. It seems, however, not to be clearly established that *Vodda-ārādhana* belongs to a period earlier than A.D. 850, the probable date of *Kavirājamārga.* In any case, these two early

Kannaḍa works must have clearly been preceded by some centuries of literary activity. Kannaḍa, as a distinct literary entity, must have taken shape at least from the time of the earliest inscriptions in that language. The Chikmagalur inscription takes us back to the fifth century, and the Śravaṇa Beḷgoḷa inscription perhaps belongs to an earlier period still. It is thus reasonable to conclude that there was an early period of Kannaḍa literature extending from at least the fourth or fifth century to the eighth or ninth, when many writers flourished and laid the foundations of the future development of the language and literature; but their works are now totally lost, and it seems unlikely that we shall recover them.

From the very beginning, Kannaḍa literature seems to have enjoyed the patronage of many kings and minor ruling chiefs. Some of these were themselves good scholars and writers. For instance, the author of the *Kavirājamārga* was the famous Rāshṭrakūṭa king, Amoghavarsha, also known by the name Nṛipatuṅga. Among the royal families that patronized Kannaḍa literature, special mention may be made of the Hoysalas, the Ṛāshṭrakūṭas, the Chālukyas, and the kings of Vijayanagar and Mysore. Gold, elephants and other costly presents were given to distinguished poets, and titles like "*kavi-chakravartī*" were bestowed upon them. Each royal court had generally its own poet, an Āstāna Vidvān. The Dravidian literatures could hardly have achieved what they have, but for liberal royal patronage all along. Many of the kings who encouraged Kannaḍa poets also likewise encouraged Telugu poets. In fact, the relation between these two literatures has been so intimate that some writers have distinguished themselves equally in both.

The early period of Kannaḍa literature, extending from the fifth to the ninth century, is well reflected in the *Kavirājamārga* and in other early works. Nṛipatuṅga mentions several of these early writers. Of these, Samanta Bhadra seems to have belonged to the sixth century, and to have been a capable Jain controversialist and a widely-travelled man. Another Jain writer, Pūjyapāda, probably belonged to the seventh century, and he seems to have been proficient alike in Kannaḍa and Sanskrit. The third, Kaviparameshṭhi, of whom even less is known than of the others, was perhaps the earliest of them all. Nṛipatuṅga also mentions such early writers as Udaya, Vimala, Jayabandhu, Durvinīta, and Śrivijaya; but these are but mere names to us, since their works are lost and are apparently irrecoverable.

Notwithstanding the references to these writers of an early age and the traditions concerning them, the starting point for the Kannaḍa literary historian is Nṛipatuṅga's work on Poetics, *Kavi-*

rājamārga, which has been mentioned more than once already. Nṛipatuṅga was a royal poet, a scholar with a mastery of both Sanskrit and Kannaḍa, and a purist who vehemently deprecated the reckless borrowings from other languages. *Kavirājamārga* contains sentiments as beautiful as they are original. It lays down that a poem, if it is to stand the test of greatness, must deal with nature, and describe the sea and the mountains, the sunrise and the moonrise, the waxing and the waning of the seasons. Other themes of poetry are heroic life, romance, adventure, games and festivities; and, of course, it is the poetic fire that in the final analysis turns the mere themes into imperishable poetry. Nripatuṅga throughout illustrates his principles by frequent citations, and it is plausible to assume that he was generally guided in his work by Daṇḍin's Sanskrit classic, *Kāvyādarśa.*

Another early writer, Guṇavarma I, was the author of *Śūdraka* and *Nemināthа Purāṇa* (also called Harivaṁśa), and was almost certainly a later contemporary of Nṛipatuṅga.

The tenth century brings us to one of the great periods of Kannaḍa literature. It was in this century that the three "gems" —Pampa, Ponna, and Ranna—flourished, and it was in this century that Nāgavarma I wrote the first Kannaḍa treatise on Prosody entitled *Chhandombudhi* or the "Ocean of Prosody," which is even now reckoned as one of the classics on the subject.

Pampa I, or Ādi Pampa, is usually regarded as the greatest Kannaḍa poet. His father, a Brahmin, was converted to the Jain faith; and the son remained a staunch Jain. Pampa appears to have been the court-poet of a minor prince named Arikesari. In A.D. 941, when Pampa was thirty-nine years old, he composed the two great poems, *Ādi Purāṇa* and *Vikramārjuna Vijaya* (also called, more popularly, *Pampa Bhārata*). The former of these is a history of the first Tīrthakara,[113] in other words, the first of the brave heroic souls who have crossed the disturbed and muddy sea of human frailty and misery, and reached the shores of unending indefinable peace. Jain chronicles name twenty-four of these Tīrthakaras, the last of them being the great Mahāvīra himself. The life-histories of the various Tīrthakaras are held in high esteem and reverence by the Jains, much as the story of the various *avatāras* of Vishnu is held sacred by the Hindus. No doubt, in these Jain Purāṇas as indeed in all Purāṇas, fact and fancy, myth and legend, mingle in curious proportions. The first Tīrthakara, for instance, is described as the father of Bharata, the king who gave his name to Bhārata-varsha, i.e. India. Pampa's *Ādi Purāṇa* tells in beautiful language the story of Ṛishabha, the first Tīrthakara, and to the Jains it constitutes an *Aeneid* and *Book of Genesis* combined.

Ponna, who was Pampa's contemporary, was also a Jain convert. His chief claim to fame is *Śānti Purāṇa,* the life-history of the sixteenth Tīrthakara, who is said to have ruled over Hastināpura and held suzerainty all over India. The third, Ranna, a bangle-seller by caste, commemorated the traditional history of the second Tīrthakara in his *Ajita Purāṇa.* This poem was composed in A.D. 993, and thus brings us almost to the close of the tenth century. A contemporary of Pampa, Ponna, and Ranna, and the patron of the last, was Chāvuṇḍa Rāya. He wrote the *Chāvuṇḍarāya Purāṇa,* a comprehensive history of the twenty-four Tīrthakaras. It is important both as hagiology and as the first—or almost the first—extant considerable work of prose in the Kannaḍa language. Chāvuṇḍa Rāya is also known to fame as the man of vision responsible for the Colossus at Śravaṇa Beḷgoḷa called Gommaṭeśvara.

Pampa, Ponna, and Ranna were preoccupied with Jain tenets, traditions, and interpretations. But they also wrote on other themes. Pampa's *Vikramārjuna Vijaya* and Ranna's *Sāhasa Bhīma Vijaya* (also called *Gadā-Yuddha*) are both secular poems based on Vyāsa's immortal epic, the *Mahābhārata.* These are no mere translations or adaptations, but independent poems by virtue of their conception and execution. While the theme is no doubt Vyāsa's, there is in Pampa's *Vikramārjuna Vijaya* a greater effort towards simplicity and concentration. This is achieved principally by identifying in the person of Arjuna the fortunes of the Pāṇḍava House. Besides Arjuna, Karṇa and Duryodhana also are very powerfully delineated in *Pampa Bhārata.* According to Pampa, Arjuna alone marries Draupadī; he is the *de facto* hero of the epic; and he and his wife Subhadrā are crowned at the conclusion of the Great War at Hastināpura. While all this makes for greater simplicity in design and clarity in presentation, Pampa's persistent identification of Arjuna with his own prince, Arikesari, produces a jarring note that somewhat detracts from the glory of this poetic symphony. It is worthy of note also that Pampa's love of his country is revealed in a passage like this: "When the breeze from the south touches me, when I hear good words from some one, when sweet music delights my ear, when I see the jasmine flower in full bloom, when I see lovers unite as if they were one soul, and whenever the spring festival is held—O! what shall I say—my mind remembers the Banavāsi land even if I am pierced with goad."[114]

Ranna too worked on the principle of deliberate limitation. The *Gadā-Yuddha* is also the *Mahābhārata* in brief, but a *Mahā-*

bhārata seen from a single angle, the hostility between Bhīma and Duryodhana. Draupadī is humiliated in Duryodhana's court; she unbraids her tresses and takes the oath that she will not gather them up again till the evil-doers are adequately punished; and Bhīma too declares that he will avenge the immitigable insult to Draupadī. The story rushes precipitately on till Bhīma and Duryodhana meet in the fatal fight with clubs.

With anger-driven blood-shot eyes, and ghastly frowns,
Fearful, immense in their aspect,
Fronting each other with their beginningless hate,
They engaged in the battle of petrifying stares.
To the four goddesses of East, West, North and South,
Bhīma and Duryodhana offered due sacrifice;
Streaming blood and glowing surging eyes
Made the crimson hibiscus of the sacrifice;
As if the sun-flushed eastern hill and the western,
flushed with the setting sun—
Two vastnesses of pent-up rage—
Dashed one against the other in mad consuming hate,
So with their giant maces Bhīma and Duryodhana charged.

"This for the pride of your erstwhile victories;
This for the killing of all my brothers;
And this especially for Duḥśāsana, the drinking of his blood":
Taunting Bhīma thus, Duryodhana dealt three successive blows.
"This for the lac-house trap, this for the poisoned food,
This for the deceitful game of dice, this for the outrage on
Draupadī,
And this for your ridiculous plight in the Hall of Mirrors:"
With these taunts, Bhīma drove at Duryodhana's feet, hands,
chest, cheeks and forehead.
When at last Bhīma struck at Duryodhana's vulnerable thigh,
He fell aslant and bit the earth, as if even then his anger had not
abated:
Like a colossal mountain torn out of the base,
Fell the Lord of the Kauravas and breathed his last.

Bhīma has fulfilled his vow, and Draupadī braids her tresses up once again. Ranna's *Gadā-Yuddha* is one of the few Indian epics that fulfils the Aristotelian canons of form and concord of parts. Ranna is an adept at exploiting the resources of onomatopoeia, and the mere recitation of his verses often suggests the full amplitude and roar and thunder of the action. As in the *Pampa Bhārata*, so in the *Gadā-Yuddha*, the hero is again and again embarrassingly identified with the poet's own patron, Āhavamalla. But, then, patronage *would* demand its "pound of flesh"—and we have no right to complain![115]

II. *Tamil Literature*

The Śaiva and Vaishṇavite revival culminated, as we saw in an earlier chapter,[116] in the celebrated *Tevaram* and *Tiruvāchakam* hymns of the Śaiva Samayāchāryas on the one hand, and the no less celebrated *Nālāyira Prabandham* of the Vaishṇava Āḻvārs on the other. The four Nāyanārs flourished in the period between A.D. 600 and A.D. 750, while the twelve Āḻvārs flourished in the period indicated by the extreme limits of A.D. 500 to A.D. 850. After three centuries of such inveterate mystical striving, punctuated by those thousands of rhapsodies of the spirit, Buddhist and Jain influence in the Tamil country declined to almost vanishing point. A period of comparative inactivity set in, and the literary development presented a bleak prospect for a time. No doubt, the Śaiva and Vaishṇava hymns were still tremendously potent influences, and there were not wanting *bhaktas* who boldly struck the lyre of devotional or mystical poetry. Some of the Śaiva hymns composed during this period were later included in *Tiru-iśaippa,* the ninth of the *Tirumurais* collected together by Nambi-Āndār-Nambi. *Tiru-iśaippa* consists of twenty-nine sacred poems, dedicated to various South Indian Śaiva temples, and comprises about 300 stanzas. The contributors to *Tiru-iśaippa* are Tirumalikai Tevar, Śenthanar, Karür Tevar, the tenth century prince Kandar-āthithan, Purushothama Nambi, and some others.

One of the poems of Tirumalikai Tevar is a fulsome eulogy of Śiva's divine personality, limb by limb, a form of praise dear to devotees, and somewhat akin to Tiruppāṇāḻvar's famous *Amalanāthippirān*. Beginning with Śiva's "lovely feet adorned with the crowns of the worshipping Deva kings", Tirumalikai Tevar proceeds to describe the legs and the navel, and ends with the lotus face and the plaited red hair mattressing the head. Śenthanar likewise sings of Śiva in picturesque terms:

> The lump white crescent, the spreading plait,
>
> The three-fold dagger, the blue neck,
>
> The sparkling eye adorning the beautiful forehead;

and the words of homage continue in strains of melting devotion.

Kandar-āthithan's intensity of devotion is no less striking, for the cry is wrung from his heart:

I cry like the separated calf from its mother!

Pattinathār, author of *Koil-nānmanimālai,* also belonged to this period—probably to the latter half of the ninth century. His outpourings on the occasion of the death of his mother, coming from a *yogi* like him, are touchingly human:

When shall I see again the mother
Who bore my burden in her aching limbs for ten tedious months,
Nursed me as a child with ambrosial milk
Holding me close with both her affectionate arms?

Pattinathār's fulminations against the tribe of Eve, whose spoilt child he had once been, may sound misogynous to modern ears; but there is a metallic ring in his clear-cut ethical asseverations in *Tiruvēkampa-mālai:*

Man is a stringed puppet that dances as long as the string is intact.

Nothing is good but the friendship of the good and devotion to God. The rest—wife, relations, children, and all life's vanities—is illusion.

Why were these people born, O Ekāmbara of Kāñchīpura?—
The cantankerous, the evil-minded, the lecherous!

Pattinathār's pupil, Pathira Giriār, exchanged in a mood of renunciation the sceptre for the begging-bowl, and moved from place to place singing divinely intoxicated verses *à la* Smart's *Song to David* or *Piers Plowman.* This rather lean period in Tamil letters was but the inevitable interregnum dividing the Age of the Nāyanārs and the Ālvārs from the great age of Kamban that was to follow not long afterwards.

1. De, "Viśākhadatta," *B.C. Law Volume,* I, pp. 50-57.
2. Keith, *SD,* p. 204.
3. He refers to Viśākhadeva who is very probably to be identified with Viśākhadatta—cf. De, *Op. Cit,* p. 57 n.
4. For an appreciation of this play read Devasthali, *Introduction to the study of Viśākhadatta and his Mudrā-Rākshasa.*

5. Vol. III, p. 17.
6. Konow, *ID*, p. 86; Keith, *SD*, p. 239.
7. Bhattanathaswami, *IA*, XLI, p. 141.
8. Keith, *SD*, pp. 225-6; Konow, *ID*, p. 83.
9. Hultzsch's view noticed by Keith, *SD*, p. 225.
10. *ID*, p. 83.
11. Durgaprasada places him in the middle of the ninth century. Cf. Winternitz, *GIL*, III, p. 241 n. 4.
12. For these, see Keith, *SD*, p. 229.
13. Krishnamachariar, *HCSL*, p. 641 f.
14. Pischel quoted by Winternitz, *GIL*, III, p. 241.
15. This is probably the first play of Rājaśekhara according to Keith, *SD*, p. 232; but Winternitz (*GIL*, III, p. 240) holds just the opposite view, *viz.* that Rājaśekhara must have composed this play after he had made a name by composing his Sanskrit plays. For the chronology of Rājaśekhara's works in general, see Mirashi, *Pathak Comm. Vol.*, pp. 359-366.
16. Also known as *Prachaṇḍapāṇḍava.*
17. See above, pp. 33, 89.
18. He is also known as Kshemendra, but not to be identified with the Kāshmirian poet of that name.
19. For several views about his identity, see Winternitz, *GIL*, III, p. 249, n. 4; also De, *NIA*, II, pp. 267-8 (*Ross Comm. Vol.*, pp. 83-4).
20. Peterson, *Third Report*, pp. 340-2.
21. For these, see Konow, *ID*, p. 89.
22. Konow, *ID*, p. 89; Winternitz, *GIL*, III, p. 242; Keith, *SD*, p. 271.
23. Winternitz, *GIL*, III, pp. 244-5.
24. For a full discussion, see Keith, *SD*, pp. 53-74; also De, *IHQ*, VII, pp. 537-8.
25. Cf. De, *Jha Comm. Vol.* pp. 139-44.
26. Keith, *SD*, p. 56.
27. *SD*, p. 185 fn. 3.
28. *JRAS*, 1926, pp. 87-8, 90.
29. *JRAS*, 1924, pp. 262-5.
30. For both Jinasenas, see Velankar, *Jinaratnakośa*, Vol. I, p. 29 (under *Ādipurāṇa*) and p. 460 (under *Harivaṁśapurāṇa* I).
31. Keith, *HSL*, p. 498; Velankar, *Jinaratnakośa*, p. 233.
32. See *NIA*, IV, p. 396.
33. Keith, *HSL*, p. 142.
34. Winternitz, *GIL*, III. p. 74, n. 4; Keith *HSL*, p. 135.
35. Krishnamachariar, *HCSL*, p. 163.
36. *HBR*, p. 310.
37. *HBR*, p. 123.
38. Keith, (*HSL*, p. 480) tacitly accepts this identity; but De expresses doubt (*NIA*. II, p. 269 n. 7, *Ross Comm. Vol.* p. 85 n. 7).
39. Ayyar, *QJMS*, XIV, pp. 302-11.
40. Krishnamachariar, *HCSL*, p. 326, n. 3; Keith, *HSL*, p. 97, n. 5 and 98.
41. Winternitz, *GIL*, III, pp. 75, 415; Velankar, *Jinaratnakośa*, p. 185; Krishnamachariar, *HCSL*, p. 169; *HSL*, p. 137.
42. Keith, *HSL*, p. 150; Winternitz *GIL*, III, pp. 43-4; also Bühler translated by Ghate in *IA*, XLII, pp. 29 ff., 137 ff., etc.
43. The work is said to have been composed about A.D. 1005—Keith, *HSL*, p. 151.
44. For details and references, see Krishnamachariar, *HCSL*, pp. 325-6, and 326 n. 3.
45. See *Āndhra Patrikā*, Annual Number (1917-18), p. 224, quoted by Krishnamachariar, *HCSL*, p. 492 and n. 1.
46. See *Jinaratnakośa*, Vol. I, p. 387 (Śobhanastuti); and Peterson, *Fourth Report*, p. cxxi (Śobhana).
47. Peterson, *Fourth Report*, p. xcii (Mānatuṅga; author of the *Bhayaharastotra*).
48. Keith (*HSL*, p. 215) holds that Siddhasena Divākara composed his *Kalyāṇamandira* in deliberate imitation of the *Bhaktāmarastotra*. But as this Divākara flourished between A.D. 650 and 750, Mānatuṅga may have to be placed in the first half of the seventh century A.D.
49. *NIA*, II, p. 268 (*Ross Comm. Vol.*, p. 84).

50. *HSL*, p. 98.
51. *GIL*, III, p. 65.
52. *HSL*, p. 98; also see Krishnamachariar, *HCSL*, pp. 236 n. 3, 169 n. 2, 271 n. 17 and 372 n. 1 for further references.
53. Gode, *JIH*, XIX, pp. 312-9.
54. Edited by Dr. F. W. Thomas from a Nepalese manuscript of the twelfth century —Keith, *HSL*, p. 222.
55. For quotations from these, see Krishnamachariar, *HCSL*, pp. 399-401.
56. Winternitz, *GIL*, III, p. 316 and n. 1 (also n. 2); Keith, *HSL*, p. 273.
57. Winternitz, *GIL*, III, p. 341.
58. Peterson, *Fourth Report*, p. lxii (Dhanapāla).
59. Keith, *HSL*, p. 331.
60. This is also called the *Dhanapālapañchāśikā*. Cf. Velankar, *Jinaratnakośa*, Vol. I, p. 58.
61. Oldenberg has adduced analogous cases in the Jātaka book. For references, see Keith, *HSL*, p. 332, n. 2.
62. *SDar*, VI, 336.
63. Devāditya according to Keith, *HSL*, p. 332, where the legend about the composition and the unfinished state of the work is also given.
64. Raghavan, *NIA*, VI, pp. 67-9.
65. Cf. *Yaśastilakachampū* (NSP), I. 17.
66. *HSL*, p. 336.
67. Ramavatara Sarma, *Kalpadrukośa*, Intro, p. XXV.
68. Bhandarkar, *CW*, II, p. 71.
69. De, *NIA*, II, pp. 272 and n. 2, 3, 4 and 6 (*Ross Comm. Vol.* p. 88 and n. 2, 3, 4 and 6).
70. Winternitz, *GIL*, III, p. 401 and n. 2.
71. Belvalkar, *SSG*, p. 91.
72. It has been necessary to use in this section many technical terms which cannot be adequately translated or explained within the short scope of this chapter. For their full significance the readers are referred to standard works on the subject mentioned in Bibliography.
73. Kane, *HAL*, pp. XLI-XCV, Revised 2nd edn. pp. 125-246.
74. See above, p. 115.
75. V. 12-14.
76. *B.C. Law Volume*, Part I, pp. 179-193.
77. Cf. *Devīśataka*, stanza 104 and commentary thereon (*KM*, IX, p. 30).
78. *NIA*, II, pp. 412-419. *Nāṭakaratnakośa* forming only a part of Kumbha's *Saṁgītarāja*, cf. Raghavan, *ABORI*, XIV, pp. 259-63.
79. *C. K. Raja Commemoration Volume*, pp. 141-152.
80. *JBBRAS*, 1935; *JUB*, 1936.
81. Keith, *HSL*, p. 511; Winternitz, *GIL*, III, p. 550. For a discussion regarding other works ascribed to this author see De, *NIA*, II, p. 274 (*Ross Comm. Vol.*, p. 90).
82. Winternitz, *GIL*, III, p. 550 and n. 4; contra, Keith, *HSL*, p. 511 and De *NIA*, II, p. 274 (*Ross Comm. Vol.* p. 90).
83. Cf. Devasthali, *Descriptive Catalogue of Sanskrit and Prakrit Manuscripts in the Library of the University of Bombay*, No. 278, p. 113.
84. Ray, *History of Hindu Chemistry*, ii, Sanskrit Texts, p. 14; Keith, *HSL*, p. 512; Winternitz *GIL*, III, p. 552.
85. Dikshit, *Bhāratīya Jyotisha Śāstra* (in Marathi), 2nd ed. pp. 229-236, and 312-315.
86. Dikshit, *op. cit*, p. 486 and n.
87. *POC*, Summaries of Papers, XI, 1943, p. 64.
88. R. C. Hazra, *Studies in the Puranic Records on Hindu Rites and Customs*, Dacca, 1940.
89. Cf. Kane, *KHDS*, I, pp. 224, 239.
90. *Festschrift Kane*, pp. 405-407.
91. Chitrav, *Madhyayugīna Charitra Kośa* s.v. Vāchaspati.
92. Also called *Tattvavaiśāradī*.
93. Read the concluding verses of *Bhāmatī*.
94. Dr. D. C. Bhattacharya gives the date as A.D. 1054 (*JGJRI*, XI, pt. 4).

95. De, *NIA*, II, p. 271 and n. 3 (*Ross Comm. Vol.* p. 87 and n. 3).
96. Winternitz, *GIL*, III, p. 466. The same Udayana is also the author of the *Lakshanāvalī* a *Vaiśeshika* work composed in A.D. 984 (*ibid*, p. 474).
97. A work in 85 *kārikās* ascribed to Ādiśesha (Patañjali) printed in *Pandit*, Vol. V, 1871, pp. 189 ff, and *TSS*, No. 12, 1911, is different from the one referred to by Abhinavagupta—cf. Winternitz, *GIL*, III, p. 446 and n. 3.
98. *Pali Language and Literature*, pp. 34-5.
99. *Saddhamma-Saṁgaha*, Ch. IX.
100. *JPTS*, 1886, pp. 60, 70.
101. *JPTS*, 1917, p. 2.
102. *Buddhaghosa*, p. 77 n. 3.
103. *PLC*, pp. 144-5; *CII*, III, pp. 274 ff.
104. *Dīpavaṁsa und Mahāvaṁsa*, p. 79; *Catalogue*, p. xiv.
105. *PLC*, p. 162; *HIL*, II, p. 223.
106. See Vol. II, pp. 221-3.
107. *Prākṛita-sarvasva*, 16.2.
107a. H. P. Sastri (*Bauddha Gān O Dohā*, Intr.) called this language *Sandhyā-bhāshā* or "twilight language". V. Bhattacharya (*IHQ*, IV. 287-296), P. C. Bagchi (*IHQ*, VI. 389-396) and F. Edgerton (*JAOS*, 1937. 185 f), however, have shown that the correct name is *Sandhābhāshā*, meaning "symbolical or intentional speech". Winternitz (*HIL*, II. 393) and De (*HBR*, I. 329), among others, accept this meaning.—Ed.
108. See above, pp. 197, 209.
109. R. S. Mugali, *The Heritage of Karnataka* (1946), p. 22.
110. E. P. Rice, *Kanarese Literature*, p. 29.
111. *History of Kannada Language* (1934), p. 56.
112. Mugali, *The Heritage of Karnataka*, p. 29.
113. Written both as Tīrthakara and Tīrthaṅkara.
114. Prof. R. S. Mugali's translation.
115. For the section on Kannaḍa Literature, I am greatly indebted to Dr. S. C. Nandimath and the late Prof. S. S. Basawanal.
116. Vol. III, Ch. XV, Sec. III.

CHAPTER X

POLITICAL THEORY, ADMINISTRATIVE ORGANISATION, LAW AND LEGAL INSTITUTIONS

I. POLITICAL THEORY

The stream of political thought which in the preceding period ran principally along the channels of the late Smṛitis and the early Purāṇas, as well as Kāmandaka's 'Essence of Polity' (*Nītisāra*), was continued in the present epoch in the Smṛiti-commentaries of Medhātithi and Viśvarūpa and the later Purāṇas, as well as 'the Nectar of the Sayings of Polity' (*Nītivākyāmṛita*) of the Jain Somadeva (tenth century A.D.). We shall attempt in the present chapter to consider some of the leading political ideas of these works, specially as regards the theory of kingship.

Medhātithi, while repeating the old Smṛiti view of the comprehensive scope of *rājadharma,* brings out clearly the dominance of the king's public functions. Explaining the term *rājadharma* in the opening verse of Manu's seventh chapter, he takes this to signify the (whole) duty of the king. This duty, he continues, comprises that which relates to visible affairs (*dṛishṭārtha*), such as the six types of foreign policy, and that which is concerned with invisible things (*adṛishṭārtha*), such as the fire-offering (*agnihotra*). It is the former, he observes, which are chiefly dealt with in the present place, for these alone are generally known as *rājadharma.* In other words *rājadharma,* while equivalent to the Whole Duty of the king, comprises chiefly his public acts, or to put it more generally, is synonymous with Politics. Corresponding to this double composition of *rājadharma,* Medhātithi indicates its twofold source. For he says in the same context, that the duties here described are based not wholly upon the Vedas, but upon other sources as well. Explaining the scope of the latter, he observes, on the authority of a text of Kātyāyana, that the duties which are not contrary to *Dharmaśāstra* are laid down here. *Rājadharma,* then, has a twofold source, namely, the Vedic and the non-Vedic (*Arthaśāstra*), the latter being subordinate to the former.

As regards the idea of kingship Viśvarūpa as well as Medhātithi introduces into the Smṛiti literature a discussion which was started by the early *Mīmāṁsā* writers in the field of Vedic ritual.

This is concerned with the question of eligibility of individuals to the royal title (*rājan*). These authorities, adopting the strict dogmatic attitude, confined the application of this title to the Kshatriya alone, though they were led by the logic of facts to recognise its extension to non-Kshatriyas in accordance with the maxim of representation. A more logical attitude is adopted by the Smṛiti writers above mentioned. Thus Viśvarūpa in one place[1] quotes Manu[2] to show that the royal title belongs to one who possesses a kingdom, and not to a Kshatriya alone. In another place[3] Viśvarūpa, after affirming on the authority of Manu[4] and Yājñavalkya[5] that the designation *rājan* belongs to the Kshatriya, adds the qualification that the title to dominion (*rājya*) belongs not to every Kshatriya, but to one who has the attributes of coronation and so forth. Very similar is the view of Medhātithi.[6] For he includes within the connotation of *rājan* any territorial ruler (*janapadeśvara*), although of non-Kshatriya caste, while on the other hand he excludes Kshatriyas who have not received consecration. Medhātithi's originality consists in his justification of this interpretation. While the use of the term Kshatriya in the text, he argues,[7] proves that a Kshatriya alone is eligible to rulership, a substitute is permitted in the Kshatriya's absence, for otherwise the subjects would perish. Again he says[8] that while according to Manu[9] the Kshatriya is to live by bearing arms and weapons, other castes who live by the Kshatriya's occupation are likewise entitled to rulership. For, as is stated by an anonymous (Smṛiti) text, whoever protects the people is known as king (*nṛipa*) and this duty has been ordained for the purpose of ensuring the welfare of the people in general. Manu's use of the generic word *pārthiva* for king, Medhātithi concludes, makes his teaching applicable not to the Kshatriya alone but to any other territorial ruler, for otherwise the kingdom would not be stable. Medhātithi, therefore, while fixing the stamp of legitimacy upon rulers irrespectively of their Kshatriya caste, bases his view upon the principle that kingship is essential for the security of the State as well as the people.

As regards the mutual relations of the ruler and his people Medhātithi[10] hints at the principle of the king's unlimited executive authority. Here, while explaining Manu's warning against incurring the king's anger, he observes that other men may forgive a fault because of difficulties in placing complaints before the king, but when the king makes up his mind to destroy a man, the latter is surely ruined because the king is all-powerful. Medhātithi, however, is careful to lay down the limitations on the authority of the king's executive edict. The 'law' (*dharma*) laid down by the king for the people's observance, he says,[11] refers to the executive arrangement (*kāryavyavasthā*) that is not contrary to the canon as well as custom. More particularly he observes that the king has no authority over the castes and orders as regards religious matters such as the fire-offering, for otherwise there would arise the occasion for conflict with other Smṛitis. In the above the author evidently applies the fundamental Smṛiti principles of the supremacy of the canon and the binding authority of custom to limit the scope of the king's executive edict. Medhātithi likewise discusses the nature of the twofold obligation of protection imposed upon the king by the old Smṛiti law. The point is fully discussed by him while explaining Manu's text[12] promising the reward of heaven to the king who protects those following the Aryan rule of life. Medhātithi's first interpretation distinguishes between the king's contractual and his general obligation of protection. It is proper, we are told, that the king should go to heaven by protecting the poor, the friendless and the learned Brāhmaṇa who pay no taxes and no duties. In the case of others, however, the king, by not performing his obligation, incurs sin, for their protection is purchased by payment of the king's means of subsistence. On the other hand the king attains immunity from sin, but not the reward of heaven, by paying the ransom in the shape of offering protection. This means that the king's contractual obligation is a compulsory (*nitya*) duty in contrast with his general obligation which is optional (*kāmya*). This is explicitly supported by the old Smṛiti argument that taxes are the purchase-money paid to the king for the service of protection. According to Medhātithi's alternative explanation, Manu's text should be understood to refer to fulfilment of the rule regarding the king's livelihood. This simply repeats the old Smṛiti conception that the king's general obligation of protection is imposed upon him by his distinctive occupation. Another view, quoted by Medhātithi, does away with the distinction between the king's contractual and his general obligation. Dismissing the reference to the king's reward of heaven as a mere declamation, this view maintains that the protection of those who do not contribute to the king's livelihood is likewise fixed by the king's occupation, for these people also form part of the kingdom (which it is the king's obligation to protect). Supporting the above by an argument from analogy, the author observes that artisans plying their craft for a living are made by the king to perform some work in lieu of taxes[13] and similarly the king, engaged in his livelihood in the shape of protection of his subjects, is made by the canon to protect the *Aryas* as a compulsory duty. Again the author applies the analogy of a householder kindling the sacred fire, who performs obligatory rites not for winning heaven or for any such reward. The king's obligation of protection, in other words, is compulsory since it is bound up with his occupation which is imposed upon him by canonical authority. Adding in this context the sanction of political danger to that of spiritual penalty for non-observance of the king's contractual obligation, Medhātithi says:[14] "He who receives taxes and still fails to slay thieves, incurs a double blame, namely in this world the disaffection of his subjects and in the next the loss of heaven: it is but proper that he who receives the taxes and yet fails to give their requital should incur (this twofold) blame".

The old Smṛiti law from the time of the *Dharma-sūtras* onwards mentions a number of civil rights of individuals which they are entitled to defend by force of arms, if necessary. These rights are explained and amplified by Medhātithi. Construing the relevant verses of Manu[15] as two different sentences, Medhātithi takes the first verse to mean that 'the twice-born classes' may take up arms on all occasions. Medhātithi rejects the contrary interpretation which would by making the two verses a complete sentence confine their scope to the specific occasions mentioned by Manu and no other. This is justified in part by the characteristics of desperadoes (*ātatāyī*) who do not wait for the other party to take up arms. The other argument is based upon the important principle of insufficiency of the State administration to ensure universal security. It may be urged, Medhātithi argues, that one may take up arms when one's religious duties are disturbed and when disorder is produced in evil times in consequence of the king's death, but at other times when the kingdom is well governed the king himself gives protection. To this argument Medhātithi replies that the king cannot stretch his arms so as to reach every man within his kingdom. There are, he explains, some wicked men who attack the most valiant of the king's officers, but are afraid of persons bearing arms. From this it follows that the people are justified in bearing arms at all times. This is evidently a plea for giving the individuals (specially of the upper classes) the permanent right to carry arms for self-defence. Continuing his argument Medhātithi puts the question whether bearing arms is intended only to strike terror, and he answers it emphatically in the negative. The slayer of a desperado, he observes, is liable neither to punishment by the king nor to penance, and he can kill the latter by all means, either publicly in the presence of other people, or secretly by administering poison and so forth. This obviously gives the individuals the fullest right to self-protection even at the cost of secret murder of their assailants. Finally Medhātithi, while paraphrasing Manu's list of occasions justifying killing of desperadoes, adds that one may take up arms for the protection of his family or property. He also quotes an anonymous view which extends this right to the protection of others as well on those occasions. One may, Medhātithi observes in the same context,[16] unhesitatingly fight for self-defence. The individual's right of self-defence, in other words, extends to the protection of his family and property and, according to one view, to the protection of others as well.

As regards the political rights of individuals Viśvarūpa assumes an attitude which brings him into line with *Mahābhārata* texts[17] justifying the subject in slaying a tyrant. When the king, we read,[18] is guilty of a grave crime, he should be slain by throwing even a mighty clod of earth against him. For, he argues, the destruction of the army, the revenue and so forth would otherwise be inevitable, as all these have their roots in the king. The people, in other words, are entitled to slay the tyrant in the interest of the State.

It will be seen from the above examples that boldness and originality of political ideas are by no means wanting in the Smṛiti commentaries of this period. Such is, however, not the case with the thought of Lakshmīdhara, author of the oldest known Smṛiti Digest called *Kṛityakalpataru.* We shall deal here with the section of this work dealing with *rājadharma* (*Rājadharmakāṇḍa*). As regards the origin of kingship, Lakshmīdhara[19] quotes Manu's dogma of divine creation of the king out of particles of the eight Regents of the Quarters, so as to make him a superman. With the same mechanical exactitude he quotes[20] the old Smṛiti texts relating to the nature of kingship. Such are the texts regarding the parity of the king's executive and judicial functions with the attributes of multiple deities and those enjoining the individual's obligation of honouring and obeying the king. To the same category belongs his quotation[21] of the *Rāmāyaṇa* text on the evils of a kingless country. The king, then, according to the author, is a superman by virtue of his divine creation, while his functions are comparable with those of various deities. The king's office, again, is the grand safeguard of security and welfare of the people. From these conceptions follows the people's obligation of honouring and obeying their ruler. As a set-off against the above principles bearing on the king's authority, the author[22] quotes the old Smṛiti passages enjoining the ruler's obligation of protection by means of the usual sanctions.

Compared with the political ideas of the Smṛiti-commentators analysed above, those of the late Purāṇas are singularly wanting in originality. As regards the origin of kingship the legends of creation of the social order in these works[23] involve the principle that the Kshatriya is divinely ordained for the purpose of protection. We are moreover specifically told that the Self-existent One created the king out of particles of the gods so that he might inflict chastisement for the protection of all creatures.[24] According to *Bṛihad-dharma*[25] Brahmā created the king's body by taking lordship from Indra, prowess from Agni, cruelty from Yama, good fortune from the Moon, riches from Kubera and goodness from Rāmajanārdana, and the king alone and no other should be recognised as Indra. Again we read[26] that the king assumes different divine forms by virtue of his different functions or attributes. The king then is a multiple deity literally by virtue of his creation out of divine particles by the Highest Deity and metaphorically because of parallelism of his attributes and functions with those of various divinities. In the composite account of the origin and nature of kingship in *Vishṇu-dharmottara*[27], the author first shows, by means of his picture of a 'State of Nature' without a king, how the king's office is the foundation of the institutions of family and property, as well as the grand security of observance of duties by the castes and the safeguard of the people against providential and human calamities. This is accompanied by the author's statement of the doctrine of the king's divinity in the literal sense of the term. The king is born among men by being strengthened with Vishṇu's lustre and by bearing the divine attributes on his person. The fundamental importance of kingship in the interest of the people is illustrated by a passage in *Garuḍa*[28] which includes a land without a king in a list of places where one should not live.

The above ideas of the king's office and functions are pressed into service in the late Purāṇas (as in the Smṛitis) for justifying the obligation of the people towards the ruler. In the extract quoted above[29] the *Vishṇudharmottara* observes in the words of a *Mahābhārata* text[30] that the chiefest duty of the people of a certain territory (*rāshṭra*) is the consecration of the king. Again we are told that honouring and obeying the ruler is the divine as well as the human obligation of the people. "When the king is pleased the gods themselves are satisfied and when he is angry the people are filled with anger: the king indeed is born because of his high spiritual merit and therefore the whole world submits to the king's command". The king, says *Bṛihaddharma*,[31] should not be harmed or reviled or slighted or abused, for the gods move about on earth in the form of kings. The same work mentions[32] propitiation of the king among the duties of the Vaiśya, while it includes[33] the act of seeing the king among the householder's daily and periodical duties.

The principle of the king's authority is balanced in the late Puranic theory (as in the theory of the Smṛitis) by that of the ruler's obligations. How protection is the divine purpose of the Kshatriya's and the king's creation is told in the stories of their origin mentioned above. The king, according to *Bṛihaddharma,*[34] is a Kshatriya devoted to the protection of the people. According to *Vishṇudharmottara*[35] the king immediately after his selection by the chief men in the State shall take the vow (*vrata*) that he would protect all of them who are righteous. As in the older thought, this obligation is enforced by the promise of spiritual rewards and the threat of spiritual penalties.[36] Some clauses of positive law in the late Purāṇas (like those in the Smṛitis) reflect the principles of the king's authority and obligation. *Agni*[37] repeats the penalties for such offences against the king's dignity and authority as violation of the Queen, miswriting the king's edict and mounting the king's conveyance. On the other hand *Vishṇudharmottara*[38] repeats the ancient Smṛiti clause requiring the king to restore stolen property to owners of all castes.

The late Purāṇa versions[39] of the old *Mahābhārata* legend of Vena and his son Pṛithu throw some light upon the authors' ideas of the nature of the king's office. It must be observed at the outset that these versions are given, not (as in the *Mahābhārata* account) for explaining the origin of kingship, but in the context of genealogical narratives of the Patriarchs, or at the most in answer to questions about the origin of the earth and the mixture of castes. Nevertheless we learn from the *Matsya* and *Bṛihaddharma* accounts that the motive for selection of the king (Pṛithu in the former and Vena in the latter case) was fear of anarchy. This of course involves the old Smṛiti view that the king's office is essential for the security of the people. In the different accounts of Pṛithu we are told that he bore the mental aspect of Vishṇu (*Garuḍa*), that Vishṇu having consecrated Pṛithu to universal lordship appointed kings over different orders of beings (*Agni*), that Pṛithu was an incarnation of God Vishṇu (*Bṛihaddharma*), and that he was Vishṇu in human form (*Vishṇudharmottara*). This involves the doctrine that the first legitimate king (or universal ruler) was created by the great God Vishṇu and was His human incarnation. The king, then, derives his authority not only from his divine creation, but also and above all from his divine personality as a representative of Vishṇu. On the other hand the story of the remonstrance of the sages addressed to the tyrant Vena implies the doctrine of supremacy of Justice (or Righteousness) or else of canonical injunctions over the king.

The *Nītivākyāmṛita* of the Jain monk Somadeva Sūri announces itself as a manual of instruction to kings and others on the subject of general morals including statecraft. The author's political thought bears little trace of his Jain beliefs and principles, but on the contrary is inspired throughout by the old Smṛiti-Arthaśāstra tradition. Somadeva[40] accepts *in toto* the ancient Arthaśāstra category of four sciences (namely, 'the Sacred Canon', 'Philosophy', 'Economics' and 'Politics') which he aptly designates as 'the royal sciences'. Explaining the place of 'the Sacred Canon' (*trayī*) in this list he says,[41] in words recalling Kauṭilya, that the castes and orders are fixed in their duties and are dissuaded from their opposites through it, and that both the king and the people attain the threefold end by avoiding confusion of their distinctive duties. This repeats the old and fundamental Smṛiti principle that Society is an association for the complete fulfilment of the individual in accordance with the law of his appointed duties and that the source of this law is the Sacred Canon.

As regards the nature of kingship Somadeva in the first place repeats the complex view of the king's origin and office found in *Manu-smṛiti* and other works. The king, we read, is a great deity and bows to none else except to his superiors.[42] Again we are told[43] that all the Regents of the Quarters attend upon the king who is therefore described as the best of his class. In another place the author exalts the king to the level of the three Highest Deities of the Brahmanical pantheon. The king, we read,[44] becomes Brahmā in his childhood when as a student he resides in his preceptor's household and studies the sciences; he becomes Vishṇu when after attaining sovereignty and receiving the ceremonial initiation at his consecration he attracts the love of his subjects by his qualities; and he becomes Śiva when with increased strength and with the possession of the highest authority he sets about extirpating thorns of the State and becomes a conqueror. Elsewhere Somadeva, applying the old conception of the supremacy of righteousness, distinguishes between the consequences of the king's attitude towards this vital principle. When the king is unrighteous, every one else becomes the same.[45] But when the king justly protects his subjects, all quarters fulfil the desires of people, the rains fall in time, and all beings live in peace.[46] The king in this sense is the cause of time.

As a corollary of his view of the king's authority Somadeva, like the authors of the Brahmanical Smṛitis, enjoins upon the people the obligation of honouring and obeying their ruler.[47] Repeating the Smṛiti view of the king's obligation towards his people the author further observes[48] that protection is the duty of the Kshatriya and that the king's duty consists in cherishing the good and chastising the wicked. Protection, indeed, is the supreme and distinctive obligation of the ruler. He is no king who fails in his duty of protection:[49] the king's *dharma* does not consist in shaving the hair, wearing matted locks and so forth. Following the same Smṛiti authority Somadeva[50] enforces the king's obligation of protection by the promise of spiritual rewards. On the other hand the author, probably under the influence of the Jain doctrine of *ahiṁsā*, so far from repeating the advanced Smṛiti ideas of resistance against the evil ruler, resigns himself passively to the latter's acts. The king's wrong-doing, he says,[51] like the ocean's crossing the shores, the Sun's causing darkness and the mother's devouring her own children, is a characteristic of the Iron Age.

II. ADMINISTRATIVE ORGANISATION—NORTH INDIA

The Pratīhāras were the most dominant political power in North India in the latter part of the ninth and the beginning of the tenth century A.D. In their stone records, they ordinarily assumed the imperial title of *mahārājādhirāja*, though in their copper-plate inscriptions they usually chose to be called by the more modest style of *mahārāja*. The territory under the direct administration of these emperors was divided into the traditional *bhuktis* (provinces), subdivided into *maṇḍalas* (districts), which were further split up into *vishayas*. Among the officers of the central government mentioned by name in their records are the *daṇḍapāśika* (police officer), *mahāpratīhāra* (chief of the palace guards), *daṇḍanāyaka* (general), and *balādhikṛita* (commander of forces). A remarkable inscription of A.D. 876[52] shows how the affairs of Gwālior (and probably of other important cities as well) were conducted in the time of Bhoja I. A certain Alla was appointed by the Emperor as the officer in charge of the fort (*koṭṭapāla*), while Tattaka was commander of the forces (*balādhikṛita*), and a Board consisting of two *śreshṭhīs* (guild-presidents) and one *sārthavāha* (caravan-leader) was apparently entrusted with the civil affairs of the town. Not only then was the civil administration of the town separated from the military, but further, the command of the fort was distinct (no doubt, for reasons of security) from that of the troops stationed thereabout. The concluding lines of the record give us some further indications of the character of the civil administration. Here we read that the whole town (*sakalasthāna*) made a gift of land in two specified villages which were in its own possession (*svabhukti*). It would therefore appear that besides the town executive just mentioned, there was a town Council (or Assembly) which owned some adjoining villages. The description of the donated land as being measured by the imperial cubits (*parameśvarīya-hasta*) suggests that the official standard was used by the town authorities for the survey of lands in their possession. In the above record, Alla is mentioned as guardian of the fort by Bhoja I's appointment. From another inscription of the same reign[53] we learn that Alla's father was born in a Brāhmaṇa family and was appointed 'Warden of the Marches' (*maryādādhurya*) by Emperor Rāmabhadra. Afterwards Alla succeeded to this office and was further appointed guardian of the fort by Bhoja I. This proves that Brāhmaṇas at that time sometimes adopted a military career and that offices went by hereditary succession.

Outside the territory directly governed by the Emperor lay the tracts ruled by chiefs belonging to various clans, such as the Chāhamānas, the Tomaras, the Chāpas, the Chālukyas, and the Pratīhāras. There were besides the great feudatory families like the Chandellas and the Paramāras who were destined for a long and independent career as ruling powers after the fall of the Pratīhāras. What is more, we find the donated village in two records of A.D. 893 and 899,[54] described as belonging to a group of eighty-four villages. This was exactly the standard size of the clan-chief's estate in mediaeval Rājputāna. In the light of the above facts it is possible to trace back the type of clan-monarchies, as they have been called by Baden-Powell, at least to the period of the Imperial Pratīhāras of Kanauj. The administration of the Pratīhāra feudatories possessed the usual complement of officers known to Northern India from older times. The list of persons receiving information of the donor's grant in the record of A.D. 893, mentioned above, consists of the *rājā* (prince), the *rājanyas* (nobles), the *rājasthānīyas* (viceroys), the *uparikas* (governors), the *amātyas* (ministers), and the *daṇḍapāśikas* (police officers). Another record of a feudatory chief, mentioned above, refers to a *sāndhivigrahika* (minister of foreign affairs) as the writer of the charter. From the well-known Siyadoni inscription[55] we learn that this town was in possession of chiefs bearing the lofty title *mahārājādhirāja* in the tenth and eleventh centuries A.D. We have some hints of the policy of the imperial government in keeping the feudatories in check. In the two records of A.D. 893 and 899, referred to above, the grant of lands by the donor required the approval of an individual described as *tantrapāla* of the reigning emperor. Probably the *tantrapāla* held an office similar to that of the Political Agent in an Indian State during the British rule. The grant by Mahendrapāla II of a village in the holding of a certain *talavargika* in A.D. 946 probably points to the Emperor's right of alienating lands in the possession of the smaller feudatories. Nevertheless we find even in the reign of Mahendrapāla I reference to a fight between two *mahāsāmantas* in a memorial tablet of V.S. 960. The decline of the Imperial Pratīhāra power gave the opportunity to many of the clans—the Kachchhapaghātas of Gwālior, the Chandellas of Jejākabhukti, the Haihayas of Ḍāhala, the Paramāras of Mālwā, and so forth—to assert their virtual independence.

The contemporary Arab observers were greatly impressed with the military strength of the Imperial Pratīhāras whom they called Ba'ūrah and kings of Jurz.[56] What concerns us here is to note the high tribute paid by one of them to the efficiency of the Pratīhāra administration. "There is no country in India," says Mas'ūdī,[57] "more safe from robbers."

By far the most important of the dynasties of Northern India contemporaneous with the Imperial Pratīhāras were the Pālas of Bengal, their rivals for the prize of empire. The Pāla monarchy was distinguished from nearly all other governments of this period by the peculiar circumstances of its origin. It was to stem the tide of anarchy that Gopāla, the founder of the line, was called to the throne by the *prakṛitis,* meaning probably the leading chiefs.[58] Such a momentous beginning failed to lay the foundation of a truly constitutional monarchy in ancient Bengal, probably because there was no permanent and regularly constituted Council of Ministers (or Assembly of the People) at that time. In the later records of the Pālas, their government is wholly assimilated to the pattern of a personal monarchy, and there is no question of any constitutional restraint upon the king's authority. The Pālas from the first assumed the usual imperial title of *parameśvara paramabhaṭṭāraka mahārājādhirāja,* for which the precedent had been set by the Imperial Guptas in their North Bengal inscriptions. As regards the offices of the central government, a *mantrī* is mentioned only in later Pāla inscriptions belonging to the times of Mahīpāla I, Vigrahapāla III, and Nayapāla. But we have the record[59] of a distinguished Brāhmaṇa family which furnished a succession of what can only be called Chief Ministers from the time of Dharmapāla to that of Nārāyaṇapāla. Making due allowance for evident exaggeration in the claims of these ministers, we may conclude that they exercised a commanding influence on the Early Pālas. But this influence was due entirely to their personal capacity, and not to the constitutional status of the office in question. From the list of officials given in the formula of the Pāla land-grants, we can infer that the central government of the early kings comprised a number of Departments. These Departments with the officials belonging to each may be enumerated as follows:—Finance (*shashṭhādhikṛita, tarika, tarapati,* and *śaulkika*), Police (*daṇḍaśakti, daṇḍapāśika,* and *chauroddharaṇika*), Army and Navy (*senāpati, gaulmika, nāvādhyaksha,* and *balādhyaksha*). Besides, there were executive officers with functions imperfectly known (*rājāmātya, dauḥsādhasādhanika, dūta, khola, gamāgamika, abhitvaramāṇa, tadāyuktaka,* and *viniyuktaka*), as well as superintendents (*adhyakshas*) of the royal herds and studs. The later records point to the creation of new officers representing the Departments of Finance (*pramātṛi*), Police (*daṇ-*

ḍika), Justice *(dāśāparādhika)*, Army *(prāntapāla, koṭṭapāla,* and perhaps *khaṇḍaraksha)*, besides the more indefinite *śarabhaṅga, kshetrapa,* and so forth. Some names like *senāpati, bhogapati, shashṭhādhikṛita,* and *daṇḍaśakti,* on the other hand, drop out of the picture altogether. The later inscriptions testify to the creation of a whole set of High Imperial officers of the type known to the Imperial Guptas. Such are the *mahāsāndhivigrahika* (minister of Foreign Affairs), *mahākshapaṭalika* (Chief Accounts Officer), *mahāsenāpati* (Commander-in-Chief), *Mahādaṇḍanāyaka* (Chief Commander of forces?), *mahākārtākṛitika, mahādauḥsādhasādhanika,* and *mahākumārāmātya* (three classes of executive officers).

Among the dignitaries mentioned in the formulas of the Pāla land-grants are included the *uparika*, the *vishayapati*, the *vishayavyavahārins* (comprising the *jyeshṭhakāyastha* or leading scribe and the *mahāmahattaras, mahattamas,* and *mahattaras* who were elders of three grades), as well as the *dāśagrāmika* (lord of ten villages), and the *grāmapati* (village headman). The *uparikas* and the *vishayapatis* were respectively in charge of provinces *(bhuktis)* and districts (*vishayas*) into which the Pāla kingdom is known from other records to have been divided for administrative purposes. The office of *dāśagrāmika* seems to show that the unit of local administration known to Manu and the *Mahābhārata*[60] existed in Bengal at this period. The *vishayavyavahārins* suggest a body of leading householders of the district. The *grāmapati* points to the continuance of the traditional village administration under a headman.[61]

In the ninth century Kāmarūpa was ruled by kings of the line of Śālastambha who are commemorated by a number of inscriptions one of which bears the date corresponding to A.D. 829. The kings adopted the usual imperial title of *mahārājādhirāja parameśvara paramabhaṭṭāraka,* or more shortly *mahārājādhirāja.* Though the succession to the throne was usually hereditary in the male line, we have a remarkable instance[62] of two Princes Chakra and Arathi being passed over in favour of the latter's son for the offence of disregarding the opinion of their elders. Among the chief officers of State are mentioned a *mahāsainyapati,* a *mahādvārādhipatya,* a *mahāpratīhāra,* a *mahāmātya,* a *Brāhmaṇādhikāra,* and a number of *balādhyakshas.* The *mahāsainyapati* and the *balādhyaksha* may be identified respectively with *mahābalādhikṛita* and *balādhikṛita* of the Gupta records, while the *mahāpratīhāra* is an old Gupta official title. The *mahāmātya* probably stood at the head of the civil administration, while the *mahāsainyapati* and *balādhyaksha* represented the military chief and his assistants. From the description of the donated land in one of the records, it appears that the kingdom was divided into the usual *vishayas*. The same record refers to rural people headed by the *vishayakaraṇas* and the *vyavahārikas*, but the precise nature of their functions is unknown.

We can form some idea of the general characteristics and tendencies of administration in Kāshmir during this period from Kalhaṇa's account. The succession to the throne was by hereditary descent, subject to breaks caused by usurpation and the like. The accession of Yaśaskara (A.D. 939) after the extinction of the Utpala line was a striking exception to the general rule. For Yaśaskara was elected by an assembly of Brāhmaṇas.[63] But this revolution was barren of constitutional results like the still more famous revolution in Bengal in the shape of Gopāla's election to the throne. As regards the organisation of the administration, we find Lalitāditya, the greatest king of Kāshmir, being credited in the *Rājataraṅgiṇī*[64] with the creation of five new offices (*karmasthānas*) over and above the eighteen older offices attributed to the semi-legendary king Jalauka[65]. The five offices were those of *mahāpratīhāra, mahāsāndhivigrahika, mahāśvaśāla, mahābhāṇḍāgarika, and mahāsādhanabhāga*. Of these, the first two, known from Gupta times, mean respectively the Chief of the Palace Guards, and the Minister of Foreign Affairs, while the last three probably mean Chief Officer of Cavalry, Chief Treasurer, and Chief Executive Officer respectively. Other State offices are incidentally referred to by Kalhaṇa in the course of his description of the subsequent reigns. Some of these like *nagarādhipa* (Prefect of the city), *pratīhāra* (Chief of palace guards), *daṇḍanāyaka* (general), and *rājasthānīya* (viceroy?) had their counterparts in the kingdoms of the plains.[66] Common to both again was the *akshapaṭala* (accounts office), although the *ekāṅgas* of the *Rājataraṅgiṇī*, forming a sort of military police attached to the same, are unknown elsewhere. Other offices like those of the *pādāgra* (revenue collector?), the *dvārapati* (commander of the frontier passes), the *maṇḍaleśa* (governor), and the *kampaneśa* (commander-in-chief) are more or less peculiar to Kāshmir.[67]

Kalhaṇa has preserved[68] anecdotes of two well-known kings, Chandrāpīḍa and Yaśaskara, testifying to the exceptional wisdom and equity of their judicial decisions. Incidentally we have in these examples a concrete illustration of the well-known Smṛiti rule requiring the king personally to look after the administration of justice. The interest that the Kāshmir kings took in works of public utility is illustrated by Kalhaṇa's remarkable account[69] of the extensive drainage and irrigation works carried into effect by an exceptionally able officer called Suyya in the reign of Avantivarman (A.D. 855/6-883). The history of financial administration, on the other hand, is on the whole a dreary record of unjust exactions inflicted by a succession of tyrants.[70]

III. ADMINISTRATIVE ORGANISATION—SOUTH INDIA

The Rāshṭrakūṭas of Mānyakheṭa were the heirs of the Chālukyas of Vātāpi in the imperial sovereignty of the Deccan. Though the Rāshṭrakūṭas were at first content with the feudatory title of *mahāsāmantādhipati,* they afterwards adopted full imperial titles. Next to the king in dignity, if not in authority, stood the Crown Prince. In contrast with their successors, the Chālukyas of Kalyāṇi, the Queens and Princesses of the Rāshṭrakūṭa line hardly exercised any political influence. We have only one record[71] of a Queen granting a village on her own authority. Among the high officers of State are mentioned those bearing the titles of *mahāsāndhivigrahika* (Minister of Foreign Affairs), *bhāṇḍāgārika* (Treasurer), *balādhikṛita, daṇḍanāyaka,* and *mahāprachaṇḍadaṇḍanāyaka* (three grades of military officers) and the officer connected with the court of justice. One record[72] mentions a *mahāsāndhivigrahika* as being the son of a *balādhikṛita,* which indicates a tendency towards the selection of high officials by hereditary descent.

The structure of local government under the Rāshṭrakūṭas partook of the regional variety of their empire. In Mahārāshṭra and South Gujarāt the donated villages are often described as lying within groups of 12, 24, and 84, while sometimes such a village is located within a *bhukti.* The numerical groups are reminiscent of the typical clan-chief's estate and its sub-divisions to which reference has been made above. The *bhukti* is the old administrative division known from the Gupta times. In the Kannaḍa region, on the other hand, the villages are included in groups having larger or smaller numerical endings.[73] These figures, as Fleet[74] pointed out long ago, refer to the real or supposed number of villages comprised within the groups. The policy of the central government often allowed combination of the larger and smaller divisions under the same officer. We also hear of separate officers (*nāl-gāvuṇḍas,* translated as county-sheriffs) in charge of smaller groups of 300 and the like. We have reasons to think that the office of the county-*gāvuṇḍa* was one of high authority and dignity. In one record[75] the county-*gāvuṇḍa* in charge of two groups of 300 each bears the title of *dharmamahārāja* known to the Early Pallava and Kadamba kings, and he expressly reserves for his own share a fixed revenue along with the king's share, while granting some lands to a temple. The county-*gāvuṇḍa,* either singly or jointly with other *gāvuṇḍas,* could endow lands, transfer revenues, and grant remissions for pious objects.[76]

The machinery of town and village administration under the Rāshṭrakūṭas was as varied as that of the administration of the provinces and districts. In North Konkan, which was ruled by the Śilāhāra feudatories of the Rāshṭrakūṭas, the towns were in charge of *purapatis* or *nagarapatis* (Town Prefects). In the Kannaḍa tract the towns were ruled by *ur-gāvuṇḍas* (sheriffs). In Mahārāshṭra and South Gujarāt the villages had their headmen called *grāmakūṭas,* the number of these in a single village being sometimes as many as six or twelve.[77] By the side of the headman there was the group of *mahattaras* (elders) with an executive board bearing the title of *adhikārins.*[78] In the Kannaḍa area the villages had their bodies of *mahājanas,* who not only attested gifts by private individuals and received assignments of local taxes from provincial and district officers, but also made grants of land for pious purposes.[79]

The feudatories of the Rāshṭrakūṭas constituted an important factor in the State administration. The great feudatory families like the Gaṅgas of Gaṅgavāḍi 96000 were invested with military commands, and they fought wars on behalf of their paramount sovereign. The court and administration of the great feudatories were modelled on those of the paramount power. Thus the Rāshṭrakūṭas of Gujarāt who bore the title of *mahāsāmantādhipati* had on their staff, as we learn from the formula of their land-grants, the *sāndhivigrahika,* the *rāshṭrapati,* the *vishayapati,* the *grāmakūṭa,* the *niyuktaka,* and the *yukta,*—a *sāndhivigrahika* (or *mahāsāndhivigrahika*) being mentioned as usual as the writer of charters. Nevertheless the status of the feudatories must have differed greatly according to their importance. While the higher class could assign taxes and alienate lands without the consent of the paramount power,[80] the lower grades had to submit to alienations of their lands at the orders of the ruling sovereign or his ministers.[81] The semi-independent position of the great feudatories is expressed by the conventional phrases indicative of their rule which differentiate it at once from the rule of the paramount Emperor and the government of mere State officials.[82]

The administration of the Eastern Chālukyas of Veṅgī, whose rule, beginning before the Rāshṭrakūṭas, survived their downfall, has some interesting features. Among their high dignitaries of State are mentioned, besides the *yuvarāja* (Crown Prince) and the *senānī* (Commander-in-Chief) known to other dynasties, a body of five ministers and the *kaṭakādhīśa* (Superintendent of the Royal Camp). The provinces were called *vishayas* and the leading member (perhaps the governor) had the title of *rāshṭrakūṭa.* We have some glimpses into the working of the village administration under the rule of this dynasty. In one case[83] the king is said to have granted the office of *grāmakūṭa* in perpetuity to an individual. This proves that the village headman, at least in some cases, could be nominated by the king. Another record[84] states that the *mahājanas* of a village elected the members of a Brāhmaṇa family on the Committee of five (*pañcha-vāra*), because of their eloquence in committee assemblies. From this it may be inferred that the Veṅgī country under the Eastern Chālukyas, like the Choḷa Empire in later times, knew self-governing village assemblies with elected committees for the transaction of business.

Few details have been preserved of the administration of the Pāṇḍya kings in the first period of their ascendancy (from the beginning of the seventh to that of the tenth century A.D.). There are, however, clear indications of the existence of a well-organised government under their rule. A distinguished family of the time of the Early Pāṇḍya king Jaṭila Parāntaka (c. A.D. 765-815) furnished a number of high officials with the titles *uttaramantrī* (Prime Minister) and *mahāsāmanta* to the State service. We hear, besides, of officers for executing the king's orders for a pious gift as well as of other revenue officers. Reference is made to the *senāpati* (general), while other records mention an officer in charge of elephants (*mataṅgajādhyaksha*) as well as troops in the service of the king or other leaders.[85] Not only therefore was the army in charge of the supreme general, but there were separate commands for its different branches, while the king as well as other leaders maintained troops in their service. The lowest unit of the local administration was the *grāmam* (village) and a number of these formed the *kuṟṟam* or *nāḍu* sometimes Sanskritized into *rāshṭra*. In the working of the village administration the assembly (*sabhā* or *ur*) played an important part. Such was the reputation of these bodies for integrity and efficiency, that kings often placed permanent endowments of gold coins in their hands for meeting the expenses of worship in temples out of the interest accruing therefrom at specified rates.[86] Again, the body of temple servants and the representatives of the village assemblies were sometimes jointly constituted as trustees for the proper administration of the temple funds.[87] The assembly also owned lands which could be granted by the great men of the village, and its approval was necessary when a Brāhmaṇa donee of a village granted lands to his kinsmen.[88] From a record of A.D. 800[89] we learn that the assembly used to meet at a stated hour in a fixed public place. According to the rules framed by the assembly on this occasion, it was to be open to all land-owners, but only those who had a certain property qualification along with the prescribed intellectual and moral attainments were to take part in its deliberations. Only those possessing the requisite qualifications were to be admitted to the committees (*vāriyams*) of the assembly. This important record proves that self-governing village assemblies with elected executive committees, such as can be traced more fully in records of the time of the Choḷa Parāntaka I, existed in the Pāṇḍya kingdom about a century earlier.

The administration of the early Imperial Choḷas assumed a high degree of complexity with the march of time. A record of the reign of Sundara Choḷa[90] points to a relatively simple administrative machinery and procedure for executing the king's order for a pious grant of land. The king's oral order was first communicated by the proper executive officer to the local authorities. Afterwards the record of the transaction was drawn up and attested by a number of witnesses who were either local magnates, or government officers. Far more complex is the process indicated in the larger Leiden plates of Rājarāja I[91] recording the Emperor's grant of a village to a Buddhist shrine. Here the king's order is successively committed to writing by the proper official, signed by four Chief Secretaries, and ordered to be entered in the Accounts Register by a Secretary and arbitrators. The entry is made by four officers of the Tax Department and three other officials called 'maintainers of tax system'. Then a Superintendent and five other officials are deputed for the marking of the donated village. Finally, the royal order is sent to the Assembly (*nāṭṭar*) of the district to present themselves on the spot and to draw up and grant the deed of assignment to the donee. The advanced organisation of the Choḷa Empire is illustrated by the fact that a general survey of lands with a record of rights was carried out about the middle of Rājarāja I's reign, while fresh surveys were undertaken from time to time thereafter. Cases were decided by the judge with the help of learned Brāhmaṇas at the *dharmāsana* (probably meaning the king's court).

The lowest unit of the local administration was the self-governing village of which there were two principal types. The first type had an assembly called the *ur* and an executive body called the *ālunga-ṇam* (sometimes shortened into *gaṇam*). The second type, which was specially represented by villages of Brāhmaṇas, had an assembly called the *sabhā* and various committees (*vāriyams*) of the same to carry out its executive work. The working of this second type is best illustrated by some records of the reign of Parāntaka I relating to the Brāhmaṇa village of Uttaramerur. At first the *sabhā* of this village by a resolution (*vyavasthā*) fixed the mode of appointment (by a mixed method of lot and election) to its five executive committees. Shortly afterwards, the *sabhā* adopted another resolution amending the rules of election. After some time the *sabhā*, by a fresh *vyavasthā*, arranged for appointment of a committee for assaying gold for the village people.[92] It was to consist of experts to be chosen by lot from those who paid taxes and lived in different quarters of the village. It was to be responsible to the Tanks and Annual Committees and (unlike the *sabhā* and its committees) was to receive a monthly remuneration. It is reasonable to think that the above method of entrusting executive work to elected committees was followed by other *sabhās* as well. The *sabhās* exercised a wide range of powers. They kept their own records relating to the rights of the villagers. They decided disputes that did not fall within the jurisdiction of other groups. They granted lands for maintenance of services and sacred teaching in the temples. They founded and maintained hospitals and took charge of all charitable endowments in the village. They controlled a number of taxes which they could assign or remit at their pleasure. They had their own staff of officials such as the *madhyastha,* who assisted in the proceedings of the assembly without sharing in its deliberations.[93]

IV. LAW AND LEGAL INSTITUTIONS

The period from A.D. 750 to 1000 is definitely associated with the works of the great Smṛiti commentators and makers of Digests in place of the metrical Smṛitis. The change, as already observed,[94] marks the advent of a new stage—the critical in place of the constructive—in the history of Hindu Jurisprudence. Among these famous Smṛiti commentators Medhātithi and Viśvarūpa, who wrote commentaries on Manu and Yājñavalkya respectively, deserve special notice. Reference has also to be made to the *Smṛitisaṁgraha,* a Digest by an unnamed author.[95]

1. *Viśvarūpa*

Viśvarūpa's opinion on the law of partition and inheritance is marked by resemblances and differences with Vijñāneśvara's thought. He anticipates Vijñāneśvara in holding that ownership does not arise for the first time on partition, but that partition takes place of what is already jointly owned. But, unlike Vijñāneśvara, he interprets Yājñavalkya[96] to mean that the father, distributing his property in his lifetime, has absolute discretion in giving equal or unequal shares to the sons. Again, he takes Yājñavalkya[97] to imply that the father, giving equal shares to the sons in the case just mentioned, shall allow the husband's share to his wives, as also to the widows of his pre-deceased sons and grandsons who have not been provided with *strīdhana.* Vijñāneśvara, on the other hand, would take the text in its literal sense to apply to the father's own wives alone. Similarly Viśvarūpa understands Yājñavalkya[98] to mean that what a man acquires by himself, without detriment to his father's interest, as well as a nuptial present and what he gets as present from a friend, shall not be shared by him with his co-parceners. He also takes Yājñavalkya[99] to mean that what was gained by learning shall not be given to the co-parceners. These views differ completely from those of Vijñāneśvara. In the case of a man without a son, Yājñavalkya[100] mentions the order of succession as follows:—wife, daughters, both parents, brothers and their sons, etc. Commenting on these passages Viśvarūpa says that the wife shall succeed if she were pregnant at the time of her husband's death, and the daughter shall do so if she was an "appointed" daughter. This is quite different from the view of Vijñāneśvara who would allow the widow to succeed without any restriction save that of chastity, and the daughters to do so without any qualification save that the unmarried has precedence over the married, and the unprovided over the endowed daughter.

2. *Medhātithi*

Passing to the views of Medhātithi, we may first notice his statements on the constitution and functions of the courts of justice. Referring to the members of the king's court, Medhātithi[101] shows by a concrete example that the Brāhmaṇas assisting the king have to be versed in polity, while he quotes an alternative view to the effect that, whereas the *mantrīs* (counsellors) should have knowledge of the details of the case, the Brāhmaṇas should have the quality of impartiality. More important than the above is the fact that Medhātithi extends membership of the court in special cases to other parties as well. For he says:[102] "Where the parties, *e.g.* traders, cultivators, and cattle-breeders belong to the same profession, and where other persons belonging to this profession feel that they would be affected by this decision, they are entitled to take part in the investigation."[103] In the same context Medhātithi throws an interesting light on the nature of the hierarchy of courts. Taking Nārada[104] as his text, he defines *kula* as 'the body of relatives', *śreṇī* as 'a body of traders and others following the same profession', *gaṇas* as 'persons who always move about in groups', and unlike *śreṇīs* act collectively. He also takes 'an authorised person' to mean 'the Brāhmaṇa learned in the Vedas.' It follows from the above that the *śreṇīs* corresponded to trade- and craft-guilds, and the *gaṇas* to wider and more closely knit Associations. The family courts, Medhātithi goes on, through fear of relations do not always exercise a check upon persons deviating from the right path. Hence a party not having confidence in them is entitled to carry his case to the Guilds. The Guilds are very jealous of their independence; in fact they take care not to let any matter within their purview go before the king, lest the king's officers should take the opportunity to interfere with their work. It is their practice to take sureties for satisfaction of judgment from both parties at the beginning of the suit, the surety being liable to a fine in the case of his party not accepting the decision. The Associations investigate cases by themselves, and they appoint committees (*upasad*) for enforcing their decision. Their practice of collective action makes them dreaded by all. The king, because of his great power, is superior to all other courts, so that a case decided by him cannot be re-opened. From the above discussion Medhātithi draws the important conclusion that the other courts ("Brāhmaṇas and others") are entitled to pronounce judgments, though the king alone has the right of inflicting punishment. Medhātithi takes this opportunity to point out the essential difference between the standpoints of the king and other authorities in judicial trials. The motive of the king, he says, in looking into cases is the proper administration of his kingdom, while that of others lies only in settling doubtful points for the benefit of the people. In another context Medhātithi[105] explains the difference between the spirit of the king's executive and judicial administration. "When he is seated upon his royal throne, the king regards wealth (*artha*) as the most important matter even in preference to morality (*dharma*). But when he is engaged in deciding suits, he regards morality as the most important thing."

The *rationale* of judicial proceedings consists, according to Medhātithi[106], in ensuring the immunity of the people from seen and unseen troubles along with preservation of the kingdom which would otherwise be destroyed. In this we have a remarkable illustration of the Smṛiti view of the identity of interests of the king and his subjects. Medhātithi's views on various points of judicial procedure treated by the older authors indicate the remarkable independence of his thought, combined with good sense and love of fair-play. Dealing with Manu's rule requiring the king to take up cases of suitors in the order of their respective castes, Medhātithi observes: "This order of investigation based upon castes is to be observed only when the troubles of all the suitors are of the same degree: when, on the other hand, the business of the lower caste is very urgent or very important, then it should be taken up first." Medhātithi justifies this rule on the remarkable ground that the public interest overrides the written text. (*Salus populi est suprema lex*) For he says: "The investigation of cases is for the purpose of maintaining order in the kingdom, so that the rules laid down need not always be followed literally." In connection with the question of time allowable for filing the plaint and its answer, Medhātithi[107] argues that the plaintiff already knows the amount of his dues or the man who has wronged him. On the other hand when the defendant is dragged before the court, he does not know the nature of the complaint against him and cannot find the right answer. The plaintiff, therefore, must complete his plaint on the same date, or he may be granted two or three days' time. The defendant should be granted a postponement which, however, must be only for the period regarded as a fair interval for the understanding of the suit and the finding of the answer. The text of Gautama[108] allowing postponement of the answer for one year, Medhātithi emphatically says, should not be followed in practice, as he pertinently asks, if non-understanding is sufficient cause for delay, why should it cease to be so after the lapse of one year only?

From the benefit of the rule allowing postponement of the answer, Medhātithi expressly excludes the group of heinous offences. His argument in support of this contention indicates his clear grasp of the essential difference between civil and criminal cases. "In the case of non-payment of debt and the like," he says, "if the parties settle it themselves, it is no business of the king to interfere. But in the case of a criminal, it is the duty of the king to punish him even though he may have come to terms with the plaintiffs." In other words, civil suits are the concerns of the private parties, while crimes are essentially offences against the State. The different procedure adopted in the two classes of suits is explained by Medhātithi while discussing Manu's text[109] which forbids the king or his servants to promote a suit. "This applies", he says, "to non-payment of debt and similar subjects: as for thieves and criminals who are like thorns in the kingdom, these the king shall capture and punish even when he catches them himself." Dealing with the law of evidence, Medhātithi categorically rejects Nārada's statement that documentary evidence is superior to witnesses. As he cogently argues, "Documentary evidence is of two kinds—those written by the party himself and those written by another person. This last again is of two kinds—(a) those written by a scribe who volunteers to do the writing, and (b) those written by an authorised scribe. Now, a document written by another person is in every way of the nature of a witness.....No reliability attaches to what has been written by a single man, just as it does not attach to a single witness. It may be argued that it is only when witnesses set down their hands to something that they become documentary evidence. But this difference cannot make the one superior to the other....'Being authorised' also cannot be regarded as a ground of distinction, because as a matter of fact all persons authorised by the king are not necessarily thoroughly tested."

Medhātithi's ideas of the law of ownership may be illustrated by one example. Dealing with the question of the king's title to the property lost but claimed by the owner thereafter, Medhātithi[110] quotes a view to the following effect:—"Even after the lapse of three years, it will not be right for the king to take or possess what belongs to another person, and hence what is meant is that after the lapse of three years, if the rightful owner does not turn up, the king shall enjoy the usufruct of the property." This doctrine which implies that title cannot be lost by any extent of adverse possession is quoted by Medhātithi only for refutation. But it was destined to be adopted afterwards by Vijñāneśvara and his school.

We have referred above to some of Medhātithi's views on partition and inheritance. But some other points may be noted. According to an unnamed authority quoted by Medhātithi,[111] Manu's rule assigning additional portions of the family property to the eldest, the middle-most, and the youngest sons at the time of partition refers to past times and is not meant to be observed during the current Age. Medhātithi rejects the above view on the authoritative ground that no such restriction as regards time is allowed anywhere. In so far as the unmarried sister is concerned, Medhātithi[112] quotes a view which objects to her being given a share in the family property on the ground that the girl is entitled by custom only to the benefit of her marriage being performed. Rejecting this view Medhātithi says: "The direct assertion of the Smṛiti is definitely more authoritative than custom. As a matter of fact, however, the custom referred to is by no means universal."

3. *The Smṛitisaṁgraha*

We may conclude this chapter with some reference to the views of the *Smṛitisaṁgraha* Digest, which are often of great historical interest. Ownership, according to the author, is indicated by the *śāstras* and is not an affair of the world—a view which was afterwards to become classical through its adoption by Vijñāneśvara and his school. Elsewhere the *Smṛitisaṁgraha* observes that the son's ownership is created in the father's property by partition—a view which was afterwards to be vigorously opposed by Vijñāneśvara. In another passage the *Smṛitisaṁgraha* takes the view quoted by Medhātithi only for refutation, namely that Manu's allowing an extra share to the eldest son at the time of partition is not followed in the present Age. In the order of heirs enumerated in the *Smṛiti-*

saṁgraha, the paternal grandmother takes the property after the mother and before the father—a view followed afterwards by Dhāreśvara. Finally the *Smṛitisaṁgraha* allows the widow of a separated co-parcener without sons to succeed only if she submits to *niyoga* under the instructions of the elders. This doctrine which was destined to be vigorously opposed by Vijñāneśvara is interesting as marking a mile-stone on the road to the childless widow's acquisition of an absolute right to succeed to her husband's property.[113]

1. *TSS* Edition, p. 98.
2. I. 109.
3. *op. cit.,* 181.
4. VII. 2.
5. I. 119.
6. On *Manu,* III. 119, IV. 84, 110, V. 93, VII. 1-2.
7. On *Manu,* VII. 2.
8. On *Manu,* VIII. 1.
9. X. 9.
10. On *Manu,* VII. 12.
11. On *Manu,* VII. 13.
12. IX. 253.
13. *Manu,* VII. 138.
14. On *Manu,* IX. 254.
15. VIII. 348-49.
16. On *Manu,* VIII. 350.
17. (Cr. Ed.) XII, 93.9; (B) XII, 92.9; XIII, 61. 32.33.
18. *TSS* Edition, p. 192.
19. *Ibid,* p. 2.
20. *Ibid,* pp. 2-6.
21. *Ibid,* pp. 7-8.
22. *Ibid,* pp. 83-86.
23. *Bhavishya,* I, 2. 120-24; *Garuḍa,* I. 217. 12.
24. *Matsya,* CCXXVI. 1; *Vishṇudharmottara,* II, 71.1.
25. *Bṛihaddharma,* III, 3, 8-9.
26. *Matsya,* CCXXVI. 3-12; *Bṛihaddharma,* III, 3.6.
27. II, 2. 2-16.
28. CX. 26.
29. II, 2. 2-16.
30. (Cr. Ed. and B.) XII, 67. 2.
31. III, 3. 7.
32. III, 4. 1.
33. *Ibid,* 6. 1, 56.
34. III, 3. 1.
35. II, 4. 2.
36. *Bṛihaddharma,* III, 3. 10-11; *Agni,* CCXXIII. 9-10; *Vishṇudharmottara,* II, 61. 18-27.
37. CCXXVII. 63-64.
38. II, 61. 49-50.
39. *Garuḍa,* I, 6. 5-8; *Agni,* XVII. 11-18; XIX. 22-29; *Matsya,* X, 3-16; *Bṛihaddharma,* III, 13. 4-59, 14. 1-74; *Vishṇudharmottara,* I. 108-09.
40. V. 55.
41. VII. 2, 3; *ibid,* 20.
42. V. 67.
43. XVII. 52.
44. XXIX. 16-19.
45. XVII. 33.
46. *Ibid,* 51.
47. XVII. 25-27; XXXII. 66.
48. VII. 8.

49. VII. 21.
50. VII. 23.
51. VII. 49.
52. *EI*, I. 159.
53. *EI*, I. 156.
54. *EI*, IX. 4 ff.
55. *EI*, I. 175 f.
56. Cf. the observations of Sulaimān (A.D. 851) and Mas'ūdī (A.D. 941-943) quoted in *HIED*, I. 4, 21, 23.
57. *HIED*, I. 4.
58. *EI*, IV. 243 f. For the above explanation of *prakritis*, cf. *HBR*, I. 98.
59. *EI*, II. 150.
60. *Manu*, VII. 118-119; *Mbh*, (Cr. Ed.) XII. 88. 3, 6; (B) XII. 87. 3, 6.
61. On the Pāla administration, see *HBR*, I. 273-80, 285-87; Benoy Chandra Sen, *Some Historical Aspects of the Inscriptions of Bengal* (*Pre-Muhammadan epoch*), Calcutta, 1942 (Part III). The most important references are *EI*, IV 243, XXIII. 290, XVIII. 304, XVII. 318, XV. 293, 304 and *JASB*, LXIX. Part I, 68. On the significance of the titles of *khola* and *khaṇḍaraksha* see U.N. Ghoshal, *The Beginnings of Indian Historiography and other Essays*, 151-153.
62. *Kāmarūpaśāsanāvalī* by P. Bhattacharya, pp. 48 ff.
63. *Rājataraṅgiṇī*, V. 476-77.
64. *Ibid*, IV. 141-43.
65. *Ibid*, I. 118-20.
66. Stein (*Rājataraṅgiṇī*) translates *daṇḍanāyaka* as 'Prefect of City' and *rājasthānīya* as 'Chief Justice.'
67. For references to the above titles, see Stein's *Rājataraṅgiṇī*, Tr. II. Index s.v.
68. *RT*, IV. 55 f., 85 f; VI. 14 f.
69. *Ibid*, V. 84 f.
70. For a detailed account of the above, see U. N. Ghoshal, *Hindu Revenue System*, 249-252 and *IHQ*, XVIII. 307-9.
71. *EI*, XXII. 105.
72. *EI*, X. 85 f.
73. Such were Banavāsi 12,000, Kundur 500, Purigere 300, and Kandarage 70.
74. *Dyn. Kan.* p. 298 f.n. 2.
75. *EI*, XIV. 365 f.
76. *EI*, XIV. 365 f; XVI. 278 f. Altekar (*The Rāshṭrakūṭas and Their Times*, 158-160) thinks that the *rāshṭramahattaras* and the *vishayamahattaras* referred to in *EI*, VIII. 186 and I. 55 (actually the former inscription mentions *rāshṭragrāmamahattaras*) refer to councils of notables and elders in the provinces and the districts respectively. But the evidence is clearly inconclusive.
77. *JBBRAS*, X. 283 f; EI, XIV. 144 ff.
78. *EI*, X. 85 f; XIV. 150; XVII. 249 etc. According to Altekar (*The Rāshṭrakūṭas*, 196) the *āyuktas*, *niyuktas* and *upayuktas* mentioned in the Rāshṭrakūṭa land-grants after the *grāmakūṭas* and before the *grāmamahattaras* were no other than village accountants and their assistants.
79. *EI*, XXI. 208; VI. 102 f. 353; VII. 201 f.
80. *IA*, XIII. 136; EI, III. 310.
81. *IA*, I. 141; *EI*, XVIII. 248.
82. The phrase applied to the feudatories is 'ruling with pleasure of agreeable or friendly interchange of communications'. This is distinguished on the one hand from the grandiloquent formula applied to the paramount ruler, namely, 'the virtuous reign, augmenting with perpetual increase, being current so as to endure so long as the moon and sun and stars may last', and on the other hand from the simple style of purely subordinate officials, namely, 'to govern with punishment of the wicked and protection of the good'. Cf. *Dyn. Kan*, p. 428, f.n. 4.
83. *EI*, VII. 185 f.
84. *EI*, V. 135 f.
85. See K. A. Nilakanta Sastri, *The Pāṇḍya Kingdom* 60-61, for references to the *uttaramantrī* and the *mahāsāmanta*, and *ibid*, 85-86, for reference to the *mataṅgajādhyaksha*.
86. In the adjoining territory under the rule of the Bāṇa kings we have similar records (*EI*, XI. 227-228) of village assemblies receiving endowments of gold from a queen and a magnate for providing worship in temples out of the resulting interest.

87. *EI*, IX. 92 f; XXI. 109 f; etc.
88. *EI*, XVII. 298 f.
89. *EI*, XXII. 9 f.
90. *EI*, XV. 50.
91. *EI*, XXII. 238 f.
92. *EI*, XXII. 149.
93. The above is based, where references are not given, upon K. A. Nilakanta Sastri, *The Cholas* II (Part I) 277 f.
94. Vol. III, p. 356.
95. According to Kane (*KHDS*, I), Medhātithi "most probably flourished between 825 and 900 A.D." (p. 225), Viśvarūpa, between 750 and 1000 A.D. (p. 261) and *Smṛitisaṁgraha* "was probably completed between the 8th and 10th centuries of the Christian era" (p. 242).
96. *Yāj*, II. 118.
97. *Ibid*, II. 119.
98. *Ibid*, II. 122.
99. *Ibid*, II. 126.
100. *Ibid*, II. 139, 140.
101. On *Manu*, VIII. 1.
102. On *Manu*, VIII. 2.
103. The present and following translations of extracts from Medhātithi are taken from the work *Manu-Smṛiti, The Laws of Manu, with the Bhāshya of Medhātithi*, translated by Ganganath Jha, (published by the University of Calcutta).
104. I. 8.
105. On *Manu*, VIII. 23.
106. On *Manu*, VIII. 1.
107. On *Manu*, VIII. 56.
108. XIII. 28.
109. VIII. 43.
110. On *Manu*, VIII. 30.
111. On *Manu*, VIII. 112.
112. On *Manu*, VIII. 118.
113. For references to the texts of *Smṛitisaṁgraha* quoted above, see *Smṛitichandrikā, Vyavahārakāṇḍa*, 257, 259, 266, 294.

CHAPTER XI

RELIGION AND PHILOSOPHY

A. GENERAL REVIEW

The fundamental features of religious ideas and practices, which characterised the previous period,[1] continue during the period under review. But the relative importance of the different religious sects undergoes a great change. The Puranic Hinduism, in the forms of Śaivism and Vaishṇavism, now gradually dominate the field, and vie with each other for supremacy. Both Buddhism and Jainism are gradually ousted from the Tamil land and other parts of South India. Jainism for a time gains an ascendancy in the Deccan, and retains its stronghold in Western India, while Buddhism, as a living force, is practically confined to the dominions of the Pāla kings in Bengal and Bihār. Both these heterodox creeds are still followed by isolated groups all over Northern India, but there is ample evidence that they were fast losing their importance, save in very restricted areas. Two notable characteristics of religious life in the preceding period, *viz.*, toleration and worship of images, not only continue in full force but are ever on the increase. The temples grow in number and massive grandeur, and the images are multiplied almost without any limit. These two features of the religion are not noticed separately in the present volume, but will be dealt with in the next, which will afford an opportunity to trace their development in an unbroken line, down to the last days of Hindu rule.

The spirit of toleration displayed by the followers of different religions led to a catholicism which overrode narrow sectarian views, and members of the same royal family are known to have been votaries of different religious cults. The most typical example is furnished by the Imperial Pratīhāras. The founder of this family was a devotee of Vishṇu, while his three descendants were worshippers, respectively, of Śiva, Bhagavatī and Sun-god. The Pāla Emperors, though staunch Buddhists, employed orthodox Brāhmaṇas as their hereditary chief ministers and attended the religious ceremonies of the latter. Many other examples of this type will be met with in the history of the different royal dynasties treated in this volume.

It is no wonder, therefore, that the period brings into prominent relief the reciprocal influence of different religious sects upon one another. Both Buddhism and Jainism develop theistic tendencies on the analogy of Śaivism and Vaishṇavism. Buddhas and Jinas are regarded as gods, and their images are worshipped in temples with devotional songs, accompanied by rites and ceremonies which clearly betray the influence of the devotees of Śiva and Vishṇu. Jina is described as the Universal spirit—a very near approach to the conception of God—manifesting itself as Śiva, Sugata, and Vishṇu, while Buddha and Jinas are accepted as *avatāras* or incarnations of Vishṇu. The idea of Hari-Hara, or personification of the two gods Śiva and Vishṇu in one image, is another illustration of the same spirit. On the other hand the cult of *ahiṁsā*, which still manifests itself in many spheres of Indian life, notably in the vegetarian diets of upper class Hindus in large areas of India, is a permanent memorial of the influence of Jainism and Buddhism upon Brahmanical sects.

One of the potent factors in the evolution of the religious ideas of this period is the emergence of the Tāntrik cult which profoundly influenced Buddhism and transformed it almost beyond recognition. The same ideas also pervaded different Brahmanical sects and radically changed their views and practices.

The fundamental unity of ideas underlying these changes not only explains the characteristics of religious transformation in general, but the gradual assimilation of Buddhism with the Brahmanical religion in particular. Jainism alone withstood these new currents and largely maintained, as before, its rigid orthodoxy. This is one of the reasons which enabled it to continue as a distinct cult while Buddhism slowly but steadily lost its separate existence in India.

While the growth of Tāntrik ideas was sapping the vitality of Buddhism, Brahmanical religion was enthroned on a high pedestal by philosophers like Śaṅkarāchārya. His triumphant career finally assured the victory of orthodox Brahmanical religion over the heterodox sects. Though he was a Śaiva by persuasion and undoubtedly gave a great fillip to that sect, his philosophical dissertations were conducive to the revival of other Brahmanical sects as well. The predominance which Śaivism acquired from this dominant personality was further helped by the growth of a special school in Kāshmir which did away with many outlandish practices that disfigured that sect. Vaishṇavism also developed an intellectual and philosophical aspect, as opposed to the emotional fervour of the preceding period, in the Tamil land. The Āchāryas took the place of Āḻvārs, and Nāthamuni, who flourished during this period, was the forerunner of a band of distinguished religious leaders who shed lustre on the succeeding age. We find already the beginnings of that great controversy about the respective place of *bhakti* (devotion), *jñāna* (knowledge) and *karma* (Vedic rites and ceremonies), in the scheme of final salvation. These three ideas which clustered round the Vaishṇava Āchāryas and the two Schools of Mīmāṁsā associated with the names of Śaṅkara and Kumārila still form the main planks or bases of the Hindu religion.

B. BUDDHISM

I. DOCTRINAL CHANGES

1. Emergence of Tāntrikism

The period under review witnessed not only the decadence of pure Hīnayāna and Mahāyāna Buddhism but also the appearance of a new phase of the religion, in which the original ethical and philosophical principles were superimposed in such a way by an esoteric Yogic system, combined with endless rituals and forms of worship, that it could hardly be called Buddhism any longer. As we have seen above, Buddha's rational and ethical teachings, free from worship and rituals, gradually gave way in the early centuries of the Christian era to a popular form of the religion with a new ethical and devotional outlook, while his philosophical teachings received a new interpretation at the hands of the masterminds like Asaṅga, Nāgārjuna, Vasubandhu, and Āryadeva. With Chandrakīrti and Śāntideva, Diṅnāga and Dharmakīrti ended the glorious days of Buddhist logic and philosophy. Then came the days of *stotras* and *stavas* begun by Sarvajñamitra of Kāshmir in the eighth century A.D.[1a] The religion lost itself in the maze of mysticism and was engulfed by a host of *mudrās* (finger-gestures or physical postures), *maṇḍalas* (mystical diagrams), *kriyās* (rites and ceremonies) and *charyās* (meditational practices and observances for external and internal purity). The teachings of one of the noblest minds were thus deformed into a system of magical spells, exorcisms, spirit-beliefs, and worship of demons and divinities.

It is strange that the promulgators of the new system sought their justification from the ancient words of Buddha and the philosophical teachings of Asaṅga and Nāgārjuna, and succeeded in conjuring up before the eyes of the masses a religion with immense possibilities. It must however be admitted that this new type of *sādhanas* or *yogic* practices did confer on the adepts some superhuman powers and also led many to the realization of high spiritual states, and that there were among the adepts some who, in purity and knowledge, ranked in no way inferior to some of the best *arhats* of the past. In fact this new phase of Buddhism was not a hocus-pocus or a ruse for debauchery but envisaged something very deep and subtle to be realized only by those who were initiated into the secrets by their spiritual teachers. At the same time it must be admitted that the human mind can be worked up into any type of perversity through faith, logic and reasoning derived from the same religion which once upheld the noblest ideals of human life and the same philosophy which unfolded the deepest mysteries of the universe. Be it ancient India or Egypt, mediaeval China or the Middle East, modern Europe or Japan, we find the same story, *viz.* that in the name of religion and philosophy, necessity and circumstances have debased human mind to the lowest conceivable vulgarity.

The mission of Buddha to wean the Indian mind from the blind faith in the efficacy of worship and rituals passed into oblivion, and the leaning of the Indian mind towards the worship of divinities and the awe and veneration for rituals and mystical utterances (*mantras*) re-asserted itself. The belief in the efficacy of the Atharvavedic *mantras,* the superhuman powers acquired by the mystics (*sādhakas*), the arts of divination, necromancy and the hundred and one superstitious beliefs could not be totally eradicated from the Indian mind, however arduous might have been the efforts of Buddha in that direction. The huge sacrificial literature (the *Śrauta-sūtras*) that grew up in the post-Vedic period permeated the Indian mind to such an extent that it was almost impossible to separate religion from ritualistic worship and mystical utterances (*mantras*). Buddha had to repeat his warnings to his disciples and devotees to disabuse their minds of the efficacy of the *mantra* rituals, but the sequel shows that he failed in his mission. In as early a text as the *Dīgha Nikāya* there is one complete *suttanta* (*Āṭānāṭiya*)[2] which is described as a *rakkhā* (protecting spell) to be memorised for averting evils from *yakshas, gandharvas* and other evil spirits. The anomaly of the occurrence of *parittās* (=*rakkhā*=protecting spells) in the Piṭakan texts has been discussed in the *Milindapañha.*[3] The *Mahāmāyūrīdhāraṇī* appears in the *Vinaya-Piṭaka* of the Sarvāstivādins. Hence it must be admitted that throughout the career of Buddhism, the use of incantations or mystical utterances was in vogue, and so Tāranātha[4] rightly said that in general the origin of *Sūtras* and *Tantras* could not be distinguished in regard to time, place and teacher, and the utmost that could be stated is that the *Tantras* (excluding the *Anuttarayogatantra*) appeared at the same time as the *Mahāyāna-sūtras.* The tradition is that the *yogic* practices propounded by Asaṅga led to the growth of esotericism, which in course of time became Tāntrikism. Tāntrikism is not confined to Buddhism and represents a common phase of development both in Buddhist and Brahmanical religions. A more detailed account of its nature and progress will be given in a later section of this chapter. Here it will suffice to note only its characteristic features so far as Buddhism is concerned.

2. *Dhāraṇīs*

The earliest literature which may be called precursor of *Tantra* was known as the *Dhāraṇīs* and formed a part of the *Mahāyāna-sūtras*. At the time of composition of the *Lalitavistara*[5] or *Sandhi-nirmochana-sūtra*[6] (about second century A.D.), the special sense of *Dhāraṇī* was unknown and its earliest use as a *mantra* was made in the *Kāraṇḍavyūha*[7] of about the fourth century A.D. It is a text devoted to the glorification of the Bodhisattva Avalokiteśvara who with Tārā formed the chief deities of worship in the early *Tantra* literature. In most of the early Mahāyāna texts, *e.g.*, in the *Suvarṇaprabhāsa-sūtra*[8] there is a section exhorting the gods and demons to protect those, who read and write the *Sūtra*, from harm. In the *Saddharmapuṇḍarīka*[9] there are a few *Dhāraṇīs* which, if uttered by the reciters of the *Sūtra*, would protect them from all harm. In course of time a large number of *Dhāraṇīs* were composed, and the utterance of these *Dhāraṇīs* not only protected the reciters from *nāgas, yakshas, rākshasas* and other evil spirits, but also from king's punishments, snakes, ferocious animals, fire, theft, diseases, deadly sins and all causes of untimely death. The utterance of *Dhāraṇīs* again conferred all kinds of blessings on the reciters like peace and happiness at the time of death, a desirable rebirth, and even a strong desire for *Bodhichitta* and ultimate emancipation.

In course of time, the *mantras* were written on birch-bark and used as amulets for particular purposes.[10] The utterance of the *Dhāraṇīs* or *Mantrapadas* was preceded and followed by an elaborate ritualistic worship of Buddhas, Bodhisattvas and other deities. These were represented either by images or by paintings, for which also there were directions in the texts. The priests, who officiated in these ceremonial worships, were called *Vidyādharas* whose function was to recite the *Dhāraṇīs* or *Mantras* which, in some special instances, were designated as *Vidyārājñī* (*e.g. Mahāmāyūrī-vidyārājñī*), for the benefit of the worshipper (*yajamāna*).

The growth of the *Dhāraṇī* literature took place between the fourth and eighth centuries A.D. A large number of manuscripts containing *Dhāraṇīs* have been discovered in Gilgit, Eastern Turkestan and Central Asia. These are written in Upright Gupta characters of the seventh ceutury A.D. Some of these appear also in the languages current in Central Asia.

The *Dhāraṇīs* or *Mantrapadas* had very little to do with the secret *yogic* practices of Tāntrikism. The efficacy of the *Dhāraṇīs* rested mainly on the repetition of *mantras* on the auspicious days of a month along with some ceremonies for the worship of Avalokiteśvara. There is no place for Śakti in these ceremonies nor in the *mudrās* and *maṇḍalas, kriyās* and *charyās.*

3. Avalokiteśvara and Tārā

The only deity invoked in most of the earlier *Dhāraṇīs* is the Bodhisattva Avalokiteśvara, who was a devotee of Buddha Vairochana. The abode of Avalokiteśvara is placed at Potalaka, a place somewhere in the south, near Śrīdhānyakaṭaka (Amarāvatī). In the *Kāraṇḍvyūha* (fourth century A.D.) this Bodhisattva is glorified as the first god to issue out of the primordial Buddha (Ādi-Buddha=Ādinātha=Vajra) and to create the universe. In this text, the goddess Tārā does not appear while there are references to Maheśvara and Umā, as devotees of Avalokiteśvara. It seems that in course of time this Umā-Maheśvara conception was superimposed on Mahāyāna and paved the way for the advent of Tantrayāna.

It is in this text again that we come across for the first time the well-known *mantra 'Oṁ maṇipadme huṁ'* with an account of the immense magical merit derived by the utterance of the six syllables. This *mantra* is said to be the innermost core *(hṛidaya)*[11] of Avalokiteśvara and the quintessence of all knowledge (including the *navāṅga*—nine divisions of the Tripiṭaka) and was known as the *shadaksharī-mahāvidyārājñī.* Repetition of these words not only conferred all the conceivable earthly and heavenly blessings, but also led to the attainment of the highest knowledge, the truth.

Thus, we see that up to the fourth century A.D., Bodhisattva Avalokiteśvara was the chief object of worship, and the goddess Tārā had not yet been included in the Buddhist pantheon.

In the *Mañjuśrīmūlakalpa,* the Bodhisattva Mañjuśrī is glorified, but the goddess Tārā is also recommended for worship by those in distress seeking relief. In the *Guhyasamāja*[12] Buddha Vairochana appears as the primordial Buddha, from whom emanated many Buddhas in the female forms of Lochanā, Māmakī, Pāṇḍaravāsinī and Samayatārā. In the *Mañjuśrīmūlakalpa,*[13] the names of different forms of Tārās are Bhṛikuṭī, Lochanā, Māmakī, Śvetā, Pāṇḍaravāsinī, and Sutārā and these are described as *Mahāmudras* (great aids for *yoga*). In the text the goddess Tārā is described as the Vidyārājñī, full of compassion and given to the alleviation of sufferings of worldly beings. Her sphere of action is the east but she wanders over the whole world.[14]

The elevation of Tārā to the position of the highest deity is found for the first time in the *Mahāpratyaṅgirā-dhāraṇī*, a fragment of which was found in Central Asia written in Upright Gupta characters of the seventh century, and transliterated in Chinese characters by the famous Tāntrik teacher, Amoghavajra (A.D. 704-774). In this treatise Tārā is described as goddess of white colour and noble mien, wearing a garland of *vajras*, holding a *vajra* in her hand, and having the figure of Vairochana on her crown, and so forth. The Kāshmirian poet Sarvajñamitra of the eighth century composed a *stotra* in praise of Tārā called the *Sragdharā-stotra*, in which the goddess is described as a giver of strength to the weak and solace to the distressed, the saviour of all beings from sufferings.

It is from the seventh century A.D. onwards that we find the exuberance of *Tārā-stotras*, and goddess Tārā (Prajñā or Prajñāpāramitā) raised to the mothership of all Buddhas and made a companion of Avalokiteśvara, the personification of love (*maitrī*) and compassion (*karuṇā*). This notion reminds us of the Hindu Tāntrik conception,[15] in which Brahman is placed as the primordial cause, the unmanifested Purusha and Śakti. Brahman, being neuter and incapable of creation, produced Śiva and Śakti, of whom Śakti is the cause of liberation (*moksha*), Śiva or Purusha, the cause of bondage (*saṁsāra*). The Buddhist conception runs almost parallel to the above and we may equate Brahman to Ādi-Buddha, Śakti to Tārā or Prajñā, the cause of liberation, and Śiva to Avalokiteśvara, the only deviation being that Śiva or Purusha is the cause of *saṁsāra* while Avalokiteśvara is the embodiment of love and compassion.

It did not take long to reach the Tāntrik conception that Tārā as such was Buddha's *śakti* and the relation of Buddha to Tārā was similar to that of Śiva to Pārvatī, the dual manifestations of Ādi-Buddha or the monistic Brahman.

4. Early Tāntrik Texts

(i) *The Mañjuśrīmūlakalpa*

The earliest works dealing with Tāntrik Buddhism are the *Mañjuśrīmūlakalpa* and the *Guhyasamāja*. The composition of both of these works took place some time after the *Kāraṇḍavyūha* and before the *Mahāpratyaṅgirā-dhāraṇī*, *i.e.* about the fifth or sixth century A.D.[16] Though both may be classified as Tāntrik Buddhist texts, the topics of the two treatises are quite different. The *Guhyasamāja* deals with *yoga* and *anuttarayoga* and incidentally with *maṇḍalas*, while the *Mañjuśrīmūlakalpa* gives an exposition of endless *mudrās* (finger-poses), *maṇḍalas* (mystical diagrams), *mantras* (mystical spells), *kriyās* (rites) and *charyās* (duties of an officiating priest in worship). This text teaches that observance of moral precepts (*śīla*), vows (*vratas*), cleanliness in acts (*śauchāchāra*), religious austerities (*niyama*), offering of oblations (*homa*), muttering of prayers (*japa*) and meditation (*dhyāna*) are the prerequisites for success in the Mantra cult. The directions regarding the above are given by the *Maṇḍalāchārya* (spiritual preceptor proficient in diagram, paintings, etc.), who gives the initiation (*abhisheka*) and then imparts the *mantra*. After a long time, when the teacher feels that his disciple has advanced spiritually, he teaches him the duties for secret *tantra-mudrā*.[17]

By far the best part of the treatise is the section devoted to *paṭavidhāna, i.e.* directions for drawing pictures of different Buddhas, Bodhisattvas, Tārā and other goddesses as also of the Krodharājas, Yamāntakas, Yakshas and Yakshiṇīs.[18] The drawing of diagrams (*maṇḍalas*) forms another important section of the treatise. Each *maṇḍala* as well as each *paṭa* is associated with certain rites and ceremonies for worshipping the deities or propitiating the evil spirits. Within and outside the *maṇḍalas*, images of deities including Buddhas and Bodhisattvas had to be painted, and the text abounds with detailed directions of the paintings of a *maṇḍala* and the group of deities to be placed within the same. Even the deities like Śiva with a trident seated on a bull, the well-adorned Umā, the ever young Kārttikeya seated on a peacock are included in the paintings.[19] This text contains *mantras* for both Hindu and Buddhist deities. It makes an important contribution to the art of painting by describing how the abstract qualities like *dāna* (charity), *maitrī* (love), and *prajñā* (knowledge) are to be depicted.

Apart from *mantras* and directions for *paṭas* (paintings) and *maṇḍalas* (diagrams) the text furnishes us with a list of the holy places for quick success in Mantra cult and recommends particularly Śrīparvata as the most suitable for such practices. This list includes all those countries which became later the chief seats of Tāntrik Buddhism.[20] In this text there is very little of the secret Yogic practices envisaged in the Tāntrik literature. The practices recommended are mostly rites and ceremonies for worship of Buddhas, Bodhisattvas, and other deities, and utterances of *mantras*. There is an admixture of Hīnayāna and Mahāyāna doctrines with *mantras* and rituals. It depicts the stage just preceding the development of full-fledged Vajrayāna or Tantrayāna and may be described in the words of Tāranātha[21] as *Kriyā* and *Karma tantras,* on the decline of which appeared the *Yoga* or *Anuttarayoga tantra.*

(ii) *The Guhyasamāja*

The *Guhyasamāja,* devoted to *Yoga* and *Anuttarayoga,* contains also several *mantras* and a few directions for *maṇḍalas,* but its chief aim is to explain the *Tathāgata-guhya, i.e.* the unknowable reality, the source of all Tathāgatas as also of the phenomenal world, and how to realise it. Its importance as an early text of Vajrayāna lies in the fact that it indicates the new ways and means for realising the reality, the *guhya,* the *vajra,* with the help of *mantras* and *maṇḍalas,* rites and ceremonies. The *Tathāgata-guhya* is so deep and subtle that it can be described as the secret of all secrets; it is the unchangeable eternal reality, the *Vajra,* the *Śūnyatā* of Nāgārjuna, and the *Vijñaptimātratā* of Vasubandhu. It is unfortunate that the word *'guhya'* has tempted a few scholars to trace in the text sexual ritualistic practices, and Dr. Benoytosh Bhattacharyya, in his introduction to the *Guhyasamāja,*[22] has done injustice to the work by isolating, from the topic and trend of exposition, the verses which have references to the conception of *śakti,* by interpreting certain verses superficially without any reference to the theme of the passages preceding and following them,[23] and also by misinterpreting a few verses.[24]

The *Guhyasamāja,* as stated above, gives repeatedly the exposition of the Truth which, according to the text, is the *Vajra,* or oneness of the universe, in which there is no distinction between a man and a woman, between a wife and a sister or a mother, between the excreta and the meat of any animal, even of a human being. The Truth or the *Vajra* is immanent in the phenomenal world of *rūpa* (from), *rasa* (taste), *gandha* (smell), *sparśa* (touch), etc., hence the adepts are asked to realise the fact that *Vajra* is as much identical with the phenomenal world as with the Truth.[25] The text[26] states that even *rāgacharyā* (acts of passion) is included in the functions of Bodhisattvas because it is not different from the Truth, the *Vajra,* just as all objects are in space and space is in all objects. *Dvesha* (hatred), *moha* (delusion), *rāga* (attachment), *chintāmaṇi* (Bodhichitta) and *samaya* (doctrine) are the five *kulas* and constitute the means of escape from *kāma.*[27] The first three as also *chintāmaṇi* (Vajra) are called *ratis,* but they are really Buddhas in female form. This imagery wants to establish that *dvesha, moha,* and *rāga* are as much emanations of Buddha or the Truth as is the Bodhichitta. The Bodhisattvas are instructed to develop their body, speech, and thought in such a way that they may become *Vajras, i.e.* remain unaffected by the worldly affairs.[28] In this text *chitta,* developed into *chitta-vajra* stage, is identified with *Bodhichitta,* and so the conception of *Bodhichitta* is different from that of the *Bodhicharyāvatāra* and other Mahāyāna texts. The *Bodhichitta* or *Chitta-vajra* in this text[29] means the realisation of the unity, the non-duality (*advayamadvaidhīkāram*) of the Truth and the universe.

5. Two Schools of Tāntrik Teachers

Among the Tāntrik teachers, the Vajrāchāryas, there were two schools of thought; one adopted the Mādhyamika and the other the Yogāchāra. The conception of Vajra, as given in the *Guhyasamāja* and in the works of Anaṅgavajra and Indrabhūti, is that of *śūnyatā* or extreme *advayavāda* of Nāgārjuna, while that in the *Dohās* and *Charyāpadas* of Lui-pā, Kāṇhu or Bhusukupāda is the idealism or *Vijñaptimātratā* or *Chittamātra* of Asaṅga and Vasubandhu. The Tibetan tradition speaks of two lines of Vajrāchāryas, one commencing with Padmavajra and the other with Saraha.[30] It is not improbable that the Tāntrik teachers had differences not only in regard to the methods of *sādhanas, i.e. kriyā, charyā, mantra,* and *yoga,* but also about the conception of Vajra.

6. Distinction between Tāntrikism and Mahāyānism

The difference between Tāntrikism and Mahāyānism (*i.e.* the Mādhyamika-Yogāchāra systems) was in the ways and methods of realising the highest truth. The Tāntrikism takes the aids of *mudrās, maṇḍalas* and *mantras* for inducing concentration of thoughts (*yoga*) and even takes recourse to *haṭha-yoga* (meditation with artificial aids). With these *mudrās* and *maṇḍalas* are associated freely the conceptions of goddesses and yoga-minded women of any caste or origin. The sole underlying object of such association was to make the adepts realise that the female sex, believed to be the source of all our worldly sufferings, was as much an appearance as the male sex, and that in the order of worldly creation, the place next to Ādi-Buddha is that of Śakti (female energy), *i.e.* Tārā of the Buddhists and Umā of the Brāhmaṇas. It is stated in the *Guhyasamāja*[31] that a few Buddhas issued out of the body of the Vairochana Buddha in the form of female goddesses as Lochanā, Māmakī, Pāṇḍaravāsinī, Samayatārā, some in the shape of *Rūpa* (form), *Śabda* (sound), *Gandha* (smell) and *Sparśa* (touch), some as *Dvesharati, Moharati, Rāgarati* and *Vajrarati,* some as the four elements, earth, water, air and fire, and others as the five constituents of a being, *viz. Rūpa* (physical elements constituting form), *Vedanā* (feeling), *Saṁjñā* (conception), *Saṁskāra* (impression) and *Vijñāna* (consciousness). In the same text[32] it is also stated that earth is represented by Lochanā, water by Māmakī, fire by Pāṇḍaravāsinī and air by Tārā, while the five constituents of a being are represented by the five

Dhyānī-Buddhas.[33] Thus an important and early Tāntrik text teaches that all the causes of our worldly attachments, *viz.* the four elements, five constituents, the objects of the organs of sense are in reality emanations of Buddhas, who are in turn emanations of the Vairochana Buddha, i.e. the Ādi-Buddha. In other words, the universe represents the variety of the unity, the Ādi-Buddha.

On account of the abuses made of the Tāntrik practices by quite a large number of religious sects, there is a general notion that all the Tāntriks advocated the use of five *Makāras, viz. madya* (wine), *māṁsa* (meat), *maithuna* (sexual union), *matsya* (fish) and *mudrā* (finger-poses). In the *Guhyasamāja* and a few other early texts, there are references to meat-eating, union with females, and finger-poses, but not to the use of wine and fish, which were probably later additions. It is a pity that a religion, with the highest monistic philosophy and the noblest ideals, recommended such ways and methods for the quick realisation of the Truth, and that it resulted more in abuses than in the proper utilisation of the aids. Although Tāntrikism has been generally condemned, it still retains its hold and works unconsciously upon the Indian mind.

II. HISTORICAL REVIEW

1. Traditional Account by Tāranātha

Tāranātha presents us with a picture of the state of Buddhism during the period which immediately preceded the reign of king Gopāla, *i.e.* the first half of the eighth century A.D., when lived and worked the famous logician Dharmakīrti. He writes that during the time of Dharmakīrti and earlier, Buddha's teaching was shining like the sun. The Āchāryas of the Mahāyāna schools were very scholarly and the members of the Saṅghas were excellent. The number of monks of the Hīnayāna schools was very large. After Dharmakīrti there appeared many distinguished Āchāryas but they could not stand in comparison with the stalwarts of the earlier period and were unable to maintain the high traditions of their teaching. He then furnishes us with a lst of such scholars. One of these was Āchārya Vinītadeva, who wrote commentaries on some of the works of Dharmakīrti,[34] and a few independent works on logic. He was also the author of the history of the eighteen sects of early Buddhism. Other teachers who dealt with logic and taught the *Sūtra* and *Vinaya* texts were Śīlapālita, Śāntisoma, Āchārya Jñānagarbha, and Āchārya Śrīgupta. In the east there were a few Naiyāyikas (Logicians) who wore pointed caps and defeated the non-Buddhist Naiyāyikas in disputations. Tāranātha speaks of a number of *Vinaya* teachers, who evidently belonged either to the Sarvāstivāda or the Theravāda sects. They were Dharmamitra, a Vibhajyavādin of Tukhāra, Puṇyakīrti of the Maru country, and Mātricheta of Kāshmir. The only Sautrāntika teacher mentioned by Tāranātha is Śubhamitra.

From the time of Ārya Asaṅga, there appeared many distinguished Mantrāchāryas, but their teaching of *Anuttarayoga* was transmitted secretly to a few deserving disciples. Though it did not spread widely, it superseded the prevailing *Kriyā* (rites) and *Charyā* (observances) *tantras*. Tāranātha[35] criticises those who are doubtful about the indigenous origin of the *Tantras* and try to trace foreign influences. He is of opinion that the *Tantras* appeared at the same time as the Mahāyāna Sūtras, but the texts of *Anuttarayoga tantra* which are full of deep meaning were produced gradually in the following order:—

(i) *Buddhakapāla-tantra* of Śrī Saraha;
(ii) *Yoginīsaṁcharyā* of Lui-pāda (or Lui-pā);
(iii) *Hevajra-tantra* of Kambala and Padmavajra;
(iv) *Sampuṭa-tilaka* of Kṛishṇachārin;
(v) *Kṛishṇayamāri-tantra* (3 sections) of Lalitavajra;
(vi) *Vajrāmṛita* of Gambhīravajra;
(vii) *Mahāmāyā* of Kukkurī; and
(viii) *Kālachakra* of Piṭo.

Tāranātha writes that at the time of Dharmakīrti there were three Āchāryas headed by Saraha and his disciple Lui-pāda, and the four distinguished Tāntrik Āchāryas, *viz.*, Kambala, Lalitavajra, Padmavajra and Indrabhūti. At that time there were two chief centres of Tāntrikism, one at Nālandā and the other at Udyāna.

Lui-pā, the head of a line of Tāntrik teachers, was also a contemporary of Asaṅga, and claimed Saraha as the founder of his line of Āchāryas. Lui-pā was born in Ujjayinī, and was a writer of a king of the west called Samantasubha.[36] He was initiated into the *Chakrasambara maṇḍala* by Śmaśānapati and reached Bhaṅgala (Bengal). He initiated the king of Oḍivisa (Orissa), Dārika, and his minister Teṅgi into Tāntrik rites.[37] In the Tibetan Catalogue, the following works are attributed to Lui-pā besides the *Yoginī-saṁcharyā* mentioned above:—*Śrībhagavadabhisamaya*, *Vajrasattva-sādhana*, *Abhisamayavibhaṅga* and *Buddhodaya*. The common practice among the disciples of adopting the names of some distinguished Āchāryas has created a good deal of confusion. It is very likely that Lui-pā of Asaṅga's time was different from the Lui-pā, the composer of *Dohās*. Āchārya Kambala attained some *siddhi*. He wrote *Prajñāpāramitā-navaśloka-piṇḍārtha* and *Svasaṁvedanaprākṛitaśāstra*.

He, along with Padmavajra, brought the *He-vajra-tantra* (*He*=*dgyes* =cheerful) from Udyāna to Nālandā. One of his contemporaries was Āchārya Lalitavajra, who was a teacher of Nālandā. He also brought from Udyāna a few *Dhāraṇīs, Kṛishṇayamāri-tantra* and a few works on Tāntrik rituals (*Kalpa-kramas*), and propagated the same in India. He taught *Vairochana-māyājāla-tantra.* Tāranātha writes that he was a contemporary of Naravarman,[38] a petty non-Buddhist prince of the West.

Āchārya Padmavajra, in one Tibetan tradition (*vide* Cordier Catalogue), is placed at the head of a line of spiritual heads (*guru*). He composed the *Guhyasiddhi*[39] in which he gave an exposition of the Vajra-conception and the means of attaining it almost on the same lines as the *Guhyasamāja,* dealt with above. He wrote *Utpatti-krama-sādhana* and a few other works.

Anaṅgavajra succeeded Padmavajra. He wrote a number of works, of which one, the *Prajñopāya-viniśchaya-siddhi,* is available in original in Sanskrit.[40] In this short treatise he explains the Truth almost in the same way as Nāgārjuna did in his works. His contribution is that the Truth can be attained only by the combination of knowledge (*prajñā*) and compassion (*upāya*=*karuṇā*), and that the adept must take the aid of a spiritual preceptor as also of *mudrās* and *mantras* to realise the same.

Āchārya Indrabhūti, who succeeded Anaṅgavajra, was a king of Sambhala, one of the two dominions into which Udyāna was divided, the other being Laṅkāpurī, which was ruled over by Jalendra. Indrabhūti took to Tāntrik practices even when he was ruling the kingdom. He received Āchārya Lalitavajra with due veneration when the latter visited his kingdom, and learnt from him more of the Tāntrik *sādhanas.* He was also the author of several works, one of which, the *Jñānasiddhi,* is available in original Sanskrit.[41] His name appears also in the *Sādhanamālā*[42] as the author of *Kurukullasādhana.* In the *Jñānasiddhi,* he points out that neither *mudrā* nor *maṇḍala* nor *japa* nor *mantra* can help one to attain the Truth. It is with the help of the *Guru,* and by following his directions that one must realise the Truth. Indrabhūti does not actually discard the efficacy of the artificial aids, but what he wanted to impress upon his disciples was that these were to be treated as mere aids and not the means for the realisation of the Truth. He composed also the *Sahaja-siddhi.*

Āchārya Indrabhūti was succeeded in the spiritual leadership by his sister and disciple Lakshmīṁkarā who had also a few works to her credit. One of her works, *Advayasiddhi,* has been found in original Sanskrit. In this work, she more or less reiterated the views of her brother Indrabhūti.[43] She is believed to be the preacher of *Sahaja-yāna.*

Lakshmiṁkarā's disciple and successor was Āchārya Līlāvajra[44] who wrote several works, some of which were on *Sahaja-yāna.* He was consecrated at Udyāna. He belonged to the Nyāya-mādhyamika school and invoked Mañjuśrī. He attained perfection and lived some time after the demise of king Devapāla, about the middle of the ninth century A.D.

2. The Patronage of the Pāla Kings

The patronage of the Pāla kings forms one of the most important factors in the history of Buddhism during the period under review. The Pāla rulers were all Buddhists, and during their long rule, extending over nearly four centuries, Buddhism found a safe refuge in Bihār and Bengal after it had ceased to have any footing in the rest of India, with the exception of Kāshmir, Nepāl, and a few isolated regions.

While the numerous inscriptions of the Pālas leave no doubt about their adherence to Buddhism, they do not tell us much about their activities in furtherance of this faith. For this we are indebted mainly to the traditions recorded by Tibetan historians like Bu-ston and Tāranātha and in texts like the *Mañjuśrīmūlakalpa.*

(i) *Gopāla*

It is said about Gopāla, the founder of the royal dynasty of the Pālas[45], that he was a devotee and benefactor of Buddhism.[46] He revived the Nālandā monastery, erected several new monasteries in his dominion, and offered lavish gifts to the Buddhist clergy. At his time Kāshmir continued to be an important centre of Buddhism to which place resorted the monks from the western countries. In the west, his contemporary king of Kachchha, Vibharatta, had Buddhist leanings, but his ministers had Brahmanic faith. For this reason the temples erected in that part of the country contained images of both Buddhist and non-Buddhist gods. Here was one famous temple, called Amṛitakumbha, consecrated by the Tāntrik Āchārya Virūpa, the junior.[47]

It is said that during the reign of Gopāla, an *upāsaka* built the towering Odantapurī (Tib. *byed ḥphur*=flying high) monastery, spending immense gold, which he obtained miraculously. The walls and the rooms of the monastery were superbly executed and the best of workmanship was displayed in the erection of the monastery. This structure served as a model for the first monastery built in Tibet.

The great philosopher and dialectician Śāntarakshita lived and worked during the reign of king Gopāla and passed away from this world at the time of king Dharmapāla. At the invitation of the Tibetan king Khri-sroṅ-lde-tsan, son of the Chinese queen of Sroṅ-tsañ-gam-po, he went to Tibet and stayed there up to A.D. 762. In Tibet he was called Paṇḍita Bodhisattva or Dharmaśāntighosha. He came of a royal family of Bengal and became a distinguished Āchārya of Nālandā. He belonged to the Svātantrika-mādhyamika school,[48] though in his work *Tattva-saṁgraha*[49] he is found to be supporting the Yogāchāra views. He wrote a commentary on Dharmakīrti's *Vādanyāya* but his masterpiece was the voluminous work *Tattva-saṁgraha* in which he discussed and refuted the views of several Brahmanic as well as Buddhist philosophers and dialecticians.

(ii) *Dharmapāla*

The next king Dharmapāla was a great admirer of the teachings of the *Prajñāpāramitā-sūtras* and made Haribhadra, the great commentator of the *Prajñāpāramitā-sūtra* and exponent of the Yogāchāra philosophy, his spiritual preceptor. He erected as many as fifty monasteries for the study and teaching of the same. In Vikramaśīlavihāra, founded by him, he granted allowance to those who studied these texts. Tāranātha acknowledges that the teachings of the *Prajñāpāramitās* spread widely under the auspices of this king.[50] After the demise of Haribhadra, Dharmapāla made Haribhadra's disciple Buddhajñānapāda his spiritual preceptor. At the advice of this new preceptor, the king supported also the study and teaching of the *Guhyasamāja.*

Āchārya Haribhadra (his full name being Haribhadrapāda) came of a royal family. He studied the Mādhyamika texts with Śāntarakshita, and the Yogāchāra texts with Vairochanabhadra. He was inspired by Ajita Maitreyanātha in a dream and preferred the Yogāchāra teachings. He wrote commentaries on the *Ashṭasāhasrika-Prajñāpāramitā* and other texts. His commentary (*Āloka*) on the *Abhisamayālaṅkāra,* a treatise interpreting the *Prajñāpāramitā-sūtras* from the Yogāchāra standpoint, bespeaks his vast and deep knowledge of the Buddhist doctrines. He resided in the Traikūṭaka-vihāra and died about twenty years after Dharmapāla's accession to the throne.[51]

One of the best disciples of Haribhadra was Buddhajñānapāda, who, after the demise of Haribhadra, became the spiritual preceptor of the king. He propagated the rituals and teachings of the *Kriyā* and *Yoga tantras* particularly of the *Guhyasamāja, Māyājāla, Chandraguhyatilaka* and *Mañjuśrīkrodha.* He performed the consecra tion ceremony of the Vikramaśīla monastery and became its spiritual head, the Vajrāchārya.

Besides these two teachers, there were a number of distinguished monks, specialising in certain branches of studies. They are as follows:—

(i) The Tāntrik Āchāryas Praśāntamitra, Buddhaguhya and Buddhaśānti, disciples of Buddhajñānapāda, Rāhulabhadra and Āchārya Padmākaraghosha of Kāshmir.

(ii) The commentator Kamalaśīla.

(iii) The dialecticians (Naiyāyikas) Kalyāṇa-rakshita, Sobhavyuha, Sāgaramegha, Prabhākara, and Pūrṇavardhana and Dharmākaradatta of Kāshmir.

Praśāntamitra was a disciple of Jñānapāda. He studied the *Prajñāpāramitās* and some sections of the *Kriyā* and *Yoga tantras* and attained *Yamāntaka-siddhi.* He built a monastery called Amṛitākara to the south of Nālandā.

Dharmapāla founded the Vikramaśīla monastery in the north on the top of a mountain near the Gaṅgā in Magadha. Around the central monastery, there were fifty-three cells suitable for Tāntrik esoteric practices and fifty-four rooms for general use of monks; in all there were 108 chambers. These were surrounded by a wall having six gates. One hundred and eight monks (Paṇḍitas) were in charge of this monastic institution; and each had a certain specified duty, *viz.* making offerings to deities, performing *homa,* giving initiation, looking after pigeons, temple-attendants, and so forth. Some of these monks were entrusted with the duties of teaching different subjects, *e.g.* grammar, metaphysics, logic, ritualistic practices, etc. Not only were these 108 Paṇḍitas maintained by the state, but even the students or listeners to the discourses were given food and money. There was provision for the award of diplomas to the monk-students who showed proficiency, and the reigning kings took interest in the award of the diplomas.[52] The income of the establishment was shared equally by the 108 Paṇḍitas.

This monastery grew up to be an important academic centre, to which flocked students not only from all corners of India but also from Tibet and other foreign countries. At this monastery many Sanskrit texts were translated into Tibetan. Jinarakshita, the commentator of Sarvajñamitra's *Sragdharā-stotra,*[53] lived in this monastery and so also did Dharma-śrīmitra, mentioned in the *Bṛihat-svayambhū-purāṇa.*[54] Dharmapāla's second spiritual preceptor Āchārya Buddhajñānapāda was put in charge of the monastery at its commencement.

In Chapter 38 of his work, Tāranātha gives an account of the succession of the Vajrāchāryas of the Vikramaśīla monastery. He writes that there were five generations of Vajrāchāryas, but actually there are twelve names, preceding the six *dvāra-paṇḍitas, viz.* Buddhajñānapāda — Dīpaṅkarabhadra — Jayabhadra — Śrīdhara — Bhavabhadra — Bhavyakīrti — Līlāvajra — Durjanachandra — Kṛishṇasamayavajra — Tathāgatarakshita — Bodhibhadra — Kamalarakshita; — then the six *dvāra-paṇḍitas* — Dīpaṅkara-Śrījñāna and others and then — Abhayākaragupta — Śubhākaragupta and others.

During the reign of Dharmapāla, the Saindhava-śrāvakas created some troubles at Vikramaśīla-vihāra. They came to the monastery soon after its erection. They destroyed the metal image of Heruka and burnt the Mantra-treatises. They preached that Mahāyānism (*i.e.* Tāntrikism) did not represent Buddha's teachings and converted many pilgrims coming from Bengal to their faith. These Śrāvakas were mostly *bhikshus* of Siṁhala. King Dharmapāla was enraged at this attempt of the Śrāvakas and was going to punish them, but he desisted from doing so at the advice of his spiritual preceptor Buddhajñānapāda.

The revival of Hīnayānism by the monks of Siṁhala and of Sindhu is an important event in the history of Buddhism. The fact that they decried the Mahāyāna and Tantrayāna teachings at such a late date as the ninth century, and still later during the rule of the Sena kings, speaks highly of their courage and firm faith. It seems that they obtained the patronage of the Gurjara rulers who asserted their sovereignty in the east during the Pāla period.

The successors of Dharmapāla did not interfere with the endowment[55] and so this monastic establishment carried on its work quietly for a century without any event of extraordinary importance. About the tenth century A.D. Vikramaśīla monastery became a famous academic centre with six renowned *dvāra-paṇḍitas,* whose function was not only to admit students into the monastery, but also to enter into controversy with the teachers of other religious faiths. The names of these *dvāra-paṇḍitas* are as follows:—

i) Ratnākaraśānti in charge of eastern gate;

ii) Vāgīśvarakīrti of Banaras in charge of western gate;

iii) Nāropā in charge of northern gate;

iv) Prajñākaramati in charge of southern gate;

v) Ratnavajra of Kāshmir, the first *Mahāstambha,* and

vi) Jñānaśrīmitra of Gauḍa, the second *Mahāstambha.*

(iii) *Devapāla*

Devapāla was a zealous advocate of Buddhism.[56] His remarkable achievement was the restoration of the sand-buried temple, Śrī Traikūṭaka, and its enlargement. This temple in course of time came to be known as the new Somapurī-vihāra the ruins of which have been discovered at Pāhārpur.[57] Haribhadra states in the colophon of his work, *Abhisamayālaṅkārāloka,* that he resided in the excellent monastery Traikūṭaka, which was adorned with learned men.

In the Nālandā stone-inscription[58] of Vipula-śrīmitra, it is stated that he was a disciple of Aśoka-śrīmitra, who again was a disciple of Maitrī-śrīmitra. The teacher of Maitrī-śrīmitra, Karuṇāśrīmitra, while residing at the Somapurī monastery, was burnt to death by an army of Vaṅgāla. At the time of Dharmapāla, the Saindhava-śrāvakas burnt the image of Heruka and Tāntrik books. The *dvāra-paṇḍita* of Vikramaśīla was Jñāna-śrīmitra, who was at first a Saindhava-śrāvaka and then became a Tantrayānist. It seems that the inscription refers to a deadly quarrel between the Saindhava-śrāvakas, whose names probably ended with the words "Śrīmitra", and the Tantrayānists of Bengal.

Another event of outstanding importance in the history of Buddhism is the communication of the king of Suvarṇadvīpa, Bālaputradeva of the Śailendra dynasty, to Devapāla, to which reference has been made above.[59] In this connection, we may refer to Chapter XL of Tāranātha's History in which it is stated that Buddhism was propagated in ancient days in the small islands called Siṁhaladvīpa, Yavadvīpa, Tāmradvīpa, Suvarṇadvīpa, Dhanaśrīdvīpa and Paṅgudvīpa. In the last two islands only there were Mahāyānists and a few in Siṁhala.

(iv) The *Successors of Devapāla*

As Tāranātha's account of the Pāla kings after Devapāla is hopelessly confused, it is impossible to give a chronological list of the Buddhist teachers mentioned by him. He refers to a number of distinguished monks. Four of them, *viz.* Sarvajñadeva, Jinamitra, Dānaśīla of Kāshmir and Dharmākara went to Tibet at the time of Ral-pa-can for translating the Buddhist texts.[60] In the colophon of *Dul-va* (= Vinaya), it is stated that in the ninth century, the text was translated by Sarvajñadeva and Dharmākara, and revised by Vidyākaraprabha. From among the Tāntrik teachers we may mention the names of Tilopā, Gambhīravajra, Amṛita-guhya, Bhaga and Ānandagarbha. Tillipā or Tilopā is counted as one of the 84 *mahāsiddhas.* He was the *guru* of Nāropā, one of the six *dvāra-paṇḍitas* of Vikramaśīla, who lived in the tenth century. It was his disciple

Mar-pā, who founded the Kar-gyu-pā sect in Tibet in the eleventh century. This line of teachers propagated the Tāntrik teachings widely in Magadha.

A king whom Tāranātha calls Mahāpāla, but whose identity cannot be established, was a supporter of the Sthavira-vādins, whose centre was in the western parts of India. They are referred to by Tāranātha as Saindhava-śrāvakas and *bhikhus* of Siṁhala.[61] Tāranātha writes that the king showed great honour to the Saindhava-śrāvakas who must have lived in large numbers in the Odantapurī-vihāra, and for whose accommodation, the king made an annexure, called the Uruvasa-vihāra. This king enlarged the monasteries of Nālandā and Somapurī-Traikūṭaka. At his time the *Kālachakratantra* was introduced by Piṭo. Among the distinguished Āchāryas of his time, the names of Jetārī and Kṛishṇasamayavajra may be mentioned. The former was a disciple of Buddhajñānapāda and was recognised as one of the his ecclesiastical successors. Āchārya Jetārī was exceedingly intelligent. He learned quickly the various scripts and sciences, the *Abhidharma*, and other works. He at first failed to obtain the royal diploma of Vikramaśīla and it was after he had made himself famous by defeating in controversies many Paṇḍitas of other lands, that he was granted the diploma of Vikramaśīla. He delivered discourses in the Vikramaśīla monastery and wrote short commentaries on Śāntideva's *Śikshāsamuchchaya* and *Bodhicharyāvatāra*, on *Ākāśagarbhasūtra*, and other texts. He wrote three treatises on logic, *viz. Hetutattava-upadeśa, Dharma-dharmi-viniśchaya* and *Bālāvatāratarka*.

III. ICONOGRAPHY

Numerous standing and seated images of Buddha of the mediaeval period have been discovered in different parts of India, his independent recumbent figure illustrating his Mahāparinirvāṇa being extremely rare. Mahāparinirvāṇa of the Master is depicted in mediaeval Buddhist art in a secondary manner. Many *sthānaka* and *āsana* types of Buddha are extant which contain on their *prabhāvalī* summary representations of seven of the principal miracles; the miracle—and every incident in the life of the Master is a miracle according to the pious Buddhists — of the great decease is invariably shown on the top centre of the back-slabs of such reliefs. The eight miracles, including that depicted by the main central seated or standing image, were connected with the four principal incidents, Buddha's birth, enlightenment, preaching of the first sermon and great decease, and the four others, such as his taming of Nālagiri, the wild elephant that was set upon him by his cousin Devadatta at Rājagṛiha, his descent at Saṅkāsya from the Trayastriṁśa heaven after preaching the law there to his departed mother, the acceptance of the honey offered by a monkey at Vaiśālī, and lastly the great miracle, in which he simultaneously multiplied himself in the presence of king Prasenajit of Kośala and a host of his own followers and other Tīrthikas at Śrāvastī. The Eastern Indian School of mediaeval sculpture contains numerous examples of such standing and seated figures of Gautama, and the Indian Museum, Calcutta, alone possesses a large number of such images, mostly hailing from Bihār and Bengal. The central figure in these compositions usually depicts Buddha seated in *baddhapadmāsana* with his hands mostly showing the *bhusparsa*, indicating that it represents the Master's victory over Māra at Bodh-Gayā preliminary to his attainment of the enlightenment, the other seven miracles in miniature being shown in well-arranged groups on his either side on the back-slab. The main image with its hands in the *dharmachakramudrā,* illustrating the preaching of the first sermon, is comparatively rare, as is also the standing type with the seven miniatures on the background. The much mutilated figure in the collection of the Vangiya Sahitya Parishat Museum, Calcutta (No. $\frac{Cc\,1}{1}$) is thus of some interest, for it shows Buddha standing in the *samapādasthānaka* attitude on a double-petalled lotus (*viśvapadma*) below which the Buddhist formula[62] is written in ninth century script, flanked on either side by three parallel rows of two scenes each with that of Mahāparinirvāṇa just on the top. The rarity of such compositions can be accounted for by referring to the artistic sense of symmetry required in the display of the miniatures. In this particular relief, if the central figure is connected with the descent from the Trayastriṁśa heaven, then the explanation of the miniature standing Buddha on the right in the middle row is difficult; the one on the left in the same row undoubtedly stands for the taming of Nālagiri, the wild elephant of Rājagṛiha, and the Saṅkāsya and Rājagṛiha miracles are the only two in which the standing posture is necessary. The birth-scene, of course, would necessitate the showing of Māyā in the same pose, but it is almost invariably carved in the right lowermost corner of the *prabhāvalī* and it does not jar at all with the artistic sense. Many standing Buddha images again, which do not contain these illustrations of the stereotyped set of miracles, fall either under the Devāvatāra or Nālagiri-taming types; the first of the two is more common and is often shown attended on either side by Śakra and Brahmā. Just to emphasise the act of descent, the artists sometimes indicate stairs beneath the feet of the three, thus reminding us of the early Buddhist convention of showing the same scene with three stairs side by side, the middle one having one footmark on its topmost rung and another on its lowermost one.[63]

Numerous seated images of Buddha have been found, which can be classified under different groups according to their association with one or other of the miracles, clearly indicated by their different hand-poses and sitting postures. The *Sādhanamālā* describes one iconographic type, named by it as *Vajrāsana* Buddha, in which Buddha is seated in *baddhapadmāsana* on a *viśvapadma* with his hands in the *bhūsparśamudrā*, attended by Avalokiteśvara on the left and Maitreya on the right, the respective iconographic cognizances of the acolytes being a lotus and a bunch of Nāgakesara flowers.[64] Other *āsana* Buddha figures, which do not contain the seven miracles in miniature in the *prabhāvalī*, show Buddha preaching the first sermon, which event is suggested not only by the *dharmachakramudrā* peculiar to this motif, but also by the presence of a wheel (*dharmachakra*) flanked by two couchant deer on the pedestal. A good many mediaeval compositions have been found in eastern India which show Buddha seated in a similar manner with his hands in the same *mudrā*, but we do not find the wheel and deer indicative of the locality of Sārnāth on the pedestal, in the place of which are shown the Nāga kings, Nanda and Upānanda, on either side of the lotus stalk; figures of miniature seated, standing, and rarely recumbent, Buddhas are gracefully arranged round the central image. These undoubtedly represent the Great Miracle of Śravastı which seems to have been a very favourite theme with the artists of mediaeval India. A comparatively rare type of seated Buddha depicts him with an alms-bowl placed on his hands, joined over his lap, and a monkey carved on the pedestal or by his side; this is nothing but an illustration of the scene of the monkey's offering honey to Buddha at Vaiśālī. An interesting relief in the collection of the Asutosh Museum, Calcutta University, depicting this variety of seated Buddha, contains an additional detail by his side, the monkey climbing a tree for bringing down the honey to be offered to Buddha. The usual sitting posture of these Buddhas is *baddhapadmāsana* or *yogāsana* in which the legs with soles upwards are interlocked on the lotus-seat. But there is another rarer sitting mode in which the legs are shown hanging down the edge of the seat, which is described by many scholars as "being in European fashion". Its textual name seems to have been *paryaṅkāsana*, different from *ardhaparyaṅkāsana* in which one leg is tucked up on the seat and the other dangles down. It was at one time the practice to name the Buddha figures shown in this way as those of Maitreya, the Buddha of the future; but this identification cannot be accepted, for the particular sitting posture is often shown in the scene of the Great Miracle of Śrāvastī where Gautama Buddha is the principal actor. Moreover, such figures are dressed in monk's robes which would ill fit with Maitreya. But a number of standing and seated Buddhas have been found in northern and eastern India, who, though attired like a monk, wear a jewelled crown and two short necklaces, no other parts of the body being adorned with ornament. These crowned Buddhas were assumed by some to stand for Ādi-Buddha who appeared late in the pantheon; but this view is hardly tenable, for most of them, if not all, are associated with the incidents in the life-story of Gautama Buddha, and are thus none but so many of his representations.[65] Another point of interest with regard to the standing Buddhas is that miniature figures of seated, and rarely standing, Buddhas are often depicted on the top section of their *prabhāvalī*, and these presumably were meant to represent some of the Dhyānī-Buddhas, whose cult, described above,[66] was further developed during this period.

The cult of the Dhyānī-Bodhisattvas also underwent a great transformation. It has already been said that the special cognizance of Maitreya, the Buddha of the future and thus a Bodhisattva, in the mediaeval Buddhist art is a bunch of Nāgakeśara flowers placed in one of his hands in place of the earlier nectar-flask. Another distinctive mark of this Bodhisattva is a miniature *stūpa* placed in his crown or by its side. This refers to the *stūpa* of Kāśyapa Buddha in the Kukkuṭapāda-giri near Bodh-Gayā; on descending to earth from the Tushita heaven Maitreya would go to it from which Kāśyapa would come out and present to him the garments of a Buddha. Maitreya can hardly be found now represented singly; he is either shown as a well-dressed secular figure in the company of the seven Mānushī Buddhas very rarely represented, or as one of the acolytes of Vajrāsana Buddha. But several of the Bodhisattvas of a different category, the Dhyānī-Bodhisattvas, were extremely popular iconographic motifs of the mediaeval age. That Padmapāṇi-Avalokiteśvara among them should be the most important one can be explained by the fact of his having been the Dhyānī-Bodhisattva of Gautama Buddha, and thus numerous varieties of him have been described in the *sādhanas;* mediaeval images, more or less corresponding to some of these descriptions, have been found mostly in northern and eastern India. If a careful analysis is made of the iconographic traits of some of them, there is hardly any difficulty in recognising in a good many of them the Mahāyānistic adaptations of two of the principal Brahmanical cult-icons, *viz.* Vishṇu and Śiva. The iconography of the general form of Avalokiteśvara and of a few others of his special ones has some analogy to that of Vishṇu, and the ideology underlying both these gods, especially relating to their character as gods of preservation and deliverance, is one and the same. But the particular aspect of Śiva, when he appears in the role of a benignant deity and a healer of diseases after proper propitiation, is none the less discernible in certain other forms of this Dhyānī-Bodhisattva; a few others of his less common ones, again, portray in a way the dire and terrific aspect of this Brahmanical deity. One particular variety among the different types of Avalokiteśvara, Hari-Hari-Harivāhanodbhava Lokeśvara, undoubtedly owes its iconographic presentation to sectarian rancour. As many as fifteen variants have been selected from those described in the *Sādhanamālā*, of which five or six at most have been recognised among the numerous Buddhist sculptures of eastern and northern India. These are Shaḍaksharī Lokeśvara, Siṁhanāda, Khasarpaṇa (named after a village in the ancient Khāḍi-*maṇḍala*, modern Twenty-four Pergannas, West Bengal), Lokanātha and Nīlakaṇṭha. The others are mostly to be found among sculptures and paintings of the northern countries like Tibet and Nepāl and they are usually dated after A.D. 1300. Shaḍaksharī Lokeśvara shows a composition with the figure of the four-armed Bodhisattva, its front hands being in the *namaskāra-mudrā* and the back ones holding a rosary and a lotus, and having a smaller male replica of him to his right and another similar but female one to the left; these two are none other than Maṇidhara and Shaḍaksharī Mahāvidyā, the respective male and female attendants of this variety of Avalokiteśvara. A very interesting mediaeval relief depicting it was discovered by Oertel in course of his excavations at Sārnāth; it was wrongly identified by him as representing the three jewels of Buddhism, *viz.* Dharma, Buddha and Saṁgha.[67] The two-armed god Siṁhanāda Lokeśvara is described in the texts as three-eyed, seated in the *mahārājalīlā* pose on a roaring lion, wearing a tiger-skin garment but no ornaments, having a miniature figure of Amitābha on the *jaṭāmukuṭa* on his head, with a trident entwined by a white serpent to his right and a sword placed on a lotus flower to his left, the lotus stalk being held by his left hand resting on the seat; the three eyes, the tiger-skin garment, the absence of ornaments, the matted locks, the snake-entwined trident, — all these traits definitely associate him with Śiva, and the *Dhāraṇīs* of Siṁhanāda refer to him as the healer of diseases. The beautiful sculpture of Siṁhanāda Lokeśvara found at Mahoba closely corresponds to the description given above. That the Khasarpaṇa variety of this god was a popular object of worship in eastern India is proved by a number of such images discovered in different parts of Bihār and Bengal. The principal type of this deity depicts him gracefully seated in the *lalitāsana* pose on a *mahāmbuja,* decked in all sorts of ornaments and holding a fully blossomed lotus flower by its stalk in his left hand, the right one being in the *varada* pose. He is almost invariably accompanied by Tārā and Sudhanakumāra to his right and Bhṛikuṭī and Hayagrīva to his left;

the five Dhyānī-Buddhas are very often carved on the upper part of the *prabhāvalī* with Amitābha, his spiritual father, placed in the centre. The finely carved image corresponding in most of its details to the above description, found at Vikrampur and now in the Dacca Museum, is a representative specimen of this type of Avalokiteśvara. Many standing images of Avalokiteśvara endowed with four and sometimes with six arms have been found in northern and eastern India; some are in the collection of the Indian Museum, Calcutta, and a few are in the Patna Museum. These have been usually described as Lokanātha, but the description given of this variety of Avalokiteśvara in the *Sādhanamālā* does not tally with the sculptures. The four-armed figures show *vara, akshamālā, bhṛiṅgāra* and *padma* in the lower right, upper right, upper left and lower left hands respectively; Sūchīmukha and Hayagrīva to the right and left are the usual attendants in these cases. The six-armed standing figures, on the other hand, have a *vara, mātuluṅga, akshamālā* in the right hands, and a *bhṛiṅgāra, pāśa* and *padma* in the left ones; here both the attending figures are female and very probably represent Tārā and Bhṛikuṭī. Standing images of Lokeśvara with more than six arms are, though rare, not unknown; reference may be made to one twelve-armed variety of this god in the collection of the Indian Museum, its additional hands holding such emblems as *aṅkuśa, kartṛi* and a few other indistinct objects.[68] The Lokanātha aspect of Avalokiteśvara, however, as described in the *Sādhanamālā*, is two-armed, the left hand holding a lotus, the right being in the *varada* pose; one of the *sādhanas* of this deity refers to the *maṇḍala* of eight gods like Maitreya, Kshitigarbha, Vajrapāṇi and others surrounding him. But Lokanātha is generally depicted alone, seated or standing, only occasionally accompanied by Tārā and Hayagrīva. Nīlakaṇṭha, as described in only one *sādhana*, is similar in appearance to his spiritual father Amitābha; he is not decorated with any ornaments, and has two serpents on his either side; the name and the iconographic traits of this type of Lokeśvara fully show that he is one of the Mahāyānistic adaptations of Śiva. Several other types of Lokeśvara images of the mediaeval period have been found, which do not conform to the descriptions of any of the varieties given in the *Sādhanamālā;* this fact proves that as in the case of the Brahmanical iconography, our collection of Buddhist iconographic texts is also incomplete, and many must have been irretrievably lost. As regards the mediaeval images of the other Dhyānī-Bodhisattvas, whose names have been already given, it may be observed that whatever literary importance they might have had in the period, they apparently had no prominence in the hieratic art of the time.

Mañjuśrī is the general name of another group of interesting Bodhisattvas who, though not strictly belonging to the category of the Dhyānī-Bodhisattvas, occupied an important place in the developed Mahāyāna pantheon. He was comparatively late in making his appearance, and his inclusion in the pantheon could not have been much earlier than the Gupta period. References in mediaeval Buddhist literature seem to connect him with China and Nepāl, and the way in which he is mentioned seems to suggest that there was some historicity behind him, and his human original was perhaps connected in some way or other with the introduction of civilisation in Nepāl from China. Thus, there was a great deal of difference between Avalokiteśvara and Mañjuśrī, the former having an abstract ideological background, while the latter a concrete human base, which was, however, subsequently assumed to stand for and illustrate some abstract qualities like knowledge and wisdom. The *Sādhanamālā* contains a number of *sādhanas* describing as many as fourteen different varieties of this god-concept, some of which were associated with Akshobhya or Amitābha, while others were either independent or had some association with the group of the five Dhyānī-Buddhas. The usual emblems of Mañjuśrī are a sword (*Prajñā-khadga* or the sword of wisdom) and a book (book of knowledge — *prajñā*), the idea being that the god severs the coils of ignorance with the sword and imparts knowledge from the book; he is thus in a way the Mahāyāna counterpart of Brahmā and Sarasvatī of the Hindu pantheon. A good many extant figures of him, including several variants, have been discovered in different parts of northern and eastern India, and this fact shows that his was a popular cult-image, specially in eastern India. Several of the mediaeval representations of this god can be identified as Mañjughosha and Siddhaikavīra (emanations of Akshobhya), Arapachana and Sthirachakra who have no definite association with any of the Dhyānī-Buddhas. These varieties are usually differentiated on the basis of particular sitting and standing postures, hand-poses and the nature of the attendants. Images of Mañjuvara and Arapachana are more numerous; the former is characterised by his lion seat and the *dharmachakra-mudrā*, with the book *Prajñāpāramitā* placed on lotus on his left, while the latter is shown seated in *baddhapadmāsana*, his right hand brandishing a sword and the left with the book placed on his breast, his attendants being Keśinī, Upakeśinī, Sūryaprabha and Chandraprabha who are shown as exact miniature replicas of the central figure. That Arapachana form of Mañjuśrī was held in great respect by the Mahāyānists of the mediaeval period is proved not only by the number of his images discovered in eastern India, but also by a few found in Indonesia. The Javanese sculpture of this form of Mañjuśrī, now in the collection of the Leyden Museum, Holland, is a fine specimen of Indonesian art. Mañjughosha, like Mañjuvara, has a roaring lion for his mount, but his other peculiar cognizances are lotus on his left side and *vyākhyānamudrā*. A very fine sculpture of the early mediaeval period in the collection of the Sārnāth Museum, unfortunately much mutilated, corresponds to a great extent to the textual description of Siddhaikavīra, who has a blue lotus in his left hand and *varamudrā* in his right. This form of Mañjuśrī, which is comparatively rare, has some similarity with the usual iconographic type of Lokanātha, a form of Lokeśvara, but the figure of Akshobhya on the crown of the former discloses his real identity. Sthirachakra is another rare form of this Bodhisattva and is characterised by a sword in his left hand and *varamudrā* in his right. The Vangiya Sahitya Parishat sculpture of Mañjuśrī, seated in *ardhaparyaṅkāsana* on a double-petalled lotus, probably depicts this variety; it, however, holds the stem of a *nīlotpala* in its left hand, over the blossom of which is placed the sword.

A reference to the images of a few of the numerous varieties of gods and goddesses who were associated with one or other of the Dhyānī-Buddhas will not be out of place here, although the concepts of many of them seem to have been subsequently added. Some of these deities again were textually connected with more than one Dhyānī-Buddha at the same time, and other images bore on their crown the miniature figures of either one or the other of these meditative Buddhas. Thus, Jambhala and Tārā (especially her form known as Mahāchīna Tārā) were emanations of Akshobhya, but the same god and another variant of the goddess, *viz.* Khādiravanī Tārā could also emanate from Ratnasambhava and Amoghasiddha respectively. Jambhala and Vajra-Tārā, again, in some of their aspects, were associated with all the five or four of the Dhyānī-Buddhas; in these cases, the miniature figures of the latter are usually shown on the top part of the *prabhāvalī* of these images. Many of these deities of the developed Mahāyāna pantheon again can be shown either from their names or their attributes to have been directly or indirectly derived from various members of the Brahmanic order. Thus the gods like Saptaśatika Hayagrīva, Heruka, Yamāri and Jambhala, the first an emanation of Amitābha and the last three of Akshobhya, have their prototypes among the various Brahmanical gods, as their names or iconographic traits show.

Hayagrīva, according to the Puranic mythology, was primarily a demon to kill whom Vishṇu assumed the form of a horse-headed man. The special cognizance of Saptaśatika-Hayagrīva is the scalp of a horse over his head; another aspect of the same god, which is associated with Akshobhya, is three-faced and eight-armed, and the number of arms as well as the emblems in the hands distinctly connect it with the Hayagrīva incarnation of Vishṇu.

The fierce god Heruka, whose two-armed varieties have been found in eastern India, is characterised by the dancing pose, a corpse below him, emblems like *vajra* and *kapāla* in his hands, a *khaṭvāṅga* along the left side of his body, ornaments like a garland of skulls (*muṇḍamālā*) and other features which leave no doubt that this particular god-concept was based on the terrific aspect of Śiva. The Dacca Museum image of Heruka, though it shows a double-petalled lotus beneath its left leg in place of a corpse (*preta*), corresponds in other respects to the textual description, and is a well-carved specimen of the mediaeval Buddhist art of eastern India.

Yamāri, as its name indicates, is based on one of the various Saṁhāramūrtis of Śiva, Kālāri or Kālāntaka-mūrti, in which form Śiva punished Kāla or Yama, the god of death, for his audacity in attempting to take the life of Mārkaṇḍeya, a great Śaiva devotee. Some of the iconographic traits of Yamāri, however, are taken from the very god of death whose enemy he is supposed to be, while others are clearly derived from the fierce form of the Hindu god. Like Yama, he has a buffalo for his mount and a mace with a skull painted on it or a *vajra* on its top as his emblem; like Śiva, he wears a tiger-skin, snake ornaments, and holds a noose (*pāśa*) in one of his hands.

Jambhala is undoubtedly a Buddhist counterpart of Kubera-Vaiśravaṇa, as some of his characteristic traits indicate. Like the latter, he is connected with wealth and treasure; mediaeval representations of him are known, in which he is shown seated in *lalitāsana* with one of his legs resting on an upturned coin-jar by the side of which are placed seven more jars. The number of the jars, eight, distinctly proves that they stand for eight treasures (*ashṭanidhi*) of Kubera; like the Brahmanical deity his figure is also pot-bellied, though the bag in his prototype's hand is replaced by a mungoose vomitting jewels. In the Brahmanical mythology, Kubera is associated with Lakshmī or Śrī, the goddess of fortune who is the presiding deity of the *ashṭanidhis*;[69] in the Mahāyāna adaptation of him, however, Vasudhārā (another name of the earth goddess, Bhūmi or Pṛithivī) appears as his consort. A good many figures of Jambhala, mostly seated ones, with many of the above-mentioned iconographic traits have been found in different parts of eastern and northern India.

Gaṇapati is another male deity recruited from the Brahmanic faith into developed Mahāyāna pantheon, and he is identical in his mediaeval iconic forms to his Brahmanical prototype. He is generally depicted as being trampled down under the feet of such goddesses as Aparājitā and Parṇaśavarī. His independent form as one-faced and twelve-armed, dancing on the back of his mount (a rat), is described in a late *sādhana*, but corresponding icons of the mediaeval period are not known; there is nothing in the texts to show that his face was that of an elephant.

Interesting varieties of goddesses are associated with one or other of the Dhyānī-Buddhas, and they seem to be more numerous than those of the gods. The worship of the female principle was comparatively more prevalent in eastern India in mediaeval times, and this fact is also emphasised by the large number of images of the Buddhist goddesses discovered there. The cult of Tārā and her various forms was strong in this part of India, and Tārā, a great object of veneration in the Brahmanical Tāntrik cult, appears to have been borrowed directly from the developed Mahayana pantheon. Mahāchīna-Tārā, one of the principal forms of this goddess, however, as her attributive epithet indicates, was an importation from Mahāchīna, a land outside India, which has been identified by some scholars with Tibet. Mahāchīna-Tārā, also known in Buddhist-Tāntrik literature as Ugra-Tārā, is an emanation of Akshobhya, and she was most probably the original deity from which various other aspects of this goddess were derived. The popularity of Tārā among the Mahāyānists is indicated by the fact that it is the common appellation of many Buddhist goddesses such as Jāṅgulī, Parṇaśavarī, Ekajatā and others. She is described in the *sādhanas* as of terrific appearance, four-armed, standing in the *pratyālīḍha* pose on a corpse, her right hands holding a sword and a chopper (*kartri*), and left ones, a lotus flower and a skull-cup (*kapāla*); a miniature figure of Akshobhya is within the 'crown of chignon' (*ekajaṭā*) on her head.[70] The iconographic trait of *ekajaṭā* of this goddess gave rise to the concept of another terrific deity of the Mahāyāna cult, Ekajatā by name, who was also an emanation of Akshobhya; several mediaeval images of her have been found in eastern India.

The most common form of Tārā, however, numbers of whose images have been found in the north and east of India, is the one which is described in the *sādhanas* as Khādiravanī-Tārā, also known as Śyāma-Tārā, an emanation of the Dhyānī-Buddha Amoghasiddha. She is depicted either standing or seated in a graceful pose, her right hand showing the *varada-mudrā*, and the left one holding a lotus with a long stalk; her two attendants are Aśokakāntā Mārīchī on her right and Ekajaṭā on her left. In the extant mediaeval representations of this variety of Tārā, sometimes curious miniature figures of eight goddesses or eight illustrative scenes are found carved on the *prabhāvalī* on either side of the principal deity. One such image in the collection of the Dacca Museum shows the former feature, and it has been suggested that these miniature goddesses individually stand for each of the syllables of the eight-syllabled Tārā-*mantra* (*Oṁ Tāre tu Tāre Svāhā*).[71] On an image of this goddess, originally hailing from Ratnagiri (Cuttack district, Orissa), we find the other feature which collectively stands for the *ashṭamahābhayas* (eight great fears) from which she saves her devotees[72].

Another variety of Tārā, described several times in the *Sādhanamālā*, is the Vajra-Tārā who is simultaneously an emanation of the groups of five or four Dhyānī-Buddhas. She is four-faced and eight-armed, and is seated in the *vajraparyaṅkāsana* on a double-petalled lotus inside a *maṇḍala* which consists of encircling attendant deities like Pushpa-, Dhūpa-, Dīpa- and Gandha-Tārās, and Vajrāṅkuśī, Vajrapāśī, Vajrasphoṭī and Vajraghaṇṭā; the *maṇḍala*, in order to be complete, should also contain the figure of Ushṇīshavijayā on the top and that of Śumbhā below. It should be noted that the number of the companion goddesses is ten, which exactly corresponds to that of the ten-syllabled *mantra* of the principal goddess, *Oṁ Tāre tu Tāre ture Svāhā*, and it is presumed that the former individually stand for the respective syllables. Another interesting feature worth noting in respect of most of these attendant divinities is the fact that they are nothing but the personifications of the *upachāras* (materials used in ritual worship) and weapons or emblems held by the principal deity in her hands (these roughly correspond to the *āyudhapurushas* of the Vaishṇavite icons). Vajrasphoṭī and Ushṇīshavijayā are, on the other hand, associated, the former with the holy sound that is uttered during the ritualistic performances, and the latter with the peculiar physical characteristic of the Buddha. Several metal images of the *maṇḍala* of Vajra-Tārā have been found in eastern India; the Indian and Dacca Museum specimens correspond fairly well to the above description.[73]

Reference has already been made to Vasudhārā, the consort of Jambhala, who is also like him either an emanation of Akshobhya or Ratnasambhava; she is the Buddhist counterpart of the Brahmanical Vasudhārā, Pṛithivī, or Bhūdevī, who, as one of the consorts of Vishṇu, holds a blue lotus in her hand. But Vasudhārā is characterised by *varada-mudrā* in her right hand and an ear of corn in her left, and the latter object fittingly symbolises her corn-producing capacity. Several stone and metal images of this goddess, both single and in the company of her consort, have been discovered in the north and east of India.

Another Mahāyāna goddess, also emanating from Akshobhya but, unlike the last-mentioned, one of a terrific character, is Nairātmā who resembles to some extent the Brahmanical Kālī. She is shown dancing vigorously with right leg raised and bent inwards, the left firmly planted on a corpse (*preta*) lying on its back, holding *kartṛi* (short sword) and *kapāla* (skull-cup) in her two hands; she looks terrible with bare fangs, protruding tongue, a garland of human skulls, and a *khaṭvāṅga* placed along the left side of her body. Her general pose and appearance remind us of those of Heruka discussed above, though their respective emblems are somewhat different. Her images are extremely rare, and the Indian Museum specimen may be regarded as unique.[74]

Parṇaśavarī, another female member of the Mahāyāna pantheon, is of great iconographic interest on account of certain features appertaining to her. She is both an emanation of Akshobhya and Amoghasiddha, and her iconography is the same in both of her aspects. The *sādhanas* describe her as three-faced and six-armed, her right hands holding *vajra, śara* and *paraśu,* her left ones, *parṇapichchhikā* (a cluster of leaves), *dhanu* and *tarjanīpāśa* (a noose round the index-finger in the *tarjanīmudrā*); she stands in *pratyālīḍha* pose either on personified representations of various diseases or pestilences or on obstacles personified (Vighnas—the same as Brahmanical Gaṇeśa, the remover of obstacles, Vighnāntaka), and is clad in leaf garments. Her *mantras* describe her as a *Piśāchī* (ogress) and *sarvamāripraśamanī* (healer of all epidemic diseases). This fact, as well as her very name which associated her with the leaf-clad Śavaras, one of the aboriginal tribes of India, distinctly proves that she was recruited from a non-Aryan cult, as a few of the particular constituents of Durgā, the Brahmanical goddess, were adapted from aboriginal cult deities. Two extant images of Parṇaśavarī found in East Bengal closely follow the textual descriptions, and both have the figure of Amoghasiddha on the top centre of their *prabhāvalī.*[75]

Prajñā-Pāramitā is a goddess of benign aspect and was held in great veneration by the mediaeval Buddhists of India and Indonesia. She was regarded as the personified form of the Mahāyāna treatise *Prajñāpāramitā,* which is said to have been recovered from the nether regions by Nāgārjuna, the principal expounder of the reoriented Buddhism. She is usually recognised by *vyākhyāna-mudrā* and the manuscript *Prajñāpāramitā* on a lotus; one of the finest images of this benign Mahāyāna goddess originally hailed from Java and is now in the collection of the Leyden Museum.[76]

A very interesting goddess of this cult is Mārīchī, an emanation of Vairochana, the first of the Dhyānī-Buddhas. Several images of her have been found in eastern and northern India and this proves that she was held in esteem in this region. Her iconographic features show that she was an adaptation from the north-Indian Sūrya and her name means 'One who has rays'. She is usually depicted as three-faced (the left one of which is that of a sow) and eight-armed, her hands holding such attributes as a needle, a string, an elephant-goad, a noose, a bow, an arrow, a thunderbolt, and a bunch of Aśoka flowers; she stands in the arrow-shooting pose on a chariot drawn by seven pigs, and driven either by a goddess with no legs or Rāhu, only a head with no body attached to it. Some of these eight-armed and three-faced figures of Mārīchī are attended by four goddesses bearing peculiar names such as Varttālī, Vadālī, Varālī and Varāhamukhī, all sow-faced and four-armed carrying several weapons and emblems similar to those in the hands of the central deity. The very fine image of Ashṭabhujā Marīchi, originally found at Sārnāth and now in the collection of the Lucknow Museum, corresponding mostly to the description given above, contains, however, the figure of the Dhyānī-Buddha Amitābha in its crown—a striking departure from the texts.[77] Another variety of Mārīchī, one-faced and two-armed, the right hand being in the *varada* pose and the left touching an Aśoka bough, is generally depicted as an attendant deity of Khādiravanī-Tārā.

Another goddess of the developed Mahāyāna pantheon, who is sometimes wrongly regarded as identical with Mārīchī, is Vajravārāhī, the chief consort of the fierce god Heruka discussed above.[78] She is either two-armed or four-armed, and her attributes and pose resemble those of her consort. Her images of the mediaeval period are not common like those of Mārīchī.

Such independent goddesses as Sarasvatī, Aparajita, Grahamatṛikā, etc. have, as their nomenclature shows, distinct Brahmanical association, but their Buddhist adaptations came to have definite iconographic re-orientation. Vajrayoginī, as the *sādhanas* describe her form, clearly reminds us of the Tāntrik goddess Chhinnamastā who was held in great veneration by the Śakti-worshippers of Bengal; she was one of the ten Mahāvidyās whose cult was an important one in mediaeval and later Bengal. In a comparatively late period the Tāntrik aspect of the Śakti worship seems to have adopted much from the Mahāyāna-Vajrayāna cult and it is sometimes extremely difficult to fix up the definite cult-association of one or other of the individual deities.

The brief study of Buddhist iconography given above shows what bewildering diversity the religious art of the later Buddhists attained in the mediaeval period. The comparatively simple and general character of the early Buddhist art was made extremely complex in its later phase and various factors were at work for this re-orientation. The most important of these was the gradual assimilation in various ways of the god-concepts of many contemporary rival sects, most, if not all, of which belonged to Brahmanical religion. Many of the numerous images of the Mahāyāna-Vajrayāna cult illustrate this fact in an interesting manner. Another important point not to be lost sight of in the study of them is the deep esoteric symbolism which underlies many of them in spite of their bizarre forms. The numerous unnamed artists, whose services were requisitioned for the satisfaction of the religious needs of the pious Buddhists, were not half-hearted in their work, and some of the specimens which they turned out were enduring works of art.

C. JAINISM

I. INTRODUCTION

As in the preceding period, Jainism lacked royal support in northern India, but this was compensated by the popularity of the religion among the trading classes in the north, and the extensive royal patronage it enjoyed in the South.

This is the most flourishing period in the history of Jainism in the Deccan. There was no serious rival for it, and it was basking in the sunshine of popular and royal support. Dr. Altekar[79] surmises that probably one-third of the population of the Deccan was following the gospel of Mahāvīra during the period under review. Jainism received a serious set-back shortly afterwards owing to rapid spread of the Liṅgāyata sect.

Important commentaries on the Digambara Canon were composed towards the close of this period.[80] During the tenth century, Uddyotana started 84 *gachchhas* through his disciples.[81] The Jain Philosophy reached its high-water mark as evidenced by the masterpieces of Akalaṅka, Haribhadra, Vidyānanda and others. Literary output also was immense. The Jain writers inaugurated an Augustan period in Kannaḍa literature, and composed outstanding works in Tamil too.

It may be noted as one of the remarkable features of Jainism of this period that it saved itself from the influence of the all-pervading Śaktism.[82] That the fortunes of Jainism were unaffected by the revival of Hinduism has been ascribed to the state patronage, and the influence of the pious Jain saints.[83]

It is interesting to note how Jain *gurus* achieved their ends by adopting well-devised and comprehensive methods. The austere routine, pious life and the absence of possessive instincts seem, in the case of Jain monks, to have always led to their being admired and honoured in the society. As king-makers they secured royal patronage for generations. By winning over generals, feudal lords and provincial governors, their success at provincial centres was assured under the aegis of these officials. By securing popular support, they had among their followers the most important section of the middle class, the Vīra Banajigas and the commercial class, whose financial help went a long way in the cause of Jainism. It enabled them to construct magnificent Jinālayas and images. Their spectacular effect, along with the active royal support, made Jainism popular and strong. These Jain *gurus* themselves owned nothing and wanted nothing. And further their insistence on the observance by the rich of the Jain doctrine relating to the four gifts (learning, food, medicine and shelter) helped a great deal in winning the allegiance and devotion of the masses, as it answered the primary needs of humanity. This resulted in drawing large sections of populace within the Jain fold.

II. JAINISM IN THE NORTH

Except in the west and perhaps Mālwā, Jainism appears to have lost its hold over the rest of the north during the period. It had already lost its importance in Magadha, the land of its origin. The Nirgranthas, who formed a dominant religious sect in Bengal in the seventh century, seem to have wielded no appreciable influence there during our period, and there is no reference to them in the numerous inscriptions of the Pālas.

The Chāpa rulers[84] were patrons of this religion. Vanarāja Chāvḍā, the founder of the line, was installed on the throne, according to the Jain Prabandhas, by his Jain *guru* Śīlaguṇasūri. Though the official religion was Śaiva and Śākta, most of the influential persons in the realm, like Mahājanas, were Jains and occupied high positions in the state. Vanarāja's prime minister was a Jain *vaṇik* named Champa, the founder of Champāner. Ninnaya, a merchant prince whom Vanarāja regarded as father, built a temple of Ṛishabha at Anahilavāḍa. Ninnaya's son Lahora was a general in Vanarāja's army. At the suggestion of his *guru* Śīlaguṇasūri, who refused the gift of the kingdom, Vanarāja built a temple known as Pañchāsarachaitya in which the idol of Pārśvanātha brought from Pañchāsar was consecrated. He and his successors also built other temples. These rulers tried to keep in check the rivalries among priests of different sects in their kingdom. The Pratīhāras also figure prominently in the Jain literature.[85] Vatsarāja (or Āma, as he is called in Jain Prabandhas) is said to have built a temple at Kanauj, 100 cubits high, and consecrated a golden image of Mahāvīra; at Gwālior he established an image of Mahāvīra, 23 cubits high. He is said to have built Jain temples at Kanauj, Mathurā, Anahilavāḍa, Modhera, etc. His son Nāgabhaṭa II is said to have been converted to Jainism and the latter's grandson Bhoja was also a great patron of the religion.

Many famous Jain writers like Dhaneśvarasūri, Dhanapāla and Śāntisūri flourished in the court of Paramāra kings.

It was during this period that in the contest between Digambaras and Śvetāmbaras, as the Prabandhas report, the sacred Girnār-tīrtha was declared to be Śvetāmbara. Pradyumnasūri is credited with the conversion of the rulers of Sapādalaksha, Tribhuvanagiri, etc. to Jainism.

III. JAINISM IN THE DECCAN AND SOUTH INDIA

Several dynasties, such as the Gaṅgas, Rāshṭrakūṭas, Chālukyas, Kadambas and their feudatories held sway over Deccan during the period under review, either successively or as contemporaries. We shall deal with the state of Jainism under these rulers in the above order.

The Gaṅga rulers were great patrons of Jainism. Nītimārga and his second son Būtuga were devout Jains. Mārasiṁha was a disciple of Ajitasena, and was a staunch Jain. He actively supported renowned Jain scholars, maintained the Jain doctrine, caused *basadis* and *mānastambhas* to be erected at several places, and, after abdication, ended his life by *Sallekhanā* (slow starvation). His minister Chāmuṇḍarāya, one of the triumvirate of the special promoters of Jainism, was a brave general and possessed several exceptional virtues including liberality. Nemichandra and Ajitasena were his preceptors. He gave many endowments for the cause of Jainism; caused the colossal image of Gommaṭa to be set up at Śravaṇa Belgoḷa; constructed a *basadi* on Chikkabetta at Śravaṇa Beḷgoḷa; and patronised the Kannaḍa author Ranna. His example was followed by his successors and feudatories.

The Rāshṭrakūṭas were tolerant of the several religious sects of the time, and many of the rulers of the dynasty were not only great patrons of, but even showed distinct inclinations towards, Jainism. The great Rāshṭrakūṭa Amoghavarsha I Nṛipatuṅga was more a Jain than a Hindu; he followed the *Syādvāda* and also revered the Hindu family deities. His chief preceptor was Jinasena and he had appointed Guṇabhadra as the preceptor for his son Kṛishṇa II. Authorship of the ritual of Jain monasteries in Banavāsi is attributed to Amoghavarsha. His other works and the literary activity of the Jains during this period will be dealt with later in this chapter. Amoghavarsha abdicated more than once, probably to observe the vow of *akiñchanatā*. How he accepted Jain-*dīkshā* is graphically described in a contemporary work *Gaṇita-sāra-saṁgraha* of Mahāvīrāchārya.[86]

The age of the Rāshṭrakūṭas (A.D. 754-974) was immediately followed by a Śaiva reaction under Tailapa II[87] and his immediate successors. It is alleged that they persecuted the Jains, but the temporary withdrawal of their patronage was due more to political than to religious causes.[88] On the contrary we read that Tailapa II had strong attachment to Jainism, and patronised Ranna, Kaviratna, the author of *Ajita-purāṇa,* who received the title *kavichakravartin* from the king.[89] Tailapa's son Satyāśraya constructed a monument (*nisidhi*) in honour of his Jain *guru.* One of his successors, Jayasiṁha III, caused a *basadi* to be constructed at Balipura.

Though the reigning monarchs of Āndhradeśa were invariably *Parama-Māheśvaras,* members of the royal family, high state officials, vassal kings and feudal lords sometimes followed Jain faith, and were either *śrāvakas* or *śrāvikās.* Some of the Eastern Chālukyas were Jains or patrons of that religion and made pious endowments to that faith. Three records of Ammarāja II speak of Jainism as a very popular religion in the tenth century, and show that the ruler, though Śaiva, extended his patronage to Jainism.

An inscription at Rāmatīrtham near Vizianagaram indicates that Jainism continued to flourish till the beginning of the eleventh century, and that the Rāmatīrtham hill was regarded as a place of pilgrimage by the Jains since early days. A Kannaḍa inscription of the reign of king Vimalāditya states that Trikālayogin Siddhāntadevamuni, Āchārya of Deśīgaṇa, who was a *guru* of the king, paid respects to the Rāmatīrtham hill. With the reign of Rājarājanarendra, son and successor of Vimalāditya, Jainism lost royal patronage and sympathy.

At Vijayawāda, the support of the Eastern Chālukyas to Jainism was counter-balanced by the Parichchhadi Paśupati rulers who followed Hinduism. These, along with Kota kings and Kākatīyas, were responsible for the disappearance of Jainism from Āndhradeśa.

Though Hindus by religion, some Kadamba rulers were also patrons of Jainism.[90]

We know from various contemporary records that the feudatories and high officials of the various ruling dynasties were supporters of Jainism. Mention may be made of a few important ladies in this connection. Jakkiabbe, who was appointed *Nāl-gāvuṇḍa* in her husband's place in Rāshṭrakūṭa Kṛishṇa III's reign, performed the vow of *Sallekhanā*. Attimebbe, daughter of Tailapa's commander Mallappa and wife of Nāgadeva, was an ideal devotee, and an exemplary patron of learning who got prepared one thousand Mss. of Ponna's *Santi-puraṇa* in Kannaḍa and had them circulated all over the country. Jakkisundarī caused a *basadi* to be built in A.D. 968. Pembabbe, elder sister of Būtuga, performed penance for thirty years.

Thus we find that during the heyday of its power there was not a single dynasty in the Deccan that did not come under the influence of Jainism at one time or another. Non Jain rulers also patronised Jainism. Ministers, generals, women—all played their part as devout Jains.

The story of Jainism in the Tamil area is one of decadence during our period. The rise of the Śaiva Nāyanārs and their organised efforts to stamp out Jainism, the conversion of Kūn Pāṇḍya by Sambandar and that of the Pallava king Mahendra-varman by Appar, led to the downfall of the Jains in Tamil land about A.D. 750. Jains were subjected to further humiliation at the hands of the Vaishṇava Āḻvārs, till in the ninth and tenth centuries, they do not seem to have enjoyed any prominence in the land. After Nāyanārs and Āḻvārs, the rise of the great Āchāryas aided the evolution of Hinduism.

As a result of all this, the Jains left the Pallava and Pāṇḍya kingdoms and migrated possibly to Koppaṇa, Śravaṇa Beḷgoḷa and surrounding territory where they were patronised by the Gaṅga and other rulers. The few that remained led an obscure life in Tamil land. A perusal of the literature produced by the Jains indicates that they generally lived in large numbers in Mylapore, Nedumbai and Tirumalai.

It may be noted that the Āḻvārs and Nāyanārs, who led the opposition against Jainism, adopted the very methods of the Jains to subvert their religion, and to attract the populace to the newly rejuvenated Hinduism. In the first place, they adopted the four-fold *dāna* (*āhāra*, *abhaya*, *bhaishajya* and *sastra*) in their system to counter the most effective missile of the Jains. Further, the Śaiva saints aimed at the highest altruistic principles, discarded caste system, and recruited people from the lowest grade in their fold. Like the Jains, the Śaiva saints instituted a hierarchy of sixty-three saints, and composed hymns in honour of local deities. Their potent weapon was the winning over the good grace of the king, thereby securing political patronage of the state. Gradually, as different kings became converts or reconverts to Hinduism, which was now made more attractive and receptive to the general public, Jainism lost its hold and receded into the background.

There were other causes peculiar to Karnātak that worked the disintegration of Jainism there. Beginning with castes and sub-castes taken over from Hinduism, Jainism was progressively adopting a number of Hindu practices and beliefs, with the result that it was gradually becoming almost indistinguishable from the surrounding creeds. It thus lost its characteristic mark, and its adherents there fell a prey to the prevailing proselytising forces.

IV. LITERATURE

The Jain literature of this period, written not only in Sanskrit, but also in Prakrit, Apabhraṁśa and the *Deśabhāshās*, is extremely rich and varied, its characteristic features being the Jain dogmatics and ethics, legendary literature in the form of the Purāṇas and didactic tales, and logic. In the south, the honour of the creation of the Kannaḍa literature and of enriching it with classics of abiding value goes to the Jains. Their contribution to the Tamil literature is also valuable; and we find that most of the major and minor epics, which are the pride of Tamil literature, are composed by Jain authors.

Haribhadra, originally a Brāhmaṇa, was the outstanding personality among the Jain writers of the period. He has written a large number of books in Sanskrit and Prakrit. He is the earliest Sanskrit commentator of the canon, and his contributions to Jain logic are outstanding. His *Dhūrtākhyāna* is a remarkable satire in Indian literature. He inaugurated a new era in Yoga literature by employing new terminology and an extraordinary and descriptive style. He has also compared the Jain terminology with the Yoga *prakriyās* in Patañjali. In his *Shaḍ-darśana-samuchchaya* he gives a brilliant exposition of the different systems of philosophy of the day. Among other Jain writers of the period, mention may be made of Bappabhaṭṭi, Śīlāṅka, Śobhana and Dhanapāla. The work of elucidating canonical texts in Sanskrit, begun by Haribhadra and Śīlāṅka, was continued by Abhayadeva (eleventh century) and Malayagiri (twelfth century). Śobhana, Dhanapāla, Devendragaṇi and Devabhadra produced innumerable romantic tales, both in Sanskrit and Prakrit, followed by Hemachandra and the writers of the Prabandhas and Charitas, who pertain to the subsequent period.

Turning to the authors in the South, we may begin with Akalaṅka, whose date has been a matter of controversy.[91] He was a great logician, whose famous works are *Rājavārttika* and *Ashṭaśatī*. Jinasena's *Harivaṁśa-purāṇa*[92] is one of the earliest Jain versions of the Pāṇḍava tale. Another Jinasena, who was the preceptor of the Rāshṭrakūṭa king Amoghavarsha, wrote the *Ādi-purāṇa,* which was completed by his disciple Guṇabhadra.[93] Amoghavarsha's reign produced a galaxy of Jain writers, including the king himself, who is credited with the authorship of *Praśnottaramālikā* on Jain ethics, and *Kavirājamārga* in Kannaḍa on rhetorics. Mahāvīrāchārya wrote *Gaṇita-sāra-saṁgraha* under Amoghavarsha. Śākaṭāyana, a grammarian, called his work *Amoghavṛitti* in honour of his patron. Vidyānanda, Māṇikyanandi and Prabhāchandra—a triumvirate of famous Jain logicians—were probably all contemporaries, and lived about A.D. 800. Under the Rāshṭrakūṭas were produced the *Yaśastilaka* (to which reference will be made later) and *Nītivākyāmṛita* of Somadeva.

To the ninth century belong the famous commentaries *Dhavalā* and *Jayadhavalā,* composed by Vīrasena and Jinasena, the latter being the author of *Ādi-purāṇa* noted above. Amṛitachandra was a brilliant commentator who expounded Kundakunda's works and also wrote the *Tattvārthasāra*, *Purushārthasiddhyupāya*, etc. Towards the close of the tenth century Nemichandra produced a number of fresh philosophic compendiums of considerable importance. It was during this period that Pushpadanta composed his monumental Apabhraṁśa work at the Rāshṭrakūṭa capital of Mānyakheṭa (or Mālkhed).

V. GENERAL OBSERVATIONS

The most important contribution of Jainism in cultural field is the principle and philosophy of *Ahiṁsā*. Though *Ahiṁsā* preached by Jainism is in a more extreme form than Buddhism, it has been duly graded for the householder and for the monk in view of the circumstances of life in which they are placed, and had no emasculating effect on the people. Jainism gave to India men who turned *Ahiṁsā* into a philosophy of action, and numerous instances on record show that the Jain generals and kings did not spare themselves on the battlefield, and were not less averse to warfare than their contemporaries of Brahmanical faith.

The Jain householders were not led astray by ascetic ideals, but they did their duties as true householders without ignoring the practical considerations. The Jain kings or soldiers, who killed their enemies on the battlefield, were following the Jain precept of doing one's duty. Such killing, as the hanging of a murderer, being in pursuance of the enjoined duty, does not constitute violation of *Ahiṁsā*, as prescribed by the code of a Śrāvaka.

It may also be noted that the principle of *Ahiṁsā* was responsible for ending the *hiṁsā* in *Yajña* and other Vedic rites, and also for introducing vegetarian diet in a large part of India.

The Jains also enriched the fine arts. The subject will properly be dealt in the Chapter on "Art". Here we may simply draw attention to the colossal image of Gommaṭa at Śravaṇa Beḷgoḷa, which is the most distinctive contribution of Jainism. Koppaṇa, Beḷgoḷa Haḷebid and other places are studded with spacious and massive temples with beautiful images, many of which belong to this period. The free-standing pillar (*stambha*), found in front of almost every *basadi* or Jain temple in Karnātak, is another peculiar contribution. Some of the cave temples of this period also show how Jainism has enriched this field.

A flood of light is thrown on the state of Jainism during the period under review by *Yaśastilaka,* a literary romance in Sanskrit prose and verse, composed by Somadeva in A.D. 959.[94] Devotion to Jina, goodwill towards all creatures, hospitality to all, and an altruistic disposition were the religious ideals of the true Jain according to Somadeva. He emphasises the four gifts of protection, food, medicine and religious instruction; but would prefer that hospitality and charitable assistance should be confined mostly to the believers in the Jain faith. The frequency with which Somadeva defends certain practices of the Digambara ascetics such as nudity, abstention from bath and ablutions, and eating their food while standing, indicates that the non-Jains looked on these as unattractive features of Jainism, and it was deemed necessary to remove all misconceptions in order to facilitate propagation of Jain faith among the masses.

Somadeva's testimony clearly indicates that though eager to propagate their faith, the Jains were opposed to admitting undesirable elements within their fold and welcomed only those who voluntarily accepted the religion. Considerable latitude, however, was shown to such converts as were unable to completely forego their former customs and beliefs. The process of infiltration of non-Jain elements in the religious practices of the Jains had already set in, and gradual transformation of Jainism was already at work, when Somadeva accorded recognition to them and tried to bring them into harmony with the orthodox position of the faith. He describes the five *yajñas* of Jain householders which are clearly modelled on the *pañcha-mahāyajñas*, though he means *dāna* by *yajña*. South Indian Jain literature shows that the Jains were not opposd to fire ritual as such so long as it involved no animal sacrifice. Somadeva sums up the position by observing that it is legitimate for the Jains to follow any custom or practice sanctioned by popular usage so long as it does not come into conflict with the fundamental principle of the Jain faith or the moral and disciplinary vows. In the light of this, the provision for *balicharudāna*, *vaiśvadeva* and *agnihotra* in some Rāshṭrakūṭa grants for Jain establishments appears to be legitimate and permissible. Despite their attacks on the Hindu caste system we find it to be prevalent among the Jains, at least in certain parts of the country, even at the time of Somadeva.

In many other respects, too, Jainism was strongly influenced by the faiths and practices of the Brahmanical religion. Jina and his mystical predecessors came to be looked upon as gods, and many hymns to Jina were sung as devotedly and fervently as the Brahmanical ones, often using similar words but with a different sense. Jainism is described along with Buddhism as a theistic religion, in the sense that it accepts God as a spiritual ideal but not as a Creator, in the *Shaḍ-darśana-samuchchaya* by Haribhadra. Further, Jina is described as the Universal Spirit who is Śiva, Dhātṛi, Sugata, and Vishṇu, possibly to accommodate Jainism to the spirit of the age.[95] *Bhakti*, again, is taken as the supreme means of salvation, and Jina became the saviour of souls, in the sense that his words lead them to *Moksha*. The temple ritual with grants for the upkeep of temples, and anointing images with milk, decorating them with flowers, etc. also speaks of the influence of Hinduism. It may, however, be noted, that the image worship and ritual indicated above arose among the laity and not among the monks. We notice the influence of Hinduism to a larger extent, particularly in the South, where we find not only the four castes, but the caste marks, prohibition of widow marriage, and such other things.

Finally, as already stated, the various *Gachchhas* originated in the north with the 84 disciples of Uddyotana. According to the *Kharataragachchhapaṭṭāvali* he flourished 550 years after Devarddhi.[96] Gāndhāṇī inscription on the back of the metal image of Śrī Ādinātha, dated V.S. 937 (A.D. 880), refers to Uddyotana's two disciples. The inscription shows that he became Āchārya in A.D. 880. *Paṭṭāvalis* give 994 V.S., *i.e.* A.D. 937 as the year of his death. The inscription does not mention *Gachchhas* as these arose after each of his disciples.[97] Most of those *Gachchhas* have become extinct, and some new ones like Tapā, Kharatara., Añchala, etc. have come into existence. Uddyotana died on a pilgrimage which he had undertaken from Mālavadeśa to Śatruñjaya to worship Ṛishabha.[98]

VI. ICONOGRAPHY

Parts of Rājputāna and Central India, Kāthiāwār Peninsula, Bengal, Bihār, Orissa and some parts of southern India (specially the central and western Deccan) possess Jain sculptural and architectural remains of the early and late mediaeval periods. There is no doubt that much of the ancient religious art of the Jains has been destroyed, and only a limited number of the extant Jain images go back to a period before the early mediaeval.

Jain images of a comparatively early period are very few in number in Bengal and certain parts of Bihār, but in other parts of Bihār and Orissa, they are fairly common. The image of Ṛishabhanātha found at Surohor (Dinājpur District, Bengal), and belonging to the tenth century A.D., is of unique iconographic interest, on account of its certain rare features. The sculpture is shaped like a shrine containing in its centre the main figure seated in *dhyānāsana*, with the miniature figures of the twenty-three other Jinas similarly seated inside small shrines all round it; the latter are also characterised by their peculiar marks which we do not find in the Lucknow Museum composition of the Gupta period noticed above.[99] The two male chauri-bearers on either side of Ṛishabhanātha, the flying garland-bearer, Vidyādhara couples on his top right and left, the two-tiered pedestal with a wheel and two lions on the upper tier and the bull and the figure of the donor on the lower, are all arranged with delicate skill and refinement. Another mediaeval composition depicting the same theme in a different manner was found at Barabhum (Midnapur District, Bengal) and is now in the collection of the Indian Museum, Calcutta.

Three other Jina images, all hailing from Bengal, are characterised by the presence of the miniature figures of the *Navagrahas* on either side of the main figure standing in the *Kāyotsarga* pose. Two of them representing Pārśvanātha with his snake-hood show four of the *grahas* on each side, the presence of the ninth in the list, Ketu, being indicated by the snake cognizance of the Jina; the third, recognisable as Śāntinātha from his *lāñchchhana*, the antelope on the pedestal, displays four *grahas* on the right and five on the left, the fifth in the left side standing for Ketu. The sculptures all belong to the late mediaeval period and their execution is not indifferent. Some mediaeval Jina images hailing from other parts of India do not fail to show the formal stereotyped character, but the attendant Jinas and other figures are displayed in different ways. Thus the seated Ṛishabhanātha from Śrāvastī (Gonda District, U.P.) shows the miniature seated Jina figures on the rectangular *prabhāvalī* in four rows of eight, two, six, and eight. The standing figures of Ajitanātha and Chandraprabhā, both from Deogarh (Jhānsi District, Central India), have only eight and four figures of standing Jinas carved on the back slab. The sculptors, however, have failed to carve the individual marks below the attendant Jinas in these reliefs, perhaps due to exigencies of space. Some other seated and standing Jina icons of the mediaeval period, though they do not contain the figures of attendant Tīrthaṅkaras, are very rich in the number and variety of other types of accompanying figures which are displayed on their *prabhāvalī* in a very interesting manner.

Reference may be made to one very well-carved seated image of Śāntinātha in the collection of the Fyzābād Museum, which shows the dancing *Navagrahas* in the lowermost section of the pedestal, the Upāsaka, Śāsanadevatā, an antelope on either side of a wheel on the *siṁhāsana* above it, two beautifully carved chauri-bearers, one on each side of the central figure, two elephants with pitchers carrying riders on lotuses parallel to the head of the Jina, and lastly on the topmost section of the rectangular *prabhāvalī* the two garland-bearing Vidyādhara couples on the right and left and one single garland-bearer over the triple umbrella above the Jina's head,—all three being depicted in the flying posture. In spite of the formal character of the principal theme, the whole composition is marked by subdued grace and beauty.

The Dilwara group of marble temples at Mount Abu, of which the most important are those of Vimala and Tejaḥpāla (c. A.D. 1032-1232), display some of the finest examples of Jain figure-sculpture, chiefly from the point of view of their exquisite delicacy of carving and severe simplicity. These images are very similar in appearance, and "representing nothing more than the skilled realisation of a fixed formula" are each a note in the whole scheme of the religious representation. What a contrast between these dream-like figures of beauty and the colossal Jain sculpture at Śravaṇa Beḷgoḷa (Hasan District, Mysore), onẹ of the largest-free-standng images in the world! The topmost section of the granite hill Indragiri was fashioned with marvellous success into this gigantic statue of Saint Gommateśvara, the son of the first Jina Ṛishabhanātha, who resigned his kingdom to become an ascetic. The saint is represented in the immovable serenity of one practising the *Kāyotsarga* austerity, undisturbed by the serpents about his feet, the ant-hills rising to his thighs, or the growing creeper that has already reached his shoulders. This huge sculpture (57 feet high), whose plastic treatment is very formal, was carved under the orders of Chāmuṇḍa Rāja about A.D. 983. Most of the extant Jain images from the early mediaeval period onwards are stereotyped in their treatment and were executed according to a set formula in which much that is common to the cult-icons of the rival Indian creeds is present.

It has already been shown that the subsidiary deities of the first class in the Jain pantheon are the Yakshas and the Yakshiṇīs, known also as Upāsakas and Śāsanadevatās. The Jain text *Pravachana-sāroddhāra* describes the Yakshas as devotees of the Tīrthaṅkaras, and they, with their female counterparts, are the principal attendants of the Jinas. Though they are usually shown as accessory figures in many medieavel Jain sculptures, separate figures of some of them were well represented in the Jain temple-carvings of the post-Gupta and later periods. Their names and their iconographic features distinctly indicate the Brahmanical association of many of them. Thus, Gomukha, the Yaksha of Ṛishabhanātha, from his bull face and bull mount as well as such of his attributes as battle-axe, noose, etc. shows his distinct affinity with Śiva; the name of his principal, Ṛishabha-nātha, and the special cognizance also prove the latter's affiliation to the same Brahmanical deity. The tenth Yaksha, known as Brahmā, is distinguished by four faces and a lotus seat and such attributes as citrus, rosary, *abhaya* or *varamudrā*, club, noose, etc.; though some of the latter attributes are foreign to the Brahmā Prajāpati of the Hindu pantheon, yet the name, the number of faces, the lotus-seat etc., closely connect him with the first member of the Brahmanical triad. Similarly Īśvara and Shaṇmukha Yakshas, the eleventh and thirteenth in the list, can be associated with Śiva and Subrahmaṇya on the basis of their names, mounts and attributes. But such association in the case of many others in the list is not apparent, though their names seem to point towards similar affiliation. A reference to the iconography of Kumāra, Garuḍa, Kubera, Varuṇa and others will prove this point. It seems that their names were adopted from Brahmanical religion, but their elaborate iconography was developed according to the ideology of the Jains. As regards many of their female counterparts also, their names alone do not always explain their Brahmanical association, though in some cases their names, attributes and mounts distinctly indicate it. Ambikā or Kūshmāṇḍinī, the Śāsanadevatā of Neminātha and consort of Gomedha, falls under the category of the latter, and her iconographic features leave little doubt that she is a Jain adaptation of the Hindu goddess of the same name. But the Jains developed a mythology of their own, which had very little in common with the stories connected with her Hindu original. She is one of the Jain goddesses whose images have been found all over India and her two-, four-, eight-, and even twenty-armed varieties of the early and late mediaeval periods are known. The wall paintings of the Vardhamāna temple at Tiruparuttikunram (Jaina-Kāñchī) in the Madras State illustrate the story of Agnitā and her two sons Śubhaṅkara and Prabhaṅkara; Agnitā was the name of Ambikā in her human birth according to the Digambara version of the story of the Yakshiṇī's origin. The Śvetāmbara and Digambara accounts taken together help to explain almost wholly the iconographic traits of Ambikā; her symbol of a bunch of mangoes and a child or sometimes two children near her with her lion mount are her characteristic cognizances. Sometimes she is shown accompanied by seven dancing female figures by her side (probably another adaptation of the Saptamātṛikā), and at other times she is seated or standing by her consort Gomedha. Several mediaeval reliefs in the collection of the Varendra Research Society's Museum, Rājshāhi (Bengal), show a couple seated underneath the spreading branches of a tree with children in their laps; miniature figures in *Yogāsana* are placed above the branches of the tree. These sculptures may be taken as the eastern mode of representing Gomedha and Ambikā, and there is little doubt that they are adaptations of the figures of Pañchikā (Kubera) and Hārītī, associated with Mahāyāna Buddhism. Padmāvatī, like her spiritual father, the Jina Pārśvanātha, is associated with snakes and her Brahmanical or popular counterpart is the folk-goddess Manasā, one of whose names is also Padmāvatī or Padmā.

D. ŚAIVISM AND VAISHṆAVISM

I. ŚAIVISM

1. *Growth and General Popularity*

Śaivism attained a dominant position in India during the period under review. This is testified to by the adherence of a large number of royal families to this faith and the building of richly endowed temples,[100] some of which have attained world-wide fame. Alongside this material manifestation of religious fervour, there was also a parallel philosophical movement which tended to fix the tenets of Śaivism. While the main principles remained the same, there were local variations and consequent doctrinal differences. It has been stated in an earlier volume that very early in the development of Śaivism there came into being several sub-sects. Most of these sects, or rather schools, were the result of different philosophical tendencies among the worshippers of Śiva. Just as in Vedānta we have Dvaita, Viśishṭādvaita and Advaita, besides many other points of view, even so in Śaivism we have schools ranging from pluralistic realism to monistic idealism.

2. *Kāshmir Śaivism*

There is a form of Śaivism, popularly known as Kāshmir Śaivism, which is a kind of monism or non-dualism. The names by which the system is known are: *Trika, Spanda* and *Pratyabhijñā*.[101] The name *Trika* primarily refers to the triple principle with which the system deals, *viz. Śiva-śakti-aṇu* or *pati-pāśa-paśu.* Though the other schools of Śaivism also accept these three categories, Kāshmir Śaivism regards the individual soul and the world as essentially identical with Śiva, and so the three, according to it, are reducible to one. The term *Spanda* indicates the principle of apparent movement or change from the state of absolute unity to the plurality of the world. And the expression *Pratyabhijñā,* which means 'recognition' refers to the way of realising the soul's identity with Śiva.

The beginnings of Kāshmir Śaivism are to be traced to the *Śiva-sūtras* whose authorship is attributed to Śiva himself. The *sūtras* are said to have been revealed to a sage by name Vasugupta who lived towards the end of the eighth or the beginning of the ninth century A.D. A succession of talented exponents of the system followed Vasugupta. Kallaṭa,[102] who was Vasugupta's chosen pupil, wrote, among other works, *Spanda-sarvasva* in which he explained the meaning of the *Śiva-sūtras* as taught by his master. Somānanda, the author of *Śiva-dṛishṭi* and a *vṛitti* thereon, was probably another pupil of Vasugupta. Among other teachers of Kāshmir Śaivism, who flourished during the period under review, we find the names of Utpala, Rāmakaṇṭha and Abhinavagupta. The last named was a prolific writer on a variety of subjects. The period of his literary activity extended over a quarter of a century, from about A.D. 991 to 1015. His best known work on Kāshmir Śaivism is the *Paramārtha-sāra* which is an adaptation of an earlier Advaita work of the same name by Ādi Śesha.

The Ultimate Reality, in Kāshmir Śaivism, as in every school of Śaiva philosophy, is Śambhu or Śiva the Supreme God. Śiva is the *Ātman,* the self of all beings, immutable and ever perfect. He is pure consciousness (*chaitanya*), absolute experience (*parā saṁvit),* supreme lord (*parameśvara*). He is the ground of all existence, the substrate of all beings. He is beginningless and one; he resides in all that moves and all that moves not. Time and space do not limit him, for he transcends them, and they are but his appearance. He is both immanent (*viśvamaya*) and transcendent (*viśvottīrṇa*). The world does not exhaust him, for he is infinite. He is called *anuttara,* the reality beyond which there is nothing. In the familiar strain of the Upanishads, the teachers of Kāshmir Śaivism tell us that the Ultimate Reality is beyond the reach of thought and language. Yet both mind and speech attempt to understand and express the Real in its relation to the universe.

The pure consciousness, which is the Supreme Reality and is referred to as Śiva, is the material as well as the efficient cause of the universe. This view is much the same as the one sponsored by Advaita-Vedānta as regards Saguṇa-Brahman. God or Reality is the substance of which the world is made as well as the instrument which makes it. Fundamentally there is no difference between the cause and the effect. But while for Advaita the manifested world is non-real, for Kāshmir Śaivism it is real.

By means of several illustrations the writers on the *Pratyabhijñā* system explain the creation of the universe from and by Śiva. The world is very often compared to the reflected city in a mirror. "As in the orb of a mirror pictures such as those of a town or village shine which are inseparable from it, and yet are distinct from one another and from it, so from the perfectly pure vision of the supreme Bhairava, this universe, though void of distinction, appears distinct, part from part, and distinct from that vision."[103] And again, "As syrup, molasses, jaggery, sugar-balls, candy, etc., are all alike juice of the sugar-cane, so the diverse conditions are all of Śambhu, the Supreme Self."[104] The illustration of the rope appearing as the snake is also employed, though not with the same implication as in Advaita-Vedānta. Another familiar analogy used to explain creation is the appearance of ideas in the mind. The creation-theory of the *Pratyabhijñā* school is known as *ābhāsavāda, i.e.* the view which holds that the universe consists of appearances which are all real in the sense that they are aspects of the Ultimate Reality.

The manifestation of the universe is effected through the Power (*śakti*) of Śiva. And Power is not different from the Possessor thereof. Śakti is Śiva's creative energy, and is spoken of as his feminine aspect. There are innumerable modes of Śakti. But the most important of them are five. They are: (1) *chit-śakti,* the power of intelligence or self-luminosity, which means that the Supreme shines by itself without dependence on any other light and even in the absence of all objects; (2) *ānanda-śakti,* the power of independence (*svātantrya*) which is bliss or joy, and by virtue of which the Ultimate Reality is self-satisfied;(3) *ichchhā-śakti,* the power of will or desire, the wonderful power of the Lord to create; (4) *jñāna-śakti,* the power of knowledge by virtue of which the objects are brought together and held together in consciousness; and (5) *kriyā-śakti,* the power of action which is responsible for the actual manifestation of objects and their relations. By these powers the supreme Śiva in his aspects as Śakti manifests himself as the universe. He manifests himself by his own free will (*svechchhayā*) and in himself as the substrate (*svabhittau*). That is, there is nothing other than Śiva. If the universe appears as if different, such appearance is a delusion. With the opening out of Śakti, the universe appears; and when Śakti closes herself up, the universe disappears. *Sṛishṭi* (creation) and *pralaya* (dissolution) alternate; and this process is without a beginning.

As in the other schools of Śaivism, thirty-six categories or *tattvas* are recognised in Kāshmir Śaivism. The *tattva* which is counted as the thirty-sixth but which is first in the logical order is *Śiva*, the Ultimate Reality, as it holds the potentiality of creation. It is of this reality, as we said, that the universe is an appearance. The *Śaiva-tattva* is the first stage in the process of world-manifestation. Of the five aspects of Śakti, *chit* or intelligence predominates over the others at this stage. The next category or *tattva* is *śakti*. It is not proper to call it the second stage, for it is by virtue of its operation that the manifestation of the *Śiva-tattva* is made possible. When *śakti* is counted separately, what is meant in reality is the manifestation of its *ānanda* aspect—the aspect of bliss and self-satisfaction which is the precursor of the manifestation of a variety of forms. The other categories need not be discussed in detail as they are mostly abstruse philosophical principles.

The supreme aim of the *Pratyabhijñā* system is to enable the individual soul to find its salvation. The salvation consists in the soul's recognition of its identity with the Ultimate Reality. As bondage is the result of ignorance, release is to be attained through knowledge. The knowledge which liberates, however, is not mere intellectual awareness; it is spiritual intuition of the fundamental unity. The intuition is gained by *dīkshā*, which is the name for the act whereby spiritual knowledge is imparted and the bondage of innate ignorance is removed. The intellectual knowledge of the *Pratyabhijñā* system is also necessary, because without it *dīkshā* will not be efficacious.

This is how the process of recognition is illustrated and explained; "A certain damsel, hearing of the many good qualities of a particular gallant, fell in love with him before she had seen him, and agitated by her passion and unable to suffer the pain of not seeing him, wrote to him a love-letter descriptive of her condition. He at once came to her, but when she saw him she did not recognise in him the qualities she had heard about; he appeared much the same as any other man, and she found no gratification in his society. So soon, however, as she recognised those qualities in him, as her companions now pointed them out, she was fully gratified. In like manner, though the personal self be manifested as identical with the universal soul, its manifestation effects no complete satisfaction so long as there is no recognition of those attributes; but as soon as it is taught by a spiritual director to recognise in itself the perfections of Maheśvara, his omniscience, omnipotence, and other attributes, it attains the whole pleroma of being."[105]

Mere human effort will not be of much avail in the path to *moksha*. What really moves here is the Divine Will. Besides the three powers of creation, sustentation, and destruction of the universe, God has the powers of concealment and grace. His real nature is concealed from the soul; and after the soul has played out its part in *saṁsāra,* God's grace descends on the individual; and the individual is released. The descent of Divine Grace is called *śakti-nipāta.*

Moksha, according to the *Pratyabhijñā* system, is a return to the original state of perfection and purity of consciousness. Abhinavagupta describes it thus: "When thus the imagination of duality has vanished, and he (the released soul) has surmounted the illusive *māyā*, he is merged in Brahman, as water in water, as milk in milk. When thus through contemplation the group of elements has been resolved into the substance of Śiva, what grief, what delusion can befall him who surveys the universe as Brahman?"[106]

3. *Śaṅkarāchārya*

In the south Śaivism received a great impetus from the life and work of a spiritual genius who was born in the Chera country about the year A.D. 788, and who, in the short space of terrestrial existence granted to him, revolutionised the spiritual outlook of men in India. Though he is primarily known as the greatest exponent of Advaita Vedānta, Śaṅkara was nevertheless the Āchārya *par excellence* who cleansed the Hindu faiths of the excrescences that had gathered round them due to accidents of history, and taught each aspirant to follow the way that was best suited to him. Besides the commentaries which he wrote on the Upanishads, the *Bhagavad-gītā,* and the *Brahma-sūtras,* he composed hymns in praise of the major gods of Hinduism. Several of these hymns glorify Śiva as the God of gods. Śaṅkara was himself a Śaiva by birth. And tradition has it that he was an incarnation of Śiva, born for the purpose of consolidating Hindu *dharma,* and in answer to the implorings of Śivaguru and Āryāmbā at Kālaḍi. In the course of his *digvijaya,* Śaṅkara met in argument several groups of pseudo-Śaivas who were responsible for the prevalence of left-handed practices, and by quelling them freed the followers of Śaivism from their baneful influence. At Ujjain, for instance, which was famous for the worship of Mahākāla, he is said to have vanquished in argument a Pāśupatāchārya. It is also recorded that he visited Kāshmir. And it is not unlikely that his doctrine of Advaita influenced, in some ways, the formulation of the *Pratyabhijñā* system.[107]

4. Iconography

The tendency to multiply the variety of Śaiva images was carried to its fullest extent in the early and late mediaeval Śaiva reliefs, most of which illustrate numerous stories current about the god. Those that do not seem to be associated with any particular mythology retain the early form, and can be generally described on the basis of later iconographic texts as Śiva Chandraśekhara. These are standing figures; seated types of such images, depicted singly or in company with Umā and Skanda, are usually known as Sukhāsana-mūrti, Umā-Maheśvara-mūrti, Somāskanda-mūrti, etc., the last of which was known only in South India. They represent the placid (*saumya*) aspect of the god, while there are other mediaeval image-types, usually designated as Bhairava, which emphasise his terrific (*ugra*) one. The numerous figures of Śiva of the post-Gupta age, hailing from different parts of India, which are illustrative of various Śaiva mythologies, can also be sub-divided into two principal groups, *viz. saṁhāra* (destructive) and *anugraha* (gracious), corresponding to his *ugra* and *saumya* aspects. These two aspects remind one of malignant-benignant concepts underlying Vedic Rudra; an epic passage refers to the two bodies of Śiva, one auspicious and the other fierce (*dve tanū tasya devasya...ghorāṁ anyāṁ śivām anyāṁ ...*). Other graceful forms of Śiva are known which are called Dakshiṇā-mūrti and Nṛitya-mūrti etc. in the Śaivāgamas like *Suprabhedāgama;* they do not illustrate any story, but portary the god as a master in various arts such as dancing, playing on musical instruments, expounding the śāstras, as also in the practice of Yoga. Reliefs depicting the themes of the marriage of Śiva and Umā (Kalyāṇa-sundara-mūrti), Śiva's expiation of the sin of Brahmahatyā (Kaṅkāla-mūrti, Bhikshāṭana-mūrti), descent of the Gaṅgā on Śiva's head (Gaṅgādhara-mūrti), granting of Pāśupatāstra to Arjuna by Śiva (Pāśupatāstra-dāna-mūrti)—really a form of Anugraha-mūrti, joint forms of Śiva and Umā (Ardhanārīśvara) and of Śiva and Vishṇu (Hari-Hara), etc., are also known from fairly early period; they usually come under the god's *saumya* form. Ardhanārīśvara and Hari-Hara motifs emphasise in their own way the attempts to harmonise different cult-deities such as Śiva, Śakti and Vishṇu. Another group of images were mostly evolved in South India in the mediaeval times, which like the Chaturviṁśati-mūrtis in the case of Vaishṇavism, were intended to symbolise some of the principal tenets of Śaivism. Sadāśiva-mūrti, Mahā-Sadāśiva-mūrti, Maheśa-mūrti, etc. belong to this category. This bewildering diversity in the anthropomorphic way of representing Śiva is all the more noteworthy when it is remembered that the principal object of worship enshrined in the main sanctum is almost invariably an aniconic symbol.

Reference has been made above[108] to the nature and significance of the Ardhanārīśvara-mūrti. The Purāpārā image in the Rājshāhi Museum shows a less common way of representing this divine aspect, where the god shown fully in the round is two-armed and ithyphallic; it is a fine piece of sculpture and can be regarded as one of the best specimens of the late Pāla period.

Mediaeval sculptures representing the marriage of Śiva and Pārvatī, usually described as Kalyāṇa-sundara or Vaivāhika-mūrti, are common in several parts of India, one of the most outstanding examples of which is the very much mutilated Elephanta relief, a fine and sublime product of the Indian artistic genius. The easy grace of the standing pose of Umā and Śiva, the tasteful grouping round them of the accessory figures, the eager and wistful attitude of the latter who appear as regular participants in the main scene, have been expressed with great skill by the unknown sculptor. The Vaivāhika-mūrtis, found in Bengal, do not stand comparison with the Elephanta sculpture in point of artistic execution, but they portray some local marriage customs. The Vangiya Sahitya Parishat (Calcutta) specimen of such an image is a representative one of this group.[109] The Dakshiṇā-mūrti types of Śaiva sculptures are principally south-Indian in character, and such figures as Yoga-, Jñāna-, Vyākhyāna-, and Vīṇādhara-dakshiṇā-mūrtis have seldom been found in northern and eastern India.[110] But if, as we have suggested above, the Nṛitya-mūrtis of Śiva are included among such Śaiva images, it can be shown that particular types of this variety of Dakshiṇā-mūrti of Śiva were fairly prevalent in other parts of India as well. The south Indian Nṛitya-mūrtis of Śiva at first show a well-marked variety which, however, came to be merged in one outstanding type, the Śiva Naṭarāja, a sublime creation in the domain of art. The Ellora and Chidambaram temples, as well as several other Śaiva shrines of the Deccan, contain figures of Śiva shown in various dance poses, such as *Chatura, Kaṭisama, Lalita, Lalāṭatilaka, Talasaṁsphoṭita*, etc.; but these gradually gave place to the ideal Naṭarāja type which, mostly in bronze and rarely in stone, became common in South India.[111] Rao says: "In all Śiva temples of importance a separate place is allotted to Naṭarāja which is known as the *Naṭana Sabhā* or simply *Sabhā*. The most important of these *sabhās* is that at Chidambaram."[112] This Nādānta dance mode of Śiva Natarāja shows him with his right leg firmly planted on the back of the wriggling Mūyaḷaka (Apashmārapurusha, the evil personified), his left leg raised high up in a slant, his front left hand in the *dola-* or *gaja-hasta* pose pointing to the lifted foot, the front right hand in the *abhaya* pose, the back right and left hands carrying a kettle-drum and a ball of fire respectively; the whole composition is placed on a well-decorated pedestal on which rest the ends of the circular or elliptical *prabhā* (*tiruvasi* in Tamil) which encircles it. The sublime ideology underlying this very characteristic dancing type of Siva images has been elaborately expounded by A.K. Coomaraswamy.[113] The Tamil text, called *Uṇmai viḷakkam,* explains the symbolism underlying the cosmic dance as follows: "Creation arises from the drum, protection proceeds from hand of hope (the *abhaya* pose in the front right one), from fire proceeds destruction, the foot held aloft gives *mukti*" (the same as *anugraha* or release). Thus, in a way, it practically embraces all the five-fold activities of the lord,—his *pañchakṛityas, viz.,* creation, preservation, destruction, grace, and obscuration, the *tiruvasi* round him symbolising the last of the activities. A different variety of Naṭarāja seems to have been evolved in Bengal and eastern India, which shows the ten- or twelve-armed god dancing in deep ecstasy on the back of his mount, Nandī, surrounded by a host of accessory figures. Such ten-armed images closely follow the description of the dancing Śiva given in the *Matsya Purāṇa,* and the Dacca Museum specimen, originally collected from Śaṅkarabāndhā, a village in the Dacca District, can be regarded as the most representative of this group. It is a fine piece of artistic work of the Pāla period and portrays with characteristic vigour the intense movement accompanied by rhythmic grace.[114] The Anugraha-mūrtis of Śiva have been found both in northern and southern India, but some of their varieties lke Chaṇḍeśānugraha-mūrti are typically south Indian in character. Ravaṇanugraha-mūrti figures are often found carved in mediaeval Śaiva temples, and one of the Ellora reliefs, depicting the theme, has been adjudged as one of the best artistic remains of ancient India.[115] Partially broken square stone pillars from Chaṇḍimau and Rājāonā (Bihār), now in the collection of the Indian Museum, Calcutta, characteristically portary the scenes of Śiva releasing the goddess Gaṅgā from coils of his *jaṭās* (matted hair) after being propitiated by Bhagīratha, and the Kirātārjuna story in which Śiva in the guise of a hunter (Kirāta) fights with Arjuna, and being satisfied with the latter's prowess, grants him the Pāśupatāstra.[116] A huge stone boulder at Māmallapuram (Madras) contains an elaborate scene carved on its surface, which was supposed to illustrate the Kirātārjuna episode; it was later explained as illustrating some phases of the story of the descent of the Gaṅgā. But it has now been proved beyond doubt that the earlier suggestion about its character is correct.[117]

Among the different types of terrific or *Ugra* forms of Siva, some of which do not seem to illustrate any particular Saiva mythology, mention may be made of his Bhairava-, Aghora-, Vīrabhadra-, and Virupaksha-murtis. The first is also sometimes described as Brahmasiraschhedaka-mūrti of Śiva, and the Purāṇas and the Agamas try to explain this aspect of Śiva, cutting off one of the heads of the polycephalous Brahmā, by different stories. But there seems to be very little real connection between these varying myths and the iconic types. The Āgamic texts enumerate as many as sixty-four Bhairavas, divided in groups of eight, each group being headed, respectively by such names as Asitāṅga, Ruru, Chaṇḍa, Krodha, Unmatta-Bhairava, Kāpāla, Bhīshaṇa, and Saṁhāra. They are the consorts or guardians of the sixty-four Yoginīs referred to in the Tāntrik form of the Śakti worship. The particular type of Bhairava commonly found in India is, however, known as Baṭuka-Bhairava (literally youthful Bhairava), who is usually shown as a nude figure, terrifying in appearance, with fangs protruding from the corners of the mouth parted in a weird smile, with eyes round and rolling, and hands holding such objects as a sword, a *khaṭvāṅga* or *Śūla,* and a *kapāla;* he wears wooden sandals and is accompanied by a dog. One Ellora stone panel is of unique iconographic interest, inasmuch as it contains a figure of Atiriktāṅga Bhairava, one of the eight headed by Saṁhāra; it shows the extremely emaciated standing figure of the god resting his weight on his three legs (the third leg is the extra limb—*atirikta aṅga*) and attended by other ghostly emaciated figures, one of whom is Kālī. Rao observes, about this remarkable relief, that "though grotesque, the sculptor has executed his work with great skill."[118] Some Aghora and Virūpāksha forms of Śiva have been found in Bengal, and one of the latter, in the collection of the Dacca Museum, depicts in a very striking manner the uncanny horror underlying such concepts of the god.[119] Another type of less terrific image of the deity is his Kaṅkāla-mūrti, in which he carries on his trident the skeleton of Vishvaksena, the gate-keeper of Vishṇu, who was killed by Śiva for his refusal to admit him into the presence of Vishnu. Such images of the late mediaeval period are comparatively common in South India. Bhikshāṭana-mūrti of Śiva, which is mythologically associated with the Kaṅkāla-mūrti is, however, of a placid type, and it shows the deity as a wandering youth of the untouchable order (the bell tied round one of his legs emphasises social degradation), usually nude, holding a *kapāla* in one of his hands, and somtimes accompanied by a frisking deer; it may be observed that the above two types do not appear to have been used as cult objects in northern and eastern India.[120] Among the images of the god portraying his terrific nature, which illustrate different episodes in his divine career, mention may be made of Gajāsurasaṁhāra-mūrti, Tripurāntaka-mūrti, Andhakāsuravadha-mūrti, Kālāri-mūrti, Kāmāntaka-mūrti, etc. The first three of these forms portray the destruction of the different demons like Gajāsura, or the demon in the shape of an elephant whose hide he wore as his garment after destroying him, the three Asuras of the three castles (*tripura*), and Andhakāsura. Some of the finest sculptures of the early mediaeval period represent these motifs, and the much mutilated Ellora and Elephanta panels, depicting the Tripurāntaka and Andhakasuravadha-mūrtis of Śiva, reach sublime heights of artistic creation; in the multi-handed awe-inspiring god in both of them is very skilfully portrayed the dynamic energy with which he destroys the demons of evil. It is worth noting, in connection with the myths underlying such images, that some of them seem to be regular developments of Vedic epithets associated with Rudra, one of the constituents of the composite god Śiva of the Epic and Puranic period. Thus, in the *Śatarudrīya* section of *Yajurveda* one of the names of Rudra is *Kṛittivāsa, i.e.* a god who has the hide of an animal (an elephant) for his garment; it will not be an exercise of our imagination, if we say that the whole episode of Gajāsurasaṁhāra-mūrti is an indirect development of the above epithet. Tripurāntaka-mūrti appears also to have developed out of some concept associated with Rudra. Gajāsurasaṁhāra-mūrti is a very favourite theme in the south, and this type of Śaiva images is also found, though comparatively rarely, in northern India. Kālāri-mūrti, in which form the god chastised Kāla or Yama, the god of death, for his attempt to take away the life of Mārkaṇḍeya, a great devotee of Śiva, while he was engaged in worshipping his deity, is fairly common in South India and reference may be made to the striking Ellora sculpture depicting the theme. Kāmāntaka-mūrti is seldom represented in mediaeval art.

There are certain types of Śaiva images which seek to illustrate some of the tenets of the Śuddha-Śaiva doctrine. As such they are not very old, for they presuppose a time when the philosophy underlying the Śuddha-Śaiva system was fully developed. A comparison can be fruitfully instituted between such Śaiva icons with the Vaishṇava ones falling under the *Vyūha* category. The latter also, as has been shown earlier, are associated with one of the principal tenets of the Pāñcharātrins: but unlike most of such Śaiva images, those of the two principal *Vyūhas* of Vāsudeva-Vishṇu, *viz.* Vāsudeva and Saṁkarshaṇa, are of a very early date. No Sadāśiva and Mahāsadāśiva-mūrtis of Śiva, which idealise the whole philosophy of the Suddha Śaiva school of Śaivism, can be ascribed to the Gupta age; all the known specimens can be dated in the mediaeval and late mediaeval periods. They are mostly of south Indian origin, being associated principally with a cult which attained its development in that region. The Āgamānta Śaivism seems to have been originally evolved in North India, for some of its ideas and concepts are closely parallel to those of the Pāñcharātra system whose northern origin is beyond any doubt. But it was subsequently fully developed in all its ideological ramifications in its south Indian surroundings, and that explains why these Śaiva images mostly hail from different parts of the Peninsula. The Sena kings, of Bengal, whose orginal home land was the Karṇāṭa country, were devout worshippers of Sadāśiva, and they used a five-faced and ten-armed figure of the god as their seal-device. It was owing to their patronage that Sadāśiva cult gained some importance in Bengal, as is proved by the discovery of several Sadāśiva images from its various parts. This variety of icons is described in the *Mahānirvāṇatantra.* the *Uttara-kāmikāgama* and the *Garuḍa Purāṇa.* The last two texts describe the god as endowed with five faces, ten arms, seated in the *baddhapadmāsana* pose, showing in his right hands *abhaya-*, and *varada-mudrā, śakti, triśūla* and *khaṭvāṅga,* and in his left ones, *sarpa, akshamālā, ḍamaru, nīlotpala* and *vījapura.* The five faces typify the different aspects of Śiva—the Pañchabrahmās or Īśānādayaḥ, viz., Sadyojāta, Vāmadeva, Aghora, Tatpurusha, and Īśāna, who in their turn are supposed to have emanated from the five particular powers of the supreme deity, Śiva, *viz.* Parā-śakti, Ādi-śakti, Ichchhāśakti, Jñāna-śakti, and Kriyā-śakti. These five aspects again are also known as five *sādākhyas* or *tattvas* such as Śiva-sādākhya, Amūrtta-sādākhya, Mūrtta-sādākhya, Kartṛi-sādākhya, and Karma-sādākhya, each being dependent on or emanating from its immediate predecessor. It will not be possible here to go into further details about the ideologies underlying the Sadāśiva-mūrti, but even a cursory study of it will enable one to be aware of the deep mysticism behind the concrete icon. The importance in which it was held in the developed cult is emphasised by the fact that its sectaries thought that all the different *'līlāmūrtis'* of the supreme god Śiva (these are the various types of *saumya-* and *ugra- mūrtis,* a brief account of which has been given above) are so many manifestations of the Maheśa-mūrti which is itself derived from a thousandth part of the last of the *tattvas,* viz. Karma-sādatattva or Karma-sādākhya mentioned just now. Rao was of opinion that the so-called Trimūrti of Elephanta cave, as well as the central image of Rāṇā Mokalji's temple at Chitorgadh (Mewār), really represents the Maheśa-mūrti of Śiva. The Mahāsadāśiva-mūrti is a further complicated aspect of Sadāśiva-mūrti, being endowed with twenty-five heads and fifty arms; each of the five heads of the latter being replaced by the same number of heads makes up the requisite number, which again symbolises the twenty-five *tattvas* of Indian philosophy. The way in which "these heads are arranged in tiers in arithmetical progression", in some of the extant south Indian specimens of this variety of a late date, distinctly reminds us of the multi-headed forms of Avalokiteśvara worshipped by the Buddhists of Tibet and Nepāl. There are other Śaiva images such as those of Ekādaśa-Rudras, Mūrtyashṭakas, Vidyeśvaras, etc., which either emphasise the Rudra or Vedic part of the composite god Śiva or illustrate in their own way one or other of the philosophic concepts of the Śaiva system. But these images are comparatively late and rare.

Mention may be made now of another image-type which does not illustrate any Śaiva tenet, but emphasises the highest position of Śiva amongst the orthodox Brahmanical Triad. This is the Ekapāda Trimūrti of the god, in which he is shown as standing one-legged, holding his usual attributes in his hands, with four-armed Brahmā and Vishṇu issuing respectively from his right and left flanks, their front hands showing the *añjalimudrā* and back ones carrying their respective emblems. If we leave out these flanking figures, the one-legged central deity reminds us of the god-concept Aja-Ekapāda, one of the eleven Rudras (*Ekādaśa Rudras*), which is one of the Vedic constituents of the composite god Śiva. This type of Śiva image, again, was at the root of another little-known Vaishṇava one in which the central figure is that of Vishṇu, the flanking ones being those of Śiva and Brahmā; there can be no doubt that it was the direct outcome of sectarian jealousy, the Vaishṇava sectary retaliating, in this curious manner, the lowering of the position of their own cult-god by the Śaivas. Another very little-known Śaiva image-type, known as Śarabheśa-mūrti, distinctly owes its origin to the sectarian rancour, for Śiva is said to have killed Narasiṁha (the Man-lion form of Vishṇu) after assuming this curious hybrid form, in which the features of man, bird, and beast were combined, when the latter got out of hand after he had destroyed Hiraṇyakaśipu, a great devotee of Śiva.[121] These two image-groups are, however, mainly south Indian in character, as are those of the sixty-three Nāyanmārs[122] or Śiva-bhaktas of the Tamil land, which were sometimes placed in particular sections of important Śaiva temples of southern India.

II. VAISHṆAVISM

1. *The Āchāryas*

We have seen how, under the patronage of the Imperial Guptas, Vaishṇavism became a great force in the religious life of both northern and southern India and how some of the Tamil saints (Āḻvārs), who flourished during that age, gave a new impetus to south Indian Vaishṇavism. In the post-Gupta period, the influence of the Vaishnava faith can be traced in every corner of northern India; some of the notable kings of various dynasties flourishing in different north Indian tracts are known to have favoured this religion. The same was also the case with South India. It must however be admitted that the greatest stronghold of Vaishṇavism in post-Gupta India was the Tamil country where it flourished at first under the impetus of the Āḻvārs up to the eighth century and then under another class of saints known as the Āchāryas. While the Āḻvārs represented the emotional side of Tamilian Vaishṇavism, the Āchāryas, who were their successors, represented its intellectual or philosophical side.

The earliest of the Āchāryas was Nāthamuni, otherwise called Raṅganāthāchārya, who was a native of Vīranārāyaṇapura (modern Mannargudi in the South Arcot District). The traditional date of his death is given as A.D. 920. This date appears to be too early for Nāthamuni's death, but may actually be the date of his birth. Another tradition makes him the contemporary of a Choḷa king residing at Gaṅgaikoṇḍachoḷapuram and thus assigns his death to a date not earlier than the reign of Rājendra Choḷa I who founded the above city in the first half of the eleventh century. This date for Nāthamuni's death is now usually accepted.

Nāthamuni lived at Śrīraṅgam and was the author of the *Nyāyatattva* which gives an elaborate exposition of the philosophy of the Viśishṭādvaita school. The essential doctrine of this school is that of the *prapatti* which is absolute surrender to God in renunciation and faith and is based on the *Gītā* and the early Pāñcharātra works. It is said that this doctrine was first brought into practise by Nammāḻvār or Śaṭhakopa and was later elaborated by Nāthamuni and his successors, the greatest amongst them being Rāmānuja. The sect founded by Nāthamuni became known as the Śrīvaishṇava. Nāthamuni was inspired by the songs of the Āḻvārs, especially by those of Nammāḻvār or Śaṭhakopa. He is said to have recovered all the songs of Śaṭhakopa and to have arranged those as well as the extant songs of the other Āḻvārs into four collections of about one thousand stanzas each.

The school founded by Nāthamuni did not approve of *Karman* done for worldly results and favoured renunciation of all results of deeds. It was a reaction against the Pūrva-mīmāṁsā school of such teachers as Prabhākara, Śabarasvāmin, Kumārila and Maṇḍana, according to which salvation may be attained by the faithful performance of ceremonial rites prescribed by the Śruti and Smṛiti literature, as well as against the Advaita (Absolute Monism) school of Śaṅkara (ninth century) which laid the greatest stress on *Jñāna*, making religion more an affair of the head than of the heart. The history of this school of Vaishṇavism under Nāthamuni's successors will be treated in the next volume.

2. *Iconography*

Images of Vishṇu and of his *avatāras* (incarnations) belonging to the post-Gupta period are found in large numbers all over India. An interesting variety of the *āsana*-Vishṇu of the mediaeval times in the collection of the Khajurāho (also spelt Khajrāho) Museum shows the god with the fore-finger of his main left hand raised to the height of his lips, with the usual accompanying figures clustering round him. The peculiar hand-pose, indicative of silence, not recorded in any of the known varieties of the Vishṇu image, reminds us of the bronze statuette discovered by Marshall at Sirkap and identified by him as the child-god Harpocrates. There is no reference to such figures as the Vishṇu *maunavratin* of Khajurāho in any of the well-known iconographic texts.[123]

Images of several incarnatory forms and manifestations of Vishṇu, whose early and late mediaeval representations are known, are of great iconographic interest. The textual description of one such, *viz.* Yajñapurusha or Yajñeśa, corresponds to a very great extent to one image in the eastern gateway (*gopura*) of the Chidambaram temple. It shows a two-headed, four-horned, seven-handed and three-legged figure with a bull by his side, and symbolises the Vedic sacrifice in a very interesting manner. In the *Śatapatha Brāhmaṇa*, Vishṇu, originally an aspect of Sūrya, is regarded identical with sacrifice, and this is why the symbolical representation of Yajña is called in some Pāñcharātra texts and Purāṇas an *avatāra* of Vishṇu.[124] Another incarnatory form of the god is Dattātreya or Hari-Hara-Pitāmaha who can be recognised among some mediaeval sculptures of India. It either shows the three members of the orthodox Brahmanical triad, namely, Brahmā, Vishṇu and Śiva, placed side by side, or it may appear as a four-armed Vishṇu whose Brahmā and Śiva aspects are indicated by their respective mounts carved on the pedestal by the side of Garuḍa. The standing and seated images of this god, hailing respectively from Ajmere (Rājputāna) and Bādāmi (Deccan), are unique specimens of the second variety of Dattātreya images.[125] Viśvarūpa and Hayagrīva are two other *avatāras* of Vishṇu, whose images, though rare, are not absolutely unknown. The former, a twenty-armed deity with various attributes in the respective hands, characteristically portrays the all-powerful and all-pervading god. A partially broken image from north Bengal, though it does not fully conform to the textual description of this aspect of Vishṇu, seems to stand for Viśvarūpa.[126] Hayagrīva or Vaḍavāvaktra, as the name indicates, is another composite form of the god, in which the head of a horse is placed on a human body. This peculiar form is said to have been assumed by Vishṇu in order to chastise a demon of that shape, who had despoiled the Vedas. Though images of Hayagrīva are comparatively rare in India, it is interesting to note that this iconic type travelled to the countries of the Far East.[127]

Kāmadeva, the same as Pradyumna, the son of Kṛishṇa by Rukmiṇī, was represented in mediaeval India. His characteristic attributes are a sugarcane bow and arrow in his hands, and his special cognizance is a *makaradhvaja;* he is usually shown accompanied by his two consorts Rati and Tṛishā.[128] Garuḍa is usually carved on one corner of the Vishṇu images with his hands in the *namaskāra-mudrā;* sometimes he is shown carrying his master on his back. But separate figures, which served as capitals of columns erected in front of Vaishṇava shrines, are also known. The Besnagar Garuḍadhvaja of the second century B.C. had one, but unfortunately it is lost. The bird-mount of Vishṇu is shown with the face and limbs of a man, stylised locks of hair rising from his head, and with the beak, wings and claws of a bird; when used as a capital piece, he is sometimes janiform. His comparatively rare four-armed types show a snake, the mortal enemy of the Garuḍa, in one of his hands. The earliest representations of Garuḍa are to be found on the coins of the Imperial Gupta rulers. A fine specimen of janiform Garuḍa capital is in the collection of Rājshāhi museum (Bengal), belonging to the tenth century A.D.; it has three eyes and snake ornaments.

Of the goddesses associated with Vishṇu-Kṛishṇa, Lakshmī, Sarasvatī (Śrī and Pushṭi) and Bhūdevī are the most represented ones. They usually appear as attending consorts of the cult-god, though their independent figures are also not wanting. In the north and east Indian Vishṇu reliefs, Śrī and Pushṭi are almost invariably shown as the principal companions, while in the south Indian ones, the place of Pushṭi is taken by Bhūdevī. Śrī or Lakshmī, when depicted alone, is usually shown as Gaja-Lakshmī, the lotus-carrying goddess bathed by two elephants, a very familiar motif which can be traced to the second century B.C., if not earlier. Other varieties of this goddess, two-armed and four-armed, are also known. Reference to one eleventh century bronze figure of four-armed Gaja-Lakshmī, hailing from north Bengal and now in the collection of the Rājshāhi Museum, may be made in this connection; one of its hands is broken, the other three hold a citron, an elephant-goad, and a jewel-basket. A Bhārhut railing pillar contains a standing female figure playing on a harp; it may be regarded as the earliest representation of Sarasvatī in Indian art. Her separate figures from the late Gupta period onwards, however, are comparatively common. Two-armed images of the goddess are shown playing on a *Vīṇā,* but in four-armed ones, the back hands carry a rosary and a manuscript; her usual vehicle is a swan, but in some Bengal sculptures of the Devī a frisking lamb takes its place.[129] One of the finest mediaeval figures of Sarasvatī is in the Rajshahi Museum; it was found in a village in the district of Bogra (Bengal).

The above brief summary gives only a glimpse of the infinite iconographic variations of one of the most important Brahmanical cults of India. There is little doubt about their evolution being gradual, but presumably by A.D. 1300, most of these came to be displayed in one or other parts of the different Vaishṇava shrines of India according to their relative importance. Rao tells us that many of the minor *avatāras* and manifestations of Vishṇu were used as *āvaraṇadevatās, i.e.,* deities placed in small subsidiary shrines in various corners of the *āvaraṇas* or enclosures of Vaishṇava temples. The Jagannātha temple at Puri and the big Śrīraṅgam temple of comparatively late date illustrate this ancient Vaishṇava practice. These iconic types may appear to the uninitiated as mere aberrations of human art instinct; but to the appreciative and the initiated they are nothing more nor less than attempts through the medium of the language of symbolism to portray the different aspects of the principal deity.

(E) TĀNTRIK RELIGION

The word Tantra has been sought to be derived in the *Kāśikā-vṛitti* from the root *tan,* to spread, with the suffix *shṭran* added. Some philosophical commentators have traced it to the root *tatri* or *tantri,* to originate or to know, while the two roots *tan* and *tantri* have elsewhere been identified and used also in the sense of spreading or weaving. In its present widely accepted sense Tantra means a literature which spreads knowledge, and particularly knowledge of profound things with the aid of mystic diagrams (*yantra*) and words possessing esoteric meanings (*mantra*), and helps the attainment of salvation. As a matter of fact, however, out of about three dozen senses in which the term Tantra may be used, quite a number is utilized in different philosophical systems in an ordinary non-religious sense, and it is only in later literature, from about the fifth or sixth century A.D., that Tantra as a special religious or philosophical concept gradually came into use. The earliest uses of the word Tantra, as in Śrauta-sūtras, the *Harivaṁśa,* Suśruta, Sāṁkhya philosophy, and didactic fables, did not bear the meaning of a special literature dedicated to the cult of Śakti. The worship of Mothers and reference to Ḍākinīs attending them may be traced to Gangdhar inscription[129a] of the fifth century A.D., and the images of Mothers are referred to in the *Bṛihat-saṁhitā.* But neither Amara in his *Kośa* nor Bāṇa in his works refers to the followers of Śakti, though both know the Divine Mothers and Amara knows also that the *mantras* have power (*śakti*).

It is necessary at this stage to issue a note of warning. Though Śāktism and Tantra are now so much identified that the word Tantra is almost reserved for the religious literature of the Śāktas, while the term Āgama is confined to the Śaivas and Saṁhitā, Kāṇḍa, or Rātra (knowledge) to the Vaishṇavas, the earlier use of the word Tantra was quite fluent, and it could be applied to Vaishṇava and Śaiva sacred literature as well. The conventional division of Brahmanical religious literature was into Veda, Smṛiti, Purāṇa, and Tantra, arranged in the chronological order and assigned to the four ages of the world. The only justification for this is that it is after the Purāṇas had established the pre-eminence of Vishṇu, Śiva, and Śakti, that the Tantras could get under way. It does not mean, however, that these different types had nothing in common between them. The contents of the Tantras were obviously modelled on those of the Purāṇas to a great extent, while some portions of the Purāṇa literature would read almost like a Tantra manual. In fact, both claimed to be in some sense the fifth Veda; but as this honour was claimed by other types of literature also, *e.g.* the *Mahābhārata,* the science of Music, and Tamil Śaiva literature (called Tamil Veda), we may understand the designation 'Tantra' as intending all sacred literature and art in which *all* could participate irrespective of caste and sex, being unlike the Vedas in this respect. While one class understood by the word *Āgama* an adventitious literature coming from non-Aryan sources, *i.e.* from outside, another class took the word in the sense of the Veda itself, which is also called *Āgama,* being revelational in character. In fact, the relation between *Āgama,* Śiva's revelation of ultimate truths through Pārvatī, and *Nigama,* Pārvatī's discourse in reply to Śiva's query, was sometimes conceived of as similar to that between Śruti and Smṛiti; naturally the Śākta Tantras could not accept this inferior position and claimed the highest authority for themselves. They claimed to have superseded all previous types of religious tenets and practices in the Kali age.

The antiquity of the Tantras, in the present acceptance of the term, is difficult to determine. We learn from an inscription in Cambodia[123b] that the Tāntrik texts were introduced there from India at the beginning of the ninth century A.D. Tāntrik manuscripts of seventh to ninth century have been found in Nepāl, and Buddhist Tantras are known to have been translated into Chinese in the eighth, and into Tibetan in the ninth century. The origin of the Tāntrik cult and the composition of special texts may thus be dated about the sixth century A.D.; some Buddhist Tantras may be even older.

Some of the Tantras themselves give their number as sixty-four, though the number of texts available is much larger. The number sixty-four is exclusive of the Śaiva Āgamas, which fall conventionally into two groups of ten and eighteen, and the Vaishṇava Saṁhitās which, though conventionally numbered as one hundred and eight, are more than double the number in available texts. The Tantras, which are extolled as the best of the four *śāstras* included within *Kalpa* (namely Āgama, Yāmala, Ḍāmara, and Tantra) and supposed to hold sway in the present Śvetavarāha *Kalpa* (the first thirtieth period of the month of Brahmā), deal with an exhaustive list of topics; namely, origination and dissolution of the universe, ascertainment of *mantra,* installation of deities, description of places of pilgrimage, the duties of the different stages of life (*asrama*), support of Brāhmaṇas, maintenance of other creatures, ascertainment of *yantras,* theogonic speculation, knowledge of trees, location of heavenly bodies, purveying of traditional history (*purāṇa*), disquisition on precious things, description of sacred vows (*vrata*), determination of cleanliness and uncleanliness, delineation of hells, description of cycles of existence (*harachakra*), signs of masculinity and femineity, duties of kings, modes of charity, contemporaneous obligations (*yugadharma*), customs (or legal procedure), and spiritual elevation. These contents are classified into four *pādas* (quarters): *jnana* (philosophical doctrines, sometimes of an occult character), *yoga* (meditation, specially meant to acquire magic powers), *kriyā* (activities connected with temple-building and idol-worship) and *charyā* (observances, rites, etc.). Some of the Tantras are credited with enormous length in later accounts, while others are said to be of moderate dimensions, but the number of *ślokas* in each, as traditionally known, is meticulously recorded in enumerative lists.

We get a fair idea of the general principles of Tāntrik belief from the *Mahānirvāṇa Tantra* which, though of later date, is one of the most popular and well known Tāntrik texts. Almost like a

Vedāntic text, it deals with Brahman, which, according to the Śāktas, is nothing but Śakti, the eternal dynamic source of all beings. It is perceived that all life proceeds from the womb of a woman; so we should think of the ultimate creative principle in terms of the 'mother' and not of the 'father'. Philosophical concepts like *Prakṛiti* and *Māyā*, and mythological figures like Pārvatī, Durgā, Lakshmī and Rādhā constitute the female principle of creation, and are merely different names of the *jaganmātā* (Mother of the World). All gods including Brahmā, Vishṇu, and Śiva, are contained in and issue out of the Divine Mother. This sect, therefore, looks upon every woman as an incarnation of the Universal Mother to whom proper respect should be paid.

The Tāntrik cult lays special stress upon the *mantras, i.e.* prayers and formulae, *bījas, i.e.* syllables of mystic significance peculiar to each deity, *yantras, i.e.* diagrams drawn on paper or inscribed in precious stone, metal, etc., *mudrās, i.e.* special positions of fingers and movements of hands, and *nyāsas, i.e.* placing the deities on the different parts of the body by touching them with finger-tips and the palm, mostly of the right hand. These are the means by which the *Sādhaka* (the aspirant after perfection) invokes, and identifies himself with, his chosen deity (*ishṭadevatā*). Though occasionally they have been utilised in dark and magical practices to control men and gods (*abhichāra*), the primary aim of the Śākta worshippers in using them has been to become one with the deity and to attain salvation.

The Tantra texts justify their existence on the plea that the Vedas are a sealed book to the majority and hence an easier cult is necessary for the people at large. Moreover, the Tantra form of worship is open to women and Śūdras also. As a matter of fact, however, it became equally popular with the higher castes and classes once the indispensableness of Tāntrik initiation (*dīkshā*) was recognised.

Perhaps no religious literature of India has raised such controversy in evaluation as the Tantras. On the one hand, they have been extolled as the repository of sublime truths, rigorous discipline, catholic outlook and indispensable means to the attainment of the highest spirituality. On the other hand, they have been branded as a type of composition containing unmeaning jargon, mysterious mummery, veiled and open obscenity, and revolting antinomianism of different kinds. Theurgy and thaumaturgy jostle with high philosophy and deep devotion, dark rites and liberal thoughts go cheek by jowl with one another, and accurate knowledge alternates with occult science. We have, in fact, a strange mixture of higher and lower thoughts, of strenuous discipline and moral laxity, of sound understanding and primitive credulity, that presents a chequered pattern, bewilders the curious in enquiry and confuses the novice in practice. The matter is further complicated by the fact that the language used is sometimes enigmatical and has both an exoteric and an esoteric meaning, and without the help of an adept or an interpreter, the proper sense is likely to be missed. Hence *dīkshā* (initiation) by a *guru* (preceptor or spiritual guide) is essential for getting access to the esoteric or real meaning of a particular word or sentence,—a meaning handed down traditionally in different Tāntrik schools and not communicated to those who would not join the particular fraternity. It is the *guru* who opens the eyes of the disciple to the true meaning of texts, guides him through dark, devious and dangerous practices to the realm of light, and anoints him (*abhisheka*) as a peer of the spiritual kingdom. Getting the better of his stupefying intellect (*tāmasa*) and unintelligent activity (*rājasa*), the bound soul (*paśu*) heroically (*vīra*) severs the bond (*pāśa*) of subjection to various restraints and, with the help of the pure element in his mental constitution (*sāttvika*), attains the divine (*divyabhāva*) that is latent in every finite spirit.

It is obvious that such a complicated system, in which the lower and the higher elements of human nature tussle with one another, could not have been a matter of sudden growth, nor could it have been derived from a single source, particularly if we consider the complexity of its practices and the diversity of the creeds involved. On *a priori* grounds it may even be surmised that systematization must have been preceded by popular beliefs and rites connected with the worship of female deities, of which the cult of the Mothers (*mātṛigaṇa*) latterly became the most prominent. These dark forces of nature embodied man's fear of the mysterious and the terrifying, without and within, and his hope that they could be pacified and controlled by appropriate incantations, sacrifices and meditations. That they appealed to something universal in man in his primitive thinking is attested by the presence of similar beliefs in many other cultures of widely distributed areas of the globe. That Brahmanism, Jainism and Buddhism should all develop or incorporate occultism in course of time and fall back upon the use of magic syllables (*mantra*) and mystic diagrams (*yantra*) proves that they had to take note of some basic needs of the human mind in a composite population drawn from different social and cultural strata and diverse tribal and racial strains. Magic, religious ministration and meditation naturally figured in an ascending order, and as intellectual coherence was demanded by the inherent logic of the human mind or by the necessity of meeting hostile criticism, methodical philosophy gradually grew in importance. The different components of

Tantra owe their existence and emphasis to these diverse needs as they developed in space and time.

It is natural that after claiming to be the final revelation for mankind in the Kali-yuga the Tantras should draw up a scale of excellence among the aspirants treading the path of spiritual progress. The successive rungs of the spiritual ladder are constituted by three states (*bhāva*) or paths (*mārga*),—the *paśu* (the natural man living a life of routine like animals) following the conventional moralities of society; the *vīra* (the bold or heroic soul) daring to indulge in antinomian rites and practices under rigid rules of discipline; and the *divya* (the divine who is above all dualities) unconcerned about all distinctions as befitting one who has gone beyond all empirical variety and attained union with the Absolute. Stated in the language of religious classification, though not meant to be taken in the literal sectarian sense, these three were supposed in later compendia to fall mainly into seven subdivisions (*āchāra*), four being included within the *paśu* stage, two in the *vīra* stage, and one in the *divya* stage. The first group of four is constituted by Vedāchāra, Vaishṇavāchāra, Śaivāchāra, and Dakshiṇāchāra (sometimes the whole group being roundly described as Dakshiṇāchara); the second group of two is made up of Vāmāchāra and Siddhāntāchāra; and the last solitary stage is constituted by Kaulāchāra. In the first group external worship, devotion to Vishṇu, meditation on Śiva, and mental approach to Devī or Śakti find respective expression in the four stages. In all these the observance of social morality and the performance of prescribed rites and ceremonies find full sway;—avoidance of cruelty to animals, abjuration of intoxicants and unlawful enjoyments, conjugal fidelity, control of the senses, austerity, practice of charity, regular worship of the gods in a pure bodily condition, etc. constitute the main elements of spiritual culture, though in the fourth stage the acquisition of magical powers by some secret innocuous Tāntrik rites is not barred out altogether. The fifth ushers in a new outlook and technique, for the correct understanding of mystic rites, generally performed in secret at night, requires proper training at the hands of a *guru* and the acquisition of the necessary courage to disregard social conventions about sexual purity, to defy taboos about food and drink, and to look upon all women as manifestations of Śakti (*kulanāyikā, bhairavī* or *yoginī*) and all males as representatives of Śiva (*bhairava*), there being no bar to the use of any married woman (*kulastrī*) for furthering personal perfection by rites, prohibited to the ordinary members of a society, which might include the use of intoxicants and of the peculiar feminine impurity as an item of bodily decoration during worship. Still, the Vāmāchāra tries to avoid publicity in the matter of disregarding fear, shame, pity, caste convention, etc. which his secret rites involve. The aspirant (*sādhaka*) practising Siddhāntāchāra, however, is not afraid of following socially disapproved practices openly. He is relentless in the pursuit of what he thinks to be true, and is not, therefore, troubled by the opinions of others regarding what he eats and drinks, enjoys or hurts, for he holds that there is nothing that cannot be purified by appropriate means. The use of the five M's (*pañchatattva* or *pañchamakāra*)—*madya* (wine), *matsya* (fish), *māṁsa* (meat), *mudrā* (parched grain) and *maithuna* (coition)—under certain prescribed conditions of discipline could be made without secrecy in appropriate places and times, and was intended to further the progress of the aspirant towards the elimination of all empirical distinctions and the attainment of complete freedom. The *Kulārṇava Tantra* virtually tells us that just as one rises with the help of the very ground on which one has fallen, so also it is through drinking life to the very lees that one has to make the spiritual ascent. A thorn has to be eradicated with the help of another thorn; similarly indulgence must be forced to yield satiety and higher value. Wine that merely intoxicates is a sinful beverage, but as the producer of a euphoric condition, in which care and anxiety are absent, it is a desirable drink. Similarly, flesh that nourishes the body, fish that increases sexual potency, grain that invigorates the system, and coition that brings about a blissful condition (*mahāsukha*) and prolongs the race at the same time, are all intended to keep the *sādhaka* in a fit condition of body and mind to pursue spiritual aims. It is obvious that in the case of some gross minds they failed to serve their legitimate purpose, specially when promiscuity was permitted with different types of women, mostly coming from lower castes and dubbed as *śaktis*. There was, however, a general prohibition against using any woman except one's wife for the purpose of the last of the five *tattvas* (*maithuna*), and there were also other restrictions. The idea was that a *sādhaka* must go beyond dualities of all kinds—of love and hate, merit and demerit, touchable and untouchable, forbidden and non-forbidden, or delectable and nauseating, in food and drink, prohibited and non-prohibited in sex relation, male and female, friend and foe, etc.,—and cultivate not only equanimity in himself but also equality towards all.

It is only when this state of mind is acquired that the last stage of sanctification is reached, namely, Kaulāchāra. This is the *divya* condition, for then the aspirant transcends the likes and dislikes of earthly life like God himself to whom all things are equal. Pity and cruelty are equally unmeaning in an ultimate reference, and so also approbated and unapprobated conduct. Just as one of the Upanishads has said that to one who has attained Brahma-knowledge no sin attaches for any kind of antinomian act, so also the Tantras place the Kaula (worshipper of *kula* or *Śakti*) above all moral judgments, and put no prohibitions and restraints in his way as being unnecessary for one who has pierced the veil of space and time, process and differentiation. A Kaula roams in all *āchāras* at will, being at heart a Śākta, outwardly a Śaiva, and in social gatherings a Vaishṇava. He sees himself in all things and all things in himself. It appears, however, that the later (*uttara*) Kaulas preferred the gross to the symbolic, just the reverse of what was fancied by the earlier (*pūrva*) Kaulas, and the Samayins alone discarded both gross sex and symbolic *yantra* and restricted themselves to mere mental imagery in celebrating the worship in a circle (*Śrīchakra*). As usual, we have very exalted explanations of the origin, nature and objective of Kaula *sādhana*, and in the *Kaulajñānanirṇaya*, which probably belongs to the eleventh century, we have a description of the various *āchāras*, which must have been crystallised some time before this work was written. In fact, we have the information purveyed by the same work that there were various Kaula schools prevalent at the time, as also that very many methods of *yoga* (*yogapraṇālī*) were followed by these schools. We have incontestable evidence also that both the Buddhists and the Nāthists, too, countenanced the Kaula method of self-realisation.

Elaborate rules are laid down as to the proper persons from whom initiation is to be taken. While the Vaishṇavas, Sauras and Gāṇapatyas can initiate one belonging to their respective sects, the Śāktas and Śaivas are privileged to initiate all sects, including their own. Orthodoxy must have been alarmed, as at the time of Mahāvīra and Buddha, by the popularity of the ascetic and homeless wandering mendicants, and so it put a virtual, though not absolute, ban on the initiation of householders by their fraternity. But it made a compromise by admitting that Tāntrik initiation was essential even for Brāhmaṇas and indispensable for women and non-Brāhmaṇas, who had no right to Vedic initiation, and it ignored, when not extolling, the union with a *śakti* (woman partner) who was not the legally married wife of the *sādhaka;* but it preferred a married man as *guru*, even though he might indulge in *vāmāchāra* practices in the mystic circle, where eight pairs of *yoginīs* or *nāyikās* and their *bhairavas* (male partners) used to meet. We are interested in the information, furnished by the *Dakshiṇāchāra-tantrarāja,* that Gauḍa, Kerala and Kāśmīra (with Kālikā, Tripurā and Tārā as goddesses, respectively, according to a later account) are the homes of the purer (*Dakshiṇāchāra*) sects. Elsewhere (*Bṛihat-Gautamīya Tantra*) it is stated that, of *gurus,* those coming from the west are the best, those from the south are middling, those from Gauḍa and Kāmarūpa are inferior to the preceding, and those from Kaliṅga are the worst. An amplified description in *Jābāla* (quoted by Vidyādharāchārya) puts the *gurus* from Madhyadeśa (Aryāvarta), Kurukshetra, Lāṭa, (Naṭa, Nāṭa), Koṅkaṇa, Antarvedi, Pratishṭhāna and Avantī at the top, those from Gauḍa, Śalva, Sūra (?), Magadha, Kerala, Kośala and Daśārṇa in the middle, and those hailing from Karṇāṭa and the banks of the Narmadā, the Revā and Kachcha, the Kālindas, the Kambalas (or Kalambas) and the Kambojas (probably in Assam) at the bottom of the scale. The *Kulālikāmnāya* mentions five celebrated seats of Tāntrik cult in different parts of the country, namely, Oḍiyāna, Jāla (Jālandhara), Pūrṇa (-giri), Mataṅga (Śrīśaila) and Kāmākhya. In the *Sādhanamālā* the four celebrated Tāntrik *pīṭhas* are Kāmākhya, Sirihaṭṭa, (with Arbuda or Jālandhara replacing Sirihaṭṭa in some texts), Pūrṇagiri and Uḍḍiyāna. Kāmākhya or Kāmarūpa in Assam is well known and Sirihaṭṭa is Sylhet. Pūrṇagiri has been identified with Poona, but location in Assam has also been suggested for it. Uḍḍiyāna has been identified with Kāshgarh (Sylvain Lévi), Swat valley (Waddell, S. C. Das), Orissa (H. P. Sastri), and Western Assam (B. Bhattacharyya). These areas for Tāntrik *gurus* of different grades of excellence, and these Tāntrik centres, throw an interesting light on the diffusion of the creed and the probable place of its origin. When to this is added the information that north-east India had active interchange of thought with the trans-Himālayan regions like Tibet, it has not been unreasonably concluded that Tantras originated in this Indian area, and foreign elements like the cult of Tārā came from Buddhism of the adjoining regions mentioned above. From about the tenth century a composite Tantra, drawing materials from Brahmanic, Buddhistic and Nāthist circles, grew up, and some deities, adepts, cults and practices became common to all of them, though the traditions did not always tally among the different communities and localities. Denominationally and geographically considered, *Vedāchāra* is patronised in Mahārāshṭra, *Vaishṇavāchāra* among the Rāmānuja and Gauḍa schools, *Dakshiṇāchāra* among the Śaṅkarites of the south, *Śaivāchāra* and *Vīrāchāra* among the Liṅgāyats and Vīraśaivas, and *Vāmāchāra, Siddhāntāchāra* and *Kaulāchāra* among the Śāktas of Kerala, Gauḍa, Nepāla and Kāmarūpa. The first three disfavour both *Vīrāchāra* and *Bauddhāchāra,* while the others extol them.

Let us turn now to certain other specific beliefs and speculations of the Tantras, and try to trace their antecedents. The Śaiva Āgamas, the Vaishṇava Saṁhitās and the Śākta Tantras agree on one point, namely, that a female principle representing the *śakti* or energy must be associated with the ultimate reality or the source or locus of power considered as male. This power is not only the cause of manifestation, but is also responsible for differentiation, and hence a diversified world in time and space, including finite individuals, comes into being because of the association of the male and the female, as in the generation of the world of living things. An elaborate philosophy developed in all the Schools—Śaiva, Śākta, and Vaishṅava, professing to explain the different types and stages of evolution, the first two approximating each other in their main outlines and the last perhaps slightly antedating them both. This origin of the cosmos is to be distinguished, however, from the birth of children to the divine pair as in Puranic accounts of the birth of Gaṇeśa and Kārttikeya, for instance, when Śiva and Śakti are considered anthropomorphically. The universe, so originated, has a systaltic process, inasmuch as the created world returns to its source in course of time, when Śakti comes to repose in the Lord, either temporarily in *pralaya* at the end of a cosmic cycle (the philosophers of *Karma* and the Paurāṇikas mostly favouring this partial dissolution), or finally by the efforts of finite souls who, by religious practice, yogic concentration, contemplation and meditation realise their oneness with God and annul their finitude. The general tendency of the Tantras is to accept the world in both its physical and mental aspects as real, only that matter or *prakṛiti,* as such, was not accorded independent existence as in the Sāṁkhya system, but was supposed to be under the control of the spirit and, in fact, the body was regarded as the seat of the divine in every part thereof.

The mystery of speech is an ancient tradition in India and from the Vedic times onwards Vāch (Speech) has been a prominent goddess and a revealer of wisdom. Transcendental and phenomenal forms of speech (*parā, paśyantī, madhyamā,* and *vaikharī*) and the association of word (*śabda*) with meaning (*artha*) were speculated upon; and as ages rolled on, the power of the spoken word, whether as boons or as curses, as prayers or as incantations, grew in popular esteem. In the Tantras and Āgamas a systematic attempt was made to relate sound (*nāda*) to reality and its different vocal symbols or seed-words (*bīja-mantra*). It was believed, in fact, that just as intense imagination might cause a kind of visual hallucination and bring about the perceptual presentation of concrete figure through thinking alone, so also intense meditation on certain mystic words, which were supposed to stand for certain deities, would produce photic phenomena and bring before the *sādhaka's* eye an image of the divinity concerned. Starting with a single letter, the *mantra* might consist of a string of such letters (*mālā,* garland). Not only each deity but each aspect of the deity has its own special *bīja-mantra.* The time and place of initiation, the initial letter of the initiate's name, and even the rosary for uttering the *mantra* have to be suited to the chosen deity.

Once it was accepted that *varṇas* (letters) are the stuff of reality, a rapprochement between the worshipper and the worshipped deity became almost inevitable. Thus the body of a deity was supposed to be composed of the letters of the alphabet (*lipi*), the number being generally fixed at fifty. A true worshipper would find a correspondence between the different parts of his own body and the letters of the alphabet that make up the divine body. By the process called *nyāsa* (placing) a worshipper would place these letters in different parts of his own body and consider himself to be possessed of a body of *mantras*. But until the necessary purification is effected one cannot divinise himself. So the purification of the elements that make up the human body (*bhūtaśuddhi*) has to be done first. The other purifications refer to the seat (*sthāna*), the words or formulae (*mantra*), the materials (*dravya*), and the image of the deity (*deva*). Surrounding himself with a circle of water, as if by a wall of fire, the worshipper is to go through the process of identification with the deity by meditating on the Vedāntic formula of Jīva-Brahman identity and by sending, by the way of the central of the three *nāḍīs* (nerves)—*iḍā*, *sushumnā* and *piṅgalā*, his finite self along with the *kulakuṇḍalinī śakti* through the six psychic centres (*shaṭchakra*) up, till she unites with the infinite Self (Śiva or Paramātman) in the thousand-petalled lotus (*sahasrāra*) in the cranium and the entire paraphernalia of finite existence is dissolved. By *prāṇāyāma* (regulation of breath) the evil that is in one's own self (*pāpapurusha*) is to be thrust out and burnt, and then alone will the body be fit to receive the 'mother' letters (*mātṛikāmantra*) in the various external (*bāhya*) parts of the body and in the differently numbered petals of the various lotus-centres or *chakras* inside (*antar*) the bodily system, and thus be entirely pervaded by the deity. No wonder that before the recognition of the fifty-one *Śakti-pīṭhas* distributed all over India, pilgrimages to sacred places should have been considered unnecessary by Śāktas, who located these symbolically within their own body.

But while *mantras* are located in the body by *nyāsa* they are also placed outside in a *yantra* (diagram) which represents, as it were, the body of the deity. The Vedic gods were invoked without any image and on the sacred grass (*barhis, kuśa*) in a sacrificial field, and the sculptured deities that followed were seated on lotuses, perhaps through a wrong interpretation of the word *padmāsana*, a bodily posture. A *yantra* has, like the sacrificial field, gates or doors (*dvāra*) and a painted or inscribed seat; and all together or in the various petals of the lotus, inscribed or drawn, or in the different parts of other types of diagrams are inserted the letters of the *bījamantra* of the deity worshipped. Coloured rice-powder is sometimes used to fill in the geometrical figures created by the drawing, just as five differently coloured substances are used to cover the ground of a *maṇḍala* (*e.g.* Sarvatobhadramaṇḍala). In Jainism small images used to be put in the spaces in a *yantra* during worship; from this the transition to the incision of figures there is an easy process; and when the letters form the body of the deity, as in Tāntrik belief, the placing of letters inserted is not difficult to explain. In Buddhism we can effectively and easily trace the process of transition from the *Sūtra* to the *Hṛidaya-sūtra,* thence to *Dhāraṇī,* from this to *mantra,* and lastly therefrom to *Bīja.* As drawings and paintings are ephemeral, it was directed that if possible a more permanent *yantra* should be made. For this purpose some metal like gold, silver and copper, or an alloy of the three metals (*trilauha*), or some precious stone like crystal, emerald, ruby, coral, etc., should be inscribed with the *yantra* and care should be taken that the *yantra* does not get mutilated, faded out by use, cracked, burnt or broken, in which case it was directed to be thrown into a sacred stream or place of pilgrimage or the ocean. Every deity has his or her own *yantra,* but the most famous of these *yantras* is the *Śrīyantra* on which lavish praise has been bestowed. In its various parts it is supposed to represent the origin, maintenance and dissolution of the world of things, the dot in the middle representing the unitary world-ground. The *bīja-mantra* of the Śakti goddess is mentally placed in the various projections of its constituent triangles and lotuses and in its circles and squares. Elsewhere we are told (*e.g.* in the *Rudrayāmala*) that the six *chakras* represent the Bauddha, Brāhmya, Vaishṇava, Śaiva, Saura and Śākta diagrams, the last being central; in later literature they have been compared to the six systems of Indian philosophy. Elaborate rules about the choice of place and the creation of a proper atmosphere of worship have been laid down, and it has been reiterated pretty frequently that external worship (*pūjā, stava,* etc.) is less efficacious than *japa* (muttering) and *homa* (oblation or dedication), and these less than *dhyāna* (meditation). Here is a fine description of Tāntrik *pūjā* from Avalon's *Principles of Tantra:* "Meditation, Worship, Japa, and Homa are the four hands of the Yajña or worship; Mātṛikā, Shoḍhā and other Nyāsas form its body; knowledge of the real truth as to Ishṭadevatā is its Ātmā; devotion is its head; reverence is its heart; and the act of performing is its eye. Knowing the body of Yajña to be composed in this manner, a good Sādhaka should perform it in all its limbs, and not divide and make it limbless....It is by His union with the supreme Śakti which arises out of the effort to accomplish all those limbs that the Yajñapurusha produces Siddhi". And here is the culminating phase of external worship with flowers: "The knowing ones regard the following as the ten flowers to be used in worship:—non-ignorance (*amāyā*), non-egoity or non-appropriation (*anahaṁkāra*), non-attachment (*arāga*), non-vanity (*amada*), non-delusion (*amoha*), non-pride (*adambha*), non-calumniation (*anindā*), non-perturbation (*akshobha*), non-jealousy (*amātsarya*) and non-greed (*alobha*). But better than these are the five virtues which make up the other group of flowers:—non-injury or non-violence (*ahiṁsā*), self-control or subjugation of the senses (*indriya-nigraha*), charity or kindness (*dayā*), forgiveness (*kshamā*) and knowledge (*jñāna*)." This surely is religious teaching at its highest. Again and again in India when the letter was threatening to kill the religious life, the spirit came to the rescue. In their attempt to provide a comprehensive scheme of social life, individual perfection, and religious devotion, the Tantras failed occasionally to keep the baser elements in proper check among a motley population of different grades of culture. But the innate moral sense operated here as elsewhere to redeem men from the thraldom of desire and selfishness. Perhaps we shall never recapture the atmosphere in which the Purāṇas and the Tantras were written, but we cannot afford to undervalue the devotion and thought that went into their composition, or their ennobling influence in the long run on the very composite population of an entire subcontinent. They certainly brought the gods nearer the hearts and homes of men and inspired their devotion, prompted their collective action for charity, and gave a fillip to the building of religious edifices all over the country.

(F) MINOR RELIGIOUS SECTS

I. *POPULAR BRAHMANICAL RELIGION*

1. *Religious Syncretism*

By the time the period opens the main elements that constitute the religious life of India have already made their entrance into popular faith. It is now a question of making alliances and settling precedence among the major gods and of composing suitable religious literature to establish the superiority, if not the supremacy, of the chosen deity. The days of the early Purāṇas are over now, but there was still scope not only for new compositions but also for working up the older literature and adding and altering contents. The religious unity of India was almost achieved; and though local tradition and patriotism were sometimes responsible for making extravagant claims on behalf of local deities and sacred spots and rivers, the different religious communities acknowledged almost the same set of major gods and made an earnest effort to make a rapprochement with other communities even when pushing the claims of their own cults in distant areas and making converts. Buddhism was dying in the south but was still a living creed in the northern part, where it became the inspirer of religious art in Bengal and Bihār under the Pālas; Jainism had still a strong following in the south and was having a running fight primarily with Śaivism. Brahmanism had to reckon with both, specially as the former was developing a well organised pantheon and the latter was trying to win and retain popular support by absorbing theistic elements from the contiguous Brahmanic culture.

Archaeological evidence is not wanting to show that the hostility of the creeds was not often quite mild and that the appropriation of the sanctuary of one religion by another and effacing the religious symbols of the former by the latter were sometimes practised. As popular instruction in religious cult extended from the scriptures to the temples, it became increasingly necessary for each major religion to possess gorgeous temples of its own to attract pilgrims and evoke religious sentiment in the faithful; and fortunately devout patrons were not wanting to endow places of religious worship and build costly and spectacular houses of gods or saints. The scribes continued their work no doubt, but the sculptor was gradually becoming a more efficient instrument of popular edification and education in religious matters. East, west, north, south—everywhere gods and saints were decently, if not gorgeously, housed and the carvers' art purveyed to the hungry souls not only delectation of the spirit but also feasting of the eye. The high aesthetic and spiritual banquet served must have whetted religious appetite and excited the spirit of imitation and emulation. From the seventh century onward temples grew in honour of different deities in different parts of India and the rock-cut and structural temples, which are at present the wonders of the world and of which Elurā (Ellora) and Khajurāho are respectively the most prominent examples, came into existence and often in close proximity to one another as a trial of artistic strength among rival faiths. And no wonder, because during this period flourished the mighty Pratīhāras, Pālas, Chandellas, Eastern Chālukyas, Rāshṭrakūṭas, Chālukyas of Kalyāni, Pallavas and Cholas who professed diverse creeds and were zealous champions and liberal patrons of their respective creeds.

But rivalry is only one of the features of the religious life of the times. Side by side there developed a syncretistic attitude in religion—a spirit of tolerance and mutual give-and-take. A modified monolatry, which maintained the supremacy of the particular supreme deity of the community while at the same time admitting the existence and right to worship of other gods, made its appearance. Śankarāchārya has been credited with the initiation of the *pañchāyatana pūjā*—the worship of the five gods Vishṇu, Śiva, Śakti or Devī, Sūrya and Gaṇeśa, the principal deity of the worshipper being placed in the middle and the other four in the four corners of a square.

But whether it is Śaṅkara or Kumārila or somebody else that introduced it, the fact remains that the idea caught the imagination of the public as the best solution of the rather perplexing problem of harmonising monotheism with polytheism and allaying communal bitterness and religious quarrel. Was the Pallava cave-temple at Trichinopoly, with Vishṇu and Śiva images inside in two sanctuaries and Brahmā, Sūrya, Gaṇeśa and possibly Subrahmaṇya sculptured outside at the entrance, an anticipation of this new cult? The Smārtas not only followed the practice of worshipping the five gods (and sometimes many more) but also compiled Puranic handbooks, in the different parts of which the major gods got their due laudations, and even an Upnishad—the *Atharvaśiras*—turned up to give the new method of worship a holy and hoary antiquity. It appears that there was some hesitation in counting the five major deities, for while the first four were almost constant features, Brahmā sometimes displaced Gaṇeśa, thereby indicating that the revealer of the Vedic *śruti* was hard to dislodge from popular veneration and Gaṇeśa was still looked upon as a plebeian god. Even in the tenth-century Choḷa temple of Koraṅganātha near Trichinopoly not only Brahmā but also his spouse Sarasvatī appears, the latter forming with Lakshmī and Dakshiṇā Kālī a trinity of divine *śaktis* as in many other parts of India. That Gaṇeśa continued to figure in the door-lintels of the temples of other gods, specially Śiva, must be regarded as a sign of his inferiority to the rest. How Kārttikeya, who appeared probably earlier and more frequently in sculpture with Śiva in the Pallava Somāskanda figures and held his own against Gaṇeśa in the period of the Bādāmi and Aihole caves, failed to maintain his position and how in the Pallava architecture Gaṇeśa began to supplant Kārttikeya from the Rājasiṁha period onward in the divine family group cannot be satisfactorily explained. It must be admitted, however, that in the Mahishamardinī *maṇḍapa* at Māmallapuram it is Kārttikeya or Mahāsena, and not Gaṇeśa, that is seated on Pārvatī's knee, and in the far-off Pāhārpur temple in North Bengal, in the scene of Śiva's drinking of poison, it is Kārttikeya who clings to the terror-stricken Durgā. It stands to reason that as Śiva's position in popular reverence increased, Kārttikeya and Gaṇeśa (and also Nandī, Ṛishabha or Vasava, the bull) also should receive popular homage, and that they should be even provided with separate buildings at a later time instead of remaining as mere ornamentations of the temple or the aureole (*prabhāvalī*) of Śiva, and thus become cult objects themselves.

One of the most noticeable features of the religious development of the period is the place found for other divinities (including those supposed to be antagonistic) in the temple of a sectarian deity. If figures of Kārttikeya or Gaṇeśa or Mahākālī or Pārvatī are found in Śiva temples, as in the Mahāliṅgeśvara and other temples near Konur and in the Bādāmi, Aihole and Ellora caves, ready explanation can be found for it in the fact that they are related to Śiva as son or wife. For the same reason the Gajalakshmī image would be quite appropriate in the Varāha temple at Māmallapuram (being, according to Burgess, the first to appear in a Hindu garb though the Buddhists had used it from the time of the *stūpa* of Bhārhut). Similarly, Kālabhairava and Saptamātṛikās (Seven Mothers) may make their appearance in Śiva temples as associated with the deity himself or Durgā. Likewise Gaṇeśa and Kārttikeya images are quite relevant as adjuncts of Devī images, as, for example, of the image from Mandoil or that from Nowgong in the District of Rājshāhi. But when Vishṇu and other gods appear in *chaitya* windows, niches and elsewhere in a Śiva temple (as, for example, in the earlier Bhūmarā temple in the old Nāgod State, or in the Kadaroli Temple in Belgāum District, or Dhumar Leṇā Cave at Ellora) or *vice versa* (as, for instance, in the Bādāmi Caves dedicated to Vishṇu), or when in a Vishṇu or Daśāvatāra temple appear the figures of many other gods and goddesses, such as Sūrya, Brahmā, Śiva, Soma, Gaṇeśa, Gaṅgā, Yamunā, etc. as in some mediaeval temples of Kāthiāwād (*e.g.*, at Kadvār) and Central India (*e.g.*, at Janjgir in Bilāspur District) and even in the earlier cave-temples of Bādāmi, Aihole, Ellora, Undavilli, etc., the motive could either be to belittle their importance by relegating them to inferior positions or reducing them to mere decorations or, what is more probable, to admit, like the tolerant mediaeval Purāṇas, that they too were worshipful, the location (whether, for instance, as a part of the deity as in Ardhanārīśvara, Trimūrti, Hari-Hara and such composite figures, or by the side of or sprouting out of the main deity, or inside the temple, or outside it in medallions in windows, or as figures in niches, or as bas-reliefs on door lintels or in architraves or in dados or in jambs of doors or windows or in ceilings) and the size and the state of fullness of the figure indicating the importance of the foreign deity. This would explain, for instance, the figures of Gaṇapati, Brahmā, Śiva, Vishṇu and Kārttikeya carved in a row on the top of the pointed stele of the two-handed Durgā image hailing from Dakshiṇa-Muhammadpur (Tipperah) and in the slab of the four-handed Ugra-

Tārā figure of Sikārpur (Bākarganj), the figures of Brahmā, Śiva and Vishṇu on the top of the Maheśvarapāsā (Khulna) Devī figure and the different divine figures in the early Durgā temple of Aihole. The figures of Brahmā, Śiva and Vishṇu on door lintels at Khajurāho, in the stele of a standing image of Vishṇu of the Pāla period in the Stuart-Bridge Collection in the British Museum, and in the panel above the door-frame in the Sandera and Ruhāvi temples of Gujarāt indicate the continuation of the conventional Trimūrti even after Brahmā had ceased to be a major deity. In fact, even in Sūrya temples of a later time, as at Modhera and Delmal, Brahmā continued to be figured. This is because in Gujarāt the cult of Brahmā continued to be a living creed at the beginning of this period, judging by the Trimūrti-temple at Kasarā dedicated to Brahmā, Vishṇu and Śiva, and the slightly later Brahmā temple at Khed-Brahmā in the old Idar State. Even now the very few Brahmā temples of North India, still used for worship, cluster in this western area, being located mostly either in Gujarāt or in Rājputāna, the other few temples being found distributed in South India.

More strange decorations are found, for instance, in the Buddhist temple of Pāhārpur (Somapura Vihāra) which was destroyed in the eleventh century. Here many Brahmanical deities — Śiva Balarāma, Kṛishṇa, Gaṇeśa, Kārttikeya, Durgā, Yama, Agni, Vishṇu, Brahmā, etc.—get artistic representation either in stone or in terracotta plaques on the outside. In Jain temples too many Hindu gods are to be found, but here they have been mostly adopted or adapted from Brahmanism by the Jains themselves, which need not have been the case with the Buddhists who had a well developed pantheon of their own and were not in need of Hindu deities as decorative motifs. We must suppose, therefore, that at this period toleration of other creeds went to the length of presenting the national religious beliefs in various works of art so that devotees visiting any temple might be *au courant* with the multiple devotion of the community at large and regaled with graphic representation of ancient religious history. It is almost like a religious art exhibition without reference to the particular deity enshrined. This will explain display of Vaishṇava and Śaiva images at Bādāmi, of Hindu, Buddhist and Jain sculptures side by side at Ellora, the co-existence of Vaishṇava, Śaiva, Saura, Bauddha and Jain temples at Khajurāho, and an almost similar group of small temples at Sarangarh in Bankura Distrct, constructed in the later part of this period. At Khera in the old Gwālior State the principal Hindu deities are similarly grouped together — Mahishamardinī, Gaṇeśa, Sūrya, Śiva and other gods. In the temples relevant figures were naturally the first to be utilised—in the Daśāvatāra temple at Ellora, for example,

Vāmana, Trivikrama, Varāha and Narasiṃha fill niches in the Vaishṇava temple. Sometimes these forms started minor religious cults —the cult of Dattātreya (the Trinity in fusion) is one such; at other times a particular form of the god was accepted as the patron deity of this or that royal family.

But composite and fused deities also made their appearance. Even in the Bādāmi and Aihole caves such fused figures are to be found, *e.g.*, Ardhanārīśvara and Hari-Hara, and the practice was continued in Elephanta, Māmallapuram and Ellora. In fact, new combinations were made in later centuries, for example, Sūrya-Nārāyaṇa of Madaun, Sūrya-Brahmā of Mahendra (Dinājpur District), Mārtaṇḍa-Bhairava of Manda (District Rājshāhi), Trimūrti Sūrya in a Delmal (N. Gujarāt) temple, at Chidambaram and elsewhere, Trimūrti (Maheśa) of Elephanta and Ellora Caves, the Ekapāda-Trimūrti of later times in which Vishṇu and Brahmā sprout forth from a central Śiva figure, and Brahmā-Vishṇu-Śiva-Sūrya of the Dula-Deo temple at Khajurāho. Outside India, at Thaton in Burma, we have the figure of Nārāyaṇa from whose navel issues a lotus stalk which branches out into three lotuses on which are seated Brahmā, Vishṇu and Śiva, just as in the Tantras they were supposed to have come out of Śakti and in Mahāyānism they were considered to be emanations of Vairochana. At the same time old associations were being broken. Vāsudeva and Saṅkarshaṇa appear now as Kṛishṇa and Balarāma; but the former gradually outdistances the latter until Balarāma becomes either an emanation or an *avatāra* or one of the twenty-four forms of Vishṇu distinguished in iconography. Dāśarathi Rāma and Paraśurāma attained some importance even in the *Mahābhārata,* and the former is mentioned, along with Bali, son of Virochana, as a subject of cult image by Varāhamihira. But though the temporary interest in the *Vyūha* doctrine had exalted Pradyumna and Aniruddha (and rarely Śāmba in the place of Aniruddha) also, it does not appear that they ever became deified—they represented philosophic concepts rather than religious objects except that they began to be regarded as two out of the twenty-four forms of Vishṇu. What is more interesting is the attempt made in the *Kūrma Purāṇa* to reduce Śiva and Brahmā to manifestations of Vishṇu when in some of the other Pūraṇas like *Mārkaṇḍeya, Brahma, Agni* and even in the *Kūrma Purāṇa* itself and in the *Pādma Tantra* the indefinite number of Vishṇu's *avatāras* was being reduced to ten and distributed among the different *vyūhas* of Vishṇu. But while popular sentiment in favour of incarnations was reflected in the increasing sculpturing of Varāha, Vāmana (Upendra) or Trivikrama and Narasiṃha, Rāma and Paraśurāma practically find no lithic representation in temples except in the Daśāvatāra group, the latter's devotion to Śiva and defeat by the former going heavily against his deification to the fullest extent. A standing figure in the Kadvār temple, which was probably a Daśāvatāra temple carrying on Gupta tradition, has been identified by Cousens as Paraśurāma and by Sankalia as Rāma, but the date of the image is uncertain. At Māmallapuram in the temple of Varāha Svāmī the figure of Rāma, worshipped by Māruti (Hanumān), is said to occur, but obviously with minor importance. What interests us more is the inscribed image of Hanumān at Khajurāho belonging to the end of the ninth century, as that indicates not only the prevalence of the cult of Rāma but also the coming importance of the monkey-god in popular devotion.

2. *Solar Cult*

Meanwhile the solar cult, of which Multān was a strong centre in the seventh century, was slowly diffusing itself all over the country. The Sun figure appears in the early Christian centuries in Gandhāra and Mathurā regions, obviously modelled on Helios-Mithra. It is found in early Buddhist monuments at Bhājā, Bodh-Gayā, Khaṇḍagiri, and Lala Bhagat near Kānpur and in Śaivite and Vishṇuite monuments like Māmallapuram, Trichinopoly, etc. Again, already in the Laṅkeśvara cave at Ellora, Sūrya is sculptured among the major gods, though not clad in the northern fashion, and he appears again in cave No. 25 (Sureśvara temple). The gift of the Rāshṭrakūṭa king Govindarāja to the temple of the Sun (Jayāditya) at Kāvi shows that princely support was not altogether lacking in later times and even the Valabhī rulers could be occasionally found to patronise this faith. Though the theory has been recently questioned, Kāshmir may have had some hand in popularising the worship of the Sun in the western part of India, the early Kāthiāwād temple-specimen in the Kashmirian style being the Sun-temple at Gop. In Kāshmir itself was built towards the middle of the eighth century the magnificent Mārtaṇḍa temple. The multiplicity of the Sun temples in the southern part of Kāthiāwād, where tribes emigrating from Kāshmir and worshipping the Sun probably lived, indicates that in this part of India the cult of the Sun was quite vigorous. The temples at Visāvāda, Kinderkheda, Modhera, Somanātha-Pattana, Thān, Sutrapādā and other places are fairly well packed in time to justify the conclusion that devotees to this deity continued their allegiance and ceremonial worship in fair numbers during a fairly long period of time in this part of India. A Sun-temple at Dholpur, perhaps of the ninth century, a tenth century temple at Osia, a probably earlier Sun figure at Hansi Fort (District Hissar), temples in the old Jodhpur, Sirohi, Bharatpur and other States, and temples found or referred to as existing in the western part of the present Uttar Pradesh indicate that the cult of the Sun was well patronised in north-western and western India during mediaeval times. Possibly the Durgā temple at Aihole and the Pāpānātha temple at Paṭṭadakal were associated with Sun worship at a slightly earlier date, and towards the close of this period the Sun temple in the Khajurāho group reared its head. Judging by the increasingly accurate reference in Indian religious literature of the time on this subject to the Persian belief, it may be presumed that the Magas, Bhojakas or Śākadvīpī Brāhmaṇas spread out over Northern India within a short time and popularised the solar cult. It should be added, however, that the southern tradition, as embodied in the Sūrya figure in a shrine near Lād Khān's temple at Aihole and Paraśurāmeśvara temple at Guḍimallam, was also not slow in diffusing itself, for in Bengal images of both northern and southern types have been found and, in fact, even earlier tradition is not unrepresented as, for instance, in the Kumārpur and Niyāmatpur reliefs. Further, in Bengal we find an evolution of newer and more complex forms; witness, for instance, the seated character of the deity in the octo-alloy miniature from Chauddagrām (District Tipperah) and the twelfth century Bāirhāṭṭā image in addition to the usual standing figure, the gradually increasing number of attendants (including Mahāśvetā or Pṛithivī), the number of hands increasing from two (as in the eighth and early ninth century figures from Bihār, now in the Indian Museum, and the ninth century figures in the Rājshāhi, and South Kensington Museums) to four, and from four to six, and even coalescence wth other deities. *e.g.* the Mārtaṇḍa-Bhairava three-headed (the fourth head being invisible in relief) figure with ten arms belonging to a later date. All this tends to prove that the solar cult was not moribund even in Bengal and Bihār. Orissa and adjoining regions took up the solar cult in right earnest during the succeeding centuries, and the many temple ruins in Orissa (*e.g.* Khiching and Konārak) and the settlement of many Śākadvīpī Brāhmaṇas (called Āṅgirasas in Orissa and Āchāryas in Bengal), who looked after the solar temples as priests and actively pursued the profession of astrologers and averters of astral influences (*grahaśānti,* which is referred to in the *Matsya Purāṇa*), bear testimony to the vigour of the solar worship in Eastern India. In Gujarāt a Trimūrti with Sūrya as the principal god is not unknown, and it appears that the *Śāradātilaka Tantra* provides even for a four-faced and eight-handed form. In the extreme south early temples to the Sun are rare, but in inscriptions of the eighth and ninth centuries solar temples (Ādityagṛihas) in the northern part of the old Madras Presidency are referred to. At a later date even an attempt to establish a trinity of Sūrya, Śiva and Vishṇu, with prominence given to the first, was made in Traipurushadeva temples. This is in accordance with the *Matsya Puraṇa* prescription that vows are to be made to Śiva, Sūrya and Vishṇu.

We may well believe that some difference of opinion existed at first about the composition of the group of major deities and that local tradition may have had some hand in fixing the number and personality. In the Pallava temple at Tiruttani near Arkonam in Madras State the deities which find a niche on the walls or the porch are Vishṇu, Śiva, Brahmā, Durgā and Gaṇeśa, which shows that in that area Brahmā was still holding his own against Sūrya who does not appear to have been a favourite god in South India. In the Goṇḍeśvara temple at Sinnar near Nāsik, on the other hand, Sūrya is included in the group and at Nālandā, Sūrya is seen with Mahishamardini figure. Sūrya is found combined with the other three major deities in different places—with Vishṇu in Sūrya-Nārāyaṇa figures (Vishṇu being himself an Āditya), with Śiva in Mārtaṇḍa-Bhairava figures, and with Brahmā in the image of a slightly later date from Mahendra (District Dinājpur). The *Matsya Purāṇa* dictum that Brahmā, Vishṇu, Śiva and Sūrya are identical or non-different *(abheda)*, the *Kūrma Purāṇa* statement that it originally consisted of four Saṃhitās—Brāhmī, Bhāgavatí, Saurī and Vaishṇavī,—and the division of the *Skanda Purāṇa* into six Saṃhitās, namely, Sanatkumāra, Sūta, Vaishṇavī, Brāhmī, Śaṅkarī and Saurī, seem to indicate that these four gods were associated together in some places and times. But this group was liable to alteration, as when the *Nāradīya Purāṇa* ascribes to the second part of the *Vāmana Purāṇa* four Saṃhitās, namely, Māheśvarī, Bhāgavatī, Saurī and Gāṇeśvarī, thus belittling the importance of Brahmā and extolling that of Gaṇeśa. The *Garuḍa Purāṇa* reserves the highest position for Vishṇu but prescribes modes of worship of Śiva, Durgā, Gaṇeśa and Sūrya also in the full Smārta manner, while the *Bhavishya Purāṇa* gives different groupings in different parts and, though conceding the importance of Sūrya in some parts, reserves pre-eminence for the old triad — Brahmā, Vishṇu and Śiva. That the solar cult was popular in Eastern India may be inferred from the fact that in an inscribed sculpture of the reign of Dharmapāla the images of Sūrya, Śiva and Vishṇu are found together, the first replacing Brahmā. Sūrya replaces Vishnu in the enormous door-lintel of the ruined tenth century Śiva temple at Tezpur in Assam with Brahmā and Śiva on the two sides.

He appears also in the much earlier pre-Ahom temple at Dah Parvatiyā near by. The deliberate attempt to lower the status of Brahmā in Śaivite literature took the form of showing him as the officiating priest in the marriage of Siva and Pārvatī, as the charioteer of Śiva in Tripurāntaka images, as punished for his moral lapse by Śiva who tore off one of his heads, and as cursed by Śiva for having falsely declared to have reached the top of the *liṅga* when Vishṇu had not reached its bottom in a contest for superiority with the latter. His origin out of the navel of Vishṇu or out of the mundane egg thrown into water by the Primal Being was exploited by the Vaishṇavas to show his inferiority. The *Padma Purāṇa* (*Sṛishṭi-Khaṇḍa*) made a belated attempt to revive the cult of Brahmā, but did not succeed in rehabilitating him in popular favour.

That Sūrya retained some importance in worship can be made out from the fact that his images are widely distributed and latterly assumed a varied character according to the diverse fancies of local potentates and sculptors, or divergent traditions of the Purāṇas and the Śilpa-śāstras. The old associates — wives and attendants — are mostly retained, and new ones, such as the Ādityas, the planets and zodiacal signs, and even the seven Ṛishis (who appear, by the way, as reliefs in a Trivikrama image recovered from Siwan and worshipped in the Kashipuri temple at Kaithal in Kurukshetra) and the seven Mātṛikās find their way into some of the images. The number of hands varies from two to ten in Bengal alone. If, as is sometimes supposed, Doṇḍa (Daṇḍī or Kuṇḍī) stands for Skanda and Piṅgala for Agni, then the superiority of Sūrya over these two is indirectly asserted by placing them as attendants by his side. Incidentally it may be observed that Sarasvatī or Śruta-Devī, the goddess of learning as depicted in Jainism, carries symbols of both Sūrya and Brahmā in her different forms (Vidyādevīs) and, in fact, in a Sarasvatī figure from Pindawara in Sirohi not only is the lotus symbol present but the Sun is represented above the crown; and occasionally in Jain Nava-graha slabs Sarasvatī appears at one of the ends, which also shows her solar association. But the wide prevalence of Navagraha figures in Jain images, specially of the Tīrthaṅkara Śāntinātha and occasionally of Neminātha, below, round or on the sides of the main image, and their presence below the figure of the Mahāyāna goddess Daśabhuja-sita-Mārīchī (Mārīchí being the Buddhist female counterpart of the Hindu male deity Sūrya and regarded as an emanation or the wife of Vairochana) indicate that they were becoming fashionable as temple decorations, for they are not only found in a panel (separate images being extremely rare) on the doorframe on the entrance door-way and sometimes on the *torana* of a Sūrya temple in Rājputāna and Gujarāt and elsewhere, but also in Śaiva sculptures (*e.g.* Vaivāhika or Kalyāṇasundara figure in the Vangiya Sahitya Parishat Museum, Calcutta) and in the Mother-and-child images. It has not been unreasonably surmised that when these figures are in bold relief, as in the Khāri (24-Paraganas) Navagraha slab, the set was regarded as a cult-object and used in *grahayāga* or *svastyayana* to avert evil. The discovery at Khiching of a Navagraha-chakra of a later date is therefore of some interest in this connection. Perhaps what happened in the case of their occasional associate, Gaṇeśa, occurred in their case also. To avert their wrath or evil influence people started with placing them outside their shrines and then they began to worship them. In this way popular devotion was canalised from the major adoration of principal deities to the channels of minor piety.

3. *Śakti Cult and the Śaiva Deities*

The most notable religious revival of the age centred round Śiva who practically swept the other gods off their feet. Sectarian Purāṇas in laudation of this divinity did not make their appearance all at once, but came in regular succession. From Kāshmir to Cape Comorin there was a stir in the religious world and some of the most famous cave temples of India owe their origin to contemporary religious fervour directed towards Śiva. Ellora, Salsette and Elephanta bear eloquent testimony to the excavator's art, while the builder's skill is manifested in the Kailāsanātha temple at Kāñchī at the opening of this period, and in the Great Temple of Tanjore at the end of this era. In Orissa also the Bhuvaneśvara group of temples dedicated to Śiva began to rear their heads in this period. As by now the affiliations of the Śaivite group of divinities had been firmly established, the stocks of this group soared high in popular estimation. Naturally, Śiva's consort and children began to shine in a kind of reflected glory—at any rate, their importance was materially enhanced. They began to be placed in independent charge of divine exploits and even some Upanishads were written to extol their power and beneficence. By the twelfth century the Śaivite momentum spent itself and Vishṇu, who never lost support at any time even during the preceding epoch, began to dominate sculptural representation. In the mediaeval temples of Rājputāna, however, the figure of Lakulīśa on the door-way continued to be a favourite device.

But there was a deeper reason for this emergence of family alliance of divinities. The period synchronised with the rise of a new philosophy and a new attitude towards divine consorts. At the root of the speculations of the period lay the philosophical theory that not God as such but God as associated with his power *(śakti)* is responsible for the creation, maintenance and destruction of the universe, and hence the mysterious association of the Supreme God with this *Śakti* must be admitted. Thus while in the Vedāntic school of Śankara it is the eternal Māyā *śakti* of Brahman that become responsible for the origin of the world of diversity, in the theistic schools of the Vaishṇavas and the Śaivas this *śakti* got greater personification and became the wife of the supreme deity. Whether this conjugal ideal was preached to counteract the ascetic tendency of Buddhism and Jainism must remain an open question, for we find that in Jainism too the *śāsana-devatās* appear in pairs and Mahāyāna Buddhism also recognised very soon female deities side by side with the male Buddhas and their emanations. It is difficult to establish conclusively the beginnings of this Śākta tendency in Śaivism, Vaishṇavism and Buddhism, for sexual esoterism is a very old phenomenon in Indian religious history. In India of the period we are discussing, popular religion influenced, and was in its turn reinforced by, speculation and mythology alike. The Vaishṇava Saṃhitās, the Śaiva Āgamas and the Śākta Tantras were tumbled down upon the votaries of the different faiths in a multitudinous heap, and for the first time the right of the language of the people to be the medium of expression for religious exaltation and religious devotion was recognised in the south. The new religious sentiment, as affected by philosophical speculations, became mellowed in temper and began to be directed to a God of grace, united with a practically eternal partner, conceived as a female principle, whether philosophically as *śakti* or *prakṛiti* or religiously as Lakshmī, Sarasvatī or Umā. The new motif appears in gradually increasing representation of Lakshmī-Nārāyaṇa, Brahmā-Sarasvatī and Śiva-Pārvatī in temple-niches, as for instance in the temple at Ruhāvi (and later in the Navalākhā temple at Gumli) in Gujarāt and in many Haihaya monuments, as for example in the Virāṭeśvara temple at Sohāgpur in the old Rewa State where over the doorway an eight-handed male figure is flanked by Brahmā and his wife, and Vishṇu and his wife, and the figures of Pārvatī and Gaṇeśa also make their appearance in the architrave. In the struggle for recognition the first bout of victory went to the Śiva-Śakti cult, strongly supported in the north by Kāshmir Śaivism and in the south by Tamil Āgamism. That there was keen rivalry among the warring creeds can be easily made out from the volume of the Saṃhitā, Āgama and Tantra literature of the time.

In the new devotion to the Śaivite household both the terrible and the benign aspect of the deities received equal and wide attention. The marriage of Śiva with Umā and the peaceful householders's life of Śiva with Pārvatī and infant Gaṇeśa or Skanda find, as in Pallava sculpture, equal lithic representation with Durgā killing the buffalo demon either as a decorative bas-relief or as a principal image in Māmallapuram in the seventh century and with Gaṇeśa, Vīrabhadra and Chāmuṇḍā appearing in the Saptamātṛikā slabs. One of the earliest dated pleasant images is that of Śarvāṇī in bronze or octo-alloy, discovered in Chauddagrām near Tipperah and belonging to an earlier period, but other benign types of Devī images, mostly with an iguana as vehicle, are also known in Bengal. It appears also that earlier Puranic motifs of art were resuscitated with greater elaboration and freer reins to fancy. Judging from images, the earlier Mahishamardinī figures seem to have had their inspiration from some other source than the *Mārkaṇḍeya Purāṇa* as the Devī's leonine mount is absent from some of the earliest images. Again, there is variation in the mode of the presentation of both the lion and the buffalo demon. Durgā sometimes fights dismounted from the lion, sometimes she sits on her mount with both legs on one side, and sometimes she sits astride the lion. The demon too is sometimes half-human and half-buffalo, sometimes he is human-bodied but buffalo-headed, and sometimes he is wholly human in appearance but with two buffalo horns sticking out of his forehead—a mode of representing theriomorphic powers of which Egyptian parallels would come readily to one's mind. Similarly, the hands of Durgā could be two, four, six, or eight, or even ten or twelve at a later time. In fact, the Devī with sixteen, eighteen, twenty and even thirty-two hands has been represented in Bengal. The ten arms may represent the combined ten hands of the four-handed Brahmā, the four-handed Vishṇu and the two-handed Śiva, seeing that Durgā was considered to be Mahā -Kālī, Mahā-Lakshmī and Mahā-Sarasvatī in one. As a matter of fact, Hemādri in his description of Kātyāyanī mentions that she should imitate the three deities, by which are obviously meant Brahmā, Vishṇu and Śiva. He also describes a ten-handed Durgā with a slightly different set of weapons and also a twenty-handed Chaṇḍī with many more weapons in her hands. As he wrote his *Chaturvarga-chintāmaṇi* in the thirteenth century, apparently he was recording later varieties of the Durgā image. But the twenty-handed image from Sirala (District Rājshāhi), belonging to the tenth century and now lost, has a good deal of resemblance with Chaṇḍī described by him. In fact, the

Purāṇas and sculptural remains vary considerably on this point of the number of Śakti's hands, and their attributes.

The *Mārkaṇḍeya Purāṇa,* which grew by accretion during the early centuries of the Christian era and is the *locus classicus* for the exploits of the Śakti goddess in the *Chaṇḍī* or *Devī-māhātmya* or *Saptaśatī* chapters, includes the Mahishamardinī episode in addition to some other accounts of Śakti's achievements as also the promise of her periodic appearance whenever the demons would threaten the peace of gods. It is also responsible for popularising the cult of the Mothers, generally seven in number, who are the energies (*Śakti*) of the different major gods that came to the assistance of the Divine Mother (Ambikā, Durgā, Chaṇḍikā, Kātyāyanī), armed with the mount and vehicles and weapons of their respective lords. Whereas the Mahishāsuramardinī was herself formed by the coalescence of the Śaktis of many more deities than seven and was endowed by them all, Chaṇḍikā maintained an independent position in her fight against Śumbha and Niśumbha and even withdrew the Seven Mothers within herself as her *vibhūtis* when taunted by Śumbha for fighting with extraneous aid. In the Saptamātṛikā slabs appear the *śaktis* of the principal gods from left to right, with occasional variations here and there, in the following order—Brahmāṇī or Sarasvatī, Māheśvari or Raudrī, Kaumāri or Kārttikeyānī, Vaishṇavī or Lakshmī, Vārāhī, Indrāṇī or Māhendrī, and Chāmuṇḍā or Chāmuṇḍī. Nārasiṃhī replacing Chāmuṇḍā (as in the *Mārkaṇḍeya Purāṇa*) or Yāmī replacing Vārāhī is not unknown. To the list is sometimes added Mahālakshmī or Yogeśvarī to make the eighth. Hemādri mentions Chaṇḍikā herself as the eighth Mother; he also gives other lists of Mothers in which abstract qualities and concrete personalities are mixed up together. Even an image with Vāgīśvarī replacing Vaishṇavī has been discovered in Bengal. The Saptamātṛikā figures are flanked on the left by Śiva (*Vīrabhadra*) or Skanda and on the right by Gaṇeśa (and occasionally by Kāla or Bhṛiṅgī), but Gaṇeśa is here not a young boy of diminutive size, as in Śiva-Pārvatī images, but is of the same size as the Mothers as befitting a leader who, alternately with Śiva, sometimes forms, in fact, the vanguard of the group of divine Śaktis. He appears as such in the Chedi country also, as in the Vaidyanātha Mahādeva temple where not only the Saptamātṛikās but also the Navagrahas figure, as they do in some other temples of this area like the temple at Marai in the old Maihar State.

The Purāṇas and the *Bṛihat-saṁhitā* had recognised the existence and worshipfulness of the Mothers; the Kadamba and Chālukya kings had worshipped them; and bas-reliefs in caves and temples had presaged their coming splendour. But the growing importance of the Śakti cult brought them into greater prominence and distributed their cult far and wide—from the Kāngra valley to Cape Comorin and from the Jhelum to Sadiya. In Eastern India specially they got independent representation. The colossi of the Eight Mothers from Muktimaṇḍapa near Jājpur (Virajākshetra) and the Eight Mothers with Śivadūtī on the bank of the Vaitaraṅī indicate their popularity in this part of East India. In Bengal also some of the Mothers have been separately sculptured and Chāmuṇḍā of various forms, such as Rūpavidyā, Siddha-yogeśvarī and Danturā, has found independent lithic representation. Even a Śakti of Gaṇeśa (Gaṇeśānī) was subsequently conceived when Gaṇeśa became a major deity.

Reinforcement to the Śakti cult came from a contemporaneous Buddhistic revival in which Tārā, the Śakti of Avalokiteśvara, played a prominent part. This goddess, of whom the nearest Brahmanical equivalent is Tāriṇī and the Jain parallel is the śāsanadevatā Sutārakā or Sutārā, was absorbed at first as a *yoginī* and then as a deity along with Ekajaṭā, Kurukullā and other Mahāyāna female divinities in the north, and found early representation in the different cave temples and also stone and metal embodiment under the Pālas (*e.g.*, the bronze eighteen-armed Tārā found in Nālandā). The adventurous mariners who carried Indian civilisation by sea to the Far East during the Pāla period invoked her as the patron of navigators through a pardonable identification of the meanings of Tārā, which signifies both a star and a goddess. In the later Tantras, which are products of the fusion of Buddhistic and Brahmanical beliefs, many of the Buddhistic female deities were identified with Brahmanical Śakti goddesses, and even the Jain pantheon, by matching each male attendant of a Tīrthaṅkara with a female, recognised the strength of the popular feeling in favour of pairing male principles with their female counterparts. In Jainism not only were Vāsudeva and Baladeva (with the snake-canopy) and Gaṇeśa and possibly also Kārttikeya taken over from Brahmanism but also Sarasvatī and Lakshmī, and its own cult of Padmāvatī became quite vigorous at a slightly later date.

That the Mothers hovered between lower *(yoginī)* and higher *(devi)* divinities is proved by the fact that, barring the Śakti of Śiva, none became a definite cult object, though isolated images of Lakshmī (sometimes Ashṭa-Lakshmī, including Gajalakshmī, corresponding to the eight Śaktis of Vishṇu, as in the *Padma Puraṇa)*, Sarasvatī, Gaṅgā, Yamunā and other female deities are found here and there all over India (*e.g.*, in the Haihaya monuments). And this is natural because the fame of most of them rested on the assistance they rendered to Durgā, Chaṇḍikā or Ambikā in her struggles against the demons that threatened heavenly peace. It is very likely also that the Śiva-Śakti cult was a federation of two originally independent faiths and Durgā had already been so separately extolled that it was not possible to bring her into a completely subservient relation to Śiva. This will explain why in the *Mahābhārata* she appears at one place as the wife of Nārāyaṇa and at another as the wife of Śiva, and in the *Durgā-saptaśatī* of the *Mārkaṇḍeya Purāṇa* she is more a Vaishṇavī Śakti than a Śaivite one, though her names betoken her Śaivite association. Sarasvatī and Lakshmī, though widely worshipped as the respective patrons of learning and riches, practically remained wives of Brahmā and Vishṇu in Brahmanism. It is really in the heterodox systems of Jainism and Mahāyāna Buddhism that Sarasvatī attained greater independence and evolved many forms and was surrounded by personified abstractions. In Jainism Lakshmī too enjoyed a similar independent status. That Sarasvatī should appear both as a śāsanadevatā and as an independent deity may provide a clue to the exact position of these minor goddesses. Like the Yakshas they never rose to the highest position in any pantheon and yet they supplied artistic models for decorating temples and even providing loci of minor veneration. Gaṇeśa, for instance, hovered between a yaksha and a deity, as when Śrī Vināyaka the deity became reduced to Gaṇeśa the yaksha door-keeper with sounding bells, both in India and outside. Kubera also hovered between a major deity (one of the *dikpālas)* and a yaksha-chief.

The name 'Mothers' had apparently something to do with the placing of children on the laps or by the side of these mother-goddesses, who were virtually looked upon as the guardian angels of small children. The Mahāyāna deity Hārītī, it may be remembered, had a similar figure and function. She had ectypes in Manasā, the serpent goddess, and also Śītalā, the goddess of small-pox, who begins to figure towards the end of this period in temples in Kāthiāwād and Gujarāt *(e.g.* at Sejakpur and Sunak). Later on the goddess Shashṭhī took over this protective function from the Mothers. The occasional absence of a child on Sarasvatī's knee or side may be responsible for the association of 'six' with the protection of children, unless we believe that Shashṭhī has something to do with the six Kṛittikās that suckled the infant Kārttikeya.

Probably the name 'Mothers' was euphemistic when extended to the Yoginīs and was designed to cover up their destructive or terrible aspect (as in the cases of Śiva and Gaṇeśa) as befitting agencies that came into existence to aid a supreme female deity in battle and to assist her in preventing the generation of new demons out of the blood-drops of the slain by licking these up, as represented in the Andhakavadha scene at Tewār. Their number was rather fluid, but when the lesser Śaktis were added to the major ones it swelled to seven or eight, and then, by the usual process of multiplication, it rose from eight to sixteen, and then to sixty-four or more in Puranic and even Jain accounts, and they were then considered as Yoginīs. In the Chausāṇṭ Yoginī temple at Bherāghāt on the Narmadā near Jubbulpore, where there is a circular colonnaded enclosure, are to be found together not only the sixty-four Yoginīs but also the eight Śaktis, three rivers, four other goddesses, Śiva and Gaṇeśa, thus making a total of eighty-one figures together with three more spaces at the entrances. At Khajurāho the sixty-four Yoginīs appear in an oblong temple, but in other places like Ranipur-Jural and Coimbatore such circular temples have been found and in Kālāhāndi there occurs the Surādā temple containing sixty-five cells. Many of these are hypaethral, which shows that the deities enshrined were of minor consideration in the devotion of men. The Bherāghāt figures have suffered, like other monuments, the fanatical fury of the iconoclasts; but most of them fortunately retain their names inscribed in the sixty-five peripheral chapels. A perusal of the names discloses the fact that they are not all canonical. Some were obviously incorporated from popular cult objects of the time and the locality, and some were actual or corrupted forms of Brahmanic originals. A comparison with the list given by Hemādri about three centuries later shows that there was no fixity in the names of the Yoginīs though their cult was fairly wide-spread. Even the eight Yoginīs now worshipped in Bengal have titles not to be found in Hemādri's list; in fact, the East Indian names of the sixty-four Yoginīs do not have any terribleness about them, being mostly names of Durgā herself, as the names in Hemādri's list have. Thus, barring the convention that the Yoginīs must be sixty-four, there is very little common in the different lists of names. What interests us in the Bherāghāt icons is the presence of Śrī-Teramvā, a Mahishamardinī figure with sixteen hands, and of Sarvatomukhī with a lotus under-seat containing the Tāntrik emblem of crossed triangles *(shaṭkoṇa)*, with the *bīja* word *Hrīṁ* in the centre. Images of Brahmā, Vishṇu, Sūrya, Gaṇeśa, Kārttikeya, some of the Divine Mothers, and Gaṅgā and Yamunā have been found in the ruins of the Bherāghāt temple, in the centre of which probably stood an Umā-Maheśvara group according to Coomaraswamy. It is probably at a later period that this Smārta method of combining the principal gods in the same sanctuary was adopted.

Once Śāktism became popular it was merely a question of time as to how exaggerated emphasis would be laid upon the diverse modes of divine manifestation. Thus Durgā might herself be conceived as many, and this gives us Nava-Durgā (of which the Nava-liṅgas of Kukkanur might be considered as the late male counterparts) or nine forms of the goddess known under different names. One set of such names—Śailaputrī, Brahmachāriṇī, Chaṇḍaghaṇṭā, Kūshmāṇḍā, Skandamātā, Kātyāyanī, Kālarātri, Mahāgaurī and Siddhidātrī—practically sketches her career and functions. Another better known set is composed of Ugrachaṇḍā, Prachaṇḍā, Chaṇḍogrā, Chaṇḍanāyikā, Chaṇḍā, Chaṇḍavatī, Chaṇḍarūpā, Atichaṇḍikā and Rudrachaṇḍā—all signifying the wrathful aspect of the deity. A rare image of Nava-Durgā in relief with an eighteen-handed central figure surrounded by eight sixteen-handed miniature figures was discovered at Porshā (Dinājpur) and is now in the Rājshāhi Museum. Nava-Durgā, Kālikā and Chaṇḍikā have been found enshrined in Jageśvara in Kumayun during this period. Similarly, just as Pārvatī was differentiated into Durgā, Chāmuṇḍā, Mahishāsuramardinī and Mahālakshmī, so also Chāmuṇḍā was herself viewed under the three forms of Karālī or Bhadrakālī, Kālabhadrā and Kālī or Mahākālī, and was endowed with various numbers of arms under different names. Reference has already been made to the diverse forms of Chāmuṇḍā in Bengal sculpture.

By the side of these major Śakti deities we have other goddesses like Jyeshṭhā, the elder sister of Lakshmī but associated with misfortune (Alakshmī), reference to whose temple is made in an eighth century inscription near Madurā. An inscribed four-handed Vāgīśvarī image of c. A.D. 940 from Nālandā, seated on a lion and tormenting a demon, is now in the Indian Museum, and another figure of the same goddess in octo-alloy, with eight hands, is in the Rājshāhi Museum. A little later than the period we are discussing came, in the wake of Tāntrik revival, the Daśa-Mahāvidyās—Kālī, Tārā, Shoḍaśī, Bhuvaneśvarī, Bhairavī, Chhinnamastā, Dhūmavatī, Bagalā Mātaṅgī and Kamalātmikā (Gaja-Lakshmī), obviously modelled on the ten *avatāras* of Vishṇu; but isolated deities like Kālī, Ugra-Tārā, Vindhyavāsinī, etc. came earlier and had other associates, both fierce and benign, like Pratyaṅgirā, Dhūmavatī or Dhūmrakālī, Lalitā, Tripurasundarī (often identified with Shoḍaśī), Rājarājeśvarī, etc. added at a later time.

It appears also that Kārttikeya was progressively losing contact with this Śakti group even though his Śakti (Kaumārī or Kārttikeyānī) forms one of the Mothers and he himself occasionally turns up in Seven-Mother slabs. Mentioned as Subrahmaṇya in the

Mānasāra, he still retained considerable popularity in the South under the titles of Velāyudha, Muruga, etc., specially with non-Brāhmaṇa classes, was assigned two wives—Vallī and Devasenā (or Devayānā)—and had many shrines dedicated to him. In the Gujarāt area too Kārttikeya or Mahāsena receives the homage of the Chaulukyas and at Ellora he finds lithic representation thrice. Judging by the Gurgi inscription, his image along with those of Umā, Umā with Śiva, Sarasvatī and Gaṇapati, was placed round a central image of Śiva in the area of the Gurgaj mound, where huge images of Durgā or Pārvatī have also been discovered. In the *toraṇa* removed to Rewa, Karttikeya and Gaṇeśa also figure with the Mothers, as do the major gods (Brahmā included) and the planets, in Śiva's marriage procession scene.

Gaṇeśa, however, retains and, in fact, improves upon his position; he not only accompanies the Mothers but also attends and imitates the dance of Śiva in sculptural representations and acts as a defender of the Brahmanical faith by guarding temples. Even a five-faced Gaṇeśa, in imitation of his five-faced *(pañchānana)* father, has been unearthed both in Orissa and in the ruins of Rāmpāl (Dacca). His figure has been found on the door lintel of one of the ruined temples at Saidābād in Kāshmir. No wonder that some terrible forms of Buddhistic deities should be represented as curbing his power in the shape of trampling upon his prostrate body (and sometimes that of his Śakti also)—Mahākāla, Aparājitā and Black Mañjuśrī being the most noted Mahāyānic oppressors of the elephant-headed god of the Brahmanical pantheon. It must be acknowledged, however, that Buddhism entertained an ambivalent attitude towards this deity, for it itself worshipped Vināyakas of different kinds. Similarly Bāla-Gaṇapati and the conch-shell symbol of some Gaṇeśa images betrayed occasional attempts at a rapprochement with Vaishṇavism, but they did not prove a very successful venture. His place in temples, however, was assured; he adorns the door lintel of practically every major god in Gujarāt —Śiva, Brahmā, Sūrya, Devī, etc.,—and also in Haihaya Śaiva temples, just as Gaja-Lakshmī did in many Chālukya temples.

Gaṇeśa's star of fortune became definitely ascendant towards the close of this period, for, under the name of Gaṇapati, he became a popular cult object, particularly in Western India, and had a distinct sect, the Gāṇapatyas, devoted to his special worship. With heads ranging from one to five and arms correspondingly increased, with one, two or more tusks with the trunk variously disposed, and with many of the ornaments, attitudes and even the shapeless liṅga-form (of red stone) borrowed from Śiva, Gaṇapati became the centre of a popular cult, open and esoteric, the rival of Śiva himself, and even superior to the other gods who sought his aid and approached and placated him when in distress. When the new fervour arose, there was a revival of the ancient number of six, of whom the five Śakti-Gaṇapatis are the most prominent, namely, the red four-armed Uchchhishṭa-Gaṇapati, the red ten-armed Mahā-Gaṇapati, the yellow six-armed Ūrddhva-Gaṇapati, the tawny-coloured six-armed Piṅgala-Gaṇapati, and the white four- or eight-armed Lakshmī Gaṇapati. Haridrā-Gaṇapati with yellow colour and four arms was also regarded as the supreme deity. In Ānandagiri's enumeration Navanīta, Svarṇa and Santāna Gaṇapatis replace Ūrddhva, Piṅgala and Lakshmī Gaṇapatis. It is probable that some of the names owe their origin to the materials with which the Gaṇapati figures were made—cream or butter *(navanīta)*, gold *(svarṇa)*, turmeric *(haridrā)*,—or to the degree of their yellowness. The devotees of these six forms formed esoteric sects. Theogonic speculations tried to give Gaṇapati a mystic origin out of Śiva, and Tāntrikism invested him with *yantras* and *mantras* suited to different purposes. The image of his Śakti, labelled as Śrī-Aiṅginī, as also his own image is to be found among the Bherāghāt icons and in the Indian Museum collection, and Gaṇeśa himself with his Gaṇas also finds sculptural representation. The five heads, as in Heramba-Gaṇapati, sometimes get separate forms under Buddhistic influence at a later time as in the Nṛitya Gaṇapati of Nepāl. In fact, images of Gaṇeśa with other Buddhistic influences, e.g. Bhūmisparśa-mudrā, are also known from other countries, which is not unnatural, seeing that latterly he became a Buddhistic loan deity. The *ashṭa-siddhis* came to be construed into his Śakti in Tāntrik belief. In the Navagraha slabs he occupies the extreme right position—just the reverse of what he does in the Saptamātṛikā slabs. His association with the Diggajas of the four cardinal points can be made out from the Ghaṭiyālā column near Jodhpur (with four Gaṇeśa images at the top facing the four quarters) with a dated inscription of the ninth century A.D., while in a slab from Sonarang (Bengal), Gaṇeśa is found sculptured on the right and the Saptamātṛikās on the left of a Sūrya temple. The Ghaṭiyālā figure installed in a market place perhaps marks his association with success in trade.

The end of this period virtually closes the origin of new divinities. Henceforward local variations, elaborations and fusions characterise the evolution of new forms. The most outstanding religious upheaval was furnished by the Tantras which necessitated an understanding with the deep-seated craving of the human heart and an acceptance of the female principle in religious worship. After

Mahāyānism had reached its zenith and given a new pantheon, a rapprochement with that cult was also found necessary, and when Buddhism degenerated and declined, its elements were utilised with suitable modifications to serve the needs of the newly absorbed Buddhist population. There was a fusion of Buddhistic and Brahmanical cults also and a revival of interest in the occult was responsible for the popularity of Gorakshanātha and other Siddhas. A new esoteric literature was born as a result of this new type of interest.

II. ICONOGRAPHY

1. *Śakti*

Images of Devī or Śakti, both of *Ugra* and *Saumya* types,[130] are met with in large numbers. Numerous eight- or ten-armed images of the Mahishāsuramardinī have been discovered in different parts of eastern India, and their principal type, with certain additional features, came to be the accepted iconic model of the composite clay image in the autumnal Durgā worship in Bengal. An image, unique of its kind, retrieved from a north Bengal village in the Dinājpur District, portrays in a very interesting manner the nine Durgās (*Nava-Durgā*);[131] the central figure of Mahishāsuramardinī is eighteen-armed with eight other sixteen-armed miniature figures of the same type grouped round it. The all-powerful and all-embracing character of the Divine Śakti is further emphasised by another unique stone image of the thirty-two-armed Devī engaged in combat with demons (not the buffalo-demon in particular), found in the said district; on the top part of its *prabhāvalī* are shown the miniature figures of Gaṇapati, Sūrya, Śiva, Vishṇu, and Brahmā.[132]

A four-armed standing figure of the goddess, of the *saumya* type, found in one of the rock-cut shrines of Ellora, exactly corresponds to the description of Pārvatī, one of the six varieties of Gaurī, *viz.*, Umā, Pārvatī, Śrī, Rambhā, Totalā and Tripurā, as described in the *Rūpamaṇḍana*. She holds in her four hands, from the lower right onwards (*i.e.* lower right, upper right, upper left and lower left), a rosary, Śivaliṅga, a miniature figure of Gaṇapati, and a water vessel, and has two pots of fire placed on her either side.[133] A comparison between this rare type of Devī image from Ellora, and a particular form of her four-armed standing figures of the mediaeval period commonly found in Bengal, will be of interest here. The latter shows her standing erect, with such attributes as a boon (*vara*) or pomegranate, a Śivaliṅga, a *tridaṇḍī* or a trident in her hands in the above order, and an iguana *(godhikā)* carved on the pedestal. There are different varieties of this type which can be dubbed Chaṇḍī on account of the *godhikā* on the pedestal of many of them (this animal had particular association with the story of Chaṇḍī and Kālaketu, current in Bengal). An inscribed stone image of the Devī, dated in the third regnal year of Lakshmaṇasena, now in the collection of the Dacca Museum, shows a couchant lion for her vehicle; she holds *vara, aṅkuśa, padma,* and *kamaṇḍalu* in her hands and like Gaja-Lakshmī, is being bathed by two elephants. The pedestal inscription describes her as Chaṇḍī; but Bhattasali denominates it as Bhuvaneśvarī on the authority of the *Śāradātilaka-tantra.*[134]

Separate images of the Devī of the *āsana* variety are comparatively rare, she being usually depicted sitting on the lap of her consort Śiva in such types of Śaiva images as Umā-Maheśvaramūrti discussed above. Several seated images, however, have been discovered in Bengal, and a few of them can be called Aparājitā, Mahālakshmī, etc., on the basis of various iconographic texts. A very interesting sculpture, found among the ruins of ancient Vikrampur (Dacca), shows a Śivaliṅga, "out of which emerges the half-length figure of a four-armed goddess, with her front hands in the *dhyāna-mudrā*, and the back right and left hands holding a rosary and a manuscript respectively"; Bhattasali identifies the image as that of Mahāmāyā or Tripura-Bhairavī.[135] The Mātṛikā group of images have been found in different parts of India, but the earliest of them does not go back to a period earlier than the Gupta. The Gangdhar stone inscription of Viśvavarman, of the time of Kumāra-gupta I, refers to the construction of the temples of the Divine Mothers, which are described as "terrible abodes' (*veśmātyugram*). The extant images of the Mātṛikās, however, with the exception of that of Chāmuṇḍā, do not indicate anything fierce or terrific; most of them are shown as exact female counterparts of their corresponding male divinities with the complete cognizances and attributes of the latter. Vārāhī and Chāmuṇḍī alone are different; the former, a sow-faced female seated on a buffalo, and the latter, an extremely emaciated figure with a scorpion mark on her shrunken belly, seated on a corpse (*pretāsanā*). To emphasise the mother-aspect, these goddesses are sometimes shown as carrying a suckling baby on their laps, and the Ellora Saptamātṛikā panel is a striking example of this type of Mātṛikā images. Figures of Vīrabhadra and Gaṇeśa are usually carved on either side of the row of the Mothers, for the myths describe them as their guardians. Chāmuṇḍā seems to have been one of the most important cult-goddesses in the Tāntrik pantheon, and this is proved by her several peculiar forms, such as Rūpavidyā, Siddha-Yogeśvarī and Danturā, whose images have been discovered in Bengal. An image of the last-mentioned aspect of Chāmuṇḍā, showing a two-armed goddess sitting on her haunches, found originally in a Burdwan village and now in the collection of the Vangiya Sahitya Parishat Museum, Calcutta, strikingly portrays the weird and the uncanny "with its bare canine teeth, rounded eyes, ghastly smile, emaciated body, lean and pendulous breasts, sunken belly, and peculiar sitting posture".[136]

2. *Gaṇeśa*

Reference has been made above[137] to the different varieties of the images of Gaṇeśa. His standing and seated figures are usually four-armed, but when he is shown dancing, he is endowed with more hands. An eleventh century six-armed stone image of the god, hailing from north Bengal and now in the collection of the Indian Museum, shows him dancing on the back of his mount, attended by two other dancing figures, one on each side, playing on musical instruments; objects like the tusk, hatchet, rosary, blue lotus, pot of sweetmeat, etc. are displayed in his hands, and there is a bunch of mangoes carved on the top centre of the pointed stele. It is a finely carved sculpture, and the artist has handled the theme of a grotesque nature with great balance and sense of proportion.[138] Another rare type of Gaṇeśa is that with five heads and ten arms seated on the back of a roaring lion; this variety is described in the text as Heramba Gaṇapati. Several such figures of the late mediaeval period have been found in India, and one unearthed from the ruins of Rāmpāl (Dacca), contains on the upper part of its stele six other miniature figures of Gaṇeśa, perhaps the cult pictures of the six sub-divisions of the Gāṇapatya sect.[139] Another type of Gaṇeśa, mostly found in southern India, is the Unmatta-Uchchhishṭa variety in which the god is shown in company with his consort in a suggestive pose; several of its extant specimens are rather of an indelicate character.[140]

3. *Kārttikeya*

The South Indian images of Subrahmaṇya display a multiplicity of forms which are given various names in the Tāntrik and Āgamic texts; but most of these are late in point of date. The Ellora stone panel shows a four-armed figure of the god with a cock placed in his front left hand, and two goat-headed attendants, one standing on either side of him. The latter evidently stand for such mythological personalities as Negameśa or Hariṇigameśi. A late relief from Tirupparankunram temple in southern India represents a unique variety of Kārttikeya figure, *viz.* Devasenā-Kalyāṇasundara-mūrti, the theme of which is the marriage of Devasenā and Kārttikeya; it is evidently based on the Kalyāṇasundara-mūrti of Śiva, as the Nṛitya-Gaṇapati figures are modelled on his dancing types.[141]

4. *Sūrya*

The iconographic representation of Sūrya came to be far more elaborate in course of time and several accessories were added. The figures of Kuṇḍī bearing pen and ink-pot, on the proper right and of Daṇḍi holding a staff on the proper left, are already present in some late Gupta reliefs of Sūrya; the figures of several spouses of the god, such as Nikshubhā, Chhāyā, Saṁjñā or Rājñī, Suvarṇā and Suvarchasā, with the goddess Mahāśvetā and other attendants, are now depicted crowding round the main deity. The legs of not only the central figure but also of those of the various attendants, both male and female, are shown encased in some sort of leggings; but the long coat has completely disappeared, and the close covering of the upper part of the body is just suggested by some delicately carved lines on the torso and the arms. The lotus flowers held in the hands are not mere buds but fully blossomed ones shown parallel to the ears, and the seven horses are almost invariably represented on the chariot. The Sūrya image, found at Koṭālipāḍā (Faridpur) and now in the Vangiya Sahitya Parishat Museum, Calcutta, dated in the eleventh ventury A.D., is a representative specimen of such icons of northern India; but it contains such additional features as *agnı-kuṇḍas* carved on the *saptaratha* pedestal, from which issue lotus-flowers whereon the god and his principal attendants are standing. Another eleventh century stone relief of the god, procured from a Dinājpur village for the Rājshāhi Museum, shows a unique mode of representation; he is depicted six-armed, his natural hands hold two fully blossomed lotus flowers, the four added ones showing *vara, akshamālā, abhaya* and *kamaṇḍalu.* The *Viśvakarmāvatāra Śāstra* description of Dhātṛi, the first of the Ādityas in the Dvādaśāditya group of divinities, partially corresponds to this type; the former, however, is four-armed, the third pair of arms showing the *vara-* and *abhaya-mudrās* being omitted. Four-armed standing and seated Sūrya images, though rare, are not absolutely unknown in northern India. If a comparison is made between the normal two-armed Sūrya figure of the north with the same of the south, both belonging to the mediaeval period, some remarkable differences may be noticed; the nature of the most important among them seems to prove that the southern Sūrya figures did not come under any foreign influence, for their legs are always left bare.[142] Seated Sun images of the mediaeval period are comparatively rare, and an inscribed one, acquired from a Dinājpur village, is all the more interesting, for the pedestal inscription of the eleventh-twelfth century A.D. refers to the god as *samasta-rogāṇāṁ harttā* (remover of all diseases). Composite reliefs of the Sun-god from northern as well as southern India, combining in them the features of several members of the orthodox Brahmanical triad, are known. These sometimes are joint representations of Sūrya and Nārāyaṇa, or Sūrya and Śiva, and very rarely the attributes of Sūrya, Brahmā, Vishṇu and Śiva are all combined in a single iconographic motif. The eight-armed and three-headed figure in the Chidambaram temple, with Aruṇa and the seven horses carved on the pedestal, and his hands carrying such attributes as a conch-shell, a discus, a pair of lotus-buds, etc. evidently represents the last. The so-called Trimūrti figures found in Bundelkhand region are really typical combinations of Sūrya and Vishṇu, and are even sometimes described as Sūrya-Nārāyaṇa. A unique three-headed and ten-armed sculpture of the twelfth century A.D., found at a Rājshāhi village, typifies in a very characteristic manner the combined form of Sūrya and Śiva; its three faces—the central one placid, and the side ones terrific—, its ten hands holding such attributes as *śakti, khaṭvāṅga, nīlotpala, ḍamaru* and the usual lotuses, and other iconographic traits closely correspond to the description of Mārtaṇḍa-Bhairava given in the *Śāradātilaka-tantra.*[143] All these composite types of images perhaps show indirectly the part which the Sun-god played in the evolution of many of the god-concepts connected with several of the important Brahmanical cults.

Several mediaeval sculptures of eastern India, showing a rider with a drinking cup in his hand and accompanied by a host of followers, were at first wrongly described as those of Kalki. But they have now been correctly identified as those of Revanta, the son of Sūrya. Both of them are shown riding on horseback, but the distinctive feature of Revanta is that he should be shown a-hunting accompanied by a host of attendants. The *Bṛihat-saṁhitā* description of the god (*Revanto-śvārūḍho mṛigayā-krīḍādi-parivāraḥ*) gives us the correct clue to his identity, and several stone reliefs depicting him have been found in eastern India, mostly in Bengal. These represent him as a rider in company with male and female followers, two-armed, booted, holding in his left hand the reins of the horse and a drinking cup in his right hand; the artists even include among the accessories a retriever dog. The late mediaeval Ghāṭnagar (Dinājpur) basalt image of Revanta, however, does not follow the above description in all its details, and presents the god in a novel manner. The *Mārkaṇḍeya Purāṇa*[144] says that Revanta was made the lord of the Guhyakas by his father, and his special task was to deliver mortals in distress "amid the terrors of forests and other lonely places, of great conflagrations, of enemies and robbers"; the Ghāṭnagar relief shows the god engaged in combat with a band of robbers who were about to disturb the peaceful pursuits of the village people.[145]

5. *Navagrahas*

The worship of the Navagrahas was also of special importance in times of danger, and they were duly propitiated by means of *grahayāga* and *svastyayana* by different Hindu sectaries. So their images were in great demand throughout India and they were usually carved in a row on the lintel of the main sanctum of a Vaishṇava or a Śaiva temple. The Śiva temples of Bhuvaneśvara (Orissa) bear this feature. Sometimes these are also shown on the *prabhā* of other cult divinities. Separate representations of these deities are, however, very rare, and the presence of two of them, Chandra and Bṛihaspati, among the basement reliefs on the main mound at Pāhārpur, are of great iconographic value.[146] The Navagraha slab in the collection of the Asutosh Museum, Calcutta University, is a very fine sculpture; it shows the nine so-called planets: Ravi, Soma, Maṅgala, Budha, Bṛihaspati, Śukra, Śani, Rāhu, and Ketu, standing side by side on lotus pedestals, holding their respective attributes in their hands with Gaṇeśa in the front of the row, and their respective *lāñchchhanas* carved below.[147] The big Navagraha slab, which served originally as the lintel piece of the Sun temple at Konārak (Orissa), shows the deities as seated ones.

(G) THE PARSIS[147a]

Numerically, the Parsi Community forms an almost insignificant element in the Indian population. But it deserves an honoured place in Indian history, chiefly for two reasons. In the first place, it is the only living remnant of Zoroastrianism,—a splendid culture and civilisation of ancient times, which has very nearly vanished from its homeland, and is to be found almost exclusively in Western India and the Bombay State. The importance of this point is further enhanced by the fact that Zoroastrianism is closely associated with the Vedic Culture of India to which detailed reference has been made in Vol. I.[148] Secondly, the Parsi Community has furnished quite a large number of eminent men—leaders in politics, and captains of trade, industry, and commerce—who have played a prominent role in the making of modern India.

Though the Parsis have made India their homeland, they have, like the Muslims, carefully preserved their separate entity. But unlike the Muslims they have not increased their ranks by local conversion and have no association—ideological or spiritual—with any community outside the boundaries of their adopted land.

The Irānians—as the Parsis were known in old days—must have settled in India in small or large bands from time immemorial. But they were thoroughly absorbed by the Indian population, and have left no trace of their existence save in such elements of culture which India might have borrowed from them. The present Parsi Community in India represents one or more of the last waves of migration from Irān (Persia) after the conquest of the country by the Muslim Arabs.

The Sasanid King of Irān, Yazdagird III, was first defeated at Qadisiyya in A.D. 637 and his power was finally shattered in the battle of Nehawand in A.D. 641. That the Muslim occupation of their country, which followed this conquest, forced colonies of Zoroastrian Irānians to seek refuge in India, admits of no doubt. There is also a general agreement that the first batch of these emigrants settled at a town called Sanjān, situated some 90 miles to the north of Bombay. But considerable difference of opinion exists about the date of their arrival.

A Persian poem, *Qissa-i-Sanjān,* composed by Bahman Kaykobād Sanjānā about the year A.D. 1600, recounts the tale of the wandering of the band of Irānians who ultimately settled at Sanjān. The author does not give any specific date, but mentions the duration of the stay of the emigrants in different places, mostly in round numbers. It would follow from this that the emigrants arrived at Diu in Kāthiāwād about A.D. 806, and after staying there for 19 years, settled at Sanjān in A.D. 825. But most scholars refuse to take the poem as historical and regard it as merely a figment of fancy.[149]

Dastur Aspandiārjī Kamdin, in a small book, published in A.D. 1826, gives a specific date, *Saṁvat* 772 (= A.D. 716), for the settlement of the Irānians at Sanjān. It is possible that he relied upon a much older tradition. Unfortunately the details about month and *tithi,* given along with the date, do not fit this year. Besides, the date A.D. 716 seems to be too early, if we are to believe in the Irānian tradition that the emigrants wandered for a considerable period in Irān before leaving for India. Hodivala, who has considered the whole question in great detail, suggests that the figure for the year is really 992, and as 9 and 7 were written very much alike such a confusion may be easily explained. The main support of his argument is that the details of the date given fit in with the year 992.[150] So it would appear that Hodivala's suggestion might be accepted and the date of the first Parsi settlement in India (at Sanjān) may, therefore, be provisionally fixed at *Saṁvat* 992 (= A.D. 936).

The earliest positive date for the settlement of these Irānian emigrants in India is furnished by two inscriptions found in Kānheri caves.[151] These record the names of two parties of Irānian tourists who had visited the caves, and like many modern visitors, chiselled their names on the rocks. The first inscription gives the names of seventeen men, and the second, of ten men, including four of the first; and these are dated respectively in A.D. 999 and 1021. The script as well as the language of both the inscriptions is Pahlavi and the personal names are, without exception, purely Irānian. As the Parsis in India freely adopted Hindu names, it has been argued that the arrival of the Irānians in India could not have been very old at the time the inscriptions were engraved. This in a way supports the date A.D. 936 suggested above.

The Parsi tradition mentions that the ruler who gave permission to the first emigrants to settle at Sanjān was named Jādi Rāṇā. According to the *Qissa-i-Sanjān,* he belonged to the race of the 'Shāhrāyas'. Neither the name nor the race is otherwise known. But here, again, Hodivala[152] suggests that the original word *Shāhrāyān* is a misreading or mistake for Shilhārāyān, which denotes the Śilāhāras. This is quite plausible. In that case we may also accept his other suggestion that the king referred to was Vajjaḍa-deva. Vajjaḍa might easily become Jādi, and as the emigrants, fresh from Irān, would not like to address their benefactor as *'deva'*, which had in the Zoroastrian literature a meaning entirely the reverse of that which it bears in Sanskrit, they added the epithet *'Rāṇā'*.

The Śilāhāra king Anantadeva made a grant to 'Kharāsān-Maṇḍalī' in A.D. 1081. Hodivala suggests that this refers to the Parsi Community.[153] As the Parsi records always speak of the first emigrants as having "come from Khorāsān", it is a reasonable presumption that for some time after their arrival they were known as "Khorāsān-Maṇḍalī".

Hardly anything is known of the Parsis in India during the period under review. Their later history will be dealt with in a subsequent volume.

H. GENERAL DEVELOPMENT OF PHILOSOPHY

1. *The Bhāshyas*

We have traced in the preceding volumes the rise of heterodox religions which crystallised into Jainism and Buddhism, their development as great and powerful sects challenging the supremacy of the orthodox Brahmanical religion, their reaction upon the latter, and the resulting contest between various schools in the arena of philosophy. This battle of wits became acute between A.D. 600 and A.D. 1000. As Winternitz remarks:[154] "The second half of the seventh and the first half of the eighth century A.D. was a period of lively philosophical disputes. Kumārila, the great Mīmāṁsā philosopher and representative of Brahmanical orthodoxy, attacked the Buddhist and Jinistic logicians, including among the last-named the prominent teachers Samantabhadra and Akalaṅka, whilst Prabhāchandra and Vidyānanda defended their co-religionists against Kumārila."

The intellectual war that was waged found expression not so much in new writings as in exegeses on old ones. It was now the period of *bhāshyas* or expositions of the *sūtras.* Less important commentaries and expository summaries were also written and bore the titles of *vṛittis, kārikās,* etc., besides the general name of *ṭīkā.*[155]

2. *Orthodox and Heterodox Schools*

Much of the philosophical discussion turned on the two main points at issue between the orthodox and heterodox schools. Heterodoxy challenged the authority of the Vedas as a source of knowledge. But, asked orthodoxy, what was its own position? The word of Buddha or of Mahāvīra was regarded as infallible and sacrosanct. But if the word of human teachers can be invested with such sanctity and infallibility, the Vedas, which are not attributed to any human authorship, must be regarded as a more authoritative source of knowledge. In popular debates and in sober arguments, this point was hammered into the minds of men with continued application and vigour.

Not only in epistemology, but in ontology also, heterodoxy had its weak points. Buddhism denied, in some form or other, a permanent soul and a permanent world. If everything was momentary as the Buddhists asserted, then what are we to deal with? And if the soul was but a stream of consciousness, if there was no permanent substance behind the changing states and processes of consciousness, whose salvation is philosophy to think of? And if, again, no definite statement — no definite affirmation or denial — about anything could be made, as the Jains said, then also how was a philosophy possible at all? Again, the Buddhist theory of the impermanance of the soul and the theory of *karma* (action) and transmigration conflicted with each other. If there was no soul that endures, to whom does *karma* cling and who is it that migrates from body to body and is born again and again? Thus the affirmations and denials of heterodoxy both contained weak points; and the battery of orthodox arguments continued to be directed against them for centuries after Buddha.

That orthodoxy eventually overcame its enemy on these points is a fact. But the heterodox thinkers developed a powerful logic—an organon of thought and debate — which could not be brushed aside. It was assimilated by those who opposed its discoverers. The development of logic in orthodox schools was considerably influenced by Jain and Buddhist writers on the subject.

It was not in logic alone that heterodoxy vanquished its victor. In metaphysics, too, its gifts were very great and largely accepted by its victor, though in a modified form. The Buddhist theory of extreme idealism and the doctrine that all is ultimately a void (*śūnya*) influenced the philosophy of the great Vedāntist, Śaṅkara, to such an extent that later critics of Śaṅkara did not hesitate to dub him as a 'Buddhist in disguise', even though he had criticised the Buddhists in his commentary on the *Vedānta-sūtras*.

Though the germs of the theory of *karma* and transmigration can be traced as early as the Upanishads, its fuller development owes a good deal to Jain-Buddhist thinkers. And a popular, though somewhat fanciful, shape was given to it in the Jātaka stories of Buddha.

We cannot attempt an exhaustive catalogue of the many ways in which the Jain and Buddhist thinkers have influenced the philosophy of the land. But there is one thing which ought to be emphasised. Their ethics have considerably influenced — may we add, and improved—the ethics of the orthodox fold. The doctrine of *ahiṁsā* or non-injury (non-violence) to the animal world is specifically a Jain-Buddhist doctrine though the Yoga system also accepts it as one of the forbearances. They regarded pure life and pure thought as a higher religion and morality than mere ablutions in water or offerings in fire. The theory of the brotherhood of man is another of their contributions. Monastic life received a new valuation and new impetus at their hands.

But with all its great contributions, heterodox philosophy had to own defeat by the end of the eighth century A.D. and, though not yet a spent force, had to be satisfied henceforth with an inferior place assigned to it.

3. *Vedānta's Bid for Supremacy*

When heterodox philosophy was a power to reckon with, all the orthodox philosophies had a common cause to fight for and they were allies. But when heterodoxy began to sink beneath the surface and was ousted from learned societies, these allies began to fall out among themselves. The differences between them were not absent before; but they were overlooked and sidetracked in face of a common enemy. When that enemy was crushed, these differences came to the forefront. The Sūtras of Vedānta attempted to refute every other system, either orthodox or heterodox, including even such minor philosophies as the doctrines of the Pāñcharātra school. Sāṅkhya-Yoga attacked Nyāya-Vaiśeshika and *vice versa.* The quarrel was mainly over the fundamentals of metaphysics. The Sāṅkhya theory of unconscious *prakṛiti* was assailed and its apparent or real godlessness received no less attention. On the other hand, the Nyāya-Vaiśeshika theory of atoms was equally castigated. The Sāṅkhya believed in what was called *satkāryavāda* or the theory that the effect was latent in the cause and was only a metamorphosis of it. The Nyāya opposed it with the theory that the effect was something *new* (*ārambhavāda*), not present in the cause. These disputes have been carried on till quite recent times.

While the different systems carried on their disputes in this way, the Mīmāṁsās made a bid for supremacy over all. They—the two Mīmāṁsās—had this advantage that they were more really loyal to the Vedas than the other systems; and the Vedas had established their right to be heard. The loyalty of Sāṅkhya-Yoga and Nyāya-Vaiśeshika to the Vedas was after all a lip-loyalty; for they did not squeeze their conclusions out of the Vedas. The Mīmāṁsās, both of them, on the other hand, were more thoroughly dependent on the Vedas, drew all their inspiration from that source and did not utter a line that was not supported by some text or other of the Vedas. This was a great advantage, specially when the Vedas, after the battle with heterodoxy, were again rehabilitated in popular esteem. To this must be added the fact that able and famous professors of these philosophies like Kumārila and Śaṅkara toured the whole country, from east to west and north to south, threw out a general challenge to all scholars of rival schools to meet them in open debate and either to vanquish them or own defeat and accept their philosophy. Half historical and half mythical accounts of these peregrinations have been preserved, and these tend to show how the philosophies emanating from the Vedas eventually triumphed over all other philosophies and conquered the whole country. Of course, it was never a complete victory, for the rival systems of thought are still alive. But the Mīmāṁsās and their source, the Vedas, had won a great position and an immense prestige in the thought of the country.

Originally the two Mīmāṁsās, as we have seen before, spoke and preached like one philosophy and with one voice. But gradually there was a split between them over an issue which was accentuated in the philosophy of Śaṅkara. The Vedas speak of two things—action (*karma*) and meditation (*jñāna*)—and accordingly there are two distinguishable parts of the Vedas. The Upanishads (or Vedānta, *i.e.* the concluding portion of the Vedas) speak of meditation more than anything else. The question arose: were the works enjoined in the earlier part of the Vedas—the rites and ceremonies—necessary for all and at all times? Two extreme views were advocated. One was that they could never be avoided; so long as a man was in his body, *i.e.* until death, the duties enjoined upon a man according to his caste (*varṇa*) and the stage of life (*āśrama*) in which he was, must continue to be performed. The other view was that these duties were only hypothetically imperative, and were indicated as means to an end. If a man wanted to live a life of happiness here and of bliss hereafter, the works should be done. But if one felt no interest in these things, if he rather desired salvation from all bondage (or *moksha*), these duties were not binding on him. Such a man should renounce the world forthwith, cut off all earthly bonds, give up all works, and live the life of contemplation and of a hermit. There was also a third view according to which it was only in the last two of the four *āśramas* (stages of life), that meditation could exclude works. The duties prescribed in the Śāstras, rightly performed, cleansed the soul and prepared it for proper meditation and intimate illumination. The beauty of the whole thing was that texts from the Vedas could be cited for each one of the extreme views; and for the third also there were authoritative sources. It was not really a philosophical question; but it meant a difference and provoked a quarrel; and separated the *Uttara Mīmāṁsā* or Vedānta from its erstwhile ally, the *Pūrva Mīmāṁsā*.

The *Pūrva Mīmāṁsā* claimed that the essence of the Vedas was directions for works. As the Upanishads did not contain such directions (*vidhis*), or very few of them, they had only a secondary importance and the philosophy based on them was of inferior value.

But the Vedānta in some of its forms brought the quarrel to a head by professing a total disregard for the works of religion which the Mīmāṁsā supported. The cleavage between the two is nowhere so sharp as in the life and teachings of Śaṅkara, the author of a celebrated commentary (*bhāshya*) on the *Vedānta-sūtras*.

4. *The Philosophy of Śaṅkara:* (c. A.D. 788-820)[156]

There are certain points on which all Vedāntists must agree. The theory of *pramāṇa* or source of knowledge is one of them. Then, the apparent discrepancies in the texts of the Upanishads can and must be reconciled; and after such synthesis they yield but one philosophy, *viz.* that of Brahman as the Ultimate Reality. Regarding the evolution and dissolution of the world, too, there is little difference among Vedāntists. There is yet another point in which they are at one. It is the superiority of the Vedānta as a philosophy as against all other philosophies. But regarding the sectarian philosophies, such as that of Vaishṇavism or Śaivism, all Vedāntists have not agreed. If a Vedāntist belonged to some such sect, as many of the later Vedāntists did, then he would urge that Vedānta was consonant with the philosophy and worship of this sect. If a Vedāntist did not belong to any sect, he would look upon a sectarian philosophy as hostile to Vedānta and, therefore, as one which must not be countenanced.

On points on which all Vedāntists agree, Śaṅkara has little original to say. The most striking feature of his philosophy, however, as he wrings it out of the *sūtras* of Vedānta, is his extreme monism which makes Brahman alone real and the self and the world of things only an appearance, an illusion of the finite mind in its state of ignorance. All that we see around us and all that we feel, consist of such stuff as dreams are made of—a stupendous *Māyā* or *Illusion*. Brahman, the one Ultimate Reality, is only an existence, without any qualities by which it could be described. Brahman is pure consciousness; not a subject knowing an object, for there is nothing other than Brahman of which Brahman could be conscious. In our ordinary knowledge there is the relation between a subject that knows and an object that is known. In Brahman's consciousness, however, such a relation was not possible; for, there was nothing that could be an object of thought to Brahman. And the *Māyā*, by which a world of things and selves was fabricated, was neither an existence nor a non-existence and was, therefore, indescribable.

Śaṅkara stands out as a notable milestone in the progress of Vedāntic thought. His style is easy and persuasive; but his personality was more persuasive and imposing. We are told by tradition and by his admiring biographers that he travelled through the length and breadth of the country, met all kinds of philosophers and pseudo-philosophers—even those who practised human sacrifices—and vanquished them all in debate, and thus spread his philosophy far and wide. He established sanctuaries in distant parts of the country, and placed some of his ablest and most devoted disciples in charge of them to propagate his philosophy from there. From philosophy it grew into a missionary movement which has not yet died. There are still well-known sanctuaries associated with the name of Śaṅkara which continued to be centres of Vedānta culture.

In his travels, Śaṅkara gained many disciples, sometimes directly by persuasion, and sometimes indirectly by defeating rivals in debate. One of the more famous of those disciples was Maṇḍana Miśra,[167] a staunch follower of the Pūrva Mīmāṁsā. Being defeated in a debate, at which his wife presided as judge, he took to the monastic life, assumed the new name of Sureśvara and wrote on the Vedānta on the same lines as Śaṅkara. How far the many anecdotes current about Śaṅkara may be regarded as historical it is, of course, difficult to say.

Śaṅkara's great claim to our recognition and to a permanent place in history lies in the fact that he created an extraordinary position for Vedānta. This is evident from the fact that he was followed by a number of able and distinguished writers on Vedānta; and gradually several different schools of Advaita Vedānta arose. What is more important is that writers belonging to established sects of religion, such as Vaishṇavism and Śaivism, began to utilise the Vedānta as the philosophical basis and background of their respective creeds. This is done by a subtle identification of the god of their creed with the Brahman of Vedānta. Thus a Vaishṇava like Rāmānuja would say that Brahman is no other than Vishṇu of his worship. Some like Vallabha would go so far as to say that Brahman is no other than Krishṇa of Vṛindāvana. And a Śaiva like Śrīkaṇṭha would say that Brahman is identical with Śiva of his worship, who is called by other names also, such as Paśupati, Rudra, etc. The actual development of these schools, however, takes us beyond A.D. 1000. The only notable commentator on the *Brahmasūtra*, other than Śaṅkara, falling within this period, is Bhāskara who taught the *Bhedābheda* doctrine (co-existence of distinction and unity in intimate relation with each other in Brahman) and severely criticised the *māyāvāda* of Advaita Vedānta. The period also saw the origin and development of the important philosophical School of

Kāshmir Śaivism, known as the Trika system, which, in spite of its theistic tendency, gradually leaned towards Advaitism.

1. Vol. III, Ch. XVIII—A.

1a. Tāranātha surveys the career of the religion in these words: There appeared more than half of the eighty-four famous Buddhist Āchāryas who had gained the *Siddhi,* after the time of Dharmakīrti down to the time of king Chaṇaka. At the time when the six jewels (Hiuen Tsang speaks of four luminaries, *viz.* Aśvaghosha, Āryadeva, Nāgārjuna and Kumāralabdha, see Watters, I, p. 245; Tāranātha perhaps added Asaṅga and Vasubandhu) stayed on earth, the Mahāyāna Āchāryas were very scholarly and apart from the fact that the monks were excellent, the number of Śrāvakayānists was much higher. Starting from this time on, the teachings growing weaker and weaker went down in a short time in the south, although in other countries it declined gradually. During the time of the seven Pālas, the religion was widely spread in Magadha, Bengal, Oḍiviśa and the other border countries and in Kāshmir. In other countries, except a few, it did not exist; in Nepāl it was much spread. In these countries the Mantrayāna and Mahāyāna were much spread; there also existed a great many Śrāvaka sects. See Schiefner, *Geschichte des Buddhismus,* 201-2.

2. Its Sanskrit version has also been discovered in Eastern Turkestan.
3. The *parittās* mentioned in the *Milindapañha* (150-51) are Ratanasutta, Khandhaparittā, Moraparittā, Dhajaggaparittā, Āṭānāṭiyaparittā, and Aṅgulimālaparittā.
4. Tāranātha, 275.
5. *Lalitavistara,* 2; *sarva-Bodhisattva-dhāraṇī-pratibhāna pratilabdhaiḥ sarva Bodhisattva-dhāraṇī-pratilabdhaiḥ.*
6. *Sandhinirmochanasūtra,* 124; *Śruta-dhāraṇī. Samādhirāja-sūtra* (p. 531) also calls itself a *Dhāraṇī.*
7. *Kāraṇḍavyūha,* ch. vii; *Taiś-ch-āpi Tathāgatair-iyam dhāraṇim bhāsitum-ārabdhaḥ.... Omchale chule chule svāhā.*
8. *Suvarṇaprabhāsa-sūtra,* Chs. XI, XII.
9. *Saddharmapuṇḍarīka,* 396, 477.
10. *Gilgit Manuscripts* by Dr. N. Dutt, I. 44.
11. Very likely *Maṇi* represents *Prajñā,* the producer of Tathāgata, placed on Padma, the Avalokiteśvara, or *Maṇi* may mean *Vajra,* the *Bodhichitta.*
12. *Guhyasamāja,* 2.
13. *Mañjuśrīmūlakalpa,* 508.
14. *Ibid,* 647-48.
15. See Avalon, *Principles of Tantra,* 324.
16. There has been some controversy over the date of composition of the *Mañjuśrīmūlakalpa* between Dr. Benoytosh Bhattacharyya and Prof. Winternitz, the former holding the opinion that the original form of this text was much shorter and was composed about the second century A.D., while the latter was inclined to the view that its composition should be placed in the sixth or seventh century A.D. The *Mañjuśrīmūlakalpa* in its present form must have been composed about the eighth century A.D., as it gives an account of king Gopāla's accession to the throne but does not refer to the activities of Dharmapāla or Devapāla. The word "Mahīpāla" occurs in two stanzas. Some provincial dialects as also some places in Bengal and Assam which became noted at a later period as most suitable for secret yogic practices are also mentioned in this text.
17. *Guhyasamāja,* 93-4. The *Guhyasamāja* is mentioned by Śāntideva (seventh century A.D.) in his *Śikshāsamuchchaya,* and by Indrabhūti in his *Jñānasiddhi.* It is listed as one of the texts of the Vajra School (Pāli Vājiriyas) in the *Nikāya Saṁgraha,* a Sinhalese work of the fourteenth century.
18. It is very likely that the Bengali artists called Paṭuyās still maintain the traditions of the *Mañjuśrīmūlakalpa.*
19. *Guhyasamāja,* 93-4.
20. *Ibid,* 87-8.
21. Schiefner, 20.
22. See *Guhyasamāja,* Intro. xiii and Text, 120.
23. See Intro. xi and Text Ch. VII.
24. See e.g., his Intro. xi; "place it (the hand of Śakti) on the hand of the dis-

ciple." The hand here is not of the Śakti but of the Guru. See 161.

25. *Guhyasamāja*, Ch. VII.
Sarva-kām-opabhogaiś=cha sevyamānair=yathechchhataḥ
Anena khalu yogena laghu Buddhatvam-āpnuyāt
This stanza should be read in the same light as the following stanza of the *Mādhyamika-Kārikā* (Ch. XXV, 19).
Na saṁsārasya nirvāṇāt kim-chid=asti viśeshaṇam
Na nirvāṇasya saṁsārāt kim-chid=asti viśeshaṇam
In other words a Bodhisattva should try to realise that there is not the slightest difference between *nirvāṇa* and *saṁsāra* (phenomenal world) as the latter is only an imaginary superimposition on the former. This superimposition appears only to the unwise and not to the fully enlightened, the Buddha. The *Guhyasamāja*, on the basis of this identity of *nirvāṇa* and *saṁsāra*, regards the enjoyment of *saṁsāra* as not harmful so long as one does not distinguish *saṁsāra* from the *nirvāṇa*.
26. *Guhyasamāja*, 37.
27. *Ibid*, 6.
28. *Ibid*, 129.
29. *Ibid*, 137.
30. *Sādhanamālā*, II, Intro., xli.
31. *Guhyasamāja*, 2-3.
32. *Ibid*, 137.
33. See Indrabhūti, *Jñānasiddhi*, Ch. II.
34. Vidyabhusana, *Indian Logic*, 321-22.
35. *Tāranātha*, 275.
36. *Mystic Tales of Lāmā Tārānātha*, 11.
37. There were more than one Dārika, and the Dārika initiated by Lui-Pā was different from the Dārika of *Dohākosha*.
38. Cf. B. C. Sen, *Some Hist. Aspects of the Ins. of Bengal*, 201; Sircar, *Sel. Ins.*, 377: Mandasor stone ins. of the time of Nara-varman (A.D. 404).
39. See *Sādhanamālā*, Intro. xlviii.
40. G.O.S. No. XLIV.
41. G.O.S. No. XLIV.
42. *Sādhanamālā*, 353.
43. See *Sādhanamālā*, II, Intro. 60.
44. This Līlāvajra should be distinguished from Lalitavajra's disciple Līlāvajra (Tāranātha, 191) who lived about the seventh or eighth century.
45. See above, p. 43f.
46. Cf. *Mañjuśrīmūlakalpa*, 631.
47. Cf. *Pag-sam-jon-zang*, 111.
48. Waddell, *Buddhism of Tibet*, 31.
49. *Tattva-saṁgraha*, (G.O.S. Nos. XXX, XXXI), 184.
50. This confirms the statement about the propagation of these texts occurring in the *Ashṭasāhasrikā* (225).
51. His colophon to the commentary (*Āloka*, 563-64, G.O.S.) corroborates the statement of Tāranātha.
52. *Tāranātha*, 232, 243.
53. Commentary on Sarvajñamitra's *Sragdharāstotra*, 50.
54. *Bṛihat-svayambhū-purāṇa*, 320-21.
55. Tāranātha, 229.
56. Tāranātha, 211.
57. Cf. Ch. XII.
58. *EI*, XXI. 97.
59. See p. 51.
60. See Waddell, *op. cit.*, 33.
61. Tāranātha, 221.
62. The formula is '*Ye dharmā hetu-prabhavā hetuṁ teshāṁ tathāgato hyavadat, teshāṁ cha yo nirodha evaṁ vādī mahāśramaṇaḥ*'. It contains one of the principal maxims of Buddhism and is very frequently found engraved on different parts of the mediaeval Buddha and Bodhisattva reliefs.
63. R. D. Banerji, *EISMS*, Pl. XXIX (a); B. M. Barua, *Bharhut*. III, Pl. XLVII.
64. *Sādhanamālā*, I, Nos. 3-5, pp. 18-25; II, Pl. I.
65. For these crowned Buddhas, cf. R. D. Banerji, *op. cit.*, Pls. XVII (b), XXI (c), XXII (b) & (c), XXIII (b), XXIV (c), XXVI (d) etc.
N. G. Majumdar identified them as Ādi-Buddha figures, *V.R.S. Annual Report*

1926-27; but A. K. Coomaraswamy challenged this interpretation, *JRAS,* 1928, 837, Pl. V, fig. 8.
66. See above, Vol. III, 393.
67. B. T. Bhattacharyya, *Indian Buddhist Iconography,* 34, Pl. XVIII a.
68. R. D. Banerji, *op. cit.,* Pl. XXXIV, fig. (a); for the four and six-armed figures of Lokeśvara, cf. *ibid,* pls. XII (a) VIII (a) and (d). The four-armed types in the collection of the Patna Museum hail from the interior of the Cuttack district of Orissa.
69. *DHI,* 116, 370-71; the *ashṭanidhis* are the concrete manifestations of the Padminī-vidyā, of which Śrī or Lakshmī was the presiding deity.
70. The description of the Brahmanical goddess Tārā as given in Brahmānanda's *Tārārahasya* and Kṛishṇānanda Āgamavāgīśa's *Tantrasāra* exactly corresponds to the above; B. T. Bhattacharyya, *op. cit.,* 77.
71. B. T. Bhattacharyya, *op. cit.,* 107, pl. XXXII (e).
72. These great fears as can be seen from this relief are *majjana-bhaya, dasyu-bhaya, siṁha-bhaya, sarpa-bhaya, agni-bhaya, yaksha-bhaya, bandhana-bhaya, hasti-bhaya;* these are depicted by miniature scenes in which the person in danger in each case is shown praying to the miniature replica of the goddess shown above.
73. B. T. Bhattacharyya, *op. cit.,* 123-26; 129-30, pl. XXXVI b; Bhattasali, *Iconography of Buddhist and Brahmanical Sculptures in the Dacca Museum,* 45-53, pl. XV-XVII.
74. Bhattacharyya, *op. cit.,* 90-2, pl. XXX (a).
75. R. D. Banerji, *EISMS,* pl. *XXXIX,* (b).
76. E. B. Havell, *Indian Sculpture and Painting,* pl. XIV.
77. B. T. Bhattacharyya, *op. cit.,* 97, pl. XXXI a.
78. For Bhattacharyya's refutation of the view that Vajravārāhī and Mārīchī were the two aspects of the same deity, cf. *op. cit.,* 93-4.
79. *AR.* 313.
80. Cf. Farquhar, *ORLI.* 218.
81. Bühler, *Indian sect of the Jainas,* 77. List of the *Gachchhas* is given on pp. 78 f.
82. *ORLI,* 213.
83. *AR.* 272.
84. See above, pp. 101 ff.
85. Above, pp. 19 ff; cf. also "Bappabhaṭṭisūricharita" in *Prabhāvakacharita* (SJS) pp. 85 ff.
86. Cf. Jain, *Jaina Siddhānta Bhāskara,* IX, No. 1, on Amoghavarsha.
87. See above, p. 15 ff.
88. Cf. Vaidya, *History of Medieval Hindu India,* III. 409; Sharma, *Jainism and Karnatak Culture,* 25.
89. Saletore, *Medieval Jainism,* 42 ff.
90. Fleet, *IA,* VI. 34.
91. Upadhye, *NIA,* II. 132 f; Saletore, *JBHS,* VI. 10-33.
92. See above, p. 181.
93. Some writers have taken these Jinasenas to be identical. But the names of their patrons and the different dates of composition prove them to be distinct persons separated by years.
94. This and the following two paragraphs are based on Dr. Handiqui's excellent monograph, *Yaśastilaka and Indian Culture,* especially Chs. 1, 6, 9, 10 and 13.
95. Cf. *IA,* VIII. 106; Rice, *Mysore and Coorg from inscriptions,* 203.
96. *IA,* XI. 248.
97. Nahar, *Jaina-lekha-saṁgraha,* III. 164.
98. The writer is indebted to Dr. A. N. Upadhye and Prof. H. D. Velankar for having gone through the section on Jainism and making a number of suggestions.
99. Vol. II, p. 420.
100. See pp. 28, 61, 89, 122, 138, 146, etc.
101. There are other names also such as Shaḍardha-śāstra.
102. According to *Rājataraṅgiṇī* Bhaṭṭa Kallaṭa, a pupil of Vasugupta, was a contemporary of Avantivarman who ruled from A.D. 855 to 883.
103. Abhinavagupta's *Paramārthasāra,* vv. 12-13; cf. *JRAS,* 1910. 723.
104. *Ibid,* 728.
105. Cf. *Sarva-darśana-saṁgraha* of Mādhavāchārya. Tr. by Cowell and Gough, p. 136.
106. *Paramārthasāra,* vv. 51-52; *JRAS,* 1910. 734.

107. For the philosophy of Śaṅkara, see below, section H. 4.
108. Vol. III, p. 435.
109. *HBR*, I. 436.
110. For such south Indian icons, cf. Rao, *op. cit.*, II. 273-92 & Pls.
111. These are described and illustrated by Rao, *EHI*, II. 108 kinds of dances carved on either side of a gopura in the Naṭarāja temple at Chidambaram correspond with 108 modes of dance as described in the *Bharata-Nāṭyaśāstra*. A book named *Tāṇḍavalakshaṇam,* published some years ago, contains a full idea about them.
112. Rao, *op. cit.*, II. 229.
113. A. K. Coomaraswamy, *Dance of Śiva*. Rao, *op. cit*, II. 231-52.
114. *HBR*, I. 443-44; N. K. Bhattasali, *Iconography of Buddhist and Brahmanical Sculptures in the Dacca Museum*, 112-13, pl. XLII. 2.
115. E. B. Havell, *Indian Sculpture and Painting*, 49-52, pl. XXII.
116. R. D. Banerji, *ASI*, 1911-12.
117. *JISOA*, XVIII. 54 ff.
118. Rao, *op. cit.*, II. 181-82, pl. XLIII.
119. N. K. Bhattasali, *op. cit.*, 118-20, pl. XLVII (a). *HBR*, I. 447.
120. For an elaborate description of the Kaṅkāla- and Bhikshāṭana-mūrtis of Śiva cf. Rao, *op. cit.*, II. 295-309, and pls.
121. For these types of images refer to Rao, *op. cit.*, I. Introduction, 44 pl. E.
122. See above, Vol. III. pp. 328 ff, 428 ff.
123. *JISOA*, I. 99-100, 103, pl. XXX.
124. For this ideology and the description of the image, see Rao, *op. cit.*, I. 248-49. Krishna Sastri who reproduces the Conjeevaram relief, is wrong in his description of this figure as Agni; *South Indian Gods and Goddesses,* 242-3, fig. 147.
125. Rao, *op. cit.*, I. 251-56, & pl. LXXII, fig. 2 and pl. LXXIII. Dattātreya concept of the god refers indirectly to a conscious attempt of harmonising the different cults.
126. *HBR*, I. 437, pl. III, fig. 12.
127. Van Guliq in his monograph on 'Hayagrīva' shows the migration of this divinity outside India.
128. For two interesting east Indian reliefs illustrative of this god, cf. *HBR*, I. 438, pls. V, 14 and 15.
129. Is a clue to this peculiar cognizance to be found in the *Śatapatha Brāhmaṇa* passages (XII. 7.1.3 and 14; XII. 7.2.3 and 7) which closely associate rams and ewes with Sarasvatī? N. K. Bhattasali refers to ram-fight and ram-sacrifice in Bengal on the occasion of the Sarasvatī-pūjā—*Cat.*, 188-190, pl. LXIII.
129a. *CII*, III. 74.
129b. R. C. Majumdar, *Inscriptions of Kambuja*, pp. 362 ff.
130. See above, Vol. III, 441 ff.
131. The nine Durgās are sometimes named, Ugrachaṇḍā, Rudrachaṇḍā, Prachaṇḍā, Chaṇḍogrā, Chaṇḍanāyikā, Chaṇḍā, Chaṇḍavatī, Chaṇḍarūpā, and Atichaṇḍikā. In the *Devīkavacha* of the *Devīmāhātmya* their names are Śailaputrī, Brahmachāriṇī, Chandraghaṇṭā, Kushmāṇḍā, Skandamātā, Kātyāyanī Kālarātri, Mahāgaurī and Siddhidātrī.
132. For these two Devī icons, cf. *HBR*, I. 453-54, pls. XIII, 35 and I, 5.
133. The *Rūpamaṇḍana* verse reads,—*Akshasūtraṁ Śivaṁ devaṁ gaṇādhyaksham kamaṇḍalum, Pakshadvaye 'gnikuṇḍe cha mūrtissā Pārvatī smṛitā*. Rao, *op. cit.*, I, pl. CVIII (fig. 1). App. C., *Pratimālakshaṇam*, p. 120.
134. N. K. Bhattasali, *Icon. Dacca Museum*, 202-3, pl. LXIX. *HBR*, I. 451, pl. LXXVII: 180.
135. *HBR*, I. 452, pl. VI. 19.
136. *HBR*, I. 455, Pl. XIV. 36. Several other figures of Dantura have been found in north Bengal.
137. See Vol. III, 444 f.
138. *ASI*, 1934-35, pl. XXIV (a).
139. Bhattasali, *op. cit.* 146-47, pl. LVI (b).
140. Rao, *Iconography,* 53-5, Pl. XI (fig. 2) & Pl. XII.
141. For the Ellora and Tirupparankunram reliefs of Kārttikeya, cf. Rao, *op. cit.*, I. 445, 448, Pl. CXXIV & CXXIX.
142. These differences have been enumerated by T.A.G. Rao, *op. cit.*, I. 311-12. Several South Indian Sūrya figures of late mediaeval period are illustrated by

him in Plates LXXXVII—LXXVIII, XCI, XCII & XCIV etc. of the same volume.

143. *Śāradātilaka-tantra, paṭala* xiv. For the Chidambaram relief, cf. H. Krishna Sastri, *South Indian Gods and Goddesses*, p. 236, fig. 144; for the Sūrya-Nārāyaṇa images cf. *IA*, 1918, 136 ff.; for the Mārttaṇḍa-Bhairava relief now in the Rājshāhi Museum, cf. *VRS*—Rep, 1929-30, 9-10, fig. 2.

144. *Mārkaṇḍeya Purāṇa*, CVIII, vv. 22-3.

145. *VRS*-Rep., 1927-28, 1, fig. 2. *HBR*, I. 459, pl. XVI. 42.

146. S. K. Saraswati, *Early Sculpture of Bengal*, 65-7, fig. 17; *MASI*, No. 55, 53-4, pl. XXX (b) and (c); Dikshit's identification of these two reliefs as Śiva and Brahmā is unacceptable.

147. *HBR*, I. 459, pl. XVII. 43.

147a. General references.

S. H. Hodivala, *Studies in Parsi History*. Bombay, 1920.

I. J. S. Taraporewala, The Exact Date of the Arrival of the Parsis in India (*Kane Festschrift*, pp. 506-514).

148. Ch. XI: "Indo-Irānian Relations".

149. Hodivala, *Studies in Parsi History*, 1-36.

150. *Ibid*, 70 ff.

151. The inscriptions have been translated in the *Zarathoshtī Abhyāsa*, III. 160; IV. 212.

152. *Op. cit.*, 74 ff.

153. *Pārsī Prakāśa*, I. 80.

154. *HIL*, II. 478.

155. Some writers of the period are:—

Buddhism: Śāntarakshita, Kamalaśīla, Dharmottara.

Jainism: Akalaṅka, Vidyānanda, Māṇikyanandī, Prabhāchandra.

Nyāya-Vaiśeshika: Vāchaspati, Jayanta, Udayana, and Śrīdhara.

Sāṅkhya: Probably the Sūtras themselves were finally redacted during this period. Gauḍapāda, the commentator of Sāṅkhya-Kārikā, belongs to this period.

Yoga: Vāchaspati, who wrote on other systems also.

Mīmāṁsā: Maṇḍanamiśra. Pārthasārathi, according to Dr. S. N. Das Gupta, flourished during this period.

Vedānta: Śaṅkara, Sureśvara (see footnote 157 below), Padmapāda, Ānandagiri, Sarvajñātmamuni, Bhāskara.

156. For various views about the date of Śaṅkarāchārya placing him between sixth and ninth century A.D., cf. *GIL*, III, 434, fn. 1. An inscription in Cambodia mentions the very interesting fact that Śivasoma, the *guru* of king Indra-varman, was a disciple of Bhagavān Śaṅkara who is presumably no other than Śaṅkarāchārya. As king Indra-varman ascended the throne in Śaka 799, Śaṅkarāchārya cannot be placed much earlier than the beginning of the ninth century A.D. Attention to this passage was drawn many years ago by Dr. R. C. Majumdar in a short note in *Indian Review* (Madras) and also by Prof. K. A. N. Sastri in *JOR*, XI. 285. But it has not yet received much attention from students of Indian Philosophy. The question has been recently discussed by Pandit B. Upadhyaya in his Hindi work entitled *"Śrī Śaṅkarāchārya"* (Ch. IV) (Hindustani Academy, Allahabad, 1950). But his arguments against the evidence of the Kambuja Ins. are unconvincing.

157. Among the disciples of Śaṅkara the most prominent are Sureśvara, the author of the famous *Vārttika*, and the *Naishkarmyasiddhi;* and Padmapāda, the author of the *Pañchapādika* which has been commented upon by Prakāśātman about A.D. 1200.

Scholars hold different views regarding the identity of Sureśvara and Maṇḍana.

CHAPTER XII

SOCIAL CONDITIONS

I. EDUCATION

1. *Courses of Study*

The old Smṛitis are completely silent about the methods and processes of primary education. But the later Smṛiti authorities introduce us to a new sacrament, significantly called *vidyārambha* (commencement of education), and alternatively *aksharasvīkṛiti* or *aksharābhyāsa* (training in the alphabet). According to them the initiation is to take place in the boy's fifth year, or at any rate before his investiture with the sacred thread. On an auspicious day, during the prescribed season, various deities and sages are to be worshipped to the accompaniment of offerings to the sacred fire, and honour shown to Brāhmaṇas. Then the teacher, seated facing the boy, is to give him his first lesson. According to an unnamed Smṛiti authority the curriculum is to consist of a primer (*mātṛikānyāsa*) and arithmetic (*gaṇita*).[1]

The ancient Brahmanical sacred law laid down a comprehensive scheme of Vedic education for students belonging to the first three classes of the Hindu social system. This is supplemented and modified in some important points by the later Smṛiti authorities who, however, often differ from one another. Thus as regards periods of study, perpetual studenthood is included by *Nāradīya Purāṇa*[2] and long-term studentship by *Āditya Purāṇa*[3] among practices to be eschewed in the Kali Age. On the other hand Medhātithi,[4] following the authority of Manu,[5] recognises two kinds of religious students, *viz.* the life-long student (*naishṭhika*), and the student who offers some return to his teacher at the end of his training term (*upakurvāṇa*).

As for the courses of study, it is strange to find the metrical *Vasishṭha-*, *Kātyāyana-*, and the *Laugākshi- Smṛitis*[6] strongly condemning the study of a Vedic recension other than one's own. This is quite unlike the catholic attitude of Medhātithi who requires[7] the pupil to study three, two, or one recensions of each of the three Vedas instead of an equal number of recensions of one single Veda. In the same context Medhātithi asks the student to undertake, in the interval between the end of his training-term and his marriage, a course of study in grammar and the like for helping him to understand the meaning of the Vedas. Turning to another point, we find Parāśara, Vyāsa, and Laghu-Vyāsa[8] insisting upon the comprehension of meaning of the Veda in place of mere reading of the text. Medhātithi,[9] however, argues that the comprehension of meaning follows naturally after hearing the text.

The Smṛiti authorities of this period, unlike those of the Gupta and preceding ages, seldom refer to technical education.[10] We have a concrete account of the training of a young merchant in the *Bhavisayattakahā,* a tenth-century Jain prose romance, but it is too exaggerated to be of much practical value. We learn from it, however, that young merchants of rich families used to be sent for residence at the teacher's house, and that not merely intellectual training but also the development of character was aimed at by the teacher.[11] We may refer likewise to Medhātithi's vivid and obviously authentic account[12] of the high technical equipment expected from a Vaiśya, the rudiments of which at least must have been acquired in boyhood from a master of the craft.[13]

Medhātithi[14] recommends the Vedic student, even after marriage, to go abroad for acquiring further proficiency in sciences (*śāstra*). The value of foreign travel as a means of general education is indicated by an expressive simile in *Kuṭṭanīmatam.*[15] Here it is averred that those who do not learn the dress, manners, and speech of other lands are like oxen without horns.

2. *Student Life*

Medhātithi insists upon the strict enforcement of the old Smṛiti law requiring a Vedic student to beg daily for his alms. The student, he says,[16] must not beg alms one day and live by them next day after mixing the same with butter and so forth; on the contrary, he is to beg for alms and partake of them the same day. For the period intervening between the end of his studentship-term and his marriage, the student, according to him,[17] shall continue to observe the vow of continence, though he need not observe other vows about abstaining from honey, meat, and so forth. A curious rule in the *Pālakāpyasaṁhitā*[18] which recalls the Smṛiti law relating to intermarriage between the *varṇas,* requires the Brāhmaṇa to teach three, the Kshatriya two, and the Vaiśya one *varṇa,* but forbids teaching even a virtuous Śūdra. A text of Yama[19] and *Kūrma Purāṇa*[20] condemn a teacher putting off instruction to a pupil who has lived with him for a year. As to the relations between the Vedic teacher and his pupil, the teacher's duty of using persuasion in the first instance and of applying the rod only in a mild form and in the last resort is inculcated by Medhātithi.[21] On the admissibility of receiving fees from pupils the Smṛiti authorities of this period are sharply divided in their views. Following the authority of Manu and Yājñavalkya, *Varāha Purāṇa*[22] includes the Brāhmaṇa teaching for a stipulated fee (*bhṛitakādhyāpaka*) among those who must not be invited at a funeral repast. On the other hand, *Matsya Purāṇa*[23] clearly sanctions the acceptance of a fee from a pupil beforehand by his teacher, for it says that one who does not teach a science (*vidyā*) or a craft (*śilpa*) after taking a fee (*mūlya*) shall be fined the whole of this sum by a just king. Medhātithi carefully distinguishes between the cases where teaching for a fee is allowable and those where it is not permitted. According to his view[24] teaching in return for a fee is blameworthy only when the payment is made a condition precedent for the teaching, while receiving instruction from a paid teacher is to be condemned only when the fee is paid by the student himself.[25] Elsewhere[26] Medhātithi declares that the conferring of some benefit upon the teacher by the pupil, prior to his return home after finishing his course of study (*samāvartana*), is not precluded by the text of Manu.[27]

As regards the service to be done by the Vedic pupil, Medhātithi[28] gives in different places examples of the kinds of household work to be performed by him as well as those forbidden to him.[29]

3. *Female Education*

Long before the present period the Smṛitis had denied the right or privilege of Vedic study to women. By progressively sanctioning early marriage of girls, they further destroyed the chances of higher education of women. How backward was the state of higher studies among girls in general during the present age is proved by the significant omission of all references to women teachers in the contemporary lexicographical works, and still more by the testimony of Medhātithi[30] to the general ignorance of the Sanskrit language among women. Nevertheless we have reasons to believe that women, including those not belonging to the higher classes, had some opportunities, as in the preceding Age, for liberal education as well as training in the fine arts. Rājaśekhara[31] refers, in justification of women's competence in poetical skill, to examples of princesses, of daughters of high officials (*mahāmātra*), of courtezans, and of concubines, who were poetesses as well as adepts in sciences (*śāstra*).[32] In Avantisundarī, the accomplished wife of Rājaśekhara, we have a striking illustration of a lady deeply learned in Sanskrit lore.[33] The dramas and prose romances of this Age also illustrate the contemporary state of learning among women. In the plays of Rājaśekhara,[33a] we find that court-ladies and even the queen's maids-in-waiting are capable of composing excellent Sanskrit and Prakrit verses. Again, we have a number of stories pointing to the skill of princesses in the fine arts, specially those of painting, music and versification.[34]

4. *Some Educational Centres and Establishments*

In Vikramaśila monastery, referred to above, we have an outstanding example of an advanced centre of learning like Nālandā and Valabhī in the seventh century A.D. We have also sufficient evidence to prove that there existed at this Age organised educational institutions which were founded and maintained by the people from the king down to humble individuals. To begin with Northern India, king Avantivarman of Kāshmir (A.D. 855/6-883) appointed a certain well-known teacher to expound grammar in a Vaishṇava temple founded by himself, while another ruler Yaśaskara (A.D. 939-948) founded a hostelry (*maṭha*) for the residence of students hailing from Āryadeśa for education.[35] Turning to Western India, we find a village-chief (*grāmapati*) in A.D. 945 granting lands to a community of scholars (*vidyārthisaṁgha*) and a dwelling house to the teacher of a school (*śālā*) which had been founded by a minister of the Rāshṭrakūṭa king Kṛishṇa III. It was further agreed that the Brāhmaṇas of this village were to contribute to the same scholarly body sums at stipulated rates on occasions of tonsure, investiture with the sacred thread and marriage, while the Parishat was to feast the same body whenever a feast was given to Brāhmaṇas. The school was afterwards rebuilt by another chief.[36] In South India the documents as usual are fuller than those of any other part of the country. A college (*vidyāsthāna*) at Bāhugrāma (modern Bāhur near Pondicherry) received an endowment of three villages from the Chief Minister of the Gaṅga-Pallava king Vijaya-Nṛipatuṅgavarman. At the time of the grant it was being continued by the residents of the village and it provided for the teaching of fourteen branches of learning.[37] At Kāñchīpuram there lay to the east of Rājasiṁheśvara temple a college (*kallūri*) which is referred to in an inscription of Rājendra Choḷa I.[38]

II. SOCIAL LIFE

1. *Social Divisions and Sub-divisions*

The old spirit of caste segregation is reflected in a passage of Medhātithi[39] which requires the dead bodies of Śūdras, Vaiśyas, Kshatriyas, and Brāhmanas to be carried out of the city by the south, west, north, and east gates respectively. As regards Brahmanical privileges, *Matsya Purāṇa*[40] prescribes for a Brāhmaṇa guilty of serious offences, banishment and branding with distinctive signs instead of the death penalty. Going a step further Medhātithi[41] forbids not only corporal punishment, but even a money-fine, to be inflicted upon a guilty Brāhmaṇa. From this he draws the corollary that if a Brāhmaṇa of learning, good conduct, and noble birth casually commits a crime, he should not be punished even with a fine for the first offence. Like Bṛihaspati and Kātyāyana before their time, Sumantu[42] forbids slaying of an *ātatāyī* (desperado) in the case of his being a Brāhmaṇa, while an un-named Smṛiti authority[43] includes the killing of *ātatāyī* Brāhmaṇas in righteous warfare among forbidden acts. Finally *Skanda Purāṇa*,[44] developing a line of thought in *Manu*,[45] observes that he who makes a gift in a straightforward fashion, without scrutiny (into the qualities of the Brāhmaṇa donee), satisfies the manes as well as the gods. While thus following the older precedent relating to Brahmanical immunities and privileges, the Smṛitis of this period equally pursue the older tradition in condemning Brāhmaṇas of particular types. Like Manu and Yājñavalkya, *Varāha Purāṇa*[46] gives long lists of Brāhmaṇas who, because of their physical appearance or occupation or conduct, must not be invited to a funeral repast. Among these is the *devalaka* (defined as a Brāhmaṇa worshipping a deity for money for three years) who, according to an un-named Smṛiti authority,[47] is so impure that a man touching him must purify himself by bathing with his clothes on. A list of six classes of Brāhmaṇas who, though born as such, are not Brāhmaṇas at all, occurs in *Śātātapa* quoted by Aparārka.[48] The Brāhmaṇas, again were degraded by residence in various foreign lands. As *Matsya Purāṇa*[49] says, Brāhmaṇas living in the *mlechchha* countries of Triśaṅku, Barbara, Oḍra (Orissa), Andhra (Telugu country), Ṭakka (Punjāb), Draviḍa (Tamil country), and Koṅkaṇa must not be invited to a funeral repast. What is more singular still, some Smṛiti authorities of this period do not exempt the *ātatāyī* Brāhmaṇa from being executed. Thus *Vṛiddha-Hārīta* and *Matsya Purāṇa* repeat Manu's famous text[50] condoning, if not enjoining, the killing even of a learned Brāhmaṇa who is an *ātatāyī*. More radical is the view of Viśvarūpa[51] who allows immunity not only to the slayer of an *ātatāyī* Brāhmaṇa, but also to one who has killed a Brāhmaṇa in battle, and one who has done so for money at the instigation of another.

We now turn to the class of Śūdras who stand at the other end of the social scale. The later Smṛitis follow and even surpass their predecessors in emphasising the social and religious disabilities of this class. Thus, according to a text of Parāśara,[52] eating a Śūdra's food, association with a Śūdra, sitting on the same seat with a Śūdra, and taking lessons from a Śūdra are acts dragging down even a 'blazing' person. An un-named Smṛiti[53] includes a Śūdra's cooking of food for Brāhmaṇas and the like in the list of practices forbidden by the consensus of virtuous men at the beginning of the Kali Age. A new departure is marked by a few texts which go to the length of declaring the touch or even sight of a Śūdra to be an act of pollution. Thus, according to an un-named Smṛiti,[54] a twice-born man, on seeing a Śūdra, must stop performance of his rite, while one touching him must take a bath. According to Gargya, a twice-born man, on touching a Śūdra or a Nishāda, must purify himself by ceremonial sipping of water.[54a] With these rules may be contrasted the texts of the ancient Gṛihya-sūtras and Dharma-sūtras which, by requiring the feet of Brāhmaṇa and other guests to be washed by Śūdras, do not at least contemplate the Śūdra to be an untouchable.[55] The old Smṛiti ban on Vedic teaching to Śūdras is repeated during this period by Laghu-Vyāsa,[56] who forbids the Veda to be taught in the vicinity of Śūdras. Similarly according to *Kāśīkhaṇḍa,*[57] a Brāhmaṇa must not let a Śūdra hear a Vedic *mantra.*

We may now turn to the views of Medhātithi which are sufficiently important and distinctive to be considered separately. Thus, as regards the Śūdra's social status, Medhātithi[58] observes that Manu's text, inculcating the Śūdra's divinely ordained duty of servitude and his incapacity for emancipation, is a pure declaration (*arthavada*), since another text of Manu declares the Śūdra eligible to release from servitude under special circumstances. Slavery, continues Medhātithi,[59] instead of being innate in the Śūdra, is voluntary with him, for he acquiesces in it only with a view to acquiring merit and, even then, he cannot be given away or pledged, unlike a bought or house-born slave. In fact, concludes Medhātithi, a Śūdra does nothing wrong if, being in possession of wealth, he lives without dependence upon a Brāhmaṇa. This discussion clearly shows that Medhātithi recognises the Śūdra's absolute right to personal freedom. What is more, Medhātithi[60] explains Manu's term *Śūdraśishya* (pupil of a Śūdra) to mean that Śūdras were sometimes teachers of grammar and other sciences. Dealing with the Śūdra's religious rights, Medhātithi, in the fashion of the *Mahābhārata,*[61] excludes the Śūdras from stages of life other than that of the householder. As he observes,[62] the Śūdra, by serving Brāhmaṇas and living as a householder, attains through service of Brāhmaṇas the fruit of all *āśramas* except salvation, which is the fruit of the fourth *āśrama* alone. As a householder the Śūdra is not entitled to perform *Smārta* rites of marriage, but he is not prohibited from uttering the name of a deity according to the views of revered teachers.[63] Again, according to Medhātithi,[64] while *Śrauta* rites are not open to a Śūdra, because of his ineligibility for initiation, there is no prohibition against his performing those that are prescribed for all in the Smṛitis. Referring to Manu, who censures a Brāhmaṇa for performing the *Agnihotra* rite with money obtained from a Śūdra, Medhātithi[65] observes that this does not apply to cases of compulsory rites already undertaken, and that it applies in fact only to the Fire-laying ceremony (*agnyādheya*) mentioned in the text. Similarly Viśvarūpa[66] observes that the naming ceremony and other sacraments are to be performed for Śūdras, but without *mantras*. In short, the Śūdra, according to Medhātithi, has limited duties corresponding to his limited rights. As he observes,[67] the Śūdra incurs sin only if he commits acts that are expressly prohibited to him; the Śūdra is not entitled to initiation and similar sacraments, and he incurs no sin for failure to bathe and fast and worship the deities.

The Smṛiti authors of this period deal also with various ethnic and professional groups known to the Brahmanical sacred law from ancient times as mixed castes. According to Medhātithi[68] sons of twice-born classes, born out of women of lower *varṇas* other than Śūdras, are entitled to the ceremony of initiation, and thence to all the privileges of a twice-born man. Among individual caste-groups the Ambashṭhas are declared by Uśanas and *Vaikhānasa-Smārtasūtra,* after Manu,[69] to be descended from the union of Brāhmaṇa males with Vaiśya females, and to have various occupations including agriculture and perhaps surgery. The Ambashṭhas are definitely included among Śūdra castes in *Bṛihaddharma Purāṇa.*[70] Uśanas[71] mentions a similar caste-group called Bhishak, which is supposed to be the offspring of Brāhmaṇa males and Kshatriya females, and to be occupied with the study of medicine, astronomy, astrology, and mathematics. The caste of Karaṇa, derived in the older Smṛitis[72] from the union of Vaiśya males with Śūdra women or in similar ways, is included among Śūdra castes in the *Bṛihaddharma Purāṇa* passage just cited. Again, the term Kāyastha, signifying a royal official in the earlier Smṛitis, inscriptions, and general literature,[73] occurs in *Vedavyāsa-Smṛiti*[74] in a list of Śūdra castes. The largest number of texts deals, naturally enough, with Chaṇḍālas known to the Smṛiti law from early times as occupying the lowest rank in the order of mixed castes. Reproducing the provisions of the older law, *Agni Purāṇa*[75] declares that Chaṇḍālas shall be employed for the execution of criminals, they shall wear the clothes of the dead, while they must live outside the village and must not touch others. Medhātithi[76] assigns to Sopākas (supposed to be born of Chaṇḍālas by Pukkaśa women) the tasks of executing criminals, of carrying away unclaimed corpses and taking their clothes, of eating cakes offered to the dead and the like. Like the earlier Smṛiti law, that of the present age lays down strict rules for preventing the pollution of other classes by the touch of Chaṇḍālas.[77] Medhātithi, again, gives examples of the distinctive signs[78] that should be borne by Chaṇḍālas when going about their business. Elsewhere[79] Medhātithi extends the rule about untouchability of Chaṇḍālas to other *pratiloma* castes such as the Sūta, the Māgadha, and the Āyogava. A new question taken up for discussion by the Smṛitis of this age, and testifying to an intensified spirit of caste exclusiveness, relates to the impurity of the Chaṇḍāla's shadow On the one hand Atri, Aṅgiras, Śātātapa, and *Auśanasa-Smṛiti*[80] go to the length of prescribing purification by bath for crossing a Chaṇḍāla's shadow, while Vyāghrapāda and Bṛihaspati[80a] would have the Chaṇḍāla kept beyond a prescribed distance. On the other hand, *Śivadharmottara*[81] says that the shadow of Chaṇḍālas or outcastes does not pollute a man. It is to the credit of Medhātithi[82] that he sides with the latter group of Smṛitis in declaring that the Chaṇḍāla's shadow cannot pollute the others.

In the Smṛitis of this period we also catch reflections of the Brahmanical view relating to social intercourse with various heterodox sects. It appears that not only the touch but even the sight of these sects was regarded by some authorities as involving pollution. Thus *Brahmāṇḍa Purāṇa*[83] enjoins that one should bathe with his clothes on after touching Śaivas, Pāśupatas, Lokāyatikas, and others. According to a similar text of *Shaṭtriṁśanmata,*[84] one should do the same if he touches Bauddhas, Pāśupatas, Laukāyatikas and others. Vṛiddha-Hārīta[85] enjoins purification by bath on touching Śaivas and on entering a Śaiva or a Buddhist temple. An unnamed Smṛiti[86] lays down that one should look at the Sun for purification on seeing Jains, Pāśupatas, Bauddhas, Kaulas and so forth, and should purify himself by bath on touching them.

Such are the scattered references found in the Smṛiti law of this period to the divisions and sub-divisions of the Hindu social system. In the contemporary historical records we have some evidence of the extent to which this law was observed in actual practice.[87] In so far as the Brāhmaṇas are concerned, the inscriptions of this period repeatedly describe the Brāhmaṇa donees of land as being devoted to the study of the Vedas and engaged in the performance of their religious rites. And yet it is remarkable that Brāhmaṇas occasionally followed occupations permitted only in times of distress or even positively degrading according to the

Smṛiti law.[88] Like the Brāhmaṇas, the Kshatriyas sometimes followed occupations not allowed to them ordinarily.[89] Other records introduce us to the various sub-divisions among the four fundamental castes. Thus as regards the Brāhmaṇas, the Nāgara (or Sapādalaksha) section of them has been traced with the help of inscriptions to the kingdom of the Maitrakas of Valabhī.[90] References to various sub-divisions of the mercantile castes have been found in the inscriptions as well as general literature of this period.[91]

Among the mixed castes, certain inscriptions of the latter half of the eighth century, belonging to the Pāṇḍya kingdom, refer to members of a Vaidya lineage (*vaidyakula*) occupying high offices of State.[92] Again, we find in inscriptions and literary works of the sixth century and thereafter, occasional references to individuals of the Karaṇa caste who filled high governmental offices, though the alternative sense of a scribe is not unknown down to later times.[93] Inscriptions and works of general literature from the latter half of the ninth century onwards refer to a caste destined to attain great importance in later times, viz. the caste of Kāyasthas.[94]

As regards the foreign races that had settled in India in the preceding centuries, the records of this period show that with the exception of the Muslims they had been thoroughly assimilated within the Hindu social system. These races, to begin with, must have adopted everywhere the indigenous language—we hear even of a Śaka poet Kapila composing a record of the Saindhavas of West Kāthiāwād.[95] Still more important is the fact, to be noted later, that the inscriptions of this time have preserved for us a few examples of Hūṇas and other chiefs being married into Brāhmaṇa families.

Compared with the abundant data of the pre-Gupta and Gupta periods about slavery, we have very scanty information about this institution in the present Age. The humane treatment of the slave as well as of his wife and son is recommended by Medhātithi.[96] In South India, under the Imperial Choḷas, not only did the temples acquire slaves by purchase, but poor people sometimes voluntarily sold themselves into slavery to temples to escape starvation during times of famine.[97] Finally we have a story in *Upamitibhava-prapañchākathā*[98] which shows that the aboriginal Bhillas traded in slaves.

2. *Marriage Rules*

The Smṛiti authorities of this period treat the older marriage rules sometimes with considerable independence. As regards inter-caste marriages, Medhātithi[99] would make marriages of

Brāhmaṇas with Kshatriya and Vaiśya women altogether exceptional, while forbidding the marriage of a Brāhmaṇa with a Śūdra girl. *Nāradīya Purāṇa*[100] declares that marriages of twice-born men with girls of other *varṇas* are forbidden in the Kali Age. In another context Medhātithi gives the general rule about the status of sons born of inter-caste marriages. In the case of marriages in the natural (*anuloma*) order, we are told, the son takes the caste of the mother, and in the case of marriages in the reverse (*pratiloma*) order, he takes the caste of the father. Marriage with the daughter of a maternal uncle is condemned both by Medhātithi and Viśvarūpa.[102] Among forms of marriage, the *gāndharva* (marriage by mutual love), which was sanctioned by some old Smṛiti authors and condemned by others, is definitely censured by Medhātithi.[103] In fact Medhātithi, following the authorities of the Gupta Age, contemplates the girls to be given in marriage, as a general rule, by their guardians.[104] As regards the marriageable age of girls, Medhātithi agrees with the views of the authorities of the preceding age. Girls, says he,[105] should be given away in marriage when they are eight or six years old and called *nagnikā*. Again he says[106] that the right time for giving away a girl in marriage is between her eighth year and her attaining puberty. The relative ages of the bridegroom and the bride laid down by Manu, says Medhātithi in another context,[107] must be taken not in a literal sense, but generally to mean that one should marry a girl very much younger than himself, such being the practice of cultured men.

When the guardian, for some reason or other, is unable to bestow the girl before her marriageable age, she is allowed by the old Smṛiti law to choose her own husband after waiting for a short term. Referring to this rule Medhātithi[108] explains that a girl should stay in her father's house for three years after attaining puberty (in her twelfth year), and then she may choose her husband without fear of sin. In case the bridegroom dies after payment of the nuptial fee, the girl, says Medhātithi,[109] should be asked to choose her own husband. In the same context[110] Medhātithi lays down appropriate rules for disposal of the fee according as the girl chooses to marry a husband other than the younger brother of the dead bridegroom, or else elects to remain a life-long celibate.

Medhātithi's rule relating to the repudiation of a girl after her betrothal reflects his view of the inviolability of the marriage sacrament. According to him[111] repudiation of a maiden suffering from physical or mental defects, even after acceptance, is allowed before the performance of the marriage. Writing in a prosaic strain, he says in another context[112] that while other commodities can be returned even after ten days with mutual consent, this rule of law does not apply to girls given away in marriage. Just as used and worn-out clothes cannot be restored to the seller even within ten days' time, so a maiden who has been married cannot be abandoned. Even when girls are given away for a fee, Medhātithi continues, they may be treated like other commodities only before marriage, while a girl who has been given away according to the approved forms cannot be revoked at all. Concluding his argument, he observes that Yājñavalkya's rule,[113] allowing a girl to be taken back for a better bridegroom even after her betrothal, holds good before and not after the seventh step (at the nuptial ceremony) is taken; when both parties have necessary qualifications, the betrothal cannot be revoked even before marriage, while even a defective wife (other than a non-virgin) cannot be abandoned after marriage.

As regards re-marriage of women, *Agni Purāṇa*[114] repeats the remarkable texts of Nārada and Parāśara permitting a woman to take a second husband in the event of five calamities, *viz.* when the husband is lost (*i.e.* unheard of), or is dead, or has adopted the life of a recluse, or is impotent, or has become an outcaste. Likewise Viśvarūpa[115] seems to sanction remarriage of women, for he quotes an authority permitting a father to give away his daughter, though no longer a virgin. On the other hand, it is forbidden by *Brahma Purāṇa* and Medhātithi.[116]

As to the custom of *niyoga,* Viśvarūpa[117] permits it in the cases of a Śūdra and a royal family without a successor. Medhātithi[118] forbids the connection of a widow with another man for the sake of her maintenance, or for progeny. But elsewhere[119] he follows the authoritative tradition in allowing *niyoga* to widows. What is more, he amplifies the law of *niyoga* by saying[120] that the elders entitled to authorise the act are the mother-in-law, the father-in-law, and other members of the husband's family, but not those of the wife's own family. The process of authorisation, Medhātithi continues, may be repeated in the event of a daughter or a blind or a deaf son being born. The law of *niyoga*, he further observes,[121] applies not only to a widow, but also to a woman whose husband is impotent, and so forth.

The general literature also reflects the current ideas and practices regarding marriage. *Abhidhānaratnamālā*[122] contains the words *varshā* and *patiṁvarā* meaning a girl choosing her own husband, as also the words *punarbhū* and *didhishu* meaning a remarried woman. We learn from a number of tales in *Upamitibhava-prapañchākathā* that while love-marriages were known, they were regularly solemnised only after approval of the girls' guardians. It appears, however, that marriages were often arranged by parents or other guardians of the parties, sometimes even before the latter were born. Sometimes girls, with the approval of their parents, chose their husbands at a *svayaṁvara* ceremony. No social obloquy was attached to marriages between first cousins. But a woman took it to be a grave misfortune to become a co-wife.[123] The historical records of this period tend to show that notwithstanding the ban of the Smṛiti-law on this point, inter-marriages of Brāhmaṇas with Kshatriya women were still prevalent.[123a]

3. *Law of Adultery*

Medhātithi's view[124] of the law relating to adultery agrees with the strict ideas of Gautama and Manu who would have the guilty pair put to death with torture. He prescribes severe punishment even for those who have just begun to make approaches to other men's wives, while he lays down the death penalty for a non-Brāhmaṇa committing adultery with a woman of the twice-born caste, as well as for a man guilty of forcible connection with a family-woman (*kulastrī*) of lower caste whose husband is alive. And yet it would appear from notices in the contemporary literature that there were, as in former times, various classes of notoriously frail women, while other women occasionally committed sin. The evil reputation of women of the former type is illustrated by *Abhidhānaratnamālā*[125] which applies to the actor (*naṭa*) a synonym (*jāyājīva*) signifying his dependence upon the earnings of his wife, as well as by *Ratirahasya*[126] which includes the wives of dancers and singers (*chāraṇa*) among those who are easily amenable to seduction. Similarly Medhātithi[127] mentions that the wives of *chāraṇas*, though not exactly prostitutes, admitted paramours into their houses with the permission of their husbands. The list of women who easily succumb to the seducer's wiles is given in *Ratirahasya* and in *Upamitibhavaprapañchākathā*.[128]

The historical records support the Smṛiti law. In an inscription of A.D. 992, belonging to the reign of the Western Chāluḳya king Āhavamalla,[129] a list of penalties is laid down for various offences according to which the adulterer is to be put to death, while the adulteress shall suffer amputation of her nose. The general application of the strict Smṛiti law in actual practice is testified to by the Arab writer Abū Zaid, who says (c. A.D. 916) that in the case of adultery both the man and the woman are put to death, while the man alone is punished if the woman is found to have been forced against her will.[130]

4. *The Position of Women*

In so far as the status of the wife is concerned, the Smṛiti authorities of the period, like their predecessors, emphasise the duty of absolute obedience and devotion of wives to their husbands. Medhātithi illustrates the wife's duty of personal service towards her husband by saying[131] that she shall shampoo his feet and render him such other service as befits a servant. But this is subject to the all-important condition that the husband follows the righteous path and is free from hatred as well as jealousy towards his wife. For the husband, so runs Medhātithi's memorable dictum, has no dominion *(prabhutva)* over his wife. The husband and the wife, says he in another connection,[132] differ only in their bodies but are entirely united in their functions. Equal right of the husband and the wife to seek legal remedy against each other in the last resort is emphasised by Medhātithi. For he says[133] that the wife, very much persecuted by her husband, like the husband very much troubled by his wife, has the remedy of appealing to the king for decision of their disputes. Other passages deal with the wife's right to maintenance by her husband. According to a verse attributed to Manu and quoted by Medhātithi and Vijñāneśvara[134] the virtuous wife must be maintained even by committing a hundred bad acts. Similarly Daksha[135] includes the wife in the list of those whom one is bound to maintain. Even the wife's fault does not make her liable to abandonment or forfeiture of her possessions. As Medhātithi says,[136] the wife, even though guilty of grievous sins, must not be turned out of the house. The punishment of confiscation prescribed by Manu for a wife hating her husband, Medhātithi continues, is meant simply as a warning to bring her to her senses, and it does not sanction the confiscation of all her belongings. After this, it is not surprising that Medhātithi[137] requires a husband, when going abroad, to make provision for his wife. Indeed, according to him, the husband must not journey abroad leaving his wife behind except for the specific purposes mentioned by Manu. The law on the subject of the wife's maintenance is summed up by Medhātithi in another context.[138] Here he says that the faithful wife must not be abandoned, even though she may be disagreeable in look, or harsh in speech, and the like. On the other hand, the unfaithful wife may be confined in a room when she has been guilty of a single act of transgression, but if she repeats the offence, she is to be abandoned. Referring to Yājñavalkya's text[139] allowing a mere subsistence to an unfaithful wife, Medhātithi observes that it applies when the husband is able and willing to maintain her, but if he is not willing she may be abandoned. The wife, concludes

Medhātithi, must be maintained even if she hates her husband, but if she becomes an outcaste she may be abandoned.

As to the husband's right of correcting his wife, *Matsya Purāṇa* repeats Manu's injunction[140] authorising the husband to beat his erring wife (though not on the head or the back) with a rope or a split bamboo. With more humanity Medhātithi[141] takes Manu to enjoin not the actual beating of the recalcitrant wife, but only a method of putting her on the right path. From this he draws the corollary that verbal chastisement is also to be inflicted on the wife, while beating may be occasionally resorted to, according to the gravity of the offence. Going a step further Viśvarūpa[142] says that the guarding of wives consists in being really devoted to them and not in beating them, and he quotes in this connection a saying of those acquainted with worldly ways about the delicacy of Pāñchāla women. That the imposition of money-fine was also one of the methods of correction open to the husband is apparent form Medhātithi.[143] Here we read that the husband, being lord (*prabhu*) of the wife,[144] may inflict the prescribed fine (of six *kṛishṇalas*) upon the Kshatriya or other wife, and a heavier fine upon a Brāhmaṇa wife, for drinking wine or for visiting shows, when forbidden to do so. Medhātithi[145] justifies Manu's rule of repudiation of a wife who is barren, or who bears only daughters, or whose children die, on the ground that the husband would otherwise violate the injunction about laying of the sacred fire and the begetting of sons. But he refuses to follow Manu in sanctioning the repudiation of a wife who is harsh of speech. In the same context[146] Medhātithi extends Manu's two conditions of such supersession (*viz.* that the wife's consent has been obtained and that she is not disgraced) from the case of a devoted and modest but sick wife to those of a barren wife and a wife bearing only daughters.

On the question of the alternatives open to a wife after she has waited for the prescribed period for her husband's return from abroad, the views of the authorities of this epoch, as we learn from Medhātithi,[147] reflected their different standpoints from one of extreme puritanism to one of considerable latitude. After the prescribed period the wife, according to one authority, must live by pursuing unobjectionable occupations. Modifying this strict view, Medhātithi urges that while she must live by unobjectionable occupations before the expiry of her waiting term, she may live by objectionable pursuits thereafter. Basing his opinion on Parāśara's text quoted above in favour of the remarriage of women, a third authority goes so far as to allow the stranded wife to deviate from chastity. A fourth author, taking the vital word *pati* in Parāśara's text in the sense of 'protector,' recommends her to accept another man's protection in the capacity of toilet-maid and the like. In such a case even if the wife has entered into six month's or one year's contract, the husband on his return from his travel may take her back immediately. The fifth and the last authority would allow the wife to marry another husband according to the practice of *punarbhūs* (remarried women), in which case the husband cannot interfere with her after his return, and she continues to be the wife of the second husband.

As regards the status of the widow, the life of strict celibacy and self-restraint enjoined upon her by the old Smṛitis was sought to be enforced during this period. As long as a widow remains faithful to her husband's memory, says Medhātithi,[147a] she deserves to have her property looked after by the king; but in the contrary case, she is not only to be disqualified for possessing property, but is to be banished (in the sense of being driven out of the main building and provided with a separate dwelling-house as well as separate food and clothing).

As in the former period, the dread rite of *satī* at this time was enjoined by some authorities, but condemned by others.[148] According to the Arab writer Sulaimān,[149] wives of kings sometimes burnt themselves on the funeral pyres of their husbands, but it was for them to exercise their option in the matter. The actual occurrence of this grim rite is testified to by a few historical examples of queens and other ladies of high families thus scarificing their lives.[150] But the view, that the custom was still mainly confined to royal families and had not yet spread among the masses,[151] is hardly supported by a passage in *Kuṭṭanīmatam*[152] which recognises it as one of the general virtues of a wife.

The custom of dedicating maidens for service in temples, which may be traced back to older times, was continued in this period. Reference to this class is found in Medhātithi[153] as well as in inscriptions of this period.[154] Abū Zaid[154a] also speaks of courtezans attached to Indian temples.

The class of prostitutes, known from early times, existed as a distinct social unit in the present age. *Matsya Purāṇa*[155] lays down a list of their duties and rights (*veśyādharma*) as well as the special clauses of law applicable to them. The deliberate settlement of such women in public places is hinted at by an early Arab geographer, while others notice it as a peculiarity of Indians that they held this profession to be lawful.[156] Several passages in the literature of this period deal with the class of accomplished courtezans (*gaṇikā*) whose virtues and vices are celebrated from the earliest Buddhist times. In two stories of *Upamitibhavaprapanchakathā*[157] we find concrete instances of the better type of *gaṇikās* as well as of those of the common variety. It is above all in *Kuṭṭanīmatam* that we have the fullest notices of the life of a *gaṇikā* during this period. It relates a story[158] which shows that connection of a Brahmaṇa with a *gaṇikā* (such as was not disapproved in the times of Bhāsa and Śūdraka) was now regarded as a disgraceful act. We may also refer to a passage in *Kuṭṭanīmatam* illustrating at any rate the author's view of the very high qualifications, both of body and mind, that a *gaṇikā* was expected to possess at this period.[159]

In general, the position of woman was patterned on the same lines as in the preceding period. Amplifying the old Smriti doctrine of the perpetual tutelage of women, Medhātithi[160] observes that women should have no freedom of action regarding the great objects of human existence (*viz.* virtue, wealth, and pleasure), but should obtain permission of their husbands or other male relations before spending money on such acts. Women who are addicted to singing and similar acts, Medhātithi continues, shall be restrained by their male guardians. Arguing that a woman's mind is not under her control, and that she lacks the requisite strength, Medhātithi[161] concludes that she shall be guarded by all her male relations at all times. Turning to the specific disabilities of women, we find Medhātithi[162] justifying their general incapacity for giving evidence as witnesses. As he observes, unlike other qualifications which are acquired and hence liable to lapse through carelessness and so forth, fickleness is inherent in women. But elsewhere[163] he admits that there are women who are as truthful and as steady as the best expounders of the Vedas, and they may appear as witnesses.

On the other hand, a more humane view is taken of the husband's authority over his wife. The wife, according to Medhātithi, must not be forsaken unless she becomes an outcaste, and 'forsaking' in this case means not that she is to be deprived of food and clothing, but that she is to be cut off from all intercourse and forbidden to do household work. According to *Matsya Purāṇa* the mother must never be abandoned, while Medhātithi observes that the mother must not be turned out of the house even for failure of her maternal duties, for to the son the mother never becomes an outcaste.[164] Medhātithi's view of the law relating to female outcastes in general follows the humane lines indicated above. Referring to Manu's penalty of banishment for outcaste women, he [165] explains it to mean that they shall be provided with a separate dwelling-place as well as food and clothes, and they may retain what they have saved. Again he says[166] that female outcastes, not performing the prescribed expiation, are to be allowed food, drink, and clothing of an inferior quality, and permitted to live in a separate hut close to the main building.

As regards the custom of Purdah, Abū Zaid furnishes the very important information that most Indian Princes, while holding court, allowed their women to be seen unveiled by the men present, whether natives or foreigners.

5. *Some Social Types*

The early Arab geographers belonging to the ninth and tenth centuries noticed the paucity of towns as a distinctive characteristic of India in contrast with China.[167] No doubt it is because of this preponderance of the rural element in Indian life that we miss in the literature of this period any special reference to the type of the city-bred man of fashion (*nāgaraka*), so well described in Vātsyāyana's standard work on erotics. We have on the contrary in *Kuṭṭanīmatam*[168] a remarkably full and vivid picture, doubtless drawn from real life, of a typical country-squire who should, according to this authority, be the first object of a courtezan's attentions.

The hero of this account is a young son of an officer (bhaṭṭa) in the king's service, who is his own master as his father constantly resides in the royal capital. His dress and manners are sufficiently showy. He wears long hair with a thick tuft, which is bound with a long-handled and sharp-toothed comb and is done up with a multi-coloured tassel. He wears finger-rings as well as ear-rings of a distinctive sort, while his neck is adorned with thin golden threads. All his limbs were dyed yellowish with saffron rubbed on his body. He wears ornamental shoes, while his clothes have a gold border and are dyed yellow with saffron. A very showy fellow, he makes his public appearance in the company of a train of attendants. In the huge dancing-hall which is crowded with guild-masters, merchants, parasites and gamblers, he sits with his followers on specially provided seats. He is served by a young betel-casket bearer with painted finger-nails, with a garland of thick glass beads around his neck and with conch-shell bangles on his wrist. He is surrounded by five or six armed attendants accustomed to speak freely and bearing a haughty mien. Equally conceited and foolish, he recites verses incorrectly and intrudes upon the conversation of intelligent people sitting by his side, while he makes known the king's confidence in his father. He inwardly enjoys the extravagant praise of his attendants for his knowledge of song, instrumental music and dramaturgy, his charities and his love of hunting. He compliments, without understanding, the performances of the female dancers.[169]

In contrast with the life-like description of the country-squire given above is the slightly idealised picture of the life and surroundings of a poet that is given by Rājaśekhara[170]—a picture which reminds us in some respects of Vātsyāyana's *nāgaraka*. The poet, we are told, should be pure in speech, mind, and body. Purity in speech and mind is derived from the *śāstras,* while for ensuring bodily purity the nails of the feet shoul be cut, betel-leaf should be chewed, the body should be anointed a little with unguents, the clothes should be costly but not gaudy, and the head should be decked with flowers. The poet's residence should be swept clean; it should have various sites suited to the needs of the six seasons; it should take away sweat and fatigue; the attached garden-house should have its awning of numerous trees. The house should have a miniature hill for sporting; it should have tanks and ponds; it should have a collection of tame birds and animals comprising peacocks, deer, pigeons, ruddy geese, swans, partridges, herons, ospreys, parrots, and starlings; it should have a shower-house with excellent floor, a creeper-bower as well as swings and hammocks; the poet's male and female servants, his scribe, his friends, and the ladies of his family should have appropriate specified qualifications and should serve him in the specified manner.

6. *Some Groups and Associations*

There are good grounds for believing that a number of groups and associations belonging to towns and villages played an important part in the social life of this age. Giving an instance of the co-operative efforts of villagers, Medhātithi[172] says that the people of one village, afflicted by constant encroachment on their grazing-grounds and their water-reserves by the people of another village, would form a compact for defence of the ancient privileges of the village *(prāktanīgrāmasthiti),* and any one breaking the compact and joining the other party would be liable to the penalty of banishment, or in the alternative, to the milder punishment of a fixed money-fine (six *nishkas* or four *suvarṇas*) as laid down by Manu. To the above we may add that Medhātithi[173], includes *saṁghas* (associations) of the same or different castes among those whose members are liable to a fine for breach of compact under Manu's law. From this it follows that not only village groups, but also associations of single and multiple castes, were engaged in collective enterprises based on mutual compacts recognised by law. The important functions performed by the organised village assemblies in South India in receiving and managing trust-funds will be treated elsewhere. But a few similar examples may be given here. From a Kannaḍa inscription of A.D. 978[174] we learn that a trust, then created in favour of an almshouse *(sattra)*, was placed under the control of thirty households of the town. Other records speak of the activities of temple committees *(goshṭhī)* whose history can be traced back to a few early Sānchī inscriptions [175] and a body now mentioned for the first time, namely, the community of goldsmiths *(sauvarṇṇikamahājana)*, placed in charge of temple funds. Purchases of house sites on 99 years' lease by the *sauvarṇṇikamahājanas* as well as the *goshṭhīs* of a certain temple out of the temple funds are commemorated in a series of documents bearing dates between A.D. 865 and 904 and belonging to the region of the Upper Gaṅgā basin.[176] An inscription of A.D. 882-83[177] mentions that the management of certain charities, made by a few horse-dealers in Pṛithūdaka (Peheva in Karnāl District), was entrusted to the *goshṭhikas*. This involved the collection of various self-imposed taxes from the horse-dealers and purchasers as well as their distribution for specified purposes. An association of weavers, entrusted with the management of a temple, is referred to in an inscription of the reign of Uttama-Choḷa.[178]

7. *Standard of Living*

The high standard of living of the people prevailing generally in earlier times seems to have been maintained during the present period. The names of a number of professions mentioned by Medhātithi[179] reveal a state of luxurious living. Such are the professions of a bath-man (*snāpaka*), a toilette-man (*prasādhaka*), and a professional cook *(pāchaka)* as well as a maid-in-waiting *(sairandhrī)*. The variety of garments and ornaments current in these times was remarkable. *Abhidhānaratnamālā*[180] gives the synonyms for an upper garment (*prāvaraṇa*) and a woollen blanket (*āvika*) as well as women's bodice (*kūrpāsa*) and petticoat (*chaṇḍātaka*), while it knows[181] technical terms *(kutha*, etc.) for blankets thrown over the backs of elephants. Similarly it refers to ear-ornaments (*tāṭaṅka*), armlet (*keyūra*), neck-ornament (*graiveya*), finger-rings, waist-bands, and women's leg ornaments (*nūpura*), In a list of things delightful to the touch found in *Upamitibhavaprapañchākathā*[182] are included couches *(śayana)* with soft cotton sheets, seats filled with goose feathers, gowns *(bṛihatikā)* and other soft garments, upper garments *(prāvāra)*, woollen-cloth (? *rallikā* or *rakshikā)*, silks, home-grown *(paṭṭāṁśuka)* and Chinese *(chīnāṁśuka)*, as well as musk, aloes, sandal, and other unguents. Girls before marriage used to wear blue bodices (*cholikā*), while after marriage they tied the knot (*nīvi*) to their garments.[183] Women's golden as well as jewelled girdles (*kāñchī* and *raśanā*) and large ear-ornaments (*tāṭaṅka*) are mentioned in verses quoted by Rājaśekhara.[184] Ladies of high families habitually delighted in the display of ornaments and the use of various unguents. In Rājaśekhara's elaborate description of the heroine's toilette, arranged by the queen just after her bath, we are told[185] that her limbs were anointed with saffron and her eyes with collyrium, her lovely locks well arranged, her hair was decorated with flowers, while her person was adorned with ear-rings, rows of bracelets, a ruby-encrusted girdle, and emerald-anklets. The same princess, while on the swing, wears a pearl-necklace, bracelets (*valaya*), a girdle with small bells attached to it, and jewelled anklets. Almost the same ornaments are worn by the heroine in another of Rājaśekhara's dramas while playing with a ball.[186] The same lady at night-time appears in a robe of Chinese silk with a pearl necklace around her neck, camphor powder on her bosom, and sandal paste thickly applied to her limbs, so that in the admiring sight of the king she looks like a goddess descended from the moon.[187]

The little cameos descriptive of the seasons and the nights that we find in Rājaśekhara's dramas also reflect the contemporary style of living. In a description of the end of the winter and the beginning of the spring season, we are told[188] that the maidens no longer put bees' wax on their lips, they do not anoint their braids of hair with fragrant oil, they do not put on a bodice, and they are indifferent to the use of thick saffron for their mouths, while they again set their hearts on sandal-juice. Again we are told in a description of the evening[189] that the jewelled roof-terraces (*maṇimayavalabhī*) and the picture galleries (*bhittiniveśa*) are being opened for pleasure, the couches (*paryaṅka*) are being hastily spread out by the attendants, and the maids-in-waiting (*sairandhrī*) are incessantly moving their fingers on the silks. At the rise of the full-moon, we read,[190] aloes are burnt as incense at the pleasure-houses (*līlāgara*), where likewise the lamps are lighted, the festoons of rare pearls are suspended, the charming pleasure-couches (*keliśayana*) are being prepared, and hundreds of female messengers (*dūtī*) are conversing together. Among the delights of summer are mentioned[191] those of rubbing sandal-paste at mid-day, playing in bathing-pools until night-fall, and drinking cool liquor (*surā*) at evening, as well as listening to the cooling sound of the flute. In a description of a dark night we find[192] that the girls then go out with garlands to seek their lovers after decking their ears with peacock-plumes, their arms with emerald-bracelets, their bosoms with sapphire necklaces and their cheeks with musk. In summer women cooled their bodies with sandal-juice.[193] To the above, may be added the evidence of *Upamitibhavaprapañchākathā*[194] according to which quantities of aloe-wood incense as well as woollen blankets (*rallaka-kambala*) were used in winter.

The description of the typical poet in *Kāvyamīmāṁsā* and of the typical country-squire in *Kuṭṭanīmatam,* to which we have already referred, widely as they differ from each other, illustrates at least the prevailing view of luxury of these classes. It was, however, in the royal palace that pomp and ostentation reached their zenith. Among the luxuries of the palace, we find a plantain-arbour (*kadalīgṛiha*) with a raised emerald seat inside,[195] a king's sleeping-chamber with perforated columns and a jewelled quadrangle,[196] and a crystal-house with picture of a king, queen, jester, betel-box bearer, chowrie-bearer, dwarf, and monkey painted on the wall.[197] The female personnel of the queen's apartment in *Karpūramañjarī* consisted of armed groups of five chowrie-bearers, five maids-in-waiting, five betel-box bearers, and five bath-keepers guarding her on the four sides, as well as a group of five overseers with golden staves in their hands.[198]

To the above testimony drawn from the indigenous literature we may add that of the contemporary Arab writers who agree in declaring the love of ornament to be characteristic of the Indians. According to Sulaimān, Indians, both male and female, decorated themselves with golden bracelets and precious stones. Indians, says Ibn al-Fakīh, used to wear ear-rings, and both males and females adorned themselves with golden bracelets. According to Abū Zaid, Indian kings wore necklaces of precious red and green stones mounted on gold, while they held pearls in the greatest esteem. Speaking of the tract from Kambay to Saimur (Chaul) Ibn Haukal says that because of the extreme heat the men used fine muslin garments.[199]

8. *Popular Amusements*

The popular amusements of these times were similar to those of the preceding period. It was the fashion for high-born girls to play with balls *(kanduka)*. Especially in the spring season and on the occasion of the Swing Festival, they used to enjoy the swing from trees in a garden. A very spectacular scene was presented by the *charcharī* (musical or dancing) performance. On this occasion maidens, richly adorned with pearls, performed various dances known by appropriate technical terms, and thereafter they sprinkled one another with water from jars sometimes adorned with jewels. Or else, suitably attired and posed, they paraded as savage mountaineers, or even enacted cemetery scenes with offerings of human flesh in their hands.[200] Dancing for recreation by ladies and dramatic representations in honour of deities are referred to in the inscriptions of the period.[201]

Other amusements described in the literature of this period

remind us of the diversions of the *nāgaraka* described in Vātsyāyana's *Kāmasūtra*. In Rājaśekhara's account of a poet's daily life[202] we read that he is to arrange a poetical assembly (*kāvyagoshṭhī*) after his mid-day meal. Elsewhere reference is made to the *goshṭhī* of persons in high life, of a queen and of other women.[203] *Abhidhāna-ratnamālā* gives us technical terms for drinking-parties (*āpāna* and *pānagoshṭhī*) as well as for drinking in company (*sahapīti* and *saha-pānaka*).[204] *Ratirahasya*[205] tells us how young pleasure-seekers used to meet their mistresses at night in well-lighted and scented houses amid amorous assemblies (*narmagoshṭhī*), to the accompaniment of sweet music. According to the same authority[206] excursions to gardens (*udyānayātrā*), excursions for drinking (*pānayātrā*), and water-sports (*jalāvatāra*) gave opportunities to unchaste wives to meet their lovers. A vivid description of the spring revels in a capital town, breathing the spirit of a true *saturnalia*, is found in *Upamiti-bhavaprapañchākathā*.[207] Describing the scene at the mythical town of Bhavachakra ('Round of re-birth') the author tells us how the people trooped out of the city into the garden and sported beneath *valuka*, *aśoka*, and other trees, while drunken revellers engaged themselves in amorous sports, and gallants took up goblets of scented wines from bejewelled drinking-vessels and placed them to the lips of their mistresses. Amid songs and dances the revellers formed themselves into numerous drinking bouts (*āpānaka*). The climax was reached when the king, mounted on a huge elephant and surrounded by a large retinue, emerged out of the town and joined in the revelry. His appearance was greeted with music from various instruments, sprinkling of sandal and saffron juice, song, dance, laughter, and other exuberant manifestations. The king, having worshipped the goddess Chaṇḍikā, strangely enough, with libations of wine, formed a drinking party with the assembled people. The end of the revels was marked by tragic scenes. Princess Ratilalitā, wife of the king's brother, being pressed by her intoxicated husband, danced much against her will in the presence of the assembly. This excited the evil passion of the king, who tried to lay violent hands upon her when all the others were stupefied by drink. Escaping from his clutches the princess sought the protection of her husband who challenged the king to a duel. In the resultant *melée* the king was killed by his brother in single combat.

9. *Lawful Food and Drink*

On the subject of lawful food the Smṛiti law of this period follows, with some explanations, the traditional lines. *Brahma Purāṇa*[208] declares a number of herbs and vegetables as well as cereals to be forbidden food. Medhātithi[208a] lays down at great length the occasions on which the eating of meat is lawful, and he seeks to define clearly the animals whose meat is or is not lawful food. From this it appears that notwithstanding Manu's general list of prohibited birds and animals, the peacock, the horse, the white ass, the female sparrow, the wild cock and the wild pig counted distinctly as lawful food, while certain kinds of web-footed and fish-eating birds were classed optionally as such. Medhātithi again gives[209] the cow, the goat and the deer as instances of animals with one line of teeth which according to the text are fit to be eaten.

As regards the use of intoxicating drinks, we seem to mark in the authorities of our times a distinct tendency towards relaxation of the strict rules of their predecessors in the case of the Kshatriya and Vaiśya castes. Both Manu and Yājñavalkya forbid the three upper classes to drink different classes of wines, and impose penances ranging up to death upon those guilty of indulging in the same. But Medhātithi[210] and Viśvarūpa[211] understand Manu's text to mean that while the three kinds of *surā (viz.* those made from rice-flour, molasses, and honey or grapes or *madhūka* flowers) are forbidden to Brāhmaṇas, the Kshatriyas and the Vaiśyas are permitted to drink the last two kinds. It is the Brāhmaṇa drinker of *surā* alone, explains Medhātithi,[212] who is guilty of mortal sin *(mahāpātaka)*, and as such is liable to corporal punishment notwithstanding the injunctions of the Smṛitis to the contrary. Summing up the settled law *(vyavasthā)* on the subject, Medhātithi[213] observes that while the penance for intentionally drinking wine made from rice-flour is death, that for intentional drinking of other kinds of wine involves performance of only the lunar penance (*chāndrāyaṇa*). Among original authorities *Āditya Purāṇa*[213a] and *Brahma Purāṇa*[214] include the drinking of wine (*madya*) among practices to be eschewed by twice-born men in the Kali Age. On the other hand *Vishṇudharmottara*[215] mentions ten kinds of wines (including those prepared from *madhūka* flower, from grape-juice, and from honey) which are forbidden to Brāhmaṇas, but permitted to Kshatriyas and Vaiśyas.

We have so far dealt with the Smṛiti rules relating to food and drink. There is every reason to believe that the old Buddhist and Jain canonical laws on this point were still regarded as authoritative during the present period. As an illustration of the continuance of the Jain ban against meat-eating and drinking, we may refer to the long and severe sermons on the evils of both put into the mouths of some observant princes.[216]

The references in the general literature and the historical records enable us to find out how far the above rules were observed in actual practice. In Rājaśekhara's description of the six seasons, partaking of pork along with newly husked rice by the people is said to be common during the cold (*hemanta*) season, while the essences of deer and quails, as also wine mixed with water, are mentioned among the dainties of the summer season.[217] But elsewhere Rājaśekhara mentions eating of pork among the practices of uncultured people.[218] The literary evidence further shows that both men and women, other than Brāhmaṇas, freely drank wine. According to a verse quoted by Rājaśekhara,[219] drinking wine (*madhu*), after partaking of pepper and betel, was the general practice among Southern (*Dramila*) ladies. Medhātithi says[220] that while Bhāhmaṇa women did not drink wine at festivals, Kshatriya and other women, to whom drinking was not forbidden, indulged in excessive drinking when they gathered together on festive occasions. In view of these statements it is reasonable to infer that the testimony regarding abstinence from wine by Indians, which is repeated by early Arab authors one after another,[221] is a rash generalisation based upon imperfect acquaintance with facts. On the other hand, we may accept the testimony of Mas'ūdī[222] about the eating of rhinoceros's flesh by the Indians to be true.

10. *Toilette and Personal Hygiene*

The high level of personal cleanliness and comfort reached in the preceding age was well maintained during this period. As regards personal hygiene, *Agni Purāṇa*,[223] lays down elaborate rules for daily observance of purification of the body (*śaucha*), cleaning of the teeth with twigs, and bathing by the householder. Bathing, again, is divided into several kinds according to its object by some Smṛiti authorities.[224] The observant Arab writers noticed these habits as distinctive of the Indian people. According to Sulaimān and Ibn al-Fakīh[225] the Indians, unlike the Chinese, cleansed their teeth with tooth-picks and bathed daily before taking meals.

As regards toilette, we have elsewhere noticed how the literature of this period refers to the use of unguents and ornaments of different kinds, especially by high-born ladies. Mention has also been made of the vivid and life-like picture of the dress of *coiffure* of the country-squire in *Kuṭṭanīmatam*.[226] We may notice here some further references to personal adornment. *Abhidhānaratnamālā* knows not only the synonyms for saffron, sandal, musk, camphor, and aloes, but also the marks (*tilaka*) made on the body with such unguents.[227] The *tilaka* and similar other decorations made on the cheeks of maidens are referred to in two verses quoted by Rājaśekhara.[228] We get a fairly complete list of unguents used in different seasons in *Kāvyamīmāṁsā*.[229] From this account we learn that sandal, agallochum, saffron and musk were used in the rainy season, saffron with bees-wax was applied to the mouth and fragrant oil to hair in the cold (*hemanta*) season, crushed saffron was applied by women to their bodies in winter, and camphor powder was used in the summer season. References are also made to the use of other artificial aids to beauty. Thus *Abhidhānaratnamālā*[230] knows technical terms (*sthānaka* and *hastabimba*) for a particular method of perfuming the body with unguents as well as those (*patravallī*) for decorations made on women's bodies by experts on beauty culture. *Ratirahasya* contains various recipes for removing bad odour from the mouth and other parts of the body, and for beautifying the complexion of men as well as women.[231] A satirical account in *Upamitibhavaprapañchākathā* shows how old men were sometimes not above using these beauty aids. Describing the attempts of old and decrepit men to appear young, the author says that they used hair-dyes of various sorts, frequently cleansed their bodies with various oils, carefully concealed the wrinkles on their cheeks, drank the elixir of life, and constantly applied cosmetics to their persons.[232] We may refer, lastly, to Rājaśekhara's works to illustrate how different fashions prevailed among ladies in different parts of the country. We learn that Marāṭhā girls specially applied saffron-paste to their cheeks and collyrium to their eyes.[233] The chewing of betel-leaf with areca-nut and camphor was the characteristic of the Kerala people.[234] The Nepalese women used musk-paste in the summer season.[235] In a description of the characteristic dress and toilette of women of different regions, we are told that the women of Bengal (*Gauḍa*) painted their bosoms with wet sandal and coloured their bodies like *dūrvā* grass with aloe, those of Kanauj (*Mahodaya*) wore large ear-ornaments and necklaces or large pearls dangling down to their navel, those of Malabar (*Kerala*) had their peculiar style of *coiffure* and method of tying up their garment-knots, while the men of Mālwā (*Avanti*) followed the style of dress of the inhabitants of the Upper Doāb (*Pāñchālas*) and their women followed the style of the Southerners.[236] Rājaśekhara, with evident partiality for his adopted country, says that fashions of dress and *coiffure* as well as ornaments of ladies of Kānyakubja were followed by fashionable ladies all over the country.[237]

11. *Beliefs and Superstitions*

The records of this period point to the continuance of the agelong belief in omens and portents. Basing its account upon the older astrological works, *Matsya Purāṇa*[238] gives a long and systematic account of omens, classifying them under appropriate heads and prescribing adequate remedies for averting their evil effects. The same work devotes a separate chapter[239] to rules for propitiation of planets. The extent of popular superstition is illustrated by a passage of Medhātithi.[240] Malevolent rites (*abhichāra*), says he, are those causing sudden death by incantations and the like, magic-spells are those meant to bring others under control, while sorcery (*kṛityā*) produces by means of magical incantations such conditions as insanity and distrust against friends and relations. The *abhichāra,* Medhātithi adds, is of two kinds, *viz.* the Vedic which is illustrated by the *śyena* and similar sacrifices, and the non-Vedic which is exemplified by such practices as taking off the dust of one's feet and pricking it with a needle. Repeatedly in the literature of this period we have concrete instances of such superstitions holding high life in their grip. In *Upamitibhavaprapañchākathā* we are reminded of the steps taken by the ministers to avert the evil eye (*durjanachakshurdosha*) from affecting a certain king and queen.[241] In the same work[242] a queen's dream, in the last watch of the night, of a handsome man entering her womb is interpreted by the king as presaging the birth of an excellent son, and the prophecy is fulfilled in due course. In *Karpūramañjarī* we read how the soothsayers prophesied that the heroine's husband would be an emperor, and the queen herself accordingly arranged her marriage with the king.[243] In *Viddhaśālabhañjīkā* we find the king using a ghost-trick with success not only against the queen's maid-in-waiting, but against the queen herself.[244] After this, it is not surprising that the restoration of the right of a village to make offering of boiled rice to ghosts should be solemnly recorded in an inscription of A.D. 958 belonging to the modern Dhārwār District.[245] The Arab writer Abū Zaid also refers to the 'most astonishing feats' of the diviners and those who drew omens from the flight of crows in India.[246]

In conclusion we may refer to a few other beliefs of the people mentioned in the records of this period. The ban against sea-voyage, which is laid down by some older Smritis,[247] is reported by *Nāradīyamahāpurāṇa.*[248] Suicide was resorted to both as a quasi-religious rite and as a relief against bodily ailments. We have an example[249] from the Kannaḍa country of a loyal subject giving up his head to a goddess on the birth of the king's son in fulfilment of his vow (c. A.D. 991). According to Abū Zaid and Mas'ūdī a body of king's companions, who had shared in taking rice with him at his coronation, would burn themselves to the last man after his death. Again, it appears from Abū Zaid and Ibn Khordādbah that persons on getting old would often commit suicide by drowning or by burning themselves.[250]

12. *Pious and Charitable Works*

The Smṛiti law of this period, following the older tradition, declared the gift of land as the most meritorious or all gifts.[251] Again *Matsya Purāṇa,* which is followed by *Liṅga Purāṇa,* describes at great length a set of 16 great gifts (*mahādānas*) involving the distribution of large quantities of gold to Brāhmaṇas.[252] The Smṛiti law of this period also follows the older precedent in enjoining upon all castes (including the Śūdras) such pious acts as digging of wells, ponds, and tanks, construction of temples, distribution of food, and laying out of gardens. These are collectively called *pūrta* by way of distinction from *ishṭa* meaning the performance of Vedic sacrifices.[253] The inscriptions and other historical records of this period offer many instances of the observance of these rules. Apart from numerous examples of construction of temples and donation of lands to Brāhmaṇas and others, we have several instances of kings performing the ceremonies of *tulāpurusha* and *hiraṇyagarbha* which are included in the list of 16 *mahādānas* mentioned above.[254] Other records refer to the construction of monasteries and almshouses, digging of wells and similar activities. We have again several instances of gift of land for the encouragement of learning.

13. *General Estimate of Character*

From the detailed survey of social conditions, it would not be difficult for the reader to form a general estimate of the character of the people during this period. Nevertheless, a few points which are sure to strike the observant critic may be emphasised. We cannot but condemn the illiberal attitude towards Śūdras, and particularly towards the Chandālas and other castes; we must also censure the illiberal treatment of women, and in particular their exclusion from Vedic sacraments and studies and the lowering of their age of marriage. On the other hand, we may well admire such features of the Indian character as the love of learning, the spirit of charity and benevolence, and the high standard of fidelity and devotion maintained by the wife. We may conclude with the remarkable tribute paid to the mental as well as physical qualities of Indians by an intelligent Arab observer whose work became, in the words of Ibn Khaldun, 'the prototype of all historians.' "The Hindus," says Mas'ūdī, "are distinct from all other black people in point of intellect. government, philosophy, strength of constitution, and purity of colour."

1. Cf. the quotations in Aparārka on *Yāj.* I. 131, *Sm. C.*, I. 26, and *Saṁskāra-prakāśa*, pp. 321-26. A connected and complete account of the *Vidyārambha* ceremony is given in the late mediaeval *Saṁskāraratnamālā* (904-07) of Gopī-

nātha Dīkshita, which also quotes a few other authorities like Śrīdhara and Garga.

2. I. 24. 13-16.
3. Quoted in *Sm.* C., I. 29.
4. On *Manu,* III. 1.
5. *Ibid,* II. 108 and 243 f.
6. Quoted in *Saṁskāraprakāśa,* 506-07 and *Sm. C.,* I. 133-35.
7. On *Manu,* III. 2.
8. Quoted in *Saṁskāraprakāśa,* 507-08.
9. On *Manu,* III. 1.
10. There are scattered references in literature, but these are not of much use.
11. In the story (*Bhav.* II. 1-3) the young Bhavisayatta, son of Dhanapati, a rich and virtuous merchant of Gajapura, is sent to his preceptor's house (*ujjhaśala*) where he learns quickly the lore of the Jain canon, grammar lexicography, astronomy, spells and charms, as well as knowledge of weapons, archery, hand-to-hand fight, wrestling, and the ways of elephants and horses. Returning from his preceptor's house he was complimented by his parents on his acquisition of knowledge and character. On the date of Dhanapāla, author of *Bhav.*, see Jacobi (*Bhav.* ed., Introd. 3 f) followed on independent grounds by C. D. Dalal and P. D. Gune (*GOS* ed. Introd. 3-4).
12. On *Manu,* IX. 329-31.
13. The Vaiśya, says Medhātithi (*loc. cit.*), shall know in what region and at what season gems, pearls, corals, metals like copper, iron and bronze, woven cloth, perfumes and condiments fetch a higher price than in another. He shall know, Medhātithi continues, what seed is sown thickly and what sparsely, what soil is suited for a particular kind of seed, what harvest is expected from a particular type of soil. He shall also know what commodities (skins and the like) are spoilt if kept for a long time, in what country large supplies of grains are available, at what season barley is profuse, what is the custom of a particular country, by using what fodder and salts cattle are likely to improve and so forth. This implies a thorough knowledge not only of the marketing conditions and other characteristics of various articles but also of much miscellaneous information.
14. On *Manu,* IX. 76.
15. *Kuṭṭ,* 212.
16. On *Manu,* II. 182.
17. *Ibid,* III. 2.
18. Quoted in *Saṁskāraprakāśa,* 513.
19. Quoted in *Sm. C.,* I. 143.
20. Quoted in *Saṁskāraprakāśa,* 515.
21. *Manu,* II. 159. Introducing the text Medhātithi explains that the author's object is to prohibit excessive chastisement in the form of beating, chiding and the like to which the teacher takes recourse on finding his pupil to be inattentive. Addressing the pupil as his child, the teacher should, according to Medhātithi, ask him gently to finish his lesson quickly so that he might afterwards play with boys of his own age. But if the boy still remains inattentive, he should be beaten with a bamboo slip as mentioned in the text. Writing elsewhere (on *Manu,* II. 70) in a humorous vein, Medhātithi observes that the boy, at the time of Vedic study, should wear light dress, because if he were to be clad in woollen clothes he would not feel the strokes of the rope administered by the teacher for inattention and, not feeling the strokes, he would not study in the proper manner.
22. *Manu,* III. 156; *Yāj,* III. 230; *Varāha Purāṇa,* XIV. 5.
23. Quoted by Aparārka on *Yāj,* II. 198.
24. On *Manu,* III. 156.
25. He who stipulates to teach the Veda, Medhātithi says (*loc. cit.*), in return for a specific payment is called a *bhṛitakādhyāpaka* ('teacher for a stipulated fee'). Such form of payment is known among bearers and others. But one does not become such a teacher, if he teaches a pupil without first making a verbal stipulation for payment of a specific sum for a specific teaching, and receives the fee afterwards. In fact teaching in return for payment of an unstipulated fee has been actually sanctioned. Similarly one is said to be taught for a stipulated fee if he studies with his teacher after paying the fee himself. But one does not incur blame if, in the absence of any other

teacher, his father or other guardian has paid the fee and placed him under a teacher.

26. On *Manu,* II. 112.
27. *Manu,* II. 235.
28. On *Manu,* II. 108, 182, 191.
29. Commenting on *Manu,* II. 108, which requires a student to perform acts of service to his teacher, Medhātithi mentions, as an example of such acts, the fetching of water in jars for the teacher's use. Again while explaining *Manu,* II. 182, Medhātithi says that the student should do all household work that is not degrading, but he must not be made to perform such acts as eating remnants of food, other than that of his teacher, and sweeping the floor. Explaining *Manu,* II. 191, Medhātithi observes that the student should do unasked such acts for his teacher as fetching water in jars and massaging his body when he is fatigued.
30. On *Manu,* II. 49.
31. *Kāv.* X, p. 53.
32. *Sūktimuktāvalī* (*GOS* Ed. 47) of Jalhaṇa, a twelfth century anthology, contains verses written by Rājaśekhara in praise of five such poetesses, *viz.* Śīlabhaṭṭārikā, Vikaṭanitambā, Vijayāṅkā, Prabhudevī, and Subhadrā.
33. In *Kāv.* (Chaps. V, IX, XI) Rājaśekhara quotes no less than thrice the views of his wife on difficult questions of rhetoric.
34. *Upamiti,* pp. 354, 453-59, 875-92.
35. *Rājat,* V. 28-9; VI. 87.
36. *EI,* IV. 60 f.
37. *EI,* IV. 180-81.
38. *ARSIE,* Ins. No. 240 of 1930-31.
39. On *Manu,* V. 91.
40. *Matsyapurāṇa,* CCXVII. 163 f.
41. On *Manu,* VIII. 124.
42. Quoted by Vijñāneśvara on *Yāj,* II. 21.
43. Quoted in *Sm. C.,* I. 30.
44. Quoted by Aparārka on *Yāj,* I. 224.
45. III. 149.
46. *Manu,* III. 150-67; *Yāj,* I. 222-24; *Varāha Purāṇa,* XIV, 4 f, *CXC.* 83 f.
47. Quoted by Aparārka on *Yāj,* III. 30.
48. On *Yāj,* I. 20. The list consists of one who has taken service with a king, one who performs sacrifices for many persons, one who performs sacrifices for a whole village, one who is in the service of a village or town, and lastly, one who does not perform the twilight ceremonies (*sandhyā*) in the morning and in the evening.
49. XVI. 16.
50. *Vṛiddha-Hārīta,* IX. 349-50; *Matsya Purāṇa,* CCXXVII. 115-17; *Manu,* VIII. 350-51.
51. On *Yāj,* III. 222.
52. *Saṁskāraprakāśa,* 513.
53. Quoted in *Sm. C.,* I. 31.
54. Quoted by Aparārka on *Yāj,* III. 292.

54a. *Ibid.*

55. Cf. *Hir. Gr.-sū,* I. 12, 18-20; *Āp. Dh.-sū,* II. 3, 6, 9-10.
56. Quoted in *Saṁskāraprakāśa,* 525 and *Sm. C.,* I. 137.
57. Quoted in *Saṁskāraprakāśa,* loc. cit.
58. On *Manu,* VIII. 413-14.
59. *Ibid,* VIII, 415.
60. *Ibid,* III. 156.
61. *Mbh.* (Cr. Ed. and B), XII. 63, 12-14.
62. On *Manu,* VI. 97.
63. *Ibid,* III. 67 and 121.
64. *Ibid,* X. 127.
65. *Ibid,* X. 42.
66. On *Yāj,* I. 13.
67. On *Manu,* X. 126.
68. *Ibid,* X, 41.
69. *Uśanas,* vv. 31-2; *Vaikhānasa-Smārtasūtra,* 10. 12; *Manu,* X. 47. etc.
70. II. 13-14.

71. Vv. 26-27.
72. *Gaut.* IV. 17; *Manu,* X. 27; *Yāj,* I. 92, etc.
73. Cf. *Vish.* VII. 3. *Yāj,* I. 322; *Mṛichchha,* IX: *Rājat,* V. 180-84; VIII. 23, 83; *EI,* XV. 130 f.
74. I. 10-11.
75. 151. 10 f.
76. On *Manu,* X. 38.
77. Cf. the quotations in Aparārka on *Yāj,* III. 292 (various penances prescribed for touching Chaṇḍālas); Medhātithi on *Manu.* V. 12 (wood and things of wood as well as walls of houses said to be defiled by Chaṇḍālas' touch); *ibid.* on *Manu,* X. 51 (vessels other than those of gold and silver in which Chaṇḍālas and Śvapākas have eaten to be thrown away).
78. *Viz.* the signs of the thunderbolt and the like fixed by the king, or else the executioner's axe or other weapon to be carried on their shoulders (*ibid.* on *Manu,* X. 55).
79. On *Manu,* X. 13.
80. Atri 288-89; Aṅgiras, quoted by Vijñāneśvara on *Yāj,* III. 30; Śātātapa quoted by Aparārka on *Yāj,* III. 292; *Auśanasa-smṛiti,* IX. I. 552.
80a. Quoted by Vijñāneśvara on *Yāj,* III. 30 and in *Sm. C.,* 1. 17.
81. Quoted by Aparārka on *Yāj,* I, 193.
82. On *Manu,* V. 133.
83. Quoted by Vijñāneśvara on *Yāj,* III. 30.
84. Quoted by Aparārka on *Yāj, loc. cit.*
85. IX, 359, 363-64.
86. Quoted by Aparārka, *loc. cit.*
87. For Arab accounts cf. *HIED,* I. 6, 16-17, 76; Hodiwala, p. 19.
88. Cf. EI, I. 186 f (3 sons of a Bhaṭṭa mentioned in list of horse-dealers. Cf. *EI,* II. 161 f (Brāhmaṇa Garga and his descendants served as ministers of Pāla kings Dharmapāla and Devapāla); *EI.* V. 123 f (a Brāhmaṇa and a Vedic scholar advised king Vijayāditya II in defeating an enemy); *EI.* XIII. 189 (Brāhmaṇa Superintendent of buildings praised for fighting an invader); *EI,* IV. 60 f (Brāhmaṇa chief minister and minister of peace and war); *EI,* XIII. 389 (two distinguished Brāhmaṇa *daṇḍanāyakas*); *EI,* II. 217 f (Brāhmaṇa *rāja-dauvārika* or king's door-keeper); *EI,* XV. 58 f (a Brāhmaṇa minister); *SII,* II. Nos. 31 and 39 (a Brāhmaṇa general).
89. Cf. *EI,* I. 159 f (son of Kshatriya mentioned as cultivator of field); *EI,* XIX. 58 f (Kshatriya merchant mentioned in record of A.D. 893).
90. It has been inferred (*IHQ, VI; IA,* 1932, pp. 43-46) from the occurrence of the same name-endings and the same tutelary deity in certain ins. from Eastern India that colonies of Nāgara Brāhmaṇas were settled in Sylhet (c. A.D. 500), Tippera (c. A.D. 750), and Orissa (c. A.D. 795). But this theory lacks confirmation.
91. Cf. *EI,* XIX. 58 f (individuals of *Vaṇik-varkkaṭa, Lamba-kañchuka* and *Māthura* castes mentioned as vendors or purchasers of lands, houses and shops in records of A.D. 864, 896 and 898). Dhanapāla, author of the *Bhavisayatta-kahā,* belonged to the *Dhakkaḍa-Baṇi* caste (*GOS* ed., XX. 9).
92. See *IA,* 1893, 57 f; *EI,* VIII. 317-21; *EI, XVII.* 291-309.
93. For the caste significance, cf. *IHQ,* VI. 53 f (*Karaṇa-kāyastha* mentioned as minister of peace and war of Gupta Emperor Vainya-gupta); *EI,* XV. 301 f (chieftain Lokanātha described as *Karaṇa*); Rāmacharita, *Kavipraśasti* v. 3 (poet's father described as foremost of *Karaṇas* and as minister of peace and war). For the professional significance, cf. *Medinīkosha* and *Vaijayantī* s.v.
94. For the earliest known epigraphical reference to Kāyastha caste, see *EI,* XVIII. 243 (writer of charter of A.D. 871 born in Valabha-Kāyastha *vaṁśa*). For other early epigraphic and literary references, *cf. EI,* XII. 61 (Gauḍa-Kāyastha family mentioned in record of A.D. 999); *Nyāya-kandalī* of Srīdhara, Benares ed. 269 (work written in A.D. 991 at the instance of Pāṇḍudāsa, head-monk of Kāyastha lineage). But Kāyastha in the old professional sense of a scribe or other official is found even in later records dated A.D. 995 (*EI,* X. 78-79); *Trikāṇḍaśesha,* II. 10.2. It has been held (*IHQ,* VI. 60 f and *IA,* LXI. 51) that the Kāyasthas of Bengal are descended from Nāgara Brāhmaṇas who had settled in Eastern India as early as in the sixth century A.D. But this startling theory, as has been rightly pointed out (*HBR,* I 589), lacks confirmation.

95. *EI*. XXVI. 200 ff.
96. According to Medhātithi (*Manu,* VIII. 299) Manu's rule, allowing an erring slave, wife or son to be beaten with a rope or a split bamboo, enjoins a method of correcting them and not the actual beating. Hence, verbal chastisement, Medhātithi continues, shall be applied to correct them, beating being resorted to only where the fault is serious.
97. For refs. cf. *ARSIE,* Nos. 216-19 of 1925, 94 of 1926, etc. These records are of uncertain dates.
98. *Upamiti,* 404-05.
99. On *Manu,* III. 14. In times of difficulty or in the event of not finding a girl of one's own *varṇa,* says Medhātithi, girls of two other *varṇas* may be married by a Brāhmaṇa but not a Śūdra girl. We learn from *Kar.* I that Rājaśekhara, the Brāhmaṇa *guru* of the Pratīhāra king, married a Chāhamāna princess.
100. I. 24. 13-16.
101. On *Manu,* X. 6.
102. Medhātithi on *Manu,* II. 18, and Viśvarūpa on *Yāj,* III. 254.
103. On *Manu,* VIII. 366.
104. Medhātithi breaks new ground when he says (on *Manu,* V. 151) that the father can give away the girl only with the mother's consent, for the husband and the wife have joint title to all things, and the daughter belongs to both.
105. On *Manu,* IX. 88.
106. *Ibid,* IX. 4.
107. *Ibid,* IX. 94.
108. *Ibid,* IX. 90-91.
109. *Ibid,* IX. 99.
110. *Ibid,* IX. 97.
111. *Ibid,* IX. 72.
112. *Ibid,* VIII. 227.
113. I. 65.
114. CLIV. 5.
115. On *Yāj,* I. 63.
116. *Brahma Purāṇa,* quoted by Aparārka on *Yaj,* I. 68-69; *Medhātithi* on *Manu,* VIII. 225.
117. On *Yāj,* I. 69.
118. On *Manu,* V. 158.
119. *Ibid,* V. 165.
120. *Ibid,* IX. 59.
121. *Ibid,* IX. 60.
122. II. 328.
123. *Upamiti,* pp. 353-64; 369-86; 400 ff; 453 ff; 872-91.
123a. *IA,* XXXIX, 191 (inscription of the Guhila Chieftain Śaktikumāra, dated A.D. 977, stating that while the founder of his dynasty was a Brāhmaṇa, his grandfather, great-grandfather and great-great-grandfather married respectively a Rāshṭrakūṭa, a Hūṇa and a Chāhamāna princess). Rājaśekhara's *Karpūramañjarī,* Act I (the author's wife belonged to Chāhamāna lineage, while he himself was a Brāhmaṇa and *guru* of the Gurjara Pratīhāra king Mahendrapāla).
124. On *Manu,* VIII. 359.
125. II. 437.
126. XIII. 29-34.
127. On *Manu,* VIII. 362-63.
128. *Rati,* XI. 31; *Upamiti,* 896.
129. *SII,* IX, No. 77.
130. For Arab writers quoted in this chapter reference may be made to *HIED,* Ferrand and Hodivala.
131. On *Manu,* IX. 1.
132. *Ibid,* I. 32.
133. *Ibid,* IX. 1.
134. Respectively on *Manu,* IV. 25; and on *Yāj,* I. 224 and II. 75.
135. II. 36.
136. On *Manu,* IX. 77.
137. *Ibid,* IX. 74.
138. *Ibid,* IX. 95.
139. *Yāj,* I. 70.

140. *Matsya Purāṇa,* CCXXVII. 153-55; *Manu,* VIII. 299-300.
141. On *Manu,* VIII. 299.
142. On *Yāj,* I. 80.
143. On *Manu,* IX. 84.
144. This contradicts Medhātithi's dictum quoted above denying to the husband dominion over his wife.
145. On *Manu,* IX. 81.
146. *Ibid,* IX. 82.
147. *Ibid,* IX. 76.
147a. On *Manu,* VIII. 28.
148. Aparārka on *Yāj,* I. 87; Medhātithi on *Manu,* V. 156.
149. *HIED,* I. 11.
150. Among the examples of *satis* during this period are a queen of king Yaśaskara of Kāshmir and a queen of his successor Kshemagupta (*Rājat,* VI. 107, 195-96); a lady probably early in the reign of the Chola King Parāntaka I (*Ins.* No. 376 of 1903); a queen of Sundara Chola (*Ins.* No. 236 of 1902 and *SII.* 393 f).
151. *AR.* 344.
152. V. 480.
153. On *Manu,* IX. 135.
154. Cf. Bayana (Bharatpur State) ins. of queen Chittralekhā dated A.D. 955 (*EI,* XXII. 122 f); Tumbagi (Bijāpur District) ins. of West Chālukya king Satyāśraya dated A.D. 1004 (EI, XVII. 8 f); Ins. No. 149 of 1036-37 belonging to the reign of Parāntaka I; Ins. of Rājarāja I, recording transfer of 400 temple women from other temple-establishments in Chola land to the king's own temple at Tanjore (*SII,* II. No. 66).
154a. *HIED.* 11.
155. LXX. 28 f; CCXXVIII. 144 f.
156. Cf. Abū Zaid quoted in *Hodivala,* 12 (Indian custom of settling prostitutes in inns built for travellers); Ibn Khordādbah, Ibn al-Fakīh, and Ibn Rosteh quoted in *Ferrand,* 28, 63, 73 (Indian custom of regarding prostitution as legal). As an illustration of the kind of service performed by this class of women in the royal household, cf. *Upamiti* (p. 385) which states that on the occasion of marriage between prince Nandivardhana and princess Kanakamañjarī the bridegroom was bathed by prostitutes.
157. *Ibid.* pp. 374 ff and 618 ff.
158. *Kuṭṭ,* vv. 256 ff.
159. In this passage (vv. 106 f) the female messenger sent by Mālatī to her lover describes not only her physical beauty in full detail, but also mentions her thorough knowledge of the works on erotics of authors like Vātsyāyana, Dattaka, Viṭaputra, and Rājaputra, as well as her exceptional skill in the dramatic manuals of Bharata, Viśākhila, and Dantila, in the science of medicine for trees (*vṛikshāyurveda*), in the art of painting, sewing and drawing lines on the person (*patrachchhedavidhāna*), modelling (*pusta*), cooking, playing musical instruments, dancing and singing.
160. On *Manu,* IX. 2.
161. *Ibid,* IX. 3.
162. *Ibid,* VIII. 77.
163. *Ibid,* VIII. 68.
164. *Matsya P.* CCXXVII. 150; Medhātithi on *Manu,* VIII. 389.
165. *Ibid,* VIII. 28.
166. *Ibid,* X. 188.
167. Ibn al-Fakīh (*Ferrand,* 63) observes with evident exaggeration that in India there are no towns unlike China where there are large towns. Sulaimān (*Ferrand,* 63 n) says more cautiously that in India, the greater part of the country is without towns, while in China fortified and large towns are found in every part of the country.
168. The following translation is based upon the Bengali rendering of Tridiva Nath Ray in his work called *Kuṭṭanīmatam,* Calcutta, 1360 B.S., pp. 12-15.
169. We have a historical reference to Bhaṭṭaputras in *ARSIE,* No. 281 of 1936-37 which mentions two groups of them as recipients of a village granted by Rāshṭrakūṭa king Kṛishna III in A.D. 964.
170. *Kāv.* X, p. 49.
171. On *Manu,* VIII. 219-20.
172. On *Manu,* VIII. 219-20. Medhātithi however adds the saving clause that the compact must be such as is beneficial to the village and so forth, is in con-

formity with canon law and custom, and is not harmful to the interests of the city and the kingdom.

173. On *Manu*, VIII. 221.
174. *EI*, XVI. 2 ff.
175. *EI*, II. 99, 100, 102.
176. *EI*, XIX. 58.
177. *EI*, I. 186.
178. *SII*, III. No. 128.
179. On *Manu*, IX. 76, 143.
180. II. 321 f.
181. *Ibid*, II. 153.
182. *Upamiti*, 220.
183. *Vid*. I.
184. *Kāv*. VI, p. 27.
185. *Kar*. II.
186. *Vid*. II.
187. *Ibid*, III.
188. *Kar*. I.
189. *Ibid*.
190. *Ibid*, III.
191. *Ibid*, IV.
192. *Vid*. III.
193. *Ibid*, II, IV.
194. *Upamiti*, 584.
195. *Kar*. II.
196. *Vid*, I.
197. *Ibid*.
198. *Kar*. IV.
199. Ferrand, 63, *HIED*, I. 39.
200. Cf. *Kar*. II; *Vid*. II; *Kāv*. XVIII; *Upamiti*, p. 354. On the significance of *charcharī* see *Kuṭṭanīmatam*, Bengali Trans. by Tridiva Nath Ray, pp. 192-3, f.n.
201. *IA*, XII. 13; *EI*, V. 23.
202. *Kāv*, X, p. 52.
203. Cf. *Vid*. I, IV; *Rati*, IV. 22.
204. II. 173-75.
205. X. 1-2.
206. *Ibid*, XIII. 93.
207. *Upamiti*, 590-603.
208. Quoted by Aparārka on *Yāj*, I. 176 and in Chaṇḍeśvara's *Gṛihastharatnākara*, 359.
208a. On *Manu*, V. 14 ff., 27, 41-2.
209. On *Manu*, V. 18.
210. *Ibid*, XI. 93-94.
211. On *Yāj*, III. 222.
212. On *Manu*, IX. 235-36.
213. *Ibid*, XI. 146.
213a. Quoted in *Sm. C.* I. 29.
214. Quoted by Aparārka p. 15; *Sm. C.* I. 12; *Par. Mādh*, I. 1. 133.
215. XXII. 83-4.
216. *Upamiti*, 603-04; 627-29.
217. *Kāv*, XVIII, pp. 102, 107.
218. *Ibid*, VIII, p. 39.
219. *Kāv*. VIII. p. 39; cf. also *Kāv*. XVIII, *Upamiti*, 590 ff.
220. On *Manu*, IX. 84.
221. For references, cf. Sulaimān (*HIED*, I. 7), Mas'ūdī (*ibid*, I. 20), Ibn Khordādbah (*Ferrand*, 28) and Ibn Rosteh (*Ferrand*, 70).
222. *Ferrand*, 105.
223. CLV. 1 f; CLVI, 14 f.
224. Cf. *Daksha* II.48. *Śaṅkha* VIII 1-17; and *Agni* P., CLV. 3-4. For fuller details see *KHDS*, II. 1. 658 f.
225. *Ferrand*, 62 and n.
226. With the above we may compare the description in *Kuṭṭ*. 149 f. of the dress and get up of a *gaṇikā* at the time of entertaining her lover. She should wear clothes that are soft, washed, and fumigated with incense; she should put on elegant ornaments, and she should perfume her mouth with a boiled decoction.

For the last-named we have a parallel in the description of the king's bath in Bāna's *Kādambarī* (cf. above, Vol. III, p. 571 n 5).

227. *Abh. Rat.* II. 386, 388-90.
228. *Kāv.* XIII. p. 70.
229. *Ibid,* XVIII.
230. II. 385, 387.
231. XV. 85-92, 94-101.
232. *Upamiti,* 545.
233. *Kar,* I.
234. *Bāla,* X.
235. *Kāv,* VIII, p. 39.
236. *Ibid,* III. pp. 8-9.
237. *Bāla,* X.
238. CCVIII-CCXXXIX.
239. XCIII.
240. On *Manu,* IX. 290.
241. *Upamiti,* 158.
242. *Ibid,* 156.
243. *Kar.* IV.
244. *Vid.* III.
245. *EI,* IX. 6.
246. *HIED,* I. 10.
247. On *Manu,* III. 158, 166-67; and *Auśanasa,* IV, 525-26.
248. I. 24. 13-16.
249. *EC.* VIII.
250. *HIED,* I. 9, 10, 164. *Hodivala,* 9-10.
251. Cf. the quotations in Aparārka on *Yāj.* I. 210, 289-90; *Agni Purāṇa,* CCIX, 23-24. The most well-known names in the list are *tulāpurusha* and *hiraṇyagarbha.* The first involves the weighing of the donor on scales against gold which is thereafter distributed among the Brāhmaṇas, while the second involves the performance of sacraments on the donor seated in a golden vessel which is thereafter broken and distributed among the Brāhmaṇas. For the complete list of the *mahādānas* and summaries of their procedure, see *KHDS,* II. 2. 870-77.
252. *Matsya Purāṇa,* II. 274-89; *Liṅga Purāṇa,* II. 28 f.
253. Cf. *Atri,* 43-46; *Likhita,* 6; *Yama,* 68-70; *Agni Purāṇa,* CCIX. 2-3 (def. of *ishṭa* and *pūrta*).
254. Cf. *EI,* XVIII. 243 f. (Rāshṭrakūṭa Dantidurga performed *hiraṇyagarbha*); *EI,* IX. 33 f (Rāshṭrakūṭa Indra III performed *tulāpurusha* in A.D. 914); *EI,* VII. 36 (Rāshṭrakūṭa Govinda IV performed *tulāpurusha*); *EI,* I. 140 f (*tulāpurusha* by Chandella king Dhaṅga).

CHAPTER XIII

ECONOMIC LIFE

1. AGRICULTURE, INDUSTRY, AND TRADE

In the records of the present period we have abundant evidence of that advanced state of agriculture which we have found to be a characteristic of the Gupta and preceding ages. *Abhidhānaratnamālā* mentions a large variety of cereals and other food-grains with their synonyms.[1] The list comprises *śāli* rice of three varieties, coarse grain (*kodrava*), mustard (*sarshapa*) of two varieties, long pepper or saffron or "Italian millet" (*priyaṁgu*), wild sesamum (*jartila*), wild rice (*nīvāra*), as well as pulses of four different kinds (*masūra, kalāya, rallā*, and *āḍhaka*). A group of 17 articles (including rice and barley) is included by the Smṛitis in the category of grain (*dhānya*), according to Medhātithi.[2] Again, Medhātithi[3] mentions sugar-candy *(ikshukhaṇḍa)* and sugar *(śarkarā)* along with sweetmeats and milk products as illustrations of the varieties of cooked food. The excellence of Puṇḍra (North Bengal) sugar-cane, which yielded juice even without a pressing instrument in contrast to a variety of sugar-cane (*kośakāra*) with its mass of flowers, is pointed out in a verse of *Kāvyamīmāṁsā*.[4] Similarly *Vishṇudharmottara,* quoted in Mitramiśra's *Paribhāshāprakāśa,* gives a list of five kinds of grains (*dhānya*), *viz.* barley, wheat, paddy, sesamum, and edible grains of two varieties (*kaṅgu* or *śyāmaka* and *chīnaka*).[5] Among other agricultural products, camphor and *aguru* are given as examples of costly articles by Medhātithi.[6] The *gośīrsha* variety of sandalwood is included in a list of specially precious products in *Upamitibhavaprapañchākathā*.[7] Other evidence indicates the knowledge of scientific agriculture. From *Abhidhānaratnamālā* we learn that soils were classified variously as fertile (*urvarā*), barren (*iriṇa*), fallow (*khila*), desert (*maru*), and excellent (*mṛitsā* or *mṛitsnā*), as well as those green with grass (*śāḍvala*) or abounding in reeds (*naḍvala*), those which were black or yellow, and those which owed their fertility to rivers or rains.[8] *Abhidhānaratnamālā* further states that different kinds of fields were selected for different classes of crops. It gives[9] synonyms for fields producing several varieties of rice (*vrīhi, śāli, kodrava* and a variety ripening in 60 days), of beans (*mudga* and *māsha*), of oil-seeds (sesame and linseed) as well as those producing hemp, barley, and vegetables. Machines (*yantra*) for crushing big sugar-canes are mentioned in a description of the winter season in *Upamitibhavaprapañchākathā.*[10] Fields irrigated by Persian wheels (*arahaṭa*) and by leather buckets are mentioned in a record of A.D. 946.[11] Again, it appears from Medhātithi[12] quoted above that the Vaiśya (the agriculturist *par excellence*) was expected to know among other things what seed was to be sown thickly and what sparsely, what soil was fitted for a particular kind of seed and what soil was not so fitted, and what harvest was expected from a special variety of seed.

The early Arab writers[13] of the ninth and tenth centuries refer to the fertility of the soil and the rich cultivation, both of grain and fruits, specially in Western India with which they were particularly acquainted. Some cities in Gujarāt grew mangoes, cocoanuts, lemons, and rice in great quantities, and likewise produced quantities of honey. One such city also grew canes and teak trees, while Malabar produced pepper and bamboo.

One of the oldest Indian industries is the textile. The progress of this industry in the Gupta epoch appears to have been continued during this period. The records of this period[13a] mention a great variety and different qualities of textiles such as woollen and hempen yarns, garments made of silk and of *Raṅku* deer's hair, and of sheep's and goat's wool. The professions of the weaver, the tailor, and the dyer (in three different colours, *viz.* red, blue, and yellow) are mentioned in contemporary literature.[13b] Medhātithi[14] says that wives, left unprovided for by their husbands, are to live by such unobjectionable occupations as spinning (*kartana*) and lace-making (*jālikakaraṇa*), and widows forced to live by their own labour are to subsist by the same occupations.

The working of metals was pursued with as much success as in the preceding epoch. The list of metals found in contemporary literature[14a] includes copper, bell-metal (or brass), iron, lead, tin, silver, and gold. Certain centres of metal industry were famous. From the synonyms given in the *Abhidhānaratnamālā* we learn that Surāshṭra was famous for its bell-metal, while Vaṅga was well-known for its tin industry.[15] No less than five centres manufacturing swords are mentioned in *Agni Purāṇa*[16] along with the distinctive qualities of their products. These are Khaṭīkhattara and Rishika (unidentified), Śūrpāraka (Sopārā), Vaṅga (East Bengal), and Aṅga (Monghyr and Bhāgalpur Districts). Ibn Haukal[17] mentions the city of Debal in Sindh as famous for the manufacture of swords. Of the metal-work of this period we have extant specimens in some of the older Choḷa bronzes. Again, the inscriptions of the Great Temple at Tanjore mention the gifts of images, ornaments and vessels of gold, copper, and silver whose recorded weight reaches a very high figure. A colossal copper water-pot weighing 3083 *palas* for crowning the copper pinnacle of the same great shrine was presented by Rājarāja I.[18]

The art of the jeweller appears to have maintained its old level. Lists of jewels are preserved in various texts,[19] the longest being found in *Agni Purāṇa* which mentions no less than 33 kinds of gems and analyses the good qualities of diamond, emerald, ruby, pearls, sapphire and *vaidūrya*.[20] The Tanjore temple inscriptions to which reference has been made above, distinguish between numerous varieties of diamonds, rubies, and, above all, pearls, and they point out the flaws to be found in these gems.[21] The lists of presents recorded in these inscriptions include various kinds of gems and indicate the uses to which they were put in actual practice. The number and weight of the objects, which are always given with scrupulous care, occasionally reach formidable proportions.[22] The list of presents given by Rājarāja I, according to one of these records, included quite a few nine-jewelled rings with one diamond, one sapphire, one pearl, one topaz, one cinnamon-stone, one coral, one emerald, one lapis-lazuli and one ruby set on each.[23]

On the extent and direction of Indian internal trade the records are almost completely silent.[24] Scattered references indicate that India's trade with the outside world was carried on both by land and sea. To the overland routes described above[25] we may add one more from India to China through Tibet.[25a] As regards maritime trade, we know that enterprising Arab merchants from Southern Arabia had built up by this time, across the Indian Ocean, extensive trade relations not only with India, but also with the countries of the Far East as far as China. Of the share of Indians in this trade we have but scanty knowledge. According to Mas'ūdī, ships from India along with those from Basra, Siraf and Oman, from Djāwaga and Champā, ascended the Khanfu river to reach Khanfu (=Canton), at a distance of six or seven days' journey from its junction with the sea. Coming to Indian sources we find in *Trikāṇḍaśesha,* as explained by the commentator, a list of names (*hoḍa, tarāndhu,* and *vahana*) for vessels plying on the high seas.[26] More important are the reminiscences of voyages made by daring Indian merchants, apparently to the rich lands of South-East Asia, which are found in the contemporary prose romances.[27]

It is chiefly from the accounts of the early Arab geographers that we get a list of the principal Indian sea-ports during the present period. On the coast of Sindh, near the mouths of the Sindhu, lay Debal, "a large mart and the port not only of this but also of the neighbouring regions." On the Gujarāt coast were Kambay,

Thāṇā, and Sopārā, and further south lay Sindān (modern Sanjān, 88 miles north of Bombay), from which was exported pepper. On the Malabar coast lay the important port of Kaulam Malaya (modern Quilon) where the ships sailing from Muscat took in fresh water before crossing the sea of Harkand (Bay of Bengal) for the journey to Kalah-bar.[28]

Turning next to articles of trade, it will be appropriate to begin with a list of India's exports. As regards agricultural products, Ibn Khordādbah,[29] writing towards the end of the ninth century, mentions Indian exports consisting of diverse species of aloe-wood, sandalwood, camphor and camphor-water, nutmeg, clovepink, cubele, cocoanut, vegetable stuffs, and textures of velvety cotton. The early Arab writers give us detailed reports of exports from different parts of the country. Thus costus, rattan, camphor-water, indigo, and bamboos were exported from Sindh. It appears that costus from the Himālayas and indigo from Gujarāt, as well as camphor and rattan, probably from Malay and Sumatra, were brought to the ports of Sindh for export. According to *Kāvyamīmāṁsā* pine and deodar trees, grapes, saffron, and jujube were products of Uttarāpatha (North-West India),[30] while birch-barks are mentioned as products of the Himālayas in a verse quoted in the same work.[31] According to Ibn Rosteh, teak was exported from the Rāshṭrakūṭa kingdom of Western India where it was extensively grown. The pepper which was exported from Sindān, and the sandals for which Cambay was famous, according to Arab writers, were sent probably from South India noted from early times as the home of these products. *Kāvyamīmāṁsā* mentions among products of Western India (Paśchāddeśa) varieties of bamboos, palm trees, bdellium, and date trees.[32] The characteristic products of Malaya Hill (Western Ghāṭs below the Kāverī) in South India consisted of sandalwood, pepper, cardamom and various perfume-bearing plants.[33] From the extensive reference to the use of sandalwood which is found in the literature of this period we can infer that a large and valuable trade in this article was carried on by South India with the rest of the country. As regards Eastern India, Pūrvadeśa (defined as the land to the east of Banaras) grew, according to *Kāvyamīmāṁsā,* different species of fragrant plants and trees (*lavalī* creeper and *granthiparṇaka* tree) as well as aloes and grapes.[34] Again, Kāmarūpa, according to Abū Zaid,[35] produced a variety of aloe-wood called *kāmarūbi* which was valued sometimes at 200 *dīnāras* per maund. It was, he says, of the highest quality, and was so tender as to retain the impression of the seal stamped on it. It was brought all the way from Kāmarūpa to the temple of the Sun-god at Multān, where the merchants bought it from the priests of the deity. If Abū Zaid's reference to Kāmarūpa is to be taken as correct, it would point to aloe having been the most valuable article of export from Assam. It should, however, be mentioned that another Arab writer Mas'ūdī, probably with better reason, substitutes Khmer (Cambodia) for Kāmarūpa in the corresponding passage. Of another kingdom called Rahma (or Ruhmi) by the Arabs, we are told that it produced Indian aloe-wood and a remarkably fine variety of cotton fabrics. The textiles of Rahma, according to Ibn Khordādbah, were of velvety cotton, while Sulaimān declared them to be so light and fine that a robe made of that cloth could be passed through a signet ring. If the identification of Rahma with the Pāla kingdom could be accepted as correct, it would follow that cotton textiles of unique fineness were manufactured in Bengal at this period and exported to other lands.[36]

As regards animals and animal products *Kāvyamīmāṁsā* includes skins and chowries made of *chamara* deer's tail among the products of Uttarāpatha, and musk among those of Pūrvadeśa.[37] In the extreme south the Tāmraparṇī river in the Pāṇḍya kingdom, at the point of its junction with the sea, was still famous for its pearl fisheries.[38] According to Medhātithi,[39] precious stones and pearls in the South, horses in the West, elephants in the East, as well as saffron, silks, and woollens in Kāshmir were royal monopolies, and private trading in them was punished with confiscation of all the property of the offender. We may refer, lastly, to the testimony of two Arab writers, Sulaimān and Mas'ūdī, that horns of rhinoceros were exported from the kingdom of Rahma to China for being made into fashionable and costly girdles.[40] The same writers supply the information that the kingdom of Ruhmi produced *"samara"* (yak-tail) hair from which fly-whisks were made.

As for mineral products, antimony (*srotoñjana*), rock-salt (*saindhava*), and beryl (*vaidūrya*) are mentioned by Rājaśekhara[41] among the characteristic products of Uttarāpatha. The rock-salt must have come from the famous Salt Range in the Punjāb. As regards precious metals, Sulaimān and Mas'ūdī[41a] heard reports of the existence of gold and silver mines in the kingdom of Gudjra (Gurjara-Pratīhāra kingdom of Kanauj), while they definitely declared that gold and silver were found in the kingdom of Rahma (Pāla kingdom?) above mentioned. These statements, vague and inconclusive as they are, lack corroboration.

We now turn to the import-trade. The paucity of horses in India has attracted the attention of foreign observers at all times. We have during this period the testimony of Sulaimān and Ibn al-Fakīh[42] that the Indians, unlike the Chinese, had few horses. The best breed of horses known to India at this period, as in former times, came from Western and Central Asia. *Abhidhānaratnamālā* mentions as examples of excellent horses those of Persia, Vanāyu, Kāmboja, Bāhlika (Balkh), Sindhu, and the land bordering on the Sindhu.[43] *Upamitibhavaprapañchākathā* singles out Bāhlika, Kāmboja, and Turushka horses as the best.[44] Horses are also included among the characteristic animals of North-West India in *Kāvyamīmāṁsā.* We may well believe that an extensive and valuable export trade in horses was carried on with India by the countries on her western frontier. The importation of wine from Kapiśa is hinted at by the synonym Kāpiśāyana given for wines in *Abhidhānaratnamālā.*[45] Ibn Said,[46] an Arab writer of later date, mentions the import of dates from Basra into Daybul in Sindh. The phrase *chīnāṁśuka* (Chinese silk), found in the literature of this period as in former times, suggests that this fine stuff was still being brought from China. It is permissible to infer from the stories in the *Upamitibhavaprapañchākathā* that gems came from South-East Asia. Again, if Abū Zaid and Mas'ūdī are correct in their statements, it would follow that the costly aloe-wood presented to the Sun-god at Multān was imported from distant Cambodia.

2. THE ORGANISATION OF INDUSTRY AND TRADE

The guilds and similar associations continued to play an important part as in the previous centuries. We learn from Medhātithi that both industrial and mercantile guilds functioned in his time, for he defines[47] the guild (*śreṇī*) as consisting of people following common professions, such as tradesmen, artisans, money-lenders, coach-drivers, and so forth. From Medhātithi's illustration of the laws of guilds in the same context we find that they sometimes compounded with the government for payment of a fixed sum in place of the usual share of their profits; in return they took advantage of the Smṛiti clause guaranteeing the inviolability of their agreement, and cornered the market for their own profit.[48] More important than the guild as an example of mercantile organisation was the *saṁgha.* In its generic sense *saṁgha* is defined by Medhātithi[49] as a community of persons following the same pursuit, though belonging to different castes (*jāti*) and regions (*deśa*). This is illustrated by the example of *saṁghas* of mendicants (*bhikshu*), of merchants (*vaṇik*), and of those versed in the four Vedas. The mercantile *saṁgha,* then, unlike the guild, was an association of traders comprising different castes and inhabiting different regions. As Manu's text[50] imposes the penalty of banishment upon those violating the compact made under oath with a *saṁgha,* it follows from Medhātithi's interpretation just quoted that the mercantile associations, like the guilds, had the right of making bye-laws that were binding on their members.

Besides the *śreṇī* and the *saṁgha* there were associations of labourers, and doubtless of capitalists as well. Illustrating Manu's law on the subject Medhātithi[51] lays down the rule that among architects, masons, carpenters, and the like the wages shall be distributed on the principle that he who does the most difficult part of the job shall receive more, and he who does the easier part shall get less.

In the inscriptions of this period we have concrete examples, not only of different classes of guilds, but also of their constitution and functions. Among the guilds specially mentioned are those of weavers, potters, gardeners, and artisans. Mention is made of single as well as multiple headmen (*mahattaras*) who evidently formed (as in the old Smṛiti law of Yājñavalkya and Nārada) the executive of these bodies. The guilds collectively made endowments for pious objects or received them on trust to provide for such objects out of the accruing interest. In either case they arranged for distributing the task among themselves, evidently in accordance with the old Smṛiti rule giving legal authority to the agreement of guilds.[52] Sometimes the guilds, no doubt because of their proved honesty, were entrusted with the task of auditing the accounts of temples.[53] Finally we have in the inscriptions of South India evidence of the working of two famous trading corporations. The first is the *maṇīgrāmam* whose history can be traced from the end of the ninth down to the thirteenth century. It was apparently a non-denominational institution open to Hindus as well as Christian settlers, and its activities were carried on in the coastal as well as in the inland towns of South India. The second is the famous Nānādeśa-Tiśaiyāyirattu-Aiññūṟṟuvar which was destined to extend its activities to Burma and Sumatra in the eleventh and twelfth centuries. There is reason to believe that it was already established by the time of the early Imperial Choḷas, Vijayālaya and Parāntaka I.[54]

While on the subject of guilds and mercantile associations we may notice the important role of the village-assemblies in the public economy of this period. Repeatedly, in the ninth and tenth century inscriptions of South India, we find village-assemblies called *sabhā* and *ur* receiving deposits of money or gifts of land on trust for pious and charitable purposes. Out of the interest accruing from these sums, or the income derived from the land, they undertook to provide for the objects stipulated by the donor. This implies that like the guilds described above, the village-assemblies often acted as bankers and public trustees.[55] We have even examples of specified markets within various town-limits functioning similarly as bankers for pious and charitable persons.[56]

3. INTEREST AND WAGES

The old legal rate of interest, laid down in Vasishṭha at 15 p.c. per annum, had ceased to be binding, and the usage had outgrown even the somewhat flexible rules of later Smṛiti texts. But Medhātithi generally upholds the older law relating to usury against later interpretations. As regards Manu's higher scale of rates (2%, 3%, 4%, and 5% per month) to be paid respectively by Brāhmaṇas, Kshatriyas, Vaiśyas, and Śūdras, Medhātithi says[57] that these alternatives are allowable to a money-lender who cannot maintain his family at the 1¼% rate, or to one who has only a small capital, or in case of the borrower not being a specially righteous person. To this, however, Medhātithi adds the saving clause that the above rate must not be exceeded by even a half or a quarter. Like the older Smṛiti writers Medhātithi permits a series of special rates of maximum interest, but unlike them he makes these higher rates dependent upon the fact (or even chance) of the debtor's success with his loan. If the money-lender, he says,[58] has been reduced to poverty and the debtor has grown opulent with the wealth earned from the borrowed grain, the interest shall be five times the principal, but otherwise it shall only be four times the same. Even where the creditor, continues Medhātithi,[59] has reason to believe that the debtor is about to carry on an extensive business with the capital lent, he may take the maximum rate of 5% irrespective of the debtor's caste and of the articles lent.

The violations of the Smṛiti law, arising no doubt from the pressing need for capital, were sometimes so frequent as to harden into regular (if unauthorised) customs. For Medhātithi mentions[60] that in some countries, grains are lent out during spring and double the quantity is realised in autumn, and sometimes a mortgaged article is enjoyed even after the value of the produce so enjoyed is equal to double the amount of the original debt. Such customs, Medhātithi adds, violate Manu's rule[61] that the accumulated debt and interest shall not exceed double the principal, as well as that of Yājñavalkya[62] limiting the amount of the accumulated interest to 80% of the principal.

The variations in the rate of interest are repeated in the contemporary historical records. In a West India record of A.D. 854, belonging to the reign of the Rāshṭrakūṭa Amoghavarsha,[63] the donor, endowing a certain sum of money in favour of a monastery, declares that after his death the interest (*kāri*) is to be fixed by competent persons. In the inscriptions of South India[64] we find a bewildering variety in the rate of interest such as 25, 20, 15, 12½ and even 5 per cent per annum.

The Smṛiti law relating to wages can be gleaned from Medhātithi.[64a] The wages which were paid in cash or in kind were fixed by contract according to the nature of the work to be done, the contract sometimes extending over a period of six months or even a year. Wilful breach of the contract rendered the labourer liable to forfeiture of his wages as well as to payment of compensation to his employer. Inscriptions of South India during the sway of the Imperial Choḷas give us lists of wages of different classes of skilled as well as unskilled labourers employed in the temples. These are specified in terms of the daily supply of paddy and the yearly allowance of coins, in the yearly supply of paddy, and so forth.[65]

4. INFLUENCE OF CANON LAW UPON ECONOMIC DEVELOPMENT

The old Smṛiti attitude, viewing the pursuit of agriculture, industry, and trade with high disfavour, is continued in the present period. This general standpoint is reflected in a passage of Medhātithi[66] where he takes the original text to mean, not that the Vaiśya shall be made, against his will, to perform the occupations of agriculture, money-lending, trade, and cattle-breeding, but that the king shall punish any other man who does this work except in times of distress. Coming to particular industries, Medhātithi[67] regards handicrafts as very low occupations, and he illustrates them by the examples of cooks and weavers. Again, with reference to Manu's text including the execution of great mechanical works among minor sins (*upapātakas*), Medhātithi[68] gives as illustrations the construction of bridges and of embankments for regulating water-flow. Medhātithi's view of the relative status of different occupations is similar to that of Manu.[69] For he says[70] that among the Vaiśya's occupations agriculture is the worst for a Brāhmaṇa, then comes trade, and next the tending of cattle and so forth.

5. GENERAL ECONOMIC CONDITION

The above survey provides broad hints of the general economic condition of the people during the present age. That the state of agriculture, industry, and trade in these times was at least as advanced as in the preceding centuries is borne out, as shown above, by the joint evidence of general literature, historical records, and foreign writings. It is worth remarking that those parts of the country like Sindh and Gujarāt, which came specially under the observation of the Arab visitors, are specially noted for their fertility and good cultivation. The variety and excellence of Indian textiles and metal-work. and above all of Indian jewellery, are attested to by literary as well as epigraphic evidence. The sea and land routes of Indian teachers visiting China, Central Asia, and Tibet, as well as South-East Asia, were no doubt followed by the Indian merchants as well, reminiscences of whose unrecorded adventures have been partially preserved in the form of stories in the contemporary Jain prose romances. The daring and enterprise as well as the profit-motive of the merchants, of which we get such vivid accounts in the Jain stories, no doubt more than compensated for the discouragement held out by the traditional Smṛiti law. About the condition of the people, it is possible to form a general opinion. The quantity and richness of the presents in gold, silver, and jewels offered by Rājarāja I to the Tanjore temple, and the fabulous wealth of Indian temples described by Muslim writers, specially in connection with Sultan Mahmūd's invasions, illustrate the high prosperity not only of the Imperial courts but also of the great shrines of this period. Some of the Imperial capitals must have attained considerable magnitude. In the reign of Rājarāja I the city of Tanjore, according to two contemporary inscriptions,[71] contained at least 25 streets, bazaars and quarters.[72] That the high level of prosperity was a fairly general one, at least in some regions, may be proved not only from the broad descriptions of the standard of living given above, but also from subsidiary evidence recorded in literature.

1. *Abh. Rat.*, II. 425-29.
2. On *Manu*, VIII. 320.
3. *Ibid*, VIII. 326 f.
4. *Kāv*, XII.
5. *Paribhāshāprakāśa*, 115.
6. On *Manu*, VIII. 321.
7. *Upamiti*, 420.
8. *Abh. Rat.*, II. 3-6.
9. *Ibid*, II. 7-9.
10. *Upamiti*, 585.
11. *EI*, XIV. 182.
12. On *Manu*, IX, 330.
13. *HIED*, I. 15-16, 24, 27-8, 35, 37-40; *Ferrand*, 117.
13a. Cf. Medhātithi on *Manu*, II. 98; VIII, 321; VIII. 326; *Kar*, I.
13b. *Abh.Rat.*, II.433 f; *Matsya Purāṇa*, (quoted by Aparārka on *Yāj*, II. 289-90).
14. On *Manu*, IX, 75.
14a. *Abh. Rat.*, II. 15-9; *Bhavishya Purāṇa* (quoted in *Paribhāshāprakāśa*, 115).
15. *Abh.Rat.*, II. 15 f.
16. CCXLV, 21 f.
17. *HIED*, I. 37.
18. Cf. *SII*, II. Nos. 1, 2, 29, 30, 32, 34, 38, 39; 42-44, 46-52, 55, 56, 79-81, 84, 91.
19. *Abh. Rat.*, II. 20-1; *Āditya Purāṇa* (quoted in *Paribhāshāprakāśa*, 115). *Upamiti*, 420.
20. *Agni Purāṇa*, CCXLVI. 1 f.
21. For a convenient summary with full references, see *SII*, II. Introd. 16-17 and *n*.
22. Thus among donations given to the temple by Rājarāja I are mentioned (*SII*, II. No. 93) gold necklaces, armlets, bracelets, arm-rings etc. set with rubies, emeralds, diamonds, sapphires, pearls, amethyst and crystals, sandalwood coated with plates of gold and set with various kinds of jewels and so forth. The gifts of Rājarāja I's queens included (*ibid*, Nos. 34, 46, 51) ornaments on which

were strung pearls, coral, lapis lazuli, and sapphire. Ornaments sets with pearls of three varieties, coral, lapis lazuli, and so forth were presented (*ibid*, No. 6) by Rājarāja I's elder sister. Presents given by Rājarāja I's general comprised (*ibid*, No. 39) golden ornaments set with pearls, diamonds, crystals and so forth. The temple manager donated to the shrine of Gaṇapati at the same temple a magnificent ring made of gold and set with eight rubies, two crystals, 14 diamonds, and 119 pearls (*ibid*, No. 86). Among presents made to the temple by a private donor in Rājarāja I's reign were included (*ibid*, No. 79) golden ear-rings set with pearls, pearl-ornaments, a gold marriage-badge set with five diamonds and one ruby, sacred foot-strings set with pearls, and so forth. In a list of treasures belonging to the same temple are included (*ibid*, No. 59) a diadem containing more than 343 *karañju* of gold, ten diamond crystals, 64 corals, and no less than 13328 pearls as well as nine golden girdles adorned with crystals, pearls, and coral. Another list of treasures belonging to the same temple dated in the reign of Rājarāja I includes (*ibid*, No. 3) sacred girdles and bracelets of gold set with pearls, a sacred crown of gold set with diamonds, crystals, and pearls, a sacred garland of gold set with crystals and pearls, and a sacred outer parasol of gold set with crystals and pearls. Many of the sacred girdles contained more than 1500 pearls each, while the outer parasol contained 1372 pearls.

23. *SII*, II. No. 93.
24. Cf. however, the story in *Kāv*. III, describing the sale of a pearl, found in S. India at Kanauj.
25. Vol II, pp. 606, 613, 617 ff, 644.
25a. Cf. Ya'kūbī's list of products imported into India (*Ferrand*, 50-52).
26. *Trikāṇḍaśesha*, I, 19.6.
27. *Bhav*. III-VI; *Upamiti*, 860-904, 996-1002.
28. For references, see *HIED*, I. 15, 37, 441; *Ferrand*, 32, 38-40, 55, 57; 64, 95. On the above see also Hobson-Jobson s.v. Cambay, Deul-Sind, Quilon, Saint-John's, Sopara and Tana.
29. *Ferrand*, 31.
30. *Kāv*. XVII. 94.
31. *Ibid*, XIV. 81.
32. *Ibid*, XVII, 94.
33. *Abh. Ratn*. II. 388; *Kar*, I; *Kāv*. XIV, XVII; *Bāla*. 670.
34. *Kāv*. XVII, 93.
35. *Ferrand*, 88.
36. Ramha identified with Pāla kingdom of Bengal (*HBR*, I. 122) but *Ferrand* (29 and 43 n) identifies it with Pegu and Çoedés (*Histoire Ancienne des Etats Hindouises d'Extrême-Orient 135*) with Lower Burma. Probably the Arab accounts have jumbled together the records of the two kingdoms of Bengal and Lower Burma.
37. *Kāv*., XVII. 93.
38. Cf. *Kāv*. V. XIV; *Bāla*, 671; *Kar*. III.
39. On *Manu*, VIII. 399.
40. These girdles were prized so highly by Chinese royalty and grandees that they sometimes fetched 2000 or even 4000 *dīnāras* each (*Ferrand*, 44, 105). To the above we may add the curious statement of Ibn al-Fakīh (*Ferrand*, 57), that perfumed rats were exported from Sindh to Zābag.
41. *Kāv*., XVII. 94.
41a. *Ferrand*, 43, 104.
42. *Ferrand*, 62 and n.
43. II. 284.
44. *Upamiti*, 474.
45. II. 174.
46. *Ferrand*, 48 n.
47. On *Manu*, VIII. 41.
48. Certain principal tradesmen, says Medhātithi (*loc. cit.*), offer to the king his royal dues fixed verbally by declaring before him: "We are living by this trade, let the tax thereupon be fixed at such and such a rate, be our profits more or less." Now on the king agreeing to this proposal, the tradesmen join together and lay down certain rules among themselves tending to bring them large profits and injure the interest of the kingdom, *e.g.* such and such a commodity should not be sold during such and such a time. If any one among them transgresses these rules, he shall be punished for breach of the guild-laws.
49. On *Manu*, VIII. 219.

50. VIII. 219.
51. On *Manu*, VIII. 211.
52. Cf. *EI*. I. 159; VI. 166; XIII. 192; XXIV. 333; *SII*. III. No. 91.
53. Cf. Ins. of reign of Uttamachoḷa *SII*, III. No. 124 (local merchants join with village-assembly as well as temple-officers in making up accounts of gifts of gold to a temple).
54. On *Maṇigrāmam* see *EI*, IV. 248 and *ARSIE*, 1926-27, pp. 93-94 giving a number of references. On Nānādeśa Tiśaiyāyirattu Aiññuṟṟuvar see K. A. Nilakanta Sastri, *The Choḷas*, Vol. II, Part I, 419-20 and the references quoted there.
55. Cf. *ARSIE*, 469-70 of 1925-26; App. B. of 958 and 963 A.D.: 109 of 1932-33; 503 of 1929-30; App. B.; *SII*, III. No. 44 of 888 A.D.. *ibid*, No. 1, *SII*, II. Nos. 7, 24, 25, 26, 27, 28, 35; *SII*, XII. Nos. 75, 87, 90; *EI*, XXVI. 234-35.
56. Cf. *SII*, II. Nos. 24 and 37. In *EI*, XXI. 109 f a pious endowment of 1400 *kāśus* is deposited by Pāṇḍya king Varaguṇa Mahārāja II with Brahmanical and non-Brahmanical village assemblies (*sabhā* and *ur*) as well as a town-council (*nagarattār*).
56a. On *Manu*, VIII. 151.
57. On *Manu*, VIII. 142.
58. *Ibid*, VIII. 151.
59. *Ibid*, VIII. 152.
60. *Ibid*, VIII. 3.
61. *Manu*, VIII. 151.
62. *Yāj*, III. 37.
63. *IA*, XIII. 134.
64. *EI*, IX. 89, XI. 228 XXI. 109; XXVI. 234; *SII*, XII Nos. 75, 87, 90; III. Nos. 94, 103, 105, 186, 190, 128; II. Nos. 6, 9, 24, 25, 26, 28, 35, 37.
64a. On *Manu*, VIII. 215.
65. For a list of wages mentioned in Tanjore Temple Inscriptions, see *SII*, II. Introd. p. 18. Also see Altekar, *AR*, 395-98, for some calculations of equivalents of salaries and wages figuring in Karnātak and South Indian Inscriptions of this period.
66. On *Manu*, VIII. 410.
67. *Ibid*, X. 99.
68. *Ibid*, XI. 64.
69. X. 80 f.
70. *Manu*, X. 85.
71. S
72. F

CHAPTER XIV

COLONIAL AND CULTURAL EXPANSION

I. THE ŚAILENDRA EMPIRE

The outstanding fact in the history of South-East Asia in the eighth century A.D. is the rise of a great empire which comprised Sumatra, Java, Malay Peninsula, and most of the islands of the Indian archipelago. The rulers of this empire belonged to the Śailendra dynasty. They put an end to the supremacy of Śrī-Vijaya in Malay Peninsula,[1] and occupied a large part, if not the whole, of it by the end of the eighth century A.D. Some time before A.D. 778 they had conquered Western and Central Java. It is generally held that they were originally rulers of Śrī-Vijaya (Palembang in Sumatra) and extended their authority gradually over Java and Malay Peninsula; but this view rests upon a very slender basis. It is equally likely that the Śailendras first rose to power either in Java or in Malay Peninsula.

We do not possess sufficient data to reconstruct an outline of the history of the Śailendras. The names of a few early kings flourishing in the eighth century A.D. may be traced in contemporary epigraphic records. One of them is probably Rājādhirāja Vishṇu. Another, king Dharaṇīndra, is described as "the ornament of the Śailendra dynasty who has conquered kings in all directions, and who has crushed the most powerful hero of the enemy." Another, king Saṅgrāmadhanañjaya, is also mentioned in a record of the last-mentioned king, but the relation between the two is not specified.

The Nālandā Charter of the reign of Devapāla, mentioned above,[2] refers to three generations of Śailendra kings. It first mentions the great king of Yava-bhūmi. His proper name is not mentioned, but we are told that it meant 'tormentor of brave foes'. The original Sanskrit expression *'vīra-vairi-mathana'* immediately recalls the epithet *'vairi-vara-vīra-vimardana'* applied to the Śailendra king Dharaṇīndra mentioned above, and the two may be regarded as identical. The son and successor of Dharaṇīndra is named Samarāgravīra. This king married Tārā, daughter of a king whose name has been read both as Varma-setu and Dharma-setu. The former reading seems preferable. Those who adopt the latter reading suggest his identification with the Emperor Dharmapāla of Bengal.

The son of Samarāgravīra and Tārā was Bālaputradeva, who is called king of Suvarṇadvīpa, a term which denotes in a general way the whole of Malay Peninsula and Malay Archipelago.

More definite information is, however, available in respect of the extent of the empire and its wealth and grandeur. This is mainly derived from the accounts of various Arab writers in the ninth and tenth centuries A.D. They refer to the country as Zābag or Zābaj and call its king *Mahārāja.* According to Ibn Khordādbah (A.D. 844-848) the daily revenue of the king amounted to two hundred *mans* of gold. Sulaimān (A.D. 851) says that Kalah-bar (*i.e.* the country round the Isthmus of Kra in the Malay Peninsula) is a part of the empire of Zābag. Ibn al-Fakīh (A.D. 902) adds that there is no country in the south after Zābag and its king is very rich. Ibn Rosteh (A.D. 903) remarks about the great king of Zābag that 'he is not regarded as the greatest among the kings of India, because he dwells in the islands.' But he adds: "No other king is richer or more powerful than he and none has more revenue."

Abū Zaid Ḥasan (A.D. 916) gives a more detailed account of the kingdom of Zābag. "The area of the kingdom," says he, "is about 900 (square) *parsangs* (1 *parsang* = 3 miles). The king is also overlord of a large number of islands extending over a length of 1,000 *parsangs* or more. Among the kingdoms over which he rules are the island called Sribuza (Śrī Vijaya) with an area of about 400 (square) *parsangs,* the island called Rāmī with an area of about 800 (square) *parsangs,* and the maritime country of Kalah with an area of 80 (square) *parsangs.*"

Mas'ūdī (A.D. 943) also gives a long and interesting account of Zābag which, he says, separates India from China and is comprised within the former country. About the extent and wealth of Zābag he remarks: "In the bay of Champā is the empire of Mahārāja, the king of the islands, who rules over an empire without limit and has innumerable troops. Even the most rapid vessels could not complete in two years a tour round the isles which are under his possession. The territories of this king produce all sorts of spices and aromatics, and no other sovereign of the world gets as much wealth from the soil".

Al-Bīrūnī (A.D. 1030) tells us that "the eastern islands in this ocean, which are nearer to China than to India, are the islands of the Zābaj, called by the Hindus, Suvarṇa-dvīpa, *i.e.* the gold islands ... because you obtain much gold as deposit if you wash only a little of the earth of that country." This common geographical name Suvarṇa-dvīpa, roughly denoting the Śailendra Empire, perhaps owes its origin to that great historical fact.

These accounts of the Arab writers, to which others may be added, leave no doubt that the Śailendra empire was extensive and powerful and comprised a large part of the Malay Peninsula and Malay Archipelago collectively known as Suvarṇa-dvīpa. There are also good grounds to believe that the Śailendras exercised supremacy over Kambuja till Jaya-varman II freed his country early in the ninth century A.D. It is also likely that the frequent Javanese naval raids on Annam (Champā) and Tonkin, to which reference will be made later, were really carried out by the Śailendras who then occupied Java. Thus the Śailendras were the leading naval power in the East, and their influence was felt on the eastern coast of Indo-China as far as the border of the Chinese empire.

This naval supremacy enabled the Śailendras to control the sea-borne trade between China and the Western countries. Mas'ūdī observes that formerly there was direct voyage between China and ports like Sīrāf and Oman, but in his time the port of Kalah served as the meeting place for the mercantile navies of the two countries. As noted above, Kalah was in Malay Peninsula within the dominions of Zābag. Abū Zaid Ḥasan also informs us that "the town of Kalah is the most important commercial centre for trade in aloe, camphor, sandalwood, ivory, tin, ebony, spices, and various other articles." He adds that there was a regular maritime intercourse between this port and Oman.

The control over the vast maritime trade of those days explains the fabulous wealth of the Mahārāja of Zābag referred to by most of the Arab writers. Several of them record a curious story which is narrated by Abū Zaid Ḥasan as follows: "There is one very extraordinary custom in Zābag. The palace of the king is connected with the sea by a shallow lake. Into this, the king throws every morning a brick made of solid gold. These bricks are covered by water during tide, but are visible during ebb. When the king dies, all these bricks are collected, counted, and weighed, and these are entered in official records. The gold is then distributed among the members of the royal family, generals, and royal slaves according to their rank, and the remnant is distributed among the poor."

The Chinese annals contain frequent references to a kingdom called San-fo-tsi which undoubtedly stands for the Śailendra empire. It sent embassies to China in A.D. 904 or 905, 960, 961, 962, 971, 972, 974, 975, 980 and 983.

The trade relations with China were also revived in the tenth century. A regular shipping house was opened at Canton in A.D. 971 and two more at a later period, which were frequented by merchants from San-fo-tsi and other places in the East Indies.

We further learn from Chinese sources that towards the close of the tenth century A.D. there were bitter hostilities between San-fo-tsi and Java. About A.D. 990 Java invaded San-fo-tsi and at first obtained some success. San-fo-tsi sought the protection of China, for she was reduced to such a state that her envoys could not voyage safely from China back to their country. But in A.D. 1003 San-fo-tsi recovered sufficient strength to send an embassy to China without any hindrance from Java. Three years later Java was completely crushed, as we shall see later, and the Śailendras were no longer threatened by that power.

The foundation of the Śailendra empire was an epoch-making event. For the first time in its history Malayasia, or the greater part of it, achieved a political unity under an empire, and a common geographical name Suvarṇa-dvīpa was applied to it. It will appear from what has been said above that the power of the Śailendras reached its zenith in the latter half of the eighth century A.D. In the ninth century both Kambuja and Java threw off their yoke as will be described later. Nevertheless the Chinese and the Arab accounts clearly show that the Śailendra empire continued to be a powerful and extensive one throughout the ninth and tenth centuries A.D.

The Śailendras introduced in Java a new type of Indian alphabet which differed considerably from the current one locally evolved from an older form of Indian alphabet. Another significant fact about this time is the adoption of a new name, Kaliṅga, for Malayasia, at least by foreigners. These seem to indicate that the Śailendras were fresh arrivals from India, but there is no positive evidence in support of this view. There is, however, no doubt that they had a close and intimate connection with India. The Śailendra rulers were devoted followers of the Mahāyāna form of Buddhism and they evidently derived it from Bengal. The Śailendra emperor, Dharaṇīndra-varman, who ruled in A.D. 782, had as his *guru* or preceptor an inhabitant of Gauḍa (a part of Bengal) named Kumāraghosha. About the middle of the ninth century A.D. king Bālaputradeva of the Śailendra dynasty, mentioned above, built a monastery at Nālandā, and requested the Pāla emperor Devapāladeva of Bengal[3] to grant five villages for its upkeep. Devapāla complied with the request, and this fact is recorded in his copper-plate grant which also gives a short account of Bālaputradeva. Similarly the Śailendras had intimate connections with the Choḷa rulers of South India in the eleventh century A.D. as will be described later.

The Śailendras introduced a new type of culture, the most prominent memorials of which are the splendid monuments in Java such as Barabuḍur which still excites the wonder and admiration of the world.

II. KAMBUJA

1. *Jaya-varman II and III*

The mighty and extensive kingdom founded by the family of Bhava-varman was split up into a number of states in the eighth century A.D. Two of these are referred to by the Chinese as 'Kambuja of the land' and 'Kambuja of the water.' The exact limits of these two kingdoms are not easy to determine. In all probability the former denoted the territory, full of hills and valleys, to the north of Cambodia proper, including a large part of Laos and touching the Chinese province of Tonkin and the Thai kingdom of Yunnan. This kingdom, which extended along the middle course of the Mekong, sent an embassy to China in A.D. 717, but five years later sent an army to help an Annamese chief who had revolted against China. But friendly relations with China were restored, and in 771 the king visited the Imperial court. The last embassy was sent to China in A.D. 799.

The 'Kambuja of the water', or Kambuja proper, comprised the lower valley of the Mekong river. A number of kingdoms flourished in this region in the eighth century, and inscriptions refer to three of them with capitals respectively at Śambhupura, Vyādhapura, and Aninditapura. The first of these is represented by modern Sambor on the Mekong. Vyādhapura was situated most probably at the foot of the hill called Ba Phnom, and possibly this kingdom represented ancient Fu-nan. The site of Aninditapura is probably to be looked for in the region east of Angkor on the northern side of the Great Lake. No detailed account of any of these kingdoms is known, though inscriptions have preserved the names of a number of kings. It is interesting to note that the rulers of Aninditapura regarded themselves as descendants of Kauṇḍinya, the reputed founder of the Hindu kingdom of Fu-nan, and Somā, the local Nāga princess married by him.

The political disintegration of Kambuja in the eighth century A.D. made it an easy victim of the neighbouring powers. King Sañjaya of Java (A.D. 732) conquered the country, and possibly the Śailendra Emperors of Java, Sumatra, and Malay Peninsula also exercised supremacy over it in the latter part of the eighth century A.D.

But Kambuja threw off the foreign yoke and rose to prominence early in the ninth century A.D. under its famous king Jaya-varman II.

This king spent his early years in Java, in what capacity we do not know. But he came to Kambuja and became its king in A.D. 802. He moved from one capital to another till he fixed it on the top of the hill called Mahendraparvata (Phnom Kulen, to the north-west of Angkor Thom). There he invited a Brāhmaṇa named Hiraṇyadāma from Janapada (probably in India) to perform some Tāntrik rites, so that Kambujadeśa might no longer be dependent on Java but have a paramount ruler of its own. Hiraṇyadāma instituted the cult of Devarāja, and initiated Śivakaivalya, the royal *guru* (preceptor), into the rituals of this worship. Jaya-varman II took a vow to employ the family of Śivakaivalya and none else to celebrate the worship of Devarāja. The king then returned to his old capital city, of Hariharālaya (Lolei, 13 miles to the south-east of Angkor) and reigned there till his death.

This short account of king Jaya-varman II is derived from a long record incised in A.D. 1052 by a descendant of Śivakaivalya, whose family had filled the post of Royal Priest from the reign of Jaya-varman II till that time,—a period of 250 years. It is a long record of 340 lines containing 130 verses in Sanskrit and 146 lines of prose text in the native Khmer language. It describes in detail the Tāntrik rites performed by Hiraṇyadāma and proves the great hold of Indian culture in these distant colonies.

Although we do not possess any record of the time of Jaya-varman II, we may form a fair idea of his life and reign from scattered notices in later inscriptions and literary traditions. It is obvious that he did not ascend the throne of Kambuja by hereditary right, though it is very likely that he was remotely related to some royal families of Kambuja. Why he went to Java and how he became the ruler of Kambuja remain unknown, but there is no doubt that he freed the country from foreign yoke. The most interesting thing in his early career is the frequent change of capitals, no less than five of which are mentioned in the record referred to above. Although the sites of all these capitals cannot be definitely determined, it appears that Jaya-varman fixed his first capital—Indrapura—not far from the ancient royal seat of Śambhupura, and that he was a native of this region. Then we find a gradual change of the royal seat towards the west, first towards Angkor, then further west towards Battambang, and lastly back again to Angkor. It is generally held that these changes were either due to royal caprices or inspired by a desire to find a suitable site for the capital of the newly founded kingdom. But it is equally likely that the changes indicate troubles which forced the king to take refuge in different parts of the country at different times. Or it may be that it took him many years to establish his supremacy over the country as a whole, and the different capitals merely indicate the different stages of political consolidation from the east to the west; ultimately, when the whole country had been subdued, he fixed his capital finally at Hariharālaya in the central part of the kingdom.

It is stated in an inscription of Hari-varman, king of Champā, dated A.D. 817, that his army ravaged Kambuja and advanced up to the very heart of the kingdom. It is not unlikely that this forced Jaya-varman II to leave the eastern and central part of the kingdom and betake himself to the western region.

On the whole, although we do not know of many specific events in the reign of Jaya-varman II, there is no doubt that he played an important part in the history of Kambuja. After a century of political disintegration and foreign conquest he restored the freedom and unity of the kingdom of Kambuja, and gave it a stability which put it on the road to a splendid and glorious career for many centuries. Posterity remembered him as one of the greatest kings, and most flattering references are made to him in inscriptions centuries after his death. Even now the Kambuja tradition represents him as a divine hero, the son of Indra. The sacred sword of Kambuja, which is still used by its kings at the ceremony of coronation and is jealously guarded by priests who claim descent from the old Brāhmaṇas, is believed to be a relic of Jaya-varman II, who remains the national hero and a great landmark in Kambuja history. Popular tradition also ascribes to him most of the grand monuments in ancient Kambuja, but we cannot definitely associate any of the existing buildings with his name. The cult of Devarāja instituted by him, which continued to be the state religion for many centuries, was a form of Tāntrik Śaivism. He died in A.D. 854 and received the name of Parameśvara after his death. Henceforth it became a fashion to give such posthumous names to the kings, and these were usually formed by adding the word *loka* or *pada* to a divine name (Brahmā, Vishṇu, Śiva, Indra, etc.). All these go to prove the thorough-going influence of Indian culture on Kambuja.

Jaya-varman II was succeeded by his son Jaya-varman III who ruled from A.D. 854 to 877. Except his inordinate passion for elephant-hunting, we do not know anything about him. With him ends the direct line of Jaya-varman II. According to a Chinese chronicler, who visited his kingdom in A.D. 862, it included the whole of Laos in the north and almost touched the frontier of Yunnan. How much of it was acquired by him or by his father, it is difficult to say. But it is fairly certain that under Jaya-varman II and his son the kingdom of Kambuja had grown into a powerful empire.

The Arab writers give us a glimpse of the history and culture of Kambuja of this period. Ya'kūbī (*c.* A.D. 875) describes the Khmer kingdom as vast and powerful, the king of which receives homage of other kings. Ibn Rosteh (A.D. 903) says that "there are eighty judges in the Khmer country. Even if a son of the king appears before them they would judge equitably and treat him as an ordinary complainant." Several Arab writers bestow high praise on the Khmers for their abstinence from drinking and debauchery in general. Ibn Khordādbah (A.D. 844-848) says: "The kings and peoples of India abstain from drinking wine but they do not consider adultery as an illicit act, with the sole exception of the Khmer king who forbids both drinking and adultery." This is repeated by several other Arab writers. It is interesting to note that in the passage quoted above, Khmer is included in India.

2. *Dynasty of Indra-varman*

King Indra-varman, who succeeded Jaya-varman III and founded a new royal line, was but very remotely related to the latter. His queen Indradevī was connected with the royal families of the three kingdoms of Śambhupura, Aninditapura, and Vyādhapura mentioned above. The mother of Indradevī, named Rājendradevī, was descended from a royal family founded by Agastya, a Brāhmaṇa from Āryadeśa (*i.e.* India). These facts. interesting in themselves, and indicating the importance of both Indra-varman and his queen, do not show that they had any hereditary right of succession. It is probable that Indra-varman was the ruler of one of the vassal states in Kambuja, and had somehow managed to secure the throne. The respectful terms in which the inscriptions of the new family refer to Jaya-varman II and III preclude the idea of any open rebellion by Indra-varman.

But the change in the royal family did not affect in any way either the extent of the kingdom or its political importance. On the other hand Indra-varman claims in his record that his commands were respectfully obeyed by the rulers of Chīna, Champā, and Yava-dvīpa. Such specific claims cannot be dismissed as mere figments of imagination. As we have seen above, Kambuja was made to suffer a great deal by both Champā and Java (Yava-dvīpa) towards the close of the eighth and the beginning of the ninth century A.D. It is very likely that she turned against her old enemies and scored some success. There are also good grounds to believe, as we shall see later, that Indra-varman extended his sway over the province of Yunnan, and it is evidently in this region that he came into conflict with China.

Indra-varman was a great builder, and the extant monuments of his reign belong to an intermediate stage between the Primitive and Classical art of Kambuja. His inscriptions refer in detail to his building activities. We are told that he excavated a big tank called Indra-taṭāka, constructed a *siṁhāsana* (royal throne) according to his own design, the vehicle called Indra-yāna, Indra-vimānaka, and Indra-prāsādaka (probably two palaces), all made of gold, built various temples and installed images therein.

Indra-varman died after a reign of twelve years (877-889) and was succeeded by his son Yaśo-varman who occupies a place of honour in the history of Kambuja. He founded a new capital city which was at first called Kambupurī and later Yaśodhara-pura. For a long time this city was believed to be the same as Angkor Thom whose magnificent ruins still excite the admiration of the world. But it is now generally held that the new capital was situated on the top of the hill called Phnom Bakhen, but it extended beyond the hill and included a large part of the present site of Angkor Thom. This region remained the centre of Kambuja power and culture till their decline and downfall.

Yaśo-varman has left quite a large number of inscriptions, which throw interesting light not only on his life and reign, but on the new type of civilisation, associated with Angkor, which was largely his own creation, and whose glory and splendour form the most brilliant chapter in the history of Kambuja.

Yaśo-varman is credited with numerous military campaigns, including a naval expedition, and is said to have reinstated vanquished kings and married their daughters. But no specific details are stated. There is, however, no doubt that he ruled over a vast empire. On the north it included Yunnan and reached the frontier of the then kingdom of China. On the west it was bounded by the mountains forming the watershed between the rivers Menam and Salween. The eastern and southern boundaries were formed respectively by the kingdom of Champā and the sea.

Yaśo-varman was not only a great patron of art and literature but was himself a great scholar. He was fond of *Śāstras* and *Kāvyas* and is said to have composed a commentary on Patañjali's *Mahābhāshya*. He was liberal in his religious views, and though a devoted follower of Śaivism, patronised Buddhism generously. He founded numerous *āśramas* or abodes of religious communities, and made elaborate regulations for them, many copies of which, engraved on stone, still exist and mark the spots where these sacred hermitages stood. These and numerous other records of the time indicate a happy, prosperous and peaceful kingdom ruled over by an able and wise monarch who took all possible measures to ensure the welfare of the kingdom in all its aspects, political, economic, religious, and social. Even making due allowances for the usual exaggerations of court-poets, we must regard Yaśo-varman as a brave general and an ideal king who excelled both in the arts of peace and war. There was undoubtedly some basis and justification for the statement in these records that the glory of Yaśo-varman was sung, even after his death, by the people "in their games, on their beds, and in their travels." It reminds us of a similar verse in praise of Dharmapāla[4] with whom Yaśo-varman may be aptly compared.

Yaśo-varman died about A.D. 900 and was succeeded by his two sons, Harsha-varman I and Īśāna-varman II. But the latter was overthrown some time before A.D. 928 by Jaya-varman IV, the husband of a sister of Yaśo-varman. The usurper removed the capital as well as the tutelary deity Devarāja to Koh Ker (Chok Gargyar), situated in a wild barren country about 50 miles to the north-east of Angkor. The only known important event in the reign of Jaya-varman IV is his successful fight with Champā, whose ruler he is said to have crushed.

Jaya-varman IV was succeeded by his son Harsha-varman II in A.D. 941 or 942. Next came Rājendra-varman, the son of another sister of Yaśo-varman. It is likely that there were struggles for succession to the throne in which Rājendra-varman came out victorious. He ascended the throne in A.D. 944 and removed the capital back again to Yaśodhara-pura which had been deserted for a long time. Rājendra-varman has left a large number of long records, which credit him with victorious campaigns in all directions. But the only specific event that we know of is his successful invasion of Champā in the course of which he advanced as far as the Khan-hoa province and desecrated the Po Nagar temple.

Rājendra-varman died in A.D. 968 and was succeeded by his son Jaya-varman V. Although Śaivism remained the official religion, the king was an ardent champion of Buddhism, and issued regulations and instructions for the propagation of that faith. He was also a great builder and led a successful invasion against Champā. He died in A.D. 1001 and with him ended the direct line of Indra-varman.

3. *General Review*

The two centuries that intervened between the accession of Jaya-varman II and the death of Jaya-varman V were marked by a rapid growth of the Kambuja empire, and constitute an important chapter in the history of Indian cultural and colonial expansion in Indo-China. In order to understand this properly we must take a bird's-eye view of the general political condition of Indo-China in the tenth century A.D.

The Chinese annals give a broad and comprehensive survey of the political geography of Indo-China about the year A.D. 960 when the Song dynasty began its rule in China. The whole of Tonkin, with the two districts in Annam immediately adjoining to the south, constituted the Chinese province of Ngan-nan; but it became an independent state under an Annamese chief in A.D. 968, and its name changed to Dai-co-viet. To the north and north-west was the independent Hinduised Thai principality of Nan-Chao or Mithilā-rāshṭra (North Yunnan) that had thrown off the Chinese yoke about A.D. 730. To the south and west of these two lay the well-known kingdoms of Champā, Kambuja, and Ramaññadeśa (Lower Burma). The central region of the Peninsula, surrounded by these states, was peopled by the Thais who had imbibed the rudiments of Hindu civilisation and set up a number of principalities which bore Hindu or Hinduised names.

The extension of the political supremacy of Kambuja beyond its northern boundary can be definitely traced as far back as A.D. 862 when the kingdom of Alāvi-rāshṭra, comprising the southern part of Yunnan, formed a part of the Kambuja empire according to a Chinese chronicler who visited these regions in that year. In the light of this we cannot dismiss, as fanciful, the claim of Indra-varman that his commands were obeyed by the king of China, and of Yaśovarman that his empire reached up to the frontier of China. Possibly they conquered Mithilā-rāshṭra or North Yunnan, and thus reached the very border of what then formed the kingdom of China. Many local chronicles have preserved reminiscences of the Kambuja rule along the valley of the Upper Mekong as far north as Yunnan.

The Kambuja kingdom also expanded along the valley of the Menam river in the west. Lavapurī, which comprised the territory extending from the Gulf of Siam in the south as far as Kampheng Phet on the north, formed an integral part of the Kambuja kingdom, which also exercised political authority over the numerous petty states in the northern part of Siam (or Thailand). The northernmost of these bore the very significant name Khmera-rāshṭra or the kingdom of the Khmers (the people of Kambuja), and touched the Kambuja kingdom of Alāvi-rāshṭra mentioned above.

To the south of Siam, the part of Malay Peninsula lying to the north of the Isthmus of Kra belonged to Kambuja. The rest of the

Malay Peninsula belonged to the Śailendras who also ruled over Java and Sumatra. Indra-varman's claim of supremacy over Java may refer to a successful contest with the Śailendras, though nothing is definitely known.

As regards the kingdom of Champā, references have been made to frequent fights between it and Kambuja almost throughout the ninth and tenth centuries A.D. There seems to be no doubt that Kambuja gained the upper hand in these struggles at least in the tenth century A.D.

It is thus apparent that under the two powerful dynasties founded by Jaya-varman II and Indra-varman, Kambuja had emerged from comparative obscurity into the most powerful kingdom in Indo-China. Its power and magnificence impressed the Arab travellers, and one of them Ibn al-Fakīh (A.D. 902) describes the Khmer kingdom as having an extent of four months' march.

III. CHAMPĀ

1. *The Dynasty of Pāṇḍuraṅga* (c. A.D. 757-860)

On the death of Rudra-varman II[5] the throne of Champā was occupied by Pṛithivīndra-varman (A.D. 757). We learn from epigraphic records that "he enjoyed the land by having conquered all his enemies by his own power", and that he destroyed all the thieves. This indicates a period of internecine war and anarchy in Champā. The express statement in the same record that he enjoyed the whole of Champā shows that he succeeded in consolidating the entire country under his authority.

Pṛithivīndra-varman was succeeded by his nephew (sister's son) Satya-varman in or some time before A.D. 774. During his reign the coast of Champā suffered a great deal from the raids of sea-men from Java, referred to as "vicious cannibals coming by means of ships." Whether these were pirates or regular mariners it is difficult to say. But they wrought great havoc. There was a sacred temple in Champā, founded, according to popular tradition, by king Vichitrasagara "in the year 5911 of the Dvāpara yuga." In A.D. 774 the Javanese raiders burnt this temple and carried away the image, *viz.* a Mukhaliṅga of Śiva. Satya-varman inflicted a crushing defeat upon them in a naval engagement, but could not recover the image as it had been destroyed. He, however, installed a new image and hence came to be regarded as the second Vichitrasagara or an incarnation of that king.

Satya-varman was succeeded by his younger brother Indra-varman. There was another Javanese raid in A.D. 787 causing the destruction of another famous shrine containing an image "established there for many thousands of years." Indra-varman re-installed the deity under the name of Indra-bhadreśvara. This Indian custom of associating the name of the king with that of the divine image set up by him was very often followed in Champā. Indra-varman himself installed two other images called after him Indra-bhogeśvara and Indra-parameśvara, and endowed many religious establishments. Indra-varman is said to have fought with many enemies and ruled over the whole of Champā. He renewed diplomatic relations with China, and sent presents of rhinoceros and buffaloes to the emperor in A.D. 793.

Hari-varman, the husband of Indra-varman's sister, next ascended the throne (c. A.D. 801). In one of his records, dated A.D. 817, he claims to have defeated the Chinese. According to Chinese history a king of Champā conquered the two Chinese districts of Hoan and Ai in January, A.D. 803, and renewed the expedition in A.D. 809; but the Chinese governor forced him to retreat by inflicting a crushing defeat upon him. Most likely this occurred in the reign of Hari-varman and forms the basis of his claim for victory over the Chinese. One of his generals led a victorious expedition against Kambuja. He seems to have advanced into the heart of the country and ravaged its towns. Its probable effect upon Kambuja has been discussed before in connection with the history of Jaya-varman II.[6] The successful aggressive policy of Hari-varman against his two very powerful rivals undoubtedly gave him justification for assuming the proud title of *"Rājādhirāja Śrī Champāpura-Parameśvara"* (king of kings, Lord of Champā).

Hari-varman was succeeded by his son Vikrānta-varman III (c. A.D. 820-860). He was the governor of Pāṇḍuraṅga during his father's reign. Since all the inscriptions of this dynasty have been found in this southern region, it has been suggested that it was probably the original seat of the royal family and the main stronghold of the rulers of this dynasty. But they ruled over the whole kingdom and had their official capital in the city of Champā. Vikrānta-varman III died without issue, and with him ended the dynasty which is usually referred to as the dynasty of Pāṇḍuraṅga.

2. *The Bhṛigu Dynasty* (c. A.D. 860-985)

The first notable king of the new dynasty that ruled Champā for more than a century was Indra-varman II. The epigraphic records give him a mythical pedigree reaching back to God Śiva. But although his father and grandfather are referred to as kings, it is explicitly stated in more than one inscription that Indra-varman gained the kingdom of Champā "by the special merit of his austerities, and by virtue of his pure intelligence, not from his grandfather or father." Most likely the immediate ancestors of Indra-varman were mere local rulers, and he made himself master of the whole kingdom by his own prowess. His original name was "Śrī Lakshmīndra Bhūmīśvara Grāmasvāmin," and after he became king of Champā he assumed the title "Śrī Jaya Indra-varman Mahārājādhirāja." The epigraphic records refer to his family as Bhṛigu dynasty, presumably because, according to the mythological account of the origin of the family, Bhṛigu was sent to Champā by Mahādeva himself.

Not much is known about Indra-varman II except his religious endowments. In spite of his faith in Śaivism the king had evident leanings towards Buddhism, for he erected a Buddhist temple and a monastery. He must have enjoyed a long and peaceful reign (c. A.D. 860-895); and he sent an embassy to China in A.D. 877.

Jayasiṁha-varman (*c.* A.D. 896-905), who succeeded Indra-varman II, was probably related to him, but nothing is definitely known. The epigraphic records give us a long list of his pious donations. Reference is frequently made to the wealth and splendour of Indrapura which was probably the real capital of this dynasty, though Champā was still officially recognised as such. The king is said to have spread his power to other lands, though no specific event is recorded except that he sent a diplomatic mission to Java. This was renewed by Bhadra-varman III (*c.* A.D. 905-910), who succeeded the son of Jayasiṁha-varman. The epigraphic records refer repeatedly to his victories over enemies and also to the multitude of royal ambassadors coming to his court from different countries. One of his ministers is expressly credited with sufficient linguistic talents to understand thoroughly the messages sent by kings from different countries. All these indicate that Champā was now recognised abroad as an important and powerful kingdom and the country played its part in international politics.

Bhadra-varman's son and successor Indra-varman III was a distinguished scholar. We are told in one of his records that he mastered the different systems of philosophy (*shaṭ-tarka*) including Mīmāṁsā, as well as Buddhist philosophy, the grammar of Pāṇini together with its commentary *Kāśikā,* and the *Uttara-kalpa* of the Śaivites. But the king could not pursue his studies in peace. The king of Kambuja, probaby Rājendra-varman, invaded his dominions, advanced far into the interior, and even carried away a golden image of the deity which the king had installed in a temple at Po-

Nagar. The invasion had no permanent result, but the kingdom of Champā suffered a great deal.

The kings of Champā had stopped their customary embassies and presents to China during the troublesome period following the overthrow of the T'ang Dynasty. Indra-varman resumed the practice and sent an embassy to China with various presents in A.D. 951. Seven more embassies were sent by him during the period between A.D. 958 and 971.

3. *The Annamese Invasions*

Indra-varman III enjoyed a long reign of about 60 years from about A.D. 911 to 971. He was succeeded by Prarameśvara-varman who sent no less than six embassies to China, between A.D. 972 and 979. As noted above, an Annamese chief had founded an independent kingdom immediately to the north of Champā in A.D. 968. This ruler, named Dinh Bo Linh, died in A.D. 979. A rival Annamese chief, who was defeated by him and had taken refuge in Champā, now planned to seize the throne of Annam with the aid of Parameśvara-varman. The latter led in person a naval expedition against the capital city of Tonkin and reached within a few miles of it. But a storm destroyed the whole fleet with the exception of the royal vessel, and though Parameśvara-varman returned safely to his kingdom, the whole expedition had a tragic end (A.D. 979). The newly elected Annamese Emperor Le Hoan sent an ambassador to Parameśvara-varman, but the latter imprisoned him against the diplomatic conventions of all ages and countries. In order to avenge this grave humiliation, Le Hoan personally led an expedition against Champā. Parameśvara-varman was defeated and killed at the first encounter, and although Indra-varman IV was hastily proclaimed king in Champā he could not save the situation. Le Hoan ravaged the capital city and occupied a large part of the kingdom. Then, after making arrangements for its administration, he returned (A.D. 982) with an immense booty, about 100 ladies of the royal *harem* of Champā, and an Indian *Bhikshu* (monk).

Indra-varman IV, who had taken refuge in the southern part of his kingdom, now sent a Brāhmaṇa envoy to the Chinese court, complaining against the Annamese occupation of Champā, but received no help from that quarter. Shortly after, internal dissensions among the Annamese chiefs enabled one of them, Lu'u-Ky-Tong, to seize the throne of Champā, and Le Hoan was unable to dislodge him. After the death of Indra-varman IV he was officially proclaimed king of Champā. But soon a national hero appeared, who freed the country from foreign yoke. He ascended the throne in

A.D. 989 under the name of Vijaya Śrī Hari-varman (II) at Vijaya, in Binh-Dinh, but later removed to the old capital at Indrapura.

Le Hoan now again ravaged the borderlands of Champā. Hari-varman sent an embassy with rich presents to the Chinese Emperor who commanded Le Hoan to keep within his own territory. Hari-varman also conciliated the Annamese king by refusing assistance to a rebel Annamese chief. Le Hoan appreciated this act and in return stopped his incursions and released a number of Cham prisoners (A.D. 992). During the same year Hari-varman was gratified beyond measure by receiving a rich present from the Chinese Emperor consisting of magnificent horses, standards, and other equipments of war. Hari-varman wrote back to the emperor that thanks to the imperial favour his kingdom was again enjoying peace, and his neighbours no longer entertained any desire of ruining him. It is evident, however, that the imperial favour emboldened the Cham king to ravage the Annamese territory to the north. although outwardly he was on friendly terms and sent diplomatic missions to Le Hoan. This undercurrent of hostility between Champā and her northern neighbour continued during the next half a century and ultimately proved her ruin. For the time being, however, things went on well, though Hari-varman's successor, called in Chinese chronicles Yan Pu Ku Vijaya Śrī, who ascended the throne some time before A.D. 999, transferred the capital permanently to Vijaya, far to the south, as a precautionary measure.

IV. JAVA

1. *The Kingdom of Matarām*

A powerful kingdom was founded in Central Java by king Sannāha in the first half of the eighth century A.D. Sañjaya, the successor of Sannāha, is known to have been ruling in A.D. 732. He is described in the Changal Inscription as "conqueror of the countries of neighouring kings"; and a literary work, composed much later, gives details of his conquests which included Sumatra, Kambuja, and probably also Malay Peninsula. It is difficult to say how far this later tradition can be regarded as historical. But Sañjaya was undoubtedly a great hero as his name figures prominently even in later epigraphic records. Some scholars have even gone so far as to regard him as the founder of the Śailendra Dynasty mentioned above; but this view rests upon very slender foundations. There are, however, good grounds to believe that Sañjaya was the founder of the kingdom of Matarām which, after a career of glory in the early period, again flourished in the sixteenth century as an important principality under a Muslim Sultan. The old capital of this kingdom was situated probably at or near Prambanan in Central Java which is famous for its big temples.

Shortly after the death of Sañjaya, if not during his reign, the Śailendras conquered Central Java, probably during the period A.D. 742-755. The successors of Sañjaya were forced to shift their headquarters about 150 miles to the east, and they ruled in Eastern Java for nearly a century. But they recovered their old capital about the middle of the ninth century A.D., evidently after the Śailendras had voluntarily left or were overthrown by them. A passage in a Chinese history describes Java as a powerful state at this period, and its supremacy was acknowledged by twenty-eight small states on all sides. Although epigraphic records give the names of a number of kings belonging to this dynasty, we know hardly anything about them till we come to Balitung. Besides his proper name Balitung which was Indonesian, he assumed different coronation names such as Uttuṅgadeva, Īśvara-Keśavotsavatuṅga, Īśvara-Keśava-Samarottuṅga, and Dharmodaya Mahāśambhu. His dominions certainly included both Eastern and Western Java, and his known regnal years are A.D. 898 and 910. It has been suggested that Balitung was originally a ruler of Eastern Java, and by marrying a princess of Matarām, became also ruler of that kingdom in Central Java. This, as well as the view that the famous temple of Lara Jongrang was the burial temple of Balitung, can only be regarded as probable hypotheses.

Balitung or Dharmodaya Mahāśambhu was succeeded by Dakshottama in or shortly before A.D. 915. He occupied a high office during the reign of his predecessor, and probably belonged to the royal family. He certainly ruled over both Central and Eastern Java, and so probably did his two successors Tuloḍong and Wawa. But the kingdom of Matarām came to an end during the latter's reign, about A.D. 928. Wawa was thus the last of a long line of kings who ruled in Java for two centuries, and for the first time, in recorded history, politically united Eastern and Central Java.

A stone inscription at Dinaya, to the north of Malang, refers to king Devasiṁha, his son Gajayāna, and the latter's daughter Uttejanā. Her son was the king who issued the inscription to commemorate the consecration of a stone image of Agastya in A.D. 760 with elaborate rituals performed by priests versed in Vedic lore. Whether the kings mentioned in this record belonged to the family of Sañjaya, or were independent of it, it is difficult to say.

2. *End of Hindu Civilisation in Central Java*

Petty dynasties were thus probably ruling in Java even during the period when the greater part, even if not the whole, of Central and Eastern Java was included in the kingdom of Matarām, which had its headquarters in Central Java, except for the brief interlude of Śailendra supremacy. But with the death of Wawa and the end of the old royal dynasty, the centre of political authority definitely shifted to Eastern Java, and what is even more striking, there was a complete collapse of culture and civilisation in Central Java. It is difficult to account for this dual change, and various theories have been put forward to explain it. According to one view, the governor of the eastern province revolted against the central authority and perpetrated massacres and ravages in Central Java on a large scale. But this can hardly account for the complete extinction of a flourishing culture, and the theory is belied by the fact that the large number of monuments in Central Java bear no signs of wilful destruction. Another theory attributes the wholesale desertion of Central Java to some natural phenomenon or visitation, like the eruption of a volcano or a violent epidemic which superstitious people might have interpreted as a sign of divine displeasure. But there are facts to prove that the migration of the people or the obliteration of culture in Java was not so sudden as the above theory would imply. According to a third view the rulers of Eastern Java deliberately laid waste the whole of Central Java in pursuance of what is now known as a 'scorched earth policy' against a possible invasion by the Śailendras. It is, however, difficult to believe that such wholesale destruction would be undertaken merely at the apprehension of an invasion.

It seems more probable that ever since the king of Matarām was forced to shift his capital to the east on account of the conquest of Central Java by the Śailendras, the centre of politics and culture was transferred to that region, and remained there, even though a vain attempt was made, after about a century, to revive the old glory of Central Java by transferring the capital back again to that region. This view is supported by the fact that even during the century that followed this formal re-transfer of capital, most of the inscriptions, so far discovered, belong to Eastern Java. Slowly but steadily the political and cultural life continued to flow towards the east, and gradually Central Java lost its political importance as well as cultural pre-eminence. This might have been obscured from the ordinary view by the glamour of the court-life, but the process of change was nevertheless a reality. Some unknown factors, such as a violent volcanic eruption, epidemic, or ravages by the Śailendras, might have hastened the progress of the decay which was in any case rendered inevitable by the original transfer of capital in the middle of the eighth century A.D.

But whatever may be the reasons, there is no dispute about the stark fact that Hindu culture and civilisation lost its hold on Central Java about the middle of the tenth century A.D., and we have here a repetition of what took place in Western Java five hundred years earlier. Since the eleventh century A.D., Eastern Java remained, for another period of five hundred years, as the only stronghold of Hindu culture and civilisation in Java.

3. *Eastern Java—Dynasty of Siṇḍok*

Siṇḍok, the first ruler in Eastern Java, was regarded as a famous king by posterity, and relationship with him was claimed, even if no direct descent was traced, by many kings for centuries. Yet Siṇḍok appears to have been intimately connected with the old royal family, and occupied such high offices of state under his two predecessors as are only held by an heir-apparent to the throne. Probably he was not the son of Wawa, but belonged to a different family, and hence, though he succeeded to the throne in the natural course, he was regarded as the founder of a long line of Javanese kings. It has been suggested that he married the daughter of king Wawa and acquired the throne by the right of his wife. But this as well as the suggestion that he was a grandson of Daksha is highly problematical.

Siṇḍok ascended the throne in c. A.D. 929 and assumed the name Śrī Īśāna-Vikrama Dharmottuṅgadeva at the time of his coronation. Nearly twenty inscriptions of his reign have been discovered so far, but they do not record any specific events of his reign. To judge from the findspots of these inscriptions the kingdom of Siṇḍok comprised merely the valley of the Brantas river, but it possibly extended far beyond this area.

The last known date of Siṇḍok is A.D. 947. He was succeeded by his daughter Śrī Īśānatuṅgavijayā, who ruled as queen and was married to Śrī Lokapāla. She was succeeded by her son Śrī Makuṭavaṁśa-vardhana, who is said to have belonged to the family of Siṇḍok and owed the throne to this king and not to the family of his own father Lokapāla. It is not likely, therefore, that Lokapāla ever ruled as king, though we possess three records issued by a king bearing this name.

King Makuṭavaṁśa-vardhana had a daughter, Mahendradattā, also known as Guṇapriya-dharmapatnī, who was married to Udayana. The princess, with her husband, ruled over the island of Bali without any royal title. The fact that her name precedes that of her husband in contemporary records proves that she ruled in her own right as the daughter of the king of Java. Incidentally it proves that the king of Java had established his suzerainty over Bali.

No other important event in the reign of Makuṭavaṁśa-vardhana is known. Nor do we know anything definite about the succession to the throne. It is known from a later record that king Dharmavaṁśa ruled in Eastern Java towards the close of the tenth century A.D., but we do not know whether he was the immediate successor of Makuṭavaṁśa-vardhana or, even, if he belonged to the same royal family. It has been suggested that he belonged to a different family but married the daughter of Makuṭavaṁśa-vardhana.

The two most important events in the reign of Dharmavaṁśa are renewal of diplomatic relations with China and the struggle with the Śailendras. The two are probably not altogether unconnected, and show an aggressive or imperial policy on the part of Java which had probably begun earlier as evidenced by the conquest of Bali.

In A.D. 992 a Javanese envoy visited the Chinese court. He represented, with the assistance of an interpreter, that a great Chinese merchant, who owned many vessels, had come several times to Java, and he availed himself of the merchant's guidance to come to the Imperial Court. This shows that Java had not been in touch with China for a long period.

The Javanese envoy to China reported "that his country was in enmity with San-fo-tsi and that they were always fighting with each other." We learn from an envoy of San-fo-tsi that he left the Chinese court in A.D. 990, but on reaching Canton learnt that his country had been invaded by Java. So he rested there for about a year and proceeded to Champā with his navy in the spring of A.D. 992. But as he did not receive any good news there he returned to China and requested the emperor to issue a decree making San-fo-tsi a protectorate of China.

As noted above, San-fo-tsi undoubtedly refers to the Śailendra kingdom. It is evident that even though the Śailendras left Java, the animosity between the two continued and broke out into open hostilities in or some time before A.D. 990. In that year Java took the offensive, invaded the kingdom of the Śailendras, and reduced them to such straits that they had to seek the protection of China. It is very likely that Java also sent envoys to China as a counterpoise to this move on the part of her rival. But though Java had achieved great success in the beginning, it was short-lived. In A.D. 1003 San-fo-tsi recovered sufficient strength to send an embassy to China without any hindrance from Java. It is evident that the Śailendra king had succeeded in his resistance and hurled back the invaders from his country.

In spite of this set-back, king Dharmavaṁśa enhanced the glory and prestige of Java in Indonesia. Unfortunately, the origin and incidents of his struggle with the Śailendras are not known, but it may not be unconnected with the tragic end of the Javanese king less than four years later. We learn from a record of his successor and son-in-law Airlangga that in A.D. 1006 Java was destroyed by a great catastrophe (*pralaya*) which overwhelmed it like the sea. "Then the flourishing capital city," so runs the record, "which was hitherto a seat of joy and merriment, was reduced to ashes, and the great king met his end in the year 929 (= A.D. 1007)."

It is held by some that the above passage refers to a natural calamity like a volcanic eruption. But this is hardly borne out by the detailed story of Airlangga's flight, his fugitive life, and the recovery of the kingdom after arduous fight with various enemies. There can be hardly any doubt that the calamity was caused by a hostile attack. It is natural to infer that the enemies who destroyed the political life of Java were either the Śailendras or some powers backed by them. But there is no evidence in support of it, and the absence of any reference to the Śailendras in the detailed account of the subsequent struggles of Airlangga makes it very unlikely. But whoever might have been the enemy, his triumph was complete. King Dharmavaṁśa died and his kingdom perished with him in A.D. 1007. The story of its recovery by Airlangga will be narrated in the next volume.

V. BURMA

The Hinduised Pyu kingdom,[7] with its capital at Śrīkshetra (Prome), was the most powerful kingdom in Burma during the period under review. According to Chinese accounts it included nearly the whole of the country, except the Mon kingdom in the coastal regions of Lower Burma, and probably also Arakan. For we are told that the Pyu kingdom touched Kambuja on the east and India on the west, extended up to the sea on the south and adjoined Dvāravatī on the south-west (evidently a mistake for south-east, if it refers to the well-known Hindu kingdom in Siam). It is said to have been 500 miles from east to west and 700 to 800 miles from north to south. It extended up to the Thai kingdom of Yunnan in the north and claimed supremacy over 18 subject kingdoms. The Chinese account also gives us a list of eight or nine garrison towns and of the 32 most important among the 298 tribes or settlements. The capital city, 27 miles in circumference, was surrounded by a wall faced with glazed bricks, and this was protected by a moat whose banks were also faced with brick. The city had twelve gates with pagodas at the four corners. It contained several thousands of families, and over a hundred Buddhist monasteries, with courts and rooms all decked with gold and silver.

The detailed account of the Pyus, particularly their sincere devotion to Buddhism, social customs, trade and currency, arts, crafts and ornaments, and high proficiency in music proves that they had attained a high degree of civilisation and had imbibed a large measure of Hindu culture. The rise of the powerful Thai kingdom in Yunnan, known as Nan-chao or Mithilā-rāshṭra, about A.D. 730 has been noted above.[8] The frontier between this kingdom and that of the Pyus on the west followed roughly the Sino-Burmese frontier of to-day. Nan-chao rapidly grew powerful, and its king Ko-lo-fong inflicted a defeat upon the Chinese in A.D. 754. He next turned his attention to his western neighbour and invaded his kingdom. The Pyu king submitted and henceforth Upper Burma was dominated by the Thais. When at the end of the eighth century the grandson of Ko-lo-fong acknowledged the suzerainty of China and sent embassies to the Imperial Court, the Pyu king also followed suit. Two more embassies were sent to China in A.D. 802 and 807. The former was led by the king's brother (or son) Sunandana, governor of the city of Śrī (perhaps Bhamo or Tagaung), who took some court musicians as a present to the Chinese emperor.

The peace with Nan-chao, however, did not last long. In A.D. 832 the ruler of Nan-chao invaded the Pyu kingdom, plundered the capital city, and took more than 3000 persons as prisoners. This was a severe blow to the Pyu power and marks the beginning of its decline. But it did not bring about a sudden end to the Pyu kingdom or its culture, as some scholars hold. For we find that even in A.D. 862 an embassy from this kingdom visited China. But little is known of its history after the ninth century A.D. It is probable that the Mons in the south grew powerful and conquered the southern part of the Pyu kingdom, forcing the Pyus to remove their capital further north to Pagan on the Irawadi. Soon a new tribe, the Mrammas (Burmans), came into prominence in this region. Pressed by the Mons from the south and the Mrammas from the north the Pyus gradually lost their power and were ultimately absorbed by their two powerful neighbours. From the eleventh century A.D. the Mrammas ruled as the dominant power in Burma with Pagan as their capital.

VI. CIVILISATION IN THE HINDU COLONIES IN SOUTH-EAST ASIA

The Hindu culture in all its aspects permeated the life of the people in these colonies to an extent which it is difficult to convey fully within the short scope of this chapter. We shall therefore confine ourselves to the delineation of a few prominent characteristics under the broad heads of society, religion, art, and literature.

1. *Society*

The caste-system, which is the most distinctive characteristic of Hindu society, and may be regarded as its fundamental basis, was introduced in Java, Madura, Sumatra, Champā and other colonies. For we have not only references to *"Chāturvarṇya"* or four castes, but there is also specific mention of Brāhmaṇas, Kshatriyas, Vaiśyas, and Śūdras, both in literature and inscriptions. This caste-system was not, however, as rigid as we find it in India to-day, but rather resembled what was in vogue here in ancient times. We can get some idea of the caste-system in these remote colonies by studying the main features which prevail even to-day in the island of Bali. Thus, as laid down in *Manu-smṛiti,* marriage among different castes is prevalent, but while a man may marry a girl of his own or lower caste, a woman may only marry one of equal or higher caste. The children of mixed marriages belong to the caste of the father, though they differ in rank and status according to the caste of the mother. The marriage of a woman with a man of lower caste is punishable with death.

In Bali the Śūdras are not despised or regarded as impure and untouchable. Nor are the castes tied down to specific occupations. Thus men of all castes take to agriculture, and the Śūdras, in addition, follow other arts and crafts. We also find another characteristic feature of ancient Indian caste-system, *viz.* inequality in the eyes of law which lays down, for the same offence, punishment in inverse ratio to the superiority of caste of the offender, and in direct ratio to that of the offended.

In some places, as in Champā, although there was a theoretical division into the four castes, practically there was no sharp distinction among the people outside the Brāhmaṇas and Kshatriyas, and even these two formed classes rather than castes. Nor did the Brāhmaṇas occupy a position of unquestioned supremacy. They enjoyed great dignity, and the murder of a Brāhmaṇa was regarded as a particularly heinous crime. But they did not dominate the king and the state to the same extent as in India. It is interesting to note that in many instances where the two classes are mentioned together, the Kshatriyas are placed before the Brāhmaṇas, as we find in Buddhist and Jain texts in India. In Bali, even to-day, the ruling princes, be they of Kshatriya or Vaiśya caste, are regarded as superior to their Brāhmaṇa subjects, and although theoretically a prince is not allowed to marry a Brāhmaṇa girl, this is often done by the legal subterfuge of expelling a Brāhmaṇa girl and adopting her in the house of the prince.

The position of woman in many of these colonies seems to have been much better than in India, at least so far as political rights are concerned. As noted above,[0] Guṇapriyā ruled in her own rights, and her name was placed before that of her husband. There are instances in later history of a daughter succeeding to the throne, although she had two brothers, and acting as regent for her mother although she had a grown-up son. Some ladies occupied the highest offices of state, and wives of officials are stated in inscriptions to have received presents from the king along with their husbands on ceremonial occasions. The old literature as well as the present day customs in Bali indicate that there was no *purdah* system and women freely mixed with men. The system of burning the widow along with the dead husband was in vogue. Sometimes even the slaves and concubines of the dead perished with him. This is now forbidden to the Śūdras, and generally the *Satī* rite is confined to royal families.

In addition to the social division into castes there was also distinction between the aristocracy and common people. The two divisions were overlapping to a certain extent, and though the Brāhmaṇas and the Kshatriyas formed the bulk of the aristocracy it certainly included other people. The external symbols of aristocracy, as in India, were (1) special articles of dress and ornaments, (2) right to use special conveyances, such as palanquins and elephants, to the accompaniment of music, etc., and (3) the claim to be seated near the king.

As regards dress, the sculptures represent, as in India the upper part of the body above the waist as uncovered, both in the case of males and females. The Chinese accounts, too, refer to similar dress. As is well-known, in Bali, even to-day, the women do not cover the upper part of the body. So this seems to be an old practice, at least in some of the colonies, and to judge from the sculptural representations, it was possibly not unknown even in India.

2. *Religion*

The Puranic religion had a strong hold on almost all the colonies. Although Brahmā, Vishṇu, and Śiva were all worshipped, the cult of Śiva was undoubtedly the most popular. Next came Vaishṇavism. As in India, the worship of Brahmā never attained great popularity. The images of Trimūrti, *i.e.* the three gods combined together, as well as of the composite god Śiva-Vishṇu, are found in Java and Kambuja. As a matter of fact the entire Puranic pantheon was known in these countries, and we come across images of Hindu gods and goddesses in their innumerable names and forms as known in India. The mystic philosophy of the Upanishads, and even later outgrowths such as Tāntrik rites, can also be traced. Indeed Hindu religion in all its aspects, both canonical and popular, appears in such fullness in these colonies, that to describe it in detail would be to recount at length the religious conditions in India.

The study of Indian religious literature was a special feature of the religious life. In Java the period under review saw the beginnings of that extensive Javanese religious literature, based on Indian texts, which will be noticed in the next volume. The inscriptions of Kambuja frequently refer to Brāhmaṇas versed in Veda, Vedāṅga, Sāmaveda, and Buddhist scriptures, and kings and ministers possessing a profound knowledge of the Dharmaśāstra. Arrangements were also made for the daily recitation of *Rāmāyaṇa, Mahābhārata,* and the *Purāṇas,* and it was considered a pious act to present copies of these texts to temples.

Buddhism was also popular, particularly in Suvarṇa-dvīpa, *i.e.* East Indies. Although the Hīnayāna form was prevalent in the seventh century, it was almost ousted in the eighth by Mahāyāna, which had a triumphal career in Java and Sumatra during the period of Śailendra supremacy. It has left undying memorials in the famous stūpa of Barabuḍur and several magnificent temples. As noted above,[10] Buddhist teachers from Bengal exerted considerable influence in Java, and the Śailendras were in close contact with the Pāla kings and such famous Buddhist centres in India as Nālandā. As in the case of Puranic religion, almost the entire hierarchy of the Mahāyānist gods make their appearance in Java, not only in identical forms and names, but also with the familiar postures called *mudrā.* We possess also an interesting work *Sang hyang Kamahāyānikan,* a somewhat free Javanese version of a Sanskrit original interspersed with a number of original Sanskrit verses, which gives an exposition of the sacred principles of Mahāyāna.

Buddhism had also prevailed in Champā. Even as early as A.D. 605 a victorious Chinese general carried away 1350 Buddhist books from this country. From the eighth century A.D. we hear of many kings constructing Buddhist temples and monasteries and installing Buddhist images. The site of Dong Duong indicates the great hold of Buddhism in this country. For its ruins contain the remains of a Buddhist temple far greater in dimensions than the largest Brahmanical temple in Champā, and a fine standing image of Buddha, which is regarded as the most artistic representation of a god so far found in that country.

The Sanskrit inscriptions of Kambuja, to which reference will be made later, throw a great deal of light on the religious developments. These inscriptions reflect the life and society in Kambuja and testify to the thoroughness of the Indian cultural conquest of these far-off lands. They prove that the people fully imbibed the tenets and practices, the theology, rituals, and the iconography of the various religious sects of India. The numerous temples, images of gods and goddesses, and pious foundations show the powerful hold which religion had over the popular mind. But the inscriptions prove something more; they clearly show that there was in Kambuja, beyond the external forms of religion, that higher and deeper spiritual view of life which is the true essence of all religions and formed such a distinctive characteristic of ancient Indian culture and civilisation. These inscriptions reveal a spirit of piety and renunciation, a deep yearning for emancipation from the trammels of birth and evils of the world, and longing for the attainment of the highest bliss and salvation by union with Brahman, the Ultimate Reality. These ideas, which form the keynote of Indian spiritual life, are frequently expressed with beauty and elegance, and in language at once stately and serene.

Generally the true religious spirit is chiefly found among the common people. But in Kambuja even the kings, high officials, and the aristocracy were inspired by the high ideals portrayed above. This is probably due to a close association between secular and spiritual heads. The inscriptions tell us that the kings usually received their early education from eminent religious Āchāryas and members of the family of hereditary royal priests.[11] There are also many instances of kings and members of the royal family becoming high priests and Āchāryas. The intermarriage between royal and priestly families was also very common. The predominance of a family, whose members supplied royal priests for 250 years in unbroken succession, is both an index and the cause of the extreme religious outlook of the king and the people.

At least two special circumstances may be pointed out as being mainly responsible for this growth of religious and spiritual life in Kambuja. The first is a constant and intimate contact with India, and the second is the establishment of a series of *āśramas* or hermitages. Both require some detailed notice.

Apart from the indirect evidence furnished by inscriptions, actual examples of contact with India are recorded in Kambuja inscriptions. Reference has been made above to Agastya, a Brāhmaṇa from India, who founded a royal family in Kambuja. Rājalakshmī, the daughter of Rājendra-varman, was married to a Brāhmaṇa, named Divākara Bhaṭṭa, who is said to have been born on the banks of the river Kālindī sanctified by association with Kṛishṇa's early life. This undoubtedly implies that Divākara Bhaṭṭa was born in India on the banks of the Yamunā river and, having migrated to Kambuja, obtained a high position there. We have similar instances, both in earlier and later times, of learned Indian Brāhmaṇas, noted for their spiritual powers, being invited to Kambuja and received with high honours. The Brāhmaṇa named Hiraṇyadāma, who performed Tāntrik rites for Jaya-varman II, has been mentioned above.[12] Another eminent Śaiva Brāhmaṇa named Sarvajñamuni, versed in all the Vedas and Āgamas, came from India, and his descendants occupied high offices. The people of Kambuja also visited India to acquire knowledge and spiritual instruction. The most important example is that of Śivasoma, the *guru* (preceptor) of Indra-varman. It is stated in a contemporary record that he learnt the *śāstras* (sacred scriptures) from Bhagavat Śaṅkara, who is undoubtedly the famous Śaṅkarāchārya.

Coming to the second factor, the *āśramas,* these hermitages were the abodes of pious devotees who dedicated their lives to study and meditation. A large number of these institutions existed all over Kambuja. King Yaśo-varman is said to have founded one hundred *āśramas,* and this is supported by the actual discovery of a large number of inscriptions recording the foundation of individual *āśramas* in different parts of the kingdom. These inscriptions are fairly long, and give detailed regulations for the management of the *āśramas* and the conduct of persons visiting them or living therein. These regulations indicate the high moral and spiritual ideal which inspired these institutions, and the great humanitarian spirit in which their actual work was carried on. These *āśramas* remind us of the hermitages in ancient India of which we get such a vivid picture in ancient Indian literature and on which they were evidently based. They formed powerful centres of Indian culture in Kambuja, from which it radiated in all directions and gained in purity, strength, and stability.

In conclusion it should be mentioned that there was a spirit of religious toleration in all the colonies. Although various Brahmanical sects flourished along with Buddhism, there was no animosity between their followers. On the other hand kings and people alike paid reverence to all religious sects. The same king endowed both Śaiva and Buddhist religious establishments or installed images of different sectarian gods. In this respect the Indian colonists maintained the best traditions of their motherland.

3. *Art*

Every Hindu colony contains numerous monuments of artistic activity in the shape of temples and images which show distinct traces of Indian influence and inspiration in varying degrees. While some are close imitations, almost replicas, of Indian models, others show refreshing development of local styles by the addition of special, sometimes characteristic, features to Indian ideas. None excels in this respect the Indo-Javanese art which reached its high watermark of glory and splendour during the period under review, and needs a more detailed treatment than the rest.

(i) Indo-Javanese Art

Art in Java, as in India and her other colonies, was the handmaid of religion. The religious structures in Java are known by the general name *Chaṇḍi,* and most of them are temples, built on a more or less uniform plan with variations in details. Each temple consists of three distinct parts, *viz.* (1) a high decorated basement, (2) the square body of the temple with a vestibule in front and projections on all other sides, and (3) the roof consisting of a series of gradually diminishing storeys each of which is a minor replica of the main temple with four turrets at four corners of the same design. The interior of the temple is a plain square chamber, whose vertical walls support a series of projecting horizontal courses of stone which form an inverted pyramid of steps and is terminated by a high and pointed hollow cone.

The decorative ornaments consist of well-known Indian motifs, and one which occurs very frequently is known as Kāla-Makara. Really Kāla and Makara are two separate motifs though they are often found united. The first is a grotesque form of Indian Kīrttimukha, and represents a conventional lion's head with protruding eyes, broad nose, very thick upper lip, and two big projecting teeth on two sides. The Makara closely resembles its Indian prototype.

The arches in these temples are constructed on the horizontal principle as in India, but columns and pillars are conspicuous by their absence. There is often a large group or cluster of temples formed by one or more big temples in the centre with numerous smaller temples surrounding them.

The earliest temples in Java are those on the Dieng plateau, which is 6,500 feet high and surrounded by hills on all sides. They are Brahmanical temples named after the heroes and heroines of the *Mahābhārata*, and belong probably to the eighth century A.D. Although comparatively small in dimensions, these temples and the sculptures in them are characterised by a sobriety and dignity which is usually associated with Indian temples of the Gupta period.

The Prambanan valley contains several groups of important temples. Among the Buddhist temples may be mentioned Chaṇḍi Kalasan, Chaṇḍi Sari, and Chaṇḍi Sevu. The first is a magnificent specimen of temple architecture, and was built by a Śailendra king in A.D. 778 for the goddess Tārā. The complex of temples known as Chaṇḍi Ṣevu contains no less than 250 temples with the main temple in the centre of a paved courtyard measuring about 600 ft. by 540 ft.

Still more famous is the Lara-Jongrang group of Brahmanical temples. It consists of eight main temples, three in each row with two between them, with three rows of minor temples making a total of 156. The three main temples in one row contain images of Brahmā, Vishṇu, and Śiva, the Śiva temple in the centre being the most magnificent. The balustrade round the temple contains a continuous series of relief sculptures in 42 panels, depicting the story of the *Rāmāyaṇa*. These exhibit a high degree of skill, and may be reckoned among the very best to be found in Java.

Midway between the Dieng plateau and the Prambanan valley stands the Kedu plain, which contains a number of fine temples, among which Chaṇḍi Mendut and Chaṇḍi Pavon deserve special mention as beautiful specimens of Indo-Javanese art.

But by far the most magnificent monument in Java is the famous Barabuḍur, a colossal structure justly regarded as a veritable wonder by the whole world. It is situated on the top of a hillock commanding a fine view across the plains of Kedu to the distant ranges of hills. This noble building consists of nine gradually receding terraces, the six lower ones being square in plan, and the upper three circular. The whole is crowned by a bell-shaped *stūpa*, which stands at the centre of the topmost terrace and is accessible from it by a series of circular steps. The three uppermost terraces are encircled by rings of *stūpas*, each containing an image of Buddha within a perforated framework. The five lower terraces are each enclosed on the inner side by a wall supporting a balustrade, and the four successive galleries thus formed contain eleven series of sculptured panels depicting the life of Buddha and other Buddhist stories. The balustrade consists of a row of arched niches resembling temples and containing an image of Buddha. There is a staircase with a highly decorated gateway in the middle of each side of the gallery leading to the next higher one.

The most notable feature of Barabuḍur is its massive proportions. It impresses the visitor with a feeling as if a hillock has suddenly come to view. It is difficult to convey an exact idea of this feeling by measurements alone, but still that is the only concrete way of expressing it. The lowest terrace, including projections on two sides, has an extreme length of nearly 400 ft., and the topmost one a diameter of 90 ft. The temple niches, each containing a fine image of Buddha, are 432 in number. The total number of sculptured panels in the galleries is about 1500.

These figures give some idea of the massive grandeur of Barabuḍur which strikes a visitor when it first comes to his view. But as he approaches closer to the structure, he is no less deeply impressed by the fine quality of its immense decorations, extensive relief sculptures, and the numerous images of Buddha. It is difficult to name any product of art, either in India or anywhere else in the world, where such a high standard of excellence has been maintained over such an extensive range. This combination of massive quantity and fine quality invests Barabuḍur with a unique character. It has hardly any parallel in the world, and it may be truly remarked of its artists that "they conceived like giants and finished like jewellers."

The construction of Barabuḍur may be roughly dated towards the close of the eighth or the beginning of the ninth century A.D. when the Śailendras ruled in Java and were the dominant political power in Suvarṇa-dvīpa. There is hardly any doubt that this great monument is the result of their patronage.

Although Lara Jongrang and Barabuḍur have cast into shade all the other structures in Java, many of them are fine specimens of Indo-Javanese architecture, and some of the sculptures, such as those of Mendut and Banon, show perhaps even a greater degree of refinement and delicacy than those of the two justly famous monuments.

(ii) *Art in Indo-China*

The art of Kambuja may be broadly divided into two classes, the primitive and the classic. The latter, which is associated with Angkor and shows the high watermark of its glory, dates from about the tenth century and will be dealt with in the next volume.

The primitive art began from the age of Fu-nan, and was developed by natural stages of evolution to the classical art. But as most of the monuments of Fu-nan were made of perishable materials like wood or brick, there are not enough remains to enable us to reconstruct the history of its art. The brick temples, roughly resembling those of Java, show some affinity with Gupta art, which is even more evident in some of the sculptures discovered both in Siam and Cambodia. It may be safely presumed, therefore, that the primitive art of Kambuja and Siam was directly derived from India. Some scholars are even of opinion that the artists and craftsmen who built the temples and made the images of gods came from India. But be that as it may, there is no doubt that the primitive art of Kambuja was purely Indian, and from Fu-nan this Indian art of the Gupta age spread over a wide territory in Indo-China along with other phases of Indian culture.

There are also a large number of temples in Champā. In addition to many isolated examples there are three important groups of temples, *viz.* those of Myson, Dong Duong, and Po-Nagar, the second being Buddhist and the other two Śaivite. These temples are generally built of brick and belong to one standard type. Their most characteristic feature is the roof which has three different forms. The first or the normal form consists of a series of four receding storeys crowned by a curvilinear pyramidal slab. The second form consists of two storeys, the upper one having the shape of an elongated arched vault with ogival ends. The third form consists of a curvilinear pyramidal dome, springing directly from the walls of the sanctuary and surmounted by an *āmalaka* such as we find in the *śikharas* of Northern India. All these forms or types are found in the rock-cut temples at Māmallapuram in Madras, and there can hardly be any doubt that the architectural style of Champā was derived from India.

Although neither Champā nor Kambuja produced during this period any structure that can even make a remote approach to what we find in Java, there was a fair amount of artistic activity in both, full of future promise. In Champā, due perhaps to the political conditions, these promises never materialised. But in Kambuja the art developed in rapid strides after tenth century A.D. and produced some remarkable monuments which almost rivalled those of Java.

4. *Literature*

The Sanskrit inscriptions discovered in Kambuja, Champā, Malaya Peninsula, and Java leave no doubt that Sanskrit literature, in all its branches, was highly cultivated in all the Indian colonies. As we have seen above,[13] we can trace its beginning to a much earlier period. But the large number of Sanskrit inscriptions—about 30 in Champā and 70 in Kambuja—during the period under review, indicate very great progress in the study of Sanskrit. Reference has already been made above to religious literature, but even in secular literature the achievements were remarkable. Inscriptions, earlier than the ninth century A.D., refer to many of its branches such as grammar and philology, philosophy, political science (Artha-śāstra), and Kāvya. The literary accomplishments of king Indra-varman III of Champā and Yaśo-varman of Kambuja have been mentioned above. Yaśo-varman's minister was an expert in astrology. All these throw interesting light on the zeal and enthusiasm with which all classes of peopl(igh and low, took to the study of Sanskrit.

The cultivation of Sanskrit language and literature reached its highest development in Kambuja during the ninth and tenth centuries A.D. This may be easily deduced from a careful study of the large number of Sanskrit inscriptions composed in beautiful and almost flawless Kāvya style. Many of these run to great lengths. Four inscriptions of Yaśo-varman contain respectively 50 75, 93, and 108 verses each, and two inscriptions of Rājendra-varman contain respectively 218 and 298 verses. The authors of these inscriptions give clear evidence of a thorough knowledge of almost all the Sanskrit metres and the most abstruse rules of Sanskrit rhetoric and prosody, intimate acquaintance with various branches of literature such as Veda, Vedānta, Purāṇa, Dharmaśāstra, Buddhist and Jain literature, different schools of philosophy, and Vyākaraṇa, specially the works of Pāṇini and Patañjali. Specific reference is made to Vātsyāyana and Viśālāksha as the authors respectively of Kāmasūtra and a book on polity, to *Manu-smṛiti*, from which a verse is actually quoted, and to the famous medical treatise of Suśruta. Both the form and contents of the inscriptions indicate a mastery of Sanskrit Kāvya. An inscription of Rājendra-varman contains four verses which are evidently copied from *Raghuvaṁśa* with slight modifications. Some inscriptions of Yaśo-varman refer to Pravara-sena and Mayūra as the authors of *Setubandha* and *Sūryaśataka*, and to Guṇāḍhya as a writer in Prakrit with an allusion to the legend about him contained in the *Kathāsarit-sāgara*. The inscriptions themselves are sometimes writtten in such a fine Kāvya style as would do honour to a reputable Sanskrit poet of India. They certainly excel in literary merits the Sanskrit inscriptions so far discovered in India. As to the legends and mythology, derived chiefly from the Purāṇas and the epics, and the allusion, alliteration, and simile etc.

which usually abound in Sanskrit Kāvyas, they occur so frequently in these records that their authors seem to be saturated with them.

Such a state of knowledge and proficiency clearly implies a close and constant contact between India and Kambuja. M. Çœdés, while editing a Kambuja inscription, has pointed out that it so strikingly exhibits all the characteristic features of the Gauḍa style, that its author must have been either an inhabitant of Gauḍa (Bengal) or one who had lived in that country for a long time. As a matter of fact similar remarks may perhaps be made in respect of many other records. On the whole the series of inscriptions may be taken as a definite evidence of the flourishing state of literature in Kambuja and her intimate contact with India.

VII. CHINA

The most active and fruitful period of intercourse between India and China came to an end with the eight century A.D.[14] The last century of T'ang rule (A.D. 618-907) was full of troubles, and the Arab incursions in Central Asia probably interfered with the free intercourse of the Buddhists between India and China. In any case we hear very little of the cultural or political relations with India about this time. But the Song dynasty (A.D. 960-1279) revived the old traditions and the active intercourse was resumed for another century.

In A.D. 972 forty-four Indian monks went to China. Next year Dharmadeva, a monk of Nālandā, was received by the emperor of China with great honours. He translated a large number of Sanskrit texts and died in China in A.D. 1001. A number of other Indian monks, including a prince of Western India named Mañjuśrī, visited China between 970 and 1036. According to the Chinese chroniclers there were never so many Indian monks in the Chinese court as at the close of the tenth and the beginning of the eleventh century A.D. A large number of Sanskrit manuscripts were brought from India by these Indian monks as well as the Chinese pilgrims. In 982 the Chinese Emperor appointed a Board of Translators with three Indian scholars at the head. They translated more than 200 volumes between A.D. 982 and 1011.

A large number of Chinese pilgrims also came to India between A.D. 950 and 1033. In A.D. 964, 300 Chinese monks started for India, and this pilgrimage lasted for twelve years. Two years later the Chinese Emperor issued an appeal to the Buddhist monks, and 157 of them went in pursuance of it to pay imperial homage to the holy places in India. They were furnished with letters patent ordering all the kings of Central Asia and Northern India to help them with guides. These monks were sometimes asked to carry out certain religious duties in India, on behalf of the Emperor.

Five of these Chinese pilgrims have left short inscriptions at the sacred site of Bodh-Gayā. One of them records the visit of the monk Che-yi in A.D. 950. Three others, dated A.D. 1022, refer to the construction of stone *stūpas* by three Chinese monks. The last inscription is more interesting. It is dated in A.D. 1033 and records the construction of a *stūpa* in honour of Emperor T'ai-tsong by the Emperor and the Dowager Empress of the great Song dynasty. We are told that the Emperor and the Empress "respectfully charged the monk Huai-wen with the task of going to the country of Magadha in order to erect a *stūpa* by the side of the Vajrāsana dedicated to Emperor T'ai-tsong." This inscription still remains as the last monument of the Chinese pilgrimage to India which began about a thousand years ago.

The last Chinese piligrim left India shortly after A.D.1033. and a group of nine Indian monks went to China in A.D. 1036. Only a single Indian monk is known to have visited China after that date, in A.D. 1053, and the official chronicle terminates its notice on India from A.D. 1036. This date, therefore, marks the close of the long and intimate cultural intercourse between India and China. The cause of this sudden end is not easy to determine, and it naturally led to a decline in the popularity of Buddhism. "The number of Buddhist monks and nuns in China in A.D. 1021 were respectively 3,97,615 and 61,240; in 1034, 3,85,520 and 48,740; but in 1068, only 2,20,660 and 34,030."[15]

There was political relation between South India and China during the Song period. A Choḷa embassy visited the Imperial Court in A.D. 1015. Details of their journey are given in Chinese annals which show that it took, in all, 1150 days, though they were actually under sail for only 247 days. The Choḷa king is said to have sent as presents, among other things, 21,000 ounces of pearls, 60 elephants' tusks, and 60 *catties* of frankincense. The envoy added 6600 ounces of pearls and 3300 *catties* of perfumes. In A.D. 1033 and 1077 the Choḷa king sent two more embassies to China.

The sea-borne trade between India and China continued throughout this period, but it is difficult to say how far the Indians took any share in it. The Song Annals do not include India among the countries whose merchants traded at Canton in A.D. 971. Chou Ku-fei, writing in 1178, refers to Quilon as an important centre of trade with China, but does not mention India among the countries engaged in that trade. It may be argued from these that the Arabs were gradually ousting the Indians from the Chinese trade.[16] But the discovery of 15 coins in Tanjore District, representing practically the entire Song period, may be cited as an evidence that the commercial relations between South India and China, which flourished in the T'ang period,[17] probably continued uninterrupted throughout the Song period.[18]

VIII. TIBET

According to the chronicles of Tibet her kings exercised political domination over parts of India during the period A.D. 750-850. The Tibetan king Khri-sroṅ-lde-btsan, who ruled from A.D. 755 to 797, is said to have subdued the frontier provinces including 'China in the east and India in the south.' His son Mu-Khri-btsan-po (or Mu-tig-Btsan-po) who ruled from A.D. 798 to 804 subjugated two or three (parts of) Jambudvīpa and forced the Pāla king Dharmapāla and another Indian king to pay tribute. The next important king Ral-pa-can (A.D. 817-836)[19] conquered India as far as Gaṅgāsāgara which has been taken to represent the mouth of the Gaṅgā.

How far these Tibetan claims of conquest and supremacy in the Indian plains can be regarded as historical, it is difficult to say. We have no reference in Indian sources to any military campaign of the Tibetans in India or to their exercising political suzerainty in any part of the country. On the other hand, Chinese sources confirm the great military strength and the aggressive military campaigns of the Tibetans both against China and India. One Chinese author says that some time about A.D. 787 the Emperor of China made an alliance with the Caliph of Baghdād and some Indian princes, for security against the Tibetans.[20] It is also to be noted that both Iṣtakhrī and Ibn Haukal call the Bay of Bengal as Tibetan Sea, thus indirectly indicating the advance of the Tibetans to the heart of Bengal. While, therefore, there may be some foundation for these claims, we cannot come to any definite conclusion, until further evidence is available.

It is interesting to note that the same period (A.D. 750-850) in which Tibetan domination in India is said to have reached its climax also witnessed the supremacy of Buddhism in Tibet. The king Khri-sroṅ-lde-btsan, mentioned above, was a great patron of Buddhism, and was regarded as an incarnation of Bodhisattva Mañjuśrī. He invited Śāntarakshita, the High Priest of the University of Nālandā, and appointed him the High Priest of Tibet. He made Buddhism the state-religion of Tibet in place of Bon, a sort of demon-worship. Śāntarakshita introduced the system of Buddhist monarchism which is now known as Lamaism in Tibet. He was helped in this onerous task of reorganising the religious system by another Indian monk named Padmasambhava. A scholar named Ananta from Kāshmir also translated sacred texts and preached Buddhism. At this time a Chinese Buddhist missionary visited Tibet and preached doctrines which were different from those of Śāntarakshita and Padmasambhava. The latter, unable to refute him, induced the king to invite the great Buddhist philosopher of Magadha named Kamalaśīla. Kamalaśīla visited Tibet and, in the presence of the assembled court, came out victorious over the Chinese sage. The king of Tibet placed Kamalaśīla at the head of the metaphysical branch of the Buddhist church. The orthodox section of the people were at first hostile to the new religion, but all opposition gradually died down. King Khri-sroṅ-lde-btsan built the famous temple of Bsam-yas in imitation of the temple of Odantapurī in Magadha. This temple still exists and is situated about 35 miles from Lhasa.

The names of a large number of Indian scholars who taught different aspects of Buddhism about this time in Tibet have been preserved. Among them may be mentioned Dharmakīrti, Vimalamitra, Buddhaguhya, and Śāntigarbha. They introduced Tāntrik ritual and taught mysticism based on Buddhist Tāntrism.

But the names of Śāntarakshita and Padmasambhava are held in special veneration. The former introduced the observance of the "ten virtues." Padmasambhava was the greatest teacher of Tāntrik doctrines which spread all over the country. He became almost a legendary and mythical figure in Tibet.

The reign of Khri-sroṅ-lde-btsan thus saw the final triumph of Buddhism in Tibet. According to Tibetan chronicles "the Bon religion was suppressed and the holy religion was made to spread and flourished" during the lifetime of this king. They quote a verse mentioning Śāntarakshita, Padmasambhava, Kamalaśīla, and Khri-sroṅ-lde-btsan as the four persons through whom "like sunrise in the dark country of Tibet, the light of the holy religion spread as far as the frontiers." "These holy men," so the verse concludes, "all Tibetans will for ever reverently salute".

The successors of king Khri-sroṅ-lde-btsan followed his policy of translating sacred books, erecting temples, and inviting *Paṇḍitas* from India. Ral-pa-can, mentioned above, was a great patron of Buddhism. As there were conflicting interpretations in the large number of Tibetan translations of sacred scriptures, he invited the

Indian *Paṇḍitas* Jinamitra, Surendrabodhi, Śīlendrabodhi, Bodhimitra, and Dhanaśīla to Tibet. He was a great lover of Indian culture and introduced even the system of Indian weights and measures in Tibet. All this provoked a reaction during the reign of his successor Glan-dar-ma who persecuted Buddhism. But he was murdered, probably by a monk, and his son, who owed the throne to the help of the Buddhist monks, restored the supremacy of Buddhism. This king (A.D. 842-70) and his successors invited Buddhist scholars from India, erected temples, and had sacred books translated into Tibetan. Eminent Tibetan scholars also visited India in order to learn the Buddhist doctrines.[21]

Tibetan Chronicles have preserved a most circumstantial account of the part played by an Indian scholar named Dīpaṅkara Śrījñāna, called also Atīśa. Even making allowances for natural exaggeration and somewhat romantic character of the story, it shows in a striking manner to what extent India was regarded as their spiritual home by the Tibetans. The story must be read in full in order to understand the reverential attitude of the Tibetans towards India. Here we can only give a summary.

Dīpaṅkara was born in Bengal in c. A.D. 980. After attaining proficiency in both Buddhist and Brahmanical philosophy and scriptures he went to Āchārya Chandrakīrti, the High Priest of Suvarṇadvīpa, and studied with him for twelve years. On his return he was acknowledged as the hierarch of Magadha and, at the request of king Nayapāla, accepted the post of High Priest of Vikramaśīla.

About this time Lha Lama Ye-śes-ḥod, king of Tibet, wanted to reform Buddhism which had become greatly debased by the admixture of Tāntrik and Bon mysticism. Accordingly he sent a number of young Tibetan monks to India to study Buddhist scriptures and to invite to Tibet renowned scholars like Dīpaṅkara, Ratnavajra and others. Out of the 21 Tibetan monks who thus came to India, only two survived and returned to Tibet after completing their studies. They made inquiries about Dīpaṅkara, but were told that any invitation to him to visit Tibet would be premature. But the king, on hearing of his high renown and scholarship, sent an envoy to Magadha with one hundred attendants and a large quantity of gold. The envoy presented to Dīpaṅkara the king's letter with a large piece of bar-gold as a present from his sovereign, and begged him to honour his country with a visit. Dīpaṅkara declined the present and the invitation. The envoy wept bitterly, but could not change the decision of Dīpaṅkara.

Shortly after this the king of Tibet fell into the hands of an enemy and died in captivity. Before his death he sent a message which so touched the heart of Dīpaṅkara that he decided to visit Tibet.

Atīśa was received with high honours at the frontier of Tibet. Four generals, with one hundred horsemen, received him and he was escorted in a procession carrying flags and playing various musical instruments. His journey through the country was in the nature of a royal tour, and he was everywhere hailed by all classes of people. The king arranged a grand ovation for him in the capital. Dīpaṅkara spent the remaining 13 years of his life in Tibet, preaching the pure doctrines of Buddhism and writing sacred texts. He reformed Buddhism in Tibet by eliminating Tāntrik elements, and wrote about two hundred books. He was the spiritual guide and teacher of Bromton, the founder of the first grand hierarchy of Tibet. He died in A.D. 1053, and is even now remembered with deep veneration all over upper Asia or wherever the Buddhism of the Tibet variety prevails.

Throughout the Pāla period Tibet was in close touch with India, particularly with the great Universities of Nālandā and Vikramaśīla. She adopted many traits of Indian culture along with religion, such as the 60 years' cycle system. Many Indian monks visited Tibet and preached the new developments of Buddhism. In particular the mystic schools of Buddhism like Vajrayāna and Sahajayāna found great favour there. The vast literature of this religion, now lost in India, has been preserved in Tibetan translations, in the two voluminous collections known as Bstan-hgyur and Bkah-hgyur. We possess only a bare knowledge of the names and general contents of the texts included in them, as most of them have not yet been studied in detail. But the systematic catalogue prepared by Csoma de Coros and Cordier, and works of several other scholars show that these works are very large in number and varied in nature. They furnish positive testimony to the intimate connection between the two countries and the profound influence exercised by India upon the development of religious thought and literature, as well as many other aspects of culture in Tibet.

IX. WESTERN COUNTRIES

We have abundant references to a very close contact between India and the Muslim world.[22] Baghdād was at this time the centre of Muslim world, and Indian culture reached it both directly as well as through Irān. Indian literature, at first translated into Persian, was later translated from Persian into Arabic. The most prominent example of this is furnished by the fables of *Kalila* and *Dimna* based on *Pañchatantra*,[23] and probably the famous medical treatise *Charaka-saṁhitā* was first known to the Muslim court in this way.

The direct intercourse between India and Baghdād is prominently noticeable during the reigns of Al-Manṣūr (A.D. 754-75) and Harun Al-Rashīd (A.D. 786-809). As Sindh was under the actual rule of Al-Manṣūr, several Indian embassies came to his court. These embassies were accompanied by Indian scholars who taught the Arabs both mathematics and astronomy, as well as various other subjects. Al-Bīrūnī tells us that the "star-cycles, as known through the canon of Alfazāri and Ya'kub Ibn Ṭārik, were derived from a Hindu who came to Bagdad as a member of the political mission which Sindh sent to the Khalif Almanṣūr, A.H. 154 (A.D. 771)."[24] Again, we learn from the same source, that the Hindu traditions regarding the distances of the stars were communicated to Ya'kub Ibn Ṭārik by "the well-known Hindu scholar who, in A.H. 161 (A.D. 778), accompanied an embassy to Bagdad."[25] Two other Indian embassies are known, from other sources, to have visited Baghdād in the year 136 (A.D. 753) and 156 (A.D. 773).[26]

The scholars who accompanied these embassies brought several works on mathematics including the *Brahma-sphuṭa-siddhānta* and the *Khaṇḍakhādyaka* of Brahmagupta. With their help these works were translated into Arabic by Arab scholars (Alfazārī, perhaps also Ya'kūb Ibn Ṭārik) and it was thus that the Arabs first became acquainted with a scientific system of astronomy. Both the works exercised a profound influence on the development of astronomy by the Arabs who learned from Brahmagupta earlier than from Ptolemy. It is probably also through these scholars that the Hindu numerals were first definitely introduced amongst the Arabs. It is well known how this new system, known as decimal notation based on the place-value of the first nine numbers and the use of zero, simplified and revolutionised the Science of Mathematics all over the world. Whether Europe derived this knowledge directly from India or through the Arabs is a disputed question, but there is a general consensus of opinion that the world is indebted to India for this epoch-making discovery. In this connection reference may be made to a remarkable statement by Severus Sebokht, a learned Syrian scholar who lived in a convent on the Euphrates about the middle of the seventh century A.D. He pays a very high compliment to the Indians for their "subtle discoveries in the science of astronomy, discoveries that are more ingenious than those of the Greeks and the Babylonians." He then refers to their system of "computing that surpasses description" and remarks: "I wish only to say that this computation is done by means of nine signs. If those who believe, because they speak Greek, that they have reached the limits of science, should know these things, they would be convinced that there are also others who know something."[27]

Without going into further details we may conclude with the following expression of opinion by an eminent European scholar: "In Science, too, the debt of Europe to India has been considerable. There is, in the first place, the great fact that the Indians invented the numerical figures used all over the world. The influence which the decimal system of reckoning dependent on those figures has had not only on mathematics, but on the progress of civilisation in general can hardly be over-estimated. During the eighth and ninth centuries the Indians became the teachers in arithmetic and algebra of the Arabs, and through them of the nations of the West. Thus, though we call the latter science by an Arabic name, it is a gift we owe to India."[28]

During the Caliphate of Harun Al-Rashīd contact with India was further promoted chiefly by the efforts of the ministers of the Barmak family, then at the height of their power. The founder of this family was a Buddhist high-priest in the Naubehar (= Nava Vihāra or New Monastery) in Balkh. Although converted to Islam they still had great leanings towards their old culture. They induced Indian scholars to come to Baghdād and engaged them to translate into Arabic Sanskrit books on medicine, pharmacology, toxicology, philosophy, astronomy, astrology, algebra, arithmetic and other subjects. Arab scholars were also sent to India in large numbers to learn those sciences at first hand from Indian authorities.

We learn from several Arab works written between the tenth and thirteenth century A.D. that a number of standard Hindu treatises on medicine, materia medica and therapeutics were translated into Arabic by order of the Caliph Harun Al-Rashīd (A.D. 786-809). These included, among others, such famous works as the *Charaka*, the *Suśruta*, the *Nidāna*, and the *Ashṭāṅga* of Vāgbhaṭa. The *Suśruta* was translated by an Indian whose name is written in Arabic as Mankh. He cured Harun Al-Rashīd of a severe illness and was appointed by the grateful Caliph the head of the Royal Hospital.

The names of a number of Indian scholars who visited Baghdād are preserved in Arabic works, but unfortunately it is hardly possible, even in a single case, to restore the original Indian form from the Arabic transliteration. Sachau's attempts in this direction are praiseworthy, but not convincing. Thus he suggests that the names of the authors of three books on 'drinkables', 'philosophy' and 'signs of swords' are respectively Atri, Vedavyāsa and Vyāghra. He also thinks that the Hindu physician who was director of the hospital of the Barmaks in Baghdād and is mentioned as the son of DHN, was probably named Dhanya or Dhanin, and connects it with Dhanvantari, the mythological physician of the gods.

Islam was influenced by India not only in literature and science, as noted above, but also in various other ways. Such influence has been traced even in religious ideas, notably in the growth and development of Islamic mysticism or Ṣūfiism. As Titus has pointed out, "here the contribution seems to be made in thought, religious imagery of expression, and pious practices, which come from both Buddhist and Vedantic sources."[29] An earlier form of such influence is manifested in *Zuhd* or asceticism, which is not identical with Ṣūfiism.[30] "The *Aghāni* has preserved for us at least one portrayal of an unmistakable Buddhistic view of life, and the *Zindīq* monks described by al-Jāḥīz (ninth century A.D.) were either Indian *sādhus*, Buddhist monks, or their imitators."[31] In any case, "the presence of wandering Indian monks was a factor of practical importance to the adherents of Islam as early as the time of 'Abbasid Caliphate".[32] No doubt they were instrumental in preaching Indian ideas which influenced even Arab philosophers. One of them, Abu-al-'Alā' al-ma'arri (A.D. 973-1057), who is described as the "philosopher of poets and poet of philosophers", was so much inoculated with Indian ideas that he adopted a vegetarian diet and a life of seclusion.[33] It is known that Buddhist works were translated into Arabic during the 'Abbasid period, specially in the reigns of Al-Manṣūr and Harun Al-Rashīd.[34] Even in building mosques they were indebted, both for craftsmen and architectural ideas, to India.[35] Early Arab geographers derived from India the notion of a world-centre, which they called *Arīn,* a corrupt form of Ujjayinī, which was famous for its astronomical observatory.[36] Many of their musical terminologies are of Indian origin.[37]

The Arab merchants visited India in increasingly large numbers, and many of them wrote interesting accounts of India, the earliest of them being dated about the middle of the ninth century A.D.[38] There were Muslims settled in India for whom mosques were built by the Indian kings.

We learn from Ibn Haukal (tenth century A.D.) that "several important cities in Western India had Jama Masjids where the Muhammadan precepts were openly observed". The same writer tells us that in the dominion of the Rāshṭrakūṭas "Musulmans lived in many cities and none but Musulmans ruled over them on the part of the ruling authority". This is a remarkable concession to the foreign settlers. It does not appear, however, that the Muslim population was quite considerable in the friendly state of the Rāshṭrakūṭas. Even in Sindh, we are told, there was a large population of infidels.[39]

1. See above, Vol. III, p. 640.
2. See p. 52.
3. See above, p. 52.
4. See above, p. 49.
5. See above, Vol. III, p. 636.
6. See above, p. 417.
7. See above, Vol. III, p. 637.
8. See p. 421.
9. See p. 429.
10. See p. 414.
11. See pp. 414, 416.
12. See p. 416.
13. See Vol. III, p. 643.
14. Vol. III, pp. 597-616.
15. *SIS*, I. 164.
16. Sastri: *Foreign Notices*, 23-25; *SIS*, II. 157.
17. Vol. III, p. 612.
18. *SIS*, I. 60.
19. The date of Ral-pa-can is given on the authority of Petech (p. 81). Francke gives A.D. 804-816 as the period of his reign (p. 80).
20. Sastri: *Foreign Notices*, 17.
21. Petech holds the view that Buddhism practically disappeared from Tibet after the persecution of Glan-dar-ma and was revived after two centuries by Atīśa (pp. 82-3).
22. For a general treatment of the subject, cf. Sachau's Eng. Tr. of *Alberuni's India*. XXX ff.
23. See Vol. III, p. 314.
24. Sachau: *Alberuni's India*, II. 15.
25. *Ibid*., II. 67.
26. *Ibid*., II. 313.
27. *JA*., II, 1910. 225-27. Also cf. *History of Hindu Mathematics* by B. Dutta and A. N. Singh, I. 95 ff; P. K. Hitti: *History of the Arabs*, 307-308, 573-4.
28. Macdonell, *HSL*. 424.
29. M. T. Titus, *Indian Islam*, 149.
30. *Ibid*.
31. Hitti, *op. cit*., 435; Goldziher, *Vorlesungen über den Islam*, Tr. by Seelye, 172-3.
32. Titus, *op. cit*., 147.
33. Hitti *op. cit*., 458-9.
34. T. J. De Boer, *History of the Philosophy of Islam*, 9.
35. Hitti, *op. cit*., 265, 417.
36. *Ibid*, 384.
37. *Ibid*., 428.
38. These have been translated in *HIED*, I.
39. *HIED*, I. 34, 38.

LIST OF BIBLIOGRAPHIES

GENERAL BIBLIOGRAPHY

I. Original Sources: Literary Texts and Translations
(1) Indian Sources:

(A) Brahmanical:

(i) Epics;
(ii) Purāṇas;
(iii) Philosophy;
(iv) Dharmaśāstra;
(v) Historical Works;
(vi) Polity;
(vii) Lexicons;
(viii) Grammar;
(ix) Astronomy, Astrology and Mathematics;
(x) Medicine;
(xi) Poetics, Dramaturgy and Metrics;
(xii) Champū;
(xiii) Anthology;
(xiv) Belles-Lettres.

(B) Buddhist:

(i) Pāli;
(ii) Sanskrit.

(C) Jain:

(D) Works in Apabhraṁśa:

(E) Muslim:

(2) Non-Indian Sources:
(A) Arabic.
(B) Tibetan.

II. Original Sources:
(1) Inscriptions.
(2) Coins.

III. Modern Works:
(1) Histories of the Period.
(2) Histories of Literature.
(3) Religion and Philosophy.

BIBLIOGRAPHY

Chapter I
Chapter II
"
"
Chapter XIV

GENERAL BIBLIOGRAPHY

I. ORIGINAL SOURCES: *Literary:*

Texts and Translations.

(1) *Indian Sources:*

(A) BRAHMANICAL:

(i) EPICS:

Mahābhārata (Bom. Ed.), with the comm. of Nīlakaṇṭha. Edited by R. Kinjawadekar. Poona, 1929-33.

(Cal. Ed.) Edited by N. Siromani and others. BI. Calcutta, 1834-39.

(Kumbhakonam Ed.) Ed. by T. R. Krishnacharya and T. R. Vyasacharya. Bombay, 1905-10.

(Southern Recension) Ed. by P. P. S. Sastri. Madras, 1931 ff.

(Critical Edition) I. Ādiparvan. Ed. by V. S. Sukthankar Poona, 1927-33.

II. Sabhāparvan. Ed. by F. Edgerton. Poona, 1943-44.

III, IV. Āraṇyakaparvan. Ed. by V. S. Sukthankar. Poona, 1941-42.

V. Virāṭaparvan. Ed. by Raghu Vira. Poona, 1936.

VI. Udyogaparvan. Ed. by S. K. De. Poona, 1937-40.

VII. Bhīshmaparvan. Ed. by S. K. Belvalkar. Poona, 1945-47.

VIII. Droṇaparvan. Fasc. 25. Ed. by S. K. De. Poona, 1953 (in progress).

IX. Karṇaparvan. Ed. by P. L. Vaidya. Poona, 1950-54.

XIII-XVI. Śāntiparvan. Ed. by S. K. Belvalkar. Poona, 1949-54 (in progress).

Eng. trans. by K. M. Ganguly. Published by P. C. Roy. Calcutta, 1884-96; New Ed. Calcutta, 1926-32.

Eng. trans. by M. N. Dutt. Calcutta, 1895-1905.

Rāmāyaṇa (Bengal Recension) Ed. by G. Gorresio. Turin, 1843-67.

(North-Western India) Ed. by Pandit Rama Labhaya and others. Lahore, 1923 ff.

(North and South) Bombay, 1902.

(South) Madras, 1933.

(Critical Ed.) Ed. by Raghu Vira. First Fasc. Lahore, 1938.

Eng. trans. by M. N. Dutt. Calcutta. 1892-94.

Trans. into English verse, by R. T. H. Griffith. Benares, 1915.

(ii) PURĀṆAS:

Agni Purāṇa — Ed. by R. Mitra. BI. Calcutta, 1873-79.
Ed. ĀSS. Poona, 1900.
Eng. trans. M. N. Dutt. Calcutta, 1901.

Bhāgavata Purāṇa — Ed. with French trans. by E. Burnouf, and continued by Hauvette-Besnault and Roussel. 5 Vols. Paris, 1840-98.
Ed. by V. L. Pansikar. Bombay, 1920.
Eng. trans. M. N. Dutt. Calcutta, 1895.
Eng. trans. by Swami Vijnanananda. SBH. Allahabad, 1921-23.
Eng. trans. by S. Subba Rao. Tirupati, 1928.
Eng. trans. by J. M. Sanyal. Calcutta, 1930-34.

Bhavishya Purāṇa — Pub. Venkatesvara Press. Bombay, 1910.

Brahma Purāṇa — ĀSS. Poona, 1895.

Brahmāṇḍa Purāṇa — Pub. Venkatesvara Press. Bombay, 1913.

Bṛihannāradīya Purāṇa — Ed. P. Hrishikesha Sastri. BI. Calcutta, 1891.

Garuḍa Purāṇa — Bombay, 1906.
Eng. trans. M. N. Dutt. Calcutta, 1908.

Harivaṁśa — Ed. R. Kinjawadekar. Poona, 1936.

Kūrma Purāṇa — Ed. Nilamani Mukhopadhyaya. BI. Calcutta, 1890.

Liṅga Purāṇa — Ed. J. Vidyasagara. BI. Calcutta, 1885.

Mārkaṇḍeya Purāṇa — Ed. K. M. Banerjea. BI. Calcutta, 1862.
Eng. trans. by F. E. Pargiter. Calcutta, 1904.

Matsya Purāṇa — ĀSS. Poona. 1907.
Eng. trans. by a Taluqdar of Oudh. SBH. 2 Vols. Allahabad, 1916-17.

Padma Purāṇa — Ed. V. N. Mandlik. ĀSS. 4 Vols. Poona, 1893-94.
Pub. Venkatesvara Press. Bombay, 1895.

Śiva Purāṇa — Pub. Venkatesvara Press. Bombay.

Varāha Purāṇa — Ed. P. Hrishikesa Sastri. BI. Calcutta, 1893.

Vāyu Purāṇa — Ed. R. Mitra. 2 Vols. BI. Calcutta, 1880-88.
ĀSS. Poona, 1905.

Vishṇu Purāṇa — Bombay, 1889.
Eng. trans. by H. H. Wilson. 5 vols. London, 1864-70.
Eng. trans. by M. N. Dutt. Calcutta, 1894.

Vishṇūdharmottara Purāṇa — Pub. Venkatesvara Press. Bombay, 1912.

(iii) PHILOSOPHY:

(1) *Mīmāṁsā:*

Nyāyakaṇikā of Vāchaspati
See below under "*Vidhiviveka*".

Prakaraṇapañchikā of Śālikanātha
Benares, 1904.

Ślokavārttika of Kumārila Bhaṭṭa
Ed. in Chowkhamba SS. Benares, 1898-9.
Ed. in *Pandit*, NS, Vols. 3-4.
Eng. trans. by G. Jha. BI. Calcutta, 1900 ff.

Tantravārttika of Kumārila Bhaṭṭa
Ed. in Benares SS. Benares, 1890.
Eng. trans. by G. Jha. BI. Calcutta, 1903 ff.
Ṭupṭīkā of Kumārila Bhaṭṭa
Ed. Benares SS. Benares, 1903.
Tattvabindu of Vāchaspatimiśra
Benares, 1870. Ed. by V. A. Ramaswami Sastri. Annamalainagar, 1936.
Vidhiviveka of Maṇḍanamiśra
with the comm. *Nyāyakaṇikā* by Vāchaspati. Benares, 1907.

(2) *Nyāya:*

Nyāyakusumāñjali of Udayana
Ed. with comm. by K. Somaśekhara Śāstrī. Tirupati, 1940.
Eng. trans. by Swami Ravi Tirtha. Vol. I. Madras, 1946.
Nyāyamañjarī of Jayanta Bhaṭṭa
Ed. by Suryanarayana Sukla. Benares, 1936.
Nyāyapariśishṭa of Udayana
Ed. with comm. by Narendrachandra Vedantatirtha. Calcutta, 1938.
Nyāyasāra of Bhāsarvajña
Ed. by S. C. Vidyābhūshaṇa. Calcutta, 1910.
Nyāyavārttikatātparya of Vāchaspati
Benares, 1898.
Ed. with notes by Amarendra Mohan Tarkatirtha and Taranath Nyaya-Tarkatirtha. Calcutta, 1936.
Nyāyavārttikatātparyapariśuddhi of Udayana
Ed. by Vindhyesvari Prasad Dvivedi and Lakshmana Sastri Dravida. BI. Calcutta, 1911-24.

(3) *Sāṁkhya:*

Sāṁkhyatattvakaumudī of Vāchaspati
Ed. with comm. by Sitaram Sastri Kelkar and Ramasastri Bhandari. Benares, 1919-22.
Ed. by Ramesh Chandra. Calcutta, 1935.

(3) *Vaiśeshika:*

Kiraṇāvalī of Udayana
Ed. with comm. by Siva Chandra Sarvabhauma. BI. Calcutta, 1911-12.
Lakshaṇāvalī of Udayana
Ed. in *Pandit*, NS., XXI-XXII.
Nyāyakandalī of Śrīdhara Bhaṭṭa
Ed. in VSS, No. 6. Benares, 1895.
Eng. trans. by G. Jha in *Pandit*, NS. XXV-XXXIV; Reprinted, Benares, 1916; 2nd Ed. with notes by H. D. Sharma. Poona, 1934.

(J) Vedānta:

Bhāmatī of Vāchaspati
Ed. BI. Calcutta, 1876-1880.
Ed. by Bala Sastri. Benares, 1880.
Ed. by Jivananda Vidyasagara. Calcutta, 1891.
Ed. with notes by Dhundiraj Sastri Nyayopadhyaya. Benares, 1935-37.
(*Chatussūtri*) Ed. with Eng. trans. by S. S. Suryanarayana Sastri and C. Kunhan Raja. Madras, 1933.

Brahmasiddhi of Maṇḍanamiśra
Ed. with the comm. of Śaṅkhapāni by S. Kuppuswami Sastri. Madras, 1937.

Brahmasūtrabhāshya of Śaṅkarāchārya
Ed. with comm. by Narayana Sastri Eksambekar. ĀSS. Poona, 1900-1903.
Eng. trans. (Vedānta Sūtras with the comm. of Śaṅkarāchārya) by G. Thibaut. SBE. Oxford, 1890.

Naishkarmyasiddhi of Sureśvara
BSS. Bombay, 1891; 2nd Ed. Ed. by M. Hiriyanna. Poona, 1925.

Pañchapadikā of Padmapāda
Ed. VSS. Benares, 1891-2.

Paramārthasāra of Abhinavagupta
Ed. with comm. Kashmir Series. Srinagar, 1916.
Ed. with comm. Benares, 1932.

Saṁkshepaśārīraka of Sarvajñātma
Ed. with comm. by Bhau Sastri Vajhe. Benares, 1913.
Ed. with comm. by S. N. Sukla. Benares, 1936.

(6) Yoga:

Rājamārtaṇḍa of Bhoja
Ed. and trans. by R. Mitra. *BI*. Calcutta, 1883.
Yogasūtras with *Rājamārtaṇḍa* and other comms. Ed. by Dhundiraj Sastri. Benares, 1930.

Tattvavaiśāradī of Vāchaspati
Yogasūtras with the comm. of Vyāsa and the gloss of Vāchaspati. Ed. by R. Bodas. BSS. Bombay, 1892; 2nd Ed. 1917.
Ed. by Gosvami Damodara Sastri. Benares, 1935.
Eng. trans. by J. H. Woods. HOS. Cambridge Mass., 1914.
Eng. trans. by Ramaprasada. SBH. Allahabad, 1910.

(iv) DHARMAŚĀSTRA:

Bālakrīḍā of Viśvarūpa
Yājñavalkya-smṛiti with the comm. of Viśvarūpa. TSS. Trivandrum, 1922-24.

Dharmaśāstra-saṁgraha
Ed. by J. Vidyāsāgara. 2 Vols. Calcutta, 1876.

Manubhāshya of Medhātithi
Manu-smṛiti with the comm. of Medhātithi.
Ed. by G. Jha. BI. Calcutta, 1932-39.
Ed. by V. N. Mandlik. Bombay, 1886.
Ed. by J. R. Gharpure. Bombay, 1920.
Eng. trans. by G. Jha. Calcutta, 1922-29.

Smṛitīnām Samuchchaya
Ed. in ĀSS. Poona, 1905.

Smṛiti-sandarbhaḥ
Vols. I-III. Gurumaṇḍala-granthamālā. Calcutta, 1952.

(v) HISTORICAL WORKS:

Bilhaṇa — *Vikramāṅkadevacharita*. Ed. by G. Bühler. BSS. Bombay, 1875.

Jayānaka — *Pṛithvīrājavijaya*. Ed. with the comm. of Jonarāja by S. K. Belvalkar. BI. Calcutta, 1914-1922.
Ed. by G. H. Ojha. Ajmer, 1941.

Jonarāja — *Dvitīya-Rājataraṅgiṇī*
Ed. P. Peterson. Bombay, 1896.

Kalhaṇa — *Rājataraṅgiṇī*.
Ed. Durga Prasad. Bombay, 1892.
Eng. trans. by M. A. Stein. London, 1900.
Eng. trans. by R. S. Pandit. Allahabad, 1935.

Padmagupta *alias* Parimala
Navasāhasāṅkacharita. Ed. by V. S. Islampurkar. BSS. Bombay, 1895.

Sandhyākara Nandī
Rāmacharita. Ed. by H. P. Sastri. MASB, v. 2nd Ed. Ed. by R. C. Majumdar, R. G. Basak and N. G. Banerji. Rajshahi, 1939.

(vi) POLITY:

Nītisāra of Kāmandaka
Ed. by R. Mitra. BI. Calcutta, 1884.
Ed. with the comm. of Śaṅkarārya, by T. Ganapati Sastri. TSS. Trivandrum, 1912.

Nītisāra of Śukra
Ed. by G. Oppert. Madras, 1882.
Eng. trans. by M. N. Dutt. Calcutta, 1896.
Eng. trans. by B. K. Sarkar. 2nd Ed. Allahabad, 1923.

Nītivākyāmṛita of Someśvara
Bombay, 1887-88.
Pub. MDJG Series, Bombay.

(vii) LEXICONS:

Dhanvantari — See below under "Medicine".

Halāyudha — *Abhidhānaratnamālā*. Ed. by Th. Aufrecht. London, 1861.

Keśava — *Kalpadrukośa*. Ed. by Rāmāvatāra Śarmā. GOS. 2 vols. Baroda, 1928, 1932.

(viii) GRAMMAR:

Kātantra — With the comm. of Durgasiṁha. Ed. by J. Eggeling. BI. Calcutta, 1874-78.

Śabdānuśāsana — of Śākaṭāyana, with *Prakriyāsaṁgraha* of Abhayachandra. Pub. by Jestharam Mukundji. Bombay, 1907.

(ix) ASTRONOMY, ASTROLOGY AND MATHEMATICS:

Bhaṭṭotpala — See below under "Varāhamihira".

Mahāvīrāchārya — *Gaṇitasārasaṁgraha*. Ed. with Eng. trans. and notes by M. Rangacharya. Madras, 1912.

Śrīdharāchārya — *Gaṇitasāra* or *Triśatī*. Ed. by M. Ramanujacharya and G. R. Kaye. Leipzig, 1913.

Varāhamihira — *Bṛihaj-jātaka*. With Bhaṭṭotpala's comm. Ed. by Sita Ram Jha. Benares, 1934.

(x) MEDICINE:

Dhanvantari — *Dhanvantarīya Nighaṇṭu*. ĀSS, No. 33. Poona. 1896.

Indu — Comm. on *Ashṭāṅga-saṁgraha*. Ed. by Rudra Parasara. Trichur, 1913-24.

Mādhava — *Rugviniśchaya* or *Mādhavanidāna*. Ed. with comm. by Kaviraj S. C. Sen. 2nd Ed. Benares, 1932.
Ed. with comms. by J. T. Acharya. Bombay, 1920.

Vṛinda — *Siddhiyoga*. ĀSS, No. 27. Poona, 1894.

(xi) POETICS DRAMATURGY, AND METRICS:

Abhinavagupta — *Lochana*. KM, 25. Bombay, 1911.
German trans. by H. Jacobi. *ZDMG*, LVI and LVII.
Lochana (VI). Ed. by S. K. De. Calcutta, 1923 (*JDL*, IX. 15-42).

Ānandavardhana — *Dhvanyāloka*, with the comm. *Lochana* of Abhinavagupta. See above under "Abhinavagupta".

Dhanañjaya — *Daśarūpa*. Ed. with the comm. of Dhanika. by F. E. Hall. BI. Calcutta, 1865.
Eng. trans. G. C. O. Haas. New York, 1912.

Jayadāman — (Comprising *Jayadevachchhandaḥ*, *Chhandonuśāsanam* of Jayakīrti and of Hemachandra, and *Vṛittaratnākaraḥ* of Kedāra). Ed. with intr., list and index of Sanskrit metres, etc. by H. D. Velankar. Bombay, 1949.

Mukulabhaṭṭa	*Abhidhāvṛittimātṛikā*. NSP. Bombay, 1916.
Rājaśekhara	*Kāvyamīmāṁsā*. Ed. by C. D. Dalal and R. A. Sastri. GOS. 3rd Ed. Baroda, 1934.
Rudraṭa	*Kāvyālaṅkāra*. Ed. with the comm. of Namisādhu by Durgāprasāda and K. P. Parab. KM, 2. Bombay, 1909.
Sāgaranandin	*Nāṭakalakshaṇaratnakośa*. Vol. I. Ed. by M. Dillon. London, 1937.
Udbhata	*Alaṅkāra-saṁgraha*. Ed. with the comm. *Laghuvṛitti* of Pratīhārendurāja. NSP. Bombay, 1915.
	Ed. by N. D. Banhatti. BSS. Poona. 1925
Utpala	*Chhandaḥśāstra*. Ed. by H. D. Velankar. *Raja Comm. Vol.* (pp. 148-152).
Vāmana	*Kāvyālaṅkārasūtra*. Ed. with Vṛitti by Durgaprasad and K. P. Parab. KM, 15. Bombay, 1926.
	Ed. with a comm. Srirangam, 1909.
	Eng. trans. by G. Jha. Allahabad, 1912; 2nd Ed. Poona, 1928.
	Ed. with German trans. by C. Cappeller. Jena, 1875.

(xii) CHAMPŪ:

Soḍḍhala	*Udayasundarīkathā*. Ed. by C. D. Dalal and E. Krishnamacharya. GOS. Baroda, 1920
Somadeva	*Yaśastilakachampū*. Ed. by Sivadatta and Parab. KM. Bombay, 1901-1903.
Trivikramabhaṭṭa	*Nalachampū* or *Damayantīkathā*. Ed. with comm. by N. K. Sarma. Benares, 1932.
	Ed. with comm. Bombay, 1885.

(xiii) ANTHOLOGY:

Kavīndravachana-samuchchaya	Ed. with intr. and notes by F. W. Thomas. BI. Calcutta, 1912.

(xiv) BELLES-LETTRES:

(*Note:* References to most important works in Sanskrit are given here. Full details will be found in the Histories of Sanskrit Literature by De and Das Gupta, Keith, Krishnamachariar, Winternitz, etc.)

Abhinanda	*Kādambarī-kathāsāra*. Ed. by Durgaprasad and K. P. Parab. NSP. Bombay, 1899.
	Ed. by Achintyaram Sarman., Lahore, 1900.
	Rāmacharita. Ed. with intr. by Ramaswami Sastri Siromani. GOS. Baroda, 1930.
Ānanda	*Mādhavānala-kathā*. Ed. by Pavloni. *OC*, IX. 1.430 ff; *GSAI*, XXII. 313 ff.
Ānandavardhana	*Devīśataka*. Ed. *Kāvyamālā*, XI. 1-31.
Anaṅgaharsha Mātrarāja	*Tāpasavatsarāja*. Ed. by Yadugiri Yatirāja. Bangalore, 1928.
Bhallaṭa	*Bhallaṭaśataka*. *Kāvyamālā*, IV. 140 ff.

Budhasvāmin	*Bṛihatkathā Ślokasaṁgraha*. Ed. with critical notes and French trans. by F. Lacôte. Paris, 1908-29.
Chaturbhāṇī	(comprising Śūdraka's *Padmaprābhṛitaka*, Īśvaradatta's *Dhūrta-viṭa-saṁvāda*, Vararuchi's *Ubhayābhisārika*, and Śyāmilaka's *Pādatāḍitaka*) Ed. by M. Ramakrishna Kavi and S. K. Ramanatha Sastri. Patna. 1922.
Hanūmat	*Hanūman-nāṭaka* (Devanāgari rec.) of Dāmodara Miśra with the comm. of Mohan Das. Bombay, 1860; 1868; etc.
	Mahānāṭaka (Bengali rec.) of Madhusūdana. Ed. with comm. by Jīvānanda Vidyāsāgara. Calcutta, 1890.
Kshemīśvara	*Chaṇḍakauśika*. Ed. by Jaganmohan Tarkalamkara. Calcutta, 1867. Ed. by J. Vidyāsāgara. Calcutta, 1884. Ed. by Krishna Sastri Gurjara. Litho. Bombay, 1860.
	German trans. (*Kauśikas' Zorn*) by Ludwig Fritze. Leipzig, 1883.
Kulaśekhara	*Mukundamālā*. *Kāvyamālā*, I. 11 f.
	Ed. by K. Rama Pisharoti. Annamalainagar, 1933.
Murāri	*Anargharāghava*. Ed. by Premchandra Tarkavagis. Calcutta, 1860.
	Ed. by Durgaprasad and K. P. Parab. NSP. Bombay, 1890.
Nītivarman	*Kīchakavadha*. Ed. by S. K. De. Dacca, 1929.
Purāntaka	*Śyāmalādaṇḍaka*. Kāvyamālā, I. 8 ff.
Rājaśekhara	*Bālabhārata*. Ed. by C. Cappeller. Strassburg, 1885.
	Ed. by Durgaprasad and K. P. Parab. NSP. Bombay, 1887 (included in the *Karpūramañjarī*).
	Bālarāmāyaṇa. Ed. by Govindadeva Sastri. Benares, 1869.
	Ed. by J. Vidyasagar. Calcutta, 1884.
	Karpūramañjarī. Ed. by Durgaprasad and K. P. Parab. NSP. Bombay, 1887.
	Ed. by Manomohan Ghosh. Calcutta, 1939.
	Ed. by Sten Konow, with Eng. trans. and notes, etc. by C. R. Lanman. HOS. Cambridge Mass., 1901.
	Viddhaśālabhañjikā. Ed. by B. R. Arte. Poona, 1886.
	Ed. by Vamanacharya in *Pandit*, VI-VII.
	Ed. by J. Vidyasagar. 2nd Ed. Calcutta, 1883.
	Ed. with comms. by J. B. Chaudhuri. Calcutta, 1943.
	Eng. trans. by L. H. Gray. *JAOS*, XXVII. 1-71.
Ratnākara	***Haravijaya*. Ed. by Durgaprasad and K. P. Parab. KM. Bombay, 1890.**

Ravideva — *Kāvyarākshasa* or *Rākshasakāvya*. Ed. by A. Hoefer. *Sanskrit-Lesebuch*. Berlin, 1849.
Ed. by K. P. Parab. NSP. Bombay, 1900.
Italian trans. by F. Belloni-Filippi. *GSAI*, XIX, 1906. 83 ff.
Nalodaya, accompanied with a metrical trans. by W. Yates. Calcutta, 1844.

Śaktibhadra — *Āścharyachūḍāmaṇi*. Ed. by C. Sankararaja Sastri. Madras, 1926.
Eng. trans. by C. Sankararaja Sastri. Madras, 1927.

Śivasvāmin — *Kapphiṇabhyudaya*. Ed. by Gaurishankar. Lahore, 1927.

Subhaṭa — *Dūtāṅgada*. KM. Bombay, 1891.
Eng. trans. by L. H. Gray. *JAOS*, XXXII. 58 ff.

Utpaladeva — *Stotrāvalī*. Ed. by Vishnuprasad Bhandari. Benares, 1902.

Vāsudeva — *Yudhishṭhiravijaya*. NSP. Bombay, 1897.

Viśākhadatta — *Mudrārākshasa*. Ed. K. T. Telang. BSS. 3rd revised Ed. Bombay, 1900. Ed. A. Hillebrandt. Breslau, 1912; New Ed. 1935.
Ed. with Eng. trans. by K. H. Dhruva. 2nd Ed. Poona, 1923; 3rd Ed. Poona, 1930.
Eng. trans. (The Signet Ring) with notes, etc. by R. S. Pandit. Bombay, 1944.

(B) BUDDHIST:

(i) PALI:

(*Note:* Important references only are given here. Further particulars will be found in Geiger, Law, Winternitz, etc. given under "Histories of Literature" below.)

Abhidhammatthasaṁgaha of Aniruddha
Ed. by Rhys Davids. *JPTS*, 1894. 1 ff.
Eng. trans. by S. Z. Aung. Ed. by Mrs. Rhys Davids. PTS. London, 1910.

Anāgatavaṁsa of Kassapa
Ed. by J. P. Minayeff. *JPTS*, 1886. 33 ff.

Gandhavaṁsa — Ed. by J. Minayeff. *JPTS*, 1886. 54-80.

Mahābodhivaṁsa of Upatissa
Ed. by S. A. Strong. PTS. London, 1891.

Telakaṭāhagāthā — Ed. by E. R. Goonaratne. *JPTS*, 1884. 49 ff.

(ii) SANSKRIT:

Abhisamayālaṅkārāloka of Haribhadra
Ed. by Giuseppe Tucci. GOS, 62, Baroda, 1952.

Advayavajrasaṁgraha of Advayavajra
Ed. by Haraprasad Sastri. GOS, 40. Baroda, 1927.

Ārya-mañjuśrī-mūlakalpa
Ed. by T. Ganapati Sastri. 3 Parts. TSS. Trivandrum, 1920-1925.

Bauddha-stotra-saṁgraha
Vol. I, consisting of *Sragdharā-stotra* of Sarvajñamitra. Ed. by S. C. Vidyābhūshaṇa. BI. Calcutta, 1908.

Guhyasamāja Tantra or *Tathāgataguhyaka*
Ed. by B. Bhattacharyya. GOS, 53. Baroda, 1931.

Jñānasiddhi of Indrabhūti
See "*Vajrayānagranthadvayam*" below.

Kaulajñānanirṇaya Ed. by P. C. Bagchi. Calcutta, 1934.

Mañjuśrī-Mūlakalpa See "*Ārya-mañjuśrī-mūlakalpa*" above.

Prajñopāyaviniśchayasiddhi of Anaṅgavajra
See "*Vajrayānagranthadvayam*" below.

Sādhanamālā Ed. by B. Bhattacharyya. GOS, 26, 41. Baroda, 1925, 1928.

Śaktisaṅgama Tantra Ed. by B. Bhattacharyya. GOS, 61, 91, 104. Baroda, 1932, 1941, 1947.

Sragdharā-stotra See "*Bauddha-stotra-saṁgraha*" above.

Tathāgataguhyaka See "*Guhyasamāja Tantra*" above.

Tattvasaṁgraha of Śāntarakshita with the comm. of Kamalaśīla. Ed. by E. Krishnamacharya with a Foreword by B. Bhattacharyya. GOS, 30, 31. Baroda, 1926.
Eng. trans. by G. Jha. GOS, 80, 83. Baroda, 1937, 1939.

Vajrayānagranthadvayam comprising *Prajñopāyaviniśchayasiddhi* of Anaṅgavajra and *Jñānasiddhi* of Indrabhūti. Ed. by B. Bhattacharyya. GOS, 44. Baroda, 1929.

(C) JAIN:

(Only important authors and works in Sanskrit and Prakrit are listed here. For full details reference may be made to Winternitz, *History of Indian Literature*, Vol. II, and Velankar, *Jinaratnakośa* Poona, 1944.)

Asaga — *Vardhamāna-charita* or *Mahāvīra-charita*. Pub. with Marathi trans. Sholapur, 1931.

Dhanapāla — *Pāiyalachchhī*. Pub. Bhavnagar, V. S. 1973. Ed. by G. Bühler in *Beitrage zur Kunde der Indoger. Sprachen*, IV. 70 ff.
Tilakamañjarī-kathā. NSP. Bombay, 1903.

Dhanañjaya — *Rāghava-Pāṇḍavīya* or *Dvisandhāna*. Ed. with comm. by Sivadatta and K. P. Parab. KM. Bombay, 1895.

Dharmadāsa — *Upadeśamālā* (Prakrit). Pub. JDPS. Bhavnagar, 1915; *Uvaesamālā*. Ed. by L. P. Tessitori. *GSAI*, 25 (1912). 162-297.

Guṇabhadra — *Uttarapurāṇa* (See under Jinasena I).

Haribhadra — *Dhūrtākhyāna* (Prakrit). Ed. by A. N. Upadhye. SJS. Bombay, 1944.
Samarāichchakahā. Ed. by H. Jacobi. BI. Calcutta. 1926.

Hastimalla	*Vikrāntakaurava* or *Sulochanā Nāṭaka*. Pub. MDJG series. Bombay, V. S. 197 (=1916).
Jinasena I	*Ādipurāṇa*. Published along with Guṇabhadra's *Uttarapurāṇa* in *Mahāpurāṇa*. Pub. Syādvāda-Granthamālā. Indore, V. S. 1973-5.
	Pārśvābhyudaya. Ed. with comm. NSP. Bombay, 1909.
	Meghadūta as embodied in the *Pārśvābhyudaya* with the comm. of Mallinātha and a literal Eng. trans. by K. B. Pathak. Poona, 1894.
Jinasena II	*Harivaṁśapurāṇa*. Pub. MDJG Series. Bombay, 1930.
Kanakasena Vādirāja	*Yaśodhara-charitra*. Ed. by Gopinatha Rao. Tanjore, 1912.
Maheśvara Sūri	*Jñānapañchamī-kathā* (Prakrit). Ed. by A. S. Gopani. SJS. Bombay, 1949.
Mānatuṅga	*Bhaktāmarastotra*. Ed. with German trans. by H. Jacobi. *IS*, XIV. 359 ff.
	Ed. with the comms. of Guṇākara, Meghavijaya and Kanakakuśala by H. R. Kapadia. DLP Series. Bombay, 1932.
Nandisheṇa	*Ajitaśāntistava*. Pub. in DLP Series, Bombay.
	Pub. by Venichand Surchand. Mehsana, 1915 (in *Pañcha Pratikramaṇādi Sūtrāṇi*).
Ravisheṇa	*Padmapurāṇa*. Pub. MDJG Series. Bombay, 1928, 29.
Śākaṭāyana	See earlier under "Grammar".
Siddharshi	*Upamitibhavaprapañchākathā*. Ed. by P. Peterson and H. Jacobi. BI. Calcutta, 1899-1914; Pub. by Devchand Lalbhai. Bombay, 1918-20.
	German trans. (Bks. I-III) by W. Kirfel. Leipzig, 1924 (*Indische Erzähler*, X).
Śobhana	*Śobhanastuti* or *Tīrtheśastuti* or *Chaturviṁśati-Jinastuti*. Pub. with the comm. of Dhanapāla. *Kāvyamālā*, VII. 132 ff.; Pub. in Āgamodaya Samiti Series. Bombay, 1926.
	Ed. and trans. in German by H. Jacobi. *ZDMG*, 32. 509 ff.
Somadeva	See earlier under "Champū".
Svayambhū	*Svayambhū-chhandas*. Ed. by H. D. Velankar. *JBBRAS*, 1935; *JUB*, Nov. 1936.
Vādirāja Sūri	See above under "Kanakasena Vādirāja".

(D) WORKS IN APABHRAMŚA:

Devasena	*Savayadhamma Dohā*. Ed. with intr., trans., glossary, notes, and index by H. L. Jain. Karanja, 1932.

Dhanapāla — *Bhavisayatta-kahū*. Ed. by H. Jacobi. Munchen, 1918.
Ed. by C. D. Dalal and P. D. Gune. GOS, 20. Baroda, 1923.

Haribhadra — *Saṇakumāra-chariu*. Ed. with German trans. notes, etc. by H. Jacobi. Munchen, 1921.

Joindu — *Paramappayāsu*. Ed. with Sanskrit comm., Hindi trans., critical intr., etc. along with *Yogasāra*, critical text, Sanskrit Chhāyā, intr., etc., by A. N. Upadhye. Bombay, 1937.

Kanakāmara — *Karakaṇḍa-chariu*. Ed. with intr., trans., glossary, etc. by H. L. Jain. Karanja, 1934.

Khanha et Saraha — *Les chants mystiques. Les Dohā-kośa (en Apabhraṁśa avec les versions tibetaines) et les Caryā (en vieux-Bengali)* avec introduction, vocabulaires et notes edites et traduits par M. Shahidullah. Paris, 1928.

Māilladeva — *Nayachakra*. Pub. MDJG Series, No. 16. Bombay.

Pushpadanta — *Jasahara-chariu*. Critically edited with intr., glossary, and notes by P. L. Vaidya. Karanja, 1931.
Mahāpurāṇa. Critically edited by P. L. Vaidya. 3 vols. Bombay, 1937-41.
Ṇāyakumāra-chariu. Critically edited with an intr., glossary, indices, and notes by H. L. Jain. Karanja, 1933.

Rāmasiṁha Muni — *Pāhuḍa Dohā*. Critically edited with intr. trans., glossary, etc., by H. L. Jain. Amraoti, 1933.

Suprabhāchārya — *Vairāgyasāra*. Ed. by H. D. Velankar. *ABORI*, 1928. 272-280.

Svayambhū — *Paüma-chariu*. Ed. by H. C. Bhayani. SJS 2 vols. Bombay, 1953 (in progress).

(D) MUSLIM:

Ashkāl ul-Bilād of ibn Hauqal
Extracts trans. *HIED*, I. 31-40,

Chach-nāma of Muḥammad 'Alī i. Hamīd i. Abū Bakr Kūfī
Trans. by Mīrzā Kalīch Beg Fredunbeg. Two vols. Karachi, 1900.
Extracts trans. *HIED*, I. 131-211.

Habīb-us-Siyar of Khond Mīr
Bombay, 1857.

Jāmi 'ul-Hikāyāt of Muhammad 'Aufī
Extracts trans. *HIED*, II. 155-203.

Kitāb Futūḥ al Buldan of Ahmad ibn Yahya ibn-Jabir al-Baladhuri
Eng. trans. by P. K. Hitti and F. C. Murgotten.

Kitāb ul-Aqālīm of Ishtakhrī
Extracts trans. *HIED*, I. 26-30.

Kitāb-ul-Hind and *Āthār-al-Bāquia* of al-Bīrūnī
Eng. trans. (Alberuni's India) by E. C. Sachau. London, 1914.

Murūj-ul-Zahab of al-Mas'ūdī
Text and French trans. by Barbier de Meynard. Paris, 1861.
Extracts trans. *HIED*, I. 18-25.

Rauzat-uṣ-Ṣafā of Mīr Khonḍ
Silsilat ut-Tawārīkh of Sulaymān
Extracts trans. *HIED*, I. 1-7.

Tabaqāt-i-Akbarī of Nizāmuddīn
Trans. by B. Dey. BI. Calcutta, 1913.

Tabaqāt-i-Nāsirī of Minhāj-ud-dīn
Trans. by H. G. Raverty. London, 1881.

Tāj-ul-Maāsir of Hasan Nizāmī

Ta'rīkh-i-Firishta — Lucknow, 1905. Eng. trans. (Rise of the Mahomedan Power in India) by J. Briggs. Vols. I-IV. London, 1829.

Ta'rīkh-i-Yamīnī of Al-Utbī
Ed. by Ali.
Trans. by J. Reynolds. London.
Extracts trans. *HIED*, II. 14-52.

Tarkhān-nāma of Saiyid Jamāl
Extracts trans. *HIED*. I. 300 ff.

Ta'rīkh-i-Ṭāhirī — Extracts trans. *HIED, I. 253-281.*

Ta'rīkh-i-Ma'sūmī — Extracts trans. *HIED*, I. 212-252.

ELLIOT, Sir H.M. and DOWSON, John. — *History of India as told by its own Historians.* 8 Vols., London, 1866-77....Vol. II. Reprinted with Introduction by Mohammad Habib, Commentary by S. H. Hodiwala, and Supplement by Khaliq Ahmad Nizami. Aligarh, 1952.

HODIVALA, S. H. — *Studies in Indo-Muslim History.* Bombay, 1939.

(2) *Non-Indian Sources:*

(A) ARABIC:

Buzurg ibn Shahriyar
Kitāb 'Ajāyab-ul-Hind or *Livre des Merveilles de L'Inde*, Texte Arabe par P. A. Van der Lith; traduction Francaise par L. Marcel Devic. Leide, 1883-86.
Eng. trans. (The Book of the Marvels of India) by L. Marcel Devic. London, 1928.

Ferrand — *Relations des Voyages et Textes Géographiques Arabes, Persans et Turks—Relatifs a l'Extrême-Orient du VIIIe au XVIIIe siècles.* 2 Vols. Paris, 1913-14. *Voyage du Marchand Arabe Sulayman en Inde et en Chine—Rédigé en 851 suivi de remarques par Abū Zayd Hasan vers 916.* Paris. 1922

(B) TIBETAN:

TARANATHA — German trans. by F. A. von Schiefner *(Geschichte des Buddhismus in Indien)*. St. Petersburg, 1869.
Eng. trans. (History of Buddhism in India) by U. N. Ghoshal and N. Dutt. *IHQ*, III. 60-68; 508-9; 803-7; IV. 530-3; V. 715-21; VI. 334-44; VII. 150-60; VIII. 247-52; X. 551-7; XXVII. 239-49; XXVIII. 41-50.
Extracts trans. into English by W. L. Heeley. *IA*, IV. 101-4; "Tāranātha's Account of the Magadha Kings" by E. Lyall. *IA*, IV. 361-7.

II. ORIGINAL SOURCES:

(1) *Inscriptions:*

AIYER, K. V. Subrahmanya. — *South Indian Inscriptions*. 2 vols. *(ASI, New Imperial Series*, Vols. 52, 53). Madras, 1928, 1933.

BHANDARKAR, D. R. — "List of Inscriptions of Northern India". Appendix to *EI*, XIX-XXIII.

HULTZSCH, E. — *South Indian Inscriptions*. 3 vols. *(ASI, NIS*, Vols. 9, 10 and 29). Madras, 1890-1929.

KRISHNAMACHARLU, C. R. — *Bombay-Karnataka Inscriptions*. Madras, 1940.

PANCHAMUKHI, R. S. — *Karnataka Inscriptions*. 2 vols. Dharwar, 1941, 1951.

RANGACHARYA, V. — *Inscriptions of the Madras Presidency*. 3 vols. Madras, 1919.

RICE, Lewis. — *Mysore and Coorg from Inscriptions*. London, 1909.

SASTRI, H. Krishna. — *South Indian Inscriptions*. 2 vols. *(ASI, NIS*, Vols. 44, 49). Madras, 1924, 26.

SEWELL, R. and AIYANGAR, S. Krishnaswami. — *Historical Inscriptions of Southern India*. Madras, 1932.

(Also *Epigraphia Indica, Epigraphia Carnatica*, etc.)

(2) COINS:

ALLAN, J. — *Catalogue of the Coins of Ancient India* (in the British Museum). London, 1936.

BANERJI, R. D. — *Prāchīna Mudrā (Bengali)*. Calcutta, 1322 B.S.

BROWN, C. J. — *Coins of India*. Calcutta, 1922.

CUNNINGHAM, A. — *Coins of Mediaeval India from the seventh century down to the Muhammadan Conquest*. London, 1894.

ELLIOT, W. — *Coins of Southern India*. London, 1896.

RAPSON, E. J. — *Indian Coins*. Strassburg, 1897.

SINGHAL, C. R. — *Bibliography of Indian Coins*. Bombay, 1950.

SMITH, V. A. — *Catalogue of the Coins in the Indian Museum, Calcutta, including the Cabinet of the Asiatic Society of Bengal*. Vol. I. Oxford, 1906.

III. MODERN WORKS:

(1) *Histories of the Period:*

AIYANGAR, S. Krishnaswami. *Ancient India.* Poona, 1941.

ALTEKAR, A. S. *Rāshṭrakūṭas and their times.* Poona, 1934.

BASAK, R. G. *History of North-Eastern India.* Calcutta, 1934.

BHANDARKAR, R. G. *Early History of the Deccan. BG,* Vol. I, Part 2. Bombay, 1896; 2nd Ed. *CW,* III. 1-198. Poona, 1927; 3rd Ed. Calcutta, 1928.

JOUVEAU-DUBREUIL, G. *Ancient History of the Deccan* (trans. from the French by V. S. Swaminadha Dikshitar). Pondicherry, 1920.

MAJUMDAR, R. C. *Ancient India.* Banaras, 1952.

MAJUMDAR, R. C. (Ed.). *History of Bengal.* Vol. I. Dacca, 1943.

MAJUMDAR, R. C. and ALTEKAR, A. S. (Ed.). *The Vākāṭaka-Gupta Age* (A New History of the Indian People, Vol. VI). Lahore, 1946; Reprint, Banaras, 1954.

MASSON-OURSEL, P. and others. *Ancient India and Indian Civilization* (Eng. trans. from original French). London, 1934.

RAY, H. C. *Dynastic History of Northern India.* 2 vols. Calcutta, 1931, 1936.

SASTRI, K. A. Nilakanta. *History of India.* Vol. I. Madras, 1950.

SMITH, V. A. *Early History of India.* 4th Ed. Oxford, 1924.

TRIPATHI, R. S. *History of Kanuaj.* Benares, 1937.

VAIDYA, C. V. *History of Mediaeval Hindu India.* 3 vols Poona, 1921-1926.

(2) *Histories of Literature:*

DAS GUPTA, S. N. (Ed.). *A History of Sanskrit Literature.* Classical Period. Vol. I. Calcutta, 1947.

DE, S. K. *Sanskrit Poetics.* 2 vols. London, 1923, 1925.

FRAZER, R. W. *Literary History of India.* London, 1898.

GEIGER, W. *Pali Literatur und Sprache.* Strassburg, 1916. Eng. trans. by B. K. Ghosh (Pali Literature and Language). Calcutta, 1943.

GOWEN, H. H. *History of Indian Literature.* New York, 1931.

KANE, P. V. *History of Alaṅkāra Literature.* 2nd Ed. Bombay, 1923; 3rd Ed. *(History of Sanskrit Poetics).* Bombay, 1951.

KEITH, A. B. *Sanskrit Drama.* Oxford, 1924. Reprint, 1954.
History of Sanskrit Literature. Oxford, 1928. Reprint, 1941, 1948, 1953.

KRISHNAMACHARIAR, M. *History of Classical Sanskrit Literature.* Madras, 1937.

LAW, B. C. *History of Pali Literature.* 2 vols. London, 1933.

MACDONELL, A. A. *History of Sanskrit Literature.* London, 1900.

WINTERNITZ, M. *History of Indian Literature* (Eng. trans. by Mrs. S. Ketkar). Vols. I and II. Calcutta, 1927, 1933.

Geschichte der indischen Literatur. Band III. Leipzig, 1920.

(3) *Religion and Philosophy*:

BHANDARKAR, R. G. *Vaishṇavism, Śaivism and other minor Religious Systems.* Strassburg, 1913; Indian Edition, Poona, 1938.

BHATTACHARYYA, H. D. (Ed.). *The Philosophies.* Cultural Heritage of India. 2nd Ed. Vol. III. Calcutta, 1953.

DAS GUPTA, S. N. *History of Indian Philosophy.* 4 vols. Cambridge, 1932-49.

FARQUHAR, J. N. *An Outline of the Religious Literature of India.* Oxford, 1920.

KANE, P. V. *History of Dharmaśāstra.* 4 vols. Poona, 1930-53.

RADHAKRISHNAN, S. *Indian Philosophy.* 2 vols. London, 1923, 1927.

VIDYABHUSHANA, S.C. *History of Indian Logic.* Calcutta, 1921.

ZIMMER, H. *Philosophies of India.* Ed. by J. Campbell. London, 1953.

BIBLIOGRAPHY

(*Note:* In the Bibliographies to the different chapters, the Original Sources and Modern Works, mentioned earlier, are not repeated save in exceptional cases).

CHAPTER I
THE RĀSHṬRAKŪṬA EMPIRE

I. *Original Sources:*

(i) LITERARY:

Kalhaṇa — See above, under "Historical Works"

Nāgavarmā — *Karṇāṭakabhāshābhūshaṇa.* Ed. by L. Rice Bangalore, 1884.

Nṛipatuṅga — *Kavirājamārga.* Ed. by K. B. Pathak.

Pampa — *Vikramārjuna Vijaya or Pampa Bhārata.* Ed. by L. Rice. Bangalore, 1898.

Somadeva — See above, under "Champū".

(ii) INSCRIPTIONS:

BHANDARKAR, D. R. *A List of the Inscriptions of Northern India written in Brahmi and its derivative scripts from about A.C. 300.* Appendix to *EI*, XIX-XXIII.

FLEET, J. F. *The Dynasties of the Kanarese Districts of the Bombay Presidency. BG*, I, ii. Bombay, 1896.

"Sanskrit and Old-Canarese Inscriptions" (dealing with the Rāshṭrakūṭas). *IA*, XI. 108-115; 124-127; 156-163; XII. 156-165; 215-225; 247-258.

HIRALAL. *Inscriptions in the Central Provinces and Berar.* 2nd Ed. Nagpur, 1932.

RICE, L. See above, under "Inscriptions".

(iii) SOME IMPORTANT RĀSHṬRAKŪṬA INSCRIPTIONS:

1. Ellora Plates, Ś.663 (=A.D. 741): *EI*, XXV. 25.
2. Samangad Grant, Ś.675 (=A.D. 753-54): *IA*, XI. 108.
3. Antroli-Chharoli Plates, Ś.679 (=A.D. 757): *JBBRAS*, XVI. 106.
4. Alas Plates, Ś.692 (=A.D. 769): *EI*, VI. 208.
5. Bhandak Plates, Ś.694 (=A.D. 772): *EI*, XIV. 121.
6. Bhor State Museum Plates, Ś.702 (=A.D. 780): *EI*, XXII. 176.
7. Daulatābād Plates, Ś.715 (=A.D. 793): *EI*, IX. 195.
8. British Museum Plates, Ś.726 (=A.D. 804): *IA*, XI. 104. *EI*, XXXIII, 327.
9. Sisavai Grant, Ś.729 (=A.D. 807): *EI*, XXIII. 204.
10. Wani Dindori Plates, Ś.730 (=A.D. 808): *IA*, XI. 156.
11. Rādhanpur Plates, Ś.730 (=A.D. 808): *EI*, VI. 242; *IA*, VI. 59.
12. Baroda Grant, Ś. 734 (=A.D. 812-13); *IA*, XII. 156.
13. Lohara Grant, Ś.734 (=A.D. 812): *EI*, XXIII. 212.
14. Surat Plates, Ś.743 (=A.D. 821): *EI*, XXI. 133.
15. Navsāri Plates, Ś.738 (=A.D. 816): *JBBRAS*, XX. 135.
16. Kavi Grant, Ś.749 (=A.D. 827-8): *IA*, V. 113.
17. Baroda Grant, Ś.757 (=A.D. 835-6): *IA*, XIV. 196.
18. Nilgund Ins., Ś.788 (=A.D. 866): *EI*, VI. 98.
19. Sirur Ins., Ś.788 (=A.D. 866): *EI*, VII. 202; *IA*, XII. 218.
20. Begumra Grant, Ś.789 (=A.D. 867): *IA*, XII. 179.
21. Sanjān Plates, Ś.793 (=A.D. 871): *EI*, XVIII. 235.
22. Begumra Grant, Ś.810 (=A.D. 888): *IA*, XIII. 65.
23. Kāpadvanj Plates, Ś.832 (=A.D. 910): *EI*, I. 52.
24. Begumra Plates, Ś.836 (=A.D. 914): *EI*, IX. 24.
25. Cambay Plates, Ś.852 (=A.D. 930): *EI*, VII. 26.
26. Sāngli Plates, Ś.855 (=A.D. 933-4): *IA*, XII. 247.
27. Deoli Plates, Ś.862 (=A.D. 940): *EI*, V. 190.
28. Karhād Plates, Ś.880 (=A.D. 959): *EI*, IV. 278.
29. Kurda Grant, Ś.894 (=A.D. 972-3): *IA*, XII. 263.
30. Gundur Ins., Ś.896 (=A.D. 973-4): *IA*, XII. 270.
31. Śravaṇa Beḷgoḷa Praśasti, Ś.904 (=A.D. 982): *Inscriptions at Sravana Beḷgoḷa*, 53, No. 57.
32. Daśāvatāra Cave Ins. (undated). *ASWI*, V. 87.
33. Jura Praśasti (undated). *EI*, XIX. 287.

II. MODERN WORKS:

ALTEKAR, A. S. "The Chronology of the Campaigns of Govinda III of the Rāshṭrakūṭas". *D. R. Bhandarkar Vol.* 153-8.

"New Light on the history of the Gujarat Rāshṭrakūṭas". *Ojha Comm. Vol.* III. 3-7.

"A Note on the date of the Manne plates of Stambha Raṇāvaloka". *EI*, XXIII. 293-4.

Rāshṭrakūṭas and their times. Poona, 1934.

AYYAR, A. S. R. "A Note on the Dates of three Rāshṭrakūṭa Kings". *EI*, XXVI. 161-5.

BANERJI, R. D. — "Northern Conquests of Kṛishṇa III". *JBORS*, XIV. 476-488.

BHANDARKAR, R. G. — See above, under "Histories of the Period".

DAS GUPTA, N. N. — "On the reign of Kṛishṇa II, the Rāshṭrakūṭa" *IA*, LXII. 134-6.

DEORAS, V. R. — "Govinda III—A Forgotten Emperor of Madhya Pradesh". *Annual Bulletin of the Nagpur Historical Society*, No. 6. October, 1951, pp. 60-75.

ELLIOT, H. M. and DOWSON, John. — See above, under "Muslim".

FLEET, J. F. — "The Family name of the Rāshṭrakūṭas of Mālkhed". *EI*, VII. 214.
"The Original Home of the Rāshṭrakūṭas of Mālkhed". *Ibid*. 223.
"The Banners and Crests of the Rāshṭrakūṭas and Raṭṭas of Saundatti". *Ibid.* 227.

GAI, G. S. — "On the Date of the Ellora Plates of Dantidurga". *IHQ*, XXVIII. 79-82.

GHANI, M. A. — See below, under Ch. V (11) "Arabs in India".

MIRASHI, V. V. — "Dantidurga, the founder of the Rāshṭrakūṭa imperial power". *JOI*, I. 31-38.
"The Dates of the Ellora Plates of Dantidurga". *JBBRAS*, NS, XXVI. 163-7.
"A further note on the date of Manne plates of Stambha Raṇāvaloka". *EI* XXIII. 295-7.
"New Light on the Medieval History of Gujarat". *D. R. Bhandarkar Vol.*, pp. 53-58.
"Two copper-plate inscriptions from Berar". *EI*, XXIII. 204-222.

SASTRI, K. A. Nilakanta. — "Amoghavarsha and Karka Suvarṇavarsha of Lāṭa". *PIHC*, X. 210-4.
"Did Dhruva abdicate?" *JOR*, XV. 9-12.
"Kṛishṇa III and the Chedis". *JOR*, XVI. 155-8.

SHARMA, D. — "The Imperial Pratiharas", *JIH*, XXXVIII, 605.

TRIPATHI, R. S. — See above, under "Histories of the Period".

VENKATARAMANAYYA, N. — "Rāshṭrakūṭas of Mālkhed". *PIHC*, VIII. 85-90
See below, under Ch. II.

CHAPTER II

RISE AND FALL OF THE PRATĪHĀRA EMPIRE

I. *Original Sources:*

(i) LITERARY:

Bappabhaṭṭicharitam — Ed. by V. Krishnamacharya. *JBBRAS*, NS, IV. 313-325.

Harivaṁśapurāṇa — See above, under Jinasena II in "(C) Jain" — General Bibliography.

Kumārapālacharita — See below, Ch. V (4).

Prabandhachintāmaṇi

Prabhāvakacharita — See below, Ch. V (2).

Vikramārjuna — See below, Ch. V (4).

Vijaya — See above, Ch. I.

(ii) INSCRIPTIONS:

LIST OF IMPORTANT INSCRIPTIONS,

(See above, p. 40)

II. MODERN WORKS

AIYANGAR, S.Krishnaswami. "The Bappa Bhaṭṭi Charita and the Early History of the Gurjara Empire". *JBBRAS*, NS, IV. 101-133.

GANGULY, D. C. "The "Gurjaras" in the Rāshṭrakūṭa Inscriptions". *PIHC,* III. 513-5.

"The Pratīhāras and the Gujaras". *JBORS*, XIV. 221-230.

HALDER, R. R. "Who were the Imperial Pratīhāras?" *IA.*, LVII. 181-4.

JAIN, H. L. "The Chief Political Divisions of India during the Eighth Century." *IC,* XI. 161-170.

MAJUMDAR, R. C. "The Gurjara Pratīhāras." *JDL,* X. 1-76.

"Some Problems concerning Gurjara-Pratīhāras." *Munshi Diamond Jubilee Vol.,* Part II (*BV,* X). 1-18.

(Both these articles give full references to earlier literature on the subject).

MUNSHI, K. M. *The Glory that was Gūrjaradeśa,* Part III: *The Imperial Gurjaras.* Bombay. 1944.

RAY, N. R. "A Note on the Chronology of the Later Pratīhāras." IA, LVII. 230-4.

RAYCHAUDHURI, H.C. "A note on the Emperor Mahīpāla of the Pratīhāra Dynasty." *PIHC,* IV. 153-5.

SASTRI, K. A. Nilakanta. "Mahīpāla of the Chaṇḍakauśika." *JOR,* VI. 191-2.

SEN, B. C. "Nāgabhaṭa II's Operations against Dharmapāla and Chakrāyudha." *PIHC,* XI. 141-7.

SARMA, Dasaratha. "The Imperial Pratīhāras—A Revised Study." *JIH,* XXII. 93-105.

"Chronology of the Reign of the Imperial Pratīhāra Nāgabhaṭa II." *IHQ,* XX. 72-75.

"A Supplementary Note on Vatsarāja Pratīhāra." *IHQ,* XXIII. 43-4.

SMITH, V. A. "The Gurjaras of Rajputana and Kanauj." *JRAS,* 1909. 53 ff; 247 ff.

TRIPATHI, R. S. See above, under "Histories of the Period".

VENKATARAMANAYYA, N. "The Rāshṭrakūṭa king Kṛishṇa II and Gurjara Pratīhāras of Kaṇauj." *PIHC,* VI. 163-70.

CHAPTER III

THE PĀLAS

I. *Original Sources:*

(i) LITERARY:

Bṛihat-Svayambhū Purāṇa
Ed. by H. P. Sastri. BI. Calcutta, 1894-1900,

Rāmacharita of Sandhyākara Nandī
See above, in "General Bibliography" under "Historical Works".

Tāranātha — See above, under "Tibetan".

Udayasundarīkathā of Soḍḍhala
See above, in "General Bibliography" under "Champū".

(ii) INSCRIPTIONS:

List of important inscriptions of the Pāla Dynasty

Abbreviations

CP	Copper-plate
I	Image
S	Stone
P	Pillar

Serial No.	Year	Find place	Name of the king.	Reference
1	26	Bodh-Gayā-S	Dharmapāla	*JASB*,IV.101.
2	32	Khālimpur-CP	,,	*EI*,IV.243.
3	..	Nālandā-CP	,,	*EI*,XXIII.290.
4	33	Monghyr-CP	Devapāla	*EI*,XVIII.304.
5	35 (or 39)	Nālandā-CP	,,	*EI*,XVII.318; Monograph No. 1 of Varendra Research Society; *JRASBL*,VII.215.
6	..	Ghoshrawa-S	,,	*IA*,XVII.307.
7	3	Bihar-I	Śūrapāla	*JASB*,IV.108. *JRASBL*,IV.390.
8	5	Rajauna-S	,,	*IHQ*,XXIX.301.
9	17	Bhāgalpur-CP	Nārāyaṇapāla	*IA*,XV.304.
10	54	Bihar-I	,,	*IA*,XLVII.110.
11	..	Badal-SP	,,	*EI*,II.160.
12-14	28,31.32	Kurihar-I	Rājyapāla	*JBORS*,XXVI. 246.
15	..	Bhatuniya-S	,,	*EI*,XXXIII.150.
16	6	Jājilpārā-CP	Gopāla II	*JAS,L*,XVII.137.
17	V.S. 1083	Sārnāth-I	Mahīpāla	*IA*,XIV.139.
18	3	Bāghāura-I	,,	*EI*.XVII.355.
19	9	Bangarh-CP	,,	*JASB*,LXI.77. *EI*,XIV.324.
20	5	Belwa-CP	,,	*EI*,XXIX, 1 ff.
21	48(?)	Imadpur-I	,,	*IA*,XIV.165 (f.n.17). *JRASBL*,VII.218; XVI.247.
22	15	Gayā-S	Nayapāla	*Pālas of Bengal*, 78.
23	15	,,	,,	*JPASB*,LXIX.190.
23a	11	Belwa-CP	Vigrahapāla III	*EI*,XXIX.9.
24	12	Āmgāchi-CP	,,	*EI*,XV.293.
25	17	Bangaon-CP	,,	*EI*,XXIX,48.
26	3	Tetrawan-I	Rāmapāla	*JASB*,IV.109. *JRASBL*,IV.390.
27	42	Chandimau-I	,,	*Pālas of Bengal*, 93.
28	8	Manahali-CP	Madanapāla	*JPASB*,LXIX Part I,68.
29	14	Jaynagar-I	,,	*ASC*,III.125; *JRASBL*,VII.216.

30	Śaka 1083	Valgudar	Madanpāla	JAS.L,XVII.27. EI,XXVIII.145.

Inscriptions connected with the Pāla Kings.

31	..	Dinajpur-P		JASB,VII.619.
32	..	Irda-CP	Nayapāla	EI,XXII.150;XXIV.43.
33	4	Kamauli-CP	Vidyadeva	EI,II.350.
34	4	Bihar-I	Mahendrapāla	ASI,1923-4,p.102.
35	5	Paharpur-P	,,	Memoir, ASI,No. 55. p.75
36	9	Gunariya	,,	JASB,XVI.278.
37	10(?)	Bihar	,,	Pālas of Bengal, 64.

Inscriptions Nos. 1, 2, 4, 6, 9, 11, 17, 19, 23, 24, 28 and 33, along with a few other inscriptions of the Pāla kings, have been edited in *Gauḍalekhamālā*, a Bengali Work, published in B.S. 1319.

II. MODERN WORKS:

In English:

BANERJI, R. D. *The Pālas of Bengal. MASB.* V. 3. Calcutta, 1915.
"Pāla Chronology." *JBORS*, XIV. 489.

BHATTACHARYA, D. C. "A Chronology of the Pāla Dynasty of Bengal." *IA.*, XLIX, 189.
"Pāla Chronology (A reply to Prof. Banerji)." *IHQ*, VI. 153.

GHOSH, J. C. "Caste and Chronology of the Pāla kings of Bengal." *IHQ*, IX. 479.

MAJUMDAR, R. C. *History of Bengal.* Vol. I. Dacca, 1943.
"Pāla Chronology." *JBORS*, XV. 643.
"The Chronology of the Pāla kings." *JASB*, NS, XVII. 1.

PAUL, P. L. *The Early History of Bengal.* 2 vols. Calcutta, 1939, 1940.

RAYCHOUDHURI, H.C. "Pāla Expansion in the Far South of India." *POC*, VIII. 537.

SASTRI, K. A. Nilakanta. "Rājendra Chola I and Mahīpāla of Bengal." *IHQ*, XIII. 149-52.
"The Battle of Venbai". *India Antiqua* (Leyden, 1947), 254-256.

SEN, B. C. *Some Historical Aspects of the Inscriptions of Bengal.* Calcutta, 1942.

SHARMA, Dasaratha. "The two white umbrellas secured by Dhruva." *IHQ*, XX. 84-5.

In Bengali:

BANERJI, R. D. *Bāṅglār Itihāsa* (3rd Edition).

CHANDA, R. P. *Gauḍarājamālā* (B.S. 1319).

MAJUMDAR, R. C. *Bāṅglādeśer Itihāsa* (2nd Ed., B.S. 1356).

ROY, N. R. *Bāṅgālīr Itihāsa* (B.S. 1356).

CHAPTER IV

EASTERN INDIA DURING THE PĀLA PERIOD

(1) NEPĀL:

Original Sources:

BENDALL, C. *Catalogue of Buddhist Sanskrit MSS at Cambridge.* Cambridge, 1883.

Historical Introduction to H. P. Sastri's "Catalogue of Palm-leaf and Selected Paper MSS belonging to the Durbar Library, Nepal." Calcutta, 1905.

Journey in Nepal and Northern India. Cambridge, 1886.

"On Some Nepalese Coins in the Library of the German Oriental Society." *ZDMG*, XXXVI. 651-2.

BHAGVANLAL, Indraji. "Inscriptions from Nepal." *IA*, IX. 163-194.

LEVI, S. "Anciennes Inscriptions du Nepal." *JA*, 1907, IX. 49-114.

SASTRI, H. P. *Catalogue of Palm-leaf and selected Paper MSS belonging to the Durbar Library Nepal.* Calcutta, 1905.

WALSH, E. H. "The Coinage of Nepal." *JRAS, 1908*. 669-759; 1132-36.

WRIGHT, D. *History of Nepal* (translated from the *Parbatiya*). Cambridge, 1877.

Modern Works

BÜHLER, G. "Bhagwanlal Indraji's Some Considerations on the History of Nepal." *IA*, XIII. 411-28.

FLEET, J. F. "Chronology of the Early Rulers of Nepal." *IA*, XIV. 342-351.

KIRKAPATRICK, Col. *An Account of the Kingdom of Nepal.* London, 1811.

LANDON, Percival. *Nepal.* 2 Vols. London, 1928.

LEVI, S. "Note sur la Chronologie du Nepal." *JA*, 1894, IV. 55-72.

Le Nepal, Vols. I-III. Paris, 1905-1908.

MAJUMDAR, R. C. "Chronology of the Early kings of Nepal." *B. C. Law Volume*, I. 626-41.

RAY, H. C. *DHNI*, I, Ch. 4.

TARANĀTHA See above, in "General Bibliography" under "Tibetan".

(2) KĀMARŪPA:

(i) *Original Sources: Inscriptions*

BHATTACHARYA, Padmanatha. *Kāmarūpaśāsanāvali* (in Bengali). Rangpur, 1931.

List of important inscriptions has been given on p. 61.

(ii) *Modern Works:*

BARUA, B. M. "Common Ancestry of the Pre-Ahom Rulers etc." *IHQ*, XXIII. 200-220.

BARUA, K. L. *Early History of Kamarupa.* Vol. I. Shillong, 1933.

BHATTASALI, N. K. "New Light on the History of Assam." *IHQ*. XXI. 19-28; 143 ff; XXII. 1 ff.; 112 ff.; 245 ff.

DUTTA, K. "New Light on the Early History of Assam." *PIHC*, XII. 154 ff.

GAIT, E. A. *History of Assam.* 2nd Ed. Calcutta, 1926.

(3) ORISSA:

(i) *Original Sources: Inscriptions*

HIRALAL. See above, in Ch. I.

"Outline of the History of Kaliṅga" and "Outline of the History of the Bhañja Kings of Orissa" by R. C. Majumdar, and *Dynasties of Medieval Orissa* by B. Misra contain complete lists of inscriptions. Inscriptions discovered subsequently are referred to in the footnotes and in *IHQ*, XXVIII. 225 ff. Some recent inscriptions are listed below.

1. Angul copperplate of Dharmamahādevī. *JAS, L*, XVIII. 245-50.
2. Baud plates of Tribhuvanamahādevī.
3. Baud plates of Pṛithvīmahādevī.
4. Bonai copperplates of Udaya Varāha Deva. *JBORS*, XXXI. 159-171.
5. Brahmeśvara Temple Ins. of Uddyotakesari. *JASB,L*, XIII. 63-73.
6. Jurada charter of Neṭṭabhañja. *EI*, XXIV. 15.
7. Khaḍipaḍā image Ins. of the time of Śubhākara. *EI*, XXVI. 247. (Re-edited in No. 10 below).
8. Madras Museum plates of the time of Narendra Dhavala. *EI*, XXVIII. 44-50.
9. Mandasa plates of Dharmakheḍi *JAHRS*, VIII. 233-7.
10. Orissa Museum image ins. of the time of Śubhākara Deva. *PIHC*, XII. 66-74. (See No. 7 above).
11. Taltali plates of Daṇḍīmahādevī. *IHQ*, XXI. 218.
12. Taltali plates of Dharmamahādevī. *IHQ*, XX. 213-220.
13. Terundia plates of Śubhākara II. EI, XXVIII. 211-6.
14. Two grants of Bhañja kings of Vañjulvaka. *EI*, XXVIII. 272-283.
15. Two Ins. from Jajpur. *EI*, XXVIII, 179-185.
16. Two plates of Devānandadeva. *EI*, XXVIII. 325-334.

(ii) *Modern Works:*

ACHARYA, P. "The Bhañja kings of Orissa." *JBORS*, XII. 92-102.

BANERJI, R. D. *History of Orissa.* 2 Vols. Calcutta, 1930-31.

CHAKRAVARTI, M. M. "Chronology of the Eastern Gaṅga kings of Orissa." *JASB*, 1903. 97-147.

CHANDA, R. P. *Bhañja Dynasty of Mayurbhanj and their ancient capital Khiching.* Mayurbhauj, 1929.

DAS, M. N. *Glimpses of Kalinga History.* Calcutta, 1949.

DAS GUPTA, C. C. "Some notes on Ādi-Bhañjas of Khijjiṅga Kotta, earlier Bhañjas of Khiñjali-Maṇḍala, Bhañjas of Bauda and later Bhañjas of Khiñjali." *ABORI,* XII. 231-245.

HIRALAL. "Bhañja kings and their country." *JBORS,* XVI. 113-116.

MAHTAB, H. *The History of Orissa.* Lucknow, 1949.

MAJUMDAR, R. C. "Outline of the History of Kaliṅga." *DUS,* II, 2.1 ff.

"Outline of the History of the Bhañja kings of Orissa." *DUS,* III. 2. 138 ff.

MAZUMDAR, B. C. *Orissa in the Making.* Calcutta, 1925.

"Sketch of the History of Orissa." *JBORS,* VI. 348-60.

MISRA, B. *Orissa under the Bhauma Kings.* Calcutta, 1934.

Dynasties of Medieval Orissa. Calcutta, 1933.

MITRA, R. L. *Antiquities of Orissa.* 2 Vols. Calcutta, 1875-80.

RAMDAS, G. "Sūryavaṁśī Kings of Orissa." *JBRS,* XXXI. 172-94.

SIRCAR, D. C. "The Bhañjas of Khiñjali-Maṇḍala." *IHQ,* XXVIII, 225-231.

"The Dhavala Ruling Family in Ancient Orissa." *PIHC,* XII. 127-129.

"Dominions of the Śulkis of Orissa." *JOR,* XVIII. 45-48.

"The Era of the Bhauma-karas of Orissa." *IHQ,* XXIX. 148-155.

"Jajpur and the Bhauma-karas of Orissa." *JAS,L,* XVII. 15-17.

"New Facts about the Bhauma-karas." *JOR.* XVIII. 49 ff.

"Some Minor Dynasties of Orissa." *OHRJ,* II, 2. 13-20.

CHAPTER V

CENTRAL AND WESTERN INDIA

Original Sources

(i) INSCRIPTIONS

(*Note:* No lists of inscriptions have been attached to this chapter in view of the facts that they are few in number and that complete lists of inscriptions will be attached to the chapter in Vol. V, which is in continuation of this chapter.)

(1) THE CHANDELLAS:

Original Sources

(i) LITERARY

Prabodhachandrodaya of Kṛishṇamiśra

Pub. *NSP.* Bombay, 1924.

Eng. trans. by J. Taylor. London, 1862.

Modern Works

CUNNINGHAM, A. *Archaeological Survey Reports*, X.

GANGULY, D. C. *History of the Paramāra Dynasty*. Dacca, 1933.

MITRA, S. K. "A Note on the Status of the Early Chandella Rulers." *IHQ*, XXIX. 304-309.

MAJUMDAR, R. C. "The Gurjara Pratīhāras". *JDL*, X. 1-76.

RAY, H. C. *DHNI*, II, Ch. 11.

SMITH, V. A "Contributions to the History of Bundelkhand." *JASB*, 1881, Vol. I. pt. 1, pp. 1-53.

"The History and Coinage of the Chandel (Chandella) Dynasty of Bundelkhand." *IA*, XXXVII. 114-148.

(2) THE KALACHURIS:

Original Sources:

LITERARY

Prabandhachintāmaṇi of Merutuṅga

Ed. Ramachandra Dinanatha. Bombay, 1888.

Ed. Muni Jinavijaya. *SJS*. Santiniketan, 1933.

Eng. trans. by C. H. Tawney. *BI*. Calcutta, 1901.

Modern Works

BANERJI, R. D. *The Haihayas of Tripuri and their Monuments*. *MASI*. Calcutta, 1931.

CUNNINGHAM, A. *Archaeological Survey Reports*, IX.

HIRALAL. See above, in Ch. 1.

"The Kalachuris of Tripuri." *ABORI*, IX. 280-295.

GANGULY, D. C. "The Early History of the Kalachuris of Chedi." *IHQ*, XIII. 482-7.

Eastern Chālukyas. Benares, 1937.

History of the Paramāra Dynasty. Dacca, 1933.

KIELHORN, F. "Kalachuris of Tripuri." *EI*, II. 300-305.

MAJUMDAR, R. C. "The Gurjara Pratīhāras." *JDL*, X. 1-76.

"The Kalachuri king Kokkalla I." *PIHC*, XII. 123-126.

MIRASHI, V. V. "Yuvarājadeva I of Tripurī." *ABORI*, XI. 361-373.

RAY, H. C. *DHNI*, II, Ch. 12.

VAIDYA, C. V. *History of Medieval Hindu India*. III. 187-192. Poona, 1926.

(3) THE PARAMĀRAS:

Original Sources

LITERARY

Auchityavichāra of Kshemendra

Ed. *KM*, I. 115 ff.

Extracts *JBBRAS*, XVI. 167-179 (Peterson).

Navasāhasāṅkacharita of Padmagupta

Ed. by Vaman Sastri Islampurkar. *BSS*. Bombay, 1895. Extract Eng. trans. *JBBRAS*, XXVI. 153 f.

Pāiyalachchhī of Dhanapāla
Ed. G. Bühler. Gottingen, 1879.
Prabandhachintāmaṇi of Merutuṅga
See above, under "Kalachuris."

Modern Works

AYYANGAR, P. T. S. *Bhojarāja*. Madras, 1931.
BÜHLER, G. and ZACHARIAE, Th. "Über das Navasāhasāṅkacharita des Padmagupta oder Parimala." *Kaiserliche Akademie der Wissenschaften*, CXVI. 583-630.
GANGULY, D. C. *History of the Paramāra Dynasty*. Dacca, 1933.
LUARD, C. E. and LELE, K. K. Paramāras of Dhar and Malwa. *Dhar State Gazetteer*. Reprint, Bombay, 1908.
MIRASHI, V. V. "Historical Data in Padmagupta's Navasāhasāṅkacharita." *IA*, LII. 101-107.
"New Light on the History of the Paramāra Dynasty." *PIHC*, V. 256-260.
RAY, H. C. *DHNI*, II, Ch. 14.
TOD, J. *Annals and Antiquities of Rajasthan*. Ed. by W. Crooke. Oxford, 1920.

(4) THE SAINDHAVAS, CHĀPAS, CHAULUKYAS, ETC.

Original Sources

Dvyāśrayakāvya of Hemachandra
Ed. by A. V. Kathawate. *BSS*. 3 Vols. Bombay, 1900-1921.
Kitāb Futūḥ al Buldan of al-Baladhuri
See above in "General Bibliography" under "Muslim".
Kumārapālacharita of Jayasiṁha
Ed. by Kantivijaya Gani. *NSP*. Bombay, 1926.
Prabandhachintāmaṇi of Merutuṅga
See above, under "Paramāras."
Prabandhakośa of Rājaśekhara
Ed. by Muni Jinavijaya. *SJS*. Santiniketan, 1935.
Prabhāvakacharita of Prabhāchandra
Ed. by H. M. Sarma. *NSP*. Bombay, 1909.
Ed. by Muni Jinavijaya. *SJS*. Bombay, 1940.
Rāsa Mālā by Forbes
Ed. by H. G. Rawlinson. Vol. I. Oxford, 1924
Vichāraśreṇī of Merutuṅga
JBBRAS, IX.
Pāiyalachchhī of Dhanapāla
See above, under "Paramāras."

Modern Works

BAYLEY, *History of Gujarat*. London, 1886.
BHAGWANLAL Indraji *Early History of Gujarat*. *BG*, I. i. Bombay. 1896.
ELLIOT, H. M. and DOWSON, J. See above, under "Muslim" in "General Bibliography".

GANGULY, D. C. *History of the Paramāra Dynasty*. Dacca, 1933.
"On the Pratīhāra Mahīpāla." *Munshi Diamond Jubilee Comm. Vol*. I. 194-201.
MAJUMDAR, A. K. *Chaulukyas of Gujarat*, Bombay, 1956.
MAJUMDAR, R. C. "The Gurjara Pratīhāras." *JDL*, X. 1-76.
MUNSHI, K. M. *The Imperial Gurjaras*. Bombay, 1944. 2nd Ed. Bombay, 1955.
OJHA, G. H. *History of Rajputana* (in Hindi). Ajmer, 1936 ff.
RAY, H. C. *DHNI*. II, Ch. 15.

(5) THE CHAHAMANAS

Original Sources

LITERARY

Dvyāśrayakāvya of Hemachandra
See above, under "Saindhavas, etc."
Hammīra-Mahākāvya of Nayachandra Sūri
Ed. by N. J. Kirtane. Bombay, 1879.
Prabandhachintāmaṇi of Merutuṅga
See above, under "Paramāras".
Prabandhakośa of Rājaśekhara
See above, under "Saindhavas, etc."
Pṛithvīrājavijaya of Jayānaka
See above, under "Jayānaka" in "Historical Works", General Bibliography.

Modern Works

GANGULY, D. C. "A Forgotten Moslem Invasion." *IHQ*, XIV 813-816.
"A New Light on the History of the Chāhamānas." *IHQ*, XVI. 567-573.
OJHA, G. H. See above, under "Saindhavas, etc."
RAY, H. C. *DHNI*, II, Ch. 16.
TOD, J. See above, under "Paramāras".

(6) THE GUHILAS

Modern Works

BHANDARKAR, D. R. "Guhilots." *JPASB*, 1909. 167 ff.
GANGULY, D. C. "Al-Biruni's Gujarat." *Islamic Culture*, III.
"A Forgotten Moslem Invasion." *IHQ*, XIV. 813-816.
"Gurjaras in the Rāshṭrakūṭa Inscriptions". *PIHC*, III. 513-515.
"History of the Gurjara Country." *IHQ*, X. 613-623.
History of the Paramāra Dynasty. Dacca, 1933.
HALDER, R. R. "The Guhila kings of Mewar." *IA*, 1927. 169 ff.
MATHUR, M. L. "Early Rulers of Mewar and their Fights with the Arabs." *IHQ*, XXIX. 315-331; XXX 31-37.

OJHA, G. H. See above, under "Saindhavas, etc."

RAY, H. C. *DHNI*, II, Ch. 18.

RAYCHOUDHURI, G. C. "Guhilot Origins." *D. R. Bhandarkar Vol.*, 311-16.

"A Note on the Early Home of the Guhilots." *IC*, III. 219-22.

"A Note on the Rise of the Guhilots in Chitor and its Neighbourhood." *PIHC*, III. 813-7.

TOD, J. See above, under "Paramāras."

(7) THE SHĀHIS:

Original Sources:

LITERARY

Jāmi'ul-Hikāyāt of Muhammad 'Aufī
See above; under "Muslim" in "General Bibliography."

Kitāb-ul-Hind of Bīrūnī
See above; under "Muslim" in "General Bibliography."

Rājataraṅgiṇī of Kalhaṇa
See above, in "Historical Works" in "General Bibliography."

Tabaqāt-i-Akbarī of Niẓāmuddīn
See above; under "Muslim" in "General Bibliography."

Ta'rikh-i-Firishta
See above; under "Muslim" in "General Bibliography."

Ta'rīkh-i-Yamīnī of Utbī
See above; under "Muslim" in "General Bibliography."

Modern Works

ELLIOT, H. M. and DOWSON, J. "The Hindu Kings of Kabul." *HIED*, II, Note A, p. 403 f.

MAJUMDAR, R. C. "Hindu Reaction to Muslim Invasions." *Potdar Comm. Vol.*, 341-351.

NAZIM, M. "The Hindu Sahiya Kingdom of Ohind" *JRAS*, 1927. 485 f.

RAY, H. C. *DHNI*, I, Ch. 2.

KASHMIR:

Original Sources

Rājataraṅgiṇī of Kalhaṇa
See above, under "Historical Works" in "General Bibliography."

Tabaqāt-i-Akbarī of Niẓāmuddīn
See above; under "Muslim" in "General Bibliography."

Ta'rīkh-i-Firishta
See above, under "Muslim" in "General Bibliography."

Modern Works

CUNNINGHAM, A. *Ancient Coinage of Kashmir*. London, 1843.
GHOSHAL, U. N. "Dynastic Chronicles of Kashmir." *IHQ*, XVIII. 195-207; 302-341; XIX. 27-38; 156-72.
RAY, H. C. *DHNI*, I, Ch. 3.
STEIN, M. A. "Notes on the Monetary System of Ancient Kashmir." *Num. Chr.*, XIX. 125-74.

(9) CHAMBĀ:

HUTCHINSON, J. and VOGEL, J. Ph. "History of Chamba State". *Journal of the Panjab Historical Society*, X. ii. 5-70.
VOGEL, J. Ph. *Antiquities of the Chamba State*. Part I. *ASI. NIS*, 36. Calcutta, 1911.

(10) KUMAUN AND GARHWAL:

ATKINSON, E. T. *N.W.F. Gazetteer*, XI. (*The Himalayan Districts of the North-Western Provinces of India*, II). 1884, pp. 469-85.
GUPTE, Y. R. "Two Taleśvara copper-plates." *EI*, XIII. 199 ff.
KIELHORN, F. "Paṇḍukeśvara Plate of Lalitaśūradeva." *IA*, XXV. 177-184.
MITRA, R. L. "Copper-plate grant from Pāṇḍukeśvar". *Proc. A.S.B.*, 1877. 71-75.
SIRCAR, D. C. "Some Ancient Kings of Kumaun and Garhwal." *BV*, XII. 149-152.

(11) ARABS IN INDIA:

ARNOLD, Sir Thomas. *The Caliphate*. Oxford, 1924.
CARTER. *A Short History of Sind*. Karachi, 1926.
DHAR, S. N. "The Arab Conquest of Sind." *IHQ*, XVI. 596-604.
GHANI, M. A. "The Advent of the Arabs in Hindustan; Their Relations with the Hindus; and the Occupation of Sindh." *POC*, X. 403-10.
GIBB, H. A. R. *Arab Conquests in Central Asia*. London, 1923.
"Chinese Records of the Arabs in Central Asia." *BSOS*, II. 613-22.
MAJUMDAR, R. C. "The Arab Invasion of India." *JIH*, X, part 1, Supplement (gives full references to authorities).
MUIR, Sir William. *Annals of the Early Caliphate*. London, 1883.
Caliphate, its rise, decline and fall. Revised by T. H. Weir. Edinburgh, 1915.
RAVERTY, Maj. H. G. *Notes on Afghanistan*. London, 1888.
LE STRANGE, G. *The Lands of the Eastern Caliphate*. 1930.
TOD, Lt. Col. James. *Annals and Antiquities of Rajasthan*. Ed. by William Crooke. Oxford, 1920.

CHAPTER VI

THE DECCAN

Original Sources:

Inscriptions

RANGACHARYA, V. *Inscriptions of the Madras Presidency.* 3 Vols. Madras, 1919.

SEWELL, R. *Historical Inscriptions of Southern India.* Madras, 1932.

(I) SELECT INSCRIPTIONS OF THE EASTERN CHĀLUKYAS:

1. Pṛithivīpallavapaṭṭana ins. of Vishṇuvardhana V. *IA,* XX. 186.
2. Masulipatam plates of Vijayāditya III. *EI,* V. 122.
3. Guntur plates of Vijayāditya III. *ARSIE,* 1912.84; JAHRS, V. 113.
4. Attili ins. of Chālukya Bhīma, *ARSIE,* 1918. 131.
5. Bezwada plates of Chālukya Bhīma. *EI,* V. 127.
6. Anakapalle ins. of Chālukya Bhīma. *ARSIE,* 1909.108.
7. Adanki ins. of Chālukya Bhīma. *EI,* XIX. 275.
8. Chevūru plates of Amma I. *EI,* XXVII. 41.
9. Pulivarru ins. of Amma. I. *ARSIE,* 1924.10, 98.
10. Masulipatam plates of Ammarāja II. *EI,* XXIV. 268-78.
11. Nandigama taluk plates of Amma II. *ARIE,* 1917.117.
12. Maliyapūṇḍi grant of Amma II. *EI,* IX. 47.
13. Kaluchumbarru grant of Amma II. *EI.* VII. 177.
14. Anaparti grant of Ammarāja II. *JAHRS,* XX. 195-201.
15. Vemalūrpāḍu plates of Amma II. *EI,* XVIII. 226-235.
16. Arumbak plates of Bādapa. *EI,* XIX, 146.

(2) SELECT INSCRIPTIONS OF EASTERN GANGAS, GANGAS OF ŚVETAKA AND EASTERN KADAMBAS:

1. Alamanda plates of Anantavarman. *EI,* III. 17-21.
2. Tekkali plates of Rājendravarman's son Devendravarman. *EI,* XVIII. 311-313.
3. Mandasa plates of Rājendravarman. *Bh. List,* No. 2051.
4. Sanskrit and Old Canarese Inscriptions. *IA,* XIV. 7-12.
5. Cheedivalasa grant. *JAS, L,* XVIII. 77.
6. Galavalli copper-plate ins. of Manujendravarman. *JAHRS,* XX. 161-170.
7. Narasapatam plates of Vajrahasta III. *Bh. List,* No. 1090.
8. Vizagapatam (Now Madras, Museum) plates of Anantavarman (Choḍagaṅgadeva). *Bh. List,* No. 1103.
9. Nagari plates of Anaṅgabhīma III *EI,* XXVIII. 235-258.
10. Palamgara grant of Anantavarman Choḍagaṅga. *ARSIE,* 1935-36.61-63.
11. Sānta Bommālī plates of Devendravarman. *Bh. List,* No. 2053. (Edited in No. 14 below).

12. Gara ins. of Devendravarman. *ARSIE*, 1932-33. 56-57.
13. Paralakimedi plates of Vajrahasta. *EI*, III. 220-224.
14. Simhapura copper-plate grant of Dharmakheḍi. *JAHRS*, III. 171-180. (See No. 10 above).

(3) SELECT INSCRIPTIONS OF THE SOMAVAMŚĪS:

1. Records of the Somavaṁśī kings of Katak. *EI*, III. 323-359.
2. Bhuvaneswar ins. *JRASB*, L, XIII. 74.
3. Mallar plates of Mahāśivagupta. *EI*, XXIII. 113.
4. Lodhia plates of Mahāśivagupta. *EI*. XXVII. 319.
5. Balangir Museum plates of Mahāśivagupta I Yayāti. *JAS*, *L*, XIX. 117-124.
6. Two inscriptions from Kelga. *EI*, XXVIII. 321-328.

II. *Modern Works*

ALTEKAR, A. S. — *Rāshṭrakūṭas and their times*. Poona, 1934.

BHANDARKAR, R. G. — See above, under "Histories of the Period" in "General Bibliography".

CHAKRAVARTI, M. M. — "Chronology of the Eastern Gaṅga kings of Orissa." *JASB*, 1903, Vol. 72, pp. 97-147.

CHHABRA, B.Ch. — "A Note on the Chronology of the Gaṅgas of Śvetaka." *EI*, XXV. 240.

CHHABRA, B.Ch. and RAO, N. L. — "Ten Years of Epigraphy (1937-46)." *Ancient India*, No. 5, pp. 46 ff.

FLEET, J. F. — "Chronology of the Eastern Chālukya Kings." *IA*, XX-XXI.

"Dynasties of the Kanarese Districts." *BG*, I, Part 2.

GANGULY, D. C. — *Eastern Chālukyas*. Benares, 1937.

MAJUMDAR, R. C. and ALTEKAR, A. S. (Ed.). — *Vākāṭaka-Gupta Age*. Lahore, 1946; Reprint. Banaras, 1954.

MIRASHI, V. V. — "An Ancient Dynasty of Mahākosala." *PIHC*, III. 319-327.

"Note on the Date of the Somavaṁśī kings." *EI*, XXVI. 227 ff.

PANCHAMUKHI, R. S. — "Badami ins. of Chālukya Vallabheśvara." *EI*, XXVII. 4-9.

RAO, B. V. Krishna — "History of Rajahmundry." *JAHRS*, III. 135-170; IV. 97-112.

"Origin and Early History of the Chālukyas." *PIHC*, III. 386-410.

"Revised Chronology of the Eastern Chālukya Kings." *JAHRS*, IX, iv. 1-32.

RAO, N. L. — "A Note on Siroda plates of (Bhoja) Devarāja". *EI*, XXVI. 337-340.

SARMA, M. S. — "Chronology of the Eastern Chālukyas." *JOR*. IX. 17-42.

"A Note on the Mandasa plates of Anantavarman." *JAHRS*, XII. 21-28.

SIRCAR, D. C. "Genealogy of the Vishṇukuṇḍins." *ABORI*, 222-228.

"Kesaribeda plates of Nala Arthapati Bhaṭṭāraka." *EI*, XXVIII. 12-17.

"Kuntala and Aśmaka." *IHQ*, XXIII. 65-68.

"Later Somavaṁśīs." *OHRJ*, I. 289-300.

"A note on the genealogy of the Somavaṁśīs." *IHQ*, XX. 76-82.

"A note on the later Somavaṁśīs." *IHQ*, XXII. 300-307.

Successors of the Sātavāhanas in the Lower Deccan. Calcutta, 1939.

SMITH, V. A. See above, under "Histories of the Period" in "General Bibliography".

SUBBARAO, R. "The Origin of the Eastern Gaṅgas." *POC*, VIII. 573-580.

"History of the Eastern Gaṅgas of Kaliṅga." *JAHRS*, VI. 193-216; VII. 57-64 (relating to this period).

History of the Eastern Gaṅgas of Kaliṅga.

SUBRAHMANIAN, K.R. "Vijayāditya III, a famous Eastern Chālukyan King." *Rangaswami Aiyangar Comm. Vol.*, 263-267.

VENKATARAMANAYYA, N. *The Eastern Chālukyas of Veṅgi.* Madras, 1950.

CHAPTER VII

SOUTHERN INDIA

Original Sources

(i) INSCRIPTIONS

AYYAR, V. V. *South Indian Inscriptions.* Vol. XII. Madras, 1943.

RANGACHARYA, V. See above, under Ch. VI.

SEWELL, R. See above, under Ch. VI.

South Indian Inscriptions.

(1) IMPORTANT INSCRIPTIONS OF THE PALLAVAS:

1. Velur Pālayam Plates of Nandivarman III. *SII* II, Part V, No. 98.
2. Triplicane inscription of Dantivarman. V. Venkappa, *EI*, VIII, No. 29.
3. Tiruvaḷḷarai ins. of Dantivarman. K. V. S. Iyer. *EI*, XI. 156.
4. Tillaisthānam ins. of Vijayanandi-Vikramavarman. Ins. No. 52 of 1895.
5. Sendalai Pillar ins. of Nandi-Pottaraiyar. Ins. No. 11 of 1899.
6. Tiruvallam ins. of Vijayanandi-Vikramavarman. *SII*, III. 93.
7. Ulagaḷanda Perumal Temple (Kāñchī) ins. of Nandippottarasar who was victorious at Teḷḷāṛu. Ins. 12 of 1895; V. Venkayya, *M.C.C. Magazine*, VIII. 102.
8. Tiruppālaitturai ins. Nandippottaraiyar, the victor at Teḷḷāṛu. Ins. No. 180 of 1907.

9. Guḍimallam Bāṇa ins. of Nandippotarasar. V. Venkayya. *EI*, XI. 224.
10. Nārattāmalai ins. of Nṛipatuṅgavarman. Ins. No. 365 of 1904.
11. Bāhūr plates of Nṛipatuṅgavarman. E. Hultzsch. *EI*, IV. 180.
12. Tiruvālaṅgāḍu ins. of Nṛipatuṅgavarman. Ins. No. 460 of 1905.
13. Kovilaḍi ins. of Nṛipatuṅgavarman. Ins. No. 300 of 1901.
14. Kaṇḍiyūr ins. of Nṛipatuṅgavarman. Ins. No. 17 of 1895.
15. Tirumukkūḍal ins. of Nṛipatuṅgavarman. Ins. No. 179 of 1915.
16. Guḍimallam ins. of Nṛipatuṅgavarman. *IA*, 1911.113.
17. Two Āmbūr inscriptions. E. Hultzsch. *EI*, IV. 182-3.
18. Copper-plate inscriptions of the 6th year of Nṛipatuṅgavarman. *Sewell's List of Antiquities*, II, No. 209, p. 30.

(2) IMPORTANT INSCRIPTIONS OF THE CHOḶAS:

1. Tirukkaḻukkuṉṟam ins. of Rājakesarivarman. V. Venkayya. *El*, III. 277-280.
2. Takkolam ins. of Rājakesarivarman (Āditya I). K. V. S. Iyer. *EI*, XIX. 81-88.
3. Tillaittānam ins. of Āditya. *SII*, III, No. 89.
4. Tirupaḻanam ins. of Rājakesarivarman. *SII*, XIII, No. 304.
5. Toṇḍaimān Nāḍ ins. Parāntaka. *SII*, VIII, No. 529.
6. Tiruvoṟṟiyūr ins. of Parāntaka I. *SII*, III, No. 108.
7. Kiḻmuttugūr ins. of Parāntaka. E. Hultzsch. *EI*, IV. 178-9.
8. Two Tamil inscriptions at Āmbūr. E. Hultzsch. *EI*, IV. 180-3.
9. Tirukkaḻukkuṉṟam ins. Parāntaka I. V. Venkayya. *EI*, III. 280-2.
10. Uttaramallur ins. of Parāntaka I. K. V. S. Iyer. *EI*, XXII. 145-150.
11. A Chola ins. from Uttiramerūr. K. A. N. Sastri. *EI*, XXII, No. 32.
12. Tirukkalithaṭṭai ins. of Sundarachola. K. V. S. Iyer. *EI*, XII. 121-126.
13. Karikāl ins. of Maduraikoṇḍa Rājakesari. E. Hultzsch. *EI*, IV. 331-332.
14. Anbil plates of Sundarachola. T. A. G. Rao. *EI*, XV. 44-72.
15. Three Tamil inscriptions of Lālguḍi. K. V. S. Iyer. *EI*, XX. 46-54.
16. Sholinghur ins. of Parāntaka I. E. Hultzsch. *EI*, IV. 221-225.
17. Museum Plates of Uttamachola. *SII*, III, No. 128.
18. Konerirājapuram ins. of Sembiyaṉ Mādevi. *SII*, III, No. 146.
19. Sembiyaṉ Mādevi ins. of Uttamachola. Ins. No. 494 of 1925.
20. Tanjore ins. Rājarāja I. *SII*, II, No. 6.
21. Melpāḍi ins. of Rājarāja I. *SII*, III, No. 14.
22. Uḍaiyārgudi ins. of Rājakesarivarman, A.D. 988. K. A. N. Sastri. *EI*, XXI. 165-170.
23. Larger Leiden plates. K. V. S. Iyer. *EI*, XXII, No. 34.
24. Tiruvālaṅgāḍu plates of Rājendra Chola I. *SII*, III, No. 205.
25. Kanyākumāri ins. of Vīra Rājendra Deva. K. V. S. Iyer. *EI*, XXV. 21-55.
26. Chārala plates of Vīra Rājendra Deva, Ś. 991. A. S. R. Iyer and V. V. Iyer, *EI*, XXV, No. 25.
27. Regulations of the Sabhā from two Uttaramallur inscriptions. K. V. S. Iyer. *EI*. XXV, No. 7.

(3) IMPORTANT INSCRIPTIONS OF THE PĀṆḌYAS:

1. Ānaimalai ins. of Neḍuñjaḍaiyan Parāntaka. K. V. S. Iyer. *EI*, VIII. 317-321.
2. Veḷvikkuḍi Plates of Neḍuñjaḍaiyan Parāntaka. H. K. Sastri. EI, XVII, No. 16.
3. Madras Museum Plates of Neḍuñjaḍaiyan Parāntaka. *IA*, XXII. 69-75.
4. Four Pāṇḍyan Records of Ukkirankoṭṭai. A. S. R. Ayyar. *EI*, XXIII. 283-289.
5. Ambāsamudram ins. of Varaguṇa I. V. Venkayya. *EI*, IX. 84-94.
6. Māṇūr ins. of Māṟaṉ Saḍaiyaṉ, K. A. N. Sastri. *EI*, XXII. 5-11.
7. Tiruchchirappaḷḷi ins. of Māṟaṉ Saḍaiyaṉ. *ASI* for 1903-1904, p. 225.
8. Tillaisthānam ins. of Māṟaṉ Saḍaiyaṉ. *SII*, V, No. 608.
9. Seṇdalai ins. of Māṟaṉ Saḍaiyaṉ. *SII*, VI, No. 446.
10. Sittannavāsal ins. of Śrī Māṟa Śrī Vallabha. Ins. No. 388 of 1904.
11. Avanipasekhara Maṅgalam ins. of Śrī Māṟa Śrī Vallabha. Ins. No. 155 of 1903.
12. Aivar Malai ins. of Varaguṇavarman. Ins. No. 705 of 1905.
13. Tirchendūr ins. of Varaguṇa Mahārāja II. K. V. S. Iyer. *EI*, XXI. 101-116.
14. Sinnamanūr Plates of Rājasiṁha III. *SII*, III, No. 206.
15. Tiruppuḍaimarudūr ins. of Vīra Pāṇḍya. Ins. 122 of 1905.
16. Suchīndram inscriptions of Vīra Pāṇḍya. *TAS*, III, Nos. 22-26.
17. Kiḻmāttūr ins. of Solaṉṟalaikoṇḍa Vīra Pāṇḍya. *SII*, V, No. 304.
18. Ambāsamudram ins. of Solaṉṟalaikoṇḍa Vīra Pāṇḍya. A. S. R. Ayyar. *EI*, XXV. 35-42.

(4) IMPORTANT INSCRIPTIONS OF THE GANGAS:

1. Jāvalī Plates of Śrī Purusha. *EC*, VI, Mg. 36.
2. Islāmpur Plates of Śrī Purusha. K. B. Pathak and Sten Konow. *EI*, XII, No. 10.
3. Hosūr Plates of Śrī Purusha. *EC*, X, Gd. 47.
4. Devarhalli Plates of Śrīpurusha. *EC*, IV, Ng. 85.
5. Manne (I) Plates of Mārasiṁha Loka Trinetra Yuvarāja. *EC*, IX, Ni. 60.
6. Manne (II) Plates of Satyavākya Koṅganivarman Rājamalla. *MAR*, 1910.
7. Galigekere Plates of Raṇavikramayya (Nītimārga I). *EC*, IV, Yd. 60.
8. Narasapura Plates of Rājamalla II Satyavākya. *EC*, X, Kl. 90.
9. Gattavadipura Plates of Rājamalla II Satyavākya and Nītimārga (Ereyappa). *EC*, XII, Nj. 269.
10. Sudi Plates of Būtuga. J. F. Fleet. *EI*, III. 158-184.
11. Keregodi Raṅgapura Plates of Rājamalla II (or his brother Būtuga II). *MAR*, 1918-1919.
12. Kudlur Plates of Mārasiṁha. *MRA*, 1920-1921.
13. Alur Plates of Mārasiṁha. *MRA*, 1923-1924.
14. Udayendiram Plates of Pṛithivīpati II. *SII*, II, No. 76.
15. Takkolam ins. of Pṛithivīpati II. *SII*, V, No. 1368.
16. Ātakūr ins. Būtuga. J. F. Fleet. *EI*, VI. 50-57.

(5) IMPORTANT INSCRIPTIONS OF THE BĀṆAS:

1. Five Bāṇa inscriptions from Guḍimallam. V. Venkayya. *EI*, XI. 222-240.
2. Udayendiram Plates of Vikramāditya II. F. Kielhorn. *EI*, III. 74-77.
3. Guḍimallam Plates of Bāṇa Vikramāditya II. E. Hultzsch. *EI*, XVII. 1-7.

(6) IMPORTANT INSCRIPTIONS OF THE VAIDUMBAS:

1. Three inscriptions of Vaidumba Mahārāja Gaṇḍa Tinetra. R. S. Panchamukhi. *EI*, XXIII. 183-193.

Modern Works

AIYANGAR, S. Krishnaswami. *Some Contributions of South India to Indian Culture*. Calcutta, 1923. 2nd Ed. Calcutta, 1942.

AIYER, K. V. Subrahmanya. *Historical Sketches of Ancient Deccan*. Madras, 1917.

AROKIASWAMI, K. *The Early History of the Veḻḻār Basin*. Madras, 1954.

CHHABRA, B.Ch. and RAO, N. L. See above, under Ch. VI.

DIKSHITAR, V. R. R. *Studies in Tamil Literature and History*. London, 1930.

GOPALAN, R. *History of the Pallavas of Kanchi*. Madras, 1928.

HERAS, H. *Studies in Pallava History*. Madras, 1933.

JOUVEAU-DUBREUIL, G. *Ancient History of the Deccan* (translated from the French by V. S. Swaminadha Dikshitar). Pondicherry, 1920.

Pallavas (translated from the French by V. S. Swaminadha Dikshitar). Pondicherry, 1917.

MAHALINGAM, T. V. *The Bāṇas in South Indian History*. Madras, 1952.

MINAKSHI, C. *Administrative and Social Life under the Pallavas*. Madras, 1938.

MORAES, G. M. *The Kadamba Kula*. Bombay, 1931.

PANDARATHAR, T. V. Sadasiva. *Piṟkālach-Choḻar-Charittiram*. Part I (in Tamil). Annamalainagar, 1949.

Pāṇḍiyar Varalāṟu (in Tamil). Madras, 1950.

RAJAMANIKKAM, M. *Pallavar Varalāṟu* (in Tamil). Madras, 1952.

RAO, B. V. Krishna. *A History of the Early Dynasties of Andhradeśa*. Madras, 1942.

RAO, G. V. Srinivasa. *South Indian Inscriptions*. VOl. XIII. Madras, 1953.

RAO, M. V. Krishna. *The Gaṅgas of Talkad*. Madras, 1936.

RAO, N. L. "Some New Facts about Chola History." *JOR*, XIX. 148-151.

RICE, B. L. See above, under "Inscriptions" in "General Bibliography."

SALETORE, B. A. *Ancient Karṇāṭaka*. Vol. I. Poona, 1936.

SASTRI, K. A. N. *The Cholas.* Vols. I, II, 1. Madras, 1925, 1937.
History of South India. Bombay, 1952.
The Pandyan Kingdom. London, 1929.
Studies in Chola History and Administration. London, 1932.

SIRCAR, D. C. *The Early Pallavas.* Lahore, 1935.
The Successors of the Sātavāhanas in the Lower Deccan. Calcutta, 1939.

VENKAYYA, V. "Five Bāṇa Inscriptions from Guḍimallam." *EI*, XI. 222-240.

CHAPTER VIII

CEYLON

Original Sources

(i) PĀLI:

(See *Dīpavaṁsa* and *Mahāvaṁsa* in General Bibliography)

Dāṭhā-vaṁsa Ed. and trans. by B. C. Law. Lahore, 1925.

Hatthavanagalla-vihāra-vaṁsa Ed. by James d'Alwis.

(ii) SIMHALESE:

Attangalu-vaṁsa Ed. by M. Kumāranatuṅga. Colombo, B. E. 2466.

Daḷadāpūjāvaliya Ed. by K. M. Perera. Colombo, 1893.

Daḷadātirita Ed. by E. S. Rajasekhara. Colombo, 1920.

Nikāya Saṅgraha Ed. by D. M. de Z. Wickramasinghe. Colombo, 1890. Trans. by C. M. Fernando with an intr. by W. F. Gunawardhana. Colombo, 1908.

Pūjāvaliya, Ch. 34 Ed. by M. Medhaṅkara Thera. Eng. trans. by B. Gunasekara *(A Contribution to the History of Ceylon).* Colombo, 1895.

Rājaratnākaraya Ed. by Simon de Silva. Colombo, 1907.

Rājāvaliya Ed. by B. Gunasekara. Colombo, 1911. Eng. trans. by the same. Colombo, 1900.

Modern Works

CODRINGTON, H. W. *History of Ceylon.* London, 1926.

COOMARASWAMY, A. K. *History of Indian and Indonesian Art.* London, 1927.

GEIGER, W. *Ceylon.* Wiesbaden, 1898.

GOPALAN, R. *The Pallavas of Kanchi.* Madras, 1928.

HULTZSCH, E. "Contributions to Singhalese Chronology." *JRAS*, 1913, pp. 517 ff.

MENDIS, G C. *Early History of Ceylon.* 9th Ed. Calcutta, 1948.

MÜLLER, E. *Ancient Inscriptions in Ceylon.* London, 1883.

PARKER, H. *Ancient Ceylon.* London, 1909.

PRIDHAM, C. *Historical, Political and Statistical Account of Ceylon and its Dependencies.* 2 Vols. London, 1849.

SEWELL, R. *Historical Inscriptions of Southern India.* Madras, 1932.

SMITH, V. A. *History of Fine Art in India and Ceylon.* 2nd Ed. Revised by K. de B. Codrington. Oxford, 1930.

TURNOUR, G. *An Epitome of the History of Ceylon.* 1836.

WIJKREMASINGHE. *Archaeological Survey of Ceylon.* Vol. I.

WIJESIMHA, L. C. *Mahavamsa.* Part I. Colombo, 1909.

CHAPTER IX

LANGUAGE AND LITERATURE

(A) SANSKRIT, PĀLI, PRAKRIT, AND APABHRAMŚA:

(*Note:* A select list of important texts in Sanskrit, Pāli, Prakrit and Apabhraṁśa has been given in General Bibliography. Further accounts of individual texts and full bibliographical material will be found in the works of Das Gupta and De, Keith, Krishnamachariar, Winternitz, Geiger, Law, and others mentioned under "Histories of Literature" in General Bibliography above).

ALSDORF, A. *Apabhraṁśa-Studien.* Leipzig, 1937.

AYYAR, A. S. Ramanatha "Nalodaya and its author." *QJMS,* XIV. 302-311.

BAGCHI, P. C. (Ed.). *Dohākośa.* Calcutta, 1938 (JDL, XXVIII).

BELVALKAR, S. K. *Systems of Sanskrit Grammar.* Poona, 1915.

BHANDARKAR, R. G. *Collected Works.* Vols. I-IV. Poona, 1927-1933.

BHATTACHARYYA, D. C. "Date of Vāchaspati Miśra and Udayanāchārya." *JGJRI,* II. 349-356.

BHATTANATHA SVAMI "Māyurāja." *IA,* XLI. 139-143.

BÜHLER, G. "The Indian Inscriptions and the Antiquity of Indian Artificial Poetry." (Eng. trans. by V. S. Ghate) *IA,* XLII. 29-32; 137-148; 172-179; 188-193; 230-234; 243-249.

CHITRAV, S. V. *Madhyayugīna Charitra-Kośa* (Dictionary of Biography in Medieval India) (in Marathi). Poona, 1937.

DE, S. K. *History of Sanskrit Poetics.* 2 vols. London, 1923, 1925.

"Bhāmaha's Views on Guṇa." *Pathak Comm. Vol.* 353-358.

"Mahānāṭaka." *IHQ,* VII. 629-643 (709-723).

"The Problem of the Mahānāṭaka." *IHQ,* VII. 537-627.

"Sanskrit Literature under the Pāla Kings of Bengal." *NIA,* II (*Ross Comm. Vol.*) 263-282.

"Viśākhadatta." *B. C. Law Volume,* I. 50-57.

DEVASTHALI, G. V. *Descriptive Catalogue of Sanskrit and Prakrit Manuscripts in the Library of the University of Bombay.* Bombay, 1944.

Introduction to the Study of Viśākhadatta and his Mudrā-Rākshasa. Poona, 1948.

DIKSHIT, S. B. *Bhāratīya Jyotisha Śāstra* (History of Indian Astronomy) (in Marathi). 2nd Ed. Poona, 1931.

DIKSHITAR, V. R. R. *The Purāṇa Index*. 2 vols. Madras, 1951, 1952.

DUTTA, B. B. and SINGH, A. N. *History of Hindu Mathematics*. Lahore, 1935.

FILLIOZAT, J. *La Doctrine Classique de la Médicine Indienne—Ses Origines et ses Parallèles Grecs*. Paris, 1949.

GODE, P. K. "Date of Rākshasakāvya or Kāvyarākshasa—Before A.D. 1000." *JIH*, XIX. 312-319.

HAAS, G. *Daśarūpaka*. New York, 1912.

HAZRA, R. C. *Studies in the Puranic Records on Hindu Rites and Customs*. Dacca, 1940.

HOERNLE, A. F. R. *Studies in the Medicine of Ancient India*. Oxford, 1907.

JAIN, H. L. "Apabhraṁśa Bhāshā aur Sāhitya" (Apabhraṁśa Language and Literature) (in Hindi). *NPP*, L. 1-8; 100-121.
"Apabhraṁśa Literature." *AUS*, I. 157-185.
"Svayambhū and his two poems in Apabhraṁśa." *NUJ*, No. 1, 1935.

JOLLY, J. *Medicin*. Strassburg, 1901 (Eng. trans. "Indian Medicine", by C. G. Kashikar. Poona 1951).

KANE, P. V. *History of Alaṅkāra Literature* (Introduction to *Sāhityadarpaṇa*, 2nd Edition). Bombay 1923; *History of Sanskrit Poetics* (Intr. to *Sāhityadarpaṇa*, 3rd Ed.). Bombay, 1951.
History of Dharmaśāstra. Vol. I. Poona, 1930.

KAVI, M. R. "Date of Sāgaranandin." NIA, II. 412-419.

KAYE, G. R. *Hindu Astronomy*. Calcutta, 1924.
Hindu Mathematics. Lahore, 1889.

KEITH, A. B. *Sanskrit Drama*. Oxford, 1924; Reprint, Oxford, 1954.

KESAVA *Kalpadrukośa*. Ed. by Ramavatara Sarma, Vol. I. *GOS*. Baroda, 1928.

KONOW, Sten *Das Indische Drama*. Berlin und Leipzig, 1920.

KRISHNAMACHARIAR, M. *History of Classical Sanskrit Literature*. Madras, 1937.

LEVI, S. *Le théâtre indien*. Paric, 1890.

MIRASHI, V. V. "The Chronological Order of Rājaśekhara's Works." *Pathak Comm. Vol*. 359-366.

MOOKERJEE, S. "A dissertation on the identity of the author of the *Dhvanyāloka*." *B. C. Law Vol*. I. 179-193.

PETERSON, P.	*A third report of operations in search of Sanskrit mss. in the Bombay Circle, 1884-86.* Bombay, 1887 (=*JBBRAS*, XVIII, Extra no. 45).
	A fourth report ... 1886-92. Bombay, 1894 (=*JBBRAS*, XVIII, Extra no. 49A).
	Three reports on a search for Sanskrit mss. With an Index of books. Bombay, 1887.
RAGHAVAN, V.	"Literary Notes. (IV) The Rasaratnakośa, the Nāṭakaratnakośa and the Saṁgīta Rāja." *ABORI*, XIV. 258-263.
	"Somadevasūri, author of *Nītivākyāmṛita, Yaśastilakachampū*, etc." NIA, VI. 67-69.
RAHULA SAMKRITYAYANA.	*Purātattvanibandhāvali.* Allahabad, 1937.
RAY, P. C.	*History of Hindu Chemistry*, etc. Calcutta, 1887.
SARMA, RAMAVATARA	*Kalpadrukośa* Intr. to (GOS, Baroda, 1928).
SASTRI, H. P.	*Bauddha Gān o Dohā* (in Bengali). Calcutta 1323 B.S.
SASTRI, P. P. S.	"Problems of Identity—Viśvarūpa, the author of Bālakrīḍā and Viśvarūpāchārya *alias* Sureśvarāchārya." *Festschrift Kane*, pp. 405-407.
SCHUYLER, M.	*Bibliography of the Sanskrit Drama.* New York, 1906.
SHAHIDULLAH, M.	"Buddhist Mystic Songs." *DUS*, IV. 1 ff.
THIBAUT, G.	*Astronomie, Astrologie und Mathematic.* Strassburg, 1889.
UPADHYE, A. N.	"Harisheṇa's Dharmaparīkshā in Apabhraṁśa." *ABORI*, XXIII. 592-608.
VELANKAR, H. D.	*Jinaratnakośa* (An Alphabetical Register of Jain Works and Authors). Vol. I. Poona, 1944.
	"Varāhamihira and Utpala (in relation to Sanskrit metres.)" *C. K. Raja Presentation Volume*, pp. 141-152.
WINTERNITZ, M.	*Geschichte der indischen Literatur.* Band III. Leipzig, 1920.

(B) DRAVIDIAN: TAMIL AND KANNADA:

AIYANGAR (IYENGAR) K. Srinivasa	*Tamil Studies.* Madras, 1914.
AIYANGAR, S. Krishnaswami	*Ancient India and South Indian History.* Vol. II. Poona, 1941.
AYYAR, C. V. Narayana	*Origin and Early History of Saivism in South India.* Madras, 1936.
DIKSHITAR, V. R. R.	*Studies in Tamil Literature and History.* 2nd Ed. Madras, 1936.
HOOPER, J. S. M.	*Hymns of the Alvars.* Calcutta, 1929.

KINGSBURY & PHILLIPS — *Hymns of the Tamil Saiva Saints.* Calcutta, 1920.

MUGALI, R. S. — *The Heritage of Karnataka.*
Kannaḍa Sāhitya Charitra (in Kannaḍa). Mysore, 1953.

NARASIMHACHARYA, R. — *History of Kannaḍa Language.* Mysore, 1934
History of Kannaḍa Literature.
Karnataka Kavi Charite (in Kannada).

PILLAI, M. S. Purnalingam — *Tamil Literature.* Tinnevelly, 1929.

PILLAI, Nallasvami. — *Studies in Śaiva Siddhānta.* Madras, 1911.

PILLAI, Sundaram. — *Some Milestones in Tamil Literature.*

RICE, E. P. — *Kanarese Literature.* Calcutta, 1918.

SHARMA, S. R. — *Jainism and Karnataka Culture.* Dharwar, 1940.

CHAPTER X

POLITICAL THEORY, ADMINISTRATIVE ORGANISATION, LAW AND LEGAL INSTITUTIONS

Original Sources

(i) LITERARY

Bālakrīḍā of Viśvarūpa
See above, under "Dharmaśāstra" in "General Bibliography".

Bṛihaddharma Purāṇa
Ed. by. H. P. Sastri, *BI.* Calcûtta, 1887-1897.

Mahābhārata — See above, under "General Bibliography".

Manubhāshya of Medhātithi
See above, under "Dharmaśāstra" in "General Bibliography".

Nītivākyāmrita of Someśvara
See above, under "Polity" in "General Bibliography".

Purāṇas — See above, under "General Bibliography".

Rājataraṅgiṇī of Kalhaṇa
See above under "Historical Works" in "General Bibliography".

(ii) INSCRIPTIONS

BHANDARKAR, D. R. — *List of Inscriptions* (See above, under "Inscriptions" in "General Bibliography".)

HIRALAL. — See above, under Ch. I.

MAITREYA, A. K. — *Gauḍalekhamālā.* Rajshahi, 1319 B.S.

SEWELL, R. — See above, under Ch. VI.

Modern Works

AIYANGAR, S. Krishnaswami — *Hindu Administrative Institutions in South India.* Madras, 1931.

ALTEKAR, A. S. *Rāshṭrakūṭas and their times.* Poona, 1934.
State and Government in Ancient India. Banaras, 1949.

BENI PRASAD *The State in Ancient India.* Allahabad, 1928.
Theory of Government in Ancient India. Allahabad, 1927.

DIKSHITAR, V. R. R. *Hindu Administrative Institutions.* Madras, 1929.

GHOSHAL, U. N. *History of Hindu Political Theories.* London 1923.

JAYASWAL, K. P. *Hindu Polity.* Calcutta, 1924; 2nd Ed. Bangalore, 1943.

MAJUMDAR, R. C. (Ed.). *History of Bengal.* Vol. I. Dacca, 1943.

SASTRI, K. A. N. *The Pandyan Kingdom.* London, 1929.
The Cholas. Vol. II, Part 1. Madras, 1937.
The Theory of pre-Muslim Indian Polity. Madras, 1912.

SUBBARAO, R. "The Administrative System of the Early Gaṅga Kings of Kaliṅga." *PIHC*, III. 187-194.

TRIPATHI, R. S. See above, under "Histories of the Period" in "General Bibliography."

VENKATESWARA, S. V. *Indian Culture through the Ages.* Vol. II. Mysore, 1932.

CHAPTER XI

RELIGION AND PHILOSOPHY

Original Sources:

(See Epics, Purāṇas, Philosophy, Dharma-śāstra, Buddhist, Jain under Original Sources and Religion and Philosophy under Modern Works in General Bibliography.)

(A) GENERAL:

Modern Works

BARNETT, L. D. *Hindu Gods and Heroes.* London, 1923.

BARTH, A. *The Religions of India* (Authorised Eng. trans. by J. Wood. London, 1882).

BHANDARKAR, R. G. *Vaishṇavism, Śaivism and Minor Religious Systems.* Strassburg, 1913; Indian Edition, Poona, 1928.

Cultural Heritage of India Published by the Ramakrishna Mission Institute of Culture, Calcutta 1937, 1953 etc.

ELIOT, Sir Charles. *Hinduism and Buddhism.* 3 Vols. London. 1921. New Edition, 1953.

FARQUHAR, J. N. *Outline of the Religious Literature of India.* Oxford, 1920.

HOPKINS, E. W. *The Religions of India.* Boston, 1895.

KONOW, Sten and TUXEN, Paul. *Religions of India.* Copenhagen, 1949.

MONIER WILLIAMS, M. *Religious Thought and Life in India.* 4th Ed. London, 1891.

(B) BUDDHISM:

Original Sources

(See "Buddhist" under "Original Sources", and "Religion and Philosophy" under "Modern Works" in "General Bibliography".)

BUNYIU NANJIO. *The Chinese Buddhist Tripiṭaka.* Oxford, 1883.

Modern Works

AVALON, ARTHUR See below, under "Woodroffe, Sir John".

BAGCHI, P. C. *Studies in the Tantras.* Calcutta, 1939.

BHATTACHARYYA, B. *Indian Buddhist Iconography.* Oxford, 1924.
"Glimpses of Vajrayāna." *POC,* III. 133ff.
"Origin and Development of Vajrayāna." *IHQ,* 1927. 733-746.

BOSE, P. N. *Indian Teachers of Buddhist Universities.* Madras, 1923.

BU-STON. *History of Buddhism.* Trans. by E. Obermiller. Heidelberg, 1932.

COOMARASWAMY, A.K. *Buddha and the Gospel of Buddhism.* London, 1928.
Living Thoughts of Gotama the Buddha. London, 1948.

DAHLKE, P. *Buddhism and its Place in the Mental Life of Mankind.* London, 1927.

DASGUPTA, S. B. *Introduction to Tantric Buddhism.* Calcutta, 1950.

DAVID-NEEL, Alexandra. *Le Buddhisme, ses Doctrines et ses Methodes.* Eng. trans. *Buddhism, its doctrines and methods,* by H. N. M. Hardy and Bernard Miall. London, 1939.

DUTT, N. *Aspects of Mahāyāna Buddhism and Its Relation to Hīnayāna.* London, 1930.
Early Monastic Buddhism. 2 Vols. Calcutta.

GRÜNWEDEL, A. See below, under "Tāranātha: Edelsteinmine."

KEITH, A. B. *Buddhist Philosophy in India and Ceylon.* Oxford, 1923.

KERN, H. *Manual of Indian Buddhism.* Strassburg, 1896.
Histoire du Bouddhisme dans L'Inde. Paris, 1901.

MITRA, R. I. *Sanskrit Buddhist Literature of Nepal.* Calcutta, 1882.

OBERMILLER, E. See above, under "Bu-ston."

POUSSIN, L. de la Vallée *Bouddhisme.* Paris, 1930.
"Tantrism (Buddhist)." *ERE,* XII. 193 f.

RHYS DAVIDS, Mrs. C. A. F. *Buddhism: Its Birth and Dispersal.* London, 1934.

RHYS DAVIDS, T. W. *History of Indian Buddhism.* London, 1897.
Early Buddhism. London, 1908.
Buddhism: Its History and Literature. New Ed. London, 1926.

SCHIEFNER, A. See below, under "Tāranātha: Geschichte."

SEN, B. C. *Some Historical Aspects of the Inscriptions of Bengal.* Calcutta, 1942.

SUMPA MKHAN PO *Pag-sam-jon-zang.* Ed. by S. C. Das. Calcutta, 1908.

SUZUKI, B. L. *Outlines of Mahāyāna Buddhism.* London, 1907.
Mahāyāna Buddhism. London, 1938.

TAKAKUSU, J. *Essentials of Buddhist Philosophy.* Honolulu, 1947.

TĀRANĀTHA. *Edelsteinmine, das Buch von den Vermittlern der sieben Inspirationen.* Aus dem Tibetischen übers. v. A. Grünwedel. Petrograd, 1914. Trans. into English (Mystic Tales of Lāmā Tāranātha) by B. N. Datta. Calcutta, 1944.
Geschichte des Buddhismus in Indien. Aus dem Tibetischen übers. v. F.A. von Schiefner. St. Petersburg, 1869.

WADDELL, L. A. *The Buddhism of Tibet or Lamaism.* London, 1895.

WOODROFFE, Sir John *Introduction to Tantra Shastra.* 2nd Ed. Madras, 1952.
Principles of Tantra. 2nd Ed. Madras, 1952.
Shakti and Shakta. 4th Ed. Madras, 1951.

[Cf. *Bibliographie Bouddhique* published by Adrian Maisonneuve. Paris, 1937.]

(C) JAINISM:

(See "Jain" under "Original Sources" and "Religion and Philosophy" under "Modern Works" in "General Bibliography".)

Modern Works

AIYANGAR, S.Krishnaswami. "Jainism in South India." *Atmananda Centenary Comm. Vol.*, 1936.

ALTEKAR, A. S. *Rāshṭrakūṭas and their times.* Poona, 1934.

AYYANGAR, M. S. Ramaswami and RAO, B. Seshgiri *Studies in South Indian Jainism.* Madras 1922.

BARODIA, U. D. *History and Literature of Jainism.* Bombay, 1909.

BÜHLER, G. *Über die indische Secte der Jainas.* Vienna, 1887. Eng. trans. *(The Indian Sect of the Jainas)* by J. Burgess. London, 1903.

DESAI, M. *Jaina Sāhityano Saṁkshipta Itihāsa* (in Gujarati) ("Short History of Jain Literature"). Bombay, 1933.

FARQUHAR, J. N — See above, under "General".
FLEET, J. F. — "Sanskrit and Old Canarese Inscriptions." *IA*, XI-XII.
GLASENAPP, H. — *Der Jainismus*. Berlin, 1926.
GUERINOT, A. — *Essai de Bibliographie Jaina*. Paris, 1908.
"Notes de Bibliographie Jaina." *JA*, XIV. 48-148.
Repertoire d'Epigraphie Jaina. Paris, 1908.
La religion Djaina. Paris, 1926.
HANDIQUI, K. K — *Yaśastilaka and Indian Culture*. Sholapur, 1949.
HAYAVADANARAO, C. — *Mysore Gazetteer*. Vol. II.
NAHAR, P.C. — *Jaina-lekha-saṁgraha*. 3 vols. Calcutta, 1918-1929.
NARASIMHACHARYA, R. — *Epigraphia Carnatica*, II, Introduction.
PARIKH, R. C. — *Kāvyānuśāsana* by Āchārya Hemachandra. Vol. II, Part 1. Intr. Bombay, 1938.
RAO, B. V. KRISHNA. — "Jainism in Āndhradeśa." *JAHRS*, XII. 185-196.
RICE, B. — *Mysore and Coorg from the Inscriptions*. London, 1909.
SALETORE, B. A. — *Mediaeval Jainism*. Bombay, 1938.
SHARMA, S. R. — *Jainism and Karnataka Culture*. Dharwar, 1940.
STEVENSON, Mrs. S. — *The Heart of Jainism*. Oxford, 1915.
VAIDYA, C. V. — *History of Medieval Hindu India*. Poona, 1921 ff.

(D) VAISHṆAVISM:

Original Sources

(See "Epics and Purāṇas" under "Original Sources" and "Religion and Philosophy" under "Modern Works" in "General Bibliography".)

Modern Works

AIYANGAR, S. Krishnaswami — *Early History of Vaishṇavism in South India*. London, 1920.
Śrī Rāmānujāchārya. (Natesan) Madras.
BHANDARKAR, R. G. — *Vaishṇavism, Śaivism, etc.* See above, under "General".
FARQUHAR, J. N. — See above, under "General".
MACNICOL, N. — *Indian Theism*. London, 1915.
RAO, T. A. G. — *History of Śrī Vaishṇavas*. Madras, 1923.
RAYCHAUDHURI, H.C. — *Materials for the Study of the Early History of the Vaishṇava Sect*. 2nd Ed. Calcutta, 1936.

(E) ŚAIVISM:

Original Sources

(As in Vaishṇavism above.)

ABHINAVAGUPTA — *Paramārthasāra*. Ed. with trans. and notes by L. D. Barnett. *JRAS*, 1910. 707-747.
ADISESHA — *Paramārthasāra*. Ed. by S. S. Suryanarayana Sastri. Adyar, 1941.

Modern Works

AIYANGAR, S. Krishnaswami	*Some Contributions of South India to Indian Culture.* Calcutta, 1923. 2nd Ed. 1942.
AYYAR, C. V. Narayana	*Origin and Early History of Śaivism in South India.* Madras, 1936.
CHATTERJEE, J. C.	*Kashmir Śaivism.* Srinagar, 1914.
KINGSBURY, P. and PHILLIPS, G. E.	*Hymns of the Tamil Śaivite Saints.* Calcutta, 1921.
PILLAI, S. Satchidananda	"The Śaiva Saints of Southern India." *Cult. Her.*, II. 235-247.
SASTRI, K. A. Nilakanta	"A Historical Sketch of Śaivism." *Cult. Her.*, II. 18-34.
SUBRAMANIAN, K. R.	*Origin of Śaivism and its History in the Tamil Land.* Madras, 1941.

(F) MINOR RELIGIOUS SECTS:

Original Sources

(See "Epics" and "Purāṇas" under "Original Sources", and "Religion and Philosophy" under "Modern Works" in "General Bibliography".)

Modern Works

BANERJI, R. D.	*Eastern Indian School of Mediaeval Sculpture.* ASI, NIS, No. 47. Delhi, 1933.
	The Haihayas of Tripuri and their Monuments. MASI, No. 23. Calcutta, 1931.
BHANDARKAR, R. G.	*Vaishṇavism, Śaivism etc.* See above, under "General".
BHATTASALI, N. K.	*Iconography of Buddhist and Brahmanical Sculptures in the Dacca Museum.* Dacca, 1929.
CHANDA, R. P.	*Mediaeval Indian Sculptures in the British Museum.* London, 1936.
COUSENS, H.	*Chālukyan Architecture of the Kanarese Districts.* ASI, NIS, No. 42. Calcutta, 1926.
	Mediaeval Temples of the Dakhan. ASI, NIS, No. 48. Calcutta, 1931.
	Somanātha and other Mediaeval Temples in Kāthiāwād. ASI, NIS, No. 45. Calcutta, 1931.
FARQUHAR, J. N	See above, under "Religion and Philosophy" in "General Bibliography".
HAZRA, R. C.	*Studies in the Puranic Records on Hindu Rites and Customs.* Dacca, 1940.
MACNICOL, N.	*Indian Theism.* London, 1915.
MAJUMDAR, R.C (Ed.).	*History of Bengal.* Vol. I. Dacca, 1943.
PAYNE, E. A.	*The Saktas.* Calcutta, 1933.
SANKALIA, H. D	*Archaeology of Gujarat.* Bombay, 1941.
SASTRI, H. Krishna.	*South Indian Images of Gods and Goddesses.* Madras, 1916.

SCHRADER, F. O. *Introduction of the Pāñcharātra and the Ahirbudhnya Saṁhitā.* Adyar, 1916.

WOODROFFE, Sir John See above, under "Buddhism".

(G) ICONOGRAPHY:

Modern Works

BENERJEA, J. N. *Development of Hindu Iconography.* Calcutta, 1941.
"Vishṇu and Sūrya—A Study in Cult Icons." *JISOA,* XIII. 55-129; XIV. 1-74; XVI. 47-100.

BANERJI, R. D. *Eastern Indian School of Medieval Sculpture.* Delhi, 1933.

BHATTACHARYA, B. C. *Indian Images:* Vol. I. Brahmanic Iconography. Calcutta, 1931; Vol. II. Jain Iconography. Lahore, 1939.

BHATTACHARYYA, B. *Indian Buddhist Iconography.* Oxford, 1924.
Ed. *Sādhanamālā.* GOS. Baroda, 1925, 1928.

BHATTASALI, N. K. See above, under "Minor Religious Sects".

COOMARASWAMY, A.K. *Dance of Śiva.* With an introductory preface by R. Rolland. Bombay, 1948.

FOUCHER, A. *The Beginnings of Buddhist Art and other Essays in Indian and Central-Asian Archaeology.* Revised by the author and trans. by L.A. Thomas and F.W. Thomas. Paris, 1917.
L'Iconographie boundhique de l' Inde. 2 vols. Paris, 1900, 1905.

GRÜNWEDEL, A. *Buddhistische Kunst in Indien.* Berlin, 1893 (Eng. trans. "Buddhist Art in India". by Agnes C. Gibson. Revised and enlarged by J. Burgess. London, 1901).

HAVELL, E. B. *Indian Sculpture and Painting.* London, 1908; 2nd Ed. London, 1928.

JOUVEAU-DUBREUIL, G. *Iconography of Southern India* (Trans. from the French by A.C. Martin). Paris, 1937.

MAJUMDAR, R. C. (Ed.). *History of Bengal.* Vol. I. Dacca, 1943.

RAO, T. A. Gopinatha *Elements of Hindu Iconography.* 2 vols. Madras, 1914-1916.

SARASWATI, S. K. "Early Sculptures of Bengal." *JDL,* XXX. 1-85.

SASTRI, H. Krishna See above, under "Minor Religious Sects."

(H) TANTRIK RELIGION:

Modern Works

BENDALL, C. *Catalogue of Buddhist Sanskrit Manuscripts in the University Library, Cambridge.* Cambridge, 1883.

GEDEN, A. S. "Tantras." *ERE,* XII. 192-193.

MACNICOL, N. *Indian Theism*. Oxford, 1915.
MONIER-WILLIAMS, M. *Brahmanism and Hinduism*. London, 1891.
SASTRI, H. P. *Catalogue of Palm Leaf and Selected Paper Manuscripts*. Calcutta, 1905.
WINDISCH, E. and EGGELING, J. *Catalogue of Sanskrit Manuscripts in the Library of the India Office*. Part IV. London, 1894.
WINTERNITZ, M. *History of Indian Literature*. Vol. I. Calcutta. 1927.
WOODROFFE, Sir John See above, under "Buddhism".

(I) PARIS:

HODIVALA, S. H. "Jadi Rānā and the Kissah-i-Sanjan." *JBBRAS*, XXIII. 349-370.
Studies in Parsi History. Bombay, 1920.
IRANI, M. S. "The Story of Sanjan." POC, X. 68-85.
TARAPOREWALA, I. J. S. "The Exact Date of the Arrival of the Parsis in India." *Festschrift Kane*, pp. 506-514.

(J) PHILOSOPHY:

Original Sources

(See under "Epics", "Purāṇas" and "Philosophy" under "Original Sources" and "Religion and Philosophy" under "Modern Works" in "General Bibliography".)

Modern Works

BHATTACHARYYA, H. D. (Ed.). *The Philosophies*. Cultural Heritage of India. 2nd Ed. Vol. III. Calcutta, 1953.
CHATTERJEE, J. C. *Kashmir Śaivism*. Srinagar, 1914.
DASGUPTA, S. N. *History of Indian Philosophy*. 4 vols. Cambridge, 1932 ff.
DEUSSEN, P. *Outline of the Vedānta System of Philosophy according to Śaṅkara*. Eng. trans. by J. H. Woods and C. B. Runkle. 2nd Ed. Cambridge Mass. 1915.
GARBE, R. *Philosophy of Ancient India*. Chicago, 1897.
GHATE, V. S. *The Vedānta*. Poona, 1926.
GROUSSET, R. *Le Philosophie Indiennes*. Paris, 1931.
JHA, G. N. *The Prabhākara School of Pūrva Mīmāṁsā*. Allahabad, 1911.
Pūrva Mīmāṁsā in its sources. Benares, 1942.
KEITH, A. B. *Indian Logic and Atomism*. Oxford, 1921.
MASSON-OURSEL, P. *Le Philosophie en Orient*. Paris, 1938.
MAX MÜLLER, F. *Six Systems of Indian Philosophy*. London, 1889.
RADHAKRISHNAN, S. *Indian Philosophy*. 2 vols. London, 1923, 1927.
SRINIVASACHARI, P.N. *The Philosophy of Bhedābheda*. 2nd Ed. Madras, 1950.
STRAUSS, Otto. *Indische Philosophie*. Munchen, 1925.

CHAPTERS XII-XIII

SOCIAL AND ECONOMIC LIFE

Original Sources

(i) INDIAN:

(See (iii) Purāṇas and (iv) Dharmaśāstra; Kalhaṇa in (v) Historical Works; Halāyudha in (vi) Lexicons; Rājaśekhara in (xi) Poetics, &c. and in (xiv) Belles-Lettres;—all under (A) Brahmanical; Siddharshi under (C) Jain; and Dhanapāla under (D) Apabhraṁśa;—in "General Bibliography" above.)

Bṛihaddharma Purāṇa
Ed. by H.P. Sastri. BI. Calcutta, 1887-1897.

Dharmakośā-Vyavahārakāṇḍa
Vol. I, Parts I-III. Wai, 1937-39.

Kṛityakalpataru of Lakshmīdhara
Vyavahāra-kāṇḍa. Ed. by K.V.R. Aiyangar. GOS. Baroda, 1953.

Kuṭṭanīmata of Dāmodara
Ed. in KM, III. Bombay, 1899.
Ed. with comm. by T.M. Tripathi. Bombay, 1924.
Ed. by Madhusudan Kaul. Calcutta, 1944.
German trans. by J.J. Meyer. Leipzig, 1903.

Parāśara-mādhavīya *Parāśara-smṛiti* with the comm. of Sāyaṇa Mādhavāchārya. Critically Ed. by V. S. Islampurkar. 3 vols. BSS. Bombay, 1893-1919.
Parāśara-smṛiti with the gloss of Mādhavāchārya. Ed. with notes by M. Chandrakanta Tarkalankara. 3 vols. BI. Calcutta, 1890-1899.

Paribhāshāprakāśa (part of *Vīramitrodaya)* of Mitramiśra
Chowkhamba Sanskrit Series. Benares, 1906.

Ratirahasya of Kokkoka
Ed. by Devidatta Sarma. 1902.
Ed. with comm. and notes. Bombay, 1922.

Saṁskāraprakāśa (part of *Vīramitrodaya)* of Mitramiśra
Chowkhamba Sanskrit Series. Benares, 1906.

Smṛitichandrikā of Devaṇṇabhaṭṭa
Ed. by L. Srinivasacharya. 6 vols. Mysore, 1914-21.
Ed. by J.R. Gharpure. Bombay, 1918.
Eng. trans. by J.R. Gharpure. Bombay, 1948 ff.

Smṛityarthasāra of Śrīdhara
Ed. by Ranganatha Sastri Vaidya. ASS. Poona, 1912.

Yājñavalkya-Smṛiti with the comm. of Aparārka. ASS. Poona, 1903-04.

(ii) NON-INDIAN:

(See Ferrand, *Relations* &c (in General Bibliography, "Arabic") especially extracts from Abū'l Faraj Muhammad bin Isḥāk, Abū

Zaid, Al Iṣtakhrī, Ibn al-Faḳīh, Ibn Khordādbah, Ibn Rosteh, Khuwārizmī, Mas'ūdī, Muṭahhar bin Tahir al-Maḳdisī, Sulaimān and Ya'ḳūbī; also, Elliot and Dowson, *History of India* &c., and Hodivala, *Studies in Indo-Muslim History*, as given in General Bibliography, "Muslim".)

Original Sources

INSCRIPTIONS:

(See inscriptions in *ARSIE, EI, IA, MAR, SII*, etc.)

Modern Works

AIYANGAR, K. V. Rangaswami — *Aspects of Ancient Indian Economic Thought*. Benares, 1934.

ALTEKAR, A. S. — *Education in Ancient India*. 4th Ed. Banaras, 1951.

Position of Women in Hindu Civilisation. Benares. 1938.

Rāshṭrakūṭas and their times. Poona, 1934.

BANERJEE, G. — *Hindu Law of Marriage and Strīdhana*. Tagore Law Lectures. Calcutta, 1896.

CHAKLADAR, H. C. — *Social Life in Ancient India*. Calcutta, 1929.

DAS, S. K. — *Educational System of the Ancient Hindus*. Calcutta, 1930.

Economic History of Ancient India. Calcutta, 1925.

HOPKINS, E. W. — *Ethics of India*. London, 1925.

INDRA. — *The Status of Women in Ancient India*. Lahore, 1940.

GHOSHAL, U. N. — *Contributions to the History of the Hindu Revenue System*. Calcutta, 1929.

The Agrarian System in Ancient India. Calcutta, 1930.

GUPTA, K. M. — *The Land System in South India between c. 800 A.D. and 1200 A.D.* Lahore, 1933.

JHA, Ganganatha — *Hindu Law in its Sources*. Vol. I. Allahabad, 1930.

KANE, P. V. — *History of Dharmaśāstra*. Vols. II-IV. Poona, 1941, 1946, 1953.

MACKENZIE, J. — *Hindu Ethics*. (Religious Quest of India Series, Oxford University). London, 1922.

PRAN NATH. — *A Study in the Economic Condition of Ancient India*. London, 1929.

SASTRI, K. A. Nilakanta — *The Cholas*. Vol. II, Part I. Madras, 1937.

SANKALIA, H. D. — *The University of Nalanda*. Madras, 1934.

SUBBA RAO, N. S. — *Economic and Political Conditions in Ancient India*. Mysore, 1911.

VENKATESWARA, S.V. — *Indian Culture through the Ages*. 2 vols. London, 1928, 1932.

WARMINGTON, E. H. — *The Commerce between the Roman Empire and India*. Cambridge, 1928.

YULE, Col. Henry and BURNELL, A. C. — *Hobson-Jobson*. New Ed. by W. Crooke. London, 1903.

CHAPTER XIV

COLONIAL AND CULTURAL EXPANSION

Modern Works

BAGCHI, P. C. *India and China*. Calcutta, 1944; 2nd Ed. Bombay, 1950.

Le Canon Bouddhique en Chine. 2 vols. Paris, 1927, 1938.

"Sino-Indian Relations." *SIS*, I. 65-84; 161-166.

BOSE, P. *The Hindu Colony of Cambodia*. Adyar, 1927.

The Indian Colony of Champa. Adyar, 1926.

CHATTERJI, B. R. *Indian Cultural Influence in Cambodia*. Calcutta, 1928.

India and Java. Calcutta, 1933.

COEDES, G. *Les États Hindouisés D'Indochine et D'Indonésie. Paris*, 1948.

Inscriptions du Cambodge. Vols. I-V. Paris.

DAS, S. C. *Indian Pandits in the Land of Snow*. Ed. by N. C. Das. Calcutta, 1893.

"Contributions on the Religion, History, &c. of Tibet." *JASB*, 1881, 187 ff; 1882, 1 ff; 87 ff.

DE BOER, T. J. *History of the Philosophy of Islam*. London, 1903.

FRANCKE, A. H. *Antiquities of Indian Tibet*. Calcutta, 1914-26.

GOLDZIHER, I. *Vorlesungen über den Islam*. Heidelberg, 1910.

GROUSSET, R. *The Civilisations of the East—India* (Eng. trans.). London, 1932.

The Civilisations of the East—China (Eng. trans.). London, 1934.

HITTI, P. K. *History of the Arabs*. 1937.

HOURANI, G. F. *Arab Seafaring in the Indian Ocean in ancient and early Medieval Times* (Princeton Univ. Press, 1951).

MAJUMDAR, R. C. *Ancient Indian Colonies in the Far East*. Vol. I: Champā. Lahore, 1927; Vol. II; Suvarṇadvīpa. Parts 1 and 2. Dacca, 1937, 38.

Kambujadeśa. Madras, 1944.

Hindu Colonies in the Far East. Calcutta, 1944.

Inscriptions of Kambuja (As. Soc. Monograph). Calcutta, 1953.

MUKHERJI, P. K. *Indian Literature in China and the Far East*. Calcutta, 1931.

OAKESHOTT, W. F. *Commerce and Society*. Oxford, 1936.

O'LEARY de Lacy *Arabia before Muhammad*.

PETECH, L. *A Study of the Chronicles of Ladakh* (Suppl. to *IHQ*, XIII-XIV). Calcutta, 1939.

Northern India according to the Shui-Ching-Chu. Rome, 1950.

SARKAR, H. B. *Indian Influences on the Literature of Java and Bali*. Calcutta, 1934.

SASTRI, K. A. N. *Foreign Notices of South India.* Madras, 1939.

South Indian Influences in the Far East. Bombay, 1949.

History of Śrīvijaya. Madras, 1949.

TITUS, M. T. *Indian Islam.* London, 1930.

WALES, H. G. Q. *The Making of Greater India.* London, 1951.

CHRONOLOGY

A.D.	
559-567	Guhasena of Valabhī (p. 214).
605	A victorious Chinese General carries away 1350 Buddhist books from Champā (p. 436).
618-907*	T'ang dynasty in China (p. 444).
c.625	Rāshṭrakūṭa family immigrates from Laṭṭalūra to Ellichpur in Berār (p. 1).
637	Defeat of Yazdagird III, the Sasanid king of Irān, at Qadisiyya (p. 353).
641	Battle of Nahawand (p. 353).
662	Jaths of Kikānan resist the Arabs (p. 127).
678	Ravisheṇa, author of *Padmapurāṇa* (p. 183).
704-774	Amoghavajra, Tāntrik teacher (p. 263).
716	Settlement of the Irānians at Sanjān, acc. to Dastur Aspandiārji Kamdin (p. 354).
717	Kambuja sends an embassy to China (p. 416).
722	Kambuja helps an Annamese chief against China (p. 416).
725	Junaid (p. 39).
c.730	Rise of the Thai kingdom in Yunnan known as Nan-chao (Mithilā-rāshṭra) (p. 433).
c.730	Mithilā-rāshṭra throws off the Chinese yoke (p. 422).
c.730-756	Nāgabhaṭa (Pratīhāra) (p. 20).
c.731-796	Nandivarman Pallavamalla (p. 168).
732	Sañjaya, successor of Sannāha in Central Java, (p. 427), conquers Kambuja (p. 416).
c.733	Accession of Dantidurga (p. 1).
c.733-758	Dantidurga, Rāshṭrakūṭa (pp. 1, 3, 20).
c.738	Battle near Navsāri in which the Arabs were worsted (p. 2).
c.739	Arabs of Sindh invade the kingdom of the Saindhavas (p. 99).
742-826	Cheraman Perumāḷ, last of the Perumāḷs of Kerala (p. 165).
c.743	Dantidurga accompanies the Chālukya suzerain in his expedition against Kāñchī (p. 2).
745	Vanarāja Chāpa builds Aṇahilapāṭaka (p. 103).
747	Death of Vikramāditya II (p. 2).
c.747-752	Devendravarman II, E. Gaṅga (p. 140).
749	'Abbasids supplant the Caliphs of the Umayyad dynasty (p. 125).
c.750-c.770	Gopāla, Pāla (p. 45).
750-850	Tibetan kings exercise political domination in parts of India, acc. to Tibetan Chronicles (p. 446).
c.752	Dantidurga overthrows the Chālukya emperor (p. 1).

*The date 618-905 given on p. 60 should be corrected accordingly.

753	Bappa, the Guhila, is said to have abdicated the throne (p. 109).
753	Dantidurga becomes the master of the whole of Mahārāshṭra, and assumes imperial titles (p. 2).
753, 771, 773, 778	Indian embassies to Baghdād (p. 450).
754	King Ko-lo-fong of Nan-chao (Mithilā-rāshṭra) defeats the Chinese (p. 433).
754-775	Caliph Al-Manṣūr (pp. 124, 125, 450).
755-797	Khri-sroṅ-lde-btsan, Tibetan king (pp. 58, 446).
756	Bhartṛivaḍḍha, Chāhamāna ruler, acknowledges Nāgabhaṭa as suzerain (p. 20).
c. 756	Hishām appointed governor of Sindh (p. 99).
757	Pṛithivīndra-varman occupies the throne of Champā on the death of Rudra-varman (p. 423).
c. 757-860	Dynasty of Pāṇḍuraṅga in Champā (p. 423).
c. 758-773	Kṛishṇa I, Rāshṭrakūṭa (pp. 3, 102).
759-765	Agrabodhi VII, Ceylon (p. 169).
c. 762	Accession of Vajrāditya of Kāshmir (p. 115).
c. 764	Death of Vijayāditya I, E. Chālukya (p. 133).
c. 764-c. 799	Vishṇuvardhana, E. Chālukya (p. 133).
765-785	Mahendra II Śilāmeghavarṇa, Ceylon (p. 169).
c. 765-815	Neḍuñjaḍaiyan (also known as Jaṭilavarman, Māṟañjaḍaiyan, Parāntaka, Varaguṇa I), Pāṇḍya (pp. 157,247).
768	Kṛishṇa I, Rāshṭrakūṭa, encamps at Manne (p 160).
768-772	Hishām ibn 'Amr at-Taghlibī, governor of Sindh (p. 115).
760	Caliph sends an expedition against Kābul (p. 126).
c. 770	Accession of Jayāpīḍa of Kāshmir (p. 116).
c. 770-810	Dharmapāla, Pāla (pp. 45, 50).
771	Kambuja king visits imperial court in China (p. 416).
c. 772	Incorporation of the whole of the modern Hyderābād State in the Rāshṭrakūṭa empire (p. 3).
c. 773	Death of Kṛishṇa I. Rāshṭrakūta (p. 3).
774	Javanese raiders burn the sacred temple in Champā and carry away the image (p. 423).
775-785	Caliph Al-Mahdi (p. 127).
775-809	Three Caliphates of 'Abbasids (p. 126).
c. 776	Arabs send another expedition against Barada p. 99).
c. 778 (or earlier)	Accession of Vatsarāja, Pratīhāra (p. 22).
778	Date of composition of *Kuvalayamālā* at Jāvālipura (Jālor) (pp. 21, 209).
778	Erection of the temple of goddess Tārā at Chandī Kalasan by a Śailendra king (p. 440).
c. 780	Accession of Dhruva, Rāshṭrakūṭa (p. 4).
780-793	Dhruva, Rāshṭrakūṭa (p. 160).

782 Dharaṇīndra-varman, the Śailendra king, has as his *guru* Kumāraghosha, inhabitant of Gauḍa (p. 415).

783 Completion of *Harivaṁśapurāṇa* by Jinasena at Vardhamānapura (pp. 21, 182).

783 Indrāyudha, the ruler of the North (p. 23).

783 Jayavarāha, of Sauryamaṇḍala (p. 102).

785-790 Udaya or Dappula II, Ceylon (p. 169).

786-809 Caliph Harun Al-Rashīd (pp. 127, 450, 451).

786 Caliph sends second expedition against Kābul (p. 126).

787 Another Javanese raid in Champā (p. 423).

c. 787 Chinese emperor makes an alliance with the Caliph of Baghdād and some Indian princes for security against Tibetans, acc. to a Chinese author (p. 446).

788-812 Śivamāra II, W. Gaṅga (p. 160).

c. 788-820 Śaṅkarāchārya (pp. 304, 358).

c. 790 Dhruva, Rāshṭrakūṭa, returns to the south from his northern campaign laden with rich booty (p. 5).

790-794 Mahendra III Śilāmeghavarṇa, Ceylon (p. 169).

793 Indra-varman of Champā renews diplomatic relations with China, and sends presents of rhinoceros and buffaloes to the emperor (p. 424).

793-814 Govinda III, Rāshṭrakūṭa (pp. 8, 160).

794-795 Conflict between Nāgabhaṭa and the Rāshṭrakūṭas (p. 26).

794-805 Agrabodhi VIII, Ceylon (p. 169).

795 Chinese Emperor, Te-tsong, receives an autographed Buddhist manuscript from the king of Wu-ch'a (Uḍra) (p. 64).

c. 795 Govinda III, Rāshṭrakūṭa, becomes the undisputed overlord of the Deccan (p. 6).

c. 796-847 Dantiga-Danti-varman, Vajrameghavarman, Later Pallava (p. 168).

798-804 Mu-Khri-btsan-po, Tibetan king (p. 446).

799 Death of Vishnuvardhana IV of Veṅgī (p. 8).

c. 799 Vijayāditya II becomes king of Veṅgī (pp. 8, 133).

c. 799-847 Vijayāditya II, E. Chālukya (p. 133).

c. 800 Durgasiṁha, grammarian (p. 190).

c. 800 Northern campaigns of Govinda III, Rāshṭrakūṭa (p. 8).

c. 800 Chitra vāhana II of Āluvakheḍa (p. 164).

c. 800-c. 1000 Dynasty of Prālambha in Kāmarūpa (p. 61).

801 Arrival of Irānian emigrants at Diu, acc. to *Quissa-i-Sanjān* (p. 353).

c. 801 Accession of Hari-varman, Champā (p. 424).

802 Jaya-varman II becomes king of Kambuja (p. 417).

802	Govinda III, Rāshṭrakūṭa, defeats the confederacy of Pallava, Pāṇḍya Kerala, and Gaṅga rulers (p. 8).
c.802	Govinda III, Rāshṭrakūṭa, defeats Vijayāditya II and puts Bhīma Salukki on the Veṅgī throne (p. 8).
802, 807	Pyu king sends embassies to China (p. 433).
803	King of Champā conquers the two Chinese districts of Hoan and Ai, acc. to Chinese history (p. 424).
c.804	Govinda III, Rāshṭrakūṭa, invades Kāñchī (p. 151).
804-816	Ral-pa-can, Tibetan king, acc. to Francke (p. 79, n. 6).
805-821	Dappula II (or III), Ceylon (p. 169).
808	Rādhanpur grant (p. 133).
c.810-850	Devapāla, Pāla (p. 50).
812	Baroda plate (p. 102).
c.813	Chippaṭajayāpīḍa of Kāshmir killed through the intrigue of his maternal uncles (p. 116).
813-833	Caliph Al-Ma'mūn (pp. 106, 126, 127, 128).
814	Death of Govinda III, Rāshṭrakūṭa (p. 134).
814-878	Amoghavarsha, Rāshṭrakūṭa (pp. 8, 11, 31, 161), 190).
815-862	Śrīmāra Śrīvallabha, Pāṇḍya (p. 158).
815	Ins. of Hari-varman of Champā mentioning invasion of Kambuja by him, and defeat of China (p. 418).
817	Vijayāditya II of Veṅgī heads a rebellion against Rāshṭrakūṭa Amoghavarsha (p. 9).
817-836	Ral-pa-can, Tibetan king (pp. 58, 79, n. 7, 446).
817-853	Rājamalla I, W. Gaṅga (p. 161).
c.820-860	Vikrānta-varman III, Champā (p. 424).
c.821	Amoghavarsha, Rāshṭrakūṭa, becomes a major and assumes reins of administration (p. 10).
821-824	Agrabodhi IX, Ceylon (p. 169).
824-825	Origin of the Kollam or Malayālam era (p. 165.
824-844	Sena Śilāmeghavarṇa, Ceylon (p. 169).
825	Settlement of Irānians at Sanjān, acc. to *Quissa-i-Sanjān* (p. 353).
829	Harjara-varman (p. 60).
c.830	Amoghavarsha, Rāshṭrakūṭa, inflicts a signal defeat on Vijayāditya II of Veṅgī (p. 9).
c.830	Death of Karkka of the Gujarāt branch of the Rāshtrakūtas (p. 10).
832	King of Nan-chao (Mithilā-rāshṭra) invades the Pyu kingdom and plunders the capital city (p. 433).
832	Charter by Jāika I, Saindhava king, as regent of his brother (p. 100).
833	Death of Nāgāvaloka (Nāgabhaṭa II), acc. to *Prabhāvaka-charita* (p. 27).

836,862	The earliest and latest known dates of Bhoja, Pratihāra (p. 32).
c.841-842	King Lakshmaṇarāja of Ḍāhala-maṇḍala (p. 87).
841	Index to the *Nyāyasūtras* by Vāchaspati (p. 204).
842	Chaṇḍamahāsena, of a branch of the Chāhamānas at Dhavalapurī (mod. Dholpur) (p. 108).
844-848	Ibn Khordādbah (pp. 413, 419).
844-879	Sena II, Ceylon (p. 170).
c.845	Dhruva I of the Gujarāt branch of Rāshṭrakūṭas killed in war against Amoghavarsha (p. 10).
c.845	Accession of Akālavarsha, Gujarāt branch of Rāshtrakūtas (p. 10).
c.845-880	Kokkalla I, Kalachuri (p. 30).
c.847	Death of Vijayāditya II, E. Chālukya (p. 134).
c.847-872	Tellāṟṟerinda Nandivarman—Kampavarman, Later Pallava (p. 168).
c.848	Death of Vishṇuvardhana V, E. Chālukya, after a rule of 18 or 20 months (p. 135).
848-892	Vijayāditya III, E. Chālukya (p. 135).
850	Vigrahapala Narayanapala.
c.850-871	Parakesari Vijiyālaya Choḷadeva (p. 153).
851	Sulaimān's Arab account of India (pp. 32, 52, 255, n. 56, 413).
c.853	Asaga composes eight works including *Vardhamāna-charita* at Dharalā in Choḷadeśa (p. 183).
853-870	Nītimārga I, W. Gaṅga (p. 161).
853-880	Pṛithvīpati I, collateral line of W. Gaṅgas (p. 161).
854	Death of Jaya-varman II, Kambuja (p. 418).
854-877	Jaya-varman III, Kambuja (p. 418).
c.855-856	End of the rule of the Kārkoṭa dynasty in Kāshmir, and the foundation of the Utpala dynasty (pp. 116-7).
855/56-883	Avantivarman, Kāshmir (pp. 117, 245, 369).
c.857	Date of Jayasiṁhasūri's Prakrit comm. on *Upadeśamālā* (p. 209).
c.860	End of the war between Amoghavarsha and the Gujarāt branch of Rāshṭrakūṭas (p. 10).
c.860	Amoghavarsha, Rāshṭrakūṭa, marries his daughter Chandrobalabbe to Būtuga, a Gaṅga prince (p. 9).
c.860-895	Indra-varman II, Champā (p. 425).
c.860-985	Bhrigu dynasty of Champā (p. 424).
861	Parabala, Rāshṭrakūṭa, rules in Central India (p. 49).
862	Embassy from Pyu kingdom visits China (p. 433).
c.862-880	Varagunavarman, Pāṇḍya (p. 159).
868-890	Vikramāditya I, Bāṇa (p. 163).

c.870 Ya'qūb ibn Layth conquers Kābul and Zābul (pp. 112, 126).

870 Jayāditya II of the Malayaketu dynasty of Vijayapura (p. 93).

870-907 Rājamalla II, W. Gaṅga (p. 161).

c.871-907 Āditya I, Choḷa (p. 153).

872-903 Ṣaffarids (p. 128).

872-913 Nṛipatuṅgavarman, Later Pallava (p. 168).

874 Rāṇaka II, Saindhava (p. 101).

c.875 Ya'kūbī (p. 419).

877 Indra-varman II of Champā sends an embassy to China (p. 425).

877-889 Indra-varman, Kambuja (p. 420).

c.878 Bāṇas and Vaidumbas defeat W. Gaṅgas and Noḷambas at the battle of Soremaṭi (p. 163).

c.878 Death of Amoghavarsha I, Rāshṭrakūṭa, and the accession of his son Kṛishṇa II (p. 11).

878-914 Kṛishṇa II, Rāshṭrakūṭa (pp. 11, 12, 31, 88).

879, Oct. 20 Epoch of the Newārī era (p. 58-9).

879-890 Udaya II (or I), Ceylon (p. 170).

879-900 'Amr ibn Layth (p. 113).

879-926 Rāghavadeva, Nepāl (p. 59).

880 Uddyotana becomes an Āchārya (p. 296).

c.880 Pallavas defeat Pāṇḍyas at Śrīpuṛambiyam near Kumbhakonam (pp. 152, 159).

880-900 Mārasiṁha II, collateral line of W. Gaṅgas (p. 161).

c.880-900 Parāntaka Vīranārāyaṇa Pāṇḍya (p. 159).

883 Death of Avantivarman, Kāshmir (p. 117).

883-902 Śaṅkaravarman of the Utpala dynasty of Kāshmir (p. 112).

c.885 Death of Bhoja (p. 33).

886 Agguka IV, Saindhava (p. 101).

888 End of the reign of Guṇaka-Vijayāditya, E. Chālukya (p. 88).

890-907 Kāśyapa IV Śrīsaṅghabodhi, Ceylon (p. 170). inscription (p. 136).

892-922 Chālukya-Bhīma I (p. 136).

893 Earliest known date of Mahendrapāla I, Pratīhāra (p. 33).

893 Balavarman, the Chālukya, in Saurāshṭra (p. 101).

c.893 Āditya I, Choḷa, defeats Aparājita, Pallava (p. 152).

c.896-905 Jayasiṁha-varman, Champā (p. 425).

898, 910 Known years of Balitung (Dharmodaya Mahāśambhu), Java (p. 428).

899 Avanivarman ruling as a vassal of Pratīhāra Mahendrapāla (p. 101).

c.900 Rājaśekhara (p. 181).

c.900 Talcher plate of Śivakaradeva (p. 77).

c.900 Death of Yaśo-varman, Kambuja (p. 421).

c.900-c.920	Māṛavarman Rājasiṁha II, Pāṇḍya (p. 159).
c.900-925	Harsha, Chandella (p. 84).
900-940	Pṛithvīpati II, collateral line of W. Gaṅgas (p. 161).
902	Ibn al-Faḳīh (p. 413).
903	Ibn Rosteh (p. 419).
904(or 905)	San-fo-tsi (Śailendra empire) sends an embassy to China (p. 414).
904, 915	Known dates of Jāika II, Saindhava (p. 101).
905-910	Bhadra-varman III, Champā (p. 425).
906	Queen Sugandhā deprived of her power, and Pārtha, ten-year old son of Nirjitavarman, placed on the throne of Kāshmir (p. 119).
907	Accession of Parāntaka I, Choḷa (p. 170).
907	Last known date of Mahendrapāla (p. 33).
907-917	Kāśyapa V, Abhaya Śilāmeghavarṇa, Ceylon (p. 170).
907-935	Nītimārga II, W. Gaṅga (p. 161).
907-953	Parāntaka I, Choḷa (pp. 154, 171).
c.908	Death of Nārāyaṇapāla, Pāla (p. 53).
c.911-971	Indra-varman III, Champā (p. 426).
c.912	Accession of Mahīpāla, Pratīhāra (p. 35).
914	Death of Kṛishṇa III, Rāshṭrakūṭa, and accession of Indra (p. 12).
914	Queen Sugandhā of Kāshmir advances towards the capital to regain her power (p. 119).
914-922	Indra III, Rāshṭrakūṭa (pp. 12-13).
914	Indra III, Rāshṭrakūṭa, performs *tulāpurusha* (p. 399 n. 255).
914	Dharaṇīvarāha, the Chāpa ruleṛ (p. 103).
c.915	Accession of Dakshottama in Matarām (p. 428).
c.915	Battle of Veḷḷūr in which the Choḷas defeat the Pāṇḍyas and the Sinhalese (p. 154).
c.915	Parāntaka Choḷa defeats the Vaidumbas of Renāṇḍu and uproots the Bāṇas with the aid of Pṛithvīpati II, W. Gaṅga (p. 155).
915-916	Visit of Al Mas'ūdī to India (p. 35).
c.915-935	Śivagupta, Somavaṁśī (p. 146).
c.916	Abū Zaid Ḥasan, Arab writer (p. 413).
916	Destruction of Kanauj by Rāshṭrakūṭas (p. 35).
917	A great famine breaks out in Kāshmir (p. 119).
917-918	Dappula III (or IV), Ceylon (p. 170).
918-930	Dappula IV (or V), Ceylon (p. 170).
c.920	Choḷas defeat and expel Rājasiṁha II, Pāṇḍya (p. 154).
920	Traditional date of the death of Nāthamuni (p. 312).
921	Nirjitavarman of Kāshmir deposes Pārtha and assumes royalty (p. 119).
922	Death of Indra III, Rāshṭrakūṭa, and accession of Amoghavarsha II (p. 13).

c.922	Death of Chālukya-Bhīma I (p. 136).
c.922	Vijayāditya IV succeeds his father Chālukya-Bhīma I (p. 137).
c.922	Death of Vijayāditya IV, E. Chālukya, after a reign of six months (p. 137).
c.922 end	Amma I, *alias* Vishṇuvardhana, succeeds his father Vijayāditya IV (p. 137).
922-929	Amma I, E. Chālukya (p. 137).
923	Death of Nirjitavarman after placing another son Chakravarman on the throne of Kāshmir (p. 119).
c.925	Accession of Yaśovarman or Lakshavarman, son of Harsha, Chandella (p. 84).
c.927-936	Govinda IV, Rāshṭrakūṭa (p. 137).
c.928	End of the kingdom of Matarām, Java (p. 427).
929	Rule of Tāla Vikramāditya (II) and Bhīma II, E. Chālukya (p. 137).
929	Kaṇṭhika-Vijayāditya IV succeeds his father Amma I, E. Chālukya (p. 137).
c.929	Accession of Siṇḍok in Eastern Java (p. 430).
930	Assassination of Bhīma II after a rule of eight months (p. 137).
930-933	Udaya II (or II), Ceylon (p. 171).
930-936	Malla or Yuddhamalla (II). E. Chālukya (p. 138).
932	Muñjāla composes *Laghumānasa* (on mathematics) (p. 200).
933	Devasena, author of *Nayachakra* and other works (p. 216).
933-942	Sena III, Ceylon (p. 171).
935-946	Period of the rule of Bhīma II, Chālukya, according to a record (p. 138).
935-970	Janamejaya Mahābhavagupta, Somavaṁśī (p. 147).
936	Amoghavarsha III overthrows Govinda IV, and occupies the Rāshṭrakūṭa throne (p. 14).
936	First Parsi settlement at Sanjān (p. 353).
936-939	Amoghavarsha III, Rāshṭrakūṭa (pp. 13, 14, 162).
937	Būtuga II ousts Rājamalla III, W. Gaṅga (p. 161).
937	Death of Uddyotana (p. 296).
937	Chakravarman of Kāshmir loses life at the hands of robbers (p. 119).
939	Unmattāvanti of Kāshmir places Śūravarman II on the throne after declaring him as his son (p. 120).
939	End of the Utpala dynasty in Kāshmir (p. 120).
939	Accession of Yaśaskara, Kāshmir (pp. 120, 244).
939	Death of Amoghavarsha and accession of his son Kṛishna III (p. 14).
939-948	Yaśaskara, Kāshmir (pp. 120, 369).

939-967	Kṛishṇā III, Rāshṭrakūṭa (pp. 14, 15, 139, 162, 171, 190).
940	Death of Pṛithvīpati II, collateral W. Gaṅga line (pp. 155, 162).
941	Pampa composes *Ādi Purāṇa* and *Pampa Bhārata* (p. 224).
941 (or 942)	Harsha-varman succeeds his father Jaya-varman IV, Kambuja (p. 421).
942	Completion of *Pāsanāha-chariu* by Padmakīrti (p. 219).
942	Bhatṛipaṭṭa, Guhila king (p. 109).
942-950	Udaya III (or IV), Ceylon (p. 171).
942-994/5	Mūlarāja, Chaulukya (p. 105).
c. 943	Kṛishṇa III, Rāshṭrakūta, and Būtuga, Gaṅga, capture Kāñchī and Tanjore (p. 14).
c. 944	Accession of Rājendra-varman and removal of the capital back to Yaśodharapura, Kambuja (p. 421).
946	Amma II succeeds his father Chālukya Bhīma II (p. 138).
947	Last known date of Siṇḍok, Eastern Java (p. 430).
948	Yaśaskara of Kāshmir poisoned by his attendants (p. 120).
948-949	Devapāla, Pratīhāra (p. 37).
949	Battle of Takkolam in which Choḷas were defeated and their crownprince Rājāditya was killed (pp. 14, 155, 159, 162, 163).
950	Death of Parvagupta, Kāshmir (p. 113).
950-953	Sena IV, Ceylon (p. 170).
950-958	Kshemagupta, Kāshmir (p. 113).
950-1000	Dhaṅga, Chandella (p. 38).
951	Indra-varman III of Champā sends an embassy to China (p. 426).
915, 953	Known dates of Allaṭa, son of Bhartṛipaṭṭa, Guhila (p. 109).
c. 953	Death of Parāntaka Choḷa (p. 156).
953-954	Vināyakapāla II, Pratīhāra (p. 37).
953-957	Gaṇḍarāditya, Choḷa (p. 157).
953-968	Rāshṭrakūṭa interregnum in Toṇḍamaṇḍalam (p. 156).
953-969	Mahendra IV, Ceylon (pp. 171, 210, 212).
955	Mahīpāla II. Pratīhāra (p. 36).
c. 956	Bādapa, son of Yuddhamalla, drives out Amma II (p. 139).
956	Krishna III, Rāshṭrakūṭa, places Bādapa on Veṅgī throne (p. 15).
956	Construction of the temple of Harshanātha by Siṁharāja, Chāhamāna (p. 107).
957-973	Sundara Choḷa or Parāntaka II, Choḷa (p. 157).
958-971	Indra-varman III of Champā sends seven embassies to China (p. 426).
958-972	Abhimanyu, Kāshmir (p. 114).

c 959 Somadeva composes *Yaśastilaka-champū* (pp. 188, 295).

960 San-fo-tsi (Śailendra) sends an embassy to China (p. 414).

c.960 Beginning of the rule of Song dynasty in China (p. 422).

960 *Mahā Purāṇa* by Pushpadanta (p. 198).

960-974 Mārasiṁha III, W. Gaṅga (p. 162).

960-1279 Song dynasty in China (p. 444).

916, 962 San-fo-tsi (Śailendra) sends embassies to China (p. 414).

c.963 Second Rāshṭrakūṭa expedition led by Kṛishṇa III into northern India (pp. 15, 38).

964 300 Chinese monks start for India on a twelve year pilgrimage (p. 444).

965 Completion of *Mahā Purāṇa* by Pushpadanta (p. 218).

966 157 Buddhist monks pay imperial homage to the holy places in India in pursuance of the appeal by the Chinese emperor (p. 444).

c.966 Bhaṭṭotpala's commentary on *Bṛihat-saṁhitā* (p. 200).

967 Accession of Khoṭṭiga, Rāshṭrakūṭa (p. 15).

968 Dinh Bo Linh, Annamese chief, founds an independent kingdom to the north of Champā (p. 426).

968 Death of Rājendra-varman, and accession of his son Jaya-varman V, Kambuja (p. 421).

969-979 Sena V, Ceylon (p. 171).

970 Dānārṇava slays his younger brother Amma II (p. 139).

c.970-1000 Yayāti Mahāśivagupta, Somavaṁśī (p. 147).

971, 72, 74, 75 San-fo-tsi sends embassies to China (p. 414).

971 Chāmuṇḍarājā of Jhālwār (p. 96).

971 Regular shipping house opened at Canton (p. 414).

971 44th Indian monks visit China (p. 444).

c.972 Taila II, Chālukya, puts an end to the Rāshṭrakūṭa supremacy in Kuntala (p. 86).

972 Death of Abhimanyu, Kāshmir (p. 121).

Sīyaka, Paramāra, captures and plunders the Rāshṭrakūṭa capital Mālkhed (pp. 15, 96, 218).

972 Sept. Death of Khoṭṭiga, Rāshṭrakūṭa (p. 15).

972-973 Dhanapāla composes *Pāïyalachchhī* (p. 187, 218).

972-979 Parameśvara-varman of Champā sends no less than six embassies to China (p. 426).

973 Dharmadeva, a monk of Nālandā, received by the Chinese emperor with great honour (p. 444).

973 Vigraharāja II, Chāhamāna (p. 107).

973	Taila II, Chālukya, rebels against Karkka. Rāshṭrakūṭa (p. 16).
973	Jaṭā Choḍa-Bhīma kills Dānārṇava in battle and makes himself king of Veṅgī (p. 139).
973-985	Uttama Choḷa (p. 157).
974	Taila defeats Mārasiṁha, Gaṅga (p. 16).
c. 974	Death of Mārasiṁha, W. Gaṅga (p. 164).
974-995	Composition of *Mṛitasañjīvinī* by Halāyudha in honour of Muñja, Paramāra (p. 190).
974-985	Rāchamalla or Rājamalla IV, W. Gaṅga (p. 162).
975	Death of Tribhuvana, Kāshmir (p. 121).
975	Vijayasiṁha composes *Bhuvanasundarī-kathā* (p. 210).
977	Śaktikumāra, Guhila (p. 109).
977	Vajradāman (p. 86).
978-1036	Bhāskara Ravivarman (p. 165).
978	Chāmuṇḍa Rāya composes *chāmuṇḍarāya Purāṇa* (p. 162).
979	Naval expedition of Parameśvara-varman of Champā (p. 426).
979	Death of Dinh Bo Linh, Annamese chief (p. 425).
979-1027	Mahendra V, Ceylon (p. 172).
c. 980	Birth of Dīpaṅkara (Atīśa) (p. 448).
980	Diddā kills Bhīmagupta and ascends the throne of Kāshmir (p. 121).
980,83	San-fo-tsi sends embassies to China (p. 414).
980-1015	Vajrahasta Aniyaṅkabhīma, Gaṅga (p. 143).
982	Chinese emperor appoints a Board of Translators with three Indian scholars at the head (p. 444).
982	Le Hoan, Annamese chief, returns with an immense booty from Champā (p. 426).
982	Chāmuṇḍa Rāya erects a basti at Śravaṇa Beḷgoḷa (p. 162).
982-1011	Board of Translators translate more than two hundred volumes (p. 444).
983	Chāmuṇḍa Rāya executes a colossal statue of Gomaṭeśvara at Śravaṇa Beḷgoḷa (p. 162).
984	Udayana composes *Tattvaśuddhi* and *Lakshaṇāvalī* (p. 205).
985	Accession of Rājarāja I, Choḷa (p. 156).
985-1016	Rājarāja Choḷa (p. 144).
985-1024	Rakkasa Gaṅga, W. Gaṅga (p. 163).
987	*Dhammaparikkhā* of Harisheṇa (p. 220).
c. 988	Accession of Mahīpāla I, son of Vigrahapāla II, Pāla (p. 55).
989	Accession of Vijaya Śrī Hari-varman (II) at Vijaya (p. 427).
c. 989	Sabuktigīn defeats the confederacy of Hindu chiefs near Lamghan (p. 86).
990	Java invades San-fo-tsi (Śailendra) (pp. 415, 431).

991	Śrīdhara Bhaṭṭa composes *Nyāyakandalī* (p. 205).
991-1015	Period of the literary activity of Abhinavagupta (pp. 206, 301).
992	Le Hoan, Annamese chief, releases a number of Cham prisoners (p. 427).
992	Javanese envoy visits chinese court (p. 431).
993	Abhinavagupta composes *Bhairava-stotra* (p. 194).
993	Ranna composes *Ajita Purāṇa* (p. 225).
995	Close of the reign of Mūlarāja Chaulukya who abdicated the throne in favour of his son Chāmuṇḍarāja (p. 105).
999	Jayapāla, Shāhi, annexes the kingdom of Lohūr (p. 114).
999	Durlabharāja, Chāhamāna (p. 107).
999	Rājarāja conquers Veṅgī from Jaṭā Choḍa-Bhīma (p. 140).
999	Śaktivarman becomes ruler of Veṅgī (p. 140).
c. 999-1011	Śaktivarman, son of Dānārṇava (p. 140).
c. 1000	Soḍḍhala, author of *Udayasundarīkathā* (p. 189).
c. 1000	End of the reign of Sindhurāja, Paramāra (p. 99).
c. 1000	Bhaṭṭa Jagaddhara and Chhichhubhaṭṭa from Kāshmir (p. 191).
c. 1000	Ugrabhūti, grammarian (p. 190).
c. 1000	Padmagupta *alias* Parimala, author of *Navasāhasāṅkacharita* (p. 184).
1001	Death of Jaya-varman V, Kambuja (p. 421).
1001	Death of Śembiyan Mahādevī, wife of Gaṇḍarāditya Choḷa (p. 156).
1001	Death of Dharmadeva, a monk of Nālandā, in China (p. 444).
1003	San-fo-tsi (Śailendra) sends an embassy to China without any hindrance from Java (pp. 414, 431).
1003	Death of Diddā of Kāshmir, and accession of Saṁgrāmarāja (p. 121).
1004	Choḷas capture Taḷakāḍ (p. 163).
1006	Destruction of Java by a great catastrophe according to a record of Airlangga (p. 432).
1007	Nirbhaya rules jointly with Rudra in Nepāl (p. 59).
1007	Death of Dharmavaṁśa of Java (p. 432).
1008	Close of the reign of Chāmuṇḍarāja, Chaulukya, according to Gujarāt chroniclers (p. 105).
1014	*Dharmaparīkshā* of Amitagati (p. 220).
1015	Choḷa embassy visits the imperial court at China (p. 445).
1015	Abhinavagupta composes *Pratyabhijñāvimarśinī* (p. 194).

1015-1016	Kāmārṇava, Gaṅga (p. 143).
1016-1019	Guṇḍama, Gaṅga (p. 143).
1019-1038	Madhukāmārṇava, Gaṅga (p. 143, 144).
1022	Three Bodh-Gayā inscriptions refer to the construction of stone stūpas by three Chinese monks (p. 445).
1027-1039	Vikramabāhu, Ceylon (p. 173).
1031	Accession of Vyāsa, Kalachuri (p. 94).
1033	Another Choḷa embassy to China (p. 445).
1033	Bodh-Gayā ins. recording the construction of a stūpa in honour of emperor T'ai-tsong (p. 445).
1036	Visit of nine Indian monks to China (p. 445).
1036	Close of the long and intimate cultural intercourse between India and China (p. 445).
1038, April 9	Coronation of Vajrahasta Anantavarman, Gaṅga (p. 141).
1039-1042	Mahālānakīrti, Ceylon (p. 173).
1042-1046	Jagatīpāla, Ceylon (p. 173).
1046-1048	Parākrama or Parākramapāṇḍya, Ceylon (p. 173).
1048-1054	Lokeśvara, Ceylon (p. 174).
1053	Death of Dīpaṅkara or Atīśa (p. 449).
1054-1055	Keśadhātu Kāśyapa, Ceylon (p. 174).
1055-1110	Vijayabāhu I, Ceylon (pp. 174, 211).
1069	Namisādhu's commentary on Rudraṭa's *Kāvyālaṁkāra* (p. 186).
1077	Choḷa embassy to China (p. 445).
1079	King Soḍhadeva, Kalachuri (p. 94).
1080-1101	Harsha, Kāshmir (p. 113).
1123-1140	Dhanañjaya, Śrutakīrti, author of *Nāmamālā* (p. 184).
1159	Sarvānanda, commentator of *Amarakośa* (p. 190).
1178	Chou Ku-fei, Chinese author, refers to Quilon as an important centre of trade with China (p. 445).
1210-1236	Sultān Iltutmish (p. 114).
c. 1211	Muhammad 'Aufi (p. 113).

GENEALOGY

1. Rāshṭrakūṭas of Mālkhed

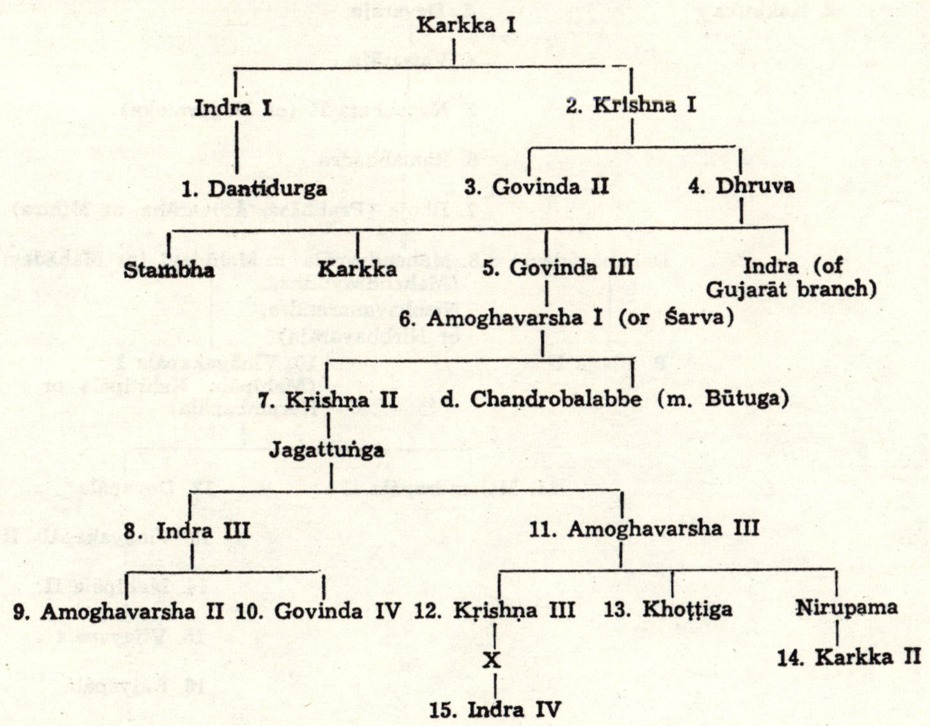

2. Rāshṭrakūṭas: Gujarāt Branch

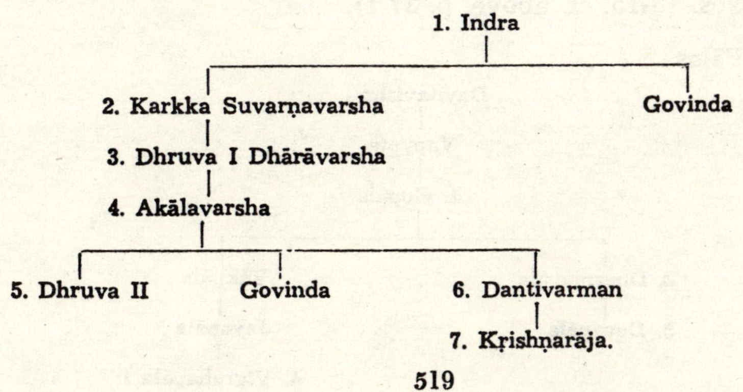

3. The Pratīhāras

X

1. Nāgabhaṭa I — X

X: 2. Kakkuka — 3. Devarāja

3. Devarāja
4. Vatsarāja
5. Nāgabhaṭa II (or Nāgāvaloka)
6. Rāmabhadra
7. Bhoja (Prabhāsa, Ādivarāha, or Mihira)

Dehanāgādevī = 8. Mahendrapāla = Mahīdevī (or Mahādevī)
(Mahendrāyudha, Nirbhayanarendra, or Nirbhayarāja)

9. Bhoja II (son of Dehanāgādevī)

10. Vināyakapāla I (Mahīpāla, Kshitipāla or Herambapāla) (son of Mahīdevī)

11. Mahendrapāla II — 12. Devapāla

12. Devapāla
13. Vināyakapāla II
14. Mahīpāla II
15. Vijayapāla
16. Rājyapāla
17. Trilochanapāla
18 (?) Yaśaḥpāla.

(N.B.—For the different views about the relationship of kings Nos. 13-15, cf. above, p. 37 f).

4. The Pālas

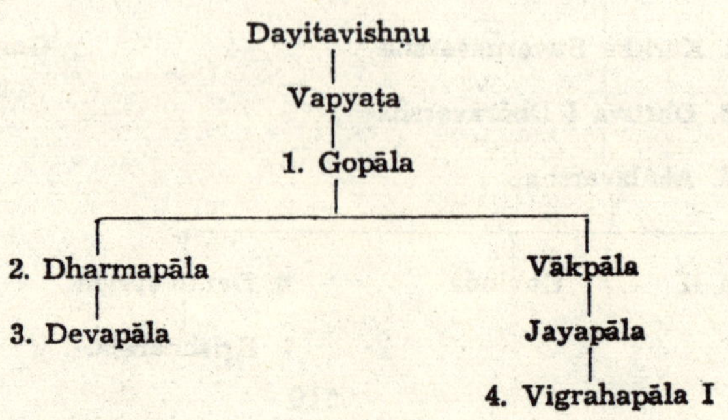

5. Nārāyanapāla
|
6. Rājyapāla
|
7. Gopāla II
|
8. Vigrahapāla II
|
9. Mahīpāla I

5. Kāmarūpa

1. Sālambha (or Prālambha)
|
2. Harjara-varman
|
3. Vanamāla-varman
|
4. Jayamāla (Vīravāhu)
|
5. Bala-varman
⋮
(? Tyāgasiṁha)

6. Nepāl[1]

1. Rāghavadeva
⋮
2. Jayadeva
⋮
3. Vikramadeva
⋮
4. Narendradeva
⋮
5. Guṇakāmadeva I
⋮
6. Udayadeva
⋮
7. Nirbhayadeva and Rudradeva

7. Karas of Utkala (See above, p. 63)

8. Bhañjas of Khiñjali (See above, p. 69)

9. Bhañjas of Khijjiṅga (See above, p. 74)

10. Śūlkis (See above, p. 77)

11. Tuṅgas

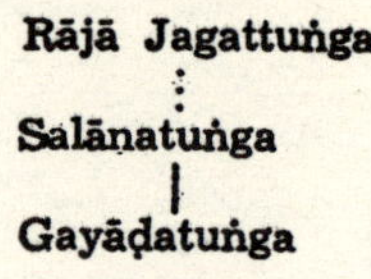

12. Mayūravaṁśa

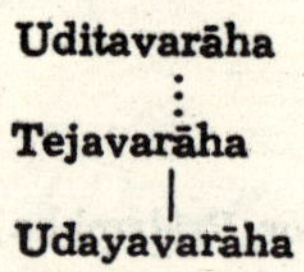

13. Nandas (See above, p. 78)

14. Chandellas of Kharjūravāhaka

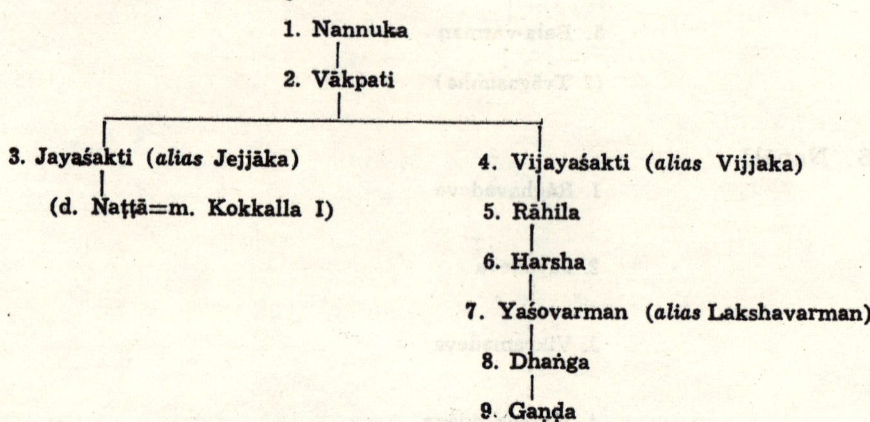

15. Kalachuris of Tripurī

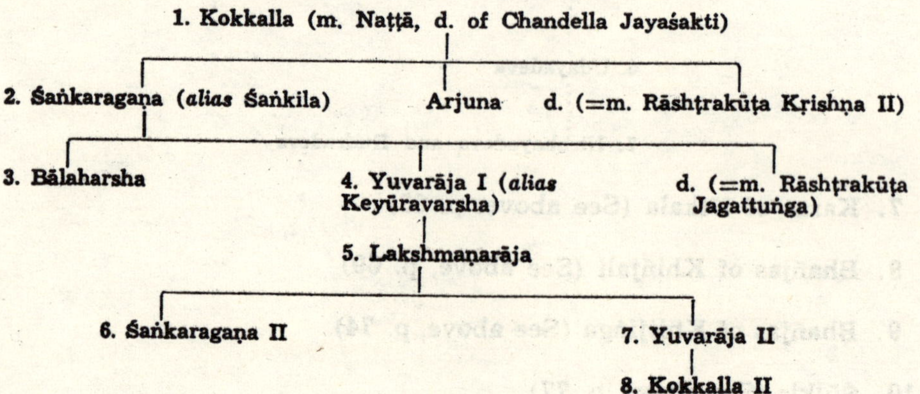

16. Kalachuris of Sarayupāra.[2]

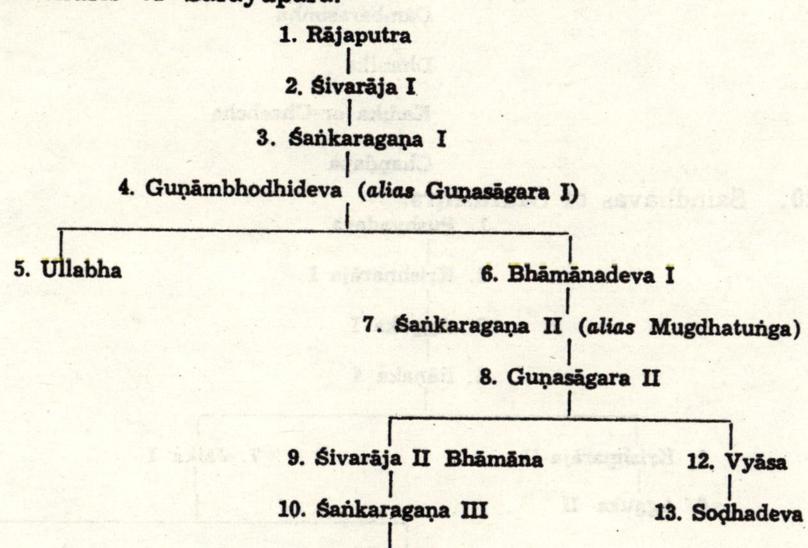

17. Malayaketus of Vijayapura.

1. Mahārājādhirāja Jayāditya I
2. „ Dharmāditya
3. „ Jayāditya II

18. Paramāras of Mālava.

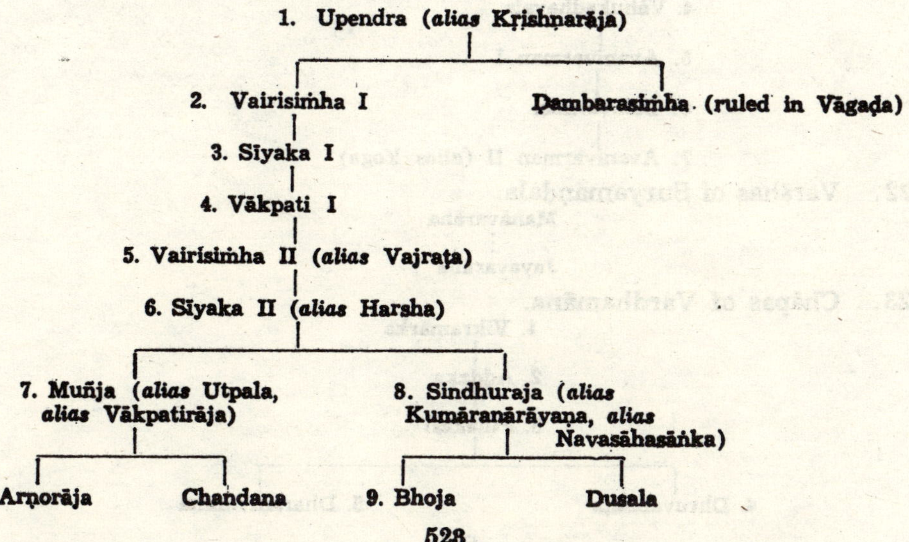

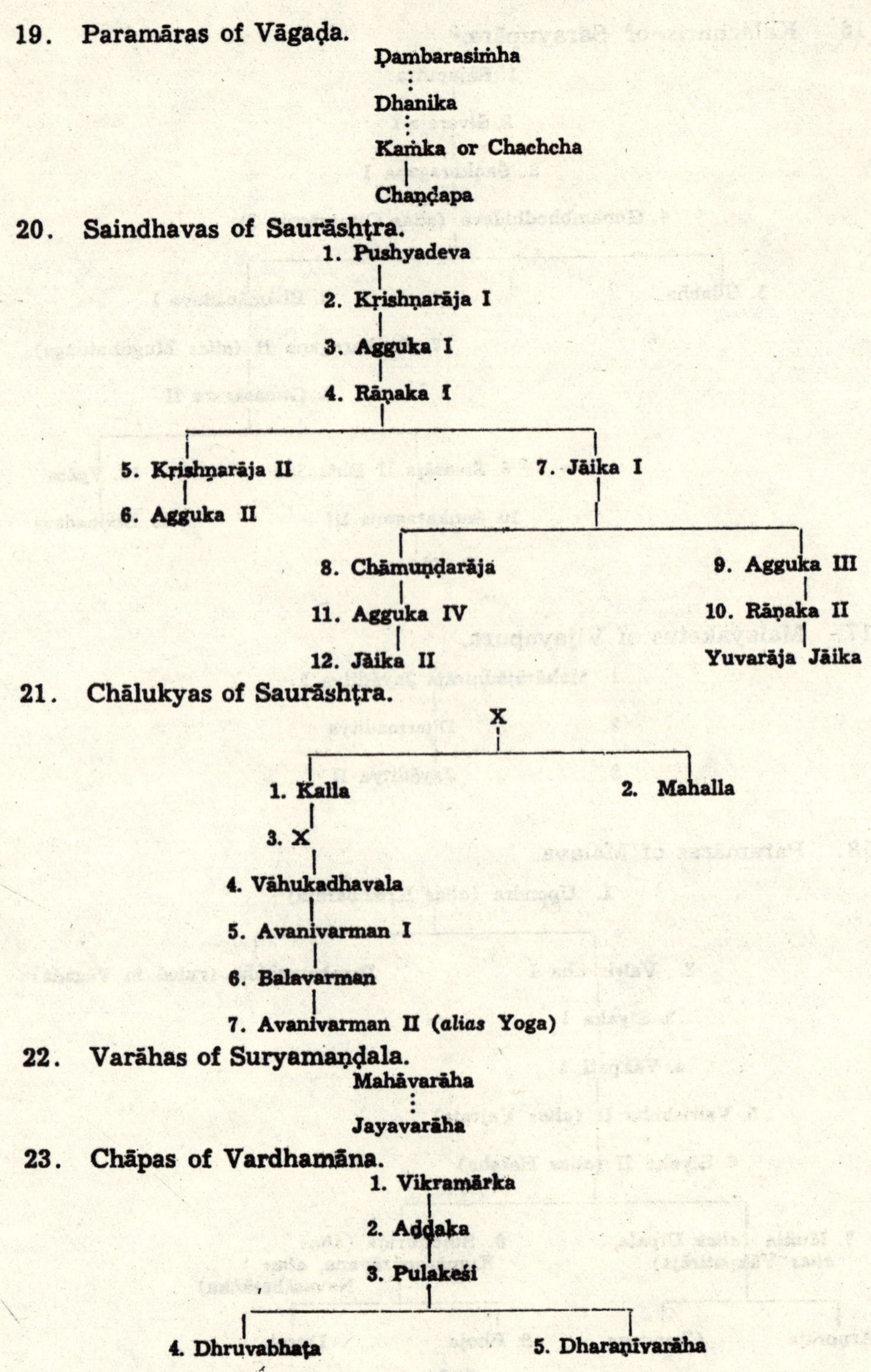
19. Paramāras of Vāgaḍa.
Ḍambarasiṁha
Dhanika
Kaṁka or Chachcha
Chaṇḍapa
20. Saindhavas of Saurāshṭra.
1. Pushyadeva
2. Kṛishṇarāja I
3. Agguka I
4. Rāṇaka I
5. Kṛishṇarāja II
6. Agguka II
7. Jāika I
8. Chāmuṇḍarāja
11. Agguka IV
12. Jāika II
9. Agguka III
10. Rāṇaka II
Yuvarāja Jāika
21. Chālukyas of Saurāshṭra.
X
1. Kalla
2. Mahalla
3. X
4. Vāhukadhavala
5. Avanivarman I
6. Balavarman
7. Avanivarman II (alias Yoga)
22. Varāhas of Suryamaṇḍala.
Mahāvarāha
Jayavarāha
23. Chāpas of Vardhamāna.
1. Vikramārka
2. Aḍḍaka
3. Pulakeśi
4. Dhruvabhaṭa
5. Dharaṇīvarāha

24. Chapas of Aṇahilapāṭaka

1. Vanarāja
2. Yogarāja
3. Ratnāditya
4. Kshemarāja
5. Ākaḍadeva
6. Bhūyaḍadeva (*alias* Bhūyagaḍadeva. *alias* Sāmantasiṁha)

25. Chaulukyas of Mattamayūra

1. Siṁhavarman
2. Sadhanva
3. Avanivarman

d. Nohalā (=m. Kalachuri Yuvarāja I)

26. Chaulukyas of Aṇahilapāṭaka

1. Mūlarāja
2. Chāmuṇḍarāja

3. Vallabharāja — 4. Durlabharāja

27. Chaulukyas of Lāṭa

Bārappa

Goṅgirāja

28. Chāhamānas of Śākambharī[3]

1. Vāsudeva
⋮
2. Sāmanta
3. Pūrṇatalla
4. Jayarāja
5. Vigraharāja I

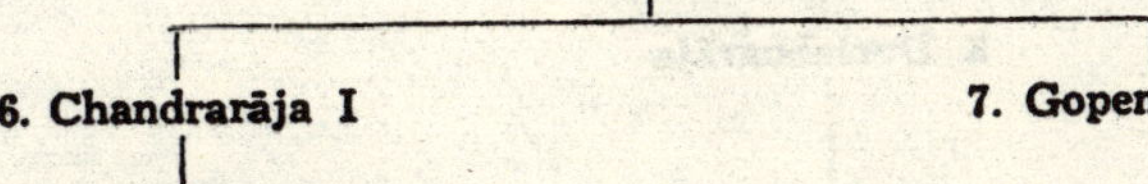

6. Chandrarāja I — 7. Gopendrarāja

8. Durlabharāja (son of 6. Chandrarāja I)

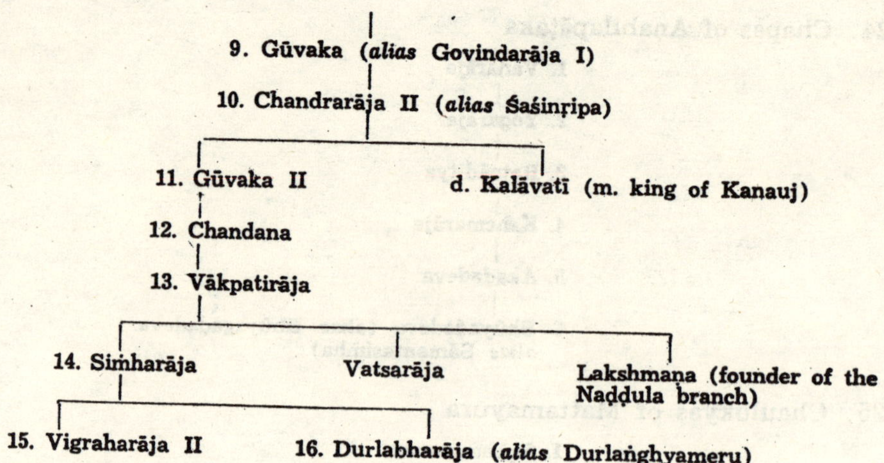

29. Chāhamānas of Naḍḍula

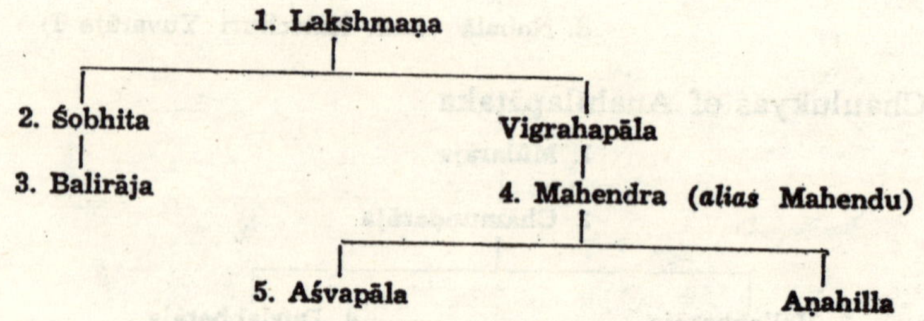

30. Chāhamānas of Dholpur

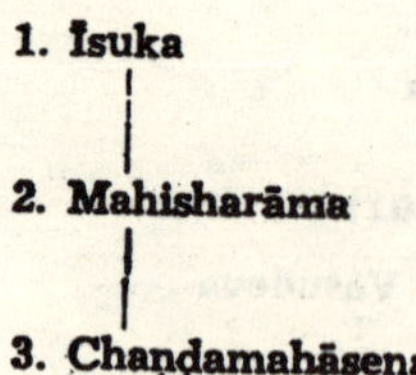

31. Chāhamānas of Partābgarh

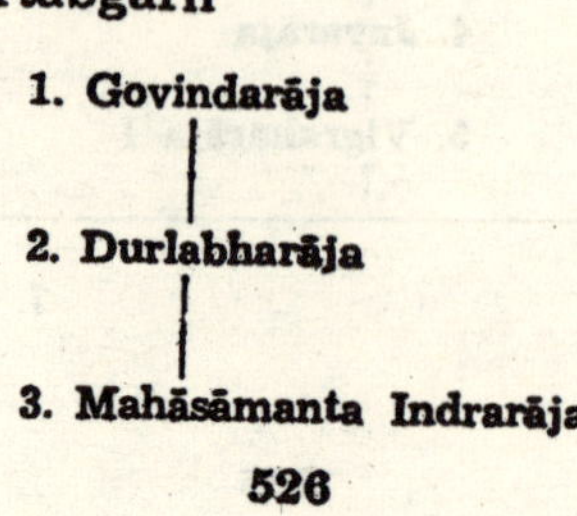

GENEALOGY

32. Guhilas of Mewār[4]

1. Khommāṇa I (*alias* Bappa, *alias* Kālabhoja)
⋮
2. Mattaṭa
⋮
3. Bhartṛipaṭṭa I
⋮
4. Siṁha
|
5. Khommāṇa II
|
6. Mahāyaka
|
7. Khommāṇa III
|
8. Bhartṛipaṭṭa II
|
9. Allaṭa
|
10. Naravāhana
|
11. Śālivāhana
|
12. Śaktikumāra

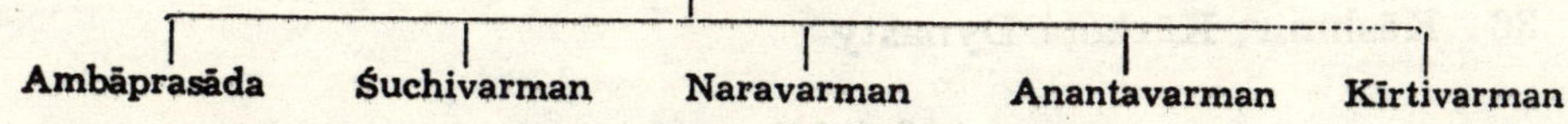

Ambāprasāda | Śuchivarman | Naravarman | Anantavarman | Kīrtivarman

33. Guhilas of Dhoḍ[5]

Guhila I
|
1. Dhanika
|
2. Āuka
|
3. Kṛishṇa
|
4. Śaṅkaragaṇa
|
5. Harsha
|
6. Guhila II
|
7. Bhaṭṭa
|
8. Bālāditya

34. Tomaras

Jāula
⋮
1. Vajraṭa
|
2. Jajjuka

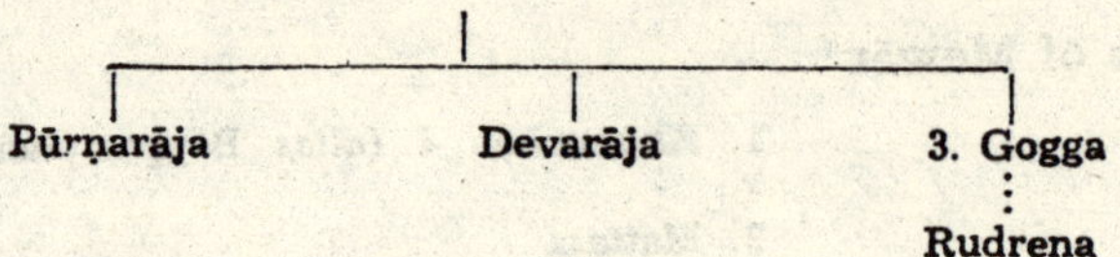

35. Hindu Shāhis

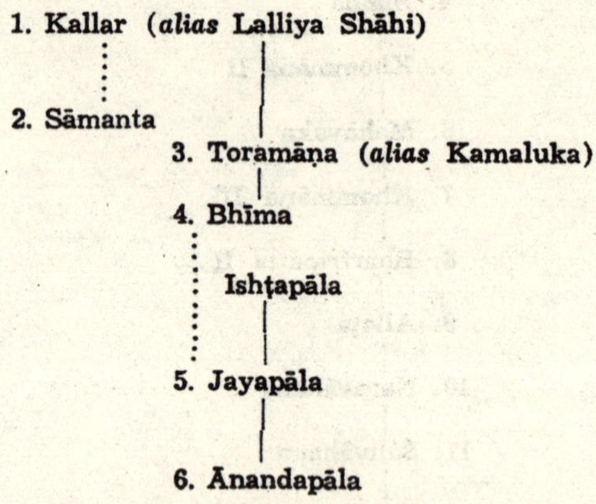

36. Kāshmir; Kārkoṭa Dynasty

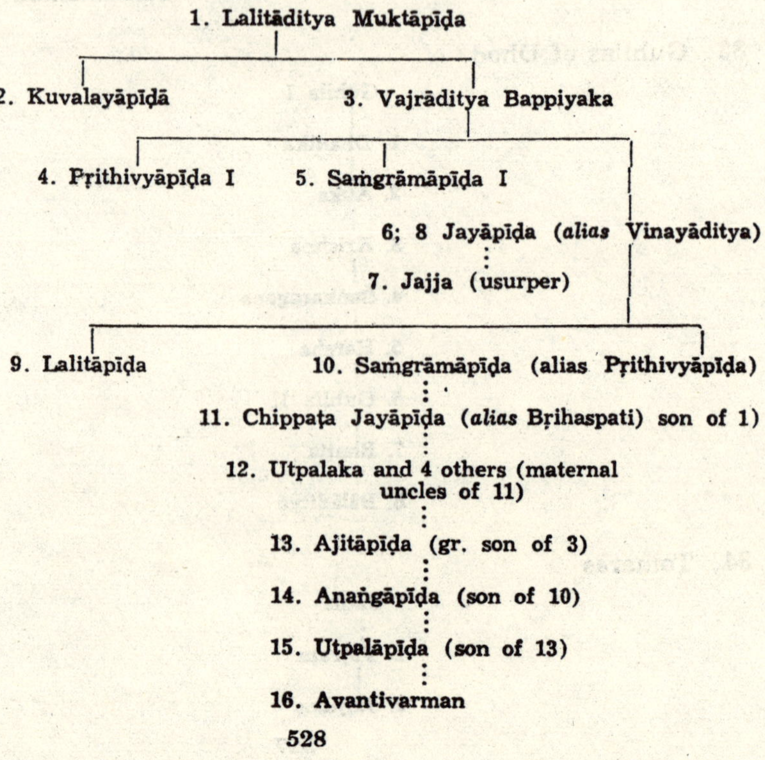

GENEALOGY

37. Kāshmir: Utpala Dynasty

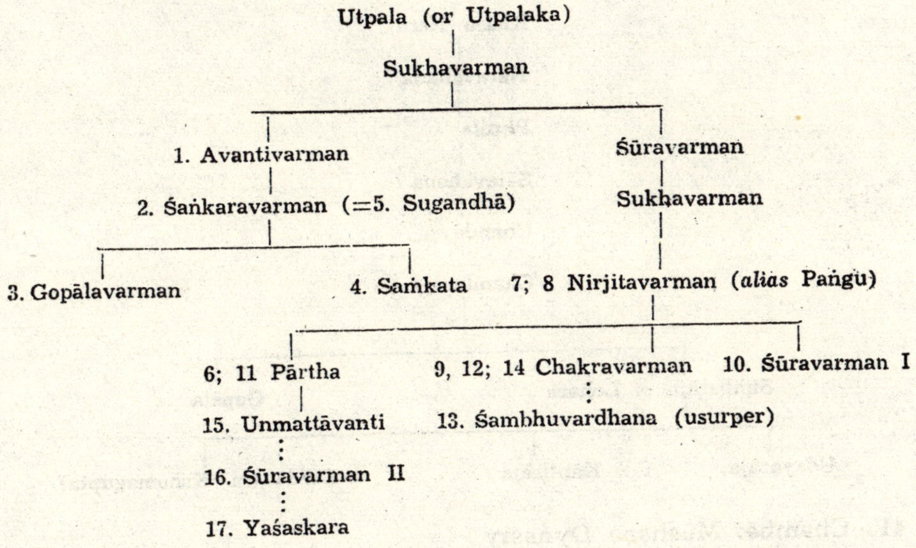

38. Kāshmir: Yaśaskara Dynasty

Prabhākaradeva
|
1. Yaśaskaradeva
|
2. Saṁgrāmadeva
⋮
3. Parvagupta

39. Kāshmir: Parvagupta Dynasty

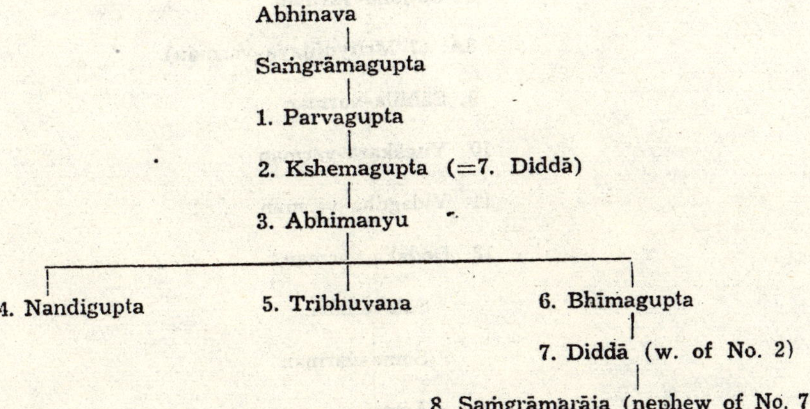

40. Kāshmir: Kingdom of Darvābhisāra and Lohara[6]

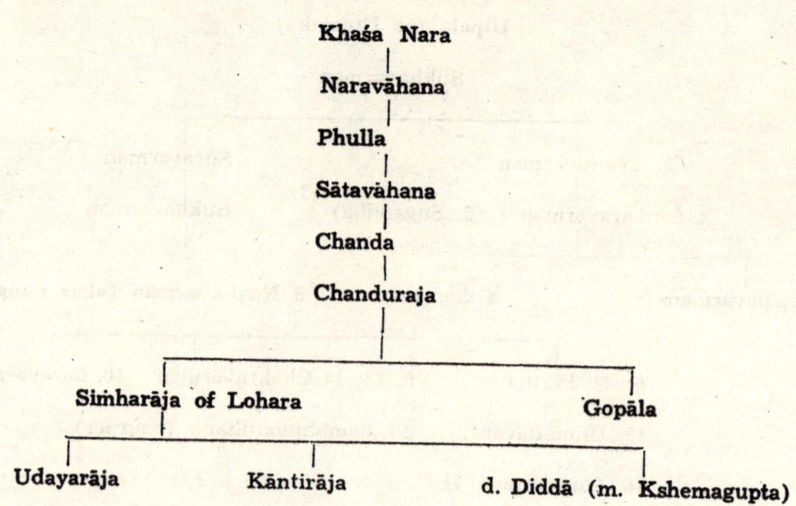

41. Chambā: Mūshaṇa Dynasty

1. Ajita-varman
2. Suvarṇa-varman
3. Lakshmī-varman
4. Mūshaṇa-varman
5. Haṁsa-varman
6. Sāra-varman
7. Sena-varman
8. Sajjana-varman

8A. (? Mṛityuñjaya-varman)

9. Sāhilla-varman
10. Yugākara-varman
11. Vidagdha-varman
12. Dodaka-varman

Sālavāhana

Soma-varman

Āsaṭa

GENEALOGY

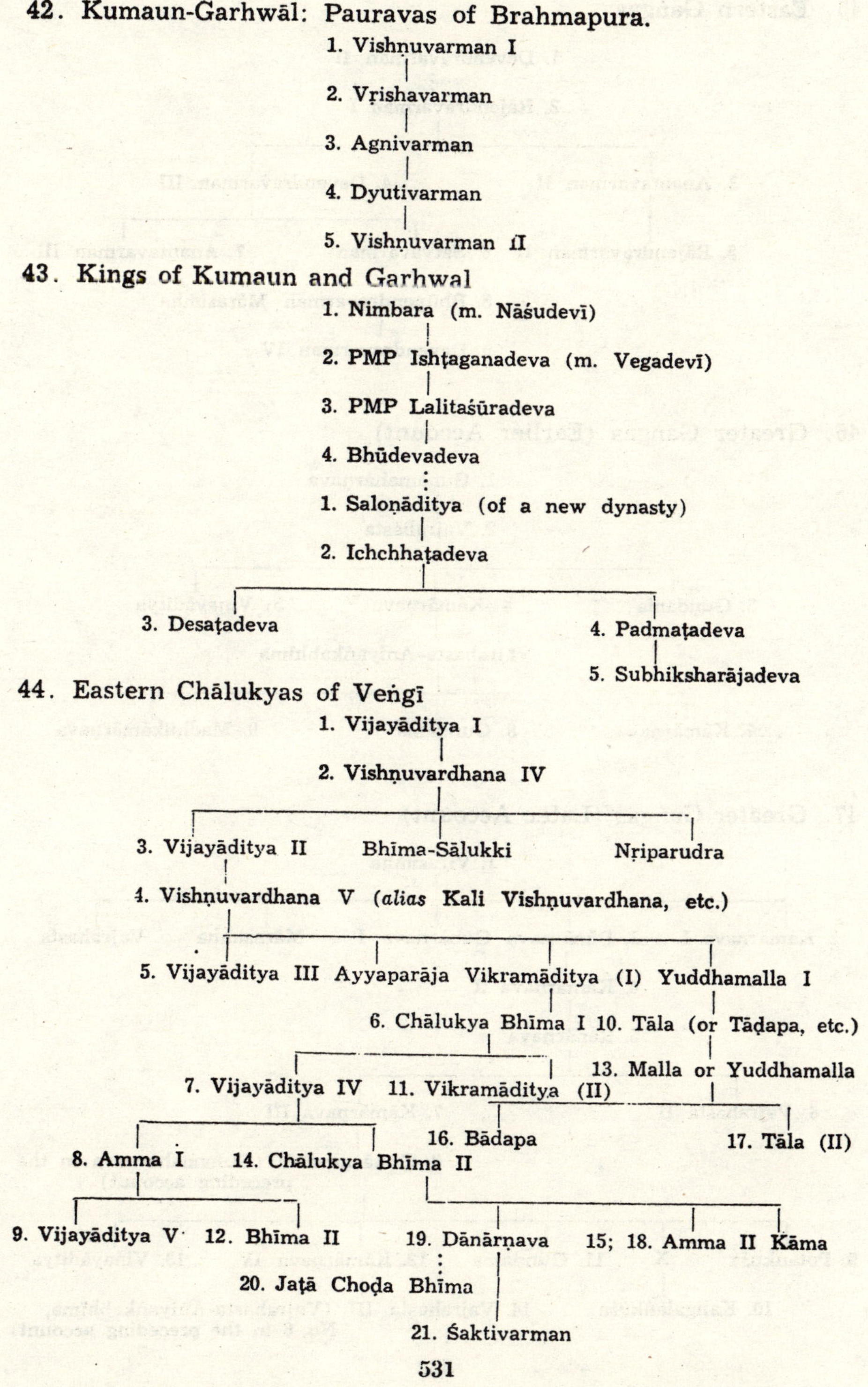

42. Kumaun-Garhwāl: Pauravas of Brahmapura.
1. Vishṇuvarman I
2. Vṛishavarman
3. Agnivarman
4. Dyutivarman
5. Vishṇuvarman II
43. Kings of Kumaun and Garhwal
1. Nimbara (m. Nāśudevī)
2. PMP Ishṭaganadeva (m. Vegadevī)
3. PMP Lalitaśūradeva
4. Bhūdevadeva
1. Saloṇāditya (of a new dynasty)
2. Ichchhaṭadeva
3. Desaṭadeva
4. Padmaṭadeva
5. Subhiksharājadeva
44. Eastern Chālukyas of Veṅgī
1. Vijayāditya I
2. Vishṇuvardhana IV
3. Vijayāditya II
Bhīma-Sālukki
Nṛiparudra
4. Vishṇuvardhana V (alias Kali Vishṇuvardhana, etc.)
5. Vijayāditya III
Ayyaparāja
Vikramāditya (I)
Yuddhamalla I
6. Chālukya Bhīma I
10. Tāla (or Tāḍapa, etc.)
13. Malla or Yuddhamalla
7. Vijayāditya IV
11. Vikramāditya (II)
16. Bādapa
17. Tāla (II)
8. Amma I
14. Chālukya Bhīma II
9. Vijayāditya V
12. Bhīma II
19. Dānārṇava
15; 18. Amma II
Kāma
20. Jaṭā Choḍa Bhīma
21. Śaktivarman

45. Eastern Gaṅgas

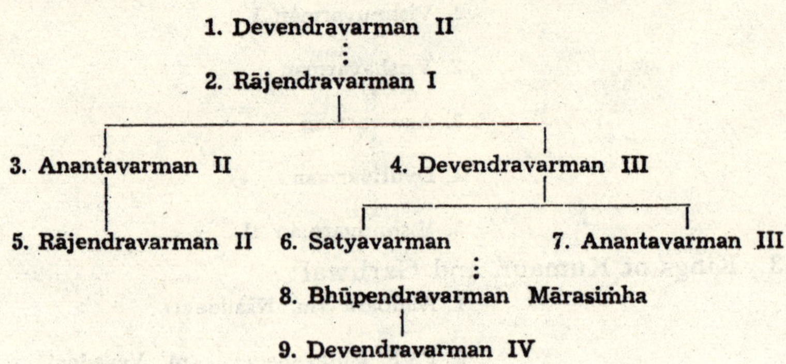

46. Greater Gaṅgas (Earlier Account)

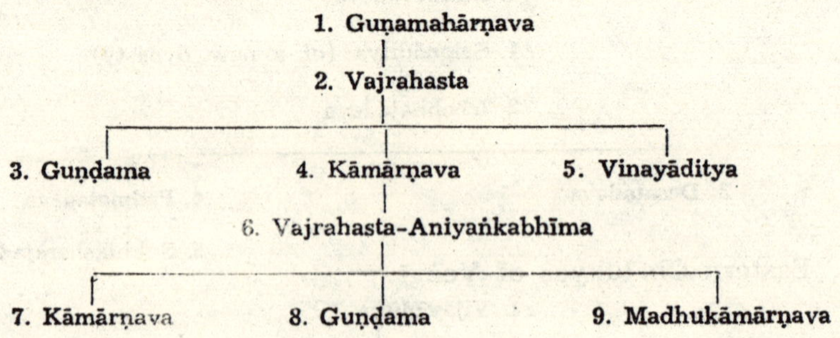

47. Greater Gaṅgas (Later Account)

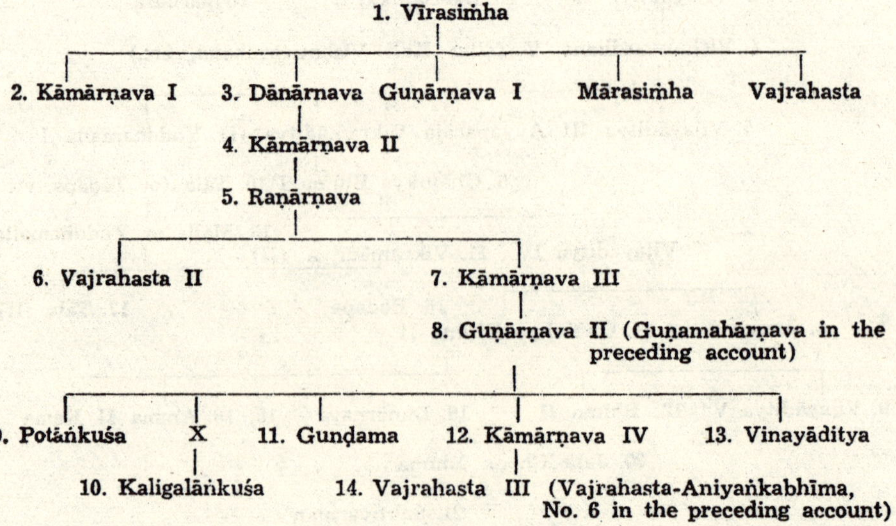

GENEALOGY

48. Gaṅgas of Śvetaka

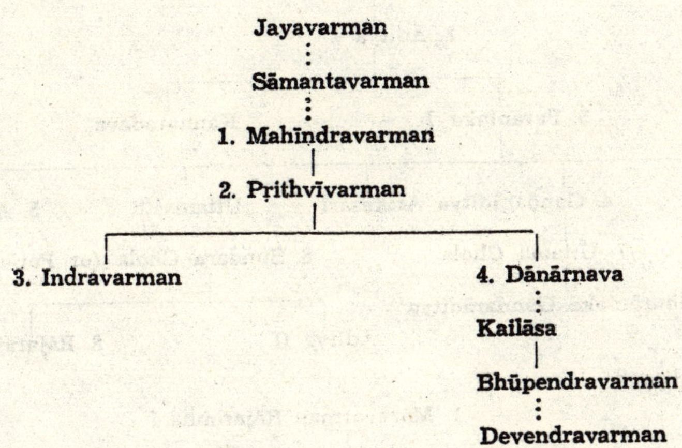

49. Kadambas of Jayantyāpura

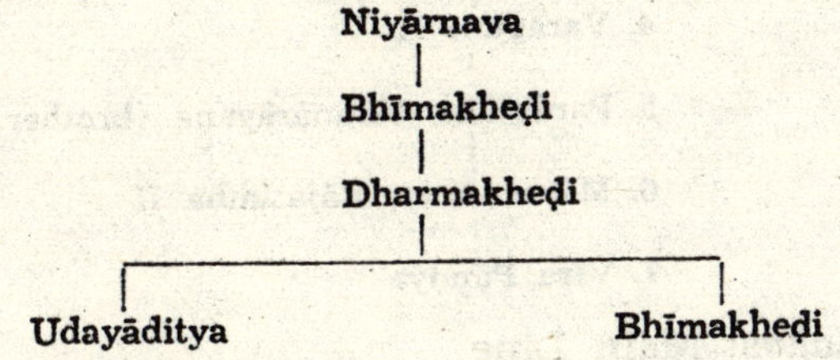

50. Somavaṁśīs of Kosala

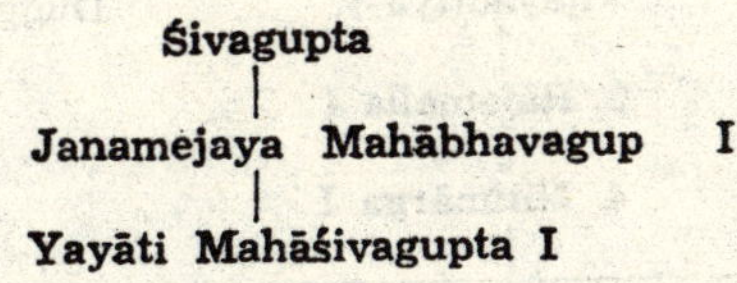

51. Pallavas[7]

1. Nandi-varman II Pallavamalla
2. Danti-varman
3. Nandi-varman III Teḷḷāṟṟeṟinda
4. Nṛipatuṅga-varman
5. Aparājita

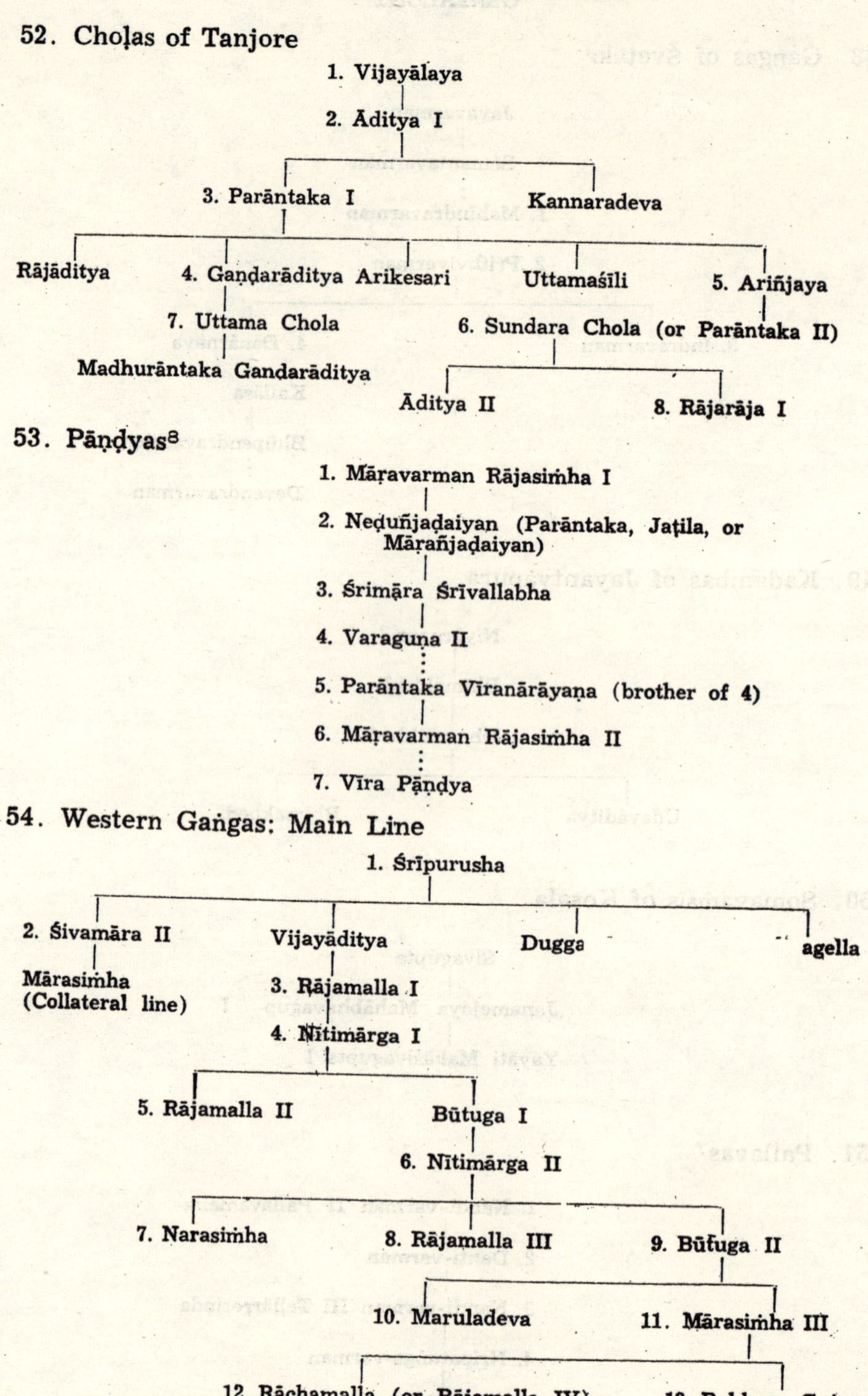
52. Choḷas of Tanjore
1. Vijayālaya
2. Āditya I
3. Parāntaka I
Kannaradeva
Rājāditya
4. Gaṇḍarāditya
Arikesari
Uttamaśīli
5. Ariñjaya
7. Uttama Chola
6. Sundara Chola (or Parāntaka II)
Madhurāntaka Gandarāditya
Āditya II
8. Rājarāja I
53. Pāṇḍyas[8]
1. Māṛavarman Rājasiṁha I
2. Neḍuñjaḍaiyan (Parāntaka, Jaṭila, or Māṛañjaḍaiyan)
3. Śrimāṛa Śrīvallabha
4. Varaguṇa II
5. Parāntaka Vīranārāyaṇa (brother of 4)
6. Māṛavarman Rājasiṁha II
7. Vīra Pāṇḍya
54. Western Gaṅgas: Main Line
1. Śrīpurusha
2. Śivamāra II
Vijayāditya
Dugga
agella
Mārasiṁha
(Collateral line)
3. Rājamalla I
4. Nītimārga I
5. Rājamalla II
Būtuga I
6. Nītimārga II
7. Narasiṁha
8. Rājamalla III
9. Būtuga II
10. Maruladeva
11. Mārasiṁha III
12. Rāchamalla (or Rājamalla IV)
13. Rakkasa Gaṅga

55. Western Gaṅgas: Collateral Line

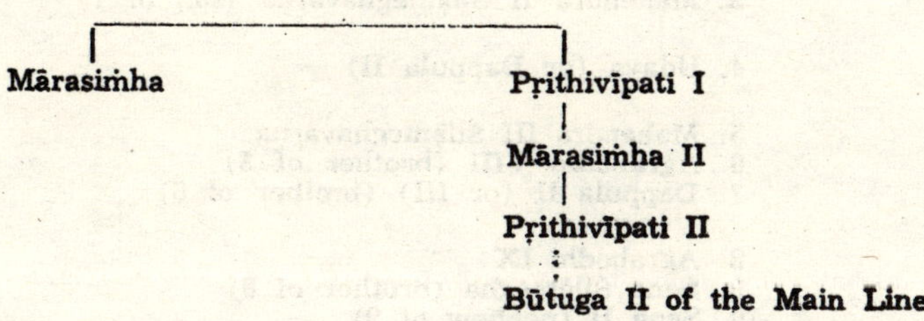

56. Bāṇas

Vikramāditya I Bāṇa or Bāṇavidyādhara
⋮
Vijayāditya
⋮
Vikramāditya II
⋮
Vikramāditya III

57. Noḷambas

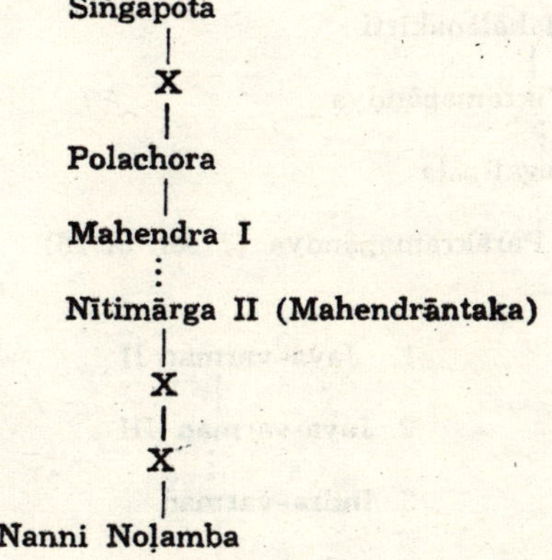

58. Vaidumbas

Irigaya
⋮
Gaṇḍa Triṇetra
⋮
Śandayan Tiruvayan I
⋮
Śandayan Tiruvayan II *alias* Śrīkaṇṭha

59. Ceylon

1. Agrabodhi VI
2. Agrabodhi VII (brother of 1)
3. Mahendra II Śilāmeghavarṇa (son of 1)
   |
4. Udaya (or Dappula II)

5. Mahendra III Śilāmeghavarṇa
6. Agrabodhi VIII (brother of 5)
7. Dappula II (or III) (brother of 6)
   |
8. Agrabodhi IX
9. Sena Śilāmegha (brother of 8)
10. Sena II (nephew of 9)
11. Udaya II (or I) Śilāmeghavarṇa (brother of 10)
12. Kāśyapa IV Śrīsaṅghabodhi (brother of 11)
13. Kāśyapa V Abhaya Śilāmeghavarṇa (son of 10)
14. Dappula III (or IV) (probably stepbrother of 13)
15. Dappula IV (or V) Śilāmeghavarṇa (probably brother of 14)
16. Udaya III (or II) (nephew of 10)
17. Sena III (probably brother of 16)
18. Udaya IV (or III)
19. Sena IV
20. Mahendra IV Śrīsaṅghabodhi (probably brother of 19)
   |
21. Sena V
22. Mahendra V (brother of 21)
   |
23. Vikramabāhu
   :
24. Kīrti
   :
25. Mahālānakīrti
   |
26. Vikramapāṇḍya
   :
27. Jagatīpāla
   :
   Parākramapāṇḍya (? son of 26)

60. Kambuja

1. Jaya-varman II
   |
2. Jaya-varman III
   :
3. Indra-varman
   |
4. Yaśo-varman.
   |
   (sons:)

5. Harsha-varman I

6. Īśāna-varman II
   :
7. Jaya-varman IV (husband of a sister of 4)
   |
8. Harsha-varman II
   :
9. Rājendra-varman (son of another sister of 4)
   |
10. Jaya-varman V

61. Champā: Dynasty of Pāṇḍuraṅga

1. Pṛithivīndra-varman
2. Satya-varman (sister's son of 1)
3. Indra-varman (brother of 2)
4. Hari-varman (sister's husband of 3)
5. Vikrānta-varman III

62. Champā: Bhṛigu Dynasty

1. Indra-varman II
2. Jayasiṁha-varman
3. Jayaśakti-varman
4. Bhadra-varman III
5. Indra-varman III
6. Parameśvara-varman
7. Indra-varman IV
8. Lu'u-Ky-Tong (Annamite usurper)
9. Vijaya Śrī Hari-varman II
10. Yan Pu Ku Vijaya Śrī

63. Central Java: Kingdom of Matarām

1. Sannāha
2. Sañjaya
3. Balitung (Dharmodaya Mahāśambhu)
4. Dakshottama
5. Tulodong
6. Wawa

64. Eastern Java: Dynasty of Siṇḍok

1. Siṇḍok (Śrī Īśāna-Vikrama Dharmottuṅgadeva)
2. Śrī Īśānatuṅgavijayā (daughter of 1)
3. Śrī Makutavaṁśa-vardhana

Dharmavaṁśa

NOTES ON GENEALOGY

1. Cf. Bendall's Historical Introduction to Sastri's *Catalogue of Palm-leaf and selected paper MSS belonging to the Durbar Library, Nepal,* p. 21.

2. According to *Bh. List,* p. 403, Vyāsa (No. 12) was the son of Śaṅkaragaṇa III No. 10) and step-brother of Bhīma (No. 11).

3. Cf. *DHNI,* II. 1062, 1137. *Contra, Bh. List,* p. 381, where Pūrṇatalla (No. 3) is omitted, and Vindhyanṛipati is inserted between Nos. 13 and 14.

4. Cf. *Bh. List,* pp. 388-9.

5. Cf. *DHNI,* II. 1208. *Bh. List,* pp. 390-1, shows no relationship between Nos. 2 and 3.

6. Cf. Stein, *RT,* I, Introduction, App. II, p. 145.

7. Cf. K. A. N. Sastri, *History of India,* I. 300.

8. Cf. *op. cit.,* p. 299.

INDEX

C

H

I

J

Q

R

S

U

V

Z